SOUTH WEST AFRICA IN EARLY TIMES

A BUSHMAN FAMILY AT HOME

Photographed by Paul L. Hoefler, F.R.G.S.

SOUTH WEST AFRICA IN EARLY TIMES

*Being the story of South West Africa up to the date of
Maharero's death in 1890*

HEINRICH VEDDER

Translated and Edited by
CYRIL G. HALL

NEW YORK

BARNES & NOBLE, INC.
Publishers · Booksellers · Since 1873

Published by Frank Cass & Co. Ltd.,
10 Woburn Walk, London W.C.1
by arrangement with Oxford University Press.

Published in the United States
in 1966
by Barnes & Noble, Inc.
105 Fifth Avenue, New York, N.Y. 10003.

First English Edition   1938
New Impression   1966

Printed in Great Britain

EDITOR'S PREFACE

THIS book was published originally in German under the title *Das alte Südwestafrika* and its sub-title stated that it was a history of South West Africa up to the date of Maharero's death in 1890. It is true that the book contains much historical information, but it is not a history in the scientific sense. The author's extensive knowledge of the ethnology of the native tribes, their languages, and customs assists in quickening the dry bones of their historical achievements, while folk-lore and tribal tradition have often been invoked in order to bridge the gaps between recent and more remote times. The original has been somewhat reduced in size for the purpose of the English edition, chiefly through the omission of numerous original letters and documents, which were fully set out in the German edition, and also through the curtailment of detailed accounts of the development and progress of individual mission stations, many of which have ceased to exist as centres of communal life. The maps and illustrations have been added, as well as a short subject index.

I wish to express my gratitude to Mr. French Trollope, the Assistant Native Commissioner at Windhoek, for his careful and efficient revision of the manuscript, which ensured that the Germanisms, which must inevitably creep into the translation of a lengthy German work, were eliminated, and that the English text was as nearly as possible 'according to Fowler'.

C. G. HALL

CHAMBERS, CAPETOWN,
January 1938.

AUTHOR'S PREFACE

THIS book should really be read only by those who love South West Africa, for much that it contains is of very minor importance in comparison with the great events of the world at large, and can only be interesting to those who have, in some way or other, become closely identified with our sunny land. Those, however, who love the country should not fail to read it, for it contains many things which are unknown even to the very people who have made the country's history, or are still making it to-day. These things they will not be able to learn anywhere else, for the history of South West Africa of earlier times has been collected, a little here and a little there, chiefly from old notes, letters, reports, and diaries and, to a lesser extent, from information given by word of mouth by Europeans and natives, who have been long in the land.

These valuable individual records have been collected for the benefit of posterity in twenty-eight volumes, and have been given the title, *Sources of the History of South West Africa*; the original manuscripts have been taken into safe-keeping by the Administration of South West Africa. They provide not only a rich store of information regarding the history of the country, but likewise as to the history of places and tribes, to which but little attention can be paid in this book.

The author's sincere thanks are due to His Honour the Administrator, Mr. A. J. Werth, for having made possible the collection and compilation of historical records of times long past, and for having done so while there was still time to prevent valuable memories of olden days from being entirely lost. My thanks are due to the Rhenish Missionary Society at Barmen for placing at my disposal the numerous reports of their missionaries, who have laboured in South West Africa since 1842, and to Miss Emma Meier of Gütersloh, one of this country's daughters, for making extracts from those reports, in a way which showed a ready comprehension of what was important, and careful attention to detail. I must acknowledge my indebtedness to the Rev. J. Olpp, Inspector of Missions, for having undertaken the examination of the records dealing with Hereroland and Namaland in the archives of the Society; to the Director of Education at Windhoek, Mr. H. H. G. Kreft, for many a useful hint and much willing assistance; to the missionaries, Messrs. Sckaer and Lehto, for valuable information regarding Ovamboland, to Mr. Paul Ribbink of

Capetown for giving me access to the treasures of the Parliamentary Library; to Dr. C. Frey of Windhoek for his capable supervision of the manuscript, and to those unknown friends of the country's history, who did not refuse their support when the Administrator appealed to them for assistance to cover the expense entailed.

The history of South West Africa up to 1890 is like a tangled skein. The author has done his best to unravel the threads of this skein and to spread them out neatly, side by side, for the benefit of those who are interested in it, in such a way that no recourse need be had to imagination in order to fill up missing gaps. Similarly, no place has been found for elegance of language, the twin brother of imagination. The aim of a history should be to present, in the clearest manner possible, occurrences and facts, and it is to the marshalling of these facts that great attention has been paid, and not to unessential ornamentation. If the reader should discover that, in the difficult processes of disentanglement, there remain still, here and there, a few knots in an occasional thread, he can temper his annoyance with the thought that the coming generation ought not to be deprived of all opportunity for research.

In a book of this kind, it is not possible to deal with important quotations from manuscript accounts and books of travel by merely referring to the literature itself, as is usually done in other books. These must be reproduced at length, because the early literature dealing with South West Africa is so difficult to obtain that far the greater majority of those who read this book will never have an opportunity of seeing it. This applies particularly to the quotations which have been taken from manuscript notes of the very earliest times, now fast becoming illegible. Maharero's letters, which he received from the chiefs of the country and from the Cape Government, or which he abstracted from the pockets of his defeated foes, have been collected and arranged in the South West Africa Administration's library. Very valuable evidence was obtained from them. Hendrik Witbooi's diary, which fell into Major Leutwein's hands during those never to be forgotten days of the Naukluft campaign in 1894, came into print through the efforts of the Scientific Society of South West Africa, and it, too, is a valuable source of historical information.

The reader should regard the click-sounds of the Nama tongue as non-existent, in so far as the spelling of the names of races and tribes is concerned, for, even if they were written with greater precision, that would hardly render him capable of pronouncing them himself.

Further, in expressing the singular and the plural, the only sensible system has been adopted, that of using simply the stems of the words, without prefixes and suffixes, and so the terms Omuherero, Ovaherero, or Hereros are not employed, but simply Herero; similarly Damara, Damra, Damaras, or Damarassen are not used, but simply Dama. The South West African Hottentot race is not called Namaqua, Namas, Naman, and so on, but just Nama.[1] It would be expecting too much of the reader to require him to learn the accidence of several of the native languages of South West Africa, as well as to peruse this book, which is not always light reading.

With the death of Jan Jonker in 1889 and of Maharero in 1890, early South West Africa came to an end. As, however, the German Empire came into South West Africa as early as 1884, the fact is referred to very briefly, although its advent belongs to a later period. The full historical importance of its coming will form the subject of a subsequent volume entitled 'German South West Africa'.

[1] This system has been departed from, to some small extent, in the translation. As it was found difficult to dispense with the plural entirely, Hereros, Damas, and Namas are used as its forms. Similarly, the term Ambo has been superseded by Ovambo and Ovambos, which are in common parlance amongst English people in South West Africa, besides which, *Ov*amboland appears on all modern maps.—*Ed.*

CONTENTS

PART III. HEREROLAND AGAINST NAMALAND

I. THE HERERO WAR OF FREEDOM AND THE ORLAM WAR

LIST OF ILLUSTRATIONS

PART I

NAMALAND AND HEREROLAND: OVAMBOLAND

I

DISCOVERY AND EXPLORATION

1. THE DISCOVERY OF THE COAST

ONE hundred kilometres north of Swakopmund in South West Africa there stands on a rocky crag a prominent stone cross. Before it stretches that mighty waste of waters known as the Atlantic Ocean, while behind it lies the terrible desert of the Namib sands. At the foot of the cross, thousands of seals bask in the sun on the white-scoured rocks. Looking southward, all that meets the eye is saltpans, stretching far away into the distance.

The meaning of this lonely cross is to be gathered from the inscription upon it in Latin and in Portuguese: 'Since the creation of the world 6684 years have passed and since the birth of Christ 1484 years and so the Illustrious Don Johannes has ordered this pillar to be erected here by Jacobus Canus, his knight.'

It was at this spot that the foot of the first European trod the shores of South West Africa. His name was Jacobus Canus (in Portuguese Diego Cão) and his King, John the Second of Portugal, had sent him to explore the west coast of Africa, which until that time had remained for the Occident a land of fable and of story. It is true that Arabian and Phoenician sailors, starting from the Pillars of Hercules and sailing southwards, had gained some knowledge of the coast of northern Africa, but their reports had encouraged no one to follow in their footsteps. Stories were told of enormous sea-monsters in the southern waters, monsters which could swallow ships whole, of heat so great that wooden ships burst into flames, of a magnetic mountain which drew the nails out of the ships' timbers and caused them to fall to pieces, of gigantic natives along the coast, who did not hesitate to devour any stranger who was rash enough to land.

If only there were accorded to the father of history, the worthy Greek, Herodotus, that measure of belief which is often squandered upon less worthy individuals, it would be learnt from chapter xlii of Book IV of his *History* that the Egyptian Pharaoh, Necho, had effectually succeeded in having the whole of Africa circumnavigated, with the Red Sea as a starting-point, 600 years before the birth of Christ. His expedition, which consisted of Phoenicians, returned after three years through the Pillars of Hercules and had nothing to relate about

these alleged dangers. What they did report, and that with considerable conviction, was that the Continent of Africa, which was called
Libya in ancient times, had a southern limit round which it was
possible to sail, and it was just this that the Portuguese wanted to
put to the test. Herodotus writes:

'It is clear that Libya, with the exception of that part which borders on
Asia, is surrounded by the ocean, and Necho, the King of Egypt, was, so far
as we know, the first to prove this. When he stopped work on the canal,
which was to have connected the Nile with the Arabian Gulf, he sent out a
ship, manned by Phoenicians, with orders to make their return journey
through the Pillars of Hercules and thus to find their way back to Egypt
through the Mediterranean Sea. The Phoenicians set out, accordingly, from
the Red Sea and sailed into the southern seas. When the sowing season
approached they made a landing, cultivated the soil just where they chanced
to be, and waited for the harvest. When they had reaped their wheat, they
voyaged further and, during the third year of their absence, rounded the
Pillars of Hercules and reached Egypt. One story which they told, however,
was—and I cannot believe it, although others may possibly do so—that upon
their voyage round Libya they kept the sun on their right hand.'

The interest which the Portuguese showed in solving the problem
of the circumnavigation of southern Africa did not spring from any
urge towards scientific exploration. It sprang rather from the desire
to acquire the riches of unknown nations and to open a trade route
to far-distant India, whose spices, silks, carpets, ivory, gold, and
precious stones were much sought after in the markets of Europe.
Until then these articles of commerce had been obtained by road
through Mesopotamia and Persia, with great danger and loss, or had
been carried in Arabian ships through the Red Sea to Egypt, whence
they were shipped to Alexandria, and thence taken to Genoa by the
ships of Venetian business houses. Portugal was anxious to secure this
trade for herself, but she could only do that if she could find a sea
route to India, with which no other power could interfere. Was not
a sea route of this kind likely to be discovered should southern Africa
prove to be circumnavigable? It was essential to make perfectly
sure on this point. Henry the Navigator had previously sent one
expedition after another to explore the west coast. By feeling their
way little by little, the Portuguese had, prior to Henry's death in
1460, become acquainted with fully 500 leagues of the coast.

In the year 1482 John the Second dispatched his knight, Jacob
Canus, and he reached the Congo and returned to Lisbon the following year with several natives from that part. Between the years 1484

and 1486, the same explorer embarked upon a second voyage, which took him as far as Cape Cross. The leaders of previous expeditions had erected wooden crosses at their landing places as tokens of the sovereignty of the Portuguese crown, and now the order was given that stone crosses should be carried to every such place and erected there as tokens of occupation. It was on this second voyage that Canus erected the first monument to European power upon South West African soil.

If one were to consider what induced him to erect the cross at just this desolate spot on the sea-shore, one could only come to the conclusion that, while sailing close to the coast, he saw that the shore was inhabited. There were not really people there, as he must have imagined, but thousands of seals, which crowded the rocks and dived about in the waves in search of food.

In answer to a further inquiry as to whether there were any natives living at Cape Cross at that time, one can deduce from the old reports, which John de Barros collected and published, that Canus made some exploratory journeys into the interior and found there several native men, whom he took with him and brought to Lisbon. All explorers had instructions to capture a few natives whenever they could and to bring them back to Portugal. The idea was that they would become acquainted with the method of living of a civilized nation, acquire its language, learn to understand the kind of wares the Portuguese were seeking in distant seas, of which gold was the most important, and that they should be taken back to their homes, supplied with this knowledge, to be available as interpreters and advisers to the ships calling there. If Canus took natives with him from Cape Cross, they must have been Saan-Bushmen or Namas, who were living by catching fish and seals in that neighbourhood, or perhaps Hereros, who had come down to the sea along the course of the Omaruru River, which forms the boundary of the southern Kaokofeld, with the object of obtaining salt from the large saltpans of the coastal area. In this instance the old records contain no precise information regarding the kind of people who were taken along.

With the passing of time the cross became very weather-beaten. In order to preserve it, it was taken by the German Government to Kiel in 1893, and it is now kept in the Oceanographical Museum at Berlin. A perfect copy of it in granite was made upon the instructions of Kaiser Wilhelm the Second, and this has been erected at the very spot where the Portuguese cross had stood.

It ought to be mentioned that the scientific adviser of Jacob Canus was the 'famous Portuguese knight, Martin Behaim of Nuremberg'. He was a pupil of the astronomer, Regiomontanus, from whom he learnt, by means of an astrolabe, to determine the situation of a ship in mid-ocean from the position of the stars. He emigrated to Portugal and accompanied Canus on his first voyage to the Congo. It is, however, very doubtful indeed whether he went to Cape Cross. After his return to Nuremberg he erected a mighty globe, upon which he mapped out the newly discovered lands of Africa, correctly as far as the Congo. Beyond this, his recordings were either taken over from older maps or freely invented and they do not stand the test of scientific investigation. Still it is to a note on his globe that we are indebted for the information that the ship in which he travelled 'continually south and then towards the setting sun' (the Gulf of Guinea) carried with it all kinds of merchandise for trade with the natives, besides 'eighteen horses with costly equipment, as presents for the Moorish kings, and all kinds of spices for the purpose of showing the Moors and getting them to understand what it is we are seeking in their country'.

Amongst the 'Moorish Kings', John the Second was hoping to find the Priest-king, John, about whom the literature of the time has so many stories. This priest-king was supposed to be a Christian and to reign over a Christian Moorish nation. John the Second was anxious to enter into an alliance with him against the Arabs and then, with his help, to make the continuance of their caravan trade between India and Europe impossible. He did not suspect that the Priest-king John, the Negus of Abyssinia, for he was the person referred to, could not possibly be reached from the west coast of Africa.

The accounts which Canus brought back with him about the coast of South West Africa, by no means discouraged King John the Second. On the contrary, they increased his hopes that a further expedition would succeed in reaching and circumnavigating the southernmost point of Africa and would thus open up a sea route to the Indies. In 1486 he sent out a further expedition. This consisted of two ships, each of 50 tons capacity, one of which was a commissariat ship, for it had been learnt by experience that the provision of a commissariat ship was essential in order to obviate a premature return from want of the necessaries of life. Bartolomas Diaz, a knight of the royal court, was given the command of this fleet. He had previously made a number of voyages along the coast of Africa and was

thus not without experience. His brother was the commander of the
commissariat ship.

On these ships were two negroes, who had been taken to Portugal,
and had to be taken back again to their homes after receiving a
measure of instruction. Diaz likewise took with him from the coast
of Guinea four negresses with the intention of landing them at convenient spots as he voyaged farther. In doing this he was actuated
by the following conclusion: the negresses, wherever they were landed,
would not run the same danger of losing their lives as would the
men; they would tell strange tribes what they had seen and heard,
and thus spread the fame of the Portuguese and their trading pro-
jects; they would allow themselves to be put ashore, with a promise
that they would be fetched again in a few months' time, more readily
than men could be expected to do, and then there could be learnt
from them what they had seen and heard regarding the native tribes
of the interior.

The first of the negresses Diaz landed at Angra Pequeña (Luderitz
Bay)—an indication that he came across some natives there. There
he made a stone cross out of shell-lime and erected it on a lofty crag
at the place which to-day bears the name of Diaz Point, and then he
sailed on to Angra das Voltas, as the mouth of the Orange River is
called on old maps. There he landed the second negress. History
does not relate what happened to these two women. Diaz was not
able to keep his promise to fetch them and take them home again.
A violent storm, which lasted thirteen days, drove him and his little
fleet far towards the west and, when he turned east again with the
object of reaching the west coast of Africa, it was not to be found.
It turned out that he had rounded the southernmost point. Steering
a northerly course, he reached the coast again and followed it as far
as the Great Fish River, and there he saw numbers of natives and
large herds of cattle, but he was forced by his mutinous crew to
return. In memory of the storm he had weathered, he called the
southern cape 'The Cape of Storms', but King John the Second
named it 'The Cape of Good Hope', because it had been established
that the continent of Africa could be circumnavigated, and he had
good hopes that a further advance (this was effected by Vasco da
Gama in 1497–9) would reveal that the way to the Indies lay open.

The cross on Diaz Point stands as a monument to this voyage,
which brought men from Europe on to the soil of South West Africa
for the second time. It is proved to have stood there undamaged

until 1821, although by that time the inscription had become obliterated, but in 1825 Capt. Owen found it thrown down and broken.
The pieces were brought to Capetown. When the Portuguese
consul at that place laid claim to them on behalf of the Portuguese
Crown, a settlement was arrived at whereby the lower portion of the
pillar was to remain in the museum at Capetown, while the upper
part was to be sent to Lisbon. It is kept there in the Geographical
Society's museum.

2. THE EXPLORATION OF THE COAST: THE *GRUNDEL*

The bays and desolate coasts of South West Africa held very little
attraction for their first discoverers and for those who followed them.
India was found and it was upon this that the real interests of navi-
gators were centred. If there were not to be found on the shores of
South West Africa even water and firewood, slaughter stock and
slaves, to say nothing of gold and gems, it was sheer waste of time to
pay it any further attention. It is therefore not surprising that
accounts of expeditions undertaken by Portugal cease with the reports
of the first two voyages of discovery. It is, however, worthy of
mention that, as early as the year 1489, a German, named Henricus
Martellus, issued a map which contains the earliest representation of
South West Africa and actually makes use of Diaz's voyages. Naturally it contains just the merest indications of the spots which had
become known on the coast, such as Cape Cross, Diaz Point, the
mouth of the Orange River, and even perhaps Walfish Bay. No information at all is given about the interior. The illustrated maps which
were published in later years give, in increasing numbers, new names
to the islands lying off the coast and to the landing-places for ships.
This proves that ships passed up and down the coast more frequently
than the lack of old records would have led one to suppose. When we
learn that 294 ships were dispatched to India and South America in
the early years of Don Manoel's reign, we must take it that the
travellers to India contributed in some measure to the further exploration of the west coast. It must likewise be borne in mind that an
extraordinarily large number of whales inhabited the coastal waters,
and an old memorandum in Janson's large Atlas (1657) makes mention
of French and English ships which set out for that coast on whaling
expeditions.

Meanwhile, the Hollanders had settled at the Cape in 1652, and
the Dutch East India Company, with its Council of Seventeen, sent

its merchantmen to the East Indian islands. With the object of supplying fresh water, vegetables, and meat for this long voyage, gardens and farms were established at the Cape and a flourishing trade with the local Hottentots sprang up. This Company showed a keen interest in the further exploration of the west coast and dispatched from Table Bay two ships for this purpose: the *Grundel* in 1670 and the *Bode* in 1677.

The captain of the *Grundel*, G. R. Muys, received orders to sail as far as the tropics, to make a careful survey of all landing-places along the coast and to ascertain how far the settlements of the Hottentots extended to the north and where the country of the Kaffirs commenced. He was also to look out for places where vegetables and firewood could be got. The cargo contained articles of barter and presents for the natives, and the order was not omitted that 'some of these natives were to be bartered or purchased as slaves, as was done by the yacht *Hasselt* in the year 1657, when she sailed from the fatherland, which slaves still serve the Honourable Company day by day'.

The *Grundel* sailed in March 1670. Mention is made in the ship's log again and again of the thick fog, which obscured the visibility for ships sailing along the coast, of the extraordinary number of whales, and of the dangerous seas. The *Grundel* reached the coast of South West Africa on the 14th April and the log records wind accompanied by heavy showers of rain. She made land on the 26th April at Angra Pequena (Luderitzbucht) but nothing particular was either seen or experienced on the shore. The bay was totally uninhabited. Sandwich Harbour was reached on the 1st May and the captain landed with two others. They saw five natives who had a dog with them. When they beckoned them to approach, they ran away. They followed them up and found between the sand dunes, which had a few green shrubs growing on them, three small native huts and, standing next to them, ten men, who waved to them with a stick to which an animal tail had been fastened. (Evidently the Hottentot's fly-swatter, which consists of a small stick with a jackal's tail attached and is still used to-day.) The natives came leaping and dancing past; they were armed with assegais, bows, and arrows. The threatening attitude which they adopted caused one of the captain's companions to point his musket at them, but the powder refused to kindle. A stab in the chest incapacitated him; he threw his gun away, pulled the assegai out of his chest with both hands and took it with him,

and the three men ran to the shore. They were pursued by the
natives, who did not, however, succeed in overtaking them. These
natives were 'very greasy and of a yellow colour; they wore skin
clothes and had their hair smeared with fat. Their words were not,
however, pronounced in the throat as is the case with Hottentots.
We could only come to the conclusion that they had never seen any
people other than those of their own tribe.' The hostile attitude
might likewise justify the conclusion that encounters with people of
other races had previously occurred and that their recollection of
what had taken place on those occasions was not a very happy one.

On 2nd May the *Grundel* sailed northwards and held that course
until the 4th of that month. The log records the following: 'We saw
land, which was very sandy, but could see no opening of the nature
of a bay or a river, and so we decided that, since with the help of God
we had got as far as this and since the land hereabouts is still inhabited
by Hottentots, we would halt and would, with God's help, commence
our homeward voyage with as little delay as possible.'

On 26th May the *Grundel* made Table Bay once again without
having effected any further investigation of the coast.

3. THE *BODE*

The results of the *Grundel*'s explorations did not satisfy the direc-
tors of the Dutch East India Company. Some seven years later (1677),
the *Bode* was fitted out with wares for trade and exchange, with iron
bars, and with provisions for six months. The captain, C. Th. Wobma,
received an advance upon the crew's wages to the amount of 200
rixdollars and a further 100 rixdollars for the purchase of vegetables
and fresh meat.

His orders were to survey the whole west coast as far as Somberia
in Portuguese Angola and to make a map of it. Most particularly
was he to have regard to the places where fresh water and firewood
were to be obtained in addition to cattle, sheep, rice, and millet. He
was likewise to bring back with him reliable information as to 'where
the Hottentots ended and the Kaffirs began, and whether these
waged war against each other, what kind of farms and houses they
had, what sort of weapons they used, what they lived on, whether
they cultivated anything and other matters of this kind'. In the
Portuguese Colony they were to let nothing at all leak out regarding
their orders and the results of their efforts, and 'always to bear in
mind that the Portuguese are false friends of ours'. Should it prove

at all possible to obtain some slaves by barter, that would be a most desirable transaction, because it would be possible to find out from them what they grew in their country and what was imported into it. The captain must employ the utmost diligence both in greeting them in a kindly manner, while ensuring that they did not have the opportunity of taking him or his sailors by surprise. He was to consult the Hottentots, who had accompanied him from Capetown, what the best way of dealing with the natives was, and what could be achieved with beads, tobacco, and strong liquors.

In this context, it sounds rather strange when the orders proceed in this wise: 'It is not to be forgotten that God's holy name must be invoked both morning and evening, for everything is dependent upon God's blessing. Steps must be taken against drunkenness, gambling, and cheating and these offences must be punished most severely. Be yourself a pattern of goodness and, then, we think that God helping you, good will prevail.' Then this warning is added: 'It is our wish that you should be imbued with heedfulness and zeal to the greatest possible extent.'

On 20th January, 1677, the *Bode* sailed from Table Bay. On the 17th February she anchored off the coast of South West Africa in a small sandy bay,

'where we landed with our men and found that there was nothing but a sandy dune country. We decided, therefore, to go inland, which we then did. After we had proceeded about half a mile, we found human foot-prints. When we had followed these foot-prints and traced them for a short half mile, we saw quite 16 to 18 people and we sent the Hottentots, who had come with us, to them. Thereupon these people came running towards our Hottentots with assegais poised in their hands, and this was a sign of courage, seeing that our Hottentots were provided with similar weapons and that we were close behind them with our well-armed followers. Then the afore-mentioned natives tried to talk and, because these people could only under-stand our Hottentots with difficulty, I took them with me to the shore, where our boats lay, and we showed them every kindness by giving them tobacco and brandy; this latter they liked very much but they had little acquaintance with the smoking of tobacco. We asked them then whether they did not possess cattle, sheep, elephants' tusks, skins, or things of this kind, and they replied, so far as our Hottentots were able to understand them, that they had not, but that there was another tribe close at hand, with whom they were perpetually at war, and that these people had recently robbed them of their cattle. They said, further, that their huts were situated fully three to four days' journey inland. Thereupon I sent for the sloop *de Haeghman* and that reached us before mid-day. At mid-day about ten or twelve Hottentot women arrived on the scene with bags made out of seal's stomachs and bladders, filled with brackish, or rather with salt, water, which they gave their men-folk to drink. After they had been with us about half an hour, they betook themselves in the direction of the interior. These aforesaid people are real Hottentots, although their language is not by any means the same as that of our Hottentots. They wore karosses of hide and of seal skins, which had been washed ashore from the island. They wore, too, some kind of thing on their heads and they had chains made of ostrich shells and threaded on thin sticks hanging round their necks; to all appearances a poverty-stricken people and an extraordinarily dry country, where there is nothing to be got; it would be possible to gather the firewood which is scattered along the shore. These said people eat stinking seals and pounded herbs and similar wretched food. Many of them had small pieces of resin, which they had brought with them from the interior, so that there must undoubtedly be some trees further inland. So far as we were able to see and judge, there is nothing to be obtained here which could benefit our lords and masters in the very slightest degree, and all that there is to be found here is sand and stones, without vegetation, and a bad anchorage with fierce, stormy winds into the bargain. . . . Wherefore, if it should happen, which God forbid, that any of the Company's ships should make a landing and be forced to go in search of food or water or anything of that kind along this coast, they ought not to venture to come here, because our most diligent researches have shown that, between this and St. Helena Bay, there is nothing in the world to be got. . . .'

After riding out a storm and losing an anchor, Luderitzbucht was reached and inspected on the 22nd February. Nothing worthy of note was discovered there, and it was recorded that Boon Island 'could not be seen for the hundreds of thousands of sea-gulls, penguins, duikers, and seals, which were making it their residence'.

Sandwich Harbour was reached on the 5th March, the place from which the *Grundel* had turned back. A landing was effected with two well-manned boats at a spot which the natives indicated.

'When we were on the point of getting out of the boats, the said people took to their heels, leaving their possessions behind, namely a pot with some sort of pips in it that looked like pawpaw pips, nor could we come into communication with these said people. The purser and the second mate were sent out to see whether they could manage to get into conversation with them, and these went fully two miles inland, where they found that the said people had taken to flight, and discovered that there was nothing else to be seen there but an ostrich shell filled with water, which was fresh, and some bladders and pieces of seal meat, which were hanging up on a pole to dry.

We did them no harm whatsoever, but, on the contrary, we left a piece of tobacco and some pipes lying in their huts as a token of friendship. We returned to the boats, and I and others set to work with nets in an estuary or river and succeeded in catching many fish of various kinds. This aforesaid estuary is salt and its waters are mingled with the sea at high tide, but, at low tide, are separated from it by a sand-bank. We went on board ship again with the fish we had caught and all our people, and when we had been on board for a little while, fully 20 to 25 Hottentots again appeared on the shore and beckoned to us. We decided to land with one of our boats only, because we were of opinion that these people got frightened when we arrived there with more than one boat. When we reached them they remained stationary but they were very shy, so much so that we laid aside our guns and they their assegais, and our Hottentots threw their assegais away, too. We likewise put on the ground some strings of beads which we had brought with us, together with some tobacco and brandy, so as to gain their good graces, and this tobacco and brandy pleased them exceedingly, far more than it had the people of Grundel Bay. When we asked them whether they had cattle, they said that they had and suggested that we should go inland with them to their huts, but, as it was already evening, we decided against that and returned to the ship.'

Next day

'we proceeded to the shore with both boats, for the Hottentots were there calling and shouting to us. When we came up to them, without waiting for us, they withdrew inland and, when we followed them, we came to their huts, which were constructed with the bones of North-Cape whales and, since the said Hottentots run further and further on, we returned to our boats and all went on board again. When we had been on board for a short time, 20 to 25 Hottentots came down to the shore, bringing 12 to 16 cows with them. We proceeded to the land with both boats, taking with us some goods for barter; in addition to the purser and Mr. Willem van Dieden, our strength was between 15 and 16 men, armed with six muskets and four pistols. When we reached the shore, I started to trade with them and when I had exchanged two cows for a few things such as iron bars and beads, they took these things away and likewise drove the cattle off, taking with them, too, a small bag containing beads. When I saw this, I held one of them fast, whereupon the rest grasped their bows and arrows with the object of shooting at me or running me through the body with their assegais, and in fact arrows began to fly.

'I had two loaded pistols with me and I shot a Hottentot in the skin, causing him to retire three paces; fully a hundred arrows were then discharged at me, whereupon the purser, the mate, and the other members of the crew, and likewise our own Hottentots, came to my aid and thereupon the aforesaid natives took to their heels; very soon, however, they came to a halt and they threatened us with bows and arrows again, while we continued to shoot at them and wounded several of them, but of this they seemed to take very little notice, trying to rub their hurts away with their hands, and attempting to cut off our retreat to the boats. Thereupon we retired to the sloop, keeping up a continuous fire, arrived there with all our men, cut the painter, and rowed to the ship. It turned out that the purser and Mr. van Dieden, as well as the second mate and three or four of the sailors, were wounded by arrows, which were poisoned, but, since they had been shot through their clothing, it seemed as if most of the poison had been wiped off, so that very little damage resulted. We found that these people were so rash, or rather courageous, that they charged in the face of fire-arms, but we doubt very much whether they will readily come to such close quarters again, seeing that they have had a pretty fair experience of muskets and pistols.'

On the 9th March the *Bode* continued her course northwards along the coast. Walfish Bay was not sighted. The log records that some green trees were seen on hills some distance inland. On the 18th March the captain landed in Great Fish Bay. There he found pieces of broken pots and human footprints and likewise four huts resembling those at Sandwich Harbour, that is to say, made out of whale ribs. It was assumed that these belonged to Hottentots. Since the crew could not discover either water or firewood, but found only an abundance of fish, the voyage was continued on the 23rd March. On the 27th March the log states that, between 14 and 15 degrees S. Lat. (the highlands of Southern Angola), 'the Kaffirs commenced and the Hottentots came to an end'. Their attention having been attracted by smoke rising from the shore, they approached the coast, but they could not land because of the surf. Three or four black Kaffirs or negroes could be plainly seen walking on the shore. Since the *Bode* had by now left the shores of South West Africa, we are not going to follow her upon her further explorations and we will just mention that she came to anchor at Portuguese Sombrera on the 30th March. The return voyage to the Cape was commenced on the 8th April, without any intermediate landing being made, and the ship arrived back in Table Bay, safe and sound, on the 26th May.

The expeditions of the *Grundel* and the *Bode* terminated, so far as we know, with practically negative results. There was no possibility of establishing trade relations with the few natives who had been encountered. Neither of the ships was able to furnish any reliable information upon the question of 'where the Hottentots ended and the Kaffirs began'. The mouths of the Kuiseb, Swakop, and Omaruru

Rivers were not discovered. A landing at Walfish Bay would have enabled them to bring back a positive answer to the question regarding the boundary lines between the races, for sometimes it was the Swakop and sometimes the Kuiseb which formed the boundary line between the yellow-skinned Hottentots and the dark-coloured Hereros. Before the latter immigrated into Hereroland, however, it was the Omaruru River which formed the southern boundary of their home in the Koakoveld.

The Portuguese seemed to have been in possession of more detailed information about the natives of the interior. On ancient maps they call the northern part the Kingdom of Mataman. 'Ma' is evidently the prefix for the plural of all nouns signifying groups of people, and presumably it originates from an Angola dialect of the Bantu language; '-taman', however, corresponds with the word Dama, the term by which the Hottentots designate both the black Bergdamas and the chocolate-coloured Hereros. The Kingdom of Mataman is likewise called the land of the Simbebas, a word which is apparently identical with Tjimbas or Schimbas. To the present day the Ovambo tribes call Hereroland Ou-schimba and the Hereros refer to their impoverished fellow countrymen, who live in the Kaokoveld, as Tjimbas. The slave trade, in the course of which the Portuguese shipped to America, 10,000 to 15,000 natives from Angola and Ovamboland every year from the west coast, seems to have increased their knowledge of the interior considerably. Besides this, there must be called to mind a man who spent a remarkable life in close association with the tribes of the interior. This was the Englishman, Andrew Battels, who was taken prisoner by the Portuguese in Brazil in 1589. He was brought to Angola, put into the Portuguese colonial forces, and rose to the rank of sergeant. He does not seem, however, to have had a great liking for soldiering. Battels fled, but fell into the hands of the Jagga tribe, who took him with them on their military expeditions. He spent sixteen long months amongst these cannibals. During this time he was in Ovamboland as well, that being regarded by the Portuguese as a part of the Province of Ohuila, but the Jagga chieftain, Mazumbo Akalunga, really governing it. In the end, Battels succeeded in escaping both from the Jaggas and from the Portuguese. He returned to England and left behind him a detailed account of the native tribes with which he had come into contact. It is from him that the earliest information about Ovamboland is derived.

4. THE *MEERMIN*

The reports which the *Grundel* and the *Bode* brought back to Capetown were not calculated to strengthen the desire for forming connexions with the native races living in the north. The travellers of other countries found and depicted the shores of South West Africa as just as desolate and unapproachable as did the commanders of both these ships, for French, English, and Americans, too, did their share of coastal exploration. We have to thank the French Count, Maurepas, for the first map of Angra Pequena, dated 1733, and also for a description of the coast.

An English expedition under Sir H. R. Popham, which cruised the west coast of Africa during the years 1784 and 1786, mentions the cross at Angra Pequena, on which the inscription had, even at that early date, become illegible.

American whale hunters came and went with numerous ships, landed in the bays and even established small settlements in Walfish Bay and Swakopmund, without having left us any written records of their discoveries and experiences.

Then, in 1793, the Dutch Government dispatched the *Meermin* in order to forestall any occupation by foreign powers. Captain Duminy proclaimed the neighbourhood of Angra Pequena and Halifax Island as the property of the Dutch Government. He then cast anchor in Walfish Bay. On account of its being so rich in whales, this large and well-protected bay had been named by the Portuguese 'Bahia das Baleas'. The Hollanders translated this designation quite correctly into 'Walvischbaai', but the English subsequently garbled the word and spelt it 'Walwich Bay', which in turn gave rise to further errors, until the correct spelling was once more restored. The oldest Portuguese name of this stormy bay is, however, Rostro da Pedra, which means the ridge of rock.

The *Meermin* effected a landing in Walfish Bay on the 23rd January, 1793, and, on the 26th February, there followed the formal act of occupation of the Bay and the surrounding country by Captain Duminy in the name of the Dutch Government.

On the *Meermin* was Sebastian van Reenen, who was desirous of searching for precious metals in South West Africa. He had suggested to the English Government that it should take possession of all the harbours. Accompanying him was the hunter, Pieter Pienaar, who was undertaking a hunting expedition in the region of the lower Swakop. We shall hear more of him in another place. When Pienaar returned with information regarding the newly discovered river, he and van Reenen proceeded together by boat from Walfish Bay to the mouth of the Swakop. On account of the heavy surf, they were unable to land, and they returned to their ship without having effected anything. The following day, they sent three men on foot along the shore to the river mouth to find a landing-place, but they, too, returned without having found one, but they were loud in the praises of the 'splendid valley' and the good water which they had found there. They spoke, too, of five old huts which they had found in this valley, which they reckoned had been erected by English or Americans, for these people, when staying in Walfish Bay, used to fetch their water from the mouth of the Swakop. These three men saw not only luxuriant vegetation in the Swakop River mouth, but likewise great numbers of wild animals, such as elephants, rhinoceros, gemsbuck, and springbuck. Pieter Pienaar reported that large thickets of trees were to be found on the banks of the Swakop and so samples of the wood were taken and it was found that most of it was red, but some of it yellow. It is quite clear that the samples in question were those of camel-thorn and Ana trees.

Sebastian van Reenen, whose search for copper and gold was not successful, wanted very much to get into touch with the 'cattle-rich Hereros' of the interior with the object of organizing the export trade in cattle between South West Africa and St. Helena. This plan, however, miscarried.

In 1795 the English coasting vessel, *Star*, followed the course the *Meermin* had taken. In that same year the English had taken over the control of the Cape. They immediately advanced claims to be the masters and commanders of the South West African wastes. Only British vessels were allowed to catch whales and seals and a small cruiser was commissioned for the protection of the industry. The captain of the *Star*, Alexander, had had instructions to take possession of all the bays and landing-places of the west coast, as far as Angola, in the name of the British Government. He touched at Angra Pequena, Spencer Bay, Walfish Bay, and two other bays to the northwards, hoisted the British flag, fired three salvoes, and turned over a few spadefuls of soil. Very few natives were met and, with these few, it was not possible to come into contact. Whaling, so far as it was conducted by foreign ships, with their headquarters on Possession Island, ceased entirely, but it flourished, under English control, for a further thirty years. In course of time, quite a considerable barter trade developed between the ships' crews and the Hottentots of Walfish Bay and Angra Pequena. During the time that Napoleon was at St. Helena, supplies of meat were imported from South West Africa. Previously St. Helena had obtained its requirements from Benguella.

As the leading facts of the history of the discovery and exploration of the South West African coastline have now been dealt with, we shall turn to the exploration of the interior.

5. JACOBUS COETSE AND HENDRIK HOP

The exploration of the South West African coast by the Portuguese, Hollanders, and other seafaring nations had revealed no road by which it was possible to penetrate the interior from the coast. The desolate waterless Namib desert had persistently barred the way. The mouths of the Orange, Kuiseb, Swakop, and Omaruru Rivers afforded the only possible opportunities for lifting the veil of mystery from the direction of the coast, but these entrance gates remained for a long time undiscovered and, after their discovery, unused.

It appeared as if the only possible approach to the interior of South West Africa was overland from South Africa. South Africa, itself, however, possessed wide areas which were totally unexplored. The boundaries of the youthful Dutch colony could be extended northwards only very gradually. The dangers to which travellers were exposed at the hands of hostile Saan Bushmen and Hottentots, and the desolate character of the northern territories placed a check upon all desire for exploration. The natives, and more especially the Hottentots, who had come from far distant parts, were very thoroughly interrogated, but anything that could be learnt from them was neither important nor encouraging. A story was continuously current to the effect that there were copper deposits in the north and that, some ten days' journey beyond the Copper Mountains, the perennial waters of the great Garib (Orange) River flowed down to the sea. The Hottentots even brought to Governor Simon van der Stel (1678–99) samples of copper ore and specimens of the sand of the 'Great River', which were highly mineralized. Thereupon Simon van der Stel himself set out, accompanied by a large escort, to make investigations at these very places. He reached the Copper Mountains of Little Namaqualand, proceeded from there to the sea and, as he found on the shore many stranded tree-trunks and great quantities of firewood, he came to the conclusion that there must be a large

CHAP. I DISCOVERY AND EXPLORATION 19

river in the vicinity. The mouth of the Orange River (Angra das Voltas), however, he did not succeed in discovering. It was only in 1739 that the 'Great River' was discovered by some of the colonists.

The stories that these people told of the existence of large quantities of game in the vicinity of the Orange River aroused in Jacobus Coetse the desire to hunt them. He was a farmer at Piquetberg and also a keen hunter. He decided to go on an elephant hunting expedition to the Orange River, for which project he obtained the Government's permission. A number of Hottentots were prepared to go with him. Amongst them was a Bastard, named Klaas Barends, who, owing both to his character and to his knowledge of languages, was specially qualified to be foreman of the Hottentots. Jacobus Coetse got through to the Orange River, found the Lion River and followed its course inland, until he reached the hot springs of the present-day Warmbad. From there he hunted for a further day's journey northwards as far as a mountain which consisted entirely of black stones. From there he turned back along his own track. He had killed two elephants only, but he brought back valuable information. The Namas told him that, some ten days' journey beyond the black mountains, there lived a black race. They were called Damrocquas (Dama implies Herero or Bergdama in the Hottentot tongue). They had long hair and wore linen clothes. The distinguishing characteristics which were given did not entirely agree, but it was interesting to learn where, more or less, 'the Hottentots ceased and the Kaffirs began'. Jacobus Coetse found the first giraffes there and became acquainted with the tree, from the leaves and tender shoots of which the giraffes obtain their food. He named it the camel-thorn tree because the giraffe was, in Cape Dutch, spoken of as the wild camel. He found the Namas in Warmbad peaceful and sociable. There was no mistaking the fact that the Cape Government had an appreciable influence right up the banks of the Orange River, for it was only when he mentioned to the Namas that he had obtained permission from the Governor to go hunting that they became somewhat suspicious of him. They were exceedingly anxious to obtain iron for the manufacture of arrow points and assegais.

The report of this bold hunter was keenly debated at the Cape and the Governor himself, Ryk Tulbagh, showed a great deal of interest in it. He decided that a visit should be paid to the 'black people with long hair and linen clothing'. Volunteers were sought for participation in a scientific expedition for the purpose of exploring the country north of the Orange River. Hendrik Hop, the captain of the Burgher Forces at Stellenbosch, was entrusted with the leadership of the expedition. The land surveyor, Brink, had to keep a diary and frame a map of the route. J. A. Auge of Stolberg in the Harz, the director of the Capetown botanical gardens, was to investigate the flora. Dr. Rykvoet (pronounced Rakefoot) was appointed as doctor and mineralogist. Marais, who had been acquainted with the Hottentot language from his earliest days, was given the post of interpreter. He and Roos were given the task of taking due note of the native tribes, their customs, and habits. Nor did the hunter, Jacobus Coetse, miss the opportunity of accompanying the expedition and of reaching once again, in the capacity of guide and hunter, the hunting-grounds of the north. The expedition was made up of 17 Europeans, 68 Hottentots, and 15 ox-wagons. A start was made from Capetown on the 16th July, 1761. They crossed the Orange River by what is known to-day as Ramans Drift and arrived at Warmbad on the 5th October. They rested there until the 10th October and on the 11th they reached the 'black mountain' where Jacobus Coetse had turned back. The route from there led between the Great and Little Karras Mountains and, on the 22nd October, they made their camp close to a Nama settlement on the Lion River. The banks of the river were well wooded: rhinoceroses, giraffes, buffaloes, zebras, quaggas, kudus, elands, hartebeests, and gnus afforded wonderful opportunities for hunting. Coetse and Marais were sent ahead, as being the members of the expedition best acquainted with the natives, to solve the problem of water and grazing for the continuation of the journey. They reached the Fish River and reported that it was quite dry. They could not get any information at all about the long-haired black people in linen clothing. The Namas on the Fish River knew nothing about them. They did say that people called the Tamaquas (Hereros or Bergdamas) lived to the northward. These bore scars on their chests and backs, wore karosses of skins, and lived in wooden huts. They heard about other races: they were called Sondamroquas (Gam-dama, i.e. Seadama, a tribe of the Bergdamas) and Birinas (*birin*, meaning a goat, implying the Bechuanas, who got this Nama name from their goat farming). Further, they discovered that smallpox, to which so many Hottentots in the Cape had succumbed in 1755, had been very bad in South West Africa.

After the receipt of this report, which was very unencouraging, the leader of the expedition decided to relinquish the search for the mythical people of the north, seeing that drought and lack of grazing were threatening disaster. The return journey was commenced on the 7th December and, after some further investigations of the copper deposits in Little Namaqualand, the travellers arrived at the Cape on the 27th April, 1762.

The results of this expedition, which had got as far as Heinabis to the southward of Keetmanshoop, were not important. In any event, the tale of the people 'with long hair and in linen clothing' was exploded and had thus lost its fascination. The cattle-breeding Herero race had taken its place.

Surveyor Brink's map must, however, be regarded as the oldest map of Namaland. It made its first appearance at a later date as a supplement to the botanist Patterson's book. Patterson, too, crossed the Orange River (14th October, 1779) and reached a spot several days' journey north of Warmbad. His remarks are of the very driest kind and are utterly useless for the purposes of this book. The map, however, though it actually contains little enough, is never-the-less interesting. At the Orange River a mighty elephant is drawn in order to indicate how rich that region was in large game of this kind. A picture of a Bushman settlement, with four huts, appears in the south west corner of the Namib. This is supposed to indicate that the map maker apportioned the south-western Namib to the Saan Bushmen. Unless appearances are deceptive, the framework which extrudes from the huts is clearly made of whale ribs, while the huts are plainly recognizable as mere protections against the wind. In an adjoining bay, seals are climbing out of the sea onto the land. To the north of the Bushmen, appears the picture of a large Nama settlement. In a circular village composed of mat huts are to be seen numbers of cattle. A large number of people, of both sexes and all ages, are engaged in a reed dance to the accompaniment of reed flutes. The mouth of the Orange River, which is called the Garieb, is not shown at all, but, instead of it, there appears in the margin this note: 'The mouth of the river may be expected to be found close to the two small mountains, which stand by themselves in flat country.' The Fish River appears as a tributary of the Orange, without any place-names, but with numerous water-holes indicated on both banks; farther on is shown the Lion River with the places Modderfontein or Heinabes, Bokkenfontein, Rhenosterfontein, Hoenderfontein, and Bergfontein on the western bank. On the eastern bank lie Warmbad, Ababeerfontein, Rietfontein, and Riet Vallei.

The Kaikaap River is drawn with special care; on it a giraffe is feeding on a camel-thorn tree and a note is made to the effect that Surveyor Brink and his comrades had given this river the name 'Great River', which does not seem to be quite correct, for 'Great River' is merely a translation of the Nama name Kaikaap (*Gei-ab*=great river). The Buffel River is shown as the northernmost water-course, and on it lies the most northerly point of Namaqualand, as it was then known, which is called Keerom (the turning-point).

6. H. J. WIKAR

For the history of exploration of South West Africa attention must now be paid to a man, who, without instructions or mission, travelled extensively, one who, most probably, did not penetrate to distant parts from a love of hunting, nor yet was driven by a scientific urge, but one who was, by the mere longing for freedom, induced to exchange the monotonous existence of a clerk in the office of the Dutch East India Company in Capetown for a freer life in the wide open spaces of Africa. The name of this man is H. J. Wikar. He was a Swede from Gothenburg. He left his clerical position in 1775, was condemned as a deserter, and was pursued by the police. Like many other adventurers of that time, he fled to the border of the Cape Settlement and lived by hunting. He passed the years 1778 and 1779 on the banks of the Orange River. He came into contact with many native tribes and he acquired an insight into and knowledge of their circumstances, such as no rapidly travelling explorer could possibly have obtained. Rumours of his experiences came to the ears of the Governor von Plettenberg (1771–85) and he decided to pardon Wikar and to obtain from him a detailed account of his experiences. He returned to Capetown in 1779. His report is to be found in two editions. The first appears to be Wikar's own record in diary form, while the second is clearly a transcript made for the purposes of the Dutch East India Company.

The reader gets a very favourable impression of Wikar's personality. From the portrayal of his associations with the natives, the conclusion must be drawn that he possessed fine mental qualities. The attention with which he recorded everything which came to his notice displayed a keen and observant intellect. The way in which he overcame difficulties, a matter which he mentions with great modesty, reveals great strength of purpose. The reasonable manner in which he represents things creates confidence, and strengthens the conviction that what he says is worthy of the most serious attention. It is true that the map of South West Africa received few additions through his efforts, but his report is a mine of information for the scholar who is seeking for knowledge of the ancient dwelling-places of Nama tribes and Hottentots and of their habits of life, views, and customs. It may be assumed that Wikar was not acquainted with the Hottentot language, nor had he the knowledge to enable him to write down phonetically the sounds of the tribe and place-names. In this respect, however, even well-educated people of that time did not do much better. The phonetic transcription of the Hottentot tongue was only accomplished about a hundred years later, after its grammar had been made the subject of careful research. It is only possible to deal here with that portion of Wikar's voluminous writings which is of particular value from the point of view of South West Africa's history. We must perforce pass over the remainder of his report, which contains observations and experiences not concerned with South West Africa, as being irrelevant.

In September 1778, in the neighbourhood of the Orange River, Wikar came into contact with some Hottentots, who were desirous of crossing the river at a place called Goodhouse (*Gu-daus* = sheepdrift) and of proceeding into Great Namaqualand with the object of exchanging beads and pearls for cattle. Klaas Barends, with whom we have previously become acquainted as the man who accompanied both the hunter, Jacobus Coetse, and Hendrik Hop's expedition to Namaqualand, was with these people. Wikar joined the party, and he was all the more welcome because his gun promised protection against the attacks of robbers. Klaas Barends became Wikar's interpreter and trusty guide. He learnt, upon many a hunting trip, to know the banks of the Orange River and the Hottentot and Bushman tribes, which inhabited them, very thoroughly. Before we proceed to group together the people of South West Africa, who came within the reach of his cognizance, it is necessary to say a few words about the correct writing down of the names of tribes, for, without a prefatory note of this kind, the names would be quite worthless. It is by no means easy to identify the races of South West Africa with whom we are actually acquainted and there is a constant temptation to give rein to the imagination concerning the tribal distinctions of early South West Africa, entirely strange and unknown to us as they are.

Note on Tribal Names

Since the earliest times it is the clicks in the Hottentot words which have made it difficult to write them. Either they have been left out altogether or they have been represented by other letters, selected quite arbitrarily, as for instance *s, t, tk, g, k, c,* &c. It is clear that this method of substitution was adopted because of the difficulty of imitating and pronouncing the clicks themselves, for which reason sounds would be produced involuntarily which differed from the sounds which were actually the original ones, and then these incorrect sounds would be reproduced on paper.

The final syllables of place and tribal names presented a second difficulty. When dealing with a language of an entirely new order, only the stem-syllable of race or place-names ought to be written; prefixes and suffixes should be omitted, for they only create confusion. It is, however, not so simple to recognize these prefixes and suffixes. It has come about, therefore, that the numerous names of the Hottentot tribes, who used to inhabit the Cape, were written in so erroneous and muddled a fashion that it is practically impossible to introduce any order into this confusion, the more so since the very word-stems were written differently by the various writers. Indeed, the very same writer frequently writes the self-same name in so many different ways that it is only after intensive study that it becomes possible to prove that he was not endeavouring to write the names of three or four different tribes, but that of one only.

One example should be sufficient to afford an insight into this confusion. The Herero race was called 'Dama' by the Namas and by the Hottentots. The Bergdamas, who lived to the north of the Kuiseb, however, were likewise called 'Dama'. Evidently, when the Namas in olden times came into contact with black people from the north, they perceived no difference between these two races. When they came to realize that, although they both had dark-coloured skins, they ought to be distinguished from each other, they added to the word Dama a qualification, and from then onwards they called the Bergdamas *Chou Dama*, i.e. the dirty Damas, and the cattle-breeding Hereros *Gomacha Dama*, i.e. the Damas who were rich in cattle.

Now, in the script of the old reports, we find the most incomprehensible forms of this simple tribal name. We read of Tma, Tama, Damra, Tamara, Damara, Damraqua, Tamracqua, Sambdama, Zountamas, Sondama, yet in each instance 'Dama' is meant.

So far as endings are concerned,

Damab means a Herero man,
Damas means a Herero woman,
Damara means two Herero women,
Damagu means several Herero men.

Damagua is an old euphonious form employed to end a sentence in place of the form Damagu, i.e. Herero men. It is to this euphonious form that the appearance of the ending *qua* in the old Hottentot tribal names is to be ascribed. When answering the question in reference to Nama men: What people are those?, the only reply which could be given to the questioner was 'Namagua', that is to say, those are Nama men. When the same question was put regarding two Herero or Bergdama women, no other answer could be given than 'Damara', which means: those are two Dama women.

From all this, it is perfectly plain that it would be entirely wrong to use the current nomenclature blindly in a scientific work and thus to perpetuate error. The same rule must be laid down for the Bantu languages, with their prefixes to nouns. Unless either the whole position is to become absurd or, through employing the prefixes correctly, the reader is to be burdened with the task of studying the syntax of Bantu speech, only the word-stems should be used and the prefixes discarded. It is, for instance, quite impossible to speak of 'one Ovambo', because 'Ovambo' is plural, the singular being Omuambo. It is far more correct to say 'the Ambo' or 'the Ambo man', 'the Tjimba' (not Omutjimba or Ovatjimba), 'the Herero', and so on.

These prefatory remarks are necessary, firstly because it was essential that what had to be said should once and for all be said, and then again because the reader is now no longer unprepared to encounter the names of the inhabitants of South West Africa, which Wikar's valuable records have preserved for our benefit. The following three Nama tribes, which were living in South West Africa in 1778, were known to him:

1. The Kamigou, who were leading a nomadic existence, some to the north and some to the south of the Orange River, on the high ground near Warmbad. These are the Gami-nun (*gami* = bundle, *nu* = black) or Bondelswarts. Wikar writes the terminal *u* of the tribal name *ou*, in the French way, as did many of his other contemporaries.

2. The Tkabobe; their dwelling-place was situated to the north of the Bondelswarts. Wikar tries to write the name Hawobe(n). This is the tribe of the Veldskoendraërs (Veldshoe-wearers), who, according to tribal tradition, were the first to acquire the art of providing sandals, which had been the usual foot-gear until then and merely protected the sole of the foot, with a skin to protect the instep, and thus to manufacture proper shoes (*hawon*).

3. The Keikao: Wikar likewise writes Keykao, Thaykoa, and Thaykao. He knew that this tribe had its grazing-grounds some seventeen or eighteen days' journey from the Company's Ford (Ramansdrift, where the Company's wagon, i.e. Hendrik Hop's expedition, crossed the Orange River). This tribe, he said, was the leading Nama tribe.

'It is only the Sandamas (which he calls in other places Sondamas, Samdamas, and Sambdamas) and those who live close to the sea, who fail to acknowledge allegiance to the chief of this tribe and even make war on him and steal his stock.' The people referred to here are the Gei-kou(n), who lived in Hatsamas and Hoachanas and called themselves 'The Red Nation'. Their chief was the superior of the other Nama chieftains. The Sandamas or Samdamas are the Bergdamas, who lived beside the sea (*gam* = water, sea) and the Saan, of whom we shall hear something later.

4. About the Thaboek, Wikar learnt that they were

'people who are poor, who lived in the bush and roamed about in all directions. There are some of these people who live amongst the Hottentots and are employed by them in various capacities, more especially as mercenaries in war, and these usually remain connected with the tribe to which they had attached themselves. If there is no war in progress, they receive remuneration in the shape of meat and other food, but in war-time they receive a share of the booty which is taken, and thus they acquire some cattle of their own. Their principal means of subsistence is, however, provided through hunting the rhinoceros, the hippopotamus, and other game, and catching fish in the rivers, and partly, too, through the theft of stock from Hottentots, other than those amongst whom they are living. Others of this race, who have no fixed abode among the Hottentots, are frightened of their fellow men and are of a murderous disposition. They are to be found chiefly in the mountains, the forests, and the deserts, where they subsist on snakes, hedgehogs, mice, and other queer foodstuffs, which other Tkaboeks (another spelling of the name!) refrain from doing. Amongst this race, which is of very small stature and rather lighter than others, many of the women and children have red cheeks. Still, because of the terrible poverty which they have to endure, they often become emaciated and often the women have hardly larger breasts than the men.'

This mysterious race, which lived partly in bondage with the Nama and partly roamed the desert as freebooters, calls to mind the tame and wild Saan Bushmen of the Cape. They were known as the Hawu(n), which means the wanderers. The people so indicated are the Saan of the Namib Desert, who were oppressed by the Namas, but yet inhabited the Namib and the areas adjacent to it in considerable numbers. To-day there are only a few miserable survivors of that race; they speak the Nama language, and they have preserved the old ideas and customs of the Namas, which the latter have abandoned and forgotten long ago. To some extent they have intermarried with the Namas but, as an independent tribe, they were almost entirely exterminated by the Namas in Bethanie, and other neighbours, during the previous century.

5. Wikar had heard of the Sambdamas and the Zountamas. He writes:

'Some old men amongst my travelling companions told me to-day that they were, as they reckoned it, still 16 days' journey further north than the place which Captain Hop's expedition had reached. They showed me some beads . . . these were of different colours, but the prettiest of them were bright green and like beaten copper ore. When I broke them to pieces, I discovered that they were nothing more than common glass. They said that they got these mostly from the Zountamas, who must live close to the sea and further to the north, like the Sambdamas. Regarding them, no further particulars are known to me, except that the Zountamas and the Sambdamas are, according to the statements of my fellow travellers, of a darker complexion than the Namacquas (Namas), but not so marked in the face as the Damracquas (Hereros), and that they are Blip or Blicquas (Bechuanas). Since the Sambdamas live nearer to the Namacquas than the Zountamas, they come to work for the Namacquas. They forge large and small beads of iron and copper. . . . For tools they employ bellows made out of a knapsack, out of which they force wind, and large stones, sharpened like axes at the upper end, which take the place of anvil and hammer. To get the forged metal smooth they rub it on stones or beat it into shape with a small axe. They say that these Zambdama smiths receive a goat from the Namacquas as a daily wage, and that they are very fond of goat meat for they are themselves very poorly supplied with it. My travelling companions told me, too, that they had heard from some of their own people, who were married to Zountama women, that the Zountamas journey every year to the Kaweps and the Blicquas, where they receive generous payment in beads for the cattle that they take with them, and out of these again they make a large profit by trading them for other cattle with the Namacquas. They say that the aforementioned northern tribes (the Kaweps) were very much inclined to come personally to the Namacquas in order to trade, but they were deterred by the Zountamas, who feared that that would put an end to their profits. They, therefore, represented to these tribes that the Namacquas were a very bloodthirsty people and they told them that the road was very long and that there was no water to be found on it, so that, if they dared to attempt the journey, their skulls would become like the shells of ostrich eggs, i.e. that they would die of thirst, and that their bare, dried-up, skulls would be found lying about the veld like ostrich egg shells.'

Wikar's Sambdamas are the Gamdamas, i.e. the Bergdamas, who lived near the sea (gam = water, sea). They inhabited the region of the lower Kuiseb and Swakop; some members of this tribe still live to-day in the Namib near the Brandberg and farther northwards. The Zountamas are the Chou-damas, that is the Dirty Damas, or Bergdamas, who had their settlements in the Auas Mountains, in the more northerly situated mountains of Hereroland, and in Erongo. Wikar tries to represent the sound *Ch*, which in Nama originates from the depths of the throat, by means of a letter and, for that purpose, he chooses the letter Z.

It is well known that the Bergdamas were the first smiths amongst the Hereros and the Namas. They did not merely make iron beads and trade in glass beads, which they had got through the Ovambos from their place of origin, Angola, but they fashioned arrow-heads, arm and leg rings, assegais, and knives. They traded the iron from the Ovambos. Wikar knew, too, that the Namas called iron *noengais* (*nu-eis* = black ore) and copper *avangais* (*ava-eis* = red ore). Many of the Bergdamas had acquired their skill as blacksmiths from the Ovambos. Indeed, it is probable that there lived amongst the Bergdamas Ovambo men, who understood the blacksmith's art. Amongst the Ovambo tribes there were many smiths, who, at certain definite times of the year, fetched their supplies of ore from southern Angola and carried on their trade in closely guarded huts. They were regarded as great magicians by the people. Upon occasion, when they had been charged with witchcraft and had been declared to be guilty of causing the death of an Ovambo, they used to come, until recent times, to Hereroland in order to escape certain death. Wikar states that smiths were likewise regarded in Namaland as magicians.

6. Now it is no longer difficult to identify the remarkable Kaweb race mentioned by Wikar; it is the Ovambo tribes. Still to this day an Ovambo man is called a Naweb in Namaland; the Seadamas, however, who cannot pronounce the click so well, say Daweb; while Wikar decides to call it Kaweb. The name is derived from the Nama word *nawe*, meaning hum. The Ovambo warriors were well equipped with assegais, which was not the case with the other tribes of South West Africa, and they had a warlike habit of whirling their assegais in the air until both blade and shaft began to give forth a muffled humming sound, and so they were called the 'Hummers'.

What Wikar states about beads, which served as a substitute for money, corresponds entirely with subsequent experiences in Ovamboland. Only thirty years ago, mean-looking glass beads were still the only form of money used by those tribes, the Portuguese in Angola being the source from which they were obtained. When the first missionaries, who were unable to buy anything with money, obtained all kinds of coloured beads from Germany and thought that they were going to purchase commodities with them, they made a great mistake. The Ovambos refused to accept them. No one knew, however, where to procure the Ovambos' miserable beads until it was discovered that, from ancient times, they had been manufactured by a glass factory in Italy. It was with these only that they could be ready for trade with the Ovambos. It is remarkable that the oldest form of coinage used in Ovamboland had to be sought for in Italy.

7. Wikar had some knowledge even of the Hereros. He called them Damracquas, in imitation of the Namas, who used to refer to them as Damas, simply because the former added to the name the word *gomacha*, i.e. rich in cattle, so as to distinguish them from the Berg-damas. He said regarding them that they lived in the north, far distant from the Namas and the Bechuanas. In stating further that 'according to hearsay another large river runs through this region' he meant evidently either the Swakop or the Kuiseb, of which nothing was known at that time. He added: 'They received a warm welcome from the Namaquas, chiefly out of fear for the magical powers with which they were attributed.'

Wikar's report contains reliable information regarding almost all the races of South West Africa. He knows about the organization of the Nama tribes and names the most powerful of them; he is acquainted with the Saan, the Bergdamas, and the Hereros, and even the Ovambo tribes are known to him. His accounts of the manner in which the Bushmen and the Namas lived are extraordinarily valuable. His description of the Saan is admirable: he mentions that they can count up to ten (the true Bushmen of the Kalahari have numerals only up to three), he depicts their joy when large swarms of locusts arrive, because they then get large supplies of food, he knows how they caught big game in game-pits and how they crossed the Orange River on a tree trunk. He depicts a hippopotamus hunt and tells how a Bushman made him a warm bed on a cold night, by making a hole in the ground, lighting a fire in the shallow cavity, and then covering him up with branches in his cosy nest.

He is still more fully informed regarding the Namas. He gives details concerning the education of children, polygamy, Levitical marriages, hunting, making war, and trading with other tribes, especially with the Bechuana. He is acquainted with their ideas regarding God and the devil, their ceremonies at the sacred fire (of

which the Namas of to-day have no knowledge), and their ceremonies
on the occasion of the holy sacrifice and the initiation of the young
men. He deals at length with the hunting methods of the Namas,
with their horrible way of making war, and with their remarkable
customs, as, for example, feeding a man with milk as a sign of prosperity, until he has an entirely misshapen body. When, however, he
said that the most potent curse of the Namas was *Ikode soreb*, meaning
'cursed be the sun', he made a mistake, for the words are *i go ge soreb*
and mean: 'the sun has gone down'. Who knows what he may come up
against in a wild and inhospitable land when the sun has gone down!

Wikar's success as a hunter will not bear comparison with his success
as an observer and an explorer. It is very much in his favour that,
although no one could have proved him mendacious had he done so,
he did not take the opportunity of ending his account with tall
hunting stories. He killed one giraffe, two rhinoceroses, one buffalo,
ten hippopotami, and two elephants, and he adds: 'I caught sight
of four herds of elephants, which were trekking out of the bush near
the river into the flats, and so numerous were they that I thought to
myself that it would be impossible to collect such a mass of them in
the whole world.'

7. GORDON, LE VAILLANT, WILLEM VAN REENEN, AND PIETER BRAND

Mention must be made of several other explorers, who made their
way to South West Africa in the last decade of the eighteenth century. The first of these was Gordon. He held the rank of captain in
the service of the Dutch East India Company and was commander
of the troops at the Cape. Upon him fell the unpleasant task of
handing the Cape over to the English in 1795. After he had done
his duty, he took his own life.

In 1779 Gordon went on an exploratory expedition to the north.
Lieutenant Patterson, of whom mention has previously been made,
was of his party. On the 17th August they reached the Orange River.
It was Gordon who named it the Orange River in honour of the royal
house of the Netherlands, the House of Orange. This name of the
southern boundary of South West Africa has survived. All other
designations, such as the Garieb (Garib), Great River, &c., are obsolete and forgotten.[1] Gordon recorded the results of his journey in

---

[1] The designation 'Grootrivier' has not been forgotten. It is the name used exclusively by the Afrikaans-speaking people of South Africa for the river which the
English-speaking people call the 'Orange'.—*Ed.*

pictures and maps, which are now preserved in a cabinet in Amsterdam. In comparison with the map of the surveyor, Brink, Gordon's maps contain no new particulars of any value.

At the time when Gordon was commander of the troops at the Cape, the Frenchman, Le Vaillant, stayed there. He, too, went on a tour and took the west coast as his route. According to his own assertions, Le Vaillant not only crossed the Orange River and made extensive journeys in Namaland, but he went as far as the Tropic of Cancer and likewise reached the hills near Rehoboth. He describes his experiences in his book, *Second Journey from the Cape of Good Hope into the interior of Africa in the years 1783, 1784 and 1785*. It has, however, been established beyond doubt that Le Vaillant left South Africa in June 1784, and returned to France. He could not have made any more journeys in Africa after that, as he states in his book. This is rather disconcerting. The descriptions of his expeditions were doubted even by some of his own contemporaries. The truth is that the geographical particulars given by this man, who intended to cross Africa from south to north, are accurate only as far as the Orange River. Beyond that, his topographical data are correct only in so far as they coincide with those appearing in the map by Hendrik Hop and Surveyor Brink. All new particulars are the product of his imagination. For example, Le Vaillant makes out that he found a Fish River (Fleuve de Poissons) in the middle of Namaland and that he travelled up and down it for some months. It is perfectly true that there is a Fish River in Namaland, and he heard about it from travellers, but he had never heard that this river came from the north and ran into the Orange River. Le Vaillant's Fish River, however, comes from the East, crosses Namaland in a westerly direction, and runs into the Atlantic Ocean at Luderitzbucht. This river, which cannot even be called legendary but rather the creature of a fertile imagination, appeared for very many years on the maps of South West Africa. It would be a waste of time to refer any further to Le Vaillant's book. The author cannot be accepted seriously as an explorer of the country. The reason why his name is mentioned here is that his book is still sought after, read, and pondered over by people who are interested in the history of the country.

'Copper is to be found in Namaland'—so ran the rumour in Capetown. There were whispers of gold discoveries. The rumour spread as far as the Olifants River, where there lived, on a valuable farm, the well-to-do family, the van Reenens. The three brothers,

Willem, Valentyn, and D. S. van Reenen, who were all bold and enterprising men, decided to investigate these matters, and more especially to go and look at the 'cattle-rich Damas', the Hereros.

Willem van Reenen obtained from Capetown the necessary official permission for a hunting and exploring expedition. He got it on the condition that he should send in a report upon the completion of his travels. This report, dated the 21st June 1792, is still available in the archives at Capetown. Seeing that it has not as yet been published, there is justification for giving a detailed statement of its contents.[1]

On the 6th October, 1791, Willem van Reenen set out from his farm for the north, taking with him two ox-wagons and several riding horses. His two brothers, Valentyn and D. S. van Reenen, originally stayed at home. Six people joined him as travelling companions, namely, Christian Eyseloor, Adriaan Louw and his son, Barend Freyn, Frederik Wysman, and Klaas van der Westhuyzen. Following Hendrik Hop's route, the travellers reached the Orange River on the 30th October and crossed it at, what is to-day, Ramansdrift through a mere thirty inches of water. They reached Sandfontein the following day and arrived at Warmbad on the 2nd November. It was there that David Freyn joined Brand. They trekked upstream along the river and reached Heinabis (van Reenen calls it Hariepbegos), but not without a certain amount of annoyance from thieving Bushmen. This was the point which Hendrik Hop had reached and from which he had turned back. They journeyed to Modderfontein, the present Keetmanshoop, and there, on the night of the 21st November, they had the misfortune of having their riding horses and trek-oxen attacked and scattered by three lions. After spending two days in searching for them, they collected them and discovered that there were twelve oxen missing. It may be assumed that the Bushmen had driven them off. Knowing that a Bastard, named Jan Sieberd, lived in the neighbourhood, Willem van Reenen sent for him and, as he had travelled widely and knew the country well, appointed him as guide to the land of the Damas, i.e. the Hereros.

Jan Sieberd had serious doubts as to the feasibility of the undertaking. It had not rained at all for three years and Hereroland could only be reached if rain had fallen farther ahead, for otherwise the watering-places would be, to some extent, dried up. The journey was resumed with Jan Sieberd as guide. One Gideon Visagie (likewise

[1] It was published by the van Riebeeck Society in 1935.—*Ed.*

written Guilliam) had settled in Modderfontein and was carrying on
cattle raising and cattle dealing there. He received his fellow countrymen in a friendly manner and they stayed with him from the 1st to
the 27th December. He supplied them with some of his native
servants, who were useful in handling the wagons and, after they had
celebrated Christmas, the journey was resumed. Once the Fish River
was behind them the difficulties of the waterless stretches were encountered. The Leber River was reached on the 9th January. Rhinoceroses, giraffes, and buffaloes were killed as food for the party.
After crossing the Sak and Bad Rivers, they reached the Rhenius
Mountains on the 23rd January. There van Reenen saw the 'valuable
mineral springs' which flow out of these mountains and in which 'a
piece of meat could be boiled'; so much water flowed from these
springs that five to six muids of seed-land could be irrigated from
them. He states that, in the neighbourhood, there is a valuable
copper mine. This reference has led some people to conclude that
it is the hot springs of Rehoboth which are being described. Others
again think that the hot springs of Windhoek are certainly indicated
by this description. One can hardly say, however, that the Rehoboth
springs flow out of the foot of a mountain; nor do the Rhenius mountains fit in with Rehoboth in any way. Van Reenen says of these
mountains: 'This mountain range lies in the land of the Heydamarassen, who are the owners of it, but recently the Goedonse became
masters of the country. It is one of the finest regions that I have
discovered in this territory.' This queer description requires closer
investigation; undoubtedly reference is made to some particular spot.

'The Heydamarassen', who occupied the mountains, are the Bergdamas, with whom we are already acquainted, and they are divided
up into Gam-damas or Seadamas near the sea, the Chou-damas or
Dirty Damas, and the Qu-damas or Mountain-top Damas. It is this
last description which is the origin of the word 'Heydamarassen', for
it is apparent that Hey is high, a translation of the Nama word *ou*,
which means top or point. The possessors of the Rhenius Mountains
were, from early times, the Bergdamas and that agrees with all the
other traditions concerning the ancient dwelling-places of the natives. But who are the 'Goedonse' by whom the Bergdamas had been
driven out? The Namas called the Hottentots, who had fled from
the Cape and wandered about amongst them, the Gu-nun in their
language, and it seems probable that Willem van Reenen heard this
name. (*Gu* means sheep and *nu* means to be far away, to be all over

the country or to be on the hunt; it likewise means people who make raids on sheep, sheep-stealers.) This expression affords a very pointed and clear way of explaining how many of these fugitives, who had found their way into Namaland, used to acquire riches. The 'Sheep-Stealers', however, only arrived in the neighbourhood of Windhoek for the first time in 1830. Prior to that they had trekked around in Namaland. At the time that Willem van Reenen went on his travels, Windhoek belonged neither to the Namas nor to the 'Sheep-Stealers', for it was the Hereros who claimed to be entitled to this place. Fierce battles were fought at a later time over the right to possess it, and much blood flowed. From the earliest times, however, Rehoboth and its hot springs had belonged to the chief Nama tribe of the Red Nation, that of Hatsamas and Hoachanas. There is corroboration of this, too, in the report of his travels. Willem van Reenen relates that on the very first night of his arrival at these hot springs, the 'Sheep-Stealers', who were living there, murdered his guide, Jan Sieberd. Their chief came next day and brought with him three slaughter oxen and four sheep by way of atonement. He stated that the murderers had fled. When van Reenen, however, came, upon his return journey, to the country of the Red Nation, on the 4th February, their chief came to him and inquired whether it was true that the 'Sheep-Stealers' had murdered one of his wagon folk. When he received an answer in the affirmative, he decided to fall upon them with an armed force and to mete out punishment. Van Reenen restrained him from putting this plan into execution, and assured him that the incident was closed, for he had the intention of travelling once more through that neighbourhood. When the chief heard this, he offered to accompany him with an armed escort so as to guard him against attack. The head of the Red Nation felt that he was responsible for what had occurred at the hot springs and was prepared to punish severely any arbitrary conduct towards a stranger in the land. He would feel that he was so responsible only if the hot springs belonged to the territory of his tribe. Rehoboth undoubtedly belonged to it, but Windhoek was generally a kind of no man's land; and, moreover, what happened to a traveller at the hot springs, served to arouse the interest of merely one chieftain of the Red Nation. Our research makes it more and more probable that Willem van Reenen's camp was at the present-day Rehoboth and not at Windhoek.

It therefore comes to this, that the travellers never came into contact with the 'cattle-rich Hereros'. It would certainly have been recorded in the account of the journey, if the Hereros had actually been encountered, and van Reenen must have found some few Hereros in Windhoek. Instead of this, information was given him (we shall hear of this later) that the Hereros were to be found very much farther to the north. This, too, points to Rehoboth rather than to Windhoek.

The camp remained at the hot springs from the 23rd January to the 14th February, 1792. The trek-oxen had to be thoroughly rested; twenty-eight of them died. As van Reenen had no longer any prospect of finding the Hereros and the prosecution of the journey seemed impossible, he sent Pieter Brand with seven Namas, mounted on riding oxen, farther to the north to make an effort to get into communication with the Hereros.

Pieter Brand set out in a northerly direction, accompanied by seven Bastard Hottentots to look for the 'cattle-rich Damaras'. It went badly with him on this expedition. All the riding and pack óxen succumbed. The land was in the grip of a severe drought. Some five or six days' journey beyond the Rhenius Mountains he came across 'wild people', who lived on roots like the Bushmen, but spoke the Hottentot language. Brand had discovered the Bergdamas. According to his description, they were blacker than the negroes of Mozambique, they possessed neither sheep nor cattle, and their food consisted of roots and bulbs out of the ground and the berries and fruit which grew wild on the bushes. 'When they want meat to eat they forge bangles and beads out of copper and exchange these with the Namas for cattle. They sometimes make useful slaves to the Namas.' He asked them why they did not keep stock like the Namas and the Hereros. They replied that they had had a large number of stock, consisting of goats, sheep, and cattle, but the Namas had taken everything away from them, and if any of them were to possess anything, they ran the risk of being robbed of it, and even of being killed. They said, too, that in former times they had defended themselves against the Namas, but that since the Namas had come into possession of iron arrow-heads and assegais, they could no longer prevail against them. Brand's guide confirmed what they stated and said that the Hereros were just as defenceless as the Bergdamas, for their only weapon of defence was the knobkerrie, while, for knives, they used hard stones, which they knew how to break off in such a way that they could use the sharp edges for cutting. Brand was astonished at this

seeing that 'this part of the country is so rich in copper'. He was told
that, from the place from which he commenced his return journey
to the camp, a journey of a further nine days was necessary in order
to reach the 'cattle-rich Hereros'. The Bergdamas said that, when
the Namas wanted cattle, they, too, got them by barter from the
Hereros, or stole them from them.

After an absence of fifteen days, Pieter Brand returned to the camp
at the hot springs. There is no means of identifying the region through
which he travelled. There is nothing stated in the account of his
journey which offers a clue by which it may be determined. No
mention is made either of mountains, rivers, or places. If the camp
was at Rehoboth, it is probable that he was in the Auas Mountains,
where many Bergdamas resided in those days. If the party was
camped at the hot springs at Windhoek, then he may well have been
in the Swakop plain. It is still inexplicable, however, why he should
have been told that the Hereros lived a nine days' journey farther
to the north. A possible explanation is that the Hereros had withdrawn, with their cattle, from their southern grazing-grounds, perhaps
on account of the drought or perhaps through fear of the 'Sheep-
Stealers'. The repeated mention of the occurrence of copper refers
to the northern areas of Rehoboth, for copper mines were discovered
there fifty years later and were worked by Europeans. They were
known to the Bergdama blacksmiths, who doubtless pointed them out.

On the 14th February, 1792, Willem van Reenen commenced his
homeward journey. He reached Modderfontein on the 14th March
and he stayed there and enjoyed the hospitality of his friend, Gideon
Visagie, until the 23rd April. Of his sixty trek-oxen, only six remained; all the others had succumbed to the drought. Unfortunately, Visagie could not help him. His wife (it is here that the first
mention is made of a white woman having her home in South West
Africa) had been to Capetown in the meantime and, as she had been
forced to spend nine months on the road, his oxen, too, were miserably
thin. Van Reenen found himself compelled to trade six of his best
guns with the natives for oxen. The Bastard, Solomon Kok, furnished
him with thirty good trek-oxen and, when the party reached Warmbad, where Barend Freyn, who had joined the travellers there some
months before, had his head-quarters, the latter helped him further.

By well-known roads, Willem van Reenen arrived at his homestead on the Olifants River on the 20th June, 1792. The very next
day he wrote the report of his journey, which forms the basis of our

description of it, for the Cape Government. He had not found the Hereros for whom he had been looking, but he had discovered the settlements of the Bergdamas instead. The new information had been obtained at the cost of considerable sacrifice: the party had lost 140 oxen on the outward and the homeward journeys. Success in hunting compensated them, however, for all their other misfortunes. Sixty-five rhinoceroses and six giraffes were killed, and, besides these, other game was shot—it was probably no inconsiderable quantity— which the big-game hunter did not regard as worthy of mention.

8. SEBASTIAN VAN REENEN AND PIETER PIENAAR

After Willem van Reenen's return from his travels, his two brothers, Sebastian Valentyn and D. S. van Reenen set out to see whether the Fates would not vouchsafe them the good fortune which they had denied his brother. Seeing that he had not succeeded in finding the Hereros by going overland, it might perhaps prove possible to do so by starting from Walfish Bay and making eastwards into the interior. There were three principal things which drew the explorers of earlier days, with magnetic force, to South West Africa, namely, its enormous wealth in wild animals, the story of the huge herds of cattle possessed by the Hereros, and the hope of discovering large copper and gold deposits. From what had been learnt from the Bergdama blacksmiths, it seemed fairly certain that deposits of copper ore were awaiting discovery in that unknown land.

Barend Freyn (pronounced Frain), with whom we have already become acquainted as Willem van Reenen's guide, and, apparently, as having his head-quarters in Warmbad, set out overland into northern Namaland, while the brothers van Reenen landed at Walfish Bay. Pieter Pienaar accompanied them, and likewise some Hottentots, who had been brought from the Cape. The ship stayed in the Bay from the end of January 1793 to the end of February, so as to be able to take the travellers back again after their investigations were concluded. While Valentyn van Reenen endeavoured, with the assistance of some of the natives, to discover the copper mines (but returned without success), Pieter Pienaar went on a hunting trip into the interior. His chief objectives were to obtain information regarding the whereabouts of Barend Freyn, to find out how far distant the copper mines were and how they could be reached, and finally to get through to the Hereros and, if possible, to trade with them for cattle.

Pieter Pienaar went from Walfish Bay in an easterly direction. His Cape Hottentots accompanied him. He soon got into difficulties in the flat country beyond the dunes. He had no more water left and he could not find a water-hole. His Hottentots sighted two 'Damaras', whom they surprised and brought to him. They were quite willing to go with him, but they advised him not to proceed with his journey in an easterly direction. They promised to show him their water-holes if he would follow them to the north-east. Pienaar agreed and, at two o'clock next morning, reached a dry river bed in which a plentiful supply of water was found in a hole dug in the bed. Pienaar had discovered the Swakop River.

He travelled inland in the Swakop valley for twelve days. He neither heard nor saw anything of Barend Freyn. He found no cattle which he could possibly buy. It is doubtful whether he saw a single head of cattle on this journey. His account of it makes no mention of his having done so. He found five 'Damara' settlements and he obtained by barter from them several copper bangles; they said that the metal of which these rings were made was found in a region lying more to the south. As the result of closer interrogation, it appeared that the mines were between the Swakop River and 'Protection Bay' (Luderitzbucht) and could be reached in twelve to fourteen stages (one stage equalled a four hours' trek in an ox-wagon). 'But the natives said that it had not rained here for five years, and it was not possible to reach the mines from here unless it had rained, for all the water-holes between here and the mines have dried up.'

The bed of the Swakop, which Pienaar did not dare to leave, because the country round was dried up and waterless, made a very good impression on him. He considered that he had never seen a finer dry river course and he waxed enthusiastic about several places, which were three-quarters of an hour (about four miles, Tr.) in width and were full of mighty trees. The enormous wealth of the fauna compensated the hunter for the explorer's lack of success. He saw over 300 rhinoceroses and even a greater number of elephants, gemsbuck, springbuck, buffaloes, and lions. Pienaar killed twenty rhinoceroses, three elephants, and much other game which he never counted. The meat served as food for the natives who accompanied him 'who fell on it like wolves and did not leave it as long as there was a bit of meat left'. This remark shows that, in addition to the two guides, many more 'Damaras' had joined his party. About a day's journey from Walfish Bay he killed another rhinoceros, which he left to the

Hottentots of the neighbourhood. With his efforts to gain information regarding the mouth of the Swakop, upon his return to Walfish Bay—efforts in which he was unsuccessful—we have dealt previously.

With regard to the natives, whom Pienaar encountered in the Swakop valley, it might quite easily be assumed that he had to do with Hereros, and in that event Pienaar was not only the discoverer of the Swakop, but likewise the first man to reach a settlement of these 'cattle-rich' stock-farmers and nomads. The report affords no solid ground whatever for regarding these 'Damaras' as Hereros, but it is both natural and possible to accept them as such seeing that both races, Bergdamas and Hereros, are denoted by the same name. Everything, however, goes to show that by 'Damaras' Bergdamas are intended, for Pienaar's Cape Hottentots were able to understand the two men they captured, as well as the natives they met later, without any trouble. That would have been quite impossible had they been Hereros, but not if they were Bergdamas, for these spoke the Nama language, too. Further, nothing whatever is said as to these natives owning cattle. The Bergdamas of former times had, as a rule, no cattle and, where they had any at all, they were limited to the very smallest numbers. The Hereros' whole existence was bound up with the possession of cattle. If Pienaar had discovered a Herero location, he would likewise have seen Herero cattle, especially as it was one of the objects of his expedition to barter for cattle. Finally, the natives, whom he met, had a fairly accurate knowledge about certain of the copper mines. The Hereros did not worry about such matters, but the Bergdamas did, for their smiths knew how to smelt and fashion the ore and carried on a lively trade with the Namas and the Hereros in the finished product. It is therefore proved that, right up to the turn of the century, this mysterious 'cattle-rich' Herero people were known in name, but that none of the explorers had seen them with their own eyes.

In our presentation of the exploration and discovery of South West Africa, we have now reached the turn of the century. Before the close of the century a great deal had been done to lift the veil of mystery from South West Africa, but more had still to be done. It was only Namaland that had become known to any extent. No explorer's eye had yet seen anything that lay northwards of the Kuiseb and the Swakop and in the distant east. Nevertheless, we leave the historical representation of the explorations of the country here and, from now onwards, we shall deal with it in conjunction with the historical development of the country as a whole.

With regard to the information which we have at present, special emphasis should be laid on the fact that, despite all effort, it is by no means complete. There is no doubt at all that very many more brave explorers, hunters, traders, adventurers, gold seekers, and copper miners reached the interior of the land than this account might lead one to suppose. The records of these men are lacking, and with these the historian cannot dispense, if he is to weave their experiences, their discoveries, and their achievements into the web of historical events. For instance, the Bergdamas in the Swakop valley told Pieter Pienaar that, in 1792, 'Christians', that is to say, Europeans, had been to the copper mines and had left again. Thus, that which Sebastian van Reenen was seeking had been discovered by these men a year previously. Hitherto, however, it has not been possible to get to know who they were and whence they came.

Many of these silent discoverers might have brought to light information in excess of that which we now possess; unfortunately it was never recorded. It is thus that rumour and story passed, in ever widening circles, from mouth to mouth, and others were encouraged to seek their fortunes as hunters and explorers in the mysterious regions of the north, until at last there came some one, who left behind him a written record for the benefit of posterity.

II

THE COUNTRY AND ITS PEOPLE

WHOEVER is desirous of reading history with insight and profit will do well to make himself acquainted with the scene of the historical events and those who took part in them.

> He must go to the poet's land,
> Who would the poet understand.

But here we are concerned with something much more than a poem. We are concerned with a history and one which, without the slightest artificial aid, presents a thrilling drama. It shows us the struggle of small, barely civilized races; a struggle forward to gain space to live, a struggle upward to gain an appointed place amongst the nations of the world. Even if this drama was acted on the far-distant stage of South West Africa, without any other countries or nations paying any attention to it, that is no good reason for regarding it as of little consequence. The same fate has overtaken many another drama. The sole duty of the historian is to give a faithful representation of the events, it is for History itself to pronounce judgment as to their value.

We shall therefore commence the portrayal of this struggle with a short description of the scene of action, and then introduce the several races individually. In both cases, however, the description will be confined within such limits as will serve the purpose of facilitating and furthering the comprehension of the history.

1. THE COUNTRY

The course of the Orange River forms the southern boundary of South West Africa; its northern boundary abuts on those perennial streams, the Kunene and the Okavango. On the west, the waves of the Atlantic Ocean beat against its thousand miles of coast line. Its natural frontier to the east is the Kalahari desert.

Three parallel strips of country divide up the territory, which is approximately 330,000 square miles in extent, into three separate, broad areas running from north to south. The coastal strip, which is from seventy to a hundred miles broad, consists of the inhospitable Namib Desert, with its enormous sand-dunes extending to the very shore. Its vegetation is scanty, its island-mountains are lofty, and its diamond mines rich. Walfish Bay and Luderitzbucht afford safe harbours for ships and provide access to the land from the sea coast.

The eastern strip of country is a part of the Kalahari, which, by reason of its lack of water and roads, effectually shuts off all approach to South West Africa from the east.

Between these two deserts lies the broad expanse of the inhabited portion of the country. From the Orange to the Swakop we find the grazing-grounds of the different Nama tribes, who in olden times trekked up and down in nomad fashion. The southern portion of Namaland is semi-desert, while the northern consists of grassy plains. Trees are to be found only on the banks of the majority of the water-less river courses.

The middle of the inhabited area consists of the Windhoek high-lands. They separate Namaland and Hereroland from each other, but a twelve mile wide valley, running from north to south, affords a means of communication between them. From these highlands, shaped like a flattened dome, river courses go out in every direction. The Auas Mountains, which rise to a height of 7,656 feet, are the principal elevation. The western side of the Windhoek highlands consists of the Khomas highlands, which are waterless and difficult of access, while the eastern side is gently sloping hill-country, with numerous river courses which carry plentiful supplies of underground water, merging into the Kalahari country. To the north the high-lands sink down, the transition being sometimes gradual and some-times precipitous. Here stretch the thorn-bush covered plains of the Herero country with its numerous island mountains (Omatako, Water-berg, Erongo) far into the immeasurable distance, losing themselves to the east in the Omaheke (Sandveld) and cut off by the dunes of Lake Ngami. It was here that, formerly, the enormous herds of the Hereros used to graze. It was here that, formerly, big-game hunters found those wide and fruitful hunting-grounds which Europe could not possibly offer them. Ivory and ostrich feathers brought them, quite frequently, considerable gains. It is here that the old historical places, Otjikango, Okahandja, Otjosazu, Otjimbingwe, and Omaruru are situated.

The farther north one goes, the more the characteristic thorn-bush of Hereroland disappears and gives place to larger trees. The river courses become fewer, until in the northern areas, the Karst-veld, they disappear altogether. The rain sinks entirely away into the porous ground. A wide, arid region, partly covered by sand and dunes, cuts off Hereroland to the north, but to the north-west a grassy plain opens to the trekker a way to the Kaokoveld with its springs, its grazing-grounds, and its mountain fastnesses.

Northwards of the arid area just referred to, the stoneless Ovamboland stretches as far as the Kunene. It is an enormous plain traversed by gently rolling hills. In good rainy seasons, the waters of the Kunene and the Okavango Rivers flow deep into Ovamboland through peculiar depressions in the land, and thus enable agriculture and fishing to be carried on there. The plains afford excellent grazing. On the higher ridges, the strongly fortified and neatly constructed dwellings of the natives are situated. Gigantic baobab trees, shady fig-trees and stately fan-palms give the landscape a picturesque and kindly appearance.

South West Africa's prosperity or misfortune depends upon its rainfall. From ancient times its inhabitants have been stock-farmers, and from those days the only food to be had consisted in the milk and meat of cattle, sheep, and goats, in addition to the hard berries of the bushes and the tubers which grow wild in the ground. If it did not rain, it was not only milk, the chief article of diet, which failed; very often the people's total possessions were endangered. In order to safeguard them, the cattle were distributed amongst different 'posts'. If the water and grazing failed in one particular area, the posts were shifted to another neighbourhood. There were chieftains who owned more than than two hundred of these cattle-posts. With unremitting toil the herds were watered from deep wells, which had been dug, with sharp sticks, in the immediate neighbourhood of the river beds. The hard conditions under which the cattle had often to be kept were cheerfully endured. If the herd was entirely lost, the whole clan lost with it its means of livelihood and its social standing. Even in olden days, it was cattle which were the only form of property, the food-supply, the old age insurance, and the inheritance for posterity, and it was the possession of cattle which alone ensured their possessor respect, power, and influence in the community.

Hence the anxious, hopeful expectation when, in December or January, the clouds appeared in the far east, when the lightning lit up the horizon of the sky at night, when the heavy rain-clouds were no longer driven away by the south-east wind in the early afternoons and, at last, a strong north-easter, accompanied by whirling wind-devils, raised mighty dust-clouds in the endless plains and drove howling through the mountain kloofs. At last the big, heavy rain drops fall. Flash after flash of lightning follow each other. The thunder rolls continuously and re-echoes from the mountains. The occasional drops increase. It is raining, pouring, the sluice-gates of the heavens seem to have opened. In a few minutes the dried-up surface of the earth is no more to be seen. A sea seems to have taken the place of a desert. Furrows fill up and become brooks. Roads are turned into rivers in a moment. The rivulets become roaring torrents. In the sand of the broad, dry river beds, the flood-waters roll down black and threatening. Three feet deep pours the raging flood, sweeping everything before it, uprooting and submerging whatever stands in its way. 'The river has come down.'

'The river has come down!' That is the most joyful message which one inhabitant of the country can give another or receive from him. It is true that the veld is usually dry again a few hours later and that it is quite easy to walk through the river bed, but the whole face of nature is changed. In a few days the grass is green, where old gnawed-off roots had before appeared to be dead. The soil of the bare flats, which was previously as hard as rock, bursts and swells, and sprouting seeds, which lay hidden underground, thrust up whole clods of earth. If further showers should fall before too long a time has passed, or even a land-rain, which is not accompanied by the tremendous downpour of the thunder-storm and thus gives the earth time to drink its fill, then in a few weeks' time, trees and bushes, grasses and herbage grow green and blossom in the bare veld and the waterless desert. A good year may be expected. The dry springs begin to run again. Hollows in the ground, in which the water cannot sink away, become broad pools (*vleis*) and hold water for many months. In olden days they formed the playgrounds of elephants and hippopotami, of giraffes and zebras, of lions and leopards.

But what becomes of the enormous quantities of water? Only a fraction remains in the country and sinks into the soil. Most of it is carried off by the rivers and borne to the sea in rapidly flowing streams. Southern Namaland is drained by the Konsib and the Fish Rivers, while the Kuiseb, the Swakop, and the Omaruru Rivers carry the waters of the midlands away to the west; the Nosob and the Omuramba Omatako drain the eastern watershed.

The yearly rainfall, which has such a varying effect upon the fortunes of the country, usually obeys the following rule: the farther one goes to the east and to the north, the better the rainfall to be expected. The Namib zone is practically rainless. Namaland can expect an average rainfall of from 3 to 10 inches a year. The midlands receive between 12 and 20 inches, while the north and east can reckon on from 18 to 25 inches. But from the very earliest times, dry periods of between five and ten years have alternated with periods of heavier rainfall. It does not seem as if any settled rule can be applied, nor can it be said that the country is gradually drying out and that the average rainfall is getting less. Very little credence can be attached to the stories of old natives, who glibly talk about the much better rainfall of olden times. Olden times in South West Africa, too, are regarded as 'the good old times', because human beings are fortunately inclined to forget the difficult days of the past more easily than the times of greatest happiness. In any case, the historian, whose task it is to preserve all the occurrences of the past, can tell of many a dry year which fell to the lot of the land in former times, side by side with happier times.

2. THE HEREROS

Owing to their number, their possessions, and their historical significance, the Hereros occupy the first place amongst the native races of South West Africa. The Hereros are mostly tall, they have well-formed bodies, chocolate-brown skins, black, crinkly hair, and a striking appearance: a real ruling race, with many of its good points and all its bad ones.

The Hereros will be depicted in this book as they were in former times, when the precepts of their forefathers prescribed the rules of their existence. In those days, the national garb consisted of the tanned skins of goats, sheep, and some kinds of wild animals. They wore an apron round their loins, which they secured by means of a finely plaited girdle. The leathern aprons worn by the women were considerably longer. They wore aprons to cover their backs as well, and these reached almost to their calves. A kind of plaited corset covered the lower part of the body and the hips; this was very artistically made out of an extraordinarily long chain, to which were attached small discs of ostrich-egg shell, which had been rounded and pierced. Neck and breast were decorated with similar chains. Iron beads threaded on leather thongs were used, as well, as jewellery for the neck, arms, and feet. The woman's leather head-dress, with its three high leather horns, edged with iron beads behind and forming a heavy protection for the neck, was a work of art. Sandals made out of giraffe skin were fastened to the ankles with leather thongs.

It was part of the woman's duty to erect the neat and roomy rondavel with its domed roof. Thick boughs were planted close to one another in a carefully measured circle and brought together in a dome at the top. Other boughs were then bound cross-ways on to the uprights with pliable bark and leather thongs, so as to give the structure marvellous stability, and this was still further increased by means of a strong pole, which was planted firmly in the ground in the middle of the hut to support the roof. The structure was then plastered with a mixture of clay and cow-dung worked up into an adhesive mass. The only tool employed for the plastering was the human hand. The floor, which was always kept clean, was made with the same mixture and, besides, it was usually covered with skins. The house which a woman had built was regarded as her own property. There *she* had the say, not her husband. Where polygamy was in vogue, the husband passed his nights in regulated sequence in his wives' huts. He possessed no house of his own. The Herero house served only as a place to sleep in. The daytime was passed in the open air. In the house were kept the household utensils: wooden bowls and milk-buckets, tubs, spoons, and other milk receptacles, which the husband cleverly fashioned with a small, curved axe. It was women's work to make earthenware pots, with narrow necks, wide middles and pointed bottoms, and to bake them in hot wood-coals.

Each family lived in its own enclosed village. The individual huts stood in regulated order at the edge of a cross-shaped piece of ground. The large house of the head wife stood in the east, and near it, to the south, stood the houses of the subordinate wives, while the huts of the growing sons, the relatives, and the servants were situated to the north and the north-west. Inside the village fence, were the cattle kraals, and, in the immediate neighbourhood of the cattle kraals, the sacred ancestral fire was tended by the head wife or her daughter. Since each village was built on the same pattern, it was very easy for a stranger to find his way about in it.

The whole establishment depended upon the possession of stock. Rich chieftains owned more than a thousand head of cattle, besides sheep and goats in great numbers. It was the task of the sons of poor Hereros, who attached themselves to the rich as servants, and of the enslaved Bergdamas, to herd the stock.

Milk was the chief article of food; it was used only when sour. The calabashes, in which the milk was allowed to curdle, were kept in the head wife's house. These were often of considerable age and, in any event, the decorations of animal claws, pieces of skin, and other objects, which were attached to particular vessels so as to distinguish them, were inherited from previous generations. Certain cows appertained to each of the calabashes, which were filled up daily with their milk. Only specially selected people were allowed to drink the milk they contained, and then only after the head of the family had, each day anew, tasted it in due ceremonial form and handed it over for consumption. A special vessel was kept for the use of strangers. Meat was eaten only when a wild animal was captured, when one of the cattle died, or when a sacrificial feast was celebrated. To sell cattle was regarded as a sin against the forefathers, from whom they had been received as an inheritance.

Veld-food, such as wild fruits, berries, and tubers, made up for the lack of fresh vegetables. The wild bees furnished a great luxury; their honey was keenly sought for and, when mixed with water, drunk with great relish until the way to make strong, intoxicating honey-beer was learnt from the Namas.

The grazing-grounds were the common property of the tribe. No individual could acquire land, nor could the chief of the tribe alienate any ground without the consent of all the men of the tribe. The boundaries of individual grazing-grounds were not fixed at all, nor were those of the tribal territories. Wealthy chiefs came together now and then for the purpose of discussing the question of grazing rights in amicable fashion, but this by no means prevented fights between the herdsmen over grazing-grounds.

The cattle owner never kept all the cattle he possessed in one place. Disease, raids by jealous neighbours, and lack of rain had taught him that it was better to establish outposts, and even to divide up his stock amongst less well-to-do relatives for use and custody, so that, if some of the cattle died, the rest survived. This arrangement had been, from olden times, the usual way of ensuring the preservation of the herd.

The Herero man devoted his entire time, strength, and personal attention—his very life in fact—to his cattle. In dry years he dug wells untiringly with a pointed stick hardened in the fire, and drew water from a depth of fifteen feet and more, pouring it into wooden troughs for his thirsty animals. All his efforts were directed to increasing the herd; his cattle were the sole object of his thoughts; his greatest pride was the good condition of his oxen; his dignity and influence increased or declined in proportion to the number of stock which he owned; even his religion stood or fell in accordance with these possessions.

The Herero of old was acquainted with the God of Heaven, who gave life and took it away, who sent health after sickness and averted misfortune. He called him Ndjambi, but had no form of worship for him; why should he when Ndjambi was kindly disposed, did no one any harm and, besides, lived in his far-distant heaven. It was the spirits of the evilly disposed dead, which were believed to haunt graves and their neighbourhoods, that were dangerous. The spirits of one's own ancestors could be dangerous too if, through oversight or negligence, their precepts were not followed. Spirits were believed to be actually near at hand. When threatened or overtaken by misfortune, it was to them that one turned for help. For this purpose the grave of one's forefathers was the appointed place for prayer, but only the head of the family dared to approach it as the representative of all the rest.

It was from the forefathers that the cattle were inherited; it was they, therefore, who could help or hinder the breeding of cattle. The ancestral fire, bringer of prosperity, was likewise inherited from the forefathers, and its extinction meant the ruin of the family. The expression 'I have extinguished his ancestral fire' bore exactly the same meaning as the announcement 'I have exterminated his whole kith and kin'. The head wife had to look after the coals of this sacred fire every night, and, in the early morning, her eldest daughter had to kindle these coals to a bright flame at the appointed spot inside the circle of the village. First of all, the flickering of the flames was the sign for the milking of the cows. It was while he sat at the sacred fireplace that the sour milk was passed to the head of the family for him to taste and give authority for its use. It was here that the elders met in council and administered justice, and here, too, the newly born children received their names. Marriages were celebrated here and the dead laid out, before they were carried away to their lonely graves. The purification ceremony for the man who had offended against patriarchal custom and command took place here, and those who were very ill were sprinkled with the sacred ashes. Ashes from the sacred fire and earth from an ancestor's grave were regarded as remedies of the highest efficacy.

The presence of ancestral spirits was indicated by means of ancestral sticks, which were planted round the fire on ceremonial occasions, but were otherwise carefully withdrawn by the head wife from the gaze of the curious and hidden in her house. The whirling stick, with which a progenitor had been wont to kindle his hunting fire, was honoured after his death as his representative and was carefully added to the bundle of the older ancestral sticks. The chief took counsel with these sticks, just as he would with a living person, and he told them everything that it was necessary for them to know regarding the weal and woe of the family. Should the fire become extinguished through lack of attention, a new one could be lighted only by employing an ancestral whirling stick in due ceremonial form.

If the family changed its dwelling-place to another locality, the greatest care was taken to bear the ancestral fire to the site of the new residence, unextinguished. The head wife or her daughter went ahead of the trek bearing a brand from the sacred fire and when the embers commenced to die down, the advance was stopped until a new fire was kindled with the coals of the last one, and the flaming brand once again made its appearance in the bearer's hand at the head of the march. When the new dwelling-place was reached, the first thing that had to be attended to was the selection of a place where the ancestral fire was to be tended for the future, and it was round this place that the new village was built.

The service of the sacred fire could only be performed by one upon whom this office had descended by legitimate succession. We find that the nation was divided into sixteen religious bodies called Oruzo. Every Herero, whether man or woman, belonged to one of these bodies. Each had its own special rules regarding food and other matters, which had to be observed by its members only. The religious ceremonies performed at the sacred fire were, however, the same in all the societies. Membership of a body of this kind descended from a father to all his children. The succession to the office of performing the rites of the ancestral fire stood in a different position. This dignity, which was very closely connected with the dignity of the chieftainship, was inherited by the eldest son of the deceased's eldest sister and, if no such son was available, it descended further in its own peculiar mode of succession in ways which it is often difficult to understand. The woman who belonged to an Oruzo different from that of her husband, passed into his on the day of the marriage. The grave of the man, who performed for the family the rites of the sacred fire and was its chief, was decorated in remembrance of him with the skulls of the many oxen which had been slaughtered for his funeral feast. It was the bounden duty of those who remained behind to send after him, beyond the grave, those favourite oxen, which had been selected by the deceased long before his death and had been given very special care, and to erect the horns on or near his grave. The Hereros, who otherwise may not kill a single healthy animal, sacrifice whole herds of cattle on an occasion of this kind and give their flesh to every one attending the funeral feast, without inquiring whether he is a member of the family, or not.

So that the ownership of cattle may be maintained and kept in the family, after the days of extreme liberality, the economic societies of heirship, called the Eanda, exist alongside the religious associations. Every Herero, whether man or woman, belonged to an Eanda. The whole nation contained eight associations of heirship. Membership was not a matter of individual choice, it was inherited and all children belonged to the Eanda of their mother. The importance of these associations came prominently to the fore twice in the lifetime of a Herero; first, in connexion with marriage, for marriage could only take place within the circle of his own Eanda, or of an allied Eanda, and, for the second time, when a death took place, and the cattle descended in the line of the Eanda, in which the eldest sister of the deceased was the first to inherit. The further processes of succession are so involved that it would require a very lengthy description to explain them and, even then, they would remain involved. Unless he possesses the most exact knowledge of the family relationship, the degrees of succession must remain a mystery for the stranger. The strict carrying out of the Eanda's regulations caused severe hardship, which we should regard as injustice. Their whole object was, however, the prevention of any splitting of the inheritance, and that object they achieved.

It remains to say a few words about the Herero language. It is extremely melodious and rich in vowel sounds. Closed vowels predominate. Strange sounds which make the language difficult to learn are few, but considerable difficulty is caused through its extraordinary wealth of words. The noun is grouped into nine classes. Special classes are provided for the designation of people, animals, plants, things singly, round things, long things, small things, abstract things and, in the ninth class, are united all the things which cannot be included in the other classes. Prefixes indicate the class to which a particular word belongs. These prefixes are repeated, with trivial changes, in adjectives and numerals, and at the same time they form the roots of the exceptionally numerous pronouns. These, when connected up with the verbs, provide such a variety of shades of meaning that the language may be regarded as a work of art of the highest order.

The wisdom of the ages is preserved in many a proverb, and fables and tales of less intellectual significance amuse the circle which, seated round the fire at night, does everything possible to impress them on the memory through constant repetition. There is, too, no lack of songs, which are sung by the performer in a monotonous sing-song. As, however, it is only the dance-song which is sung in the presence of big gatherings, the knowledge of these little songs has been poorly preserved, for, in ancient times, they used to be sung only by the bards, who used to go from village to village and make their living by their singing. If any one wished to collect the songs, he could fill a large volume with them. The purport of them is very destitute of ideas. The Herero song deals with two subjects only: the deeds of great men and the colours and qualities of outstanding oxen, about which every village could boast; on this account every locality had the privilege of being called in jest by the first word of the song of its oxen instead of the place-name, by which it was known to the uninitiated.

3. THE NAMAS

The Namas, whose ancient grazing-grounds lay in the southern portion of the country between the Orange and the Swakop, belonged to the Hottentot race, which, in far-distant times, inhabited the whole of southern Africa. They were nomads and they lived by stock-raising, hunting, and from what they could collect in the veld.

The Nama does not possess the striking appearance of the Herero. Physically he is of medium height, but there is a certain number of tall people amongst them. In those cases where there is a strain of Bushman blood, the majority of Namas do not reach the average height of 5 ft. 8 in. The colour of the skin is yellow and it becomes reddish with some of the tribes. The skull is fairly well rounded and is regularly covered with soft, crinkly hair, which is bunched up into separate little knots in such a way that the scalp is everywhere visible in the spaces between them. (This is known in South Africa as 'pep-percorn hair', Tr.) The nose is broad and barely distinguishable at its base. The bold, prominent cheek bones and the pointed, retreating chin give the faces of older persons a triangular shape, which appears ugly to us. The lips are pale red and fleshy, the eyes dark brown and the eyelids often slightly oblique. The elegant hands and feet of both sexes are very noticeable, as is the large deposit of fat (steato-pygy) on the posteriors of many of the married women.

The tribal dress consisted of a leather apron, to which was added, in the case of the women, a large skin which passed under the left arm and was knotted above the right shoulder, thus protecting the back. It likewise served as a receptacle for edible roots and berries, and left the right arm free for the work of collecting them.

Caps were employed as headgear, and these were often made out of the skins of jackals or other animals, in fantastic shapes. Leather sandals on the feet completed the clothing. Jewellery consisted in leather rings, rings made out of ostrich-egg shell and, later, of metal, worn on the wrist, upper arm and ankle. The body was smeared with an ointment from red iron-stone and fat, and a powder made out of sweet-smelling herbs, woods, roots, and fruits was employed to conceal the smell of perspiration emanating from the body.

The Hottentot werf, a circular village, consisted of from five to thirty, or more, mat huts, which were built in the shape of bee-hives and had their doors facing the middle of the circle. The huts combined the properties of a permanent home with those of a movable tent. Spars, which had been carefully prepared and bent into shape, were planted in small holes in the ground in a circle with a radius of between four and five feet; these were brought together at the top to form a flat dome, bound together by cross bars and then covered with rush mats of considerable length. These mats, which were about a yard in width, were made by the women with bone needles and with thread made from animal sinews. The reeds were arranged one by one and laid on the thread to the width of a span, with long and patient labour, and then the threads were not sewn round the reeds, but each of these was carefully threaded through. In hot weather, these reed huts afforded a fair amount of play to any cool breezes which might blow, while providing, at the same time, protection against the inclemency of an African rain storm, for even a moderate wetting made the reeds swell and closed up all the intervening spaces and made the whole water-tight. The huts could be taken to pieces within an hour's time, including the rolling up of the mats and the tying together of the framework. On the backs of pack-oxen they could be very easily transported to a new place, where they could be erected again in less than a day.

The places in which the occupiers of the huts slept at night were indicated by hollow depressions in the levelled earthen floor. The blankets, which were made out of dressed skins from which the wool had not been removed, were aired daily in the morning sunlight.

The utensils for domestic use were hung up on the rafters. A special rack made of sticks was sometimes provided for them. On this stood the powder-boxes made out of the shells of small tortoises. Here hung the rouge-pots on leather thongs; these were made from pieces of ox horn, rather more than the length of a finger, to which had been fixed tops and bottoms of softened leather. There was generally to be found there, too, a tobacco-pipe made out of animal bone or soapstone. What was generally smoked in preference to tobacco was a kind of intoxicating hemp, called dagga, which was originally the only plant grown for use by the Namas in their own gardens, until gradually they learnt to grow calabashes, mealies, and melons. The men's bows and arrows, and also their spears, were stowed between the frame of the hut and its mat covering, so that the children could not play with them and hurt themselves. Against the wall of the simple hut and on the floor, stood earthenware pots laboriously fashioned by the wife, milk buckets hewn out of wood by the husband, and ostrich-egg shells with small openings, in which the drinking water was kept.

Stock-farming was the principal source of food. Cattle, sheep, and goats were raised. Unlike the Hereros, the milk was generally drunk before it went sour. Butter-making was a well-known art, the cream being put into a calabash of the largest possible size, which was suspended by means of a leather thong and swung backwards and forwards until the butter formed. Whenever possible a meat diet supplemented the milk, but as there was too much meat when an ox was slaughtered, and it so readily went bad, more time was devoted to sheep and goat farming. For the preservation of their herds and likewise out of love of hunting, the men often went out hunting in great numbers and, with bows and arrows and their spears, they ventured to attack even elephants, giraffes, rhinoceroses and buffaloes. These hunting expeditions extended as far as Lake Ngami and into Ovamboland, and the Nama hunters put forward claims to the ownership of these territories on the ground of these hunting trips.

Just as it was the husband's duty to provide the family with meat, so it was the wife's to furnish them with everything edible that grew on bushes and shrubs, on runners above ground or as roots below the surface. The greater portion of this vegetable food was obtained from small starchy tubers growing in the veld. These were dug out of the ground with a sharp stick, which had usually been hardened in the fire and was frequently weighted by means of a stone, as big as one's fist with a hole through it, Bushman fashion.

The herding of the cattle and the harder tasks of the household were performed, when possible, by domestic servants, who were either Bergdamas, Bushmen, or captured Hereros, with the assistance of the growing sons of the family.

The clans used to live separated from each other in enclosed circular villages. Just as Europeans assign to their sons, to their growing daughters, and to relations who have joined the family circle, separate rooms of their own, the Namas built a special hut for each particular family in the clan and, while the European has a common dining- and living-room, the Namas had the common use of the open spaces within the village circle.

In the Hottentot werf, the word of the head of the clan was law. His rule was patriarchal. Several clans formed a tribe, and at its head was a chief, whose office passed from father to son. One of the men of the tribe was chosen as counsellor for life to assist the chief. The tribal territory, the boundaries of which were never clearly defined, belonged to the whole tribe and could not be alienated without its consent. The cattle belonged to the family. The only property regarded as personal was that which had been made by its owner with his own hands.

The parental control extended to sons and daughters, even long after they had grown up. Children did not become majors, in the sense that they do with us, as long as the elder members of the family were still alive. In the case of marriage it was customary for the parents of the young man to make the arrangements with the parents of the lady of his choice. They made the agreement as to the marriage settlement, which consisted of stock, and fixed the wedding-day. This was celebrated with an abundant feast of meat. The parents of both parties had to contribute towards the feast and all the relatives took part in it. A goat or a sheep was set aside for those who were absent and killed for them when they arrived. Participation to any extent in the wedding feast was regarded as consent to the wedding. After the wedding, about which there was nothing very particular except the feast, the young husband had to stay for a year with his parents-in-law, in order that they might get to know him well, might instruct him in the care of stock and, principally, so that they could make him work for them. After this year of service was at end, he returned to his own people. His wife was then brought to him by her relations and she was handed over to him formally with the following gracious words:

'Here we bring you our daughter. We know that she is an ill-bred, worthless creature. She possesses no common-sense, she is incapable of hard work, and she is unhandy and obstinate as well, but you worried us so continuously to give her to you that we at last consented. If you do not like her, do not ill-treat her and do not kill her. Give her back to us uninjured as we have handed her over to you to-day.'

As was the case with the Hereros, the position of the Nama wife was quite good. She was mistress inside her house, for the house belonged to her and it was regarded as rude to ask her for even a drink of water without courteously saying please. As, however, polygamy was a recognized practice, jealous quarrels often arose. Naturally, each additional wife had her separate hut.

Lamentation for the dead accompanied funerals. A funeral feast, consisting of the flesh of several goats, had to be provided for the morticians, who made the grave and carried the corpse to its burying-place. The whole family had to be present at the funeral, and even small children had to throw a handful of earth into the grave as a last farewell. The women threw a little buchu powder into it. The body was sewn up in skins and, after it had been covered up with branches, the grave was filled up and packed with heavy stones to protect it from wild animals. The care of graves was unknown. A traveller passed close to a grave only if he was compelled to do so. To point at a grave, to tread on it, or to pass over it, were forbidden. Whenever a traveller's road led him past a grave, he saluted it from afar, picked up a twig, a stone, or a tuft of grass, and laid it on the grave. When leaving it, he did not dare to look back and he held one hand behind his head as a shield.

Upon their return from the funeral the relatives formed themselves into successive groups and all partook of a small quantity of the blood of the animals which had been killed for the funeral feast. With the rest, mixed with the intestines, an old woman besmeared those present in the region of the heart and the small of the back in order to counteract the harmful effect of the mourning and the strain of the lament for the dead. Further, it was very important to open everything closed which had belonged to the deceased, such as powder-boxes, rouge horns, tobacco pouches, and such like, and to take a little of the contents out of each of them. This ensured the safety of the closed grave, for it was considered dangerous if wild animals should open the grave and the spirit of the deceased should escape. If he got restless, he could take it into his head to return to his former dwelling-place and to take the spirits of his relations back with him. To make quite certain, the huts were moved soon after the death of a relative, and they were either erected again close by or in a different locality.

The father's eldest brother was entitled to the custody of the estate. If disputes as to the division arose, the chief acted as arbitrator. All the possessions of the deceased belonged to his estate, including his clothes, which were only buried with him if he had died from an infectious or loathsome disease. His children of both sexes were given equal shares and his relations were not forgotten.

The Nama is intelligent, grasps and learns a thing quickly, has a good memory, and is handy and skilful in performing light tasks. All that has been written in old books about the stupidity of the Hottentots only applies when they have been taken into an entirely strange environment. As the result of very close study, it can be stated that this race is the most gifted of all the South West African peoples. Their feelings are easily moved and they are very easily swayed for good or evil. Hatred makes the Nama a dangerous opponent and a merciless enemy. Endurance of any kind is not one of his hereditary characteristics, nor is careful thrift with a view to the future within the category of his virtues.

The Nama language has a wonderful structure. While the musical Herero language passes clumsily from sentence to sentence in obedience to the rigid rule for the sequence of words, the Nama language has the knack of always giving a sentence a new turn, while it possesses a flexibility which makes it possible to express the very finest shades of meaning. It is just this, however, which makes it so difficult to learn. It is possible to speak Herero when a knowledge has been acquired of the innumerable forms and of a fixed vocabulary, because the speaker can think in his own language and then translate the separate words into Herero at lightning speed. The Nama language can only be spoken fluently by a person who actually thinks in it, for the Nama puts at the end of the sentence the part which, in European languages, usually comes at the beginning, and separate parts of speech have a way of assuming this inverted shape. The learning of the language presents another difficulty because of the many strange

sounds it possesses; these can be uttered only by people who
have vocal organs specially adapted to the purpose, and the gift of
tongues is of no assistance. The vowels which are spoken through
the nose are amongst the easiest of these queer sounds. They are to
be found in European languages, French for example, although not
in such frequency. It is the four clicks of the Nama tongue that
have, for the last three hundred years, been the obstacle in the way
of all attempts to learn the language. One has only to read what the
early colonists of South Africa had to say about it! As the Nama
names of places and persons will frequently be used in this book, this
seems a convenient place to prepare the reader by saying something
more about them. If closely investigated, the clicks are far easier to
pronounce than most of the sounds of our alphabet. How much
preparation and movement of the vocal organs does not the production of a 'b' or an 'm' demand? No one even notices that. A click
requires merely two movements of the tongue with the lips fairly
well open. The tongue is pressed up against some particular part of
the mouth and then withdrawn either slowly or suddenly. The
throat, the lungs, the vocal cord, and the lips remain entirely inactive.
The first click, which is written as a vertical stroke (|), is produced
by pressing the tip of the tongue against the base of the front teeth
and drawing it slowly back; by doing this the very same sound is
produced as that which old women use to express their astonishment
when they hear of anything dreadful having happened. The second
click, which is represented by two vertical strokes (||), is known to
us as the sound of encouragement with which the rider urges on his
horse. To produce it, the front part of the tongue is laid flat so that
its edges touch the teeth on both sides. The rear portion, however,
is raised, pressed against the palate, and then slowly withdrawn. That
is how the smacking sound now under discussion is produced. The
third click, which is written as the exclamation mark (!), required
for its production the pressing of the tongue into the alveolus and its
quick withdrawal to the back. It has a dull sound, not unlike the
noise made when a cork is forcibly drawn from a bottle. The fourth
click, which usually causes the student the greatest difficulty, sounds
like the hard clear snapping sound, which is made with the thumb
and middle finger when one person snaps his fingers at another. The
point of the tongue is pressed up against the alveolus and then brought
violently downwards with a sudden jerk. It is written as a cross with
two cross-bars (‡). These four sounds, which were probably taken

over from the Bushmen in the dark ages, were always analogous to consonants; they stood only at the beginning of words and never as middle or final sounds. As it was sought in the old records to employ a letter of the recognized alphabet to represent a click-sound, it follows that this method of recording the actual sound which represents a particular word could only be reproduced very imperfectly and ambiguously. The old names of places, tribes, and people can usually be traced back to their phonetic origins and accounted for only with reservations and hardly ever with any certainty. It is to the Nama missionaries of early days, especially J. M. Kroenlein (Bersheba 1851–77), that the credit is due for having given the Nama language proper written characters and for having investigated its grammar.

The ancient linguistic monuments of a nation which knows no writing are preserved through the handing down of proverbs and songs. Any kind of verse is transmitted from generation to generation much more accurately than the prose narration of legend and story. There are very few proverbs in the Nama language. There are, however, in existence numerous little songs, which are no longer generally known, but which are sung on great occasions, even up to the present day, by an individual, but never by a number of people together, the monotonous tune to which they are sung being apparently left to the ingenuity of the singer. These songs bear, both from the point of view of their language and their form, the unmistakable stamp of great age and they are well worth preserving as linguistic monuments of times gone by. While the Herero song merely lauds the praises of the distinguished man and the most wonderful of oxen, the Nama song extols everything in heaven and earth which arouses the contemplative faculties of the observer: thunder and lightning, drought and rain, wind and cloud, cow and calf, bird and beast, mountain and stream. People are practically never the subject of these songs.

The religion of the ancient Hottentots was not investigated timeously. It is possible to reproduce only the merest sketch of it out of the fragmentary memories which still survive, and by the comparison of these with the religious ideas of the Bergdamas, the black servitors of the Namas, and the Saan, a race closely related to them. The highest divine being known to the Hottentots, amongst whom we include the Namas, was probably Gâuab; they looked to him principally for the thunderstorms, with the blessings for man and beast

which flowed from them in a drought-stricken land. It appears, however, that the worship of Gâuab gave place to the worship of a popular
hero, who likewise played a part in the myths of other African races.
His name was Tsui-goab, which means Wounded Knee. He got this
name because he was wounded in the knee when fighting hard for
his people. The divine attributes of Gâuab were transferred to
Wounded Knee and he was regarded as almighty, ever-present, and
immortal. The influence of the earliest missionaries had a further
effect: Tsui-goab was recognized by them as the name of God, while,
from then onwards, Gâuab became the evil spirit, the devil. The
demi-god, Heiseb, enjoys considerable popularity, even to the present
day. His name means tree-like. His human birth took place in
wonderful circumstances, he distinguished himself through his wit
and cunning, and even death itself had to surrender to him. Whenever Heiseb died, he rose again from the dead and his merry song
rang out from his seat in the trees and bushes. Everything which,
from olden times, seemed to be inexplicable in mountain and kloof
was ascribed to Heiseb's skill; for example, the numerous rock-
paintings of past ages, the footprints of men and animals impressed
in the rocks, and more especially the so-called graves of Heiseb.
These consisted of enormous piles of stones and no one, who is a
heathen, passes them without a salutation, which takes the same form
as that which is offered to an ordinary grave. Under each one of
these heaps of stones, which often reach enormous dimensions, Heiseb
was once buried, and from every one of these graves he has risen again.
But the story is likewise current that these rock-piles are not graves
at all, but that another explanation is possible. In any event, when
search has been made, human bones have never been discovered
beneath them.

   Apart from Heiseb's spirit and the spirits of deceased ancestors,
the Namas peopled the mountains and the valleys, the streams and
the plains with spirits of different kinds. Belief in their harmful
influence was much stronger than it was in their good intentions.
Shadows were greatly feared by any one who had a guilty conscience.

   On bright moonlight nights regular dances were organized and, on
these occasions, a soloist sang old songs verse by verse while the
dancers answered him with loud 'ho-hoes'. The opinion is expressed
in old reports that the origin of the word Hottentot, as the name of
the race, might be traced to this shout of the dancers. It is certain

that this name did not originate from the language of these people. How it is to be explained, no one can say with any degree of accuracy.

4. THE BERGDAMAS

In describing the natives of South West Africa we must take the Bergdamas after the Namas. They were, from ancient times, the servants of the Namas, and even to-day, a Bergdama will address a Nama with the title, 'Mister', although he has long been released from his ancient domination, the reason being either that all recollection of the earlier condition of servitude has disappeared, or that he intends, by employing a different form of address, to show that the old days are past.

The Bergdamas call themselves Nu-khoin, i.e. the black people. All other names, which are to be found in books, are founded upon misunderstandings, to which travellers, who spend but a short time in the country, are naturally more liable than are people who have spent several decades working amongst the people and learning their language. The Namas gave these black people the name of Dama, which appears in the earlier literature in the plural form, Damara, a form which ought only to be used when either two women, or a man and a woman, are being referred to. The correct way is to use just the stem of the word as the name of the race and to say simply Dama. As, however, the Namas used the same word to indicate the Hereros, it was necessary to add to it some qualification in order to distinguish the Hereros from the Bergdamas. In the case of the Hereros, with their herds of cattle, a designation naturally followed; they were called the Cattle Damas. The black race, however, who had taken refuge in the mountains when the Namas and the Hereros pressed them, received the name of Bergdamas. A more contemptuous name was often used for them, a name which arose through its being noticeable that excrement was not carefully buried in the neighbourhood of the Bergdama villages, in accordance with what was thought to be decent manners with the Namas and the Hereros; they were called Dung Damas (Chou-damas). The Hereros simply called them Ovazorotua, meaning black slaves.

It is almost unnecessary to call particular attention to the fact that, of all the inhabitants of South West Africa, the Bergdamas are striking because of their black skins. Sturdily built, of medium height, with brown eyes, coarse features and crinkly hair, which hangs in a tangle over the forehead, they present no very attractive appearance. Cultural influences have turned them into quite different people to-day. As we, however, have to do with the history of early South West Africa, it is the Bergdamas of former times whose characteristics must be described here.

The clothing of both men and women was made of leather, tanned from the skins of wild animals. A grown-up man's clothes consisted of a short apron in front and a longer one behind, supported by a leathern thong for a belt. The women's apron at the back was considerably longer and hung down as far as the calves of her legs. In addition to this, the women wore a soft skin fastened on the left shoulder in the Nama fashion. This covered the back and, as it was held together by means of a riem round the body, it served both as a covering and a receptacle. Sandals were often worn and the men affected the embellishment of a cap made out of some wild creature's skin.

The decking out of the person was practised only by those who had learnt its merit from other races. The true Bergdama male despised it and wore no ornaments except a couple of shells in his matted hair. The women, however, decorated themselves with leather rings on arms and ankles, and perhaps with iron beads as well, these being threaded on thin leather riems. The Bergdamas, as has been remarked before, were people who understood the working of iron from the earliest times, and the iron beads with which the Hereros used to ornament themselves, sometimes using as much as 10 lb. weight of them, must have been made by the Bergdamas.

The simplicity of the Bergdama huts was only exceeded by that of the Bushman windbreak. They were erected in sheltered places in the mountains or in thorny thickets. In a roughly measured circle of three to four paces in diameter, branches of trees with any useful twigs left on them, were planted in the ground close together. The boughs were joined together at the top without an effort being made to form a proper domed roof. The cross supports were tied to the superstructure with bark, and the gaps were filled with twigs and tufts of grass. The huts were usually so low that it was scarcely possible to stand up inside. Seen from a distance, a Bergdama house of the old style, which is still occasionally to be found to-day, looked like a large heap of hay. The huts were regarded merely as a resting-place for the night. The days were spent in the open air.

A Bergdama village consisted of only a few huts, for it was usual for a single family to found it. The eldest member of the family was the person in authority, while an elder acted with him as steward. This chieftain decided matters of hunting and raids, of staying in a place or trekking away from it and he bore the responsibility for the welfare of his little community. There was no such thing as combining with another family. The Bergdamas first obtained one chief over them all through the influence of the German Government.

Their domestic economy was very simple. The man was first of all a hunter, and as a secondary pursuit many of them went in for farming with goats, which they traded from the Bechuanas. A family which possessed a few cattle was to be found occasionally, but the Bergdama never became a proper stock farmer, and that was all the more reason why the Hereros' cattle and the Namas' sheep proved such an attraction for him. He did not reckon it wrong to prey on them. For this reason the Hereros and the Namas became more and more hostile towards him, and there were times when, out of dread of the roving Hereros, the Bergdama in the open veld had to make himself understood by his mates by barking like a dog or a baboon. If the Hereros found him, they either killed him on the spot or they carried him off to a lifetime of hard work, as their slave.

The women's work was to provide the family with wild berries, roots, bulbs, and everything edible which nature provided in the shape of frogs, lizards, birds' eggs, young birds, and so forth.

In spite of this simple method of living their intellect was not entirely stunted. This is shown by the numerous proverbs which reveal a sound wit, and the little songs with which they were wont to improve the lonely hours. The long dance-song and the funeral dirges display a wealth of thought and conception which could hardly be expected from so poverty-stricken a race. The little songs were passed down from mouth to mouth in their ancient settings. They were sung with the strumming of the hunting bow for an accompaniment, and the art of producing various notes through the pressure of the fingers on the bow-string in different places was well understood. Another musical instrument was made, with a hollowed tree bole for a sounding board, having five fairly long bow-shaped pieces of wood projecting from one end of it; strings made of animal sinew were attached to these bows and they were drawn taut, fiddle fashion, so that the required sounds could be produced by them. After the singer had worked himself up to the right pitch through a little preliminary strumming, he sang a sentence of his song falsetto to the accompaniment of his harp and then, after a little intermezzo, he sang a little more, never getting tired of his alternate playing and singing. Quite often he worked himself up into such a state of emotion that the tears coursed down his black cheeks. The dance-song must be regarded as a form of prayer, for dancing had, as a rule, a religious significance. For Bergdamas of the old stamp the only kind of religious ceremony he knew was the dance. A leader, either male or female, directed the ceremony, sang the dance-song sentence by sentence, and allowed time, in the pauses, for the dancing community to express their concurrence through loud shouts and with violent stamping on the ground. The death dirge was sung in the same manner by a woman as leader, line for line, while the mourning women answered with long drawn-out wails and violent weeping. This song, which contains many obsolete forms of speech, is likewise a reflection of the life of the Bergdamas in ancient times, for all the joy and sorrow which man, woman, and child experienced in the course of his life is minutely dealt with in the funeral dirge. The leader has the right to adapt the song to the circumstances of the particular case, in which event the new matter had to be fitted into the old form.

For a long time it was thought that the Bergdamas had no religion and no actual conception of God. There was considerable justification for this assumption. Wherever the Bergdamas have come into close contact with the Hereros and the Namas, and have learnt a higher culture at one or other of the bigger centres in the land, it is useless to ask them about the religion of their forefathers. Just as they have substituted for their own language that of their masters, the Namas, they have surrendered too the spiritual inheritance of their race. A successful search was made and there were found in the kloofs of the Otavi Highlands several Bergdama families, who were quite unaffected and were living in the manner of their forefathers. From information obtained from them, it was apparent that the philosophy of life of this needy race could well be called rich in comparison with the religious ideas of many other tribes, who regarded the Dung Damas with contempt.

The Bergdamas acknowledge a supreme being whom they called in their language Gamab. Heaven is his dwelling-place. There he has his head-quarters and there he gathers all the essentials, so far as the Bergdamas are concerned, for a happy existence after death. Nor does he have any regard for moral superiority or inferiority; whoever is a Bergdama is entitled to a place in the Bergdama heaven. All the things which are to be found on earth are there in perfection. It is only while they are there that they can likewise appear on earth. There is the perfect hunting-ground, the perfect fruit tree, and the perfect tuber. There is no anxiety about food there, for everything can be eaten. When the human spirit leaves the dead body, it finds itself on a broad way which leads to Gamab's home. Departed spirits meet him on this road to lead him safely on. One danger threatens the dead man, but this he can escape. Along the road there is a deep pit, which glows like a red-hot fire. Whoever ventures too near to this pit falls into it and is doomed to destruction. Whoever escapes it reaches Gamab's abode. At its entrance he finds a hollowed tree trunk filled with melted fat, for it is not with a drink of water but with a ladleful of melted fat, which the new arrival greedily drinks, that the Bergdama god welcomes his earthly children. After this refreshment the traveller lies down to rest under a large and shady fig-tree. It is there that Gamab's true holy fire burns, for it is only because there is a holy fire in heaven that one is kindled in every Bergdama village, after many prayers and incantations. It is, moreover, only because the perfect fig-tree casts its shade over the blessed ones in heaven, that every head of a family chooses, as his dwelling-place on earth, a spot in the midst of which there stands a shady tree. When any one is sufficiently rested he goes out into the heavenly country-side, perhaps in pursuit of game, perhaps with the object of enjoying the delicious berries, plums, or ground fruits. The gathering place for them all is once again the fig-tree, beneath which the holy fire burns and where Gamab himself lies at his ease on the ground. All around him squat or lie the old men who were the forefathers of the race in the dim and distant past. The greatest luxury they can have is human flesh. Like as the hunter slays with his bow and arrow the game of the open veld, and thus satisfies his children's hunger, so is it Gamab's privilege to treat the world of men as his hunting-ground. When an old man grows hungry he takes his bow and arrow in his hand and he speeds, with deadly aim, the arrow of death into a human body. The stricken man falls ill; he feels the arrow in his body and knows that he is sick unto death. It would be useless and impious indeed to offer any resistance. The man who feels Gamab's arrow in his body eats and drinks no more, nor do the members of his family make further provision for him. It is not wise to seek to stay Gamab's hand. Since the arrow of death often strikes small children, who still require a woman's care, the spirits of dead women regard it as a special honour to cherish and protect these children until they are grown-up. They are zealous in carrying out their task, and they feel unhappy when their foster-children grow up and no longer require their care. Then they besiege Gamab with their importunities until he causes the death of many children on the earth. This explains why, however careful a mother may be with the rearing of her babies, such a large number of children die while they are growing up. It is no wonder that there was a dread of the departed spirits!

This dread was still further increased by the fact that it was not every dead person who found his way to Gamab's abode just after he had died. Many a man held so fast to his family and his worldly goods, that his spirit wandered about for days in the neighbourhood of his old home. As a measure of protection against this visitation, the dying man is either carried out into the bush and left there to breathe out his spirit with his dying breath, or the body is dragged out of the hut through a hole in the side, the door is built up, the hole filled up, and a new door made, so as to prevent the spirit from finding its way properly if it seeks to visit the family. In all cases the wisest course is to leave the hut or to burn it, and to move to another place. There had likewise to be taken into account the fact that the new arrival in Gamab's village might not find the company round the fire to his liking. Under such circumstances, Gamab was wont to take pity upon him and to give the spirit permission to pay the earth a visit, so that he could carry off one of his relations or friends for company. This was the explanation of the position, which it was otherwise impossible to understand, that after one death, a second and even a third often occurred.

The old men, who had their place of honour at the holy fire on high, could likewise interfere dreadfully with the life of the Bergdamas on earth. If Gamab's arrow did not bring them enough human flesh, they tried to provide it themselves. In some mysterious way, they hid an object, the effect of which was deadly, in a human body, and while the person was still alive, they ate up quite a large part of his flesh, as his getting thinner plainly showed. These objects were of many different kinds, such as little knives, thorns, small stones, splinters, scorpions, mice, lions, and leopards in miniature, and so forth. Seeing that this took place without Gamab's permission, remedies might be used to combat diseases of this kind. Indeed, Gamab himself had made provision for people to help these sick folk. These helpers were the sorcerers, who were in direct communication with Gamab, could talk to him, and could be called by him. They understood the art of assembling the cause of the sickness at one particular place, by drawing it together with the hands. When they had done this they applied the mouth to the place and sucked out the cause. Then they showed those who were sitting round the object which they had removed from the body. If, however, the cause was a living animal, the sorcerer spat it into the shell of a tortoise, held the hand flat upon it to prevent its escape, and put some red-hot coals into it, thereby killing the little animal. He then held the shell outwards and committed it in a short address to those who had been the authors of the mischief, after which all present were allowed to examine the now empty shell. Since there was no longer any trace of the cause of the illness in the shell, the operation had a very convincing effect.

But how was any one to know whether it was Gamab's arrow or the wantonness of his old men which had been at work? It was only the diviner who could give information on that score, and he was prepared to disclose the secret for three or four iron beads or two pieces of leather cut in the shape of shoes. Before calling in the sorcerer, it was necessary to approach the diviner, who discharged the duties of his office in return for food and presents.

They believed, too, that the entire atmosphere, the valleys, mountains, and watering-places, were inhabited by spirits who were inimical to mankind. Luckily these were thought to be blind. While his old men were eating up dead men's bodies, Gamab had taken away their eyes and had fixed them in the skies at night, from where they looked down upon the earth as stars. Special care had to be taken to guard small children from the spirits which were flitting all about. They were very fond of children's flesh and they used to feed on it secretly, as the falling off of babies showed when they were weaned and had to go over from a milk diet to one of raw meat and hard food from the veld. The Bergdama mother very much disliked hearing any stranger praising her well-nourished infant. There might be a spirit in the neighbourhood, to which this praise might betray the fact that here was fine prey for him. She would not hesitate for a second to pinch her little darling hard, so that his loud cries could apprise the spirit of the fact that it was not going nearly as well with him as the statement it had heard might have led it to expect. If, however, the child grew thinner in spite of all possible precautions, the spirits were then clearly at work and an attempt was made to satisfy them by sacrificing the little finger of one hand. The father chopped it off with a heavy blow with a stone on the back of his knife, took the finger

into the veld and called the spirits together, telling them that he
gladly gave them his child to appease their appetites. The blind
spirits were deceived by this portion into thinking that it was the
whole and, when the baby had got used to the change, it would, in
course of time, thrive again. There are, even to-day, many Bergdamas of both sexes who have lost the little finger of one hand.

It was thus that the Bergdamas of olden times loved and lived.
They lived in the Otavi Highlands, in the Paresis Mountains, in
Erongo, and in the Auas Mountains. From the Orange River to the
Kunene, members of this race were to be found in the service of the
Namas, the Hereros, the Bushmen (Saan) and the Ovambos, per-
forming domestic tasks and herding stock without any wages at all.

5. THE OVAMBO TRIBES

Numerous tribes, which we call the Ovambo tribes, had made
their homes in the north of Hereroland, between the Kaokoveld in
the west and the Okavango in the east.

The following Ovambo tribes, each of which lives in its own territory and had, in earlier times, its own chief, belong to South West
Africa, namely: Ukuanyama, Ondonga, Ukuambi, Ongandjera, Ukualuizi, Ombalantu, and Ukolukazi. Eunda, which is likewise sometimes
referred to as a tribal territory, is a piece of country belonging to
Ukolukazi.

Every tribe has its special characteristics, its organization, and its
own particular customs. As, however, all that is required here is to
describe the Ovambo race to an extent which will enable the reader
to understand the history of the country, everything which differen-
tiates the tribes from each other will be left out, and mention will
be made only of the things which they all have in common. In doing
so, no regard can be had to the way in which this community of
interests is stressed or treated in each of the particular tribes.

In their physical appearance, build, colour, and the growth of their
hair, the Ovambos resemble their southern neighbours, the Hereros.
It is remarkable that with them a thick-set build predominates, while,
in the case of the Hereros, tall people are more usual. A leather belt,
as broad as the hand, supports an apron made out of the stomach of
an ox. In addition to this, the women wear a covering for the back,
made out of the skin of a black ox, and a hat, which, in olden times,
was so plaited on to the owner's head by means of threads of sinew
and her own hair that it could not be taken off. Leather sandals

completed the dress. The man kept his knobkerrie, his pipe, and his horn snuff-box under his belt, and in it was stuck his double-edged, dagger-shaped knife in its wooden sheath. A corset made out of ostrich shells served the woman both as clothing and as an ornament; this covered the lower part of the body and the hips in artistic and graceful turns, and its length indicated the social standing of its possessor. The ankles were decorated with copper rings as thick as the thumb, and the arms as well were sometimes covered with rings as far as the elbows. This finery was given to the women by their husbands and remained the property of the giver.

The man's finery was his weapons. Without them he never appeared outside his house. Bows were made from the centres of the leaves of fan-palms. Arrows of different shapes, some with iron points and some without, were carried in a quiver. A dagger, with its sheath, in the belt, a knobkerrie and an assegai with an iron blade completed his armoury. Many of the Ovambos bore in olden times, in the manner of the Hereros, a tribal token on their eye teeth. The chiefs did not have them, as it was strictly prohibited that the blood of a chief should be allowed to flow. The token was affixed as soon as the child had lost its milk teeth.

Since the Ovambos were always agriculturists, their dietary was richer than that of the Hereros, the Namas, or the Bergdamas. Their chief food, which was a thick porridge, was made out of Kaffir-corn and millet which they grew themselves, and they had milk, meat, beans, pumpkins, melons, and ground-nuts as well. They had, too, a better supply of wild fruit than was to be found in the Herero and Nama countries. They were particularly fond of palm-tree fruit, wild figs, and marula nuts. Their stock farming was restricted to the keeping of cattle and goats, as the country was not suitable for sheep, and horses and mules were unknown in early times. The tilling of the ground was the women's task. Hoeing was the only known method of cultivation. Besides this, the wife had to grind the meal in the early morning hours, to see to the preparation of the food and to make the beer, of which every hut had to have its supply. Its alcoholic content was very weak, and it was brewed from millet with various ingredients added. Plates, bowls, and baskets, which were both ornamental and useful, were made from palm leaves. The making of pots was likewise understood. The corn was stored in extraordinarily large baskets, which were raised up on poles as a protection from termites, while a wicker-work roof warded off the sun

BERGDAMA WERF WITH A HOTTENTOT WOMAN STANDING IN THE CENTRE OF THE HUT

A BABOON IN THE FOREGROUND

By courtesy of F. Nink, Windhoek

and the rain. In this way the wife was kept busy the whole day, but the husband's work was not so hard, nor did it occupy him throughout the daytime. His task was to look after the stock, to clean out the water-holes, to fix handles to the hoes and axes, to see to the repairing of the hut, to go out hunting, to manage the flocks, and to provide the family with meat. For this purpose, the wealthy might perhaps slaughter their cattle, but poor folk never permitted themselves this luxury.

The werfs[1] of single families were scattered throughout the settled part of the country. There were no enclosed villages. The dwellings stood either in the middle or at the edge of the cultivated land. They differed from the huts of the southern people in arrangement and construction. The husband had his own sleeping hut; the head wife and the secondary wives each had their own. The growing boys had their sleeping-place in a hut specially erected for them. Even sleeping accommodation for guests was not forgotten. These huts were built circular in shape with poles and were covered with an artistically fashioned roof like a peaked hat, the edge of which projected over the walls. The huts were surrounded with a pallisade sufficiently high that no one could see over it. The settlement consisted of an enclosed homestead, which could be entered only through a very narrow gateway which was closed up with a thorn bush at night. But even inside the courtyard it was difficult to pass freely from one hut to another. Pallisaded passages separated the dwellings, which seemed like a labyrinth to the uninitiated, for it was only the householders who could find their way about in them. Apparently it was the insecurity of life and property which had led to the invention of a homestead arranged on this system, in the construction of which several thousand tree trunks were required.

The chief's werf differed from that of his subjects by virtue of its enormous extent, the height of its pallisade, the large number of huts—he had usually more than a dozen wives—and by the intricacy of the inside passages. In these werfs there was community of goods. The corn-bins, the calabashes which served as bottles, the beer vats, the pestles and mortars were all kept in their special places; even the stock kraals[2] lay inside the outer circle of the pallisades. Order reigned in an Ovambo werf.

The life of the whole family ran its course in this remarkable small

[1] *Werf* is the South African word for a dwelling place with the land immediately surrounding it—*Ed.*

[2] *Kraals* are cattle pens, often made of poles or thorn bush, in which the cattle are kept at night—*Ed.*

world. Before the birth of her child the mother was excused from heavy labour and she was given better food. A few days before the birth her nearest relatives were allowed to come and stay with her, and it was duly displayed to them after it was born. An old woman took it and carried it round to the scenes of its future labours. A girl was taken to the corn-bins, stampers, and beer casks. A boy was shown the stock kraals and the milk tubs, and was also carried to the entrance of the werf and given a brief view of the outside world. Neighbours and friends, as well as the relatives, came to attend the naming ceremony, which took place a week after the birth. They all brought beer and food for the festive occasion. The father received the child from its mother's arms, laid it on his lap, passed his hands caressingly a few times over its body, and pronounced its name. The name of one of the father's friends was usually selected, and he became, in a certain sense, the child's god-father. It was his duty, in years to come, to make it small presents and to keep a watchful eye on it. Names which, by their form or sound, distinguished boys and girls from each other were unknown.

The birth of twins occasioned great dismay, for it was regarded as a misfortune. Both children were stifled soon after birth by closing their mouths and noses up with clay. The mother had then to be purified by means of a special ceremony before she could be permitted to see other people.

The growing child had to undertake its share of the work at the earliest possible time. The girls helped their mother in all her tasks and the boys were employed by their father.

When the boys were between fifteen and twenty years of age and so were approaching manhood, they were taken to an initiation ceremony, which was held near the chief's residence. There they had to stay for three or four weeks. Boys of the same age, belonging to many families, were gathered together in huts specially erected for this purpose. Their parents had to maintain them. They were circumcised with a stone knife by a skilful practitioner from another tribe. Every bit of boy's clothing had then to be burnt, and the circumcised youth returned home in the new clothes of a grown-up man. It was not for every one that attendance at this feast was compulsory. The poorer classes of the people took no part in it.

Matters were somewhat different with the girls. They were not allowed to marry until they had gone through the special initiation ceremony for girls. This took place every second year and was regulated by the chief. He selected a spot where it was to take place in narrow little huts, and he appointed the people who were to conduct the almost month-long ceremony. When the first crescent of the new moon appeared the festival began, and it only ended with the last days of the month. One part of the solemnities was the testing of capacity for enduring hard work and privations of all kinds. The girls were compelled to pass the nights herded together in narrow rooms and then to stamp corn at the very break of day. Alas for her whose strength failed her. She was driven away and had to bear the most bitter consequences. Then again they had to sit on the ground for hours at an end in the fierce heat of the sun, or to show their endurance by dancing the whole night through. Their whole bodies were covered with white ashes, and they wore fantastic clothes or coverings made of palm fronds and fearsome head-dresses. Towards the end of the festival the girls used to go in troops out into the country and woe betide the man who fell into their clutches. He was beaten unmercifully and dared not defend himself. This month was not exactly in the nature of a school of instruction for married life, but whoever endured to the end was considered marriageable.

A young man did not personally pay court to the damsel of his choice; he sent a friend to her. If her answer was favourable, it was for her to acquaint her mother with the position, and for the latter to tell her father. If the young man was acceptable to the family, he visited her home as a guest. This visit could take place long before the young girls' festival, but he was not allowed to be too friendly with her. Pregnancy before the festival was punished with death in earlier days; the unfortunate girl was swathed in dry grass and burnt. If a marriage was arranged, the father of the bride invited the guests to the wedding. The bridegroom brought his future step-mother an ox as an ante-nuptial gift. The marriage was solemnized in the presence of the parents and relations. The ceremony consisted in the bride and bridegroom sitting opposite one another and rubbing each other's breasts with ochre salve; that was all. The mother-in-law served her guests with meat, corn porridge, and plenty of beer. In the evening the young bridegroom went back to his own parents. It was only some days later that he sent a girl of his acquaintance to fetch the young wife to her husband's home. The marriage of subsequent wives took place in exactly the same manner. They all did their share of the work of the house and the fields and they remained subordinate to the head wife.

The families were divided up into the families of chiefs, those of the old landed nobility and those of the common people. In accordance with the fixed rights of succession the chieftainship passed to the chief's younger brother when the elder brother died. If there was no brother, the deceased's nephew, i.e. his eldest sister's son became heir. The chief's own sons were regarded as common people; they neither belonged to the aristocracy nor did they have any privileges at all. The reason for this was that chiefs married women of the people, who had no honourable position which their sons could inherit from them.

The chief was an autocrat in the widest sense of the word. The whole of the tribal territory belonged to him. Whoever occupied a district, or a werf with farm land attached, did so merely on loan, and it could be taken away from him at any time. The chief exercised rights of ownership over the herds of cattle and of life and death over his subjects. The chief's mother was the only person who dared to voice her opinion freely. Even the nobility were subordinate to him in respect of their persons and their property. They were not allowed to marry among themselves. The sons had to marry the daughters of respectable common folk and the daughters had the right of choosing husbands for themselves from the people. Succession amongst the nobles was, however, in the female line.

The tribal land was divided into districts, in each of which there were between fifteen and twenty farms. The headman of the district got his appointment from the chief in consideration of his paying a recognition fee, but the position could be conferred upon him as a favour without any such fee. He was responsible for the keeping of order in his district, and it was to him that the chief's commands were issued when he required the men of the district for labour, war, or hunting. He had to see to the tributes of corn and cattle being regularly delivered. The occupiers of werfs had actually to pay their rent to the headman of the district, but he was open to receive gifts of all kinds as well.

Chiefs were allowed to travel about within the boundaries of the tribal territories accompanied by an armed bodyguard, and then banquets were held and riotous feasting was resorted to, but ancient custom forbade them to pass beyond the boundaries of the tribe's possessions. Ovambo chieftains were not allowed to visit each other. It was generally believed that, in that case, one or other of them would die very soon. The principal pleasures were raids and hunting expeditions, and the relation of stories of the raids of former times. It was decided by the chief, in secret conclave with his advisers, upon which of the neighbouring tribes a raid was to be made, with the object of capturing people and cattle. An armed force was assembled and they proceeded secretly, in the dead of night, to an unsuspecting werf and fell upon it in the grey of dawn. Those who offered any resistance were killed. The cattle were driven off, the people, bound together, driven after them in haste, while an armed rearguard saw to their safe passage. The cattle became the chief's property, while the people became slaves to those who took them prisoner; they could, however, be ransomed afterwards by their kindred by the payment of cattle. Naturally, revenge on the part of the neighbouring tribe was soon forthcoming. This custom filled the history of ancient times with stories about robbery, murder, and other atrocities. A chief sometimes despoiled his own rich subjects in a similar manner.

Hunting expeditions often lasted for weeks in the uninhabited parts of the tribal territory. Huts were erected there and the hunters who accompanied their chief to the hunting-grounds took their wives with them to look after them.

The chief's power was terribly displayed when he sat in judgment. It was not his custom to hear the cases himself; one of his counsellors was appointed to do that. It was the chief, however, who pronounced judgment, and the life of a man meant less to him than that of a beast. He kept, as executioners at his court, men of another tribe, or Bushmen; a nod sufficed and they dragged the victim away to throttle him, stab him, beat him to death, or shoot him, just as it pleased them. A man who had been executed was not allowed to be buried; his body was thrown into the bush as food for the hyenas.

Revenge at the hands of his victim's relatives pursued the man who murdered or struck another down, without recourse to law. He had, however, four sanctuaries to which he could flee and so save the life he had forfeited. He could take refuge at the grave of the last chief who had died; he could try to embrace the knees of the reigning chief, or, if he could not succeed in doing that, he could seize one of his milk calabashes. An occasion is known of a chief himself pursuing a murderer with his armed followers, but of giving up the pursuit when the murderer reached a chief's grave in the course of his flight. Naturally, the fugitive was safe only so long as he remained at the sanctuary. If his pursuers left him, he could not stay in that country any longer. He either fled to another Ovambo tribe or to Hereroland.

As a fourth place of sanctuary with some tribes there was a huge pot, which stood in the chief's werf, and was so large that an ox could be roasted whole in it. The killer did not flee to the pot, but contrived to hide himself somewhere or other; his father or uncle then took a red ox to the chief, told him about his relative's guilt and his danger, slaughtered the ox and cooked the meat, with the blood, in the pot, whereupon those who were present consumed it. If atonement had been made in this way, the murderer went free and revenge could not be taken upon him.

The procedure upon the death and at the funeral of a chief differed with different tribes. With the Ukuanyama in olden times, the successor often strangled his dying predecessor. This was not done out of cruelty, but with the object of keeping the soul in the body. A huge grave was then dug in the cattle kraal and the skin of a freshly slaughtered black ox was laid in it. A female slave seated herself on the skin and the chief's corpse was placed on her lap; both were then covered up in the skin and the grave was filled in. The same day the deceased's head wife and his counsellors were strangled. This was done with the idea of affording him service and company in the hereafter.

A protective monument made of heavy tree trunks was erected over the grave. These were planted in the ground leaning one against the other in such a way as to form a pyramid of considerable height. After the death of a chief, the burial of the body of a common person was not allowed until some member of a noble family had died. Until then the bodies were thrown out into the bush. The graves of the common people were made inside the werfs. The children were buried in the huts of their mothers, the women close to the stampers, and the men in the cattle kraals. For the latter, a black ox, a dog, and a cock were killed on the burial day.

This shows how the idea of a life after death and a world to come occupied their thoughts and influenced their lives. Something more of these conceptions and the things associated with them ought to be explained. So as to be able to understand them something must be said about their philosophic outlook. They believed that there is not only one world, but that there are three. The first is above us and it is pleasant to live there, for droughts and hunger are unknown. It rains quite frequently and sowing and harvesting is unceasing. It is there that Kalunga, the highest divine being, dwells. The nobles of the land gather round him. A man of the people has little prospect of reaching this upper world. The second world is that on which we live. It receives from above just a little of the surplus rain, only that which oozes through and falls on the ground. But still it is sufficient to give man the chance of producing the means of existence in good years and to afford him grazing for his stock. The worst world is the third, which is to be found under the earth. It is only the surplus rainfall of this earth which percolates through to the lower world. The departed souls of the common people are to be found there. They live in poverty and suffer hunger. The poverty leads to their waging endless wars amongst themselves. Their hunger is so great that they even catch flies for food. It is therefore easy to understand why the spirits of the dead feel a strong urge to get back to earth again. Many succeed, and then they become a source of danger to mankind, especially to the relatives, for every spirit clings particularly to those members of his family who are still living on earth. Since human beings are partly good and partly bad, the same applies to spirits. The good spirits, however, keep themselves apart from the wicked ones; they do not live all mixed fortuitously together, like the people on earth. They are present after sunrise and they shine forth like the light. The time of the evil spirits is after sunset and they look like the approaching shades of night. The good spirits promote human effort in the daytime, while the evil spirits are particularly dangerous to human beings at night. People do not go into the open at night. It is fortunate that the spirits cannot get into a werf. They are all forced to turn back at the narrow entrance. The worst that can happen is when an evil spirit takes possession of any one. He then falls ill and, if assistance is not forthcoming, he dies.

There are simpler ways of propitiating or exorcizing these spirits. It is a simple matter to feed them, for they live in great necessity. The father of a family, who occupies a werf, never fails to remember the spirits at the beginning of seed-time and at the end of harvest-time, and on many another occasion too. He has food prepared and, with his whole family sitting round him in the open fields, he throws the contents of the dish, bit by bit, first to the east and then to the west, saying: 'Receive this from my hands, ye spirits of the east! Take this as a gift from me, ye spirits of the west!'

Should a member of the family fall ill, the first duty is to have inquiries made as to the cause of the sickness. Wise women, and wise men too, do this for a fee. They rub ashes between the palms of their hands and, by observing carefully the formations which result, they learn the secret. They then advise as to what must be done. In the case of severe illnesses, a skilful witch-doctor must be fetched; he sucks out the cause of the sickness, which the spirit has introduced into the body, and produces it. Small stones, thorns, bits of wood, and things of that kind are removed in this manner.

It can happen, too, that a living person, who is an enemy, can go to a wicked witch-doctor and get him to pronounce a curse upon the sick man. The sickness can then be cured only by means of a stronger counter-spell, and this costs a goodly number of cattle.

It is likewise possible, however, that certain people, who themselves are perhaps unaware of it, are possessed of evil powers and that other people, who come into contact with them, thereby become fatally ill. These are the sorcerers and witches in which the Ovamboland of former times was so extraordinarily rich. Indeed, in the case of every death, this formula was employed: 'Kalunga', that is God, ' has taken him away.' In spite of this, however, the evil custom universally prevailed of accepting that, as a fact, a sorcerer or a witch had a hand in every death, and a terrible fate awaited all those whom the witch-doctor indicated as witches. He went to work in the following manner: seated at the fire in the deceased's hut, surrounded by the sorrowing relatives, he placed his double-edged dagger in the fire and, chewing a ground-nut fine, he smeared the palm and the inside of the fingers of the left hand with it. When the knife was hot enough, he passed the edge of it over the palm as if he were scraping it and uttered the names of the different districts of the country. If the knife slipped unchecked over the skin, this implied a negative, but if it stopped suddenly, the district was discovered. In a similar manner he found out the werf and, amongst the inhabitants of the werf, the guilty person. The latter, who suspected nothing, was seized and brought before the chief, who had the circumstances investigated once again, in the same way, by his court witch-doctor. If the latter's dagger confirmed the declaration of that of his colleague the person was declared to be guilty and the most terrible tortures were applied to force him to confess. The upper portions of his arms were tied behind his back with riems, a stick was pushed through the riems with which these were twisted until the arms were torn out of their sockets. Another way was to tie a bow-string round the upper jaw and behind the head, passing it beneath the nose and fastening a small stick to the string at the back. By twisting this stick, unspeakable pain was caused and it made the victim willing to confess anything. Otherwise two thick sticks were placed on either side of the head and bound together, both back and front, with riems; a small piece of stick was inserted and this was twisted until the skull cracked and the eyes burst from their sockets. Similarly bow-strings were tied tightly round the breasts and fingers of women to force a confession of guilt from them. When this had been accomplished the wretched victim of human imbecility was borne off and put to death. In the tribe of the Ukuanyama, it was essential that, with every death that took place, a woman had to lose her life in this manner, because she was a witch.

What an atmosphere of calm and comfort must have been created by an institution like the sacred fire, which had been received from Kalunga for the purpose of bestowing protection, happiness, and blessing on the house. This fire used to burn at the chief's place of residence near to where he slept. It had to be carefully tended by his principal wife or her daughter and, if it went out, it meant that the whole tribe was doomed to destruction. It was not to be allowed to flame, and it was essential that it should be fed with green wood from special trees. The district headmen obtained glowing coals from this fire for the making of their own fires in their werfs, and they passed it on to the inhabitants of their districts. Nothing might be cooked on a fire of this kind, except the parting meal of a man who was leaving for war. No one was allowed to sit at it or to warm his hands over it. Thus there burnt throughout the tribal territory the fire from a single hearth, a fire from which nothing but advantage and good were expected, but which assisted nobody to escape from an evil fate.

And Kalunga, the God of heaven? He appeared to be connected with the aristocracy. It is true that it was known that he showed himself, at different places, as an old man in shabby clothing. It was likewise told of him that he carried two baskets on his arms; in one of them he carried happiness and in the other misfortune, and he distributed the contents of these baskets according to people's conduct and his own discretion. As, however, Kalunga worship was unknown, the idea of a godhead remained quite dormant in the daily life of the people, and it was merely expressions which were in frequent use amongst them that served to call to mind a time when it was recognized that the governance of this world was in his good hands, and that there was no need to fear the witchcraft of wicked people and the influence of evilly disposed spirits.

6. THE BUSHMEN

The Bushmen are the scarcest and most interesting natives of South West Africa. From the earliest times they were despised, hated, and fiercely persecuted by all other natives, and so the only dwelling-places left to them were inaccessible hiding-places in the mountains and just as unapproachable hidden refuges in the trackless thorn bush of the plains. Distrustful of every one who belonged to another tribe, suspicious of the members of their own unless they belonged to their own clan, they avoided all contact with the outer world, and they live, even to-day, their miserable Bushman life, just as their ancestors have lived it for centuries. With extraordinary natural capacity they adapted themselves to the region in which they struggled to keep body and soul together by hunting and collecting roots. Where a native of another race could no longer eke out a living, the Bushman felt at home; he knew precisely the spots where water was to be found, he knew the trees and bushes from which he might expect to get wild fruits, and he was always able to find the plains where the starchy veld-tubers grew.

We do not intend to weary the reader by requiring him to commit to memory the names of the different branches of the Bushman race. It is sufficient to state that two groups ought to be distinguished from each other. The first group consists of the Saan; that is to say, 'the gatherers'. The name itself makes it plain that their chief article of diet is the food which grows wild in the veld. They are to be found in the Namib and roaming about the Orange River; small groups of them inhabit the mountains of Namaland and they exist in larger numbers in the districts of Outjo and Grootfontein. There they are called Heikom, which means 'people who sleep in the bush'. The Namas, Hereros, and Ovambos used, of course, when compelled to spend a night in the open, to seek out a high-lying sleeping-place without any trees, from which they could look out over the surrounding country and become aware of approaching danger. The Bushmen, however, differed from them in that they had the contrary habit of concealing themselves in the bush at night. These groups speak Nama. Every Hottentot is able to understand them easily. They have, however, preserved archaic forms, which have already disappeared in Hottentot. The Saan stand in close relationship to the Namas in religion, law, and custom, and there are clear indications on the borders of their territories that there has been interbreeding. Where even pure-bred Saan are met with, a skilled observer can scarcely distinguish them from Hottentots. One astonishing feature deserves particular notice. Just as the Hottentots had a predilection for forcing people from strange tribes to take service with them, to make them herd their cattle and perform all the heavier tasks, so too the Heikom used to collect Bergdamas, in days gone by, to help them with their hunting.

The Kalahari Bushmen, whose hunting-grounds lie to the east, are to be distinguished from the Saan in the west and middle of South West Africa. It is no task of ours to acquaint the reader with all the Bushman tribes of the Kalahari; the only ones which interest us are those who live within the boundaries of South West Africa. Their distinguishing features are their light yellow skins, their very small stature, and their extraordinarily neat hands and feet. Individuals with a height of 4 ft. 6 in. are often to be found, but the majority are taller than this. There are Bushmen who reach 5 ft. 6 in. in height. The longish flattened head, covered with dark curly hair, which is a mixture of knotted balls and short strands, has in front, rather strangely, a bold but narrow forehead. The nose hardly protrudes at all and is plainly recognizable only through its broad nostrils. Brown eyes blink anxiously and shyly through nearly closed eyelids. An astonishing feature with children is the ungainly protruding stomach; and with adults the more hideous contraction of the stomach, the skin of which lies in deep folds, both long-ways and cross-ways. The fatty buttocks, which are found in Hottentot women, are extraordinarily prevalent with Bushman women.

It is quite possible to trace some of these characteristics back to the influence of environment and mode of living. The blinking eyes may be ascribed to the life in the open under the bright African sun and the looking out for game and for threatening dangers. The child's distended stomach is surely to be attributed to the lack of nourishment in the veld growths used as food, of which the developing body requires a large mass to enable it to thrive. It reminds one of the 'potato stomach' of the poor children of other lands. The stomach of older persons of both sexes, with its large overlapping folds, forms apparently a special provision for the days of heavy feeding, which arrive when the hunter captures big game. How easily meat goes bad in a hot country! The Bushman has not discovered a method of preserving it. All that there remains for him is to eat it. That he succeeds in doing without any trouble or difficulty; and, after he is successful in his efforts, the ugly folds in his stomach disappear.

Kindly Mother Nature has provided him with a receptacle, which renders him the same good service that the store-room of his house affords the European. The fatty buttocks may be explained in a similar way. The body collects, at a spot where movement is least impeded by it, the fat which is not required for immediate use, so as to be able to draw upon it in time of need. If this explanation is accepted, it is then easy to understand why this remarkable feature is mostly in evidence in the female sex. Pregnancy, birth, and the suckling of a child prevent a woman from getting her regular supply of food, and a rich supply of fat in the store-house of the body comes to her assistance. Against this the argument might be advanced that this fatty deposit is much more strikingly developed amongst the Hottentots, but that can be ascribed to the fact that the Hottentots, as stock breeders, have much more opportunity of getting fatty food. Without doubt, the steatopygy of the Bushman women would show the same proportions if the same way of living were possible to them. The remarkably pronounced development of the masticatory muscle is generally a noticeable bodily characteristic. People are apt to ascribe this to the heavy demand upon the chewing mechanism, but that is probably not correct. This swelling forms only when meat is scarce and when a diet consisting only of veld-tubers and roots is resorted to. When the missionaries of Barmen did not have sufficient provisions in the years 1844 to 1850, and at a later period too, and they were forced to use roasted and stamped tubers as a substitute for meal, these swellings, which are so noticeable in the Bushmen, formed on their faces too. A racial feature of the male sex, which ought not to be overlooked, is the penis continuously standing in semi-erection. Even the rock-paintings throughout South Africa display this characteristic very plainly indeed, and when any question of their authorship arises, this peculiarity is worth consideration.

The Bushman clothing is simplicity itself. A narrow apron, made of dressed animal skin and held in position by means of a leather riem, comprises the dress of both sexes. The woman wears as well, as a covering for her back, the brayed skin of a wild animal. The neck, arms, and ankles of the girls and married women are ornamented with leather rings and chains made from ostrich egg-shells. These leather rings are the hunting trophies of the husband, who provides the family with meat. In more recent times, rings of iron, copper, and brass are met with. The men wear no ornaments at all. It is remarkable how some of the tribes constrict the upper arm and the higher part of the thigh by means of a leather ring, which is forcibly pulled on and sunk deep into the flesh. This is not regarded as an ornament but as a means of enabling its wearer to run better. A Bushman never dares to wash himself. He declares that his luck in hunting will desert him directly he cleanses his skin with water. Encrusted dirt is removed with animal fat or vegetable oil.

The poverty of the Bushman existence is very clearly indicated by their huts. It is the women's task to erect them. At a distance of from 6 to 8 feet apart, two strong poles are planted in the ground in such a way that the points meet at a height of about 5 feet. The tops are tied together with the soft bark of a tree. This archway forms the door to the Bushman hut and it is never closed. Further poles are now planted in an irregular semicircle and joined at the top to form a sort of domed roof. This framework is covered with branches with the leaves on, and dry grass, and the Bushman hut is complete. It matches its surroundings so marvellously that it can scarcely be seen from a distance, probably because the Bushman is forced to settle on the open plains. At a casual glance, the grass, bushes, and Bushman huts blend together in such a way that the discovery of a hut in the open veld always comes as a surprise.

In a werf there are always several huts. The arrangement of them is supposed to be in a circle, but this is by no means always adhered to. Only members of the same family live together. As they seldom have more than three children, this membership is usually small. A settlement containing twenty people is quite a big one. There is no chief or headman in control of it. The highest authority known to a Bushman is the head of the family. Several families join forces in times of the greatest danger only. The head of the family decides the spot where the huts are to be erected. If it is in any way possible, a shady tree must occupy the centre of the site, so that he can kindle in its shade the sacred fire, upon which good fortune in hunting and in the collection of veld-food depends. The building of the huts can only start when the fire is alight. A werf seldom comprises more than from ten to fifteen shelters, for that is all they can be regarded as. The number varies according to the number of members of the family present. Each wife, and each aunt, has her own hut; and even the sons and daughters live by themselves. When they marry, the men do not possess huts, but old men who are left alone in the world do.

All property is, nevertheless, common. The head of the family is regarded as the owner of the water-holes, the hunting-grounds, and the sacred fire, for he has inherited all that from his ancestors, and he will leave it as an inheritance to his eldest son. Every family tries with all its power to preserve these rights. The boundaries of the hunting-grounds are carefully fixed and recognized. The boundaries of the food-gathering area coincide, and beyond these boundaries no one is permitted to hunt or gather veld-food. Whoever is found in a strange district can be summarily knocked on the head or shot with a poisoned arrow. For this reason a broad no-mans-land is usually to be found between the holdings of two different families. In spite of this, by far the greater number of families are antagonistic to each other; a Bushman hardly ever dares to leave his own territory. The women go out in the early morning with their digging-sticks and their skin collecting bags to gather veld-food. Nothing that can be eaten is despised. Frogs, mice, and lizards are welcome additions to the wild vegetables, and so are birds' eggs, fat grubs, and snakes. If the distance is not too great, they return home early in the afternoon, collect some dry wood for the fire, and each of them roasts on the glowing embers of her own fire the results of her diligent search.

At the same time the men go out after game. Only the very old ones stay at home and look after the sacred fire, feeding it with roots and special fuel so as to ensure good hunting. The men are equipped with bows and arrows. One of them at least carries an assegai, which, in earlier times, had a bone point, but more recently has an iron one, obtained by barter from some neighbouring tribe. The arrows are carried behind the back in a quiver of bark or skin. Many Bushmen carry arrows in their hair. The old Bushman arrow is a work of art. Beside the iron-tipped arrows of recent times there are still to be found in every quiver old arrows with long sharp bone points, which can be affixed to shafts made of reed. This point is very much more effective when it has on it a potent, quick-working poison, which the Bushman gets from plants and certain small insects. A knobkerrie for throwing completes his hunting outfit. When he sees an animal he stalks it; he gets down on the ground, raises his body, while resting his weight on his hands so that he can advance both feet at the same time, and then he stretches forward slowly with his arms again. In this way the animal does not notice the hunter's movements. He discharges his poisoned arrow only when he gets as near as possible; a Bushman is not nearly such a good shot with a bow and arrow as he is generally stated to be. The stricken animal rushes off in terror. If it should make its way through the bushes, the arrow shaft may fall off, but the arrow tip sticks fast. That is what the hunter aims at when he constructs his arrows in three parts, i.e. the shaft, the middle section, and the tip. Now the poison can do its work. The hunter lies down quietly under a bush and lets time work for him. A young Bushman, however, must take the good news as quickly as possible to the old men and the womenfolk. When he reckons that the poison has done its work, he follows up, with his companions, the spoor made by the animal in its flight. He reads the spoor much more readily than a European can read a book. If the animal has gone over the boundary, it is unfortunate; a wise hunter will follow it no further. As a rule, however, he finds it lying stretched out somewhere within his own territory. His hunting companions have not been idle; it is their duty so to shape the course of the fleeing animal that it remains, if in any way possible, within the family territory. Now the assegai does its work. The shrill note of a small hunting whistle summons the hastening women to the spot. The carcass is cut up; the women and children carry the skin, entrails, head, and legs, while the men carry the flesh of the carcass. Upon their arrival at the huts the men assemble immediately at the sacred fire. After the head of the family has partaken of the meat, all the hunters begin to cut it into flat pieces, as large as the hand, and to roast it in the glowing embers, a process which seasons it somewhat at the same time. Some families possess earthen pots, in which the meat which is very fatty, is cooked. The hunter, whose arrow hit the quarry, receives the piece of meat with the wound in it; this he carefully cuts out and he then eats the rest without any danger. This piece is specially effective in ensuring him further success in his hunting. The women and children eat those parts which they carried home, after cooking them on the fires in their own huts.

But it is not with bow and arrow alone that the hunter gets the better of his prey. He knows how to capture it by using a sling and by means of a pit-fall. Sometimes he may even pursue, with his knob-kerrie in his hand, a fleeing animal which he cannot wound with an arrow; he proceeds at an easy trot and scares it up time after time until he tires it out after hours of running. A blow with the knob-kerrie then puts an end to it.

A boy starts at an early age to shoot birds and lizards with his little bow. When he has attained some skill in the handling of weapons, he can accompany the men and help with the hunting. The more skilful he shows himself, the sooner dawns for him the day on which he, usually in company with some of his comrades and with due ceremony, receives the rank of hunter and, with it, recognition of his attainment to manhood. Permission to marry is accorded him at the same time, and he is granted the right to a seat at the sacred fire. Far away from the location a hut without a roof is erected under a tree; often the hut embraces the tree like an enclosure. There the old men go with the initiates. The festival begins on the day when the first quarter of the new moon becomes visible and it can last until the end of the month. Careful provision is made for meat. The women provide veld-food, but this is brought to the place by men, because no female is allowed to go near it. So that plenty of both shall be available, the ceremony of the hunters' initiation is generally held at the end of the rainy season, for it is then that the earth and the hunting-grounds are most productive. The first operation to which the young men are subjected is the smearing and painting of their whole bodies with black oil, obtained from the stones of a kind of wild plum. These kernels, which are white in their raw state, are roasted and they then turn black. They can then be rubbed in a thick film over the skin, like grease. A second part of the performance consists in making the initiates smoke wild hemp out of stone pipes, or pipes made from hollow bones, which has an intoxicating effect upon them. This is regarded as the action of the deity because the stupefied smokers, in the course of their vivid and delightful dreams, see and experience things which are not visible to them when they are in their sound and sober senses. When they are all sober again, the third act begins. The youthful hunters must learn that hunting can only be successful when the deity opens the eyes and directs the hand. They have therefore got to know how to render this spiritual Being favourably inclined. That is effected by dancing. All the possible kinds of animals, which they may one day hunt, are imitated in their walk and behaviour. God is pleased by this and, at the same time, it shows him what the heart's desires are. The dance is the Bushman's way of worshipping God, and the dance is his form of prayer. There are more than a dozen dances of this kind, and it is no simple matter to master them all. That is nevertheless required of any one who wishes to be acknowledged as an expert hunter. The same dances can likewise be performed purely for recreation, for the mere pleasure of movement and from erotic motives, but in that case they may not take place at the real dancing place, and the ornaments of the men, which consist of a peculiar kind of rattle, must be discarded.

When the dances have been learnt a painful operation, which with some tribes is accompanied by circumcision, follows, and it is performed in the following manner: One of the old men sits down flat on the ground. The young hunter lies down between his open legs on his back with his face turned towards the old man. The latter makes an incision in the skin between the eyes at the root of the nose with a stone knife, or a sharp arrow-point. After the blood has stopped flowing, he fills the wound with a powder made from small particles of the flesh of all kinds of wild animals. These particles are ground between two stones after having been well roasted. This 'medicine' is to increase the budding hunter's powers of vision and to enable him to descry the game betimes and to hit it correctly. Almost every Bushman carries the sign of the hunter between his eyes. Directly the wound is healed, the final act can begin. The hunter is eager to get married. He must, therefore, undergo a test to show that he is capable of providing meat in a short time, should his wife express a desire for meat during her confinement, or require it to restore her strength after her delivery. Failure to respond to a wish of this kind at that time brings ill luck both to mother and child. This test consists of bringing in an animal within a prescribed time and, when it is passed, the month of the hunter's initiation draws to a close. Bows and arrows are given to the young men as their own property, the small aprons, which they wore as boys, are burnt, the men's aprons, which are drawn through between the legs and fastened again to the girdle are put on and, with much shouting, the old men return to the huts accompanied by the young ones. The adult circle round the sacred fire has increased in size.

When the growing girl notices for the first time that she has become a young woman, the mother erects a small lodging for her, with an entrance made of branches, behind her hut. There the daughter remains hidden from the eyes of men and boys. No male is allowed to go near the hut. He would forfeit entirely his success in the hunt if he contravened this ancient usage. The only food which the young girl may eat at this time is such as had been brought home by women in their collecting skins. Each day a dance of the women takes place. The girl has to attend these dances, but she has to cover up her face and her body with a large skin. After the dance is concluded, some of the older women sit with the young girl in the hut to explain things to her and to instruct her properly. How a wife should treat her husband is the subject of the instruction. She must be kind to him, must conscientiously provide wood and drinking-water, must gather veld-food and, in his absence, must be faithful to him. He would quickly discover infidelity. Upon the slightest suspicion, he would plant in the ground before her hut the root which reveals the truth, and he would set it on fire. The flames of the burning root tell him whether she has been faithful, or not. If they turn towards the hut, a stranger has gone in to her and her life is forfeit; he has the right to pierce her heart with an arrow without any further investigation. If the flame turns away from the hut, her innocence is proved. When the days are past, the girl goes into the veld accompanied by two women, who have good reputations and are not quarrelsome, to gather veld-food. What she gathers that day may only be eaten by older women. The following day she goes collecting wood with two other women. In the meantime her mother is erecting a hut for her daughter's separate use. Then the girl receives recognition as a food-gatherer and she becomes marriageable.

Marriage within the family circle is strictly forbidden. The young Bushman may only marry a woman from a friendly family, but he seldom proposes personally to the girl of his choice. Such cases do occur but they are contrary to the usual rule. A sound custom requires that one of the young man's friends should approach his future mother-in-law. If she is agreeable, the young man himself puts in an appearance one day. Without looking at her or greeting her, he hands her his bow for safe-keeping during his short visit, and he joins the men at the sacred fire. If she accepts the bow, an engagement ensues. The mother takes it quietly to her daughter's hut. When she returns from her work, she knows by the presence of the bow that a stranger has proposed to her. She takes it unostentatiously to her mother's hut and by doing so she signifies her consent. The surrender of the bow means to the mother-in-law, 'I will serve you for your daughter for a whole year with my bow, and I will deliver to you everything I gain from hunting', while for the daughter it implies a promise to provide for her in future. If the young man is acceptable, his bow is given back to him again without a single word being spoken, and nothing stands in the way of the marriage. After a successful hunt, the young man and his friends bring the meat to the location of his bride's family, and it is silently deposited at the hut of his mother-in-law. The male and female relations come on the scene likewise. Now matters become serious. The engaged girl is questioned by every one. She suddenly takes to her heels and hides herself in the bush. The women of both families pursue her and bring the resisting fugitive back. This is what custom requires; to fail to observe it and to display wedding-day gladness on this occasion would be a serious insult to her parents. By doing so, the girl would make it clear that she was glad to exchange her life in her own family circle for life with another family. The wedding feast is celebrated. The bride takes no share in it, for she is required to show sorrow in consequence of the change in her life. It is only when the dance begins that she takes her place in the ranks of the women. While the dance is in progress, the young bridegroom advances out of the ranks of the men and, still dancing, approaches his chosen one, who along with the other women is accompanying the dancing with clapping and stamping in unison and with a monotonous sing-song. With his eyes fastened upon her, he retreats, dancing backwards, into the ranks of the men. A little later the bride comes forward circumspectly from the ranks of the women, singing and clapping her hands, and she goes up close to the bridegroom with her eyes riveted upon him, and then falls back into the ranks of the women again. In this way they pledge their troth in the presence of many witnesses.

The young bridegroom's relatives return to their location without him. The young son-in-law is bound to stay with his wife's parents for a full year and to work for them with his bow and arrow. He delivers all the results of his hunting expeditions to his mother-in-law, but he never speaks to her, never looks at her, never calls her by her name, and he is treated by her in the selfsame way. When the year of service is ended, he takes his wife to his own family and lives with her there.

Only when his young wife is expecting a child, is she allowed to go to her mother for the confinement. If it is in any way possible, the birth of the child must not take place within the circle of the huts. Outside, in the protection of the bush, the Bushman child sees the light of the sun for the first time. A branch stuck in the ground, or a carefully placed tuft of grass, warns every one to keep away from the spot. The mother and some other old women act as mid-wives. The young mother often returns to her mother's hut with her child the very same evening. If, however, the mother dies and there is no one available who can suckle the child, the living child and the dead mother are buried together. This is a bitter necessity, for there is no milk or similar food to hand with which a motherless child can be raised. A baby, too, which will not thrive and as to whose survival the mother is doubtful, is often buried after the older women have carefully considered the matter. The same fate overtakes a child which is born while an older brother or sister is not in the position to exist upon tough meat and hard veld-food. Long before the birth the whole family knows that this child cannot be allowed to live. Without any lamentation at all the child is put away immediately it is born. The mother does not even see it. In this case too there is no deliberate cruelty. There is a choice between two alternatives: either both the children must die little by little through lack of food, or the younger must be sacrificed for the preservation of the elder. These circumstances compel a man to take a second wife, while he still has the first. As a result of strict domestic arrangements, provision is made for the mother of a child to have a rest of at least three years. In spite of the position, many monogamous marriages are maintained and, in the southern Kalahari, to have only one wife appears to be the fashion.

The keeping of a watchful eye over the observance of inherited customs and rules is, in the first instance, the duty of the head of the family. His strongest ally is the fact that the Bushman is thoroughly religious by nature. Whoever transgresses the customary law, sins both against the spirits of his forefathers and against those invincible forces which he knows are round about him with every step he takes. Punishment at the hands of these powers pursues and overtakes him, and not only him alone, but all the members of his family as well. It is the duty of each and every one of them not to incur such penalties, which take the form of lack of success in hunting and on the gathering-grounds, and of sickness, accident, and death. The highest divine being, who is known by different names in different regions and where differences of language occur (Thora, Hue, Huwe, Gâua), is really not to be feared so much as a sinister, impersonal, spiritual force, to which no name is given, but which acts with the sureness of a law of nature. We call this force Fate, and it is this conception which comes nearest to the Bushman idea. No one can defend himself against Fate, nor can he escape it. It is only the witch-doctor, who, by means of his incantations, his unguents and his dances, knows how to protect any one from danger, by drawing round him a magic circle into which the threatened evil cannot penetrate.

Besides this, the Bushman firmly believes that mountains and valleys, plains and lowlands, springs and rivers are inhabited by spirits

SAAN OR HEIKOM BUSHMAN

Photographed by Paul L. Hoefler, F.R.G.S.

of some kind. It is not the best kind of spirit which wanders about restlessly everywhere. The spirits of kind relations usually have their dwelling-place in the moon, and they never worry people; but the spirits of wicked people are dangerous. Without rhyme or reason, they implant in people's bodies causes of sickness, in the shape of small scorpions and snakes, thorns, arrow-tips, stones, and bits of sinew; these can only be extracted by getting a skilled witch-doctor to suck them out, and he takes them out of his mouth and shows them to the sufferer. They are the people, too, who can see with the naked eye into the spiritual world, and can give timely warning to folk of the evil which is threatening them.

When left to his own resources a Bushman is still not entirely helpless, even if he does not possess the witch-doctor's knowledge and skill. There are two things which help him to avoid or ward off the threatened misfortune. Every hunter carries in his belt a means of foretelling the future and of discovering what is hidden. This consists of long pieces of skin, animal claws, or knuckle-bones. When he wishes to consult the oracle, he throws them one after another on the ground, after having rubbed them with fat and having exhorted them at length to tell him the whole truth. There is no question which agitates the Bushman's mind that cannot be answered in this manner. The second is a queer one, and it is peculiar to the Bushman. It enables him to drive off evil spirits and to kill people who are ill-disposed towards him. A miniature bow of the length of a finger is made out of horn by men who command exceptional powers of magic, and some twenty tiny arrows are made too out of hard grass stalks and horn. A small finely worked leather bag, shaped like a quiver, serves to keep them safe. They are fastened to the girdle or to the knee with a leather thong, or kept in a leather purse, which is attached to a riem and carried under the left arm. A 'Bushman revolver' of this kind can be obtained from a witch-doctor for one head of big game. When terror assails a Bushman, when he is wandering alone in the veld by day or by night, so that he realizes that evil spirits are in the vicinity, he fires off some of these arrows with his small bow in all directions. In this manner he drives the demons away. Indeed, these arrows can find their mark upon a far-distant enemy, who is sitting unsuspectingly in his hut making wicked plans. All that is necessary is to shoot them off in the direction of his hut to the accompaniment of evil wishes. Sooner or later the enemy falls ill and no witch-doctor can help him. He feels the arrow-points boring into him, generally in the shape of inflammation of the lungs, and he dies a miserable death.

A counter remedy for all these powers pregnant with evil, which threaten the Bushman's happiness, is to be sought in the sacred fire (Gâua-d'a), which burns beneath the tree round which the huts lie. Benevolent influences proceed from this fire; the family health and success in the hunting-fields and in the gathering-grounds must be ascribed chiefly to this fire. But it is not every one who is permitted to kindle it. It is true that every one is able to kindle a fire with two sticks, but the head of the family alone is allowed to light 'God's fire', and it is only from his mouth that the words of the prayer, which he offers up to Huwe and Gâua, are effective. The principal wife has the duty of tending the embers of this fire from the evening to the following morning, in order to make sure that it shall flame up again, when it is light, beneath the tree. It is regarded as a misfortune if the embers in the woman's hut are extinguished. If the head of the family is absent, no one dares to light the fire without proper religious observances. A messenger is sent to call him back; and only after he has kindled the family fire again is fresh fire fetched from it for each hut. It is the task of the old men, who can no longer go hunting, to tend 'God's fire'. They have not only to supply it with fresh firewood, but also with tough roots, which have to be broken and scraped into small pieces while the hunters are away in the veld. In this way they help the success of their hunting. Should they prove to be unlucky, it is probable that some one has transgressed the laws of hunting, and then the fire is offended, and the best thing to do is to let it go out and to replace it with a new one.

In any event, the life of 'God's fire' lasts only for a year. The new year begins at the end of the rainy period, sometime in April. Then the veld-food gets ripe, but no one may eat it until the New Year feast has been held. The head of the family appoints New Year's Day. The previous evening the old men cover the glowing embers of the old fire with ash and smother it. The following morning all the members of the family gather in a wide circle and squat round the patriarch on the ground. He squats on a piece of soft, grooved wood, which he grips fast between his feet, and he holds in his hand a long, hard kindling stick about fifteen inches long. The palms of his hands glide industriously up and down the stick, maintaining it in rapid, twirling motion, until the point of the stick bores a hole in the soft

wood beneath. Like a worm, the black sawdust issues from the hole.
The old man prays:

> Father, I come to thee,
> Give me food, I pray
> And all the things that needful be
> To help me on life's way.

On the black worm there appears a red glowing point. It is the spark.
With touching tenderness and care it is introduced into the softest
of grass-fluff and fanned with the gentlest breath. In a very short
time a tiny tongue of flame appears. It is fed little by little with
coarser grass, then the thinnest wood is given to it, and soon the fire
is blazing merrily. Thereupon the signal is given for the women and
girls to go out into the gathering-grounds and to look exclusively for
veld-tubers. Nothing of what is gathered may be eaten, everything
must be laid down at the sacred fire. The old men roast the first
yields of the new year's harvest. The first portion is taken by one of
the old men to a nearby ancestral grave, and only when he comes
back, does the head of the family eat a small piece. Now the tubers
and the other kinds of veld-food with them become free for the consumption of all. The new year has begun.

Mention was made of the graves of ancestors. Bushman graves,
more especially in parts where there are no stones, are very difficult
to find, and they are known only to the initiated. New graves are
protected either with thorn-bushes or stones. Graves are always put
in remote places. They are dug with a digging stick to a depth of
rather less than four feet. The body is buried sometimes in a squatting
position and sometimes on its back with its knees drawn up. If the
deceased was a scoundrel, and every one is afraid of his restless spirit,
his back is broken first. By doing this his resurrection is prevented.
It may happen that the body cannot be moved. Then it is left in
the hut, the sides of which are pushed inwards, and the place is deserted, for it is dangerous to stay in proximity to a hut of this kind,
or to live near a grave. After a death, it is always advisable to trek
away and to seek a new place in which to live. The souls of the dead
are believed to haunt the immediate neighbourhood of their graves
and their huts are regarded as still belonging to them. It is dangerous
to disturb their rest. Without a very good reason no one walks past
a grave. If any one is compelled to do so, he timidly lays a stone or
a twig on the grave by way of greeting, and he hastens away from it.
Not even those dead people who conducted themselves decently in

life and whose souls are believed to be in the moon are trusted. The dead are spoken about with the utmost reluctance, and the name of a dead man is never uttered again.

The conception of a happy life in the moon for the souls of good people seems to have been more strongly held in earlier days than it is now. In practically all the Bushman tribes it is a tradition that the object of the moon is to keep death away from the human race. It was only through her message to human beings having been falsely transmitted that death came, as a sort of mistake, into the world. Variations of this theme are, however, not lacking, such as, for example, the ascribing of human death to the fact that people do not believe in the moon's message.

It might appear to be improbable that the miserable Bushman, whose thoughts and efforts seem to be directed solely to the satisfaction of his bodily needs, should try to solve the problem of the origin of death. But any one who has delved into multifarious myths and fables, many of which have already been collected, realizes that the question of the origin of death is only one of the many which exercises his mind. He can tell remarkably sensible mythical stories about the birth of the sun, the moon, and the stars, about the origin of the wind, the clouds, and the rain, and about the creation of mountain, spring, and plain. Such a wealth of legends is unknown amongst any other race south of the Zambezi and the Kunene. This is not meant to imply that there is very much more in the Bushman than a hasty regard for his wretched exterior might lead us to think, but to show that there survives with him a very ancient tradition, which he continually repeats in the warmth of the sacred fire, and one which provides his intellect with more plentiful food than the fields, which he has inherited from his forefathers, can offer his needy body.

III

MIGRATIONS AND DWELLING-PLACES

1. THE INHABITANTS OF OLDEN TIMES

EVEN nations settle and migrate, come and go, arise and disappear again. It is seldom that the places they lived in, and the routes they took in their wanderings in the dim and distant past, are recognizable in the clear light of history. The student of history is forced to fall back upon suppositions founded on deficient tradition and obscure legends. There are certainly no written records available to him. He must look back along the thousands of years that are past for other evidence. Every reminder arising from sound or stone, insignificant though it may be, is of value to him. Every trace of the creative human hand serves as a pointer to him. It is to language that attention must specially be paid. Speech is an ancient inheritance moulded by past generations. Every considerable change in the universe has left clearly recognizable traces behind. Through the contact of one race with another, foreign sounds creep in and foreign words are borrowed. They enable conclusions to be drawn regarding the relationships and connexions between peoples, which have long disappeared. Myth and saga, proverb and song, philosophy of religion and life, custom and law, dwelling and manner of living, weapons and utensils, family control and tribal divisions, and many other things have to serve as sources, from which the drops which often drip so meagrely must be collected so as to form the streamlet of a history, which bears but little resemblance to the clear mountain stream hurrying in its busy course to join the broad river of the history of the human race. When he correlates his work scientifically the historian finds perhaps that one of his sources lies upon a watershed; technically it should have taken a northerly course, while nature has given it a southerly one. As his eyes become sharper he learns to view old discoveries in a new light, while new ones cannot be brought into the preconceived line. Finally, there dawns upon him the conviction that, before the race in which he is interested and to which he was prepared to award the birthright of the first-born, there existed in the dim past another race, regarding which nothing more can be said than that it actually existed.

In this respect what is the position in South West Africa? We are wont to regard the Bushmen as the oldest inhabitants and, after them, it is the Saan, the Hottentots, and the Bergdamas who claim our interest. We would like to get to know whence and at what period of time they found their way in, but it is recognized by the silent consent of every one that the Bushmen were most probably the first people to enter into occupation of the country, unhampered, in ancient times. It would require an enormous amount of labour to obtain an unequivocal answer to this question. At various places, in caves and holes in the rocks, at springs and ancient water-holes, old utensils and stone implements have been found. Is this to be taken to prove that South West Africa likewise had its Stone Age? Its Stone Age is not at an end even to-day. There live to-day in inaccessible places Bushmen, Bergdamas, and Tjimbas, who are still in the Stone Age. By merely breaking a particular piece of stone, preferably one with sharp edges, they manufacture their cutting implements without any further process, and they throw them away when they no longer require them. Experts are unanimous in declaring that it is very difficult to say with any degree of certainty whether stone implements, which are found on the surface, are very old or new. It must be borne in mind that the manufacture of a stone knife in ancient times con-sisted solely in the fracturing of a larger stone, from the fragments of which some particular piece with sharp edges was taken for use, without further preparation. The process of working up the stone, which gives prehistoric investigators something reliable to go upon, was a later development. It is only the study of the country itself and the depth at which an article is found that can be looked to in order to determine the age. For the layman, however, there are many pit-falls. For instance, a friend sent me a piece broken off an earthenware pot lid. It had been found while digging at a depth of sixteen feet. This circumstance alone indicated that it was of quite a considerable age. Warned by hundreds of previous experiences not to base, even upon exact observation, a rule-of-thumb explanation, but, as far as possible, to obtain first the opinion of intelligent natives, who often instinctively possess more correct powers of judgment in matters concerning the country than the European, who has been bred in quite a different environment, I showed the find to a gathering of Hereros, Bergdamas, and Namas. They looked at the fragment of pottery with great interest. The Hereros saw at once that they had to do with the cover of a Herero pot. Now the Hereros have hardly been 250 years in South West Africa. How could the top of a Herero pot have been found at a depth of sixteen feet beneath the surface of the ground ? They insisted that, at the place where it was found, there must have been an old Herero well, into which the top fell while water was being drawn and then was covered up. Investigation showed that the Hereros were quite correct in their opinion, in spite of the fact that there were no longer any visible signs of the existence of a well. The place where the cover was found was, however, situated in close proximity to a river bed, and it was at this very spot that the Hereros of former days used to dig their wells.

Technical men of experience do not easily fall victims to deceptions of this kind. Much sound work has been done by them in South Africa and in South West Africa of an informatory nature. We can place reliance upon their judgment, when they say that many of of the stone implements, which are to be found in public museums or in the possession of private individuals, are several thousands of years old, and that South West Africa has a long history behind it. It is, however, remarkable that it has been noticed that the really old stone implements in South Africa are those which show the most careful manufacture, and it is believed that the same can be proved of South West Africa. That goes to show that, before the advent of the old inhabitants of South-West Africa, that is before the Bushmen, Hottentots, and Saan, there was probably another race, whose name we do not even know.

There are other circumstances pointing in the same direction. In South Africa, graves are occasionally to be found on the sea-shore. The human remains which they contain show that the people who were buried in these graves cannot be reckoned as belonging to races who inhabit southern Africa at the present time. Careful calculations made in respect of some of these graves, which at the present day lie some considerable height above sea-level, but could only have been very little above sea-level at the time they were made, give them an age of from fifteen to twenty thousand years at least. Graves of this kind are not known in South West Africa. We may, however, presume that there were some here too. First of all, let us look round for other proofs of the traces of prehistoric man.

In the Orange Free State, Bechuanaland, and the Western Trans vaal, there are often to be found on exposed rock surfaces all sorts of rock drawings, representing elephants, giraffes, rhinoceroses, ostriches, &c., although it is often difficult to recognize them. These rock drawings are not painted but they are obviously engraved, with much

patient effort, with a hard, pointed stone tool, in the process of which
the rock is broken and removed bit by bit through carefully directed
blows. These pictures are likewise to be found beyond the Zambesi.
They even make their appearance in the Atlas Mountains and the
Nubian Desert. In its northern part, South West Africa is exceptionally rich in them. In the Otavi Highlands, the Waterberg, the
Paresis Mountains, the Erongo Mountains, and in the Brandberg, as
well as in the neighbourhood of Omaruru and Franzfontein, pictures
of this kind are to be encountered. In Namaland, on the contrary,
they are very rare. There the rock-faces usually show just a small
number of clumsy geometrical figures. Many of these engravings are
quite large. Most of them vary in size from 12 to 24 inches. It is remarkable that the animals are generally portrayed in profile and
seldom appear in pairs or mixed up together. Nor was it the artist's
intention to create a scene to depict animal life or hunting. He must
have been actuated by some other purpose. Alongside these pictures
of animals, more especially in South West Africa and in some other
isolated cases too, numerous round holes, with a depth of about half
an inch and a diameter of from 1 to 2 inches are found. They are
dotted about without any recognizable regularity wherever there is
room for them. Further, there are often to be found upon the very
same bench of rock the footprints of giraffes, zebras, kudus, buck, &c.
These spoors are sometimes so carefully made that one is led to
think that the animals trod upon rock that was not yet quite hard,
that their feet sank in slightly and so produced a spoor, which the
fully hardened rock preserved unchanged. But spoors which were half
made, or spoilt in the making, soon show the uninitiated that this is
the work of human hands. In long defiles hundreds of footprints and
hundreds of round holes, too, are to be found. Usually, however, only
a picture of animals occurs, with sometimes a human foot, the heels
and toes of which are very clearly delineated. The animal figures,
holes, game spoors, and human footprints are not brought together
so as to make a composite picture. Every figure stands by itself in
isolation, and it can be found standing isolated, under other circumstances, upon different rock-faces. Places are known where there are
only animal pictures, while in others there are only round holes, and
in others again exclusively footprints. In places, however, where the
drawings are very numerous indeed, all four of these forms make
their appearance, and irregular geometrical designs are apt to occur
as well. These rock engravings have obviously nothing to do with

the Bushman paintings found in caves and hollows in the rocks. The latter are done with colours, while the former have no colour about them and are cut into the rock. The latter portray scenes from human and animal life, in which a single idea dominates the whole picture; the former show the figures close to each other without any guiding idea, and each individual figure, if taken out of its surroundings, has, as nearly as possible, the same significance. The latter are to be found in caves and rock hollows, where climatic influences cannot damage them very greatly and where it is difficult to find them; the former avoid caves and are drawn on open rock-faces, which may be either horizontal or perpendicular, where they can hardly fail to be noticed. The latter are hidden away and are to be sought far away from roads; the former are, clearly of set purpose, placed either in the middle of ancient footpaths or in their immediate neighbourhood, so that a passerby can easily discover them.

Any question regarding the age of these engravings can only be answered by saying that they must be very old indeed. When they were made, the age patina of the rock must have been removed in drawing the first lines. Almost all the pictures show that the indentations are once again covered with a patina and it is this circumstance which causes many people to pass these rock-drawings by to-day without even seeing them. The drawing and its surroundings are once more of the same colour, namely that of the patina of old age. To re-create this patina requires enormous periods of time. This proof of great age does not brook contradiction.

There remains for solution the riddle of the meaning of these drawings. They must have had a meaning. They cannot be regarded as mere senseless scrawlings, for they are too true to nature for that. They can hardly pass for manifestations of the artistic instinct, for then what would be the object of the hundreds of repetitions of the selfsame idea in the round holes and the animal spoors. We have not the courage to try to endow them with a magical meaning by taking it that the artist was trying to bewitch the game with his spoors, so as to be able to catch them, for what would he then be trying to bewitch with the round holes and with the small human footprints?

The advisory measure: 'Ask the natives, and in the first instance the Bushmen, as to the meaning of these engravings', has often been employed, but it has always led to a negative result. I repeatedly took Hereros, Bergdamas, Ovambos, and Hottentots to a place I had chosen and, after a close inspection of all the drawings there, I got them to express their opinions as to the meaning of them and their authorship. They declared unanimously that neither they nor their fathers had drawn things of this kind on the rocks and that they had no idea at all what the drawings meant. The Namas and the Berg-damas were of opinion that the author could only have been either Gâuab (Gamab the god of the Bergdamas and the devil of the Namas) or Heiseb (a demigod of the Hottentots). That too points to great antiquity.

At last I decided to make a test with Kalahari Bushmen. I took fifteen of them to the place and left them to look at the drawings for half a day, giving them the opportunity of discussing the authorship and meaning of them amongst themselves. The result was the same. They denied steadfastly that any Bushman could make pictures of that kind, nor could they contribute anything to the explanation of them. I thought, however, that I could see a slight difference in the result of my questioning them. I gave them my own explanation which was founded upon the disposition of a race, which necessity had compelled to live, isolated, shut within the bounds of a tribal territory. The Bushmen seized upon the idea immediately, expressed lively concurrence with it and behaved like persons, who have a word on the end of their tongue but cannot express it, or like some one who is burdened with a feeling to which he is unable to give adequate expression, until some one else comes along and says the word which brings the obscure feeling to the point of clear expression. I know that no great weight can be attached to this. The excitement, which the solution of the riddle aroused, may have led them to feel that my explanation was a satisfactory one. It is nevertheless well worth considering that the Bushman, who still knows to-day what the territory and boundaries of the clan mean, and what hunting crimes and thefts of veld-food, what watering-places and animal totems imply, should have, out of the depths of his subconscious experience, have signified his concurrence, and that without any objection.

The explanation which has been tested over and over again from every possible point of view is the following: these rock engravings are signs of ownership. Similar marks are still to-day placed upon pots, dishes, and other articles of daily use by different tribes. Who-ever lays claim to a particular wild fruit-tree in the veld ties a shred of his clothing to one of its branches. Whoever finds a bees'-nest, puts a stick into the hollow of the tree or into the ground. Whoever has killed a head of large game and is forced to leave it for the purpose of summoning his companions for the disposal of the meat, sticks a tuft of grass into the animal's mouth or lays a green branch on its body. Whoever in the course of his ranging finds a water-hole, puts his foot down in the sand or dust of the road, in such a way that it indicates the direction of the water, in order to attract the attention of any of his people who may follow him. Every human spoor made distinctly on the edge of a road draws attention to something or other. Bushmen of the Kung tribe make long walking-sticks, which are decorated with circles, leaves, human figures, and the spoors of animals. When they send a messenger to another tribe, the possession of this stick serves as confirmation of his words. The making of marks of ownership, and the calling of attention to them, is still observed to the present day. It is not as if any particular race practises that method of communication—all the races of South West Africa do the same thing or something very much the same, for the nature of the country makes it necessary for them to do so.

Let us explain more fully: If the country has not altered since it was first trodden by human beings, then it is probable that, in the far distant past, there was a tribe which could get the means of existence only by hunting and finding veld-food in its tribal territory, that tribal boundaries were respected, and that hunting offences and the theft of veld-food were prevented. The tribal territory is, however, extensive and the settlements do not remain confined to one spot. Even if the hunter is not a nomad, he has to erect his huts where the hunting is most productive and the task of collecting food is easiest. Where should he then set up his mark of ownership. The most suitable spot is the narrow native pathway, which is as old as the hills. A path of this kind, running over the hills, is to be found between Grootfontein and Korab in the District of Grootfontein. The path is plainly trodden in the rock itself and shows an actual depression, which could only have come about through continuous use. How old may this footpath not be? We actually find these ownership signs on these old paths, and the explanation is this: it is not unreasonable to presume that the animal spoors signified to a wanderer from a strange clan: 'Do not dare to kill the game, the spoors of which you see here; this territory has its owner.' The round holes may have pointed out to him: 'The round veld-food and the bulbs in the ground have their owner too; keep your hands off them.' Seeing that a human footprint always shows the direction in which water is to be found in the rocks or in which there is a spring, the explanation of this is by no means difficult in this context. It implies: 'The water which may be found when any one goes in that direction likewise has its owner.' The complete picture of an animal would appear to serve as an answer to any question regarding the tribal name of the occupier. It appears to have been the totem animal of the clan, which placed its notice board on the road and said to the stranger: 'Here you have to do with the Elephant Clan, or with the Giraffe Clan, or with the Ostrich Clan.'

Whether a key is the right one, or not, can only be discovered by using it to unlock some particular lock. Many problems are quite easily solved by accepting the explanation of the engraved rock-pictures as marks of ownership and warning notices as being correct. Some of these problems may be mentioned here. Why is it that in some rock-defiles there are hundreds of round holes and animal spoors? Why this waste of labour and time? Some of these holes and spoors are so old that they are recognizable only to practised eyes, while others are clearly of more recent date. All are, however, already covered with a perfectly formed age patina. Was it not necessary for the stranger, when passing through another clan's territory and seeing the ownership marks, to ask: 'Is the clan still here or has it died out, or has it given up this territory and gone elsewhere? The signs are still there; are their authors there too?' Thus there arose the necessity for each succeeding generation to make a few new holes and a few new spoors, for in this manner alone could the question of the existing ownership be answered.

The composition or collection of groups of animals is never to be found in these engraved rock-pictures, but there are nevertheless to be found, here and there, two or three different animals placed close to each other. According to our idea, where more than one animal is portrayed, one clan, that of the Ostrich for instance, has left the territory permanently and that of the Bushbuck, let us say, has inherited it. The latter therefore added to the picture of the ostrich that of the bushbuck.

But seeing that all over the world striking signs invite imitation, it may be well, too, that other artists of a later race attempted to imitate the warning notices of the ancient tribal lands. To this may possibly be attributed the fact that there are occasionally to be found on the rock surfaces figures which do not fit properly into their actual frames. A close investigation of the age patina and the execution ought to make it perfectly evident, which of these are really old and genuine, and which must be taken to be later additions.

It is extremely unlikely that the forefathers of any of the present-day native races of South West Africa could have been the authors of these pictures. The very earliest people to be considered are the Bushmen. The Bushman paintings and rock engravings are usually spoken of in the same breath. When the arguments for and against are weighed, we are forced to the conclusion that, probably long before the coming of the Bushmen, another race came in and disappeared again. This race was compelled by the nature of the country to lead a Bushman's existence, without having any racial connexion with the Bushmen, and it has left nothing behind it except some stone implements and some rock inscriptions, concerning the meaning of which we have busied ourselves without any desire to maintain that, with the explanation we have given, the last word has been said.

2. THE BUSHMEN

It is the pictures painted in the caves which next deserve our attention, after the pictures engraved on the rocks. The northern part of South West Africa is exceptionally rich in these paintings. They may be successfully sought not only in the Erongo and the Otavi Highlands but likewise in the northern Namib. The further we go to the south, the scarcer they become. In contrast with the engraved rock-pictures, where a preference is shown for exposed positions near or on footpaths, the cave paintings are only to be found where the overhanging rock affords a protection against the weather. These caves would appear to have always been used as human habitations, and so, when looking at these pictures, it is difficult to resist the conclusion that, whatever else they may imply, they were made with the object of decorating the dwelling-place of the painter. The colours which were selected were usually red, brown, white, and black, but other colours are not entirely absent. The figures are often of considerable size and painted surfaces 9 to 12 feet square sometimes occur. Just as isolated figures of animals, holes, and geometrical designs appear as the motive of the rock-pictures, so it is plain that composition is the aim of the cave-paintings. There is an underlying idea, which actuates and controls the individual figures. Hunting, dancing, and fighting scenes are most frequently depicted. Nature, with its mountains, lakes, and trees, plays a subordinate part. The costumes of the human figures are often strange. The manner of dressing the hair usually differs, where it is recognizably depicted, from that which is adopted by the tribes living in South West Africa at the present time. Where Bushmen are meant to be represented the plain indication of the sign of the male sex, which has previously been discussed, is not lacking. Pictures are to be found of every single animal of South West Africa which was of any value to the hunter. The animal figures are almost always clearly recognizable, and they are quite often very true to nature, while the same can seldom, if ever, be said regarding the way in which the human figure is portrayed. While the rock-drawing shows animal figures at rest, the cave-painting represents both men and animals in vigorous movement.

South West Africa possesses several hundred cave-pictures, which are already known, and there certainly must be many more which have not yet been discovered. Cave-pictures are to be found, in just such large numbers, throughout South Africa and Rhodesia, and in the Central African lake regions and elsewhere. It is desirable that a comprehensive purview of the whole art of rock-painting should be obtained, so that individual pictures may be the more readily understood. In order to get a really general idea as to the occurrence of pictures in grottoes and caves, it must be accepted that five different provinces, are to be distinguished, in which coloured pictures play a part. The first province stretches over southern France and eastern Spain; the grotto-paintings at Altamira in Spain have become famous throughout the world; they date from palaeolithic times. The second province embraces the Atlas country and the Sahara. The pictures which are found there resemble somewhat those of the first province. The art of making these pictures did not die, as it did in Europe, with the passing of the Stone Age, but continued, with the result that, in Africa, old and new examples are undoubtedly to be found in juxtaposition. The third province is that of Nubia, the Lybian Desert, and the Nile Valley. According to Frobenius the ancient form ends in the wall decorations of the Egyptian temples and dies out there only after the Semitic incursion. Tanganyika and Rhodesia belong to the fourth province, while the fifth province covers the Union of South Africa and South West Africa.

The cave-pictures which are of especial interest to us are those of the fourth and fifth provinces. Much toil and energy has already been devoted to discovering them and making copies of them. The valuable collections of G. B. Stowe, D. F. Bleek, and L. Frobenius afford us a glimpse of a peculiar world which is full of riddles. Firstly, a few words about the style and whether such a thing is recognizable in cave-pictures. Undoubtedly it is, and so clearly that any one who has looked at a cave-picture carefully, will easily distinguish the copy of it from another one. Frobenius distinguishes two styles of painting, and calls the style of the Rhodesian pictures the northern style, while he designates the style of the coloured pictures in South and South West Africa as the southern style. He explains some variations in the styles through their having been influenced by both kinds. A thorough examination of the available material will assuredly prove that he is right.

The northern style has the silhouette painted in red (iron oxide) only, and has the details drawn in with water-colour. Where people are depicted, the outline is shown in profile. The upper part of the body is always wedge-shaped and, for the sake of clarity, we will call this style the wedge style. The limbs are always poised at sharp and extravagant angles. This acuteness in the drawing of the angles of the limbs is reminiscent of the ancient way of representing people in Egypt and the countries of the Euphrates, but it bears little resemblance to the style of the western European Stone Age.

The southern style may be described as the rounded style, since its most striking characteristic is the representation of the human body in cylindrical form, with an exaggerated length and without any waist. The angles of the limbs are shown in proper proportion. The movements of persons walking or running often appear as excessively vigorous, while the wedge style adopts a more restful attitude. Von Luschan saw a resemblance between this style and that of the discoveries at Altamira, and Frobenius says: 'These presentations of animal pictures are allied to the Franco-Cantabrian style. Many of these figures are as like to the human pictures of the Eastern Spanish style, in contour, attitude and gesture, as one egg is to another.' Naturally they are not as old; what has died in Europe, lives on in Africa.

Many burial scenes, processions, and battle scenes are to be found in the wedge style. The human figures walk, lie down, sit about, take strides and fall down, but they seldom run and, where they are shown as running, all exaggeration of movement is avoided. Every sort of large game is represented there in paint, but there are no cattle. Rain, river, and lake are painted as well, and it can likewise be seen that trouble has been taken to bring into the picture, a tree here, a mountain there, or something else out of the landscape.

In the rounded style people are depicted in the same bodily postures, but it is hunting and dance scenes which predominate. There are people shown in long, queer garments. Human beings are often portrayed with the heads of animals, or horns, or with long protruding ears. Most of the pictures show people naked with an apron suspended from the hips. Ornaments are often drawn with special care. Almost all the animals are represented, including cattle.

The question of the age of the cave-pictures has received several different answers. The reference to their relationship to the grotto-pictures of southern Europe has clearly been responsible for an age of several thousand years being attributed to them. The realization, however, that well-known pictures, which were admired half a century ago for their freshness and distinctness, have, since then, partly or entirely disappeared, has caused many people to estimate their age in centuries. In addition to this, there are actually some pictures in which a person riding on horseback is shown, and the horse was totally unknown before 1820.

Those who argue in favour of old age ought not to forget that, while age may make a thing interesting and venerable, the real value of these cave-pictures consists principally in showing that an art, which in Europe disappeared with the people of the Stone Age, was preserved in Africa up to modern times. But those, who wish to deny the pictures any value because they are not very ancient, may bear in mind that there are often two or three pictures painted on the top of one another, and that, of these, the underneath ones, which are painted over but still clearly recognizable as pictures, may well have a quite respectable age. In addition to this the fact must not be lost sight of that, in these hustling times, the cave-pictures are exposed to quite different dangers from those to which they were exposed in the centuries gone by. The frequent visiting of the caves, the deliberate destruction of pictures, the superstitious scratching off of the paint by the natives for medicinal purposes, intentional deletion, with the object of being rid of troublesome visitors, rubbing off by grazing cattle and other similar occurrences, may have been more harmful to them than the gentle passing of the centuries of quieter times. For the investigator it is, however, worth while knowing that pictures, which have entirely disappeared from sight, can be made visible again by applying a moderate quantity of water to the painted rock-face. The rock, owing to its being impregnated with the oiliness of the colours which have been obliterated or have disappeared, then shows again quite clearly the old picture as a dark shadow. Any one in calculating age is oft-times, therefore, confronted with the fact that, alongside the pictures of recent times, old and very old pictures appear. It may generally be observed that pictures which are known to be old are more true to nature than those of more recent date and that, again, those of the rounded style are truer to nature than those of the wedge style.

If our explanation is the correct one, then the engraved rock-pictures served a practical purpose. Probably innate artistic instinct was responsible for the painting of the cave-pictures. At the same time it was impossible to deny that neither imagination nor actual experience have had full play in the grouping and portrayal of human beings. It can likewise not be denied that a mythical and magical trend of thought often led the painter to present figures otherwise than they actually appeared to him. Animal heads on human bodies and the spirit forms done with faint lines, which so often occur, are evidence of this. There is something touching about it, when one imagines the miserable dweller in inhospitable and comfortless caverns trying to make his dwelling-place more homely with bright colours.

The authors of these painted cave-pictures have been thought to be an art-loving and talented race, which was in some way related to the Stone Age people of southern Europe, but which has disappeared here as it has there. There are, however, others, and they are greatly in the majority, who call the cave-paintings simply 'Bushman-paintings', and say that they are produced by the Bushmen who are known to us. But they contend, further, that this race is a very ancient one, that it most probably inhabited the whole continent of Africa many thousands of years ago, that it was in some manner connected with the Stone Age people of Europe, and that it consists to-day of a residue, a mere racial fragment, in the African forests, the Cameroons and in East Africa, where its members are called pygmies. Most of them have exchanged their own language for that of the surrounding Bantu peoples. Other groups, however, still speak to-day a language with clicks, like the Bushmen in the Cape Province and the Kalahari. The mere fact that the Bushman has been thrust into the background by all other races may have made him forget his ancient skill in painting, which he still knew how to exercise scarcely a hundred years ago. This is the reason why the Bushmen of our day cannot paint any more.

It seems that, despite expressions of opinion to the contrary, this view ought to be adopted. It has so much in its favour. Now that

Bleek, Dornan, and others have produced the proofs, which were repeatedly demanded, that, a mere generation ago, Bushmen were seen
in the very act of painting by reliable Europeans, there is no longer
any reason, to my way of thinking, for refusing to agree with what
has been popularly asserted for the last three hundred years, namely
that the cave-pictures are Bushman paintings. In South West Africa
the old Bushmen have entirely disappeared from the places in which
cave-pictures are to be found. They had to give way for the Saan,
the Namas, and the Hereros. The Kalahari Bushmen have no opportunity for making pictures in the old way. They live in a country in
which not only caves are usually lacking, but where there are no
stones, so much so that the indispensable grinding stones, with which
they break up the hard veld growths, have to be fetched from a great
distance, or to be obtained by barter. But there still seems to lie
dormant within them an old talent for making pictures. I found that
they had the 'message-stick', which is known to the Hottentots as
well. When a messenger is sent, he is given a walking-stick to take
with him, which is as thick as the thumb and about 5 to 6 feet long.
The custom was so deeply rooted with the Hottentots of past times
that, even to this day, they speak of sending a message by using the
word *hei-si*, which means to send a stick, and this despite the fact
that a messenger no longer carries a stick with him. Pioneers in South
West Africa remember the custom of inserting a letter, which a native
had to deliver, in the top end of a cleft stick. This custom undoubtedly originated from the Nama one. I was surprised to find
the messenger's wand in use with the Kalahari Bushmen too. It was
the decorations on the stick that aroused my interest. It was covered
over its whole length with tokens, such as animal spoors, human
figures, rings, leaves, worms, and snakes. In answer to my question
as to the meaning of these tokens they said that every head of a family
made a stick of this kind, and, when he sent a messenger to a friendly
family, the well-known stick was satisfactory proof that the messenger had really been sent, and that his message was true. So that no
one could abuse this custom by bringing any sort of stick with any
kind of message, it was essential that every head of a family should
have a stick marked by his own hand. I had the opportunity of
watching one of these artists at his task. He took a stick from a
rhenoster bush, the bark of which adheres very fast to the wood, and
turned it in hot ashes until it began to sweat, when the bark came
off very easily and the white wood became soft. The artist now made

little holes, about one-twentieth of an inch deep, in the soft surface of the wood, with a nail which had been made into a sharp punch. By putting rows of holes close together, he made lines, and figures, which could plainly be recognized as actual spoors, human bodies, and so on. When a figure had been perfectly pricked out, he took the roasted kernel of the *erop* plum, which, when roasted, can be rubbed on like tallow and is black in colour. He rubbed the fatty kernel over the whole surface, through which some of the vegetable oil penetrated the holes. He then wiped the painted places with a piece of leather, removing all the superfluous paint, and the figure stood out on the white wood with astonishing clearness. This was an instance of genuine, uninfluenced Bushman art.

Does not the production of these figures remind one very much of the manner in which the animal-pictures and spoors were produced on the warning notices of the rock-drawings of ancient times, which were likewise made with a sharp stone, gradually, blow by blow? Does not the use of colour serve as a reminder of the cave-dweller's habit of decorating his inhospitable habitation with paintings? Has not perhaps the prehistoric race passed over into the Bushman race which followed it up, so that the Bushman stick, in which we catch a glimpse of the artistic achievements of both races, is to-day some evidence of the fusion process, and that it thus affords us information regarding occurrences about which neither history nor fable can tell us anything? Imagination! Without imagination a work of art can neither be understood, judged, nor appreciated.

3. THE BERGDAMAS

Impenetrable darkness lies over the origin and descent of the mysterious race of the Damas. Many people regard them as the original inhabitants of South West Africa, and they may possibly be right, although it is much more probable that the Bergdamas had found their way into the country before the Saan and the Hottentots came on the scene. In that case they had only to share the mountains and the plains with the Bushmen, between whose family holdings such wide spaces intervened that there was room enough for both of them.

It has often been the case that a historian has been able to find his way in the confusing maze of fable, myth, and ancient memories by means of the fine Ariadne's thread of language, so as to make it possible for him to pass an opinion, at least by venturing to make a presumption, as to whence the people he is interested in may have come, and the roads by which they reached the country they settled in. May it not be possible to solve the riddle of the Bergdamas in the same way? This thread was unfortunately broken long before we got hold of it. The Bergdamas have forgotten their ancient speech. In the northern part of South West Africa, where they still live undisturbed in their old way, they speak the dialect of the Hottentot Saan, and in the south they talk pure Nama. It has been pointed out that their way of speaking Nama is much less accomplished than that of their former masters. It is suggested that that may be a proof that the change of language does not lie very far back in point of time. That is, without any doubt, a wrong conclusion. Children, who have grown up from their earliest days in a country where a foreign language is spoken, learn that foreign tongue perfectly. Bergdama children are no exception to this rule. The awkwardness, which prevents them from using the Nama language like a Nama, has another origin. It is the mental clumsiness of the Damas showing itself in this particular way. This race stands far below the Hottentots in its natural proclivities and talents, and that is the reason why it is unable to master the fine, flexible language of the Hottentots to the same degree as they can. One has only to hear how a Bergdama, who has been raised to a high mental level through many years of schooling or service with a European, masters the Hottentot language, to recognize that there is very little difference between him and a true Nama.

Even if we have to admit that our Ariadne's thread was broken when the change of language took place, another thread has been joined on in the shape of the Nama-Saan language. This affords us proof that, in former times, there must have been a very much closer contact between the Damas, on the one hand, and the Saan and Hottentots on the other than was the case at the time when Pieter Brand, in 1791, brought to South Africa, from the mountains of Windhoek or the lowlands of the Swakop, the first reliable information about them. By this time there were already many free Damas in the land, and the assumption that this race was conquered and enslaved by the Namas, and lost its speech in that way, cannot be right. It cannot be accepted that, in an immense territory such as South West Africa is, an ancient, thinly scattered population could be so completely reduced to slavery that practically every single individual should be enslaved. Many a family could undoubtedly have concealed itself in the impassable mountain ranges, and we should have been able to find to-day Bergdamas, who had preserved some recollection at least of their ancient tongue. But that is not the case; the most diligent search for families having their own language has proved futile. Wherever Bergdamas of any kind have been sought out in the most remote parts of South West Africa, they have been found speaking Nama, or some dialect of that language. It has never even occurred to them that it is remarkable that they, as 'black people', as they are so fond of calling themselves, have a common language with the 'red people', as they call the Namas. It was the searching questions and investigations of Europeans which first drew their attention to this problem, which is a proof that the change of language must have occurred imperceptibly and not catastrophically.

I succeeded in collecting from the Damas of the Otavi Highlands a dozen words which are not indigenous to the Nama language. It might conceivably be taken that these words possibly belong to their own forgotten language, seeing that these particular words are not to be found in any language which is spoken in South West Africa, or its surrounding territories. Dr. B. Struck discovered that they bear some relationship to words in the language of the Sudan.

May not the wandering Nama tribes have picked up, in the course of their migrations in Central Africa, servants of a negro tribe, who went with them because it was to their advantage to stay with masters, who were wealthy in cattle, seeing that a plentiful supply of food is guaranteed in the service of a rich cattle owner? May it not be that, through close contact between these negroes and their yellow-skinned masters, their own language was gradually forgotten, with the succeeding generations, and the speech of their masters was adopted in its place? If this is the answer to the riddle, then it would explain too why the Bergdamas speak the Nama language to a man. It would explain at the same time how the remarkable physical differences of this race arose, and why its members vary between the true negro type and the fine Herero type. It may well be that these are people from different African tribes who, in the course of centuries, attached themselves as servants to the nomadic Hottentots. The remarkable fact that the very humblest race of South-West Africa understands the art of melting and working iron may throw some light on the matter. It is not as if every Bergdama understood this art or practised it, but the fact remains that the Bergdamas were the first blacksmiths of South West Africa. May they not have brought their skill with them from the northern regions of Africa, the home of the blacksmiths, and have employed it in the service of their masters, who had no knowledge of it, but required its products in the form of assegais and arrow heads?

If, however, the Bergdamas were already in the company of the Namas at the time they invaded South Africa, it ought to be possible to discover some mention in the old accounts of the fact that black people were with the Hottentots as servants. I have searched in vain for any such statement. Professor von Luschan seeks to connect with our Bergdama legendary stories about a South African race of pygmies, called Katteas, and says:

'In the stories of the Boers, the Katteas play a considerable role as well as the Bushmen. These must be pygmies, living in the Northern Transvaal, smaller than the Bushmen and quite dark in colour, who are often described as negroid, and sometimes even as "pitch-black". I have many a time done my best to ascertain on the spot something further about these people, who must differ in their colour and size, just as much from the light-complexioned, little Bushmen as they do from the dark, tall Kaffirs, but I have not only failed to catch sight of these small Katteas myself, but I have failed to find any one I could believe who knows of them except by hearsay. It is only the old stories that are dished up to me, as, for instance, that they feed on carrion for preference and are therefore called by the Kaffirs dogs and vultures, while the Bushmen call them apes and accuse them of cannibalism. It would appear as if any of these characteristics, which are not entirely imaginary, are the result of mixing these people up with the Bergdamas, about whom we likewise know very little indeed. It really seems, however, that they must be small and very dark. Passarge describes two people with skin "of a dark-bluish colour, such as I have never even seen in the case of negroes", and with very ugly, "exaggerated" negroid features; he suggests the possibility that "in the Bergdamas we have really a relic of the prehistoric negroes, for whom South West Africa was the furthest limit of dispersal".'

Now there are, amongst the Bergdamas, two clearly distinguishable racial divisions, namely the Hom-damas (*hom* meaning mountain) in Erongo, the Auas Mountains, &c., and the Ou-damas (*Ous* meaning mountain-top), who have their true home in the Otavi Highlands. They are known there by the name of 'Honey-kings'. The Mountain-top Damas are despised by the Bergdamas and marriages between the two divisions rarely take place. The higher class, the Bergdamas, higher in this case in a restricted sense of the word, keep, under normal conditions, a few goats. The lower class have no inclination for stock-raising and lead a purely Bushman existence. In some cases, of which I myself have been a witness, they outdid even the Bushmen by showing so little daintiness in their methods of getting meat that, without any real need, they dug up the carcases of animals that had died and ate them after they had been buried for days, and that they even resurrected buried after-births in the cow-kraal and found them palatable. According to the assertions of the higher class of Damas, it is for things of this kind that they are shunned. May it not be that the story of the Katteas and the Bergdamas is that of the black race, which the Hottentots, or the Namas, had as servants, of which the ancient accounts are missing? We do not know and we are forced back upon pure supposition. It remains to add that, beside these two classes of people, the Bergdamas and the Mountain-top Damas, there is, in the Brandberg and to the north of it, an isolated Bergdama tribe which is called the Dauna-damas or Ao-guwu. This tribe has obviously withdrawn itself from all contact with any other members of its race for a long period of time, for it speaks a dialect of the Nama language, which the other Damas find it difficult to understand.

Let us now turn to tradition, which has so often proved to enshrine matters of historical significance and to provide a pointer for the solution of racial riddles. Among the Mountain-top Damas of the Otavi Highlands who are, generally speaking, smaller than the other members of their race, there runs a legend, which on the one side seeks to explain why they are smaller than other people, and on the other to show that an ancient relationship exists between them and the Ovambo tribes, something which is also asserted in Ovamboland. It is as follows: Two sisters came from the east. They journeyed through Grootfontein to the north. That happened at a time when Ovamboland was still uninhabited. When they reached the bare plains beyond Namutoni, the smaller sister said, 'Come, let us turn back; I am afraid of the desert.' The taller sister said, however, 'If you are afraid, turn back; I shall then go on alone.' The smaller sister then turned back and stayed in the mountains of Otavi. She became the progenitor of the Mountain-top Damas. The taller sister, however, reached the land beyond the desert and became the progenitor of the Ovambo tribes.

Another legend treats of the same theme: the origin of the small, lowly race and that of the superior and taller one. Once some people were travelling about. Amongst them was a woman heavy with child and her little daughter, Aga-abes. For the woman the way was hard so she sat down at the wayside to rest awhile. But a woman who devoured human beings lived close by. When she saw these two

she said to the woman: 'What are you doing here in my territory?'
She replied, 'I am weary from the long journey because I am with
child, and I sat down to rest awhile.' The devourer of men said,
'Come to my house; I will nurse you there until you are well again';
and the two went with her. When they came to the house, the
woman took the expectant mother into the house and said to Aga-
abes, 'Go and fetch me water from the well.' The well, however,
was a long way away, and the girl did as she had been bidden. Then
the woman rubbed Aga-abes's mother very vigorously until she
brought forth twins. These were very tiny and they were put into
a little skin bag and hung behind the door. Then the woman ate the
mother up. When Aga-abes came back from the well she asked,
'Where is my mother?'. The woman-eater said, 'Your mother is
quite well again and hastened after the other people some time ago.
You must stay with me'. Aga-abes did not believe it, but she stayed
with the woman. The two children started to grow in the little skin
bag; they were boys and the bag began to get too small for them.
One day it burst. The woman took the boys and put them into an
ostrich egg. When some time had passed, and they were fully grown,
the ostrich egg burst too, and they came out as if out of their mother's
womb. The boys began to walk, and they imagined that the little
skin bag, out of which they had first come, was their mother. But
when they were out in the veld one day, Aga-abes recognized them
and said: 'You are my brothers! Our mother was eaten up by the
cannibal woman, she is trying to kill me with all the work she forces
me to do, and she will eat you up one day, too.' They then put their
heads together and discussed what course they should take. When they
got back to the house, Aga-abes refused to fetch water and to sweep
the house out. The woman was then forced to go and get the water
herself. In the meantime the brothers fetched brush-wood and
packed it round the house. When the woman returned it was dark.
She went into the house and went to bed. Then the boys set fire to
the heaps of brushwood and the house caught alight. The woman
woke up and started screaming. The children said: 'Now give us our
mother's heart.' She threw a heart out, but it was her own. When
the children saw it they saw that this was not their mother's heart
and said: 'What is this? What does it mean? This is not our mother's
heart! Give us our mother's heart immediately!' Then she gave
it to them. They took it and they threw the other heart into the
fire and there it was burnt together with the cannibal woman. The

children laid their mother's heart in the warm embers and sprinkled it with sweet-smelling herbs. They then went to the veld to look for veld-food. When they returned in the evening, their mother had come to life again, being reborn out of her heart. Then the mother said to Aga-abes: 'Our people are gone. The men who could have married us are no longer to be had. You take your smaller brother as a husband and I will take the bigger one'; and they did so. When they begat descendants, the small Mountain-top Damas were the progeny of Aga-abes's children, while her mother's children were the progenitors of the larger Bergdamas.

Even if the relation of this legend is to be regarded only as a sample of the rich fund of legends which this insignificant-looking little race possesses, it still serves the purpose of showing something of what it thinks itself about its origin. It believes that it once had another home, somewhere in the east, and it thinks, too, that it has been living in South West Africa for a very long time, a time indeed when there were neither Ovambo tribes in the north, nor was there a Herero race in the midlands.

There is another folk-story, which indicates a close communal life with the Hottentots: In the days when people were not as yet red (Hottentots) and black (Bergdamas) they once upon a time slaughtered an ox. Then a woman came there to select a piece of meat for herself. First she took the lungs, but these she put on one side and she seized the liver, carried it off and ate it up. But the liver had the effect of colouring black all the children she bore. In that way she became the mother of the black Bergdamas. Another woman, however, took the lungs and ate them, and the lungs gave their colour to all the children whom she bore. So she became the mother of the Namas, who were called the *awakhoin*, or red people.

The Bergdamas of the Erongo Mountains have their own folk-lore and they say that their proper home is in Kanubes (Okanjande in the District of Otjiwarongo). There, before any other race had put in an appearance in South West Africa, a rock burst open and the first Bergdamas came out of the crack. They spoke the same language and lived in peace and concord together. Then a rumour reached them that Death was stalking through the land, and the families fled in different directions into the mountains. Some fled to the Erongo, some to the Waterberg, and some again to the Auas Mountains.

There are likewise stories told amongst these same dwellers in the Erongo, which sound like real historical memories and point to a close relationship between the Bergdamas and the Ama-Xosas. Dr. Lebzelter, who had the opportunity of investigating these legends in Okombahe, writes about them as follows:

'Above all, there is deeply ingrained in their racial consciousness the conviction that they are connected with the Ama-Xosas in the south-east. There are different opinions as to the way in which the Damas and the Ama-Xosas parted from each other. According to one story, the forefathers of the Damas had gone with the Ama-Xosas as far as the present Xosaland, or perhaps into the Free State. At some time there was a report that there was a place, far away in the north, where there was a great deal of game. A big hunting expedition, consisting only of young men, was organized. They trekked as far as the Gariep River. That could have been the Orange, which still bears that name to-day, but it might likewise have been the Zambesi, which could have had that name, too, in ancient times. The expedition remained there for a long time and some of the members took wives in the north. When it came to returning home, the married ones stayed in the north, while the rest went home. As those who stayed behind soon quarrelled with their neighbours, they trekked with their wives and children through the desert into Ovamboland.'

'According to another version, the Xosas were said to have lived in the east in earlier times. One day a number of children and young people were sent over the dunes to keep a look out. When they came back the others had gone away. They chose from amongst their number a clever youth who understood how to make iron weapons as their leader. This was the first chief A-a-nanub. He brought the children through the desert into Ovamboland. A-a-nanub taught the Ovambos the art of working iron, and the poor Damas became the slaves of the Ovambos and made iron beads, swords, and spears for them. Some of them stayed with the Bushmen. The Damas increased rapidly in numbers in Ovamboland, and since they wanted to be free they trekked to the south.'

Dr. Lebzelter then gives a list of twenty-one names of ancient Dama chiefs. I have, unfortunately, not had the opportunity of verifying the list myself, so I give it just as my informant, Dr. Lebzelter, gave it to me. Although the Bergdamas had no chiefs at the time the Europeans came on the scene, but only family elders in the same way as the Bushmen, it should not be lost sight of that these people were probably a conglomeration of several races, and that it is quite probable that the recollection of important events in the past may have survived with some section of them. In order to render this list of chiefs more or less chronological, I put it in an

order which goes back from the son to the father and then back to
the grandfather. Seeing that the Bergdamas used to marry early, we
may take it that, on an average, to every father an eldest son was
born when he was twenty-five years old, and in this way we get the
following chronological table of successive chieftains:

Name	Probable year of birth	Name	Probable year of birth
1. Hosea Goreseb	1890	12. Aruseb	1615
2. Judas Goreseb	1865	13. Kudeb	1590
3. Cornelius Goreseb	1840	14. Goseb	1565
4. Abraham Seibeb	1815	15. Uru-ge-heib	1540
5. Hoeseb	1790	16. Owo saub	1515
6. Gaoseb	1765	17. Hau-karib	1490
7. Tsaoseb	1740	18. Kari garub	1465
8. Nawaweb	1715	19. Gei garub	1440
9. Tsowaseb	1690	20. Saub	1415
10. Gariseb	1665	21. A-a-nanub	1390
11. Narirab	1640		

The above list can only be accepted with the greatest possible reser-
vation. To those who are really interested in the problem of the
Bergdamas it will undoubtedly be welcome. Of course, the very fact
that even the very oldest names are derived, both in form and meaning, from the Nama tongue gives rise to suspicion, for this language
was certainly not spoken by the Damas in very early times. A-a-nanub
means 'the widespread thunder cloud'; Saub means 'grass seeds collected by the ants'; Gei Garub means 'the great leopard'; Kari Garub
means 'the small leopard', and so on. Confidence in the reliability of
this traditional record would be considerably increased if the oldest
names were to belong to some other African language, even if their
grammatical forms were derived from the Nama tongue.

Dr. Lebzelter's account then proceeds as follows:

'For a long time the Damas stayed in the area south of Ovamboland undisturbed. It was under Narirab that a great war with the Ovambos took
place. Narirab fell and most of the Damas fled into Namaland, while the
Ao-guwun withdrew into the fastnesses of the Brandberg. Some of the others
reached the Gariep River, where Gariseb was chosen as leader, but under
him the Damas were scattered in every direction. With a small residue,
Gariseb went northwards and settled in Kanubes, i.e. Okanjande. There the
nation grew strong again.'

The author adds this to his account:

'The results of my anthropological investigations support the correctness of this tradition', namely, the acceptance of an association between the Damas and the Ama-Xosas.

In confirmation of the foregoing, it might be as well to give a short account by the mission teacher at Grootfontein, Jacobus Neib, who states as follows:

'One of my forefathers was the ancient Neib. He brought the Damas of the Swakop back from Namaland into Hereroland. This happened at a time when the Hereros were already in the country. In very early times, the Damas of Okombahe (Erongo) lived in Namaland. They drank the waters of Berseba, Bethanie, and Rehoboth, for this was also Bergdama territory in times gone by. But whenever war broke out between the Hereros and the Namas, the Bergdamas always kept in with the side which was victorious. When the Hereros overcame the Namas many of the Bergdamas fled to the Hereros, and if the Namas were victorious, many of the Damas ranged themselves on the side of the Namas. If any one did not want to do that he hid himself in the mountains while there was a war being waged. My grandfather was half Bushman. When the Bergdamas came up from Namaland under his father's leadership he took a Bergdama wife of the tribe of the Geio-damas. The Bergdamas were in former times of the same class as the Bushmen, or even somewhat below them. The original territory occupied by the Geio-damas lay between the Waterberg, Otjiwarongo and the Paresis Mountains. That was their old home. They were not under the domination of the Namas, nor were they their servants. The Hereros came there and started quarrelling with them. Then many of them fled to Namaland and became the Namas' servants. Others again, who did not flee to Namaland, hid themselves in the mountains and lived with the Bushmen, that is with the Saan Bushmen. I am inclined to think that the Damas of olden days, who forgot their own language, acquired the Nama language which they speak now, not from the Namas but from the Saan Bushmen, for the latter speak Nama too.'

Coming back to the question of where the Damas came from and what caused their change of language, we do not suggest that a study of their folk-lore can provide a solution of the entire problem. That purpose is just as little effected by the view, which I expressed, that the Bergdamas were collected by the Hottentots from different races of Central Africa, and were the ancient servants of these nomads, although this solution solves the problem of the change of language easily and satisfactorily. Unfortunately there is no confirmation for it in the history of the Hottentots. In the old accounts there is not the slightest trace to be found of the Hottentots of the Cape having had a negro race as their servants. The scanty accounts of the

Katteas do not suffice. Still, the acceptance of the alternative theory, which is to be found in the early literature, that the Namas conquered the Bergdamas, and that their enslavement and, with it, the replacing of their own language by Nama were a consequence of that, is just as unsatisfactory. That leaves unanswered the question as to how it was possible for the conquerors to bring a race, which was thinly scattered throughout an extraordinarily wide area, to such a degree under their influence that, to the very last man, it adopted their language and forgot its own.

This additional fact must be noticed, that the Nama tribes know for a certainty that it was only the 'Red Nation' of Hatsamas and Hoachanas, that is to say, the oldest and the ruling tribe of the Nama people, who possessed a large number of Dama slaves. The other tribes did not depend upon Bergdamas for help in their stock-farming, although they may not have refused to allow fugitives of that race to stay in their kraals. It seems out of the question that there was a time in South Africa when all the Bergdamas were Nama slaves. The historical origin of this enigmatical people seems to be something of the following nature. The prehistoric Bushman race of South West Africa was joined by a dwarf, negroid, prehistoric race from Central or North Africa. This latter race differed from the Bushmen by reason of their very dark colour, but they were, in common with the prehistoric Bushmen, of very small stature. The character of the country forced both races to adopt the same mode of living. The Bushmen and the ancient Damas must have lived by hunting and collecting food. The Ou-damas, or Mountain-top Damas of the Otavi Highlands, are a relic of these Damas of prehistoric times. Other fragmentary remains of them may have survived near the sea, in the Brandberg, and to the northwards of it, in the shape of the Dâunadamas and the Ao-guwu. It seems, too, that there were such people in the Swakop Valley and in the Auas Mountains a century or two ago.

At some later time there joined these Ou-damas, or prehistoric Damas, some wandering folk from eastern Bechuanaland, Ama-Xosas and the like. But it was more especially fugitives from Ovamboland, who tried to save their threatened lives amongst the Damas of olden times, just as, in our times, Ovambo fugitives have made use of the country lying to the south of Ovamboland as a sanctuary and a hiding-place. It is practically certain that the fugitives who could never return home again mingled with the Damas, and became fused into one race with them, and exactly the same thing may well have happened in regard to the small numbers of Bechuanas and Ama-Xosa people, who came in from the east. These strangers from the north and the east were skilled in the working of metal. Blacksmiths were regarded in Ovamboland as marvellous magicians who carried out their secret tasks in the darkness of their huts, lit only by flickering flames. Even if the fugitives, who practised this black art, were cut off from the mines of South Angola, they searched for ore in South West Africa, and they discovered it in the Otavi Highlands, in the Auas Mountains, at the Kuiseb and in Namaland. We shall, at a later stage, see that it was, in every instance, the Bergdamas who told the first discoverers and explorers of the land about the copper deposits and showed them where they were. Bergdama blacksmiths were people who went right into southern Namaland to ply their trade in the making of bangles, arrow-heads, assegais and knives. They obtained the iron from outside, but their own land provided them with copper.

With these prehistoric inhabitants of South West Africa, i.e. the Bushmen and the pre-Damas, strengthened through accretions from the north and east, were associated the Saan, who were so closely related to the Hottentots as to speak their language, but were not stock-raisers and were compelled to depend upon hunting and food-gathering, just as were both the races of the ancient inhabitants with whom they allied themselves. Mentally, however, they were distinctly superior to the Bergdamas, and that is probably why the Bergdamas became subject to the Saan. The Saan could find a living wherever the Bergdamas managed to do so. This might likewise afford an explanation as to how it became possible that the old Bergdama language came to be entirely forgotten, and the Hottentot language of the Saan to be adopted. This process of association may not have taken place in a perfectly peaceable way. Until quite recent times, the Saan of the northern districts have understood how to keep and treat Bergdamas as slaves. If it were asked how a hunter and food-gatherer could employ a servant and make him work for him, I would point to the custom of the Saan and the Bushmen, under which they kept a son-in-law with them for a full year after his marriage before they allowed him to return to his family with his young wife. Whatever he killed with his bow and arrow during this year he had to deliver to his parents-in-law. I would likewise point to that old Bergdama, who once showed me in Otaviland an old ele-

A GATHERING OF HEIKOM BUSHMEN AT KEIBEB, GROOTFONTEIN, SOUTH WEST AFRICA

Photographed by Paul L. Hoefler, F.R.G.S.

phant pit, saying, 'In this pit I killed an elephant with my assegai, but I ate none of its meat for I was then in the service of a Saan Bushman.'

When, in the course of time, the Namas came to join the Bushmen, the Bergdamas and the Saan, then there began for the Bergdamas, who had not succeeded in creating any tie between these races, a fugitive existence. Their dwelling-places in the South West Africa of olden days are to be found everywhere within the boundaries of the land as far as the Orange River. The roads by which they wandered and fled could not be traced without writing a history of every separate family, and that would merely be a series of stories of stock-raiding, pursuit, massacre, and flight into inaccessible mountain fastnesses.

4. THE HOTTENTOTS AND THE SAAN

There are three races with light yellow skins living in South West Africa. The Bushmen, the colour of whose skin especially in childhood, could almost be described as white, have already been dealt with. The Saan Bushmen, too, are light-coloured in varying degrees, as are the Hottentots, of whom the so-called Nama tribes in South West Africa consist, although in days long gone by they had their grazing grounds in the Cape Province. A thorough examination of these three groups raises a presumption that they must, at some period of time, have been closely connected with each other. They all three speak a click-language. The Bushman language, it is true, is richer in clicks than that of the Hottentot and the Saan. The former has five or six different clicks while the latter has only four. It is, however, remarkable that the Bushman language represents a language family which has disappeared. The Saan-Hottentot language, however, belongs to the Semito-Hamitish language group of North Africa. The two languages are no more connected with each other than are, for example, German and Chinese, in so far as the grammatical construction of their form and syntax is concerned, but they correspond to a marked degree in vocabulary. It is obvious that there occur in the Hottentot language many root words derived from Bushman and that, in the Bushman language, similarly, many Hottentot words have intruded themselves. The differences and the resemblance between these two languages can be illustrated by means of a few examples. For this purpose, let us take first of all the different Bushman languages which are spoken in the Kalahari. The noun of these languages, which possesses only one form for the singular and the plural, makes no distinction between classes like the Bantu languages do, and none between the sexes like the Indo-Germanic tongues. The stem of the noun can be used both as an adjective and as a verb, according to its position in the sentence. The numerals generally consist of the numbers one to three, sometimes they go as far as five, but very seldom up to ten, in which latter case foreign influence is traceable. The verb has no inflexions, but expresses the different tenses by adding particles, so that the Bushman verb is simplicity itself. The syntax is as simple as it can possibly be. One principal clause is placed next to another, while subordinate clauses are hardly ever used. Besides this, among the sounds there are five, six, and sometimes seven clicks, with the peculiarities of which we have previously dealt at some length, and these cannot be regarded as prefixes or factors which produce changes in sense, despite the fact that they are placed at the beginning of words. They have to be treated just like other consonants, with the result that the Bushman languages comprise vowels, consonants, and clicks. The vowels can be pronounced freely or nasally, and although the same sounds are used, the meaning of the words will be quite different. Besides this, every word has its special tone, and although one word may be made up of exactly the same sounds as another, a variation in the tone it is expressed in changes the meaning completely.

The various dialects of the Hottentot language possess a well-constructed accidence. So far as the noun is concerned, they distinguish not only the male and female genders, but they have a neuter form as well for those cases in which the gender cannot, or need not, be expressed. The assignment of a noun to a particular gender is not hard and fast, as it is with the Indo-Germanic languages, but with many words the gender is variable. In the naming of things, large, strong objects are usually masculine, while delicate, fine, or thin things, are usually feminine, and through this peculiarity the language becomes very expressive. Besides this, the noun and the pronoun have, as well as a singular and a plural, a form for the dual; and, with the pronoun, this shows very clearly whether a person who is spoken to is regarded as included in what is said, or not. 'Sage' meaning 'we men' implies all of us who speak and are being spoken to, while 'sige', which likewise means 'we men', implies those who are speaking, and not those who are being addressed. Moreover the pronoun can be used as a suffix to both the noun and the verb, as is the case in Semitic languages. The syntax is extraordinarily complicated, and compound sentences occur so frequently that only a person who is able to think in Hottentot can speak the language. This is a position entirely different from that of the Bushman languages. Hottentot has, however, four of the same clicks as Bushman has, and it has the same nasal pronunciation of vowels and varying intonation of words. Any one who wishes to study a Bushman language would be wise to make a preparatory study of Hottentot, seeing that this can be dealt with scientifically, and it really makes the process of grasping the phonetics of Bushman easier. Mention may be made of the fact that there is a considerable number of Bantu languages which have two or three click-sounds, and from this the deduction can be drawn, not that they were all derived from one original language, but that they have been borrowed.

Comparative philology makes it appear probable that the Hottentot language belongs to the Hamito-Semitic language group. This probability is increased by the fact that numerous words occur in it which are entirely without click-sounds, and the roots of which indicate clearly that they belong to Semitic languages. Of course, it must necessarily remain an open question whether we have to do with a process of borrowing, so far as these words are concerned, or with actual prehistoric possession. I regard some of these words as borrowed from Arabic, but I am inclined to consider the majority as having belonged to a prehistoric Hottentot language. The Bushman languages cannot, with any measure of certainty, be placed in any language group. They stand all by themselves distinguished by their click-sounds.

When we come to review everything which is useful for our purpose in all these observations and considerations, we feel inclined to agree with those people who think that, between 15,000 and 20,000 years ago, the continent of Africa was inhabited by a race bearing a close resemblance to the Bushmen, of which only small fragments still survive to-day, that this race has changed to a very great extent, in its physical characteristics owing to the introduction of foreign blood, and in its language and customs through foreign influences, but that it may have remained practically unchanged where circumstances have been favourable to its preservation, for example, in the case of the pygmies of the African forests and, in South Africa, in the Kalahari. This does not prevent the acceptance of the theory that these two races adopted, in prehistoric times, two routes for their migrations, one from the north-west, i.e. those of the dancing-style, from the Atlas, and the other from the north-east, who were the people employing the wedge-style, from the Euphrates.

We learn from a number of Greek and Latin writers, of whom Herodotus, as the Father of History, is entitled to first place, that an ancient African race, which spoke a wonderful click-language, aroused attention and astonishment in olden times. Herodotus tells of the cave-dwellers of Ethiopia that they have a language which resembles no other on earth, because they speak with hissing sounds which are very much like the squeakings of bats. This description could hardly have been intended to apply to anything but click-sounds.

It seems probable that some thousands of years ago a Hamitic stock from the north came into very close contact with the prehistoric Bushman inhabitants of Africa, and that this contact took place somewhere in Central Africa, probably in the lake region. This race would seem to have spoken a language, which in its construction and form reminds one, on the one hand, of the Hamitic, and indeed to some extent of the Indo-Germanic languages, but, on the other hand, displays peculiarities which are recognizable as of Semitic origin. Unless all this is quite wrong, this Hamitic race mixed freely with the Bushmen and the consequence was that their physical shape assumed certain Bushman characteristics, as for example steatopygy, hair, facial expression, and the delicacy of hands and feet, that the language remained intact so far as its grammatical construction was concerned, but that it took over from the Bushman language a number of new words, as well as the four click-sounds, and that this race was very considerably influenced by the Bushmen in its religion, its myths, and its customs. In this Hamitic stock we recognize the forefathers of the Hottentots. It would be misleading to say that the close association between the Hamites and the Bushmen probably took place in the Kalahari or in South Africa at all. If that were so, the language of the Hottentots would have shown a much greater similarity in vocabulary to that of the Bushmen of the Kalahari than is actually the case. In the Bushman language of the Kalahari there occur words which have been borrowed from Nama, while the converse is not the case. The contact between the two races must have taken place with some other Bushman stock which possessed quite a different vocabulary from that of the Kalahari Bushmen.

After a period of the closest association and mingling (Thiel considers that it took place somewhere in Somaliland and regards the Hottentots as a race sprung from the association of Egyptian fugitives with Bushman women), there appears to have supervened a period during which the new races developed upon new lines. As Hamites they were stock-farmers and they probably possessed, even at that time, the Syrian fat-tailed sheep, a possession which they looked after with the greatest care; it seems as if the Hottentot fable about *Sore*-sheep, the slaughtering of which entailed the direst punishment, can be traced back to this. There were, however, always two kinds of blood in their veins, the Hamitic blood, in which lay the urge to stock-raising and the love for animals, and the Bushman blood, to which stock-raising was something entirely foreign but, for this very reason, made them all the keener upon hunting. That is why, in the case where the Bushman blood persisted, there is still to-day an aversion to stock-raising and, accompanying it, a propensity to despoil the flocks of others and to treat them as wild game. When the no-madic stock-farmers found that they could not live in harmony with their dangerous hunting brothers, they tried to get rid of them by force. It may be presumed that they drove them out. Seeing, how-ever, that the way to the north was barred by Bantu races, it was only the way to the south that remained open. Taking this, the Hottentot hunter forced his way through to South Africa and occu-pied wide areas in the Cape and the surrounding country out of which he drove the ancient inhabitants, the Bushmen, so far as he was able. Whether this immigration took place a thousand years ago, or before that, cannot be established. It is, however, certain that it was not very long afterwards that the stock-raising Hottentots fol-lowed them by the same routes and, pouring into these very same lands, penetrated to every part of them. Probably they had been pressed by Bantu tribes. The fact that these two migrations into southern Africa cannot be very far distant from each other in point of time is based upon differences in language between the hunting and the stock-raising Hottentots. The difference in speech between the hunters and the other Hottentots is quite unimportant; they speak different dialects of the same language and can understand each other without any difficulty. The hunters were called Saan by their brethren, but the early Hollanders, who emigrated to the Cape in 1652, did not distinguish them from true Bushmen, for they called every human being who lived in the bush by means of hunting and gathering wild growths a Bushman. There were a number of people who were inclined to speak of tame and wild Hottentots and this expression was certainly much more correct. It was Lichtenstein

who first recognized the real difference between Bushmen, Saan, and
Hottentots. The word Saan is derived from the Nama word *saa*,
which Dr. Hahn translates as 'to settle or rest' and finds in that
meaning proof of the fact that the Saan were the prehistoric inhabitants of South Africa, and the very first people to settle in the
country. He has, however, overlooked the fact that *saa* only means
'rest' when it is pronounced nasally. This is not the case with the
tribal name 'Saan' (-*n* is the communal inflexion and is not a part
of the stem of the word); it is pronounced openly and without any
nasalization, both by the Hottentots and by the Saan themselves.
The verb *saa*, spoken freely, means to pick out, gather or collect, so
that the Hottentots who gave this name showed correctly by it the
essential difference between themselves and those they gave it to, for
the Saan differ from the Hottentots in that they depend upon the
collecting of wild things for their existence, while the latter, although
they are not averse to gathering in the veld a certain amount of vegetable
food, rely upon stock-farming as their principal means of subsistence.

It might thus have been thought possible for the Bushmen, the
Saan, and the Hottentots to have lived together side by side in the
wide stretches of South Africa, for what the Hottentots wanted, i.e.
grazing for their stock, was required neither by the Saan nor the
Bushmen. But the Hottentots had to water their stock, and for that
they required the springs and water-holes. These, however, the Bushman guarded most jealously, and whoever went to his water-hole or
spring he regarded for ever after as his deadly enemy. Nor would
the Hottentots refrain from hunting, and this affected the Bushmen
and the Saan in the same way. More important still, were the Saan
and Bushmen to leave the Hottentot's flocks untouched, when the
latter shot down their game? The stock-raiser was, however, an
implacable foe when any one touched his stock. Thus it was that
the first Europeans, who settled at the Cape, found the Hottentots
in irreconcilable enmity with the 'Bosjesman', i.e. the Saan and the
Bushmen.

Through the coming of the Europeans the position got worse
instead of better, for they, too, settled near the springs and organized
hunting expeditions of no inconsiderable magnitude as well, so that
very soon it became impossible for the native hunter to get what he
required. He did no damage to the stock of the European farmer, but
he raided the flocks of the Hottentots who lived in peace with the
white man and became his servants. Within thirty-six years of the

advent of the first settlers (1688), a fierce struggle between the farmers and the stock thieves arose; the men were shot down and the women and children taken as slaves. No improvement in the relationship between them took place; the Europeans continued to go hunting and the 'Bushmen' to steal stock. The position finally became so impossible that, in the years 1786 to 1796, commandos were sent into the country to exterminate the Bushmen, seeing that it had become apparent that it did not help to declare them outlaws. The Hottentots were taken as auxiliaries to these commandos. It has been calculated from the official figures that, in this period of ten years, 2,700 Bushmen were killed and 700 women and children enslaved. That solved the Bushman problem for South Africa, however negative the solution may have been. It is only fair to say, however, that the Government first took a great deal of trouble to try and accustom the Bushmen to a different way of life. They furnished them with farms and breeding stock in an effort to get the roaming hordes to settle down and to adopt a peaceable manner of living, but the Bushmen killed and ate the breeding stock and then returned to their thieving ways.

We have gone too far ahead and we must now go back again to the times when the Bushmen, Saan and Hottentots were in sole occupation of South Africa. The Bushman lived in small family communities, scattered throughout the hunting and gathering grounds which they had inherited from their ancestors. They had no chiefs. The Saan likewise lived in family communities and they had to be content with the no-man's-land which must have existed in all directions between the areas occupied by the Bushmen, as is the case to-day in the Kalahari. They, too, had not become united under the actual rule of a chief. The Hottentots, however, reached a higher stage of development in the course of time; there were twenty to thirty different chiefs, and it has been calculated that there were between twenty and thirty thousand Hottentots in the Cape alone. With these powerful brothers of theirs the Saan had no chance of competing and, if they did not want to be exterminated, they had to give way. It may well be that they were actuated by the hope of finding, somewhere or other, a free country where they would not be harassed by troublesome neighbours and rival hunters. A land of this kind lay to the north. Beyond the Orange River lay South West Africa, in the southern portion of which there were hardly any Bushmen, the northern part being only very thinly populated with them. (The proof for this conclusion is to be found in the fact that there are in Namaland hardly any Bushman pictures, and that they only occur in certain parts of Hereroland.) Many Saan then trekked across the Orange River and settled in Namaland, while others pushed forward across the Kuiseb and the Swakop and came to a halt only at the borders of Ovamboland, for it was thus far only that the Bantu tribes had reached in their southernward thrust. The saltpans of the north, with their inexhaustible wealth of wild animals, attracted a great many families. Where the Bushmen were few in number, the Saan appear to have exterminated them.

But roaming Hottentot tribes ventured farther and farther north. The increase of their stock and the search for new grazing grounds may have been partly responsible for this. The desire to get away from the immediate neighbourhood of the Saan, numbers of whom still made the Cape unsafe, may have actuated them as well. Little Namaqualand, which lies south of the Orange River, could not hold them except while they were passing through it; the area is too rainless and has sufficient water and grazing for large herds only in times of heavy downpours. So they crossed the Orange, too, or trekked up and down its banks, until they found permanent grazing grounds in the territories which lay to the north of it.

The first tribe, which settled permanently in Namaland, found, after trekking about for a considerable time, that the veld of Hatsamas and Hoachanas was suitable for its purpose. It bore the Hottentot name Kouben. The stem of the word 'Kou' means 'to defend' when it is spoken in a high pitched tone; if it is uttered in the middle pitch, it means 'to invite'. Seeing that the Namas still use the high intonation, the name of the tribe can be translated as 'the defenders'. They called themselves Awa-khoi, or red people, since they had dull red complexions. They are known in the history of later times as 'The Red Nation'. When, in the course of time, the tribe grew larger, and a part of it trekked into the territory which is to-day Rehoboth, and to the upper Fish River, the old tribe in Hoachanas came to be called the Gei Kou, which means the great defenders, while the section which had left the parent stem got the name of Kou-gôa, meaning children of the Kou. The children were likewise called, from the name of their leader, the 'Swartboois'. In this history of ours we shall refer to them by this name, while we shall call the old tribe 'The Red Nation'.

The Red Nation considered itself to be the owner of the whole of Namaland and it could put forward a valid claim to the title. Before its arrival the country was inhabited by Bergdamas and Saan. It took it away from them during many years of petty warfare and thus gained for itself the name of 'the defenders'. It stood to reason that other Nama tribes, who wanted to come and settle in Namaland, had first to arrive at an understanding with the Red Nation, lest they should find themselves at war with the latter from the start. Thus it came about that a small yearly tax had to be paid in sheep and cattle to the chief at Hoachanas in recognition of his suzerainty.

The first tribe to join the Red Nation and to recognize their own chief as being subordinate to the latter's was that of the Hawobe, who have become known in literature by the name of the 'Veldskoen-dragers', i.e. those who wear veldshoes. They introduced into the country a new idea, that of providing better protection for the feet by fixing to them a thin skin to protect the rest of the foot. They found the grazing which they wanted to the south of the present Keetmanshoop.

With the leave of the Red Nation, the Fish River was occupied by the Kara-gei-khoi, which means the quite tall people, so there must have been exceptionally tall people amongst them. They have been called the 'Frenchmen Hottentots'. A branch of this tribe gained their independence and wandered about near the Lion River. It got the name Kara-oan, which calls to mind their relationship with the 'quite tall people'.

The upper reaches of the Fish River and the territory between that and the Kuiseb were occupied by the O-gei, or Groot-doden who in later times were completely wiped out by other tribes.

These four or, if you like, six tribes compose the real Nama race, whose heart was the Red Nation with its suzerain chief at Hoachanas. For fear of him the Saan and Bergdamas withdrew into the mountains, hid themselves in the inaccessible kloofs of the Orange River, went out into the inhospitable Namib Desert, or fled to the north. The Red Nation reduced the numbers of the Bergdamas very considerably. They had taken Hoachanas away from them and killed their menfolk, making their women and children their servants, so much so that it is still to-day a common saying that the Bergdamas were the Namas' slaves. This applies, however, only to the Red Nation, not to the others who came into the country later and the tribes associated with them. When these arrived the Bergdamas had disappeared altogether, and it was chiefly with the Saan that they had to do. Many of these preferred to take service with the Namas, without payment. These are the 'tame Bushmen' of whom Wikar writes. The Bergdamas, however, maintained their freedom and roamed about in the mountains as troublesome stock thieves, or kept to themselves in the Namib, in the south-western corner of the country.

Besides these four (or six) older tribes, who stood together under the leadership of the Red Nation, there were still two others who never joined the tribal community. The first of these two to come in was the tribe of the Ouni, or Topnaars, which means the 'sharp people', who were clearly distinct from the other tribes and had to be satisfied with the territory of the lower Kuiseb, which was quite unsuitable for stock-farming. It located itself at Rooibank and Walfish Bay, where a little stock-raising was possible and where the fish in the lagoons and the nourishing wild melons of the Namib afforded a plentiful food-supply in addition. As this race has, from the very earliest times, intermarried with the Saan of the Namib and possesses no recollection whatsoever of a period of migration, it can be taken to be one of the oldest of the Nama tribes.

The second tribe, which laid claim to entire independence, is the tribe of the Bondelswarts. Its name is Gami-nun, i.e. *gami*, meaning bundle and *nu*, meaning black. For a long time this tribe wandered up and down the banks of the Orange River, until, under the influence of the missionaries, it settled down permanently on the right bank at Warmbad. The hot springs of that place have, since that time, served their first discoverers as the centre of their territory.

Amongst the things that tradition has preserved concerning the history of the five allied and two free tribes, that which is of the greatest interest to us is what it has to tell about the ruling tribe, the Red Nation. Its first chief was called Hab. It was he who took a firm hold upon his own tribe and bent the different clans to his will with a stern hand, and then succeeded in making his fellow men recognize him as the chief of the oldest and most powerful of the tribes. It seems as if the Saan and the Bergdamas were the cause of this happening. The land was still full of them and they were extremely troublesome as neighbours. They were at war with the newly arrived flock-owners, who were disputing the possession of the land with them.

In war, however, the thing is to damage one's adversary in such a way that one gains for oneself some advantage or other, and so the stealing of stock went on continually. A single family could not protect itself very well against this practice; it was only by joining forces that the despoilers could be overcome. It appears to have been Hab's task to clean up the land by employing the united forces of the tribe. It is for that reason that it is said regarding him 'Hab made the Nama a nation', the word 'nation' being used to imply the union of the tribes who stood under the leadership of the Red Nation.

Hab's successor was his son, Hanab, of whom nothing more is told than that he had five sons, of whom Gao-karib was his successor. He had no difficulty in keeping up the high position which his predecessor in office had occupied. He is depicted as a friendly and peace-loving chief who did not oppress his subjects. During his chieftainship a great drought occurred in Namaland. The necessity for shifting the cattle-posts to the north had to be considered. Nama hunters had been in those parts long before and had talked about the plentiful springs of water and the extensive grazing-grounds, which they had discovered on the northern side of the mountains. The hot springs of Ai-gams, i.e. Windhoek, were known to them. They had been at Gei-keis (Okahandja), had seen the springs at A-tsâb (Otijimbingwe), and they had even explored the veld and the springs of the Waterberg. They knew, too, all about the Bergdamas in the Auas Mountains and in Okahandja, and about the Bergdamas and the Saan in the Waterberg. Any danger that could threaten the flocks could only come from the side of the Saan and Bergdamas, but to employ force against them seemed hopeless for they were very numerous. Gao-karib, in keeping with his character, undertook to find a solution for this problem in a peaceable way. He summoned a number of his reliable men, had his riding oxen saddled, loaded his pack-oxen with a goodly stock of dagga and tobacco and set out to visit the Bergdamas and the Saan. He was well received in the Auas Mountains, for the present of dagga inclined the hearts of the Bergdamas towards him. They entered into a treaty of friendship with the kindly, powerful Nama chief and acknowledged his supremacy. He had the same success in Okahandja. The Saan of the Waterberg made a great feast in his honour, crowned him with a wreath of red lucky-beads, which grew like hard beans in those parts, performed a dance in which they sang the praises of their new suzerain and sent him away in peace. Thus it was that Gao-karib became, in his own eyes and those of his people, the rightful suzerain chief of the whole of the north, right to the Waterberg. There was no need to make any sacrifice on either side, for the Namas did not want what the Saan and the Bergdamas required, and the new grazing-grounds, which the Namas wanted, the Saan had no use for. The consequent security to life and property was a gain to both parties. Gao-karib returned to Windhoek and there he fell ill. The care and attention given him by his men, which is described in moving terms, were unavailing. He was brought home ill to Hoachanas and he died there shortly after his return.

Unfortunately he had no son of the same disposition to follow in his footsteps. A substitute had to be chosen to govern until a son from the chief's family should come of age. The choice fell on a rich cattle owner named Haromab. He trekked with his cattle most of the time up and down the Fish River, busied himself with his own possessions, and neglected the interests of the Red Nation. Finally, he became arrogant and antagonized the people by his rude behaviour. One particular incident did him a great deal of harm. A lion had taken three of his cows and he decided to kill it. There were three of his people who had guns, and he took these and some others with him to kill the lion. The first of them found the lion, shot at him but missed, and was mangled by the lion. The second ran to the spot, missed too, and was severely wounded. The third took aim as well and shot past the lion, which sprang on him. Haromab then ordered his men to catch hold of the lion with their hands and to stab it to death. They did so, but they always bore the wounds it inflicted on them. Then they said, 'Our chief is too hard with his people; we will not stay with him'. They left him and joined other tribes. When, however, they failed to return when Haromab sent for them, he called his men together and inflicted punishment upon some of the minor chiefs who had received the fugitives. He took their stock away from them and forced those who had fled from him to return. This was the first time that war broke out amongst the Namas themselves. Haromab remained chief as long as he lived, and the period of his reign was about thirty years.

When he died there were two male descendants of the ancient ruling house who could be his successors. The older of the two had an unpleasant disposition, for he was avaricious and arrogant, so they chose the younger, who is known as Nanieb I. In his time the Nama hunters went as far as the Swakop and Okahandja, and there they saw strange black men of fierce appearance with their teeth filed into points. These were clearly Herero hunters who were rendering the Swakop country unsafe. Some of the Namas were killed and the others escaped. They brought back terrible tales of the appearance of cannibals at the Swakop River.

In dry years the cattle had long grazed undisturbed in Windhoek, Okahandja, and on the Swakop down to Otjimbingwe, but now it was dangerous to send them there. Soon afterwards the cattle-herds of this strange people came in from the east and unconcernedly grazed the northern parts of Namaland. These were the herds of the Mbanderu.

Nanieb II followed Nanieb I, but he did not live long and he left behind him a minor son called Oasib. As, however, there was no desire to appoint a substitute for the chief again, seeing that the time of Haromab's ungracious rule was still fresh in the people's minds, the choice fell upon Games, the sister of Nanieb I, and a remarkable woman she must have been.

This would seem to be a strange measure. In the old accounts of the period her name always appears in the male form, Gameb, but there is no doubt whatsoever that, from about 1800 to 1835, the affairs of the Red Nation were in women's hands. This choice con-flicted in no wise with the views of the Nama people, for the whole history of the country knew neither her prototype nor her imitator. The 'eldest sister' is held by them in such high esteem that an oath taken in her name is of more binding effect than one taken on any other sacred object in the world.

Here we break off, for the turn of the century brought in its train a new phase into the history of the Nama nation, by reason of that exceedingly important occurrence, the incursion of the Orlam tribes.

5. THE HEREROS.

Just like the majority of nations, the Hereros have a tradition regarding their descent in which myth, fable, and history are all mingled together, but which now and again contains pointers to which the historian should pay attention. Their story is that the original parents of mankind came out of a tree.

'Near the south of Ovamboland there stands a large Omumborombonga tree (*Combretum primigenum*). Except for the wild fig-tree, it is the only tree in Hereroland which gives real shade. It was out of this tree that the first human beings came forth. The man's name was Mukuru, which means "the ancient one". [Later on this word was used as the name of God.] His wife was called Kamangarunga; *Mangara* means "she is like Karunga", which was the name of God amongst the Ovambo tribes. The wild animals of the veld, as well as the cattle and sheep, came out of this tree, too, but the Bergdama came out of a rock which split open, as did goats and baboons. The first people were white, but when an ox was slaughtered Kamangarunga took the liver for herself and cooked and ate it. From this her children became reddish-brown and got the colour which the Hereros still have to-day. Another woman took the blood, prepared it and ate it, and that made her children red. She was the ancestress of the Red Nation, the Namas. The progenitor of the Hereros and the Bergdamas lived next to each other and their cattle grazed the same veld. On a certain night, when both of them were asleep, the thuds of passing animal's hoofs were heard. The Herero woke the Bergdama up and said: "Get up! the cattle have broken out and are running away; bring them back!" The Bergdama got up and ran after the animals, but he could not catch up with them, for they were not cattle but zebras, as the Herero knew very well. While the Bergdama was away, he got up and made himself scarce taking all the cattle with him. That is the way it came about that the Bergdamas have no cattle, and that they steal some from the Hereros, for they reckon that they have a rightful claim to them.'

Because the story states that the first people had white skins there is no need to regard this as being a recent fabrication on the ground that the Hereros of olden times never saw a white man. The fact that Herero children are born with virtually white skins, and that only after the lapse of several days, or perhaps weeks, does the dark pigment show itself, must be taken into account. It is remarkable that the ancestral tree is still to be found on the borders of Ovamboland. Some of the old men claim to have seen it growing, but now it is dead. Only the stump still survives, and in it there are deep knot-holes. All Hereros and Ovambos who passed close to the tree took a bunch of leaves, or some grass, spat on it, rubbed their foreheads with it and then thrust it into a hole with these words: 'I greet thee, O my father; grant me a prosperous journey.' At a later period the veneration of this tree was extended to all Omumborombonga trees in Hereroland and, when any one came across them in the veld, he addressed them in a similar manner. The Tjimbas of the Kaokoveld, who were impoverished Hereros and did not raise cattle as those who live in the Koakoveld do to-day, venerate the Omutati tree instead of the Omumborombonga, a tree which resembles the latter in many respects.

Something in the traditional story which is worthy of notice, in so

far as the subsequent relationship between the Hereros and the Bergdamas is concerned, is the fact that, from the very beginning, the
Hereros appear as the masters of the Bergdamas. The Bergdama is
the servant who is roused in the night and sent off to look for the
cattle while the Herero stays at home.

The same story appears in another form which has the appearance
of being spun from the threads of exuberant phantasy. It is as follows:

'When the forefathers of olden times came from the east they did not
travel by themselves, for the Ovambos accompanied them. At the large
Omumborombonga tree, on the southern boundary of Ovamboland, the
Ovambos turned to the north and settled in Ovamboland, for the Ovambos
were tillers of the soil and that country was suitable for agriculture. But
the Hereros trekked farther to the west and reached the Kaokoveld. They
stayed there for a time, but not for very long, and then they went to grazing
grounds in the south whence they set out once again and found their way to
their present locations.'

It may well be that we find here, side by side with the correct
recollection that the roads they travelled led them from east to west
until they came to a preliminary standstill in the Kaokoveld, that
another historical fact has been remembered, and that is that there
travelled with the Hereros some kind of Ovambo tribe, which may
not have been a real Ovambo tribe at all, but some of the Hereros
who settled at the Kunene, for there are many tribes living at the
Kunene who come very close to the Hereros both in language and
customs. In 1915 Chief Tjiute of Kaoko Otavi gave me the names
of the following tribes, living in southern Angola, saying that they
must be regarded as belonging to the Herero race: the Ngambue,
Ngumbi, Ndjondi, Nguvare, Nona, Ngoroka, Hakaona, Tjerenge,
Kakuu, Karundu, Karunga, and Tjiku.

It has been stated previously that the river which forms the
country's northern boundary owes its name, Kunene, to a misunderstanding. The river is called by the Ovambos 'Omulonga', which
means 'stream', and the Hereros called it, correspondingly, 'Omu-
ronga'. It is a peculiarity of the Hereros that they have given none
of the numerous rivers of their land a name. The river courses are
named sectionally according to the places which lie on the banks. The
name Kunene applies to the country on the right side of the northern
river (*okunene* means 'the wide or right side'), by which is meant
southern Angola, whereas the land on the left side of the river was
called Kaoko from *okaoko*, which means 'the small or left arm'.

Where did the Hereros probably come from? Some of the old men amongst them profess to recollect things, but these are really nothing but fable. Their recollections are family tradition with the names of places and people included. Tradition of this kind is to be found preserved very faithfully in the old ruling families, which always saw to it and still see to it to-day, that succeeding generations are marvellously well versed in family history. By collecting this traditional information and piecing it bit by bit into a comprehensive whole, a historical picture can be conceived.

According to the Hereros the race did not exist in ancient times; their forefathers were not then called Hereros. The name of the race was Mbandu or, as others called it, Mbundua. The people of Mbandu lived in a land where water was plentiful and where much sedge and reed grew. It was called the Reed-Land (*ehi raruu*). Some of the cattle owners did not like the country any more, but it is not known what really actuated them in leaving it. Amongst those who went to look for other grazing-grounds were Huru, the son of Mungava, and two others called Tjivisiua and Kamata. They trekked into the land of the Bechuanas and were well received by them. At that time Bechuanaland was considerably larger than it is to-day. Its western boundary stretched right to Oviombo (District Okahandja) in the present-day Hereroland. That was how the emigrants of long ago came to arrive in those grazing-grounds of South West Africa, which afterwards became their own property but then belonged to the Bechuanas. The Herero cattle grazed in the Omuramba Omatako, when neither Okahandja or Otjiwarongo or Omaruru had been reached.

In the course of time, however, misunderstandings arose between the Bechuanas and the forefathers of the Hereros. The herdboys of both races began seizing each others' cattle, and hostility between the Bechuana chief Kavitine and a section of the new-comers arose in consequence of this. It ended in a bitter struggle in which the ancestors of the Hereros were worsted. In order not to lose their cattle they proceeded west past Grootfontein and Outjo, but not daring to cross the borders of Ovamboland, which was held by powerful chiefs. There remained nothing for them to do but to trek into the empty Kaokoveld and to graze their herds in the plains, advancing gradually southwards through the country which stretched as far as the Omaruru River. Otjitambi, which is now Schlettwein's farm, was a central place for these wanderers, for there lived there a man whose sacred fire was of very great repute.

Kamata's people did not leave with the others. There was no trouble between them and the Bechuanas. They trekked about with their cattle, as they had hitherto done, in Ovitore, the watershed to the eastwards of Gobabis. When the Bechuanas asked 'Will your other people come back to us again', they said '*Va hererera okukara*', which means 'They have decided to stay where they are'. (*Okuhea* means 'they have decided', while *Okuhererera* means 'to have finally made up one's mind'. It was thus that the inhabitants of the Kaokoveld came to be called 'Hereros', i.e. 'those who have decided'. Previously they had been called 'the people of Reed-land' (*Ovandu varuu*), because they had come from there. This name continued as the tribal name of those who had remained with the Bechuanas, who are still to-day called Mbanderu, and this name indicates the fact that they belong to the race of the Mbandus, while pointing out that they formerly lived in Reed-land (*oruu*).

The forefathers died in Kaoko and the people increased in numbers and spread out to the north. Excellent grazing was discovered near the Kunene. The people could brag to those who lived in the south about the number and sleekness of their cattle. They got the name of the Himbas, which means 'those who boast'. In the mountains of the west, those who were not so well off found enormous herds of game and beautiful springs of water, and so they became skilful hunters. They kept goats and even tried to farm with cattle, but these they always lost, either through wild animals, or through droughts, for it rains less in the Kaokoveld than in other parts of the land. As many of them lived from what they could pick from the bushes and dig out of the earth, they got the name of Tjimbas, or 'the poor people from Ondjimba', which means 'ant-bear', an animal which likewise scratches its living out of the ground. This mean name was originally given them by the Ovambos, who, to this very day, call all Hereros 'Shimbas'. The Hereros, however, apply it only to the poorer inhabitants of the Kaokoveld. The places are still known to-day in the Kaokoveld where their fellow countrymen, the Hereros, trekked about in former times in the south or in the middle of that territory, or where they made their homes for a short while. The ancestors of the Hereros of Okahandja, for instance, lived for a long time at the springs of Otavi and Ombombo. The chief of Otavi showed me a spot, close to the spring, where no grass grew 'because it was here that the people, who afterwards went to Omaruru, had their goat-kraal, and, where a goat-kraal has stood for any length of time, grass does not grow any more.'

As soon as they became prosperous they became arrogant. They felt that they were strong enough to try a fall with the Ovambos who lived to the east of them. A raid was made into Ovamboland to get Ovambo cattle. But the Ovambos were stronger than the Hereros, for the separate tribes had chiefs whom all the people obeyed to a man while the Hereros did not have a common commander or leader. The raid was a failure and the Hereros were driven back with great loss. The iron assegais of the Ovambos inspired terror in the Hereros, for they were unacquainted with iron and fought with wooden arrows and knobkerries. Once the friendly relationship between them and the Ovambos was broken they were compelled to endure repeated raids at the hands of the neighbouring tribes. If they did not want to lose everything they had to look for new pastures. According to the stories of their fathers they knew that there lay to the south-east a large uninhabited territory. This country was called Oukuruha, and the few people who lived in it were called Ovakuruha, i.e. Saan Bushmen. (The word is made up from *Ova*, the prefix to the human class of nouns, *ehe*, meaning 'the home', and *Kuru*, which means 'old', thus implying the ancient inhabitants.) The reason that the Bergdamas were not looked upon as owners of the land arose from the fact that the Saan were regarded as the masters of the Bergdamas.

They possessed a good deal of other information about this country, for Herero hunters had already discovered and opened up the game paradise of the Swakop River. Only a few of them had returned to the Kaokoveld. Most of them remained in the Swakop, lived upon game and stock which they stole from the Namas, who had already crossed the Kuiseb and the Swakop with their most advanced cattle-posts. In later times these hunters gained a great reputation amongst the Hereros for bravery and courage, even when these characteristics were displayed to their own discomfort. These people are likewise a ruling race, and a masterful appearance makes an impression upon them. The most famous hunters and raiders of that period were called Hembapu, Kauapirua, Ngava, Mberijandja, and Kausengua. Since Hembapu had time and again done much harm to the Namas, these decided to wipe him and his followers off the face of the earth. It did not avail him at all that he fled to the mouth of the Swakop with the cattle he had stolen and tried to settle there. He actually constructed an encampment and, for lack of wood, he used whale bones from the shore. But if he wished to escape from his doom he had to find some other place of refuge, for the Namas had arrows with iron points, and many of them even had assegais. He did not feel that he was capable of dealing with people who were so well armed. He decided to return to the Kaokoveld, but it seemed too dangerous an undertaking to pass through the Erongo Mountains. There Bergdamas lived, who had not the slightest respect for a Herero's cattle, and somewhat farther ahead he would have to pass the boundaries of the Saan in the Paresis Mountains. He therefore decided to drive his cattle northwards along the sea-shore, and to take them through to the Kaokoveld along the next river-bed, that of the Omaruru River. Upon arriving at the mouth of the river, the Hereros saw in the distance some queer creatures, of whom it was difficult to say whether they were men or animals. They finally decided that they must be human beings because they only had two legs. They went nearer to them and found that they were two white men who had no clothes on them at all. On the shore lay the remnants of a boat. Both these men joined the party and got sour milk from the Hereros, but one of them died, probably owing to the effect of the sour milk to which he was unaccustomed. The other one wanted to go with them, but the Hereros would not agree to that. They gave him some of the stolen oxen and left him to his fate and they brought their booty safe and sound to the Kaokoveld.

The rich, fearless Tjiponda, with a large following of brave men came back along Hembapu's spoor from the Kaokoveld to the Swakop River. Even to-day a Herero's face lights up when Tjiponda's name is mentioned. When his thirsty oxen caught sight of the blue waves they rushed down to them, but shook their heads when they found that they had been cheated and that the water was undrinkable. Tjiponda, who was following them, did not know that the blue plain was the sea. He thought that the blue sky must have fallen to the ground and he called out *ejuru*, which means 'the sky'. He kept his wits about him, however, and drove his cattle southwards to the Swakop valley. There a solitary Huni tree was struggling for its existence in the sand flats. The Bergdamas had already given the spot the name of Hunidas, which means 'the little Huni tree'. At a later time this name became Nonidas through wrong pronunciation. There Tjiponda set up his first dwelling-place, and because he could not find any building material he used tree trunks washed up by the sea, of which he found a plentiful supply in the mouth of the Swakop River. He called the place Orovihende in memory of this (*Ovihendi* means poles). On the shore, where in later years Swakopmund was to be built, he found quantities of round shells, which were regarded by the Hereros as jewellery and signs of dignity. Three of these shells were woven into the hair of favourite children on either side, and another one on the forehead. Rich people wore one on the forehead as a sign of their wealth. The priests of the sacred fire wore one of these shells on a riem round their necks. Until then these shells had been bartered from the natives of southern Angola, and a young ox had been given for each shell. Here they lay in heaps on the shore. Tjiponda named the place of this valuable discovery Otjozondji or 'the place of shells'. But he did not stay very long in the lower bed of the Swakop; travelling inland up the river he came to the veld of Otjimbingwe. A spring (*omusema*) was discovered at the place where a small tributary joined the Swakop with luxuriant grass and bush round about it. There the zebras came to drink and the lions threatened both man and beast with danger. This place got the name of 'the living fountain' for it was said of it: '*Omundu ma zingua momutima*', which means 'The sight of this spring refreshes the heart of man'. From *zingua*, which means 'is refreshed', the place-name Otjizingwe was formed; this became Otjindingwe later, and it is to-day written as Otjimbingwe.

Tjiponda journeyed on from there and went right to the upper reaches of the Swakop. The thievishly inclined hunters, or such of them as lived near the Swakop, left him alone. Indeed it would not have been very wise of them to try to set on him and rob him. He travelled into the veld of Windhoek and as far as the Nosob district, where he found the junction of the two rivers and called the place Epako; the place where the two rivers form a fork is still called by this name to-day. There, however, he came up against the Mbanderu at a place which is to-day called Gobabis (i.e. Goabes, which in Nama means the houses of the elephants). He had no liking for being confined or hemmed in from any direction, so he turned back and went into the country round about the little and great Waterberg, where the Saan lived with their servants, the Bergdamas. They would not allow a stranger to water his cattle at the strong spring which they had inherited from their forefathers, but it was just this fine spring that attracted Tjiponda. He had no comprehension of rights of inheritance and, when the Saan stole some of his oxen, he decided to kill them. He set out to attack them armed with bows and arrows, but they greeted him with a poisoned arrow, which took effect upon him and he died. They buried him at the Waterberg. The greater part of his cattle fell into the hands of the Saan; and his followers, such as were not killed off, were scattered in all directions. Some of them returned to the Kaokoveld and told of the wide pastures through which they had trekked. This encouraged others who travelled, not along the coast, but gradually deeper and deeper into the centre of the country and finally reached Okahandja and Windhoek. Others again remained in the northern territory.

Nandavetu, the son of Kandjou, trekked to the large spring in the north, which reminded him very much of the strong springs at Kaoko Otavi. So he called the place Otavi, for it struck him, cattle farmer as he was, that the water gushed out with jerks, and this reminded him again of the actions of a calf drinking from a cow, when it jerks its mother's udder with its mouth to make the milk flow. The Hereros call this jerking *tava* and from this the word Otavi was formed, a word which ought really to be written Outavi. Nandevetu lived in Otavi and pastured his cattle in that neighbourhood, but he did not approve of his neighbours, the Saan, in Tsumeb. Whether they had done him harm is not known, but, in any case, he set out with his men to make an end of them. The same fate overtook him as had overtaken Tjiponda in the Waterberg, for a poisoned arrow slew him. Severely wounded as he was he wished to be carried to Otavi but he died on the road, at a place called Ondjora (really Ondjoura, which means 'abundance', i.e. of water and pasturage). The Bergdamas and the Saan have named this place Korao, or 'the rough, stony place', because a strong stream of water runs in between rough limestones. Nandavetu was buried there and a mighty heap of stones was piled on his grave, some twenty feet in length and three feet in height. It can still be seen to-day close to the railway line.

Katauu sought to achieve from the east what Nandavetu had not succeeded in doing from the west. He had trekked round with his cattle for some time in the southern part of the country and then he trekked right up the Omuramba[1] Omataku until he came to the flat country round about Grootfontein. The Saan and the Bushmen called the springs at Grootfontein Gei-ous, or 'the great springs'. Katauu gave the place the name Otjivanda Tgongue, which means 'the leopard flats', for leopards molested his cattle there. He should have been satisfied with the wide, grassy flats, but he was attracted by the waters at Gaub and Nosib, which lay along the road to the

[1] An Omuramba is a shallow river-bed, in which water flows only in times of heavy rain.—*Ed.*

green mountain of copper at Tsumeb. He tried to get possession of these also, but the Ovambo chief of Ondonga set great store upon the possession of these rich copper deposits. His kraals only began at Namatoni, but his blacksmiths fetched their copper ore from the copper country near Tsumeb. At Nosib stood a stone out of which in earlier days a Bergdama blacksmith had made copper bangles, and this stone was always regarded as sacred. Whoever passed by it made it his duty to place upon the stone a small offering of dagga. When Katauu tried to conquer this district he came up against both the Ovambos and the Bergdamas. The Ovambos fell upon him with a powerful force and wiped him out with his following. This is how it came about that, in later times, the Hereros considered that they had a right to possess the northern section of the country, although they did not exercise their rights by trekking there with their cattle. The country round Outjo remained free of Hereros for some time for fear of the Saan.

During this period Mutise moved away from his location. He was the grandfather of Tjamuaha, whose son was to be the most powerful of all the Herero chiefs and their liberator from the hands of the Namas. He left the Kaokoveld, in the southern part of which his father lay buried, with all his people and trekked into what is to-day the district of Okahandja. Tjiraura brought his people into the same neighbourhood. He had suffered severely at the hands of the Herero hunters in the Swakop River, who were not prepared to allow any one to seize and occupy the neighbourhood of the Swakop. He became very much annoyed and he attacked these impious fellow countrymen of his, who possessed nothing and yet dared to forbid a wealthy cattle-king to use the pasturage. He made such a clean sweep that hardly any of the hunters remained alive, and these had to find occupation as cattle-herds. These hunters got the name *ovanate voma-runga*, or 'the children of the robbers'; 'children' because they had no chief and 'of the robbers', because they inflicted a great deal of damage on the Hereros through stealing their cattle. Tjiraura lived for a time in Okahandja where there was, during good rainy seasons, a flowing spring in one of the Swakop's tributaries. As this tributary was much wider than the main stream, the Namas had given it the name of Gei-keis, i.e. 'the large sand-flat', meaning by the name the sandy river-bed, where no one lived but in which the Namas had found a resting-place. The Hereros gave this river-bed, with its lofty trees, the name Okahandja which has the same meaning.

Tjiraura then left the spring at Okahandja and went farther south where there was said to be a much stronger spring. He looked for this and found it on the side of a hill. The Namas had already given it the name of Ai-gams, or 'the hot water', for it was a hot spring. Tjiraura was considerably astonished by the steam which rose from the spring and he called it Otjomuise, which means 'the place of smoke'. It is round this spring that the town of Windhoek was built in later times. But Tjiraura was not at all pleased with the presence of thieving Bergdamas, who lived in the nearby Auas Mountains, and on that account he turned back again and went to Otjosazu close to Okahandja.

Mutjise's son was called Tjirue. His cattle grazed unmolested far to the east in the Sandveld. He had his kraal in Otjikune, which is the farm Schenkswerder to-day. He failed to have regard for the fact that the boundary of the Bechuana country was still in its old position and that it went beyond Oviombo, and the Bechuanas took offence at this. They had found herds of Herero cattle in the Omaheke and, in Ghanzie, those of the Namas and the Boers. It is hardly necessary to stress the point that the process of 'finding' implied, in the parlance of that period, not merely seeing, but actual seizure, and this naturally led to friction. The Bechuanas carried off any Herero cattle which they found on their pasturage, and the Hereros raided the herds of the Bechuanas in return. The hatred between them grew apace and war ensued. In Etemba and thereabouts the Hereros and the Bechuanas fought fiercely for many weeks and the water-holes were bloody. Then the Matabele hastened to the assistance of the Bechuanas. They had barbed assegais and large oxhide shields, while the Hereros had no weapons of that kind. Behind the bogs of Lake Ngami they constructed barrages of thorn bush and when the Hereros advanced to the attack they stuck fast in the quagmires. Flight was out of the question. They bore themselves bravely and slew the Bechuana leader, whose name was Kavarure, but many of the foremost warriors amongst the Hereros fell too. In spite of this they remained the victors and, when the attack upon them was abandoned, they retired from the field of battle. They had won by force of arms grazing-grounds of their own. The Bechuana chief was called Tjekeue. Some time afterwards (1820) he came to Okahandja, bringing with him a white ox as a token of peace and a horse as well, an animal with which the Hereros were as yet quite unacquainted. The fact that Tjamuaha, Maharero's father, took part in this battle as a young man is helpful in fixing its date. For the Hereros, however, the battle of Etemba remained a painful memory, although they were actually victorious. Even to-day the proverb which is used when any one is suddenly overtaken by misfortune is *Onganda jetu ja tire Otjekeue*, which means 'Our kraal is plunged into misery by Tjekeue'.

It is hardly necessary to state that struggles of this kind have the necessary effect of weakening the combatants. Tjirue's herdsmen, whose cattle the Bechuanas had carried off, escaped to Gobabis and others brought the news to Otjikune, but it was only after the cattle had been lost that a large body of men set out to punish the raiders. After the war was over and the Hereros were able to call the enormous extent of pasturage their own, Tjirue was gathered to his fathers and his son took his place at the sacred ancestral fire. He was not, however, of much account, and thence comes the Herero saying that Tjamuaha was no chieftain at all, but that it was his son who really attained to that dignity by virtue of his great deeds. In fact he was no chief in the sense that he was the possessor of large herds of cattle, but he was none the less a chief for the simple reason that he was his father's successor to the office of the sacred fire. But still the sacred fire is of no very great importance if the herds of cattle, which are the adjuncts of this fire, are lacking. Then the ancestors have proved themselves weak, for they had not the power to protect the sacred herds from loss and the ancestral fire is not of much account if it fails to help its children to increase their material possessions. Tjamuaha was eager to become rich again at all cost, and we shall be able to recognize this bent of his very clearly later on in our story, for every means of getting possession of cattle became the same to him. At first he tried lawful methods. He sent a message to his friend, Tjipangandjara, who lived in the Sandveld and begged him to transfer to him some of his numerous followers. Presumably he wanted to use them for the purpose of enriching himself by forcibly despoiling other wealthy cattle owners. Tjipangandjara sent him back the reply that he required his people himself, but he was sending his friend a number of oxen as a present; with these he could buy wives and breed children of his own, and then he could soon build up a tribe again, which would not leave him in the lurch, as so many of his people had done when they saw that his father, Tjirue, was reduced to poverty. Tjamuaha accepted the oxen, acted upon his friend's advice, and achieved some measure of success.

The tidings that the Hereros had acquired by conquest a land of their own spread through the Kaokoveld. One cattle-post after another was gradually advanced with the object of getting a share of the newly acquired territory. It was very necessary to be cautious about this, for it was not only the thieving Saan and the Bergdamas who had to be reckoned with, but their own fellow-tribesmen, too, who had not always been courteous enough to send their relations in the Kaokoveld an invitation to the feast. A new movement ensued on the old migratory routes along the sea-coast. The forefathers of the Otjimbingwe and Omaruru tribes came down along them. Timorously they tried to establish themselves, with their small herds, at the mouth of the Swakop, the reason for their fear being that, after the destruction of the Herero hunters, the Bergdamas had once again settled there and they made the country unsafe for others. When it was realized that it was dangerous to stay in the lower course of the Swakop in dry years the exploration of the lower Kuiseb valley was undertaken. A Bergdama woman, who was in service with the Namas at Walfish Bay, found the Hereros wandering helplessly about in the plains, and took them to Awa-haos, which means the 'Ridge of Red Rock' and became afterwards Schleppmansdorp and Ururas. As both banks of the Kuiseb were well covered with vegetation in which numbers of ant-bears (*ombinda*) lived, the Hereros called the place Otjombinda, meaning 'ant-bear houses'. There both water and pasturage were to be found and the old men know for a fact, from what their forefathers told them, that, in those times, there were no sand-dunes between Walfish Bay and Swakopmund, that the whole of the Kuiseb mouth was free from dunes, and that grass grew luxuriantly on its broad plains.[1] The Hereros and the Namas lived there amicably together, but, as time went by, the Namas began to covet their neighbour's cattle and they devised a scheme for getting possession of them. A match in which Herero and Nama cattle were the stakes was arranged. The match developed into a brawl and the Namas alleged that their cattle had been taken by force. They had surreptitiously brought bows and arrows with them and they killed many of the Hereros who were watching the match. Those of the Hereros who escaped being killed had to flee back to the Swakop River and they could take only very few of their cattle with them. For long years they lived in the lower Swakop. Their chief was the

---

[1] The area described here is to-day entirely occupied by large sand-dunes, on which nothing grows.—*Ed.*

father of Zeraua, who subsequently came to be known as the chief of
Otjimbingwe and Omaruru. When quite a young man he realized
that the possession of a gun would mean much to himself and his
tribe. Taking some of his friends and a number of oxen with him, he
left the others at the Swakop mouth and proceeded to Walfish Bay.
He had heard that it was possible to buy a gun from the white people
there. Good fortune attended him for the Namas did not molest
him; he obtained a gun and ammunition from the traders in exchange
for fifteen oxen, learnt how to handle the weapon and set out for
home. Somewhere on the road he saw a large bird and he was seized
with a desire to try out his new gun. He killed the bird with the very
first shot. In his joyous mood he took with him one of the bird's
talons and, when he got back home, he tied it to the neck of a new
calabash, giving orders that the milk of that calabash was to be drunk
only by himself and the friends who had gone with him. He set
aside, too, for the supply of milk to this vessel a special cow, which
was taken out of the profane herd and transferred to the inviolable
herd belonging to the sacred ancestral fire. This event is mentioned
here for the purpose of affording a historical instance, illustrating the
relationship between the profane herd and the sacred one. The
profane herd remained the property of the Eanda heir in the female
line, while the sacred herd of the ancestral fire, on the other hand,
passed from father to son in the male line. Women, children and
strangers might drink the milk of the profane herd, but no one might
drink the milk of the sacred herd unless he had the right to a seat at
the ancestral fire. The circle could, likewise, as in this case, be arbitrarily confined to particular people. When the herd increased the
consecration and selection applied to the progeny, and, in a similar
manner, the right which a particular individual had to use the
milk, passed to the sons of him who had first possessed that right.
This custom of establishing special rights of use is to be found every·
where in hundreds of different forms, and a whole book could be
written about the Herero calabashes, relating the history of the
causes which actuated the founder of particular calabashes to ensure
that the recollection of some important event should be preserved in
the memories of succeeding generations. Happy and impressive
family recollections are in this way renewed day by day. Should a
calabash of this kind break, it is mended with thongs of sinew or bark, or
a new one is provided to which the old name is given and the old token
of memory fastened, for every milk calabash has its own particular name.

Zeraua's people wandered about for a long time in the region of the middle Swakop, until at last the missionary Rath persuaded them to settle in Otjimbingwe, but, when the dry years came, part of them trekked to Omaruru. The place did not, of course, bear that name then: better pasturage was expected there, but the cows fed on the bitter bush, and the milk became bitter (*ruru*) in consequence, and so the Hereros called the place ever afterwards 'the place Oma-ruru' (from *Omaere omaruru*, meaning 'bitter curds)'.

It would only be tiresome to follow up the wanderings of the various tribes, and nothing of historical significance could be gained by doing so. When I questioned an eighty-year old Herero of Otjimbingwe about the happenings of early times, he replied:

'Have not the Hereros been cattle-breeders ever since God created them? As a cattle-breeder, does not one always live in the selfsame way? One treks with the herd wherever water and grazing are to be found and, in the meantime, the cattle increase. Sometimes they are stolen by our enemies; sometimes no thefts take place for many years at a time. That is the life of a Herero; that was the life my great-grandfather lived, that was the life my grandfather lived, and my father lived it too. When we all live in exactly the same way there is not much to be told. Some people are surprised that we have so little to tell about our leaving the Kaokoveld, but I am not a bit surprised about it. Was not the whole land actually one land? The people of old trekked about just where they pleased. Wherever water and grazing were plentiful they stayed for some considerable time, but when these were scarce they soon trekked away. They, therefore, drove their cattle southwards out of the Kaokoveld and, when it did not suit them there any more, they often trekked back to the Kaokoveld again. When it was no longer convenient for them to stay there, they came back into Hereroland until, at last, they stayed here for good. So it never really occurred to the old folk that anything great had occurred when they left the Kaokoveld and sought new pastures here. This country had no owners then, unless we are to regard the Bergdamas and the Bushmen, who lived in the veld like wild animals, as owners?'

After possession of the land had been taken from every side, an energetic cleaning up of the mountains and the bush was undertaken. The Bergdamas and their masters, the Saan, were regarded by the Hereros as having no right there at all and they were looked upon as pests. They were killed wherever they were encountered. Women and children were carried off and put to work at domestic tasks and as herdboys. It is because of this that the Bergdamas say that it was through them that the Hereros first became numerous and powerful. Most Hereros of ancient lineage are thin and tall, while the common people are of smaller stature; it seems possible that this difference arose through miscegenation with the Bergdamas. The only refuges which finally remained for the Bergdamas, after the Saan had been utterly destroyed as far as their most northerly habitations and hunting-fields, were the inaccessible mountain ranges of the Auas, the Erongo, the Paresis, the Waterberg and the Otavi Highlands. In the plains the Herero lord (*Omuhona*) reigned supreme.

This may be a good place to quote some of the sayings of intelligent old Hereros to show what the people themselves thought about their old chiefs, for some of them called themselves chiefs but were not chiefs, while others were chiefs in fact, but were never regarded as such. The following are three statements, which are literally translated:

1. The chiefs of early times did not live as chiefs ought to live. A chief ought to work in his people's interest and see that they are safeguarded and fed. But that the old chiefs did not do. Every one looked after himself and, if any of the smaller people had any cattle but had a few followers only, then a stronger man came and took his cattle away. If he was dissatisfied about it he was promptly killed. Every one was covetous of his neighbour's property, and whoever thought that he was powerful enough to do so took the next man's property away from him, and the latter could be very glad if he escaped with his life.

2. If, in olden times, any one was robbed of his cattle, it was not the chief's (*Omuhona's*) duty to help him. He was only too pleased that he had not suffered loss himself. It was left to the man who had been robbed to take his own revenge. He, however, had become poor; the people who had gathered round him in good times, so that they could live at his expense, left him and attached themselves to others instead of helping him to attack and punish the robbers.

3. In former times the Herero had no chiefs by birth. The matter was regarded in this way: To be a chief, a man must have two qualifications: he must own many cattle and he must have a numerous following. When these two attributes were combined, then a chief came into being. A man who had many cattle but no following, was not a chief, and the man who had a large number of followers but lacked cattle was not a chief either. It was only the man who possessed a hundred head of cattle and round about a hundred followers

in addition, who thought that he had become entitled to illtreat and oppress others and to call himself *Omuhona*, or chief.

In these sayings one thing particularly has been overlooked, and that is the sacred fire and its significance in the life of the race. This has been previously explained. The man who tended the sacred fire was, by virtue of doing so, the possessor of the sacred herd, which was closely connected with it, and of the calabashes from which the consecrated milk was drunk. It was a man of that kind who was a chief 'by birth'. Now the Herero race had sixteen religious groups and every Herero belonged to one of these groups. They were all alike and they had the same object in the service of the sacred fire, but the different groups had their special food laws which were most rigorously observed. There could thus, at any particular time, have only been sixteen chiefs, for there was only a single man in each of these religious societies who could succeed to the position of priest of the sacred fire, by way of inheritance from father to eldest son. The dying father took his son's hands in his, rubbed them several times as if he were handing something over to him, and said 'Receive this, receive this! Fulfil faithfully your duty to the sacred fire of your forefathers'. Then, uttering the words again, he spat into his mouth and, with the spittle, the father's spiritual powers passed to the son. After this, the latter was capable of communing with his ancestors in prayer at the sacred fire and at their graves. No one else had this right or possessed this power. From that time onwards his person was just as sacred as the sacred fire itself, or the ancestral staffs, or the graves of his forefathers. If the herd of the sacred fire was large he had nothing to worry about, for people gathered round him and he was then a powerful chief, a chief 'by birth'. But if the sacred cattle were stolen, or they died through sickness, then others who were wealthy came to the fore and called themselves chiefs; but they were not chiefs in the real sense of the word, and it is from this that the saying originates that the chiefs of former days were not chiefs at all, but upstarts, who gave the poorer people no protection, but oppressed and robbed them on every side.

It is a matter for real surprise that it should be possible to discover, at the present day, so much information regarding the happenings of past times in the form of Herero traditions. They are entitled to be regarded, not as mere imagination, but as of real historical value, and for this reason: it is not every Herero who is able to impart information regarding the ancient history of his race. The ordinary man usually knows little about it. There are, however, amongst them human repositories of tradition, who, although they may take much time for thought, possess a marvellous recollection of the things which were in former times impressed upon their memories. This preservation of ancient tradition is always to be found amongst the families and descendants of those whose forebears were guardians of the sacred fire and, as such, 'chiefs by birth'. They know the names of succeeding generations of ancestors often as far back as the seventh, and sometimes even to the twelfth degree. They preserve this knowledge in the form of old songs, of which the finest ox of every place forms the subject (*omitandu viozongombe*) and in which their owners play a certain part. I know a Herero, who is descended from Tjamuaha, whose mother imprinted into the mind of her small son, in his earliest youth, the songs of his ancestors and their oxen before he could even understand the meaning of them. If he is asked to-day, now that he has learnt to think, a question regarding persons and things of the past, he is not capable of giving an immediate answer. He first recites the song which he thinks must contain the information, with the object of listening for the answer and getting it from the sound of the words which he causes to pass as it were in review before him. He is not in a position to recite these songs in deliberate speech, but he has to babble them just in the same way as he learnt to repeat them in his youth in order to grasp the present import of them, and to discover, by testing the single sentences and names, whether they contain answers to the questions which are put to him. These songs contain a wonderful store of information which throws light upon the early history of the country.

The religion of the Hereros is, moreover, ancestor worship. No particular form of worship has ever been evolved for the service of the highest god, Ndjambi Karunga. Ancestral worship took place at the ancestral fire by arranging in circles the fire sticks of all the ancestors, which were so carefully looked after, and talking to them just as if they were human beings. To be able to do this it was essential that the ancestors' names should not be forgotten. In times of great need the 'chief by birth' went to pray at the graves of his forefathers and, to be able to do this, it was necessary that the name of the ancestor in each grave should be remembered. From this arose the astonishing knowledge which the Hereros possessed of ancestral names and graves.

Finally, the Hereros did not count the years like we do, but gave every year its special name in accordance with some remarkable or important thing which took place in it. Even at the present time a year is never referred to in conversation by its number. The counting of the years has actually begun, but it has not come into general usage yet. The names of the years were often revealed during the feast of the circumcision of the young men. These names are not always quite the same. It is often the case that, alongside a particular name, another name has made its appearance. Even if it is not absolutely dependable, for the purpose of deciding the date of a battle, or the death of a prominent individual, &c., to arrange the names of the years in order, by comparing the years which precede or follow any one particular year with each other according to other evidence, still the historian derives a great deal of assistance through a knowledge of these names.

Since, in the course of this book, we shall deal with the history of the Herero people between the years 1830 and 1890 (the year of Maharero's death), it may be advisable to set out here the names of those sixty years, always bearing in mind that small errors are possible and even probable. The prefix *oj*- should be translated 'the year of'.

1830. Ojozombunga, the year of the wild dogs.
1831. Ojombua ja Mbundu, the year of Mdundu's dog.
1832. Ojongombondo, the year of the black and white oxen.
1833. Ojomeva, the year of waters.
1834. Ojozombahe, the year of the giraffe.
1835. Ojondonambe, the year of the good milch-cow.
1836. Ojakatjititjimue, the year of Katjititjimue.
1837. Ojetemba, the year of the large drinking-trough.
1838. Ojondjuuo, the year of the house.
1839. Ojorukui, the year of the flute.
1840. Ojekuva, the year of the axe.
1841. Ojorukoro, the year of the breast.
1842. Ojohera, the year of the false rumours.
1843. Ojongungo, the year of the rushing sound.
1844. Ojondukua, the year of the buttermilk.
1845. Ojokajambi, the year of Kajambi.
1846. Ojokakuoko, the year of Kakuoko.
1847. Ojovihende, the year of the poles.
1848. Ojomeva omanene, the year of the mighty waters.
1849. Ojorupera, the year of the leather cloak.

1850. Ojomandjembera, the year of the berries.

1851. Ojonganga, the year of the magicians.

1852. Ojohange, the year of peace.

1853. Ojorukata, the year of the drying-up.

1854. Ojotumbo, the year of the leg.

1855. Ojoukoze, the year of jealousy.

1856. Ojondema, the year of the heifer.

1857. Ojonganda ja Hejuva, the year of Hejuva's kraal.

1858. Ojakamaue, the year of Kamaue.

1859. Ojondujondiuo, the year of the sheep bell.

1860. Ojepunga, the year of the lungs.

1861. Ojokakuoko, the year of Kakuoko (Jonker Afrikander).

1862. Ojeue ra Tjamuaha, the year of the stone or mountain of Tjamuaha.

1863. Ojokurondeue, the year of climbing the mountain.

1864. Ojorupoko, the year of the kloof.

1865. Ojotjikoroha, the year of the smallpox.

1866. Ojorupati, the year of the ribs.

1867. Ojerambu, the year of the drought.

1868. Ojomukaru, the year of the thorn bush (*omukaru*).

1869. Ojongava, the year of the Rhinoceros (*ongava*).

1870. Ojohange, the year of peace.

1871. Ojoheo, the year of the arrowhead, namely of chief Kandiri-kirira in Okahandja.

1872. Ojotjiruiju, the year of the hot hole in the ground.

1873. Ojomatupa, the year of the bones.

1874. Ojomuambo, the year of the Ovambo.

1875. Ojejuva, the year of the sun.

1876. Ojotjikesa, the year of the coffin.

1877. Ojorungara, the year of the sacrificial charger.

1878. Ojozombaue, the year of the hail.

1879. Ojeraka, the year of the tongue.

1880. Ojongombe inganga, the year of the ox with the white spots.

1881. Ojohara, the year of the large army.

1882. Ojomativa, the year of the worms.

1883. Ojonjose, the year of the comet.

1884. Ojorutjindo, the year of the campaign.

1885. Ojovitenda, the iron year.

1886. Ojokondjuu, the year of the house.

1887. Ojorundumba, the year of the rabies.

1888. Ojondimbu, the year of the stump tail.

1889. Ojongamero, the year of the camel.

1890. Odjondjendje the year of the shell from the forehead.

With this list of the names of the different years, it becomes possible, with some trouble and care, to fix the date of historical events fairly closely, and to bring it into line with our chronology, although dislocations and other small sources of error must be taken into account.

But what is the position as to the fixing of dates in earlier times, when the names of the years have been either very imperfectly remembered or forgotten altogether. Questions which are of very great interest to us are: when did the Hereros migrate from the swamp country to Bechuanaland; how long did they stay in the Kaokoveld; and when did they enter into occupation of the territories which they occupy, more or less at the present time?

Only approximate answers can be given to these questions and those only on the strength of the numerous genealogical tables, in the repeated study of which and the constant testing of their genuineness one must not allow oneself to become discouraged. The names of the ancestors are known to the descendants, especially in the families of the chiefs, and the situation of their graves is usually known as well. If it is assumed that the father begat his eldest son when he was about thirty years of age, and one knows more or less the age of the grandson who is descended in a direct line from the grandfather ascribed to him, a fixed date is arrived at from which the genealogical table can be historically compiled with an approximation to accuracy. So that the reader may not become bored we shall give two only (see pp. 152–3) of the most trustworthy of these genealogical tables, namely the sequence of Maharero's ancestors, and those of a talented Herero teacher, who has taken a great deal of trouble to investigate his own descent.

Genealogical Table of The Chief Maharero, compiled by Tjamuaha's descendants.

Name of ancestor	Approximate date of birth	Where buried	Remarks
1. Maharero	1820	Okahandja	
2. Tjamuaha	1790	Okahandja	
3. Tjirue	1760	Otjikune, Dist. Okahandja	
4. Mutjise	1730	?	He died in the neighbourhood of Okahandja. Grave unknown.
5. Mbunga	1700	Otjitambi Kaoko	
6. Tjituka	1670	Karuporiro Kaoko	
7. Tjoutuku	1640	Otjombande Kaoko	
8. Kasupi	1610	Otjozongondi Kaoko	
9. Mbingana	1580	Okangundumba Kaoko	He gave the Oruzo or society of the Kudu the command that they were not to eat a hornless animal. A *kudu* head had to be put on a grave instead of an ox's head.
10. Batje	1550	Grave forgotten	Batje's uncle was called Kaundja and he led his people into the Kaokoveld.
11. Kengeza	1530	Karuporiro Kaoko	

Note.—According to this table the exodus from Bechuanaland to the Kaokoveld must have taken place about 1550, for it must be assumed that Kengeza, Batje's father and Kaundja, his uncle, were of more or less the same age. It would appear, however, that Kaundja was older, for he was appointed as leader of the emigrants. The Hereros had the Kaokoveld as their pasture land for about 200 years and they entered upon the present sphere of occupation from 1750 onwards. This does not make it impossible that particular cattle owners did not leave the Kaokoveld prior to this date, for Maharero's ancestors were by no means the first immigrants. The hunters of the Swakop were earlier comers, and so were Tjiponda and others.

Genealogical table of Kamatoto's family, compiled by the mission teacher Gustav Kamatoto of Windhoek.

Name of ancestor	Approximate date of birth	Where buried	Remarks
1. Gustav	1870	Still living	Teacher
2. Kamatoto	1840	Waterberg	
3. Mbaurua	1810	Waterberg	
4. Mukuruue	1780	Waterberg	
5. Tjavene	1750	Kaoko	
6. Tjitio	1720	Kaoko	
7. Ngavete	1690	Kaoko	
8. Kamaendo	1660	Kaoko	
9. Ngautje	1630	Kaoko	
10. Tjitumba	1600	Kaoko	
11. Ngondera	1570	Kaoko	
12. Kahuiko	1540	Kaoko	

Note.—Kahuiko came into the Kaokoveld. His father's name is not known. His grave must be in some unknown spot to the east. If we assume that Kahuiko accompanied his family when he was a boy of ten, we again arrive at the year 1550 as the year of leaving Bechuanaland, and we find as well that the change from the Kaokoveld to the present Hereroland began with the period 1750, on the same assumption as to Mukuruue.

The reason why no Herero, whom I know, can trace his ancestors back farther than the migration into the Kaokoveld may well be that the withdrawal from Bechuanaland may have been caused by a war, in which many of the older people were killed and found an unknown grave, or died, perhaps, owing to hardships suffered during the flight. It then became impossible to go to the graves of these ancestors to pray, and thus the names of their occupants were no longer kept in remembrance.

We shall not be far wrong if we take it that the migration from Bechuanaland took place round about 1550, that the Hereros stayed in the Kaokoveld for about 200 years, and that the infiltration into the Hereroland of the present day began somewhere about 1750.

6. THE OVAMBO TRIBES

The sixteen religious societies of the Hereros, with the addition of the seven amongst the Mbanderus, correspond to some extent to the Omapata of the Ovambos, except that the latter are not centred round religion. Just as amongst the Hereros the guardians of ancient family traditions are to be met with in close association with the priests of the sacred ancestral fire, the Ovambos have, too, a special association of *Ovakuanahungi*, that is to say people whose profession

it is to preserve the history of the tribe. They are said to come together at nights to discuss the events of olden times with the idea of
keeping their memories green. There are many guilds or castes
amongst Ovambos, for instance, those of the chiefs, the landed nobility, and the carriers who have to carry the chief's luggage when he
goes on a journey; then again there are the tillers of the fields, the
wood-cutters, and the artists in ostrich egg-shell, and again the zebra
hunters, the lion hunters, and those who hunt with the hounds, and
finally the societies of the men of the holy fire and water, the rain-
makers, and the makers of amulets.

What interests us principally is what the 'story-tellers' know about
the history of earlier times. It is only natural that their oldest stories
should appear in the guise of myth and fable. The story runs that
Kalunga, the highest deity of the Ovambos, summoned forth from
the earth a man and a woman. The man was called Noni, which
means 'the lance-bearer'. These first human beings had four children,
three sons and a daughter. The first son was called 'Cattleman' and
it was his task to herd and breed cattle. The second son was called
'Husbandman' and it was his work to cultivate cereals in the fields.
The third son was named 'Fireman'; he had to look after the fire and
herd the sheep. Noni's daughter was given the name of Janoni and
she became the mother of the 'Hali', that is to say the male mourners
to whom reference is made later on.

These people lived in a country where there was a large lake, on
the banks of which there were many elephants. For some unknown
reason they were forced to leave this country and they decided to
go to the west. As they were tillers of the soil they looked for a
country which was suitable for making gardens. They set out and
passed through many places, the names of which have been forgotten.
They never followed a straight path; their road took them this way
and that, but always westwards. They did not journey on continuously. When it pleased them they stopped a while; when they
did not care to stay they went on their way. At last they came to
the Okavango at the place where the Nano live to-day. They crossed
the river and found a branch of the stream, which turned to the
south and ran into the Etosha Pan. They followed this river channel
southwards. At that time it was full of water. Later on, after the
earth had had a trembling fit (the recollection of an earthquake), the
water grew very much scarcer. On this road they encountered a
number of small lakes formed by the river. The names of these lakes

were Omulavi, Osimolo, Omanonjeno, Elundi, Okuambili, Omuandi, Onenja, Omatemba, Oengue, Kapako, and Hakafia. At this last lake the water spouted out of the ground.

The wanderers settled down at Osimolo on this branch of the Okavango. A quarrel arose over fishing and two parties came into existence and they did not want to live close to each other any more. Sitenue had been chief of the whole tribe until then. He trekked away with those who had remained true to him and went to live at the Kunene River, at the place where its course takes its turn towards the west. The other section trekked away to the Hakafia lake, where the water spouted out of the ground. For both sections Osimolo remained a sacred place.

When it turned out that Hakafia did not come up to expectations, the people began to trek about in all directions. There were all kinds of folk amongst them. Besides the descendants of 'Cattleman' there were people of the hunter's caste and of the wood-cutter's caste. They all made special claims regarding the sort of country in which they desired to settle. Their leader was Kambungo, a cattle-man. He first of all came to Nameva with his people, he then trekked to Nambabi, and from there he reached the Kunene where it was flowing in a westerly direction. At this spot the Kunene likewise has a secondary channel, just as the Okavango has. This course used formerly to carry water from the Kunene to the Etosha Pan. This also forms certain lakes in its course, called Sekediva, Njokolulu, Nambeke, Olufa, and Ekuma.

Although the whole area was uninhabited, Kambungu and his people did not stay there. He went on until he reached what is to-day the middle of Uukuanyama and he built his kraal in Nehula. The 'Stone of the Country', near which the chief's kraal was erected, is still there to-day. This stone is one of the most famous things in Ovamboland, for the reason that at no other place in the whole country is there any stone which can be put to use. But here there is one on which axes could be ground and knives sharpened. If any one wanted to sharpen iron implements, he was forced to come to this place, and so the stone came to be called the 'Stone of the Country'. Close to it one part of the wanderers found a new home.

The other half of the tribe who had gone to Hakafia did not stay there very long. They owned a large number of cattle and, where there are cattle breeders, there is usually trouble. There were five leaders and each of them had his following. They were Kanene, Omundongo, Hamangudu, Hamukuambi, and Hamu-ngandjera.

Kanene set out with his people into the forest country on a hunting expedition. There they found a great deal of game and good soil for tillage as well, and so they decided to stay there. Kanene wanted to see how cultivation would answer. They had brought only a small quantity of grain with them on their hunting expedition and this was used for seed. No one was allowed to eat any of it. While one part of the people prepared the soil, the rest went hunting and provided food for them all. The numerous wild fruits growing on the trees and the bushes proved a great help in these difficult days. When the first harvest was reaped it became possible for every one to resume a normal way of living, for meal was once more to be had and without that no Ovambo could be content. The time had now arrived to set about fetching the cattle, which had been left behind in Hakafia. Kanene sent some of his men to fetch them, but the gathering and division of the cattle was done in a manner which was neither brotherly nor honest. Kanene's people took all the cattle they could lay hold of and drove them off. It was more like a raid than the peaceable dissolution of a partnership. The others did not, however, dare to use force against their fellow tribesmen, because there were a number of experienced hunters amongst them. They allowed them to trek away unmolested, but they gave them the uncomplimentary name of Ova-kua-njama, which means the 'the meat gorgers'. This description has become the tribal name of to-day. (According to others it was not the snatching of the cattle which was the origin of the name, but the fact that the region in which the new settlement was made was so rich in game that it turned into meat-eaters people who had hitherto eaten cereals as their principal food.)

Hamangudu, the second of the five headmen, collected the best of the cattle which Kanene had left behind and trekked away with them. He, however, went to the south and came to the plains. His cattle could live here very well, but he was too much accustomed to porridge, beer, and the like to be content to go without them, so he went looking for another place in which agriculture, as well as cattle farming, was possible. He felt that he was poor, despite all his wealth in cattle, and he said to his children, 'Am I then become a Schimba?' (*Schimba* means an impoverished man). He trekked back again, turned to the west and settled down at the springs in the Kaokoveld. From this the people who live in the Kaokoveld are still called Schimba to this day.[1]

After these two headmen had departed from Hakafia with their people, a third, Hamungandjera, decided to break away with his followers. He trekked westwards until he found a place which was in accordance with his requirements and liking, and he became the first chief of Ongandjera, the whole tribe becoming known by the name of its first leader. The inhabitants of Ukualuizi broke away from this tribe at a later date.

The fourth headman, Hamukuambi, followed Hamungandjera and settled in the district of Oukuambi. His tribe, too, took its name from that of its first leader. The fifth headman, Omundgo, remained in possession of the territory of Ondonga and became the first chief of this tribe.

All these immigrant tribes were, from the time of their arrival in their new homes, in possession of iron, and there were amongst them smiths who understood how to work it. They forged axes which, from their description, must have consisted of a handle and head in one piece. They made long spears with iron shafts and also short spears with wooden hafts, as well as the so-called Ovambo knives, which were double-edged and spear-shaped and almost a foot long. They made, too, iron arrow points and hoes for the cultivation of the fields. They made arm-rings and leg-rings out of copper and they likewise understood how to protect and decorate the young men's fore-arms, from wrist to elbow, with a spiral of thick copper wire. Tradition tells even of iron bows and pots which were fashioned by these artisans. There can be no question about it that the art of working metals could not have been originally acquired in Ovamboland, for this country possesses neither mountains nor stones, nor has it either iron or copper mines. The knowledge of working metals went much further back and a mine was discovered in Angola, from

[1] The Schimba or Tjimba of the Kaokoveld are Hereros. The name, Schimba, was given them by the Ovambos. They call themselves Hereros; they have the religious customs of the Oruzo, just as their fellow tribesmen in the south have, and they inherit their cattle and other possessions according to the laws of the Eanda succession. It is, however, remarkable that the Ovambos say that the ancestors of the Tjimba were once upon a time of their company. We should remember that the Hereros likewise have a story according to which the Ovambos and the Hereros parted company at an Omumborombonga tree on the southern boundary of Ovamboland.

which the blacksmiths were wont to fetch, after the harvest each year, a year's supply of iron, by smelting it out of the ore on the spot. It was the general opinion that these blacksmiths were mighty magicians, who plied their craft by firelight in huts which were otherwise quite dark. There were others, however, who laid no claim to the title of great magicians, but made useful things in the open air with primitive tools, and travelled about the country with them and traded them with other tribes. They went into Hereroland, stayed amongst the Bergdamas, and even visited Namaland. They made such an impression that, for example, the year 1840 is called 'The year of the axe', because it was in this year that the Herero, Tjizenga, learnt the blacksmith's craft from an Ovambo blacksmith and made his first axe with his own hands.

A proof that the blacksmith's craft amongst the Ovambos goes back to the time of their arrival in the country can be found in the fact that all the ancient iron utensils, dating from the time of their arrival, were subsequently collected by the chiefs and stored in huts which were especially well-built, as if in a treasure house. They were collected in Ondonga by the chief, Nembungu. The strong hut, in which the chief kept them, was regarded as a tribal sanctuary and no one was allowed to go near it. The men who had built the hut and had stored this treasure of iron in it killed Nembungu after they had finished their task. Tradition states that the iron utensils were, in like manner, collected in Uukuanyama, but that they disappeared and no one knows what became of them. The story goes that a baobab tree grew in the hut in which they were stored, and that the iron vessels were all swallowed up by this tree in the course of its growth and disappeared.

Let us now see what happened afterwards to these immigrant tribes. The 'meat-gorgers' in Uukuanyama left their first place of residence and went in a westerly direction. A large territory was there at their disposal. Kanene, the first leader and chief, died and his successor, Omusindi, considered it wrong to continue to live near his predecessor's grave, so he changed his kraal and placed it near to that of the chief Kambungu, of whom we heard previously. The latter still lived close to the 'Stone of the Country'. This stone was very valuable to him, even more valuable than a strongly flowing spring or a fine well, but it did not supply him with water. His oxen bellowed from thirst, and even to the present day when thirsty oxen bellow the proverb in general use is, 'The oxen bellow like Kambungu's'.

Omusindi found plenty of water. His neighbour, Kambungu, heard of the former's successful well-making and he went to him and told him of his own lack of water. Omusindi made no objection to Kambungu sinking a well close by. His men went briskly to work and, within a short time, they opened up a strong water supply. The cattle were brought over and the lack of water was at an end. Kambungu liked it so much at his friendly neighbour's place that he asked whether he might not stay there. Omusindi was willing, so the chief's kraal was enlarged, a dividing wall was made in the middle of it, and Omusindi lived in the eastern and Kambungu in the western portion. The 'husbandman', Omusindi, hung a hoe over the entrance to his part of the kraal, while the 'cattleman', Kambungu, decorated the entrance to his part with an iron axe.

In course of time, however, each of them wanted to be sole ruler, and they recognized the fact that it could not go on like that. Like sensible men they decided to settle the question peaceably and to leave it to the judgement of the gods to determine which of them should have the supreme command. The 'husbandman', Omusindi, was to boil beans and the 'cattleman', Kambungu, had to strangle an ox and to boil certain parts of it. This ox had to be strangled and not slaughtered because slaughtering was forbidden when the killing was for religious purposes. The office of the chieftainship for the future was to fall to him whose pot boiled first.

They both went to work, but the judgment of the gods never eventuated. The young men of both parties were by no means in agreement with this scheme, so they directed their efforts to making the judgment ineffective. They hid in the bush and waited until the fire had been lighted under both the pots. They then rushed out and raised the death-cry 'One of our men is dead'. The two old men were frightened for they understood very well what that death-cry implied. They realized that there was a revolution on foot. Kambungu fled with his comrades and his cattle back to the place he had come from. He saw from the spoors of the cattle that no one else had entered into occupation of his former territory, and he was glad that, in escaping from one danger, he was not running into a new one. It is for this reason that the Ovambo cattle herds, when they see that the old spoors of their oxen have not been obliterated by strange spoors, still sing to-day:

> The cattle spoors which we see here
> are those of our own cattle.

Kambungu was, however, no longer able to maintain his position as independent chief of his own tribe.

Omusindi fled too. He did not feel himself capable of putting down the revolution of the younger generation. He departed with a few trustworthy companions and erected a new kraal, but he did not succeed in regaining esteem. The young men who had followed neither Kambungu nor Omusindi now chose the 'cattleman', Kavengelo, as chief. His family were given the name of the death-cry, because the revolution which had resulted in his becoming chief had begun with the death-cry (*Ovakuananali*). The 'cattlemen' from whom he was descended still form the ancient nobility of the land.

Thus Ovamboland got its population, and Sitenue's headmen, who had lived with their paramount chief in Osimolo, became chiefs in their turn each over his own tribe. This did not, however, destroy the idea of a united nation, nor did Sitenue surrender his rights as paramount chief. He still lived on in Ositeve, where he finally died. His successors, as well, regarded themselves as paramount chiefs of all the Ovambo tribes and no one challenged their right. Their especial privilege consisted in their installing the young chiefs in their offices when predecessors had died. The act of installation was performed by sending him a symbol of authority. A magic staff, a bow with three arrows and a chief's chair made of iron were dispatched to the new chief from the court at Ositeve. As furnishings for the chair three sheep skins were sent with it, one for the back, another for the seat, and the third for the feet. In Ovamboland a sheep skin was a valuable possession, which only a chief was allowed to have. Sheep did not thrive there at all; if any one succeeded in breeding them the animals were regarded as inviolable. No one dared to kill a sheep for the penalty for doing so was death. It was only the little successor to the chieftainship who was allowed to be, and had to be, carried about by his nurse wrapped in a sheep skin. When he no longer required it, it was carefully put away with the other sacred objects in a special room. The sheep here referred to were the Syrian fat-tailed sheep, which the early Hottentots likewise had, and this reminds us of the Nama myth about the 'Sheep of the sun', the killing of which was prohibited; if any one transgressed this commandment, he ran the risk of dying miserably from thirst.

When a chief died, the symbol of authority which had been sent him, had to be returned to the paramount chief at Ositeve. A number of delegates took the staff, the bow, and the chair back to him. A young girl, decked out with valuable jewellery, had to accompany them. Forty round shells, each of which was worth as much as a young ox, had to be included in her finery. (This reminds us of the use to which these shells were put amongst the Hereros, who wore one single shell as the insignia of a wealthy man or a priest of the sacred fire; they obtained one of these shells in Angola in exchange for a young ox, until Tjiponda found them in large quantities on the shore at Swakopmund.) When they had delivered the dead chief's symbols of authority at the court at Ositeve the men returned home, but the girl had to stay at the court of the paramount chief for the rest of her days. This custom persisted up to modern times. The young chief, Uejulu of Uukuanyama (1884–1904), received the last iron chair, but now the ruling family of Sitenue has become poor and of no further account.

Tradition has not preserved very much regarding the lives and deeds of the chiefs. It is chiefly acts of cruelty which are related about them, and these are unimportant from the point of view of the country's history. A few samples of these should suffice. The story is told of the first chief, Kavangeko of the cattlemen caste, that he had an enormous kraal erected for him by his subjects, and gave the order that the poles of the palisade should not be planted with the bark of one pole touching the other, but that each of the many thousand poles had to be carefully cleaned off with the axe, which was truly a colossal task. He premised his right to make use of his people's labour with the words, 'The land is mine and every man who lives in it is my slave'. After his kraal had been built, he had the whole neighbourhood cleared of trees and bushes so that he, in his greatness, could have a wider field of vision.

It is said of Haita that he surpassed his predecessors in cruelty. He tortured his subjects in a more refined way. Once he took away from them all the iron hoes with which the lands had to be cultivated just at seed time, but he nevertheless issued a command that the fields were to be cultivated in spite of this, and that the soil was to be turned over with the fingers. The consequence was that a bad famine ensued. He treated his own headmen with the same degree of cruelty. He ordered them to fell a large boabab tree with their teeth and their finger nails, but the tree is still standing to-day, for it proved impossible for them to carry out the order. A deep groove in the mighty trunk of the tree, which has almost closed up, is still pointed out to-day as the mark made in the effort to carry out the chief's impracticable order.

It is indeed no wonder that people, who for some reason or other were forced to pay a visit to the chief's kraal, provided themselves with every possible kind of amulet and charm to ensure their safe return home. Nor was it a wonder that many of the Ovambos of this tribe fled secretly from the land and sought a refuge amongst the poor Bergdamas of the southern mountains. It seems as if Haita set an example with his cruelty to the chiefs of other Ovambo tribes. Other stories of the same kind about the cultivation of the soil and the felling of great trees are told.

Haita did not die a natural death. A poor woman came to him one day and begged for food. Haita had an ox slaughtered, a large quantity of porridge cooked and plenty of beer prepared. Enormous plates of meat and porridge were brought and placed in front of the woman. Haita ordered her to eat everything even to the last crumb, and seated himself opposite her to gloat over her discomfort. When she could not do so he drew his knife with the intention of killing her. The woman defended herself and the chief's knife pierced his own throat and he bled to death. The woman disappeared without leaving any traces. Throughout the length and breadth of the land the people said 'The cry of the poor made Kalunga hasten'.

It is surprising that thousands of subjects put up with tyranny of this kind. Did not the chieftainship ever pass from one caste to another owing to a revolution? There are stories to the effect that the harassed subjects tried to free themselves by force. One of the chiefs had a heavy canopy made and this was fixed to four poles so that it could be carried round. When the chief wanted to go for a walk, several powerful men had to carry the canopy so that the sun should not worry him. It was made of dry straw. The four men who had to carry this tremendous sunshade got so annoyed that one day, after making secret preparations, they let the heavy roof fall onto the chief, held him down under it and, setting fire to the straw, they burnt him to death, sunshade and all. The horror with which the Ovambos of to-day tell of a treacherous act like that shows how utterly unthinkable was the taking of a measure of this kind against a 'sacred' person. So sacred was the chief that no subject might touch him under pain of the severest punishment, and it was like the granting of an order of distinction if the chief unbent so far as to lay his hand on the shoulder of one of his subjects, or to touch him in any way.

The first considerable war which broke out between the Ovambo tribes took place in Omutota's time. The chiefs of Ukuambi, Ondonga, and Ongandjera combined and attacked him. Omutota was taken prisoner and tortured to death. A fig-tree grew out of his grave and is still pointed out to-day as Omutota's tree. His relations fled across the Kunene and took refuge in Evale. This is the reason why, in later times, the woman who was to conduct the girls' initiation ceremony had to be fetched from Evale. It was there, and there only, that the persons lived who knew how to conduct a ceremony of such importance properly and in due form, owing to the fact that they alone were endowed with the necessary supernatural powers.

Tradition points to Haimbili as the chief who was most kindly disposed towards his people. He is always spoken of with respect and veneration. He had actually driven his predecessor out of the country and there was famine in the land. He was a just man and he loved his people, and so he made a number of raids into his neighbours' territories and, by this means, brought a large number of cattle into his own country. It happened in his time that a soothsayer called Sisaama arrived in Uukuanyama and foretold the coming of evil days. His prophecy passed from mouth to mouth and it has come down through the ages intact. We think it worth while to give a free translation of it here.

Sisaama's prophecy

Passing through our veld I see an elephant,
Approaching Haimbili's gardens, green with corn-ears,
His coming bodes us evil; he will die
In Haimbili's fields. Why must that happen?

Mighty men are coming down our highways,
Making for our land, where they wish to dwell,
Coming from the lordly kraals of Pamba,[1]
Where they once lived, but now I see them here.
I cannot see the reason of their coming
And yet I see their houses in Ondonga.
They look towards Ukuambi and Ongandjera,
And they soon will come to Uukuanyama.

[1] Pamba is the name of a god.

Has only one man come without his wife and children?
It seems that Pamba ordered him to hurry.
Does this portend our chieftain's early death, or
Does this person bring him many blessings
As does the bat which haunts the chieftain's dwelling?
Strangers will point the way and those unborn
Will see it. The skunk[1] shall lose its skin.

A cry for help re-echoes through our country.
All hear it and hasten to the great one's aid.
All hear it, and each one whispers to his neighbour:
'We are weary of our chieftain's household'.
The chief's kraal—Look, the fire has caught its roof-trees
And those who did it wander far from home.
Still, Haimbili will not live to see it,
Nor will Nangoro ever see it happen.[2]

It is a difficult and venturesome undertaking to compile a table of the ancient Ovambo chiefs, for there is greater risk of inaccuracy than there is in the case of the genealogy of the Herero chiefs. Amongst the Hereros, the office of chief, with its duties at the sacred fire, descended from father to eldest son, while those who were not chiefs by birth left their property to their nephews, that is to say to the son of their eldest sisters, in accordance with the rights of succession in the Eanda. The succession to the chieftainship is differently regulated amongst the Ovambos, and it is the nephew who is the important person. Commencing with a fixed point of time, we have always assumed that, amongst the Hereros, a father begat his eldest son when he was about thirty years of age, and we therefore considered ourselves justified in reckoning a period of thirty years between each generation so as to get an approximately correct chronological table: It may be taken that the average period of an Ovambo chief's rule was twenty years, although it is known that Haimbili was chief of the Uukuanyama for forty-five years, and we know that Muesipandeka, whose kraal in Uukuanyama the Missionary Hahn visited in 1866, ruled from 1852 to 1882. In order to have a round figure, we will take the year 1850 as the date from which our calcu-

[1] The skunk means the tyrannous chief.
[2] Nangoro died in 1857 from a heart attack on the very day that he gave the order to murder the Missionary, Hahn, and his companions, who were on their first visit to Ovamboland.

lations are to commence, and then the chronological table of the
chiefs of Uukuanyama runs as follows:

Name	Year of succession	Remarks
1. Muesipandeka	1850	Of the house of
2. Sifeni	1830	the 'Cattleman'
3. Haikukutu	1810	..
4. Haimbili	1790	..
5. Hamangulu	1770	..
6. Haihambo	1750	..
7. Simbilinga	1730	..
8. Sikumanga	1710	..
9. Omutota	1690	..
10. Haudolonde	1670	..
11. Haita	1650	..
12. Kapuleko	1630	..
13. Kauengeko	1610	..
14. Omusindi	1590	Of the house of
15. Kanene	1570	the 'Husbandman'
16. Sitenue	1550	..

It is remarkable that this simple calculation, which is by no means
without a good foundation of fact, should bring us once again to the
year 1550, as the year of the exodus from the old home. Of course,
many objections can be made to it and it has been admitted before
that a table of this kind is really of little scientific value. When, however, the historian cannot possibly offer exact dates both he and his
readers must fall back upon probabilities, and it remains open for any
of them to fix other dates in accordance with their own points of
view.

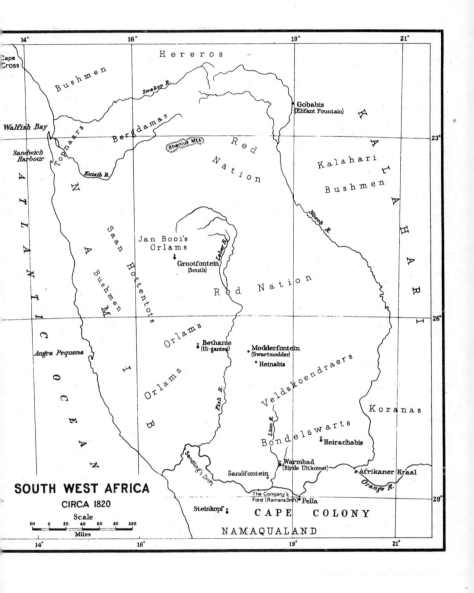

14°   16°   19°   21°

Cape Cross

Bushmen

Hereros

Swakop R.

Gobabis
(Etifant Fountain)

Walfish Bay

Bergdamas

K

23°

Sandwich Harbour

Topnaars

Kuisib R.

Rhenius Mts.

Red

Nation

Kalahari

Bushmen

A

L

A

N

A

Saan Hottentots

Jan Booi's Orlams

Grootfontein
(South)

Leber R.

Red Nation

Noob R.

H

A

R

I

26°

Angra Pequena

Bushmen

Mt.

Orlams

Orlams

Bethanie
(Ui-gantes)

Modderfontein
(Swartmodder)

Heinabis

Koranas

Orlams

B

Fish R.

Lion R.

Veldskoendraers

Bondelswarts

Heirachabis

O

C

E

A

N

A

T

L

A

N

T

I

C

Sendling's Drift

Sandfontein

Warmbad
(Blyde Uitkomst)

Afrikaner Kraal

Orange R.

29°

SOUTH WEST AFRICA

CIRCA 1820

Steinkopf

The Company's Ford (Ramans Drift) • Pella

CAPE COLONY

Scale

10 0   20   40 60 80 100
Miles

NAMAQUALAND

14°   16°   19°   21°

PART II

NAMALAND AGAINST HEREROLAND

I

INVASION AND WARFARE

1. THE NAMA INVASION

The spreading of the old tribes

THE Namas of earlier times were not only nomadic stock-farmers but were hunters as well. The land's enormous wealth of game was itself an invitation to the chase, which provided the family with nourishing food. Besides that, the flocks could be spared when the hunting-grounds provided flesh food. They possessed very few fire-arms but they had made the acquaintance of the horse, for which they willingly gave fifty oxen when they got one from the east or the south. With a horse it was possible to get close up to the larger wild animals and to deal them deadly wounds with an assegai. The meat was then cut into thin strips on the spot and hung on the bushes to dry in the heat of the sun. It could then be loaded onto pack-oxen and sent to the place where the trekking family had halted with its flocks. A considerable number of men usually took part in these hunting expeditions. Those who had horses undertook the killing of the game, while those who accompanied them on foot cut up the meat, dried it and saw to its transportation. The European hunter made his appearance in their hunting-grounds. As it was ivory that he was after and not meat, the Namas did not regard him as a competitor. Whole villages trekked along with him; the foreigner had a gun and that ensured good results. He set no store on the meat and that made them sure of the booty. It necessarily followed that the game began to be killed off. Giraffes and elephants became much scarcer.

The hunters ranged always farther north. In those early days the Swakop River made a tremendous impression on them, for whole herds of kudus, rhinoceroses, and elephants were to be found there. But the Herero hunters drove them away and so they turned in a north-easterly direction and travelled as far as Lake Ngami. The country which the Nama hunter's foot had trodden was, however, regarded as Namaland. It is on this that the saying of the Namas is based that, in former times, their country stretched to Lake Ngami. The game in Namaland actually decreased, but the herds of cattle increased. The people, too, increased in number and it was not long before grazing had to be sought for in the less populated areas. The Red Nation established outposts in the Karras Mountains. Kanebeb occupied the position of lesser chieftain of this offshoot of the great tribe. His successor was Tsâuchap and the latter's son Haobeb followed him in the chieftainship. During his rule an open breach between the tribe and its branch took place. The 'Children of the Red Nation' (Kougôan) separated themselves from the Red Nation, which was from that time onwards called the Gei-kou, or the Great Kou, and trekked to the Fish River. Haobeb's son, Willem Swartbooi, assumed the leadership of the tribe after his father's death, about 1835. His tribe was from that time called 'The Swartboois'. He took them to the northerly part of the Fish River and to the Kuiseb.

Another rich cattle owner, named Zeib, left the Red Nation and trekked to that part of the country which is now known as Keetmanshoop. His people became known as 'The Tseib Hottentots'.

A new Nama tribe

The valuable part of Namaland was now occupied, but people who were related to the Red Nation lived in the lower reaches of the Orange River. They had previously lived in the Cape Colony, and in 1710 they had sent the Governor a present from the Elephant River. At a later date they trekked from one water-hole to another, exchanged their cattle with European traders for tobacco, brandy, iron, and beads, and became very poor. They eked out a miserable existence on the banks of the Orange. The chief of the Red Nation allowed them to settle at Ui-gantes in his territory. This spring, which 'could not be closed up with a stone', and the surrounding country, received later the name of Bethanie. The chief of these impoverished relatives of the Red Nation crossed the Orange River and established himself at this strong spring. He wore trousers made of untanned leather and, on that account, he was called Amab (*ab* means 'untanned leather'), although his proper name was Garib. In consequence, his tribe was called the Aman or Amain. They had to pay the price of their admission in assegais and knives. The grazing grounds allotted to them stretched as far as the Useb in the north and the Fish River in the east. To the south and to the west the boundaries of the new tribe's territory were the Orange River and the sea. In this history we shall refer to this tribe as 'The tribe of Bethanie'.

The incursion of the Orlam tribes

The most important event of this period is the incursion from the Cape Colony of a number of new tribes, who had no connexion whatsoever with the original Nama tribes. The leaders of these tribes were not pure Hottentots. There generally flowed in their veins the blood of Europeans who had cohabited with Hottentot women at the Cape. They had acquired considerable knowledge from their European masters, either as slaves or workmen. They spoke, for the most part, Cape Dutch, while many of them wore European clothing, and there were even some Christians amongst them. The heavy tasks of slavery, the urge for freedom, or, with many of them, an evil conscience and the fear of the police, caused them to leave the Cape in small bodies and to settle down, first of all, in the neighbourhood of the Orange River. These wanderers and fugitives were called Orlams.[1]

Missionaries followed them up and founded a mission station in Little Namaqualand for the purpose of gathering the stragglers together and getting them to settle down. The Government gave a helping hand and granted land to several mission stations for the purposes of cultivation. The rainfall was, however, too scanty in that part of the country; successive periods of continuous drought forced the occupants of the mission stations to scatter far and wide over the veld, in order to get sustenance for themselves and their cattle.

One of these collecting stations was Pella, where the missionary Heinrich Schmelen laboured. In a dry year his congregation, too, decided to leave the place. They knew the people who had formerly lived lower down the Orange River and had trekked to the 'unquenchable spring', and so they decided to follow them. In 1815 Schmelen reached there with about 150 Orlams and gave the settlement a name, which has since become, so common, i.e. Bethanie. To the Nama tribe, which was living there at the time, he was neither unknown nor unwelcome. In 1812 their chief had gone to Capetown to ask that a missionary might be sent to his people.

Once the doors of Bethanie were opened, many more Orlams put in an appearance. Amraal[2] Lamberts came with his following; he

---

[1] Orlam is a word of Malay origin, derived from the Malay *Orang lama*, an old person, and came to mean 'one who has been a long time in the land', thus 'one who knows the world thoroughly', and so 'one who is wide awake'. According to Velk, *Uit Oost en West* (Arnheim, 1889), p. 10, the Hottentot tribe of Orlams adopted this name because they had a great opinion of their own abilities.—*Ed.*

[2] Amraal is a contraction of Admiral.—*Ed.*

was born in Clanwilliam and was for many years a slave in Worcester. Amraal was wise and upright, but the people who had joined him were uncontrollable and rapacious.

Dietrich Isaak came, too, with his people. He crossed the Orange River at Warmbad and settled down in the Karrasberg. When he died, his son-in-law, Paul Goliath, became the leader of the tribe. Amraal's and Goliath's people were related to each other. They could have formed a united tribe. In the course of time, however, Amraal trekked eastwards and, after long years of wandering about, found what he sought in Gobabis. Goliath's people, however, who were originally not averse to uniting with the tribe of Bethanie, settled finally, after much fruitless searching, at the foot of Mount Brukkaross, and, owing to the efforts of the mission, established the centre of their tribal existence at the spring in Ou-tsaweis, or Berseba.

Another arrival at Bethanie was Jan Boois with his lawless following. He settled down there at first, but he later found grazing in the veld to the west of Rehoboth, without ever succeeding, however, in establishing a permanent dwelling-place as a tribal centre.

It may be mentioned here, although this anticipates the actual historical development, that the Afrikander tribe likewise came into the country during this period under the leadership of Jonker Afrikander; this was the tribe which in later years was, from its centre at Windhoek, to exercise such a great influence upon the history of the country. The last people to arrive were the Witboois, who rose to importance later on. After trekking about for a great many years, they settled down in Gibeon in the year 1863.

The Orlam tribes which were of any importance were, then, the following:

1. Jan Boois and his people who arrived in 1815.
2. The Hei-khaua, who entered the country in 1816, and were first in the Karasberg, then at the Lion River, and finally at the Fish River and in Berseba.
3. The Gei-khaua under Amraal, who came in in 1815 by way of Bethanie and afterwards went to Gobabis. (This tribe was called the Khaua from *khau* to 'break up'; the tribe, which was united in Pella, divided. The Hei, which means 'light brown', were Goliath's people, and they were so called because of the light brown clothing which their leaders wore. Amraal's people were called Gei, meaning 'great', because of their numbers.)
4. The Aich-ai (the 'warlike people'), the Afrikanders of Windhoek.

5. The Khowese (beggars) of Gibeon, who became known as the Witboois.

In this book we shall not make use of the tribal names in the difficult Nama language. Having set them out this once, we shall in future speak about

1. The Boois' tribe,
2. The tribe of Berseba,
3. The tribe of Gobabis,
4. The Afrikanders, and
5. The Witboois.

In order to obtain grazing and water these five Orlam tribes had to come to an understanding with the Red Nation in Hoachanas. Both of these were granted to them against the payment of twenty heifers a year. Particular grazing-grounds were not pointed out to them; they found grazing for themselves. No steps were taken, however, to admit the new tribes to the alliance of the old tribes. The reason for this may be that, just in these critical years from 1800 to 1835, the Red Nation was ruled by a woman, Games by name, as the future chief, Oasib, was not as yet old enough to be ruler. The appearance of the more sophisticated Orlams had an intimidating effect on the old inhabitants. They felt that they were by no means the equals of the new-comers, even if some of their own people were in possession of guns and knew how to use them. They were forced, too, to recognize their intellectual superiority. In spite of this, the Orlams contributed very little indeed to the intellectual or moral advancement of the old tribes. Materially impoverished and morally neglected as they were, they became a danger to the country. The chiefs and headmen, who owned small numbers of cattle, had no idea of keeping their subjects in proper order through strict tribal control. They stole many a sheep from the Namas, and it was no calumny, nor was it due to malice, that they gave the Orlams the name of *Gu-nu*, or 'sheep-hunters'. It was not very long before the sheep-hunters got to know that, in the Kuiseb and Swakop River beds, there were grazing not only sheep but the Hereros' large herds of cattle. The Namas of Bethanie and Hoachanas had stolen many an ox from there. Hunting Herero cattle was a paying proposition. A man set out for the north quite poor and returned from there as the owner of a herd of cattle. Very soon the sheep-hunters became the keenest cattle-hunters, and lawless bands of the old inhabitants cheerfully followed their example. A position like this could only lead to serious conflict with the Hereros.

2. THE HERERO INVASION

In their own country

The Hereros called a wide area their own. It had been wrested by them from the Bechuanas after a hard struggle. Their task now was to consolidate their position there. All the Herero tribes from the Kaokoveld had not as yet put in an appearance. The tribe which was later to settle in Omaruru was not there yet. The Waterberg was, too, still unoccupied, but the Okahandja District had its owners. A firm grip of the Swakop country was gradually being obtained, and the reckless robber bands along the Ondondu Jomarunga, the 'Robber River' as the Swakop was called, were being driven out. Then Kandjizei, the father of chief Ndjiharine, later of Omburo near Omaruru, came into the country, and likewise Kaneena, the son of Kuaiima, who settled in Osona near Ohahandja. Oseu, the father of the mighty chief Kandjii made his appearance and lived for a considerable time between Okahandja and Windhoek on the farm known to-day as Düsternbrock. Tjamuaha, Maharero's father, settled at first at Otjikune, now the farm Schenkswerder, and there his son was born in 1820. As, however, he had become very poor, his relatives trekked back to the Kaokoveld with their possessions and stayed there for a long time. Kavarikotjiuru, an uncle of Tjirue's, came in, too, and settled at the hot springs in Windhoek. Mungunda, who was of the same family, chose the hot springs of Otjikango as the site for his kraal. On the east, the Mbanderu encroached upon their brothers, the Hereros. Epako (Gobabis) was in their possession and their cattle grazed in the bed of the Nosob River.

There was really no such thing as established boundaries. The limit of Hereroland to the south was taken to be the line Leuwater–Klein Nauas–Rehoboth, while, to the north, claim was laid to all the country over which the Herero cattle had grazed, that is to say, as far as Grootfontein. The eastern boundary remained an uncertain quantity, for the closely related tribe of the Mbanderus moved up and down on that side and lived in amity with the Bechuanas.

It was very necessary for the owners of such an extensive piece of country to get rid of the original inhabitants, those troublesome folk, the Saan and the Bergdamas. Wherever it was possible to lay hands on them a thorough business was made of it. Ruhaka attacked the more advanced tribe of Bergdamas who lived in Okahandja and Otjiwarongo. This tribe owned goats and had a chief who kept law and order. His name was Haramab and his descendants know to-day that their ancestors emigrated from Bechuanaland 'not in peace, but probably because their forebears had stolen goats, for Bechuanaland is the land of goats, and is called Birin or Goatland'. Haramab was killed and those of his tribe who escaped hid themselves in the Erongo and the mountains of the Swakop River. Other fugitives tried to take refuge in the Omaheke, but they were followed up by Nama hunters and driven out, so they fled to the Auas Mountains. Many others escaped into Namaland and found a refuge in the kloofs of the mountains along the Orange River.

Then the Bergdamas in the Paresisberg were set upon. They did a regular trade with the Ovambo tribes, from whom they got cows, goats, iron, and copper in exchange for dagga, for 'dagga was at that time the Bergdamas' money, with which they could buy anything'. They grew this strong, intoxicating herb, which could be smoked, worked it up into cakes and used it in this form as a means of exchange. Dagga cakes had to be paid yearly as tribute to their overlords, the Saan. The Hereros did not succeed in driving all the Saan and Bergdamas out of the Paresis Mountains. They made, however, a raid into Ovamboland and succeeded in stealing several herds of cattle. In 1830 the Ovambos made a punitive raid into Hereroland as far as the Omuramba Omatako. The rains had set in already and the Omuramba was full of water, and so many of the Ovambo warriors were killed in the marshes.

At the beginning, the Hereros did not dare to attack the Bergdamas and the Saan of the Waterberg. Whenever the Herero herdsmen, explorers, or hunters came across the Bergdamas, a bloody conflict ensued. Finally, all that the Bergdamas ventured to do, when they were forced to leave their hiding-places in their search for food and they came face to face with Hereros, was to have recourse to loud shouting with the object of calling attention to the danger which was threatening. They warned each other, in accordance with an agreed scheme, by imitating the bark of a baboon or a dog, or the cry of a bird.

It must not be thought that, in taking the steps that they did, the Hereros were bringing a cruel fate upon an entirely innocent people. The Bergdamas stole large numbers of Herero cattle, and they practised a kind of religious ceremony in the dispatching of their young warriors, when a raid on the Herero's cattle had been planned. A Bergdama song of those uncivilized days might well prove of interest. It tells of the efforts of the young men to capture some Herero cattle

for a comrade's wedding feast. The one who was to have been married
is killed in the raid, and his comrades bring the cattle home without
him.

> Hard as it is with one's bare hands
> The mountain kranz to break away,
> As hard is it to take away
> His cattle from a Herero.
>
> She, who scarcely had arrived
> At a proper age to marry,
> Is a widow, for her loved one
> Fell in the fight for cattle.
>
> Still, we made a successful raid.
> Look how his sister's children
> Gaze with greedy eyes upon
> The cattle we brought back with us.
>
> Far he travelled after saying
> 'Oxen for my wedding banquet
> Will I fetch from distant places';
> Now he lies in death's dark cavern.
> All of us must hasten homewards
> And none can stay to dig his grave.

But it was not only the cattle stealing which was so annoying to
the Hereros, for there was another particular act of the Bergdamas
and the Saan which aroused their keenest displeasure. During the
months which immediately preceded the rainy season, the Bergdamas
had a way of setting fire to the dry grass and burning the grazing
throughout the whole countryside. This they had learnt from their
forefathers. When the high grass is burnt off, young green grass
sprouts immediately. This attracts the game, and the hunter, who is
no longer impeded by the high grass, can count on easier and more
successful hunting than he could had the high grass been left standing.
The women, too, regarded the removal of old grass as a measure
which was necessary to produce a good crop of roots and wild tubers.
The Hereros, however, were placed in an extremely difficult position
through these sudden grass fires, for it often happened that, in a single
day, all the grazing they had for their large herds of cattle went up in
flames.

In Namaland

It was not only veld-fires which brought despair upon the cattle
owner. Far worse for him were the times of drought, when hardly

any rain fell and the wells ran dry. When this happens, a Herero, who will do or suffer anything to save his cattle, does not worry a bit about boundaries, and he has no regard whatsoever for his neighbour. A drought of this kind occurred in the years 1829 and 1830. The cattle of the midlands and the eastern portion of the land were food-less, but there had been good rains to the south of the Swakop and the Kuiseb. What was to stop them from transferring their cattle to that part? Surely not consideration for the Namas who had stolen so many Herero cattle? One knew very well that the cattle posts would be in constant danger of being raided, but by providing the herdsmen with strong bodyguards, it would be easier to protect the cattle against Nama raiding parties than it would be to preserve them from the danger of dying from hunger and thirst in their own country. So thousands of cattle set out on their southward trek and, out of the north-east, came the Mbanderu cattle as well. The Herero cattle grazed in the Rehoboth veld. The Namas were very annoyed at this. The Red Nation collected their forces and fell upon the intruders. They took several thousand cattle away from the herdsmen. This was fatal for the owners, but the other cattle owners did not worry their heads about the losses of those who had not shown them-selves strong enough to protect their own possessions. Soon after-wards herds of Herero cattle, accompanied by strong guards, pushed their way into the veld of Gibeon. Tradition even relates that one bold cattle owner ventured right down to the present-day Keetmans-hoop. The danger arising from this position of affairs did not consist merely in the fact that the veld had been entirely grazed off for that year by strange cattle, but it arose from the recognition of the fact that the grazing of any particular veld went hand in hand with a kind of ownership through seizure. Just as the Nama said: 'Where my hunter's foot treads is Namaland', so the Herero said: 'Where my cattle have grazed is Hereroland'.

The Namas could perhaps have warded off the threatening danger if they had combined their forces, but it was a woman, Games, who ruled the Red Nation, with her council of men. The tribal discipline had become slack, the coherence between the old tribes had weakened, and the 'sheep- and cattle-hunting' Orlams, while providing the country with an increase of revenue, did not make for an increase of strength. Any of those who suffered loss and dared to take their revenge on the Hereros had to pay dearly in the end. The big Hereros were not a bit frightened of the little Namas. They did just as they liked, and if any one offered any resistance they beat him to death. These circumstances were bound to lead, in the long run, to fierce conflict with the Namas.

3. THE STRUGGLE: JONKER AFRIKANDER

The Koranas

The power of the Europeans in the Cape increased in the seventeenth and the eighteenth centuries, and the Hottentot tribes began to feel the pressure. Through trade they lost their cattle, through the increase of settlers they lost their best water-supplies, while through being forced into service, they lost their freedom. Many of the tribes trekked back again to the north. They found in Little Namaqualand sufficient grazing and water for the needs of their few stock. Amongst those who left were the Koranas. Following the course of the Orange River they finally found a resting-place between it and the Vaal River, established about twenty small chieftainships, and regained their prosperity. If any of them were without cattle, they tried to acquire some by stealing them. Their neighbours on the middle and lower portions of the course of the Orange River and likewise the Namas, who lived to the north of them, had a very hard time. A Korana horde descended upon what is to-day the farm Blau in the District of Keetmanshoop, with the object of making raids from that point upon the Nama tribes, who lived farther to the north. No one dared to attack this horde for they were terribly revengeful. Besides this, the Namas were by no means displeased to see that the Koranas directed their special attention to the Herero cattle, which were grazing in large numbers in the Kuiseb valley, and were even to be found to the south of this excellent grazing country. The leader of these Koranas was called Eiseb. On several previous occasions he had carried out successful raids against the Hereros, and he now returned to Blau with greater spoils than usual. On this occasion he had robbed, as well, a Nama tribe which he had met with in the veld of Gibeon. Now the spoils had to be divided. The leaders had already picked out for themselves the best of the cattle and sheep. The rank and file were then free to divide the balance amongst themselves in conformity with the usual custom of the Namas and Koranas. On this occasion things went badly with the division and a free fight ensued. Suddenly some shots went off and several wounded Koranas fell to the ground. They were all panic-stricken and they left the

cattle where they stood and took to their heels. Eiseb then collected
his horde and retired to the Orange River whence he had come. He
had realized that he had to do with a terrible foe, the tribe of the
Afrikanders, and that he could not afford to interfere with them.
This tribe was not only in possession of numbers of guns, but it had
an energetic and prudent leader, one Jonker Afrikander, whose name
had been known, for some time, throughout the length and breadth
of the land.

Games and Jonker

Jonker Afrikander was the son of the famous Jager Afrikander, who
had his head-quarters at Afrikanderkraal, about 100 miles eastwards
of Warmbad on the Orange River. He had formerly lived at the
Cape but, after he had murdered his master and carried off his stock,
made for the Orange River in order to escape the attentions of the
police. He had gathered together into his Afrikander tribe all the
rogues he could find and, well-armed with guns as he was, he was
the terror of both banks of the river. A missionary came to stay with
him and he turned Christian, was baptized with his whole family,
and renounced his evil ways. To the end of his days in 1823 he remained faithful to the principles he had adopted, and the fierce Jager
Afrikander died as Christian Afrikander, in the odour of sanctity.

Christian's sons did not follow in his footsteps. The crooked ways
of Jager were much more to their liking. Their father was no sooner
dead than a fierce quarrel arose as to which of them was entitled to
the chieftainship. According to the ancient law of the Namas, the
eldest brother was entitled to be chief and many members of the
tribe supported his claim. Jonker, however, Jager's younger son,
knew very well that his father had chosen him as his successor, and
he too had his following. As he would not forgo his claims, a feud
arose which ended in Jonker leaving the tribe, together with his supporters and a small number of stock. In his father's lifetime he had
taken a prominent part in some of the raids, and now he became a gang
leader such as the Orange River had never yet known. He undertook
numerous plundering expeditions on both banks of the river and, in
dividing the spoils, he made his chief objective, in the beginning, not
the acquisition of property, but the equipment of his men. The
greater part of the loot went into the hands of traders, who delivered
to him in exchange guns, powder, and shot. With every fresh gun he
acquired his strength increased and, as it increased, the loot increased
too and he procured more and more guns with the proceeds of it.

Games sent to Jonker Afrikander two of her counsellors, Haromab and Aoemab, to ask him to assist her and her people against the trespassing Hereros. Jonker let the messengers wait for three days without an answer, and in the meantime he summoned his uncle, David Afrikander, who lived on the south bank of the Orange. After consultation with him, Jonker gave the messengers a promise of immediate assistance upon the condition that the Red Nation would grant him the free choice of a place of residence and grazing in their tribal territories. The delegates gave him this assurance, for Games was prepared for anything if only the threatening danger from the Hereros could be averted. Jonker's men were speedily equipped and ready for the road, and the trek first took the direction of Keetmanshoop. On the way Jonker met a hunter from the Cape, called Jan Swart, who encouraged him in his venture, saying that it was only right and proper that one chief should support another and one tribe help another.

At Blau near Keetmanshoop the collision with the Koranas, which was referred to above, took place. Jonker took the cattle which they left behind for himself and set out for Gibeon, for it was in that neighbourhood that he expected to come down upon the Hereros. At Aris close to Gibeon, he found the Nama tribe, which had been robbed by the Koranas, in a sorry plight. Their cattle were gone and they had no other means of subsistence. When Jonker saw the difficulties these people were in, he took pity on them and divided the small quantity of provisions he had with him amongst the sufferers.

Jonker and the Hereros

Jonker came upon the Hereros to the north of Gibeon. There they were grazing their cattle under a strong guard. He suddenly fell upon the unsuspecting herdsmen, and those who did not run away were shot down. The cattle remained in Jonker's hands. He did not trek back to the Orange River with the wealth he had gained, for there was nothing more that he could get there. His brothers and their followers had settled in Warmbad. They had no intention of living a rover's life. In the shadow of the mission, however, it was quite impossible for Jonker to live, for he had a very bad reputation with people of that kind, and so he stayed where he was and, from then onwards, it was no longer the Herero herdsmen who were to be seen driving the cattle out to graze, but the Herero cattle grazing the same veld under the supervision of Jonker's herdsmen. And thus the years went by.

With brooding anger the Hereros realized that a knobkerrie was of no avail against a gun, and they ventured no farther than the neighbourhood of Rehoboth. As soon as Jonker found it convenient, he made a surprise attack on them there and struck them a second blow, with the same success. In this way the old northern boundary of the Kuiseb River was once again restored. Jonker had every reason to be satisfied with his success, as were Games and her counsellors, and for a long time he did nothing more. Games, however, became tired of her regency and Oasib had reached the age of majority. She laid down her office and the tribe of the Red Nation chose Oasib as its chief. A great feast took place in Hoachanas, oxen were slaughtered and game-meat was provided for the guests. Jonker did not worry his head about that; what was troubling him most was that his stock of powder was becoming exhausted. Seeing that he had shot his ammunition away in driving the Hereros back to their proper boundaries, it was only right that they should pay the cost of the war.

He struck them a third blow, and this time he chased the Hereros to beyond the Auas Mountains. It was then that he saw for the first time the hot and cold springs of Ai-gams, or Windhoek. At Windhoek there lived at that time the Herero, Kavarikotjiuru, who was an uncle of Tjirue, Tjamuaha's father. When Jonker advanced on Windhoek, Kavarikotjiuru sent an urgent message to his relations in Okahandja and advised Tjamuaha, saying, 'I have got hold of a rhinoceros with both hands. Send me help or it will break through right to Okahandja!' Neither his own hands nor those of his relatives in Okahandja were of any avail. The rhinoceros stormed through Windhoek, destroyed Kavarikotjiuru's huts and kraal, and suddenly appeared in Okahandja, where all the inhabitants had fled into the mountains.

Jonker returned to Windhoek. The valley which is now called Klein Windhoek pleased him very much. Shut in by mountains as it was, it must have reminded him of his early youth, which he had spent in Roode Zand (afterwards Tulbagh), where his father had been the head of the Afrikander family. Close to Tulbagh stands the Winterhoek, a mountain which is often covered with snow in the cold time of the year. According to an old document, it was said to have been called Winterhoek on this account.[1] It seems that Jonker gave

[1] The Winterhoek is a kloof from which the adjoining mountains take their name. The kloof was so named because, in times of severe cold, the farmers in the neighbourhood were able to find sheltered places in the big kloof where their stock could graze in comfort and safety.—Ed.

his place of abode a new name in remembrance of that mountain. In the valley at Windhoek he established his home, and the Hereros were very annoyed about it. Windhoek was old tribal property of theirs and was the gateway to the south, which they did not want to see closed. They were wont to say that wherever the Herero cattle have grazed is Herero country, and on that ground they laid claim to the southern territories. The Namas were likewise wont to say that wherever the Nama hunter has set his foot is Nama country, and upon this they based their claim to the northern territories.

Little by little the Hereros recovered themselves. The mighty Mungunda lived between Windhoek and Okahandja. Kahitjene was there too and, although he was no great chief, he was a hero 'like Major Franke', as the Hereros say to-day.[1] Fear was to him unknown. But fearlessness alone was not of very much use in those difficult times. Jonker had guns while Mungunda and Kahitjene had none at all. They had to give way before the firearms, and so Jonker stayed in Windhoek. From here he could provide himself with cattle, at the expense of the nearest Hereros whenever he needed them. From here he might well succeed in making himself chief of Namaland. He did not lose sight of either of these points of view. Was he not the saviour of Namaland, whom the Red Nation itself had summoned to its assistance, and, as such, was he not entitled to become its over-lord? None of the Nama chiefs had given him any reward for all the trouble he had taken on their behalf. It was the Hereros who had had to pay him recompense, and they were going to pay him a good deal more as time went on. Jonker's goal was the supremacy of the whole of South West Africa. It seemed to him that Windhoek, lying as it did in the middle of country between the Namas and the Hereros, was the right place from which to achieve his purpose.

It is not possible to assign actual dates to Jonker's different campaigns. The missionary Schmelen encountered him, when on his travels in 1825, in the Siebel Mountains and, in 1837, Captain J. C. Alexander found him at Niais in the district of Rehoboth. It would serve no useful purpose to try to assign particular dates to Jonker's history between the time of his father's death in 1823 and his settling down in Windhoek about 1840, for there are no contemporary records.

---

[1] Major Franke was the commander of the German troops in many a struggle with the natives in South West Africa. At the beginning of the Great War, he became Commander-in-Chief, and was finally forced to surrender to Union forces, which outnumbered his by 10 to 1. He was a fine soldier and a brave man.—*Ed.*

Hardly any record of his campaigns remains, and the historian has in most cases to rely upon the traditional recollections of the Hereros and the Namas.

4. PROGRESS IN EXPLORATION

Missionaries and travellers as explorers

It is only natural that, once missionary work had commenced, the missionaries played the chief role in the exploration of the country. Seeing that they had little interest in discovering mineral wealth and in opening up new markets for European wares, they were able on their journeys to add considerably to the geographical and topographical knowledge of the country. They, too, were the men who were best qualified, and had most time and opportunity, to study the native languages, their tribal systems, religions, laws, and customs. It is by no means right to measure their services towards the acquisition of knowledge of the country from the amount of their writing of books and reports. At that time the oral relation of experiences and occurrences, of discoveries and observations, served just as useful a purpose as a written record of them. A great many things were reported by them to the Government and other interested parties, of which no written record was kept, and the knowledge of South West Africa was more extensive at the Cape than the available literature would lead us to suppose. All that remains to-day at the disposal of the historian is what the ancient documents have preserved for him. In setting out the separate steps which were made in the exploration of the country between 1800 and 1840, we must confine ourselves to these.

The Albrecht brothers were the first people who had the opportunity of making a careful study of the part of South West Africa in the neighbourhood of Warmbad and along the Orange River. They left us a fairly exact knowledge of the tribes of the Bondelswarts, the Veldskoendraers and the Groot-doden, the last of whom lived in the Karras Mountains. Some mention is made, too, of the Swartboois. They lived precariously in the mountains and kloofs in the south, which is a sign that the separation of this tribe from the Red Nation happened only a short while ago.

Besides dealing with these South West African tribes, Albrecht mentions the names of twelve other Hottentot tribes, who wandered about on the Orange River and with whom he came into less close contact. They belonged to the nomadic race of the Koranas.

Albrecht's companion, Seidenfaden, went on an excursion to the northern parts of the country shortly after he came to Warmbad. He was in the Karras Mountains and found 'tame Bushmen' there, who, from the form of their greetings, must plainly have been Saan. Seidenfaden writes that they greeted him with the words, '*Twee, twee*'. The word is really *tawe* or *tawete*. It is of Malay origin and came with the Hollander's servants from the Malay Archipelago to the Cape. There it was adopted by the Hottentots as a form of greeting and it spread to the Saan Bushmen, who spoke Hottentot.

Campbell, who during his stay in Pella in 1813 collected information about the native tribes of the Orange River, draws a broad distinction between the rich and the poor Damas. The poor Damas are the Bergdamas and the rich ones the Hereros. He was told that the poor Damas were often to be found in the service of the Namas.

In 1820 Barnabas Shaw of Lilyfontein and James Kitchingman of Pella accompanied Heinrich Schmelen on a journey to the Fish River. Their road passed over the Hanami Flats (Hanami means flats, on which, *am*, there are tubers, *han*) to the great Brukkaros Mountain. On their journey they came upon the chief of the 'Sheep-hunters', who said that he lived a month's journey to the north. Shaw was able to state, in his report, that the country to the north-east was not mountainous, and that grass-covered plains and plentiful supplies of water were to be found there. He mentions the Nosob River.

We learn for the first time, in 1821, through Archbell, something about the Hudub River and Grootfontein South, and also about the war of extermination which the western Nama tribes were then waging against the Bushmen of the Namib. He was the first person to undertake a journey by sea from Luderitzbucht for the purpose of reaching Capetown.

George Thompson, who was born in Capetown, paid the western part of the country a visit in 1824 and collected information regarding Namaland and Hereroland. He it was who established the fact that the Fish River did not run from west to east and reach the sea at Luderitzbucht, as Le Valliant's statements had led people to believe, but that it was a tributary of the Orange River. He named it after a business friend in Capetown, Borradale, but the old name did not permit the new one to supplant it. He was of opinion that the language of the Hereros was probably related to that of the Bechuanas, and he had a great deal to say about the wealth which the Hereros possessed in the form of cattle.

Heinrich Schmelen traversed the whole of Namaland in the course of his various missionary journeys. He reached in 1814, according to his own estimate (for from lack of instruments he could not make exact calculations) the 22nd degree of latitude. In 1824 and 1825 he reached the Kuiseb, followed its course to Walfish Bay, and stayed for a considerable time in the area westwards of Rehoboth. It is of some historical importance that he found the Orlam chief, Jonker Afrikander, in this neighbourhood.

Sir J. E. Alexander's Expedition

The journey which Sir James Edward Alexander made, in the years 1836 and 1837, from Capetown to Walfish Bay, by way of Warmbad and Bethanie, is of special importance. He was acting upon the instructions of the Royal Geographical Society of London in making it, and he hoped to do a service to science and to the inhabitants of the country through his efforts. He was very successful in both respects. His party consisted of seven people, whose names deserve mention. They were: (1) An Englishman, Charles Taylor, as naturalist; (2) an Englishman, Robert Repp, as overseer of the oxen; (3) an Irishman, John Elliot, in charge of the armament; (4) a Portuguese servant of Alexander's named Perreira; (5) a Bengalee, who had formerly been a slave and had been eighteen years with the Kaffirs; (6) a Baster, named Hendrik, as wagon driver, and (7) a Baster, called Willem, as wagon leader.

The expedition left Capetown on the 8th September, 1836. Alexander went past Kommagas in order to get the benefit of the missionary Schmelen's knowledge of the country in selecting his route. There the missionaries Leipold and Terlinden came to meet him, and invited him to make an excursion to the mouth of the Orange River. He set out on this journey on the 27th October and, upon his return, remained in Pella for several days. There he recognized that it was an unsatisfactory arrangement that a Field Cornet, to whom all the farmers were related, should be the sole Government representative in this unsafe neighbourhood, and he was of opinion that it was desirable that an independent magistrate should be appointed, seeing that the nearest magistrate was stationed at Clanwilliam. Accompanied by twelve farmers, he crossed the Orange and reached Warmbad. He states that Abraham Bondelswart, the chief, was one of the most comic figures he had ever seen. Tall and well-built as he was, his face, with its flat nose, broad mouth, hollow

cheeks, high cheek-bones, and eyes set closely together, made a rather
unpleasant impression. He was wearing leather trousers and a red
coat. Here we see the close observer, whom nothing escapes, and one
who omits nothing from his descriptions. This attribute of the real
explorer, which he possessed, makes the reading of the account of his
journey, which was published in London in two volumes in 1838,
not only a pleasure, but also an inexhaustible fund of very many carefully observed details, which are of interest to all those who have
any regard for the South West Africa of days gone by. Without
going deeper into his experiences we must be content with saying
that he proceeded farther on his journey, passing through Nanebis
to the Fish River, which he crossed close to what is to-day Seeheim.
His other camps were Naiams, Kosis, and Bethanie, which latter he
found in ruins. He then passed over Suurberg, Goais, and Remhoogte
to Grootfontein, where Archbell had laboured for fifteen years. Continuing his journey Alexander passed the Naukloof, reached the
Tsondab River at Bulpoort, followed its course to Ababis and crossed
the Gansvlakte to the Kuiseb River. He followed the course of the
Kuiseb to Walfish Bay, where he arrived, after unspeakable difficulty
and danger, on the 19th April, 1837.

Alexander stayed with his company in the Bay until the 3rd May,
making observations. He viewed, too, the mouth of the Swakop
River and he made the acquaintance of an American captain, whose
ship was anchored in the Bay. He had to give up all hopes of getting
into touch with the inhabitants of the northern part of the country.
His draught oxen were in poor condition and he lacked a leader who
was acquainted with the conditions of the country. He set out on the
return journey, but did not direct his course to Bethanie, for he had
heard that the famous, but dreaded, Jonker Afrikander was living in
the high country, where Rehoboth is to-day. He was anxious to see
him and to gain some knowledge of the country from him. Possibly
he might, with his assistance, get through to the cattle-owning
Hereros and open the road for the export of cattle from Walfish Bay
to St. Helena.

Alexander reached Jonker's place about 300 miles east of Walfish
Bay. He had advised Jonker that he was coming and so Jonker's
brother met him and took him to the settlement of the Afrikander
tribe. To his great astonishment, Alexander found a small, well-
ordered township, in which he estimated that there were 1,200 people
living. It was quite easy to distinguish between the huts of the

Namas and those of the Bergdamas, who were living amongst them. The Namas had dome-shaped huts covered with reed thatch. The Bergdamas lived in round huts, which were pointed, and were made out of branches and grass. Jonker came to greet him and he made a good impression upon Alexander. He described him as a small man, of friendly appearance, with the usual Nama type of face, thick lips, but a well-formed nose. (There was European blood in Afrikander's family for some generations.) By his dignified carriage and his energetic movements, he showed that he was a man used to giving orders. Alexander passed an opinion on him which was greatly in his favour.

Alexander felt himself perfectly safe in Niais, as Jonker's village was called. He was provided with everything which Jonker had, and Alexander, on his side, was not grudging with presents. Needles with large eyes were specially desired by the Afrikanders as articles of exchange. Alexander was anxious to find out from Jonker what the eastern part of the country was like, and whether it was possible for him to get through to the Hereros. Jonker gave him a careful description of the eastern areas, but he told him that it was impossible for him to reach the Hereros. The road to them went past Ai-gams, i.e. Windhoek, and he was so loud in his praises of its fine situation and wonderful water-supply that Alexander gave it the name of Queen Adelaide's Baths without even having seen it. There would, however, be no Nama or Bergdama who would be willing either to take a message to the Hereros or to act as guide, for he had defeated the Hereros at Windhoek and driven them out of it. They were determined, however, to take the place back again. For this reason he could not settle there himself, for he would always be fearing that they would attack him or carry off his cattle.

Even if a visit to the Hereros was out of the question, it was exceedingly useful for Alexander to see the numerous Herero prisoners whom Jonker had. They impressed him by their well-built, muscular bodies, the pleasant expression of their faces and their melodious speech, with its wealth of consonants. It is quite plain, from what he says about the Hereros, that there was much more known in Capetown in the year 1837, through the medium of verbal communications, than such documents of the time as are available to us would lead one to understand.

Alexander states that the Hereros say that they call themselves Oketenba Kacheheque, and that another name for them is Omotorontorondoo, but this was due to misunderstanding on both sides.

The Herero whom he questioned had clearly taken it that it was his own name that was asked and he therefore replied 'O *Katemba ka Heheke*', which meant 'I am Katemba of Heheke', thus giving his own and his father's name, according to the usual custom. The second so-called name of the race would be written more correctly as Omuzorozorondu, and it signified 'a perfectly black person'. (*Omundu* means person; *zora* is to be black, and *zorazora* to be very black.)

Here was another opportunity for solving the old problem of the race in the north 'with long hair and cotton clothing'. Alexander had been told by a chieftain in Walfish Bay that these people were to be found near the sea a month's journey northwards. The chieftain had been there himself, had been treated by them kindly, had been able to understand them although they spoke a different language, and had himself been astonished at their long hair. Alexander was not able to get any further information from the chieftain.

At Niais, however, a distinguished looking Herero woman told him that she had once, in the company of other women, met these mythical people on the sea-coast. The men had driven the cattle down to the sea, at a place where there was a bay. The men stayed with the stock, while the women were taken in a boat to a white man's camp, where the people wore hats on their heads. They exchanged their cattle for iron, copper, and knives. These people were called Obatchna and another name for them was Obantoobororontoo. The headman of the bay was called Oban.

So far as all these names are concerned, to any one who has a knowledge of the Herero language it is clear that the name Obatchna is a distortion of the Herero word *Ovatua*, which is even to-day their collective name for all foreign people. Europeans, as well as Bergdamas, were called *Ovatua*, or foreigners, by the Hereros. Oban is just a Namaization of this Herero word. Obantoo is recognizable as an English transcription of the word *Ovandu*, which means people. Bororontoo has its own peculiar explanation. When a Herero wishes to tell any one that he does not understand their language, he puts his fingers in his ears and says '*Poroporo*'. The Nama have taken this word over and, in similar circumstances, they say '*Buruburu*'. The Hereros call the Bushmen, by reason of their incomprehensible speech, Butootoo, 'i.e. the little people, whose speech cannot be understood'. The word *Bororontoo* is thus just an exclamation to which a person gives vent when he is confronted with a language which he cannot understand.

Alexander thought that the people they were referring to were

most probably traders of Portuguese origin, who traded with the
natives of South West Africa in former times by coming to the Great
Fish Bay in Angola, and exchanging for the stock, which the natives
brought there as their only medium of exchange, iron and copper.
The people 'in the cotton clothing with long hair', whose reputation
had crossed the Orange River and reached Capetown, must then have
been the Portuguese, the first Europeans to settle on the West coast
of Africa. Moreover, it seemed as if it was not quite as the Herero
woman had told Alexander that it was only the Hereros who went to
these men, but that they were not permitted to enter the Herero
country. The Bergdamas of the north-west told a story that, in
ancient times, before any Europeans had come into South West
Africa, people with white skins had been seen, and that, in the Namib
somewhere near the Okambahe hills, there were some graves in which
white men lay buried, which had been there long before the African
races had been visited by the hunters and explorers of more recent
days.

After spending a week with Jonker, Alexander set out on the 3rd
June, 1837, pointing his wagon-pole to the south. Prior to his departure he was besought by Jonker and a number of the women to
send them a missionary, and he promised to lay this request before
the Wesleyan Missionary Society. Jonker took his guest to a valley
which he had specially chosen as a residence for himself. Namas had
lived there before, but they had been attacked by the Hereros and
killed. A plentiful water-supply and rich soil made it easy to lay out
a garden. Jonker had had a small dam made, in which he collected
the water from the spring, and used for irrigating tobacco and pumpkins. As he had promised to show Alexander a copper mine, he took
him to the Swartmodder River, where the explorer took some
samples. Then Jonker turned back and Alexander took the road for
his journey back. He passed through the territory of the Red Nation,
and there he found Amraal Lamberts with his followers. Jonker had
asked Alexander to use his influence to prevent these people from
attacking him. A quarrel between the Afrikanders and Amraal's
people seemed imminent, and Alexander tried by means of a letter
to settle the dispute.

The travellers reached Bethanie on the 13th July and returned to
Capetown on the 21st September, 1837, after an absence of a year.

The topographical material collected on this expedition was worked
up by Arrowsmith into a map, which was published in the account

of Alexander's travels, entitled *An Expedition of Discovery into the Interior of Africa* (London, 1838). It is the oldest map of Namaland, embracing the whole country. Earlier maps included only particular portions.

Alexander had covered about 4,000 miles on his journey. The objects of scientific interest collected on the expedition consisted of rock samples, plants, skins of unknown animals, 320 birds' skins, weapons, and other Nama and Herero curios, important descriptions of the native tribes, and a list of fifty words of the Herero language, which had hitherto been totally unknown.

5. THE BEGINNINGS OF CIVILIZATION AND ITS OBSTACLES
The beginnings of civilization

It is very interesting indeed, just at the close of this account of the period from 1800 to 1840, to take one more look at the beginnings of cultural development in a land which had hitherto been untouched by European civilization, and to consider what the chief obstacles in the way of such development were.

It is a fact of no inconsiderable significance that a day-school, with more than sixty pupils, was kept going at Warmbad under exceedingly difficult circumstances. A matter which is well worth mentioning is the fact that a man like Jager Afrikander placed an order for books, which would gladden the heart of any present-day bookseller, and that he himself learnt to read when he was forty-four years of age. The fact that the women of his son, Jonker's, people exerted themselves to get education for their children and made, jointly with their chief, a request to Alexander that he should obtain a teacher and a missionary for the tribe, shows that they had a strong desire for cultural progress, something which might hardly have been expected of them, seeing the difficult years of unrest and warfare through which they had passed. Of course, it should not be overlooked that the Nama character was such that they could not apply themselves faithfully and consistently to the attainment of a great purpose, but the fact remains that the urge for cultural advancement was obviously present. Captain Alexander's accounts of the impressions which he received from the Afrikanders show, by the very warmth of their expression, that he felt at home amongst them and that he was surprised at the degree of civilization attained by a tribe, which was always described as a mere band of robbers. The reports made by Schmelen during the early years of his missionary work in Bethanie show that, not only the

Orlams, but the Namas also were capable of being raised to a higher religious and moral standard.

We catch a glimpse of the very beginning of material civilization in the shape of the first house built of burnt bricks by the brothers Albrecht at Warmbad. The school children shaped the first bricks for it on the 3rd February, 1806. In the first brick house there stood shortly afterwards the first piano, which suffered the fate of being dug up by Jager Afrikander and his band of ruffians in 1811, and broken into small pieces so that it could be divided as spoil.

The very first garden ever made in South West Africa was made in Warmbad. Christian Albrecht writes about it in 1806 as follows: 'The inhabitants of this country have to live entirely without bread, for the land is unsuitable for the cultivation of grain. We intend to lay out a vegetable garden with their assistance, so that, if we should be successful, we can provide food both for ourselves and our community.' It was not only oats, barley, and rye which were sown and reaped, but he writes in 1808: 'We have likewise planted cotton, which grew well, but as we have no spinning-wheels and looms, we are unable to make any use of it.' To this he adds: 'We should very much like to have a printing press and some glass for windows.' The only plant which had been cultivated by the natives of South West Africa up to that time was dagga, a kind of hemp, which was smoked on account of its intoxicating effect. The cultivation of tobacco, which ought really to have been a much better proposition, was taken up very gradually.

There were no roads in the South West Africa of those days; there were just narrow footpaths, which very often coincided with the tracks made by the elephants. Elephants tramp out clearly defined pathways between one water-hole and another, and roving natives have a way of trekking from water-hole to water-hole. It was the dependence of elephants and human beings upon water that made it essential to provide roads. An old Tjimba of the Kaokoveld said to me 'If you are ever without water on a journey, look for an elephant path and follow it in one direction or the other, and you will come, in due course, to a water-hole.' When the ox-wagon made its appearance in South West Africa, the old footpaths were no longer of any use. It was not only that they were too narrow, but they often went over lofty mountain ranges and so compelled the wagon driver to make a new road somewhere else. The next wagon generally followed the spoors of the previous one, for wagon spoors remain visible in

Africa for a long time. There is every justification for doing this, for if the first wagon reached its destination the one that follows it has a very good prospect of reaching it too. It was thus that the first roads came into existence and these were the road to Warmbad and from Warmbad to the north, and the road through Sendlingsdrift over the Orange River and from there along Schmelen's roads, which Alexander took, also, to the Kuiseb River and Walfish Bay. Schmelen laid down, too, the first part of the road to the sea at Luderitzbucht. To the Bushmen of the north his wagon seemed like some large animal which was respectfully given a wide berth. If one of the wheels broke, he left the wagon in the veld and had recourse to his more reliable riding oxen. The Bushmen were afraid to tread on his wagon spoors and took great leaps across them.

The first beginnings of business could only take the form of trading by exchange of goods. The Orlams knew what money was from their days in the Cape Colony, but the Namas and the Hereros did not. What was most sought after was iron, from which arrow-heads and assegais could be made, and iron beads and knives were likewise in demand. Nails were much sought after, for they lent themselves very easily to the fashioning of arrow-heads and awls for working leather. Copper was used for bracelets and anklets, and glass beads were employed as jewellery. At first there was no demand for European dress materials, nor bindings for the head[1] and suchlike. It was only the Orlams who had any use for hats, coats, and trousers. The 'wearers of hats', however, had an evil reputation, for other people had met with unpleasant experiences at their hands. In a Nama gathering, which Seidenfaden had convened in 1806 on the occasion of his visit to the Veldskoendraers, for the purpose of discussing the question whether they wanted a missionary, or not, these hard words were uttered:

'We Namas are not regarded by the Colonists as human beings, but as animals. They come here to attack and kill us and the officials do not worry one jot about it. A farmer, named V., was here in the country and how did he treat us? He shot at us and stole our stock and we did not dare to offer any resistance. This man (the missionary) has come here in the disguise of a teacher. When he has been here for a time, he will do the same thing.'

The accusation that the Cape Government had failed to enforce

---

[1] The Nama and Herero women of South West Africa all wear head-dresses, or *kopdoekke*. These are usually of a very bright coloured material. The Herero women of to-day usually wear silk ones, often a foot high.—*Ed.*

the law and order proper to a civilized state along the Orange River and in Namaland does not even require refutation. The borders of the Colony came nowhere as far as the Orange River and the road to the nearest Magistrate lay very far from there. For the purpose of keeping some kind of order on the borders, a farmer at Lilyfontein had been invested with police authority. The Government, therefore, refused to grant any protection to missionaries and travellers beyond the northern boundaries of the Cape Colony. In spite of this, they were forced to interfere in several cases, as Jager's story and that of Threlfall's murderer show. In any case, what happened on the Orange River and in Namaland held considerable interest for the authorities at the Cape. When Albert Albrecht went to Capetown in 1807, the fiscal, Rhyneveld, demanded from him the delivery of a written account about the people at Warmbad and his work amongst them for the information of the Government. He was, moreover, invited to trek to the Colony with the Nama tribes who were under his influence. The Government was prepared to grant extensive areas for settlement, free of charge.

Obstacles in the way of civilization

This touches the problem upon which the best friends of South West Africa have laboured for very many years, a problem upon the solution of which so many have exhausted themselves with the result that, when they thought that they had solved it, they saw everything they had achieved vanish in smoke. This problem is: how can a nomadic people be turned into a settled one? It is quite plain that, by answering it, the way is opened to raising a race with a low standard of civilization to a higher one. There are in South West Africa two causes for nomadic existence. One lies in the natural inclination of its ancient inhabitants to go searching for things, thus leading them to a frequent change of habitat, and the other arises from the fact that the people obtained their subsistence from the natural products of the land, and that this becomes exhausted in the effort to preserve live stock. The keeping of stock is possible only where water and grazing is sufficiently plentiful. The best grazing in the country is quite useless if there is no water within reach of it. It is, of course, possible to keep a large number of people with their stock at a tribal centre in years when the rains are good, but the greater the number of the inhabitants of this centre, and the more animals they possess,

the sooner the surrounding country is denuded. Then there soon
arises a necessity for sending some of the cattle to outside posts,[1]
while the members of the family keep at the village only such cattle
as are essential to maintain their food-supply. When the grazing no
longer suffices for this smaller number of animals, then the whole
family is forced to go out to the outside posts, and in the village
where, whenever possible, the whole tribe gathered together and enjoyed the pleasures of social intercourse, only the broken stock-kraals
and empty huts bear witness that this was once a place of human habitation. The need for tribal centres of this kind seems to have been
recognized, to a less or greater degree, by the nomads from the
earliest times, and Warmbad, Hoachanas, and Hatsamas were such.
Amongst the Hereros the position had not developed to the extent
of the formation of fixed residential centres. While they were living
in the Kaokoveld, Otjitambi was a fixed centre, and, after they left
there, it seemed as if Okahandja, or Otjikango, and Windhoek might
possibly have become so. With these as starting-points, the men who
made it their life's work to raise these people higher tried to establish
new centres at suitable places. The attainment of a higher degree of
civilization is bound up entirely with fixity of habitation. We find
the first missionaries, therefore, at the tribal centre of the Bondelswarts in Warmbad. For that part of the tribe which could not be
provided for there, Heirachabis was designated to serve as a centre.
Schmelen went to a great deal of trouble to create a fixed centre at
Bethanie for the mixture of Namas and Orlams who had gone northwards. His efforts met with good results when the rains were good,
but, when the drought set in, the very man who was most anxious to
get the tribe to settle had himself to become a wanderer, if he wished
to remain faithful to his calling. He trekked with a portion of his
congregation from one water-hole to another in Namaland and along
the Orange River, and visited, with untiring energy, the tiny communities which had gone wandering in other directions; and he sorrowed
over the increasing barbarity of those very people, over whose former
progress he had so greatly rejoiced beside the fountains of Bethanie.
How much might not have sprung from the devotion of this man to
his duty, if he had had under his influence for so many years a settled
people instead of a wandering one!

[1] Throughout South West Africa the places at which sheep and cattle are regularly watered and kraaled, when situated elsewhere than at the homestead, are called
'posts'.—Ed.

The first forty years of the history, which we are doing our best to portray, reveal merely the beginnings of cultural development; definite progress is not recognizable. The obstacles which had to be overcome, such as the lust for plunder, war's confusion, a vacillating national character, and, above all, nomadic proclivities, were altogether too great.

UNDER THE DESPOTISM OF WINDHOEK

The position in 1840

JACOB IRLE says in his book about the Hereros:

'Any one who wants to give a description of the Hereros finds himself in much the same position as that of a photographer, who comes out to Africa from Europe and is unfamiliar with the light and shadow effects. It is very easy for him to get perfectly black negatives through over-exposure, with the result that the dark negroid faces come out almost white. In describing them there is a danger of painting the picture in too glowing colours, while, on the other hand, it may easily happen, and it has very often happened, that it is only the Hereros' bad characteristics which are disclosed and the possibility of their possessing noble ones is overlooked.'

These words do not apply only to the dark-skinned Hereros, whose ancient history it is only too easy to depict in bright colours—for who does not involuntarily range himself on the side of an oppressed and conquered people—but it applies, too, to the light-coloured Namas and Orlams, whose history offers only too great an inducement to emphasize the dark side of the picture. We shall strive to control the effects of light and shadow so as to attain the most suitable exposure, so that a picture of both races, which is true to nature, may result. The history of the Bergdamas and the Bushmen is entirely interwoven with that of the Namas and the Hereros during the years 1840 to 1880. We shall first deal with the period between 1840 and 1850.

The Hereros had been so thoroughly trounced by Jonker that they surrendered the Rehoboth country with its splendid grazing lands, and the Swakop River came to represent the boundary of their country from then onwards. Since they had lost the major portion of their vast herds of cattle to Jonker, there was for the time being no urgent reason for them to go beyond this boundary line. Many cattle owners went down the Omuramba Omatako, or spread themselves over the Sandveld, or returned once again to the land of their forefathers, the Kaokoveld. Yet the upper reaches of the Swakop River were by no means uninhabited, for the cattle kings, Tjamuaha, Kahitjene, Omuiniuouje and Mungunda were in temporary occupation of them. Tjamuaha was the least important of them, for he was not so wealthy as the others, but he had four sons, Kavezeri, Hirapi, Kavikunua, and Maharero, all of whom were courageous youths. That has made him of special importance from an historical point of view. Besides that, he was the guardian of the sacred fire of an ancient generation, and that ensured him a certain amount of dignity. The springs at Okahandja and those at Otjikango near by were the centres of a very large Herero population, which had gathered round these headmen, but they, again, were not in good odour with the rest of the Hereros. Tjamuaha's and Kahitjene's possessions were not entirely derived from their energy and skill in raising stock; they had not hesitated to attack weaker members of their race and to take their cattle away from them. This was the reason why it did not seem advisable to them to retreat to the north before Jonker's onslaughts, for they would then have run the risk of falling into the hands of their enemies and of losing all their cattle again. They therefore preferred to stay where they were and to come to terms with Jonker. If they could succeed in placing themselves under Jonker's protection, they would escape the danger with which their own people threatened them from the north, as well as that with which the Namas and Orlams threatened them from the south.

The conditions under which Jonker was living prevented the carrying out of this scheme. After his last battle with the Hereros, he had allowed his troops to take a good rest in Windhoek, and then had returned once again to his grazing-grounds in the Rehoboth area, leaving a small number of his Afrikanders at the Windhoek springs, as a garrison. As early as 1837 Jonker had told Alexander that he would very much like to go and occupy Windhoek with his whole tribe, but that he feared that the Hereros would worry him too much. He would have to build enormous stone kraals if he wanted to be sure of protecting his cattle from their depredations.

There was a further consideration. Jonker had been sent for by the paramount chief of Namaland. The Red Nation of Hoachanas would likewise have something to say if he were to occupy Windhoek. It was quite true that he had been given the right to choose a place of residence according to his liking, and Oasib, who was also called Kornelius, as the suzerain chief of Windhoek and Okahandja had made him some promises. Now, however, Oasib was toying with the idea of going to Windhoek himself, and the Orlam, Amraal, who lived with his following at Oasib's place, was rather inclined to settle at Windhoek as well. If that happened, then nothing would come of Jonker's idea of uniting all the Nama tribes under the leadership of himself and his Afrikanders. It would not then be Oasib who was living with Jonker, but Oasib who would be taking Jonker and his tribe to live with him in Windhoek. Although he might often turn it over in his mind, Jonker could not seriously entertain the idea of a war against the Red Nation. His tribe was not large enough for a venture of that nature. How easy it would be to destroy him utterly in Windhoek, if the Red Nation from the south and a number of Hereros from the north attacked him simultaneously. Jonker knew perfectly well that Oasib had no right whatever to keep him out of Windhoek, which had belonged to the Hereros since the earliest times, so he took steps to find out what the Hereros thought about it, and he sent to ask Tjamuaha whether he had any objection to his settling in Windhoek. Tjamuaha, who felt himself honoured by the request, gave a favourable reply. Jonker realized at once that he could come to an arrangement with this man. Messages went backwards and forwards but what was discussed and agreed upon was never recorded in writing. The consequence was that Jonker proceeded to Windhoek. It is not possible to ascertain for a certainty in what year this took place, but it is probable that he entered into possession in the last months of 1840, and that the different families of the tribe followed after him one by one. The Hereros were glad that Jonker was leaving them in peace. Willem Swartbooi, who was likewise trekking around in the Rehoboth country, was pleased when Jonker's cattle departed; in order to improve his position, he made a raid on Walfish Bay and robbed the Topnaars of almost everything they possessed.

The peace of Christmas Eve, 1842

Missionaries belonging to the Rhenish Missionary Society went to stay at Windhoek. Jonker had asked Capt. Alexander for them and Schmelen had promised him that he should get them. Their names were Heinrich Kleinschmidt and Hugo Hahn. Charles Bam of Capetown, a brother of the missionary Schmelen's second wife, came with them as assistant. They arrived in October 1842 and Jonker gave them a friendly reception. Bam, who had remained in Windhoek while the two missionaries made their first journey, noticed that negotiations between Jonker and Tjamuaha were in progress. Tjamuaha had sent two men and a woman from Okahandja to tell Jonker that, if he really wanted to make peace with him, he should give the messengers his drinking-mug, his wash-basin and his knife as pledges of his good faith. Jonker had willingly sent along a tin bucket, his tin mug and his knife, and there was now nothing to prevent the chiefs of the two peoples from coming together and concluding a treaty of peace and friendship. Bam, however, had his own ideas. He proposed to Jonker that he should say nothing to the missionaries regarding the peace negotiations, but that he should invite the Hereros to come to Windhoek on the holy night so as to give the former a pleasurable surprise for Christmas. Jonker gladly fell in with the suggestion. Hahn had in his pocket the consent of his Society to his founding a mission station amongst the Hereros directly it became possible, but how was he to do it while the position was so uncertain. Until peace had been concluded between them and Jonker, there was absolutely no possibility of getting into touch with the Hereros, much less of settling amongst them. A Christmas in Africa celebrated under circumstances of this kind was calculated rather to lower one's spirits than to raise them. The two men went to bed on Christmas Eve with anything but a Christmas feeling. 'Peace on earth' was what the angel had once sung on this very night, but his notes had not yet managed to reach Windhoek.

In the middle of the night a great shout suddenly arose: 'The Hereros are here! The Hereros are here!' was heard from every side. The two men thought at first that it was an attack. Kleinschmidt rushed out to find what the shouting meant. He returned quickly to tell Hahn the joyful news that the Herero chiefs, Tjamuaha and Kahitjene, had just arrived, and that Jonker was prepared to make peace with them on the Christmas holiday. Hahn could not possibly have imagined a finer Christmas present. He had no idea whither this peace was going to lead. He was convinced that peace with Tjamuaha and Kahitjene meant rest and security for the whole Herero nation.

After service had been held on the Christmas morning, Jonker came with the two Herero chiefs to the missionaries to cement the bonds of friendship over a cup of tea. They were all in good spirits. The Hereros said that, as peace had now been made, Jonker must come to Okahandja and pay them a visit in return for theirs. Unfortunately there fell, in the course of this conversation, a drop of bitterness into the cup of friendship. Jonker would not accept the invitation. Despite the conclusion of peace his suspicions were not

completely lulled. He was afraid that they might set a trap for him. The
Hereros had meant it fairly and Hahn felt the jar which his refusal
caused. Since he felt for the Hereros, he tried quickly to remove the
unpleasant impression which Jonker's refusal had created. He promised the two chiefs that he would come to see them during the
coming weeks instead of Jonker. But that was not at all to Jonker's
liking. He was afraid lest this strong-willed individual should supplant
him in the good graces of the Hereros, and, moreover, he did not
want to see the Hereros helped forward through their accepting a
missionary. He then stated that whoever came to stay at his place
had to submit to his orders. Hahn regarded himself as a free agent
and said that no one could prevent him from acting according to
his Master's command to preach the Gospel to all nations. Jonker
immediately veered completely and said that he was really concerned
about Hahn's safety. If he were murdered by the Hereros, he, Jonker,
would get the blame for it. He would only consent to his visiting
Okahandja if Hahn would give his colleague, Kleinschmidt, a written
certificate, before he set out on his journey, stating that Jonker was
in no manner of means responsible for whatever might happen to
him on the road. Hahn agreed to this, but it was fortunate that
the unsuspecting Hereros could not understand anything of this conversation. Early in January 1843 the two Herero chiefs went back to
Okahandja satisfied, and Hahn followed them on the 8th February.
He had an excellent reception and he reached Windhoek again unharmed. Jonker could now be sure that the Hereros were really in
earnest about the conclusion of peace. Some time later he paid a
surprise visit to Okahandja, and it never occurred to anybody to do
him or his people the slightest harm.

The peace treaty had now to be turned to some practical value.
It was not sufficient for Jonker merely that he was no longer permitted
to raid Tjamuaha's and Kahitjene's cattle. He arranged with
Tjamuaha and Kahitjene that they should come to see him in Windhoek. He wanted to present Tjamuaha's sons with guns as a token of
his friendship and confidence and to give Kahitjene one too. He
was anxious to train the young Hereros in preparation for times of
mutual danger, and Maharero ought to be in command of them.
Tjamuaha was quite pleased with the idea. What Hereros would
dare to attack him if he stayed in close proximity to the powerful
Jonker, and if his sons learnt how to handle firearms? Jonker, however, felt like a man who is surrounded by the flames of a veld-fire,

HERERO WOMEN IN ANCIENT TRIBAL DRESS

By courtesy of E. B. Schoenfelder, Grootfontein

but has made a protective ring round his wagon by burning the grass close to it. The raging flames could not reach him any more. What Jonker thought at that time of the security provided by the Hereros who lived round about him we do not know. He never spoke about it. Probably he was really concerned to maintain peace. The efforts of his missionaries were bent in this direction, and he showed in every respect that he, too, as a great chief, wanted the whole country to be converted to Christianity.

The growth of the Afrikander tribe

The Herero says, 'Two things make a chief; a large number of cattle and a numerous following. A man who has many cattle, but few followers, is not a chief at all, and the man who has a large following, but no stock, cannot maintain his followers and they leave him.' Another Herero proverb runs: 'Employ people for your undertakings, for you will never achieve anything with cattle alone.'

Jonker recognized that this saying was applicable to him, the Orlam, as well. He had plenty of cattle, but he wanted very much to strengthen the Afrikander tribe. He turned to Cupido Witbooi, who was still living with his people in Pella, but was considering whether he would not look about in Namaland for some better veld as the Orlam tribes of Bethanie had done. He advised him to leave the Orange River and to come to Windhoek. Cupido was in favour of this plan, but the majority of his followers were against it. They did not trust Jonker. Jonker then took a step which probably went against the grain. He sent an invitation to his brothers and his uncle, David, from whom he had formerly parted in anger. Their people lived partly in Blydeverwacht and partly in Warmbad, and they stood under the influence of the Wesleyan Mission. His brothers Jonas, Valtyn, and Adam, who was nicknamed Kraai, were by no means disinclined to share Jonker's good fortune in Windhoek. Valtyn was a habitual dagga smoker, and he had already sacrificed his health and sanity to his craving. His uncles David and Titus made conditions. They said that they had grown accustomed to their own missionary at Warmbad and that they would only go to Windhoek if they might bring a Wesleyan missionary with them. Without saying a word to the two Rhenish missionaries, Hahn and Kleinschmidt, Jonker accepted this condition and replied that the missionary, Haddy, would be welcome to come. He considered it possible for a number of missionaries from different societies to work amongst his Afrikanders.

In the meantime Tjamuaha and Kahitjene went to Windhoek.
Jonker kept his promise to give Tjamuaha's four sons guns, and
Kahitjene received his as well. The young Hereros were formed into
sections with Maharero as their captain, but they all stood under
Jonker's command. They were to act whenever he needed them.
Tjamuaha settled in Otjipuna, which became known afterwards
as Pokkiesdraai long after the Hereros had abandoned it. The missionary, Eich, when on his way to Windhoek in his ox-wagon,
discovered here that small-pox (*pokkies*) had broken out in Windhoek
and he was forced to turn back (*draai*) again. The new settlement
was named after Tjipuna, because he was the oldest man amongst
Tjamuaha's followers. Kahitjene erected his huts and kraals at the
place where, in these latter days, the aerodrome has been constructed.
Tjamuaha made preparations to stay permanently and there was to
be seen at Otjipuna something which had never before been seen in
South West Africa. In place of a thorn fence, he fortified his whole
kraal by means of a circular palisade. He was still afraid of the
revenge of the Hereros he had despoiled, and to the old fear there
was probably added the new one that his friend, Jonker, might some
day become his enemy.

Jonker lived with his tribe in what is to-day Klein Windhoek. The
church and the mission house were there too. The missionaries had
actually given the place the name of Elberfeld, but it did not take on.
About 800 members of the Afrikander tribe lived with Jonker. There
settled, on the western side of the mountains, an unruly element,
drawn from all the Nama tribes, who looked for booty and a good
time under Jonker's leadership. Their number was the same as that
of the Afrikander tribe. The Bergdamas crept out of their hiding-
places in the Auas Mountains and offered their services to both
parties. They were so numerous that they exceeded the combined
numbers of the Afrikanders and the Namas. They made excellent
herdsmen and domestic servants, for they expected no wages, but
required only protection and food, and in this latter respect the veld-
food, which they gathered for themselves, and small game were the
principal items.

So as to avoid giving the impression that perfect peace reigned in
Windhoek in those days, the following characteristic incidents are
mentioned. Some Namas, who did not live in Windhoek, killed three
Hereros and stole their cattle, and Tjamuaha told Jonker what had
occurred. Jonker felt that he was bound to protect this friend against

Nama attacks. He followed the Namas up and had the huts in which they lived surrounded, but the culprits were never caught.

The punitive commando was hardly back before the Mbanderu, or eastern Hereros, killed four of Kahitjene's men. Kahitjene was of the opinion that he ought to deal with the matter himself and, when five Mbanderus came to Windhoek to buy tobacco, he had them seized and was on the point of putting them to death. Jonker heard of this and, since these men had had nothing to do with the murder, he took them away from Kahitjene and placed them under his own protection. He then went out himself to the east, with some 200 men, to punish the Mbanderus properly. As a reward for his trouble in carrying out the dictates of justice, he brought back with him some Mbanderu cattle, whose owners were entirely innocent and had therefore not fled upon Jonker's approach, for the very reason that they had clear consciences.

The Afrikanders could never overcome their fear that danger was threatening them from the side of the friendly Hereros. One night in May 1843 a panic arose. A noise had been heard and some people were suspicious that Tjamuaha's and Kahitjene's people were on the point of attacking them. Jonker sent for Tjamuaha who replied without any embarrassment: 'If a rumour of this kind gets about again, then you should stone the Herero, who carries the tale over to you, to death. We can then see who brought it. We have become your servants. If any one kills you, he must kill us too. We want to live with you and to die with you. What reason have we for breaking the peace? Are we not far better off than we were previously?'

Jonker's plans for the future

The country could not possibly permit of so many people living close together, so Jonker started to look about him for outside places, in which he could take refuge in the event of Windhoek's veld becoming totally grazed off. His restless spirit even conceived that there might be glorious, well-watered pasture land somewhere in the north, where he could live more comfortably than he could in Windhoek. From the stories that the Hereros told, he had heard that there were such places, and imagination added to their desirability. He set out in June 1843 with a reliable and well-armed force to make an inspection of the country, as became its lord and master, as he conceived himself to be. After some months he returned home. He had discovered two good places where water was plentiful, and he had found trees at these springs which five men were unable to span completely with their outstretched arms. (These were Ana trees, which sometimes have an enormous circumference.) The springs were on the slope of a steep mountain range, which was inhabited by Bergdamas. It seemed probable that this area was free from horsesickness, and he decided to send his horses there during the coming rainy season. Jonker had reached the Erongo and it is not unlikely that he had found the springs at Ameib. He said later that he had found a river bed, which broadened out to the north, and that there was a wrecked ship lying at its mouth. He would very much have liked to search the ship to see whether he could get anything useful from it, but the waterless wastes of the Namib Desert had prevented him from reaching the sea. His ideal from then onwards was to live at a place from which he could get to the sea easily and quickly. It was not at all to his liking that Windhoek was such a long way from Walfish Bay. The road which he had had made for his missionaries over the Auas Mountains, between Windhoek and Walfish Bay, was a useful link between the two places, but how easily could it not be severed in troublous times, and it was just in troublous times that supplies of arms and ammunition had to be ensured.

For the time being he did nothing to alter the fact that he was living in Windhoek and that he had not discovered a more satisfactory place in which to live elsewhere. It was possible to make some other arrangement. He could try to get some traders to stay in Windhoek. These people understood business and saw that necessary supplies reached the places where there was a demand for them. People of that kind were to be found at the Orange River, and it was from there that he was expecting the Afrikanders, who had remained behind with his brothers, and the missionary, Haddy, as well; that was the place he would get traders from too. Jonker wrote a letter on these lines and it was well received in Warmbad. By Easter 1844 the traders had come to Windhoek, and the other half of the Afrikander tribe was on its way to join Jonker. The missionary, Haddy, and his family arrived with the traders. A blacksmith made his appearance in Windhoek and began to put old guns into proper order, to forge weapons, to import quantities of iron and to make himself generally useful. In order to avoid any unpleasantness, the Rhenish missionaries came to an agreement with Haddy, and after handing their charge over to him, left for Otjikango, to which they gave the name of Barmen. Both names have persisted to the present day. They founded the first mission amongst the Hereros close to the hot springs. Jonker was satisfied with the arrangement. He had himself recommended the founding of a settlement at this spot, and the Hereros regarded themselves as still being under Jonker's protection.

Considerable activity developed in the conditions of life at Windhoek. Everything that the heart desired could be obtained from the traders. Jonker's wife went about arrayed in silks, and expensive sunshades bobbed up on every side, but it did not stop there. The traders' brandy was very much to the liking of the menfolk and the whole stock was speedily sold out. The traders had to devise the shortest and cheapest way of getting new stock to Windhoek and of finding a market for the cattle for which they had bartered their goods. The best way was to have the goods sent to Walfish Bay and to fetch them from there by ox-wagon, but the simplest way of fixing up arrangements of that kind with Walfish Bay was to go there and see to things themselves. The traders, therefore, decided to go to Walfish Bay and they took Jonker, who was well acquainted with the lie of the land, with them to the sea. They knew just how to interest him in their plans, and they did not neglect to supply him plentifully with brandy. Jonker returned to Windhoek an entirely changed man —changed for the worse. His craving for liquor mastered him and his Afrikanders followed his example. Windhoek became a business centre, to which large herds of cattle and sheep were driven. Guns and powder were to be bought there and lead and bullet moulds. There was a plentiful supply of iron. Spears with short iron heads and long wooden shafts disappeared entirely, and shaft and head were made in a single piece. The cattle and sheep, which had been taken in exchange for goods, were sent out of the country in enormous herds, some to the Cape by way of the Orange River, and some to St. Helena through Walfish Bay. With Jonker's assistance that which Captain Alexander had striven for hardly ten years before but had not achieved, was brought to fruition, but the trade was not of a kind which an honourable man like Alexander would have contemplated.

Jonker and Oasib

The chief of the combined Nama tribes regarded Jonker's good fortune with envious eyes. He had given up the idea of trekking to Windhoek with his people. He began to consider ways and means of getting rid of Jonker, or of injuring him, and showing him who was really master in the country. Since, however, he had himself given Jonker a free hand, he had lost much prestige as paramount chief. All eyes were fixed on Jonker and when Jonker spoke the whole of Namaland gave ear. It was not as if they loved and admired Jonker, for all the Nama chiefs hated him. Even his own brother-in-law, the chief of Warmbad, could not forgive him for weakening his tribe by getting his brother, with whom he had lived in harmony, to go and live in Windhoek. Oasib took advantage of this and he proposed to him that they should make a combined raid against the Hereros. He did not dare to attack Jonker, but he reckoned that he had the right to take steps against his friend Kahitjene, to compensate himself somewhat for all the losses he had sustained through the long continuance of peace. Jonker got to know of these plans and he gave the Bondel chief such a lively warning that he lost all his keenness for any further association with Oasib, and so Oasib proceeded to the execution of his plan alone, at the end of 1844. He had worked out a scheme which, if it succeeded, would bring him considerable booty. He decided to pay Kahitjene a friendly visit, accompanied by his followers. It was just at dusk; the cattle were all in the large kraals and the cows were being milked. Kahitjene knew what was required of him as a Herero. He had all the men served with milk out of the calabashes, which were kept specially for guests. They drank their fill of the milk and then suddenly attacked the unsuspecting owners of the werf,[1] killed all who offered any resistance, and drove Kahitjene's stock to the south that same night. Jonker, however, did not intervene on his friend's behalf. He hoped that Oasib would be satisfied, for the booty was considerable. Besides that, a little setback would do his friend, Kahitjene, no harm, for he did not show very much subservience, but acted much as a Herero does when he is dealing with a chieftain of his own standing.

If Jonker could not protect his friends better than that, there was very little object in staying with him any longer. This was the conclusion to which Kahitjene came, and he left Jonker, but no quarrel took place. Kahitjene had a large number of cattle left, and he had to

---

[1] Werf is an Afrikaans word meaning the dwelling-place on a farm, with all its surrounding buildings, kraals, and sheds, and likewise the spaces in between. There is no farmyard as in Europe. It has been taken into use in English like other Afrikaans words, such as trek and kraal. When used in connexion with natives it implies the whole of the premises used by a chief or headman for the accommodation of his family and dependents.—Ed.

go and see to them. In those times, no Herero used to keep all his possessions in one place.

But it was not only against Kahitjene that Oasib was so hostile. His displeasure was directed against all the Orlam tribes. He could not overlook the fact that they would not join in a general expedition against the Hereros. He was angry with the people of Bethanie, because their missionary, Knudsen, restrained them from committing any acts of violence. He was annoyed with the tribe which lived along the Fish River, and afterwards made its tribal centre at Berseba, because they were, from the very beginning, averse to stock-raiding. It was only Tseib in Keetmanshoop who was his supporter, for he had much the same ideas as his suzerain had. Knudsen writes regarding this period:

'The Red Nation is very arrogant and is exceedingly annoyed with all the rest of the Namas and with the Orlams, who left the Cape Colony and have done them a certain amount of harm. Although they are not, on the whole, much stronger than our Namas, they stand together much better than we do, and, even if we were superior in numbers, we know that man-power alone is not very effective against a people, which, to a man, nourishes its claims to supremacy upon fierce national pride and hatred.'

Jonker's breach of the peace

Jonker's prosperity collapsed. His needs were greater than the natural increase of his possessions, and, in addition to that, he drank heavily. Brandy had to be paid for in cattle, and his Afrikanders made constant demands upon him. Then a brewery was established in Windhoek and a strong, intoxicating beer was brewed from honey or sugar with the addition of wild raisins. A wild way of living became the order of the day. Hahn went to Windhoek in 1845 and took very sad impressions back with him. He writes, 'Elberfeld looks as neglected as a vineyard overrun by wild hogs.' Tjamuaha's Hereros learnt how to make honey beer from Jonker's people, and they began to search keenly for honey and wild raisins in the veld round about Windhoek. This made Jonker angry. If the Hereros were too stingy, despite their ever-increasing herds of cattle, to buy sugar for beer-making, they were at any rate not going to do him an injury by taking away all his honey and raisins. He proclaimed a law to the effect that honey and raisins were an Afrikander monopoly, and imposed a severe penalty upon any one who contravened it by taking them. That was hard upon the Bergdamas, who were fonder of honey than of anything else, and hard, too, upon the Hereros, who thought that, under their treaty with Jonker, they were entitled, not only to grazing and water, but to everything which the veld contained. They persistently defied the new law. Then Jonker had pieces of rag tied to all the raisin bushes, so as to mark them with the tokens of ownership according to ancient custom, but that did not help in the least. When Jonker wanted raisins, he found that other people had been to the bushes previously and had stripped them of fruit. The spoors round the bushes showed, however, that it was not Nama feet that had made them; their size proved conclusively that the big Hereros were the thieves. When Jonker wanted honey his servants found nothing but empty bees' nests. The spoors betrayed the fact that Herero hands had carried the honey-comb away. Jonker had the spoors traced up and he had the suspected thieves severely punished. Several Berg-damas forfeited their lives. The Hereros became annoyed at the treatment thus meted out to them by their friends, but they were by no means overawed and they became only more obstinate.

Now Maharero was the Hereros' responsible headman. It was to him that Jonker turned when evil-doers amongst the Hereros had to be traced, but he was not so accommodating as Jonker, and perhaps Tjamuaha, wanted him to be. Jonker had a way of calling his head-man 'Tjamuaha's calf' and, when a fit of anger took him, he used to order the Namas to 'bind my friend's calf to the wagon wheel', and Maharero had then to stand, for days and nights at a time, with his feet and arms bound with riems to the wheel of an ox wagon. In spite of its progress there was no prison in Windhoek as yet. Any one who had to be punished was either thrashed, or branded with a burning stick, or even maimed, but punishments of this kind could not be inflicted upon the sons of chiefs. Binding them to wagon wheels served to punish them by restraining their liberty. The friendship between Jonker and Tjamuaha received many a jar through occurrences of this kind, but it held for the nonce because Tjamuaha had one fixed idea, and that was to preserve and increase his cattle; everything else had to give way to that. Thus it was that the year 1845 came to a close and the eventful year 1846 began.

Jonker had incurred a considerable debt to his trader, Morris, and could not pay it. Morris demanded 800 cattle and a large number of small stock from him, but Jonker did not possess more than half the number. Jonker's people, too, were similarly in debt to Morris. The trader had exercised a great deal of patience and had given lengthy credit, but at last he required his money. It appeared that he had entered into an agreement that he would send a large consignment of cattle to St. Helena by a certain ship, and he found that he was therefore compelled to put considerable pressure upon Jonker for the payment of his debts. When the latter told him that he could not possibly pay everything at once, Morris pointed out to him that the Hereros had a very large number of cattle, and it did not matter one bit to him where Jonker borrowed cattle from, or where he took them from. Jonker took the hint. He had his brother, Adam Kraai, summoned with his men. He told him that the Hereros were restless and that he expected trouble, but he did not let him know what his real scheme was. He was actually planning a cattle raid on a large scale. An unexpected event was the cause in deciding where it was to take place in this critical time.

For some time past, the Mbanderus, or eastern Hereros, had been in the habit of submitting their tribal disputes, not to their own chiefs, but to Jonker, for decision, and there had been disputes between the Mbanderus and the Hereros for a considerable period. The Hereros went farther and farther eastwards into the Sandveld with their cattle, and so cramped the Mbanderus. With the object of getting more room and likewise of adding to his own possessions, the Herero, Katuneko, resorted to a treacherous trick. He invited all the wealthy Mbanderus, into whose area he had trekked, to a great feast, and the representatives of five kraals accepted the invitation. During the course of the feast, Katuneko's followers fell upon the Mbanderus and killed them. Their kraals were then destroyed and their stock driven off. The relatives of the victims were so weak that they were powerless to revenge themselves, so they turned to Jonker and begged for his assistance. This coincided most luckily with Jonker's own ideas. Now he knew where to go. Luckless Mbanderus, who had been robbed, sought his protection, and every one must surely sing his praises for granting them this protection. No one could possibly blame him if he made these presumptuous Hereros pay him an indemnity in cattle on an occasion of this kind. He could always avail himself of arguments of this kind, if he were accused of having broken the peace with the Hereros.

In March 1846 Jonker set out with a large force. He had under his command the Afrikanders, his brother, Adam Kraai's men, Maharero with his body of Hereros, and many of his Bergdama servants.

The march to the north took five days and, when they reached Katuneko's kraal, it was deserted. Katuneko had fled with all his people and had taken his loot to a safe place. Jonker was beside himself with rage. He had no desire to return to Windhoek without having secured some booty. A wealthy Herero, named Kahena, lived close by. He had had nothing to do with the matter at all, and he had remained in his kraal, secure in the possession of a clear conscience. Jonker fell upon him and took possession of more than 4,000 oxen. Morris's share was put aside immediately and driven to Windhoek. The rest were divided. Jonker returned to Windhoek. The peace was broken.

The results of breaking the peace

Jonker had got rid of his debts and he breathed once more. He could buy on credit again and he made good use of his new facilities. He was satisfied with his success. Kleinschmidt journeyed from Rehoboth to Windhoek to speak to Jonker personally. Jonker expressed surprise that Kleinschmidt did not commend him for what he had done, seeing that he had merely done his duty as a chief. When Kleinschmidt drove him into a corner, by pointing out that Kahena, whom he had robbed, had been entirely guiltless, Jonker turned away and admitted roundly: 'I did wrong deliberately.' That was on the 2nd April, 1846.

Like a veld-fire the words sped through Namaland: 'The peace is broken. The Herero cattle are free game again.' The paramount chief of the Red Nation was annoyed with Jonker for not taking him with him. He was determined to secure the loot, which he had now missed, on the first possible occasion. Knudsen's position in Bethanie was a very difficult one. Part of his congregation left him. They refused to recognize that participation in a raid brought with it exclusion from the congregation as a consequence. Knudsen was openly accused of trying intentionally to keep the people in poverty, so that he could have a better hold over them. The old doctrine 'It is permissible to do evil if good comes of it' was resuscitated and proclaimed. It was the same in other places. Even old Willem Swartbooi was restless and Kleinschmidt had great difficulty in restraining him from the evil ways to which the Herero cattle lured him on.

In September Jonker went to the north with a trustworthy bodyguard. No one knows what the object or purpose of his journey was. It was probably to the Waterberg, in order to discover whether it was possible to establish a settlement there in the rear of the Hereros, for they were constantly getting farther and farther out of his way to the north. It may well have been that, on this occasion (there is no written record about it), Jonker established a kind of security and observation post, where he left a number of Namas and they joined up with a Baster from the Cape Colony named Kruger, who had made himself chief of the Bushmen and the Bergdamas there. This troop had orders to exert pressure from the north upon the Hereros if difficult circumstances arose. This little tribe settled later at Gaub near Grootfontein.

While Jonker was on this expedition, Oasib, the paramount chief, likewise made a move. He had to abandon his scheme of allying himself with Willem Swartbooi for the purpose of attacking Jonker and annihilating him completely and then combining to march against the Hereros, because Willem would have nothing to do with it. He had not the courage to attack the Hereros alone, for he knew very well that Jonker would not regard that lightly, not because he regarded himself as their protector, but rather in the light that Jonker would lose whatever Oasib seized. He, therefore, turned his attention to the Mbanderus on the east, and he came back home with rich spoils. Jonker took no interest in this arbitrary action of Oasib's, but he wrote to Kleinschmidt: 'You are always making charges of robbery against me, and I only take from those who took from me first. You should prevent the Red Nation from doing things of this kind.'

War with Kahitjene

In December 1848 Jonker went to Walfish Bay. He had heard that there was a ship lying wrecked there, and he wanted to secure its cargo. It was, however, impossible to reach the ship and he was annoyed at his failure. He had expected to return home laden with wealth, but he now found himself on the way home, empty-handed. That did not suit him at all. He passed near to some Herero villages and this put evil ideas into his head. Towards evening he sent an invitation to one of the wealthy Hereros. He was very pleasant to him and he got him to tell him how many Hereros lived in the neighbourhood, where the cattle kraals were and various things of that kind. He then invited his guest to spend the night with him. This guest's name was Kamukamu and he was Kahitjene's half-brother. Jonker had him murdered in the night and, at break of day, he wiped out the kraals of Kamukamu, Katjari, and Muhako, by killing every single human being and driving the cattle away to Windhoek; so he did not return with empty hands.

Kahitjene heard of the raid. He learnt that about sixty people had been put to death and that his half-brother was amongst the number. In a case of this kind the duty of taking revenge fell upon him. Jonker knew very well what that implied. Kahitjene was not the man to let the matter rest. It was not very long before Kahitjene attacked Jonker, but without much success. Jonker scarcely excelled his former friend where bravery was concerned, and he did not surpass his skill in taking care of his cattle to any extent, but Kahitjene was no general. He was defeated and he lost his best warriors and a large number of cattle. In this battle Jonker's son, Christian, who was to have been Jonker's successor, was wounded, but Kahitjene's brother, Kanja, was killed. This was a fresh ground for a vendetta against Jonker.

An exceedingly difficult existence began for Tjamuaha and his Hereros in Windhoek. Even if the friendship between Kahitjene and Jonker had changed to open hostility, Tjamuaha did not dare to take his relation's part. He thought of his cattle which would assuredly fall into Jonker's hands. Then one of his sons was killed by Jonker's people, without Jonker taking the matter up. That gave him good cause to declare the friendship at an end. He refrained from doing so and explained to Jonker that the veld round Windhoek was no longer sufficient to provide his cattle with proper grazing, and that he was forced to return to Okahandja for a time. Maharero would stay with Jonker. Jonker was content and let him go.

For some time past Jonker had not had a good word for Maharero. 'Tjamuaha's calf' was growing too big, and weaning it did not make it any the tamer. He often did things which aroused Jonker's displeasure. For instance, Jonker had sent his Afrikanders out one day to kill a lion, which had destroyed some of his cattle. After the hunters had found the spoor and followed it for a distance, they came upon the lion. Maharero and a few of his followers had been sent to accompany the Afrikanders as helpers and servants. When the lion threatened to attack the hunters they ran away. They returned to Windhoek without effecting anything and gave Jonker a number of fabricated excuses. Maharero, however, stayed behind, killed the lion, skinned it, and brought the lion skin back to his lord, Jonker.

In the eyes of the Afrikanders, however, the lion was a noble animal, and it might not be killed by the hands of servants, and so Jonker regarded Maharero's act as one of unpardonable insolence, and 'Tjamuaha's calf' was given three days on the wagon wheel to reflect upon the rights of a lord and the duties of his subjects. Similar occurrences frequently took place and Maharero tired of being Jonker's Herero headman.

After Kahitjene had been so sorely defeated and despoiled by Jonker, he sought fresh pastures for the cattle that remained. He went to the missionary, Hahn, at Barmen, who was regarded as the chief of that place, seeing that he had established it. There were, however, other cattle owners, who had trekked there previously, living with Hahn. In order to provide space for himself and at the same time to balance his losses to some extent, Kahitjene made sudden attacks on Hekununa, and then on Mungunda and others. This did not happen without Tjamuaha knowing about it beforehand, for he was annoyed that these men, who had before been quite poor, should have attained comparative wealth and thus have become sharers of the pasturage, which he would much rather have kept for himself exclusively.

But even Tjamuaha was not going to get off scot-free. It cannot be proved, but it seems more than probable, that Jonker took a hand in the game. One of Oasib's commandos made a surprise attack on one of Tjamuaha's outposts and drove him out of it. Tjamuaha complained to Jonker about Oasib's action. Jonker sympathized with him and promised to compensate him out of oxen raided from the Hereros at the first possible opportunity. His son, Maharero, could undertake the raiding expedition. The raid was made in due course and Tjamuaha received his compensation.

This, however, increased enormously the exasperation of those Hereros, who had no ties of friendship with Jonker. The following is an illustration of this. An Herero, who was not acquainted with recent events, went through Okahandja to Otjikango (Barmen). He was asked what road he had travelled by. This question is a part of the usual form of greeting amongst the Hereros. He replied that he came from Tjamuaha. He was immediately surrounded by men and women who wished to kill him, and it was only Hahn's authority which saved the man's life.

Raiding and plundering became general. Nama hordes came up

from the south and seized cattle. The Hereros who had been robbed
had recourse against their own people in order to rehabilitate themselves. Those who had nothing more fled to Hahn at Barmen, or to
Kleinschmidt at Rehoboth.

But Kahitjene was not afraid of fighting, and Jonker knew what
to expect from him. The lust for revenge may remain concealed for
some time like a smouldering fire, and then it suddenly bursts into
an all-destroying flame, when the time and the opportunity are ripe.
It was, therefore, advisable to get rid of the man and to render his
followers harmless, but Kahitjene did not dare to attack Jonker and
neither did Jonker dare to come to grips with Kahitjene. It was
Jonker's servants, the Bergdamas, who had to pay the penalty for
all the atrocities they had committed against the Hereros in the
course of the fighting. Kahitjene took punitive measures against
them, and Jonker did not go to their assistance. He did not wish
to take the field until he was thoroughly prepared, so that he could
make absolutely sure that Kahitjene would not escape. As a preliminary measure, he ordered forty horses from the Cape Colony
through his traders, and these he received in December 1849.

Jonker was thinking, moreover, of making an alliance once again
with the Red Nation. All the other Nama tribes were to be included
in the alliance, if they approved of his plans, which were to attack
not only Kahitjene, but the whole Herero nation, and to destroy
them utterly, root and branch. The children could be spared and
incorporated into the Afrikander nation. If this plan succeeded,
it was not only that the danger of the Herero race would be removed,
but, through the addition of so large a number of children, the
Afrikander tribe would, within a reasonable period of time, become
so strong, that it would be in a position to exercise unlimited authority
throughout the land. Against a scheme of this kind, the plan which
had been made by Amraal and Willem Swartbooi, with the assistance
of Haddy of Windhoek and Tindall of Naosanabis, could not possibly
prevail. They wanted to form an association of the chiefs for the
maintenance of law and order, but they met with no support.

Jonker went to Walfish Bay to provide himself with the arms and
ammunition necessary for putting his plan into execution, but he
never reached the Bay. An urgent message from Windhoek recalled
him. The Mbanderus had surprised one of his posts, had killed the
herdsmen and driven the cattle away. Every one expected that
Jonker would march against these eastern Hereros and take a terrible

revenge, but Jonker did nothing. While Kahitjene was alive he did
not dare to deprive Windhoek of its protective garrison, but he was
actuated by this in taking a step which he otherwise would not have
taken: he made an alliance with Oasib, the chief of the Red Nation,
and entrusted him with the punitive expedition in the east. Oasib
had got what he had been wanting badly for a long time. He summoned all the Nama tribes to come and join in this expedition.
Tseib came from Keetmanshoop. A small number of the Namas from
Bethanie and Berseba took part. Both these tribes were so much
under the influence of Christianity that blind participation in this
warlike expedition was out of the question, for it was well known
that it was not a question of punishing those who were guilty, but of
the complete annihilation of every one, including those who were
innocent. A portion of Amraal's people joined up, and Jonker sent
a division of his Afrikanders. This commando did its best to make a
clean sweep. All the men upon whom hands could be laid were
killed. According to Jonker's instructions, the young women and
children were spared and carried off as slaves. As, however, the women
and children were unable to last out on the long homeward march,
they were dispatched as well. That happened in December 1849
and January 1850.

Early in February we find Oasib in Rehoboth. He had gone there
to make an alliance with Willem Swartbooi, and that against Jonker.
From his point of view a great wrong had been done him. Jonker
had laid claim to the lion's share of the booty and had sent the paramount chief away with almost empty hands. Willem Swartbooi
would not take any part in Oasib's schemes.

Oasib was very dissatisfied. In the east there was nothing left to
be got. He did not dare to attack Jonker alone and force him to
surrender his share of the spoils, so he decided to recoup himself at
the expense of the Hereros by attacking them single-handed. He
reckoned that Jonker would not oppose him in this instance. He felt,
however, that, for his missionary's sake, he had to have a good excuse
for a raid, and he found this excuse. The trader, Thomas Morris,
who had taken over his uncle's business, came to stay with the Red
Nation at Hoachanas. He had been to Windhoek shortly before and,
by way of introducing himself to his business friends there he had
expended a whole cask of brandy and had sold some powder and shot.
While he was there, however, his trek oxen ran away. It seemed as if

they had gone northwards to the Hereros, but no one could say where they were. Morris was acquainted with Oasib's intentions and schemes. He suggested to him that he should go and look for his oxen, and that he should seize this opportunity to take for himself whatever took his fancy. This seemed to Oasib quite a bright idea. Who could have any objection to his looking for a trader's oxen? It was a pity that his horses were not there. He had left them with Willem Swartbooi at Rehoboth, so he sent a messenger to Willem Swartbooi with instructions to fetch the horses. But Willem Swartbooi took a hand in the matter. The messenger had told him what Oasib intended to do. For the first time in his life, he sat down and dictated to a Nama, who was able to write, a letter to Oasib, directing it at the same time to the trader. This letter has been preserved and it reads as follows:

Rehoboth, the 17th May, 1850.

Dear Brother Cornelius (Oasib),

You must not shoot the Hereros down. No one has stolen the oxen, for they simply ran away in the night. You must send some one from Jonker's area.

Cornelius, you must consider the matter carefully. You are the chief. I am opposed to your doing things of this kind, and it is your duty to stop others who do them. I pray of you to do what your brother (Willem Swartbooi) says. You simply must do it. I am a man of peace. I accepted your horses in peace, and if you insist upon having them, I will restore them in peace again.

Thomas Morris, you are a trader. You have no right to encourage people to shoot each other. I am expecting you. I want to buy a bag of powder from you. When your cattle get lost you should tell the Captain about it, so that he can have a search made for them, and then you can go on your way.

I am, Yours truly, Freiderik Willem Swartbooi,
Captain.

The horses were not sent back. Instead of them Willem gave the messenger the following warning for Oasib: If Oasib attacks the Hereros, I shall follow him with my men on foot. Oasib thereupon abandoned his scheme, with the intention of taking it up again upon a more convenient occasion.

The massacre at Okahandja

Kahitjene had thought it wise to trek from Barmen to Okahandja. The veld was better there, Tjamuaha lived there, and a mission station was soon to be established. He erected his principal kraal to the west of the place under a high hill. New additional kraals were erected at Otjihua, Osona, and Okakango near by. Tjamuaha was living on the eastern side of Okahandja at the foot of a high mountain. Kahitjene paid the missionary, Kolbe, a visit and the latter was favourably impressed by him. Kolbe describes Kahitjene as a tall, distinguished-looking man with piercing eyes. 'He is certainly one of the most sensible men of his race. His behaviour is modest and unassuming and he is never officious or tiresome. He decorates his person lavishly with bead and iron ornaments.'

Kahitjene, from now onwards, not only sent his children to school, but himself attended church on Sundays. The reason for his doing so is evident from some of his sayings, which it is worth while relating. On Sunday, the 7th July, 1850, the Hereros collected for the service. There were as yet no Christians amongst them. Kolbe, who could speak Herero, had just opened the Bible to read out his text. Kahitjene demanded of him that he should tell him out of the book what Jonker's intentions were; whether he was going to make war against him, or not.

Kahitjene was in church again on the following Sunday. As he had no bell, Kolbe had, in the beginning, hoisted a flag to show that it was Sunday, and this was flying gaily in the breeze. Kahitjene looked at this strange object and remarked contentedly: 'Peace will continue. The flag points to the south and wards off the danger.' Windhoek lay southwards of Okahandja, and that was where Jonker lived.

It was just at this time that David Cloete, an Orlam assistant of Hahn's, came to Windhoek to find out how much truth there was in the rumours which were going about the country. He found Maharero in durance vile. Jonker had once again had 'Tjamuaha's calf' tied to the wagon wheel. Cloete wrote a hasty note and sent it by messenger to the chief, Zeraua, at Otjimbingwe. It read as follows: 'Maharero is constantly being tied up and ill-treated by Jonker. Is he your relative, or is he not?' Zeraua had the note read out to him and said: 'I know what I have got to do.' Then he sent his strongest man, Tjiuhundja, with a number of brave warriors, to take Maharero out of Windhoek.

Maharero, however, did not wait for the arrival of these people. When he was freed from his bonds and went home to his young wife, she greeted him with the bad news that, while he was under arrest, Jonker's people had stolen all their cattle. Then Maharero, with his

family and his Herero followers, made haste to get away and they went
to the missionary, Hahn, at Barmen as refugees. That was on the 5th
August. His intention was to stay at Barmen. When Hahn asked
him whether he was not afraid that Jonker would try to kill him, he
replied: 'I do not think so. I have saved Jonker's life three times.'
Then Tjiuhundja came there with his companions, and Maharero
went with them to his uncle, Zeraua, at Otjimbingwe.

Then Jonker began determinedly to rid Windhoek of all Hereros.
Those who did not escape immediately were dead men. Hereros
fleeing from Windhoek passed through Barmen daily. These were
the Hereros who had previously separated from their own people
and linked up with Jonker. The other Hereros, who had had nothing
to do with Jonker, hated the fugitives intensely, and they killed them
wherever they could lay hands on them.

Kahitjene's doom crept nearer. He knew very well that he would
get no help from Tjamuaha when Jonker appeared on the scene. On
the 21st August, Kahitjene went to Hahn to ask his advice. Hahn's
diary contains the following remark on this date: 'It is said that
Jonker Afrikander has made extensive plans and that he is equipping
a strong force. Kahitjene intends to leave and I feel that I cannot
dissuade him, although I can hardly think that Jonker would be so
wicked as to attack a mission station.' Kahitjene returned to Okahandja. He had made up his mind, he was going to take refuge with
Hahn at Barmen.

He left Okahandja with his cattle and all his people on the morning
of Friday, the 23rd August. The march was well regulated. The
children even went and said good-bye to Kolbe. The long column
had hardly disappeared from sight when heavy firing was heard.
This was about 9 o'clock. Jonker was there. Everything that Kahitjene had in Okahandja fell into his hands, i.e. his people, his cattle,
and his children. He himself, with a bodyguard of some twenty men
escaped, and reached Kolbe. The latter advised him to take refuge
in the church, as Jonker's men would respect this as a sanctuary.
Kahitjene followed this advice and was not set upon by Jonker's
fighting men, but when they discovered that Kahitjene was in the
church, they employed a ruse. They pretended to go away, so as to
tempt him to come out. The ruse succeeded. Kahitjene left the
church and hid himself behind some large stones. There they set
upon him. He defended himself bravely. He shot a Nama off his

horse with an arrow. While the others were attending to their wounded comrade, Kahitjene escaped. Then the murdering and robbing of the Hereros, who did not belong to Kahitjene's following, began. Women's hands and feet were hacked off to enable the copper bangles to be pulled off more quickly. Children were beaten or stabbed to death. It was only Tjamuaha's village that remained untouched. About 350 men, consisting of Namas, Bergdamas, Mbanderus, and Afrikanders had taken part in the attack, and they were armed with about 150 guns and had about 40 horses. Jonker came next day only to see the scene of the massacre. He was completely intoxicated.

Kahitjene fled during the night succeeding the attack to Hahn at Barmen. Soon after his arrival a messenger came from Kolbe saying that Jonker was at the missionary's house and that he was searching for Kahitjene. Hahn gave him the message and Kahitjene left Barmen the same night to go to his outposts, which were near the Omatako. Kahitjene had hardly left when Kolbe and his family reached Barmen. All his household effects were destroyed. Jonker's people had not laid hands on them, but some Hereros had broken the doors of his house open, had taken away everything made of iron, and made everything else utterly useless. As far as it was possible to do so, the wounded were brought into Barmen and attended to there.

After the massacre

Tjamuaha was now alone in Okahandja. He was no longer troubled by Kahitjene's cattle. It cannot be proved that he had a hand in the latter's downfall. Until to-day, however, rumour has it that he knew a great deal more than he thought it advisable to tell his rival, Kahitjene. Other tribes in that neighbourhood shared the same fate. Katjikuru, Katjikununa, and Mungunda lost the greater part of their people and their cattle. Tjamuaha always had a finger in the pie. It has been quite correctly said that, at this time, the flower of the Herero race was destroyed.

Jonker stayed for a few days with the cattle, as they trekked slowly along the road to Windhoek, and he was back in Windhoek again on the 1st September, 1850. The process of cleansing Windhoek of Hereros was resumed. Then he had all his own relatives, who had begun to get scattered, called back. Titus, his uncle, was already on the road to Blydeverwacht on the Orange River. They were all dissatisfied with Jonker. His cruelty was repellent to them. Haddy, who had brought them to Windhoek, had some days before the massacre

at Okahandja given up his work amongst the Afrikanders and gone
back to Capetown. Tindal at Naosanabis did the same. They handed
over their task to the Rhenish Mission. The fact is well worthy of
note, and undoubtedly redeems the good name of Jonker's relatives,
that, seeing that they had made it a condition of their going to
Windhoek that their missionary, Haddy, should go with them, they
left Jonker when Haddy gave up his work. This was not, of course,
the only reason for their departure. Jonker, the younger brother,
who was not entitled to the chieftainship of the Afrikander tribe,
did not permit either his brothers or his older relatives to occupy
any position next to himself. He stood upon 'his rights', which he
maintained and asserted when he commanded others to do things.
He based his claim to absolute sovereignty over the Afrikander tribe
on the ground that, when his father Jager went to Capetown with
Moffat, he took him with him. As has been told elsewhere the
Governor of the Cape Colony had this notorious man from the
Orange River introduced to him. He took his son, Jonker, with him
and the Governor asked the father, who was to be his successor in
the chieftainship after his death. Jager replied: 'The legal heir will
be my eldest son, but I do not fancy him. This one here (pointing
to Jonker) will be my successor.' The Governor expressed his agreement with this. Jonker based his rights on this incident, and he
allowed no one to dispute them.

2. MISSIONARY EFFORTS

Two missionary societies began their labours in South West Africa
in 1840. The London Missionary Society had its station in Bethanie,
and it was there that Schmelen collected the first Nama congregation.
After his unhappy departure the work was discontinued and, in 1840,
the London Society transferred its rights to the Rhenish Missionary
Society in Barmen.

The Wesleyan Missionary Society had already taken over, in 1834,
the work of the London Society in Bethanie, and the missionary,
Cook, laboured amongst the Bondelswarts and that part of the Afrikander tribe, which had stayed behind at the Orange River after
Jonker's campaign against the Hereros, and had made Blydeverwacht
its tribal head-quarters. Cook, however, was concerned about Jonker's people. In 1841 he journeyed to Windhoek and paid them a
short visit. The missionary, Tindall, established another station at

Naosanabis[1] on the Nosob, for Amraal's people, and some thirty miles south of Warmbad lay the station Hoole's Fontein. Thus, between the years 1840 and 1850, the Wesleyan Mission worked the three stations Warmbad (Nisbet's Bath), Hoole's Fontein, and Naosanabis (Wesley Vale), and regarded Windhoek as a branch institution.

Now Captain Alexander had, at Jonker's instance, gone with the request for a missionary for Jonker's Afrikanders both to the Rhenish and the Wesleyan Missionary Societies, and, in addition, Jonker had requested Schmelen to get him a missionary. Schmelen wrote very emphatically to the Rhenish Missionary Society at Barmen, asking them not only for a missionary for Jonker, but urging them to take up missionary work amongst the Namas and more especially amongst the Hereros. At their general meeting, held on the 4th March, 1841, the Society passed a unanimous resolution to send the missionary, Hugo Hahn, from Riga in Livonia out to Africa, with instructions that he should settle in Bethanie for a while and work in conjunction with Heinrich Kleinschmidt, who was going out from Blasheim in Westphalia. From there he was to look for an opportunity of establishing a mission amongst the Hereros.

Hahn and Kleinschmidt arrived in Africa. They went first to see Schmelen at Kommagas. The latter was able so to direct the movements of them both that Kleinschmidt, who became his son-in-law, settled first of all in Bethanie, but went from there, in company with Hahn, to Jonker's tribe at Windhoek, when the missionary, Knudsen, was capable of carrying on the work at Bethanie. Hahn and Kleinschmidt arrived in Windhoek on the 9th December, 1842. Johannes Bam from Capetown, the Catechist, was already there. They stayed there until October 1844, when the missionary, Haddy, of the Wesleyan Missionary Society came to Windhoek. The political considerations which led Jonker to thrust on one side the Rhenish missionaries, whom he had originally greeted with pleasure, have been dealt with previously. To avoid discord, Hahn and Kleinschmidt handed over their work to Haddy and tried to establish themselves in Okahandja. Continuous drought compelled them to go to the strong springs at Otjikango, where they established the first mission station amongst the Hereros on the 31st October, 1844, and called the place Barmen.

After the preliminary work of establishment had been done, Kleinschmidt left his colleague, Hahn, and proceeded to Anis, or Rehoboth,

[1] Naosanabis or Wesley Vale adjoins the present hamlet of Pretorius on the Nosob River.—*Ed.*

in order to labour amongst the Swartbooi tribe there. He reached there on the 11th May, 1845.

Further missionaries arrived. Rath and Scheppmann were the first of the Rhenish missionaries to land at Walfish Bay, and from there they travelled to Otjikango (Barmen), which now served as the mission centre of Hereroland, while Rehoboth served the same purpose for Namaland. Scheppmann founded a mission station for the Topnaar tribe, which lived in the dunes round Walfish Bay, at Rooibank near Walfish Bay, in the year 1845, and, in 1849, Rath established a second mission station for the Hereros at Otjimbingwe. At the same time Kolbe settled amongst the Hereros at Okahandja, and the missionary, Samuel Hahn, began in October 1850 to collect the tribe of the Orlam chief, Paul Goliath, in Berseba, at the foot of Mount Bruk-karos.

3. THE PROGRESS OF CIVILIZATION AND ITS OBSTACLES

So it was that the Rhenish Missionary Society extended, in the short period of ten years, a network of mission stations throughout that part of South West Africa which was then known. In 1850 the problem of settling the Namas and the Hereros had been theoretically solved by establishing tribal centres at particular places, where each tribe had its spiritual and intellectual home in the shape of its church and its school, and this solution had been tested out in practice. The Nama tribes of Walfish Bay, Bethanie, and Rehoboth, soon became quite accustomed to the idea of this home. The Orlam tribes, that is Paul Goliath's and Amraal's people and Jonker's Afrikanders, recognized the fact that they belonged to Berseba, Naosanabis, and Windhoek, respectively. The Bondelswarts clung to Warmbad. In 1850 there were only two centres for the Hereros, Otjikango (Barmen) and Otjimbingwe. The people who were still without tribal centres at this time were the Veldskoendraers and Tseib's people in the south of Namaland, and Jan Booi's tribe and the Grootdoden in the north. The Red Nation at Hoachanas, which had provided itself with a tribal centre without any intervention on the part of the missionaries, was on the point of taking to itself a missionary. The Mbanderus in the east, and all the Herero tribes living north of the Swakop River, were still entirely nomadic in their habits.

Road-making

It only pays to make roads where there are permanent centres of habitation. It follows naturally that the progress of civilization in

South West Africa is measurable by the number, length, and nature of the roads. The missionaries used roads for getting by ox-wagon those necessaries of life which the sterile land did not afford them. The Orlams used roads, for they had learnt the value of the ox-wagon during the time that they lived in the Cape Colony and on the banks of the Orange River. Roads were used, too, by traders, who traversed the country with wagons and carts after it had been somewhat opened up. Seeing that the whole country is to-day a network of roads, which are either good or not too good, it may seem of minor importance to inquire who the makers of the earliest roads were, but it is not right that a history of the country should pass by, without mention, those pioneers who found how the ways went and made them into roads.

Schmelen's old road to Oas had been washed out by the rains, but it was still quite recognizable. Samuel Hahn repaired it in 1849, by cutting down the bushes, which had grown in it in the meantime, and filling up the pot-holes, which had been washed out by the running water. In South West Africa a heavy rainstorm turns every road into a running river, scouring the wagon spoors into deep ruts, and tearing huge holes in the rained-soddened soil. Hahn, too, made a road from Bethanie to Guldbrandsdalen, and from there to Berseba. It is true that it was exceedingly difficult to travel, for there was one spot where a steep ascent could not be circumvented. All the goods had to be off-loaded there, the empty wagon had to be dragged up the mountain, and the goods had to be carried up by pack-oxen or on human backs; but the important thing about it was that it was the link between Bethanie and Berseba.

Jonker at Windhoek was likewise amongst the road-makers. When he was expecting the missionaries, Hahn and Kleinschmidt, in 1842, he made a road through the Auas Mountains. Even if it fell far short of the perfection of a European highroad, it was a great help to travellers. We must not forget that the road through the Auas Mountains had until then been an absolute bugbear to transport riders. Kleinschmidt writes in 1842:

'In the Siebel Mountains (the Auas Mountains had been named the Siebel Mountains after a merchant in Elberfeld called Siebel, who was the treasurer of the Rhenish Missionary Society at that time) we reaped the fruits of Jonker's praiseworthy efforts, for he has had quite a good road made, where it was otherwise practically impossible to get through; those who made it consumed two oxen and seven sheep in the process.'

Jonker proceeded to make a road to Walfish Bay. He began the first stretch of it from Windhoek in 1843. He then set the Namas and Bergdamas, who lived in the country through which the road was to go, to work on it, and by 1844 it was finished. Hugo Hahn, who used this road to go to Walfish Bay, writes about it:

'Jonker has made, by a remarkable effort, a highroad through this part of the country, which was formerly impassable for a wagon. I must confess that, nowhere in the Colony, have I seen a work of this sort being undertaken. It is scarcely credible that people with hardly any tools, or generally with none at all, could have carried out a task of this magnitude. Enormous rocks have been dug out, others have been shattered with loose stones, trees and bushes have been rooted out, and so on. This road, which is between twenty-five and thirty feet broad, will connect the interior with Walfish Bay.'

Jonker's road to the Bay ran from Windhoek in a westerly direction, over Heusis and Kurikaub, to the southern bank of the Swakop and, then without crossing the river, turned southwards over Onanis, Tsaobis, and Tinkas to the Kuiseb River, in the bed of which it went down to Rooibank and Walfish Bay. When it was finished, Jonker busied himself with plans for constructing a road from Windhoek to the Waterberg, but the sudden change in his way of living, and the way in which he developed, prevented these plans from ever being executed.

Hahn and Kleinschmidt, however, made a road from Windhoek to Okahandja, and from there to Otjikango, which was improved by Kolbe.

Thus was the pioneer work in road-making accomplished, and that part of South West Africa which was explored was opened up for wagon traffic as early as 1845. Bethanie could be reached through Sendlingsdrift or Ramansdrift,[1] along Schmelen's or Hendrik Hop's routes. From there one might travel, without any great danger to wheel or wagon, through Rehoboth to Windhoek, and from Windhoek the Bay road led to Walfish Bay, and there was likewise a road to southern Hereroland.

It was, however, a great waste of time for people living at Otjikango to go to the Bay via Windhoek. The conference of missionaries, which sat at Otjikango in 1845, decided that the young missionary, Scheppmann, who was to be stationed in the district of Walfish Bay,

---

[1] A 'drift' means a ford in a river, through which a highway passes. These two drifts through the Orange River formed the earliest approach to South West Africa and they are still used for wagon traffic to-day.—Ed.

should try to find a short cut through to Jonker's Bay road, somewhere near Kurikaub. The experiment failed for Scheppmann came to grief on the road and was brought back to Otjikango badly hurt. After his recovery he had to travel to Rooibank and Walfish Bay by way of Jonker's road, and it was left to his colleague, Rath, to open up the road from Otjikango to Otjimbingwe, and from there to Walfish Bay, in 1850.

The new Bay road brought considerable relief. It now became possible to fetch foodstuffs from the Bay when a ship touched there. Up to now everything had had to be fetched from Capetown by ox-wagon. It had taken Rath eleven months on the road to get provisions from there, and he had naturally had to load all kinds of goods for Rehoboth, Bethanie, and Berseba as well, and fully half of the provisions were used up for the wagon boys, because he did not know how to keep them in food with his gun. In the meantime, the people in Otjikango had had to live on meat, milk, and veld-food, for the garden had proved a failure. Hahn writes in the famine year, 1846:

'The locusts are doing their utmost to destroy the little that the rains are causing to grow. There is no part of the world which is so thoroughly cursed as South West Africa. Thorns are its shield; the trees and bushes are full of them. Even on the plains, where there are neither trees nor bushes, one's feet are often badly hurt by the thorns of creepers, which are hidden in the grass.'

On the top of all that a hail-storm swept over Otjikango, and then the river came down and destroyed the last hope of any possibility whatever of getting through without provisions from outside. Once the Bay road was opened up, their needs never became so urgent as they had been in former years.

Postal arrangements

When villages and roads have been established, it becomes possible to organize and arrange a system of postal communication of a simple kind. The post plays an unobtrusive, but very important part in the process of civilization. The beginnings of postal arrangements in South West Africa belong to the history of the development of its civilization. Any one who wanted to send or to receive a letter in very early days, had to send a messenger to Capetown at his own expense. Many letters were, of course, sent when opportunities arose, and, after they had passed through many hands, they might perhaps reach their addressees after the lapse of years. The earliest missionaries complained that they often received letters which were two years old and that that had to be altered. The question was discussed at the conference and a post was established, in the working of which the chiefs of the different tribes took part. Letters from Europe were brought by the postal authorities to Kommagas south of the Orange River. The post from South West Africa had to be sent there and the European mail fetched from there. Two messengers, duly provided with food, went by stages from Otjikango to Windhoek, and then from Windhoek to Rehoboth. Willem Swartbooi saw to the postal arrangements between there and Bethanie, and David Christian had the post taken to Kommagas. Traders, travellers, and hunters were all allowed to make use of this system. Orlams and Namas had, too, the opportunity of sending letters to their distant relatives, if they were able to write, or some one in their neighbourhood could write letters for them. The charge on this side was, in the beginning, very small.

A new arrangement functioned from about 1848. Kolbe writes from Otjikango during this year:

'It is the fate of my letter to traverse the whole of Namaland in a Nama's rawhide wallet, and then to find its way through the length of the Cape Colony, where it finally gets to a proper post office in Cape Town. It is very fortunate that the Namas have such great respect for a letter that they look upon it as something sacred, and that they would rather lose their last shred of clothing than the letter. The bigger the seal is, the greater their respect for it. This is the reason that the missions in the interior of Africa receive their letters as regularly as the missionaries in the Cape Colony.'

Of course it might sometimes happen that the post would go wrong. For instance, in 1848, the post was given to two Namas in Bethanie to take to Kommagas. One of the two post boys was killed by a lion, while the other lost his way and was never heard of again, with the result that the whole post was lost.

The whole arrangement, which had been organized with so much difficulty, almost came to grief in 1848. Willem Swartbooi of Rehoboth refused to send the post on. Letters had come to Rehoboth from Bethanie about the evil-doings of Jan Booi, who had stolen some cattle from the Hereros. This caused a great deal of feeling in Rehoboth against their dishonest neighbour. But Willem had been going about with the very same ideas in his head, and Kleinschmidt had, time and again, dissuaded him from pursuing them. He now regarded the post as a betrayer of people's thoughts, and, as chief, he at least wanted to know what the letters contained before he was going to send them farther. It was war-time and the fact that a chief, who could neither read nor write, wanted, of his own initiative, to set up a censorship of all letters, shows what progress civilization had already made in this respect. Actually the censorship was never imposed.

Tribal organization

In the very early days, the old form of tribal organization, with its transmission of traditional laws and customs by word of mouth, served its purpose. When more modern times had set in, neither the law, nor the tradition of it, remained effective. In Bethanie, the arising of a question about the succession to the chieftainship showed that there was need for written laws, and for proper guardians of the law, elected by the tribe. Some fixed regulations regarding judicial decisions and punishments had to be framed, unless the law, and all decisions and punishments under it, were to be left entirely to the arbitrary discretion of the chief. The real chief of Bethanie was a minor, and an uncle was acting as regent for him. It was then decided that, on the day the legitimate heir took up office, a new constitution should be introduced, and that a 'Statute Book',[1] containing all the necessary regulations, should come into effect in all matters concerning the tribe. Knudsen undertook to compile a book of this kind. This tribal statute was passed on the 17th and 18th October, 1848, and the chief and his tribal council were solemnly installed in office.

The Statute Book, which is still in existence and of which the principal laws are still effective, consisted of three parts. The first part comprised a history of the tribe, with provisions regarding the succession to the chieftainship. The second part contained the laws, and the penalties for their transgression. The third part consisted of commentary, and was undoubtedly so planned that necessary amendments could be made, and new provisions added, as time went on.

Some of the regulations are worth mentioning. The eldest son followed his father in the chieftainship. A woman could never become chief; the experience which the Red Nation had had with Games was clearly the reason for this provision. The chief must appoint two intelligent men as judges, and he himself sits as president of the court in court cases. The people must elect seven members of the tribal

---

[1] In the text this book is described as a 'Reichsbuch', or book of government. The term 'Statute Book' seems to describe it adequately.—*Ed.*

council, at a general meeting of the tribe, and one of these must be
able to interpret from Dutch into Nama. Another member must be
chosen from amongst the elders of the congregation. The chief and
the two judges become members of the tribal council *ex officio*. The
chief acts as chairman of the tribal council. On the 2nd January in
every third year the seven elected members of the tribal council must
either be re-elected or newly elected.

Further statutory provisions are as follows: Murder is punishable
by death. Dagga may not be either smoked, planted, or dealt in.
Men and women may not settle their differences by personal conflict,
but must lodge complaints with the judges. Polygamy is forbidden.
A man is allowed to have only one wife. If any one steals a cow, he
has to compensate the person from whom he stole it by giving him
five cows. Those suffering from venereal disease are not allowed to
live in the village, but must put their huts right away in the veld
until they are well again.

The Superintendent in Capetown, Hahn, who was in charge of the
Nama mission, makes the following remark about this tremendous
task which was so well-meant: 'The Statute Book saw the light of
day too soon. It is time and circumstances which make laws. The
person who makes them before their time must be omniscient.' The
passing of the years has proved that he was not entirely wrong, but
in the beginning it had the effect of arousing the public conscience and
consolidating the tribal morality.

As the inhabitants of Berseba were well acquainted with and, to
some extent, related to the tribe of Bethanie, they likewise adopted
this system of tribal law, with some minor alterations. Rehoboth,
too, did not want to be left behind. The discussions over particular
provisions turned into angry debates. It seemed too severe, for instance, that the penalty for murder should be death, and finally the
disputants agreed upon the ambiguous formula that murderers and
homicides should be punished according to their deserts. In Rehoboth, too, a distinction was drawn between burgesses, who were entitled to vote, and mere inhabitants, who were not so entitled. It was
decided that only those who owned at least five cows and fifty sheep
should have full rights of citizenship. Those who could not show
property to this amount were not eligible for election, nor could they
take any part in one. The constitution was adopted in general
meeting of the tribe, on the 24th and 25th August, 1849, and the
elections were held on the 27th August.

The laws had, in one respect, a very important result, even if many of the provisions turned out to be inoperable, and this was that in Bethanie, Berseba, and Rehoboth blood-feuds became a thing of the past. Until then, it had been a duty, amongst people of Nama race, for the nearest relatives of a man who had been killed by violence to avenge his death, at their own convenience, without the chief having anything to do with the proceedings. From then onwards, matters of this sort were brought before the judges of the tribe. The Statute Book of Bethanie was, for this reason alone, very helpful in the cultural development of the tribes which adopted it. We shall see that, in the course of time, the fact that the three tribes were governed by the same laws had the effect of bringing them closer together in times both of war and peace. These laws, of course, applied to the whole tribe and not merely to the small section which was Christian.

Trade and traders

Under normal conditions, every European in an uncivilized country is a pioneer of civilization. In dozens of ways the natives notice things about him which are strange to them. His actions are peculiar, and make them think, and his mere presence leads them to imitate his clothes, his ways of living, and his conduct. He is, moreover, the representative of a race, the superiority of which is undoubted, and one which is constantly imposing its will upon them. It is a sorry business, when there happen to be amongst these Europeans people whose influence is bad, as appears so clearly to have been the case with Jonker.

But South West Africa has, to some degree, to thank these men for its development, for it was they who forced their way through the country in all directions as explorers, hunters, traders, and prospectors, and it is for that reason that history has to take them into account. It is not possible to compile a complete list of all the Europeans who came to South West Africa between 1840 and 1850, but the names of such as are known are mentioned here.

A farmer, named Visagie, was living at 'Swartmodder, the present Keetmanshoop, with his wife and son round about 1830, or even, perhaps a little earlier. When Titus Afrikander went to join his nephew, Jonker, at Windhoek, he tried to attack and loot the Namas who had settled in Visagie's vicinity. Visagie succeeded, however, with the aid of his son and his rifle, in beating off the attack, and Titus had a narrow escape from the bullets which were intended for him. The inducement to settle at Swartmodder and to live there for very many years (Willem van Reenen found a Gideon Visagie in Swartmodder in 1792, and perhaps it is the same man who fought Titus Afrikander, or even his father) may have been that excellent pasturage for horses was to be had round about this spot. There was no horse-sickness there, and the breeding of horses was a paying business at that time when the price of a horse was thirty oxen. The chief, Tseib, who belonged to the Red Nation of Hoachanas but lived in the same part, made use of this advantage by taking and grazing the Namas' and Orlams' horses in the rainy season, when danger threatened them. He wanted, however, such a high price for the service that Tibot of Goliath's tribe, for one, refused to send his horses there in 1842, and lost them all in consequence.

Traders turned up at Bethanie in 1842 and did a brisk business in brandy. As they not incorrectly regarded the missionary as their enemy, they tried to bring him into discredit with the Namas. Their strongest argument was that the Namas ought to be very careful of him as he was trying to make English subjects of them.

The traders, Morris and Lewton, were living at Walfish Bay by 1845. Morris had lived previously in St. Helena and he carried on the business of exporting Herero oxen to the island, but this came to an end in 1846. The Cape Government probably put a stop to it when they heard of the way in which Morris got hold of the supplies of oxen which reached Walfish Bay. This is a pure supposition which is not supported by documentary evidence. As a matter of interest, it may be mentioned that Morris was for a little time in occupation of the house on the estate at Longwood, in which the Emperor Napoleon formerly lived. He used to tell the story of how Napoleon had had a way of annoying the Governor, Sir Hudson Lowe, by insisting upon eating nothing but ox-tongues, which could only be obtained with great difficulty and expense.

Mr. Dixon had built a house close to the shore at Walfish Bay and lived there with his wife and family. Captain Grayburn, too, had his home there, and his house was placed at the disposal of travellers who landed at the Bay, and had to wait until an opportunity occurred for proceeding up-country. It was from Walfish Bay that traders set out on their trading trips into the interior, and the natives often came there from far distant parts of the interior to make their purchases, amongst which arms and ammunition figured largely.

In 1848, Messrs. Ridge and Noblenoon took Jonker's Bay road to

Rehoboth, and went from there to Bethanie, returning to Capetown
via Angra Pequena, for the purpose of getting to know something of
the country.

James Sherman and Stewardson, Morris's son-in-law, made the
first trading trip to the Hereros without Windhoek's sanction. They
ventured to go to Otjikango in 1849, by way of Rath's Bay road, with
guns and iron spears, and to push forward from there northwards, in
the direction of the Omatako Mountains, into unexplored country.
They found there an outpost belonging to Kahitjene, and the
Hereros were very pleased with guns and spears as a medium of
exchange. But Jonker took this trading expedition of theirs very
much amiss.

Hans Larsen stayed for some time, from 1850 onwards, with Rath
at Otjimbingwe and helped him to lay out the mission station. He
later joined Andersson in his exploring expeditions.

Two sailors lived for some time alone on the lower Swakop river.
Thirst for adventure had led them to desert from their ship. They
had made their way into the interior in the company of some traders
and had acquired some fifty oxen there. Jonker ordered them to
remain down in the Swakop valley. One of them was called Bill and
hailed from Hamburg.

Trading brought with it all kinds of changes. Clothing and tools
came into the country. Those Namas and Orlams who thought anything of themselves, adopted European clothing. Even if these clothes
were worn only on Sundays, to church, or when a traveller paid the
village a visit, the process of clothing the body made great progress,
and the mission encouraged it in every way. Trade brought, too,
large numbers of guns into the country, and we have seen that it was
not only for hunting that they were used. The unconscionable introduction of guns, ammunition, and bullet-moulds intensified the
carrying on of the one-sided warfare against the Hereros until they
were almost exterminated, for Jonker became very angry if his traders
sold them guns. The trade in liquor became an evil and a danger to
the community. The history of the Bethanie and the Afrikander
tribes affords sad proof of this statement.

The considerable traffic, which trading brought in its train, produced unexpected results, of which the following is an example.
When Hahn paid the Red Nation a visit at Hoachanas in 1843, he
found a new institution there, about which he tells as follows:

'During the last year a kind of police service has been established by the

Red Nation, which has for its object the provision of every possible comfort for strangers, whether Namas, Basters, or Europeans. When the traveller dismounts or outspans there, he finds some officials waiting to take his horse or his oxen, to lead it until cool, unsaddle it, water and graze it, and to bring it home of an evening, so that it is safe from the lions. They see that he is duly provided with milk, water, and wood, and often with meat, and they make sure that the children do not annoy him. A roomy, clean mat house is given him to live in. If the stranger is alone, some one has to sleep with him to keep the fire going, or perform other services for him. A special sleeping-place was put up for me, as they know how we dislike bugs. Directly the traveller wants to leave, he tells the official, who advises the chief, and his horse or his oxen will be there at whatever time he fixes, even if it should be the very middle of the night. It never enters anyone's head either to ask for payment or to offer it.'

Another improvement, which accompanied increasing business, was the introduction of ox-wagons and carts. The time when people jumped over a wagon spoor in superstitious fear, and regarded the wagon itself as a great big animal, was past. Even the trekkers recognized that this movable house offered considerable advantages. The pack-ox had to learn to become a trek-ox. When Goliath's and Swartbooi's people gave up their nomadic way of life, the former entered Berseba with all their possessions in four ox-wagons, and the latter went into Rehoboth with three. Jonker had dozens of ox-wagons, and Amraal's people went to Capetown in 1849 to buy four new ones. An ox-wagon could be procured for from forty to sixty large oxen.

The country's exports consisted of ivory, cattle, and sheep. Cattle were chiefly exported to St. Helena, but the Cape Colony provided a good market, too. A beginning was made, in a small way, with the exportation of other things. In 1843 Bam took a load of skins down to Capetown and got forty-two Cape dollars for it. For two young lions, which he took down with him at the same time, he got the goodly sum of 600 Cape dollars.[1]

The white trader's example started the natives trading amongst themselves. In Otjikango, for instance, the impoverished Hereros grew tobacco and calabashes. The latter were quite indispensable in every Herero household for the preparation of sour milk. Hereros then came from far and near to Otjikango and gave stock in exchange for both these necessary commodities, thus restoring the inhabitants

[1] The Rixdaler of the Cape had, in those days, a purchasing power of from 3s. to 3s. 6d. of our present money.—*Ed.*

to some degree of prosperity. Those who had no cattle brought steel beads, copper rings, spears, axes, and knives for sale. As things sometimes became rather too lively owing to the haggling over prices, Hahn saw the necessity for establishing a market place with some measure of stricter control. A cattle-kraal was erected and strangers who wanted to sell stock, had to put the animals into it. The people who wished to do business met together under a large camel-thorn tree, and concluded their transactions there. Perfect peace reigned on market days. No one dared to make trouble, strike any one else, or steal from him, lest he should be turned out and chased away. A similar market was in existence for a time amongst Jonker's people at Windhoek.

Obstacles to civilization

The dawn of civilization was, for South West Africa, the gloaming of the Stone Age. Speaking generally it is correct to say that the Stone Age in South West Africa was past in 1850, although many a stone knife must have been fashioned and used after that date. It was not nearly so difficult to use a stone knife as one is inclined to think. On Bam's first journey to Windhoek in 1842, he came across some people along the road who had killed two hippopotami. The hunters, who were Namas, loaded four pack-oxen with meat and left the remainder to the Bergdamas 'who were there when the meat was cut up, and were as handy with their stone knives as our people are with their steel ones'.

Since everything can become a blessing or a curse, according to the use it is put to, iron, powerful factor for promoting civilization though it may be, may likewise prove an obstacle in its path. North and south could never have started a war of extermination, with all its deplorable results, had it not been for metal fire-arms. The uneven struggle, which was accompanied by serious moral and economic crises throughout the whole country, would not have brought in its train the dreadful consequences it did, had it not been that, both in north and south, the Stone Age came up against the commencement of the Iron Age.

The superiority of the south resulted in the despoiling of the north and east. The Mbanderus especially were massacred, robbed of all their possessions, and carried off into slavery by the Red Nation. That was a very significant retrogression. Until then the Namas had had Bergdamas as their overseers; and Bushmen, belonging to the

Saan tribe, as their servants; but the Herero prisoners were borne off into actual slavery.

With regard to the taming of the Bushmen, Bam tells of an incident, which took place in 1842, which, even if it was not the general practice, shows that there was a considerable modification of the rude way of doing it in some parts of the country. He writes: 'If the Namas see Bushmen, when they are out hunting, they chase them until they catch one; they then treat this one well, give him presents and send him back to his own people. In this way they gain their confidence and get them to come and stay with them.'

In the selfsame year, however, the chief of Bethanie was occupied with the idea of exterminating the Bergdamas to the west of Bethanie, not because they had done him any harm, but because they occupied a piece of country which the chief wanted for his own tribe, and cultivated tobacco there. It annoyed him that the Bergdamas should acquire, through their trade in tobacco, small flocks of goats, while the Namas' goats decreased in number. He absolutely refused to allow the missionary to visit these Bergdamas, and he made it impossible for him to go to them, as he had intended to do, by issuing an order that no one was to go with him to the Bergdama settlement. It was impossible to visit them without Namas as guides. The Bergdamas have, however, disappeared since then from the country round about Bethanie. No one knows what has happened to them.

The procedure which Bam mentions was not that which most of the Namas adopted with regard to the Bushmen. In 1859 a wealthy Nama called Umab was living to the west of Rehoboth. His son died, and in accordance with ancient custom, Umab called in a sorcerer to determine the cause of his son's untimely decease, and he attributed it to the Bushmen. Umab had a number of Bushmen servants. He had three of the men seized, flogged them unmercifully, and then threw them into a fire which had been made in a game pit. When these three had succumbed in the fire, he had four more Bushmen killed in the same way. Shortly afterwards, Kleinschmidt arrived at Umab's werf, where he found three Bushmen women and eleven children in a very sorry state. He could not carry out his intention of taking these poor creatures with him to Rehoboth, as Umab asked too large a sum for freeing them. The tribal council, however, took the matter up and sent fifteen armed horsemen to Umab, had the Bushmen women and children taken away from him, and divided them amongst the more kindly disposed Swartboois in Rehoboth. Soon afterwards the Red Nation carried off everything Umab possessed. We have here a good example of, on the one side, the enslavement and ill treatment of the defenceless and, on the other, of the liberation and protection of members of another tribe.

Alcohol, in the form of honey- and sugar-beer and of the more expensive luxury, brandy, was a great obstacle to the progress of civilization, and there is no need to waste words about it, and the smoking of dagga can be placed in exactly the same category. It is hardly possible to form any conception to-day how universal the craving for dagga was amongst the Bergdamas, Namas, and Saan. It brought many of them to financial ruin, for dagga was expensive and had to be paid for with stock. Beside this, it undermined the whole physical system and many people lost their reason through its poisonous effect. While the fight which the missionaries made against alcohol had little effect, their struggle to suppress the cultivation of dagga met with considerable success. Hugo Hahn took up the fight against dagga with an almost excessive zeal. At the time that he first came to stay in Windhoek he had, with Jonker's permission, systematically removed every dagga plant from the Afrikanders' gardens and had them burnt. His journey to Walfish Bay in 1844 was in the nature of a dagga campaign. At one of Jonker's outstations which he passed, he collected all the herdsmen, lectured them as to the dangers of the weed, and succeeded in having all the gardens cleared of it without encountering any resistance. He repeated his discourse at another of Jonker's sheep posts with the same result. According to his own calculation and to the statements of the people there, dagga to the value of a hundred sheep was burnt. The same thing happened at a Bergdama werf some distance farther on. The Bergdamas were the chief growers of dagga and they carried on a trade in it as far as Ovamboland. When he came to Tsaobis his reputation had spread to such an extent that the Bergdamas pulled up their dagga without any demand being made upon them and threw it into the river, which was in flood at the time. His actions were undoubtedly too drastic, and the burning of the dagga at Windhoek, without the consent of those who had grown it, helped very little, while it had the effect of making a section of the community his enemies. There are occasions, however, when one who is really anxious for the public weal, is forced to take strong measures, when he is in the position to carry them out, and when the wise teacher is compelled to think and act for the people, when they lack understanding, provided they recognize him as their mentor as was the case with Hahn.

The advance of civilization is along a road which leads, not only forward, but upwards as well. The path which leads upwards cannot be followed, especially with people of the kind that the Namas, Bergdamas, Bushmen, and Hereros were in 1850, without the devotion of an immense amount of energy, effort, and toil. Knudsen, writing in 1842, says that he met a Nama on his travels, who, so far as he could recollect, had only washed himself twice in thirty-five years, and Kolbe writes about the inhabitants of Walfish Bay in 1848: 'No trace is to be found amongst them of any ancient heathen religion. It is true that they talk about evil spirits, but they know no higher being than tobacco, i.e. dagga. Tobacco is their god and their heaven. The man who has plenty of tobacco is, in their estimation, the wealthiest and luckiest person on earth.'

4. THE EXPLORATION OF THE COUNTRY

The extension of geographical knowledge

It might have been expected that, after Captain Alexander's successful explorations in 1837, at least one explorer of note would have made South West Africa, with all its unsolved riddles, the object of his investigations during the following ten years, but that was not the case, The country, barren, dry and war-stricken as it was, did not offer sufficient prospects of safety and success for exploration on a large scale. The task of exploring the country devolved upon the men who had come to settle there and were compelled by their calling to increase their knowledge of the country, to study the languages, customs, and habits of the natives, and to convey to the outside world what there was to be found in South West Africa and what went on there. We possess very few accounts by the traders of that time of their experiences and observations, but the reports and diaries of the missionaries contain a great deal of information about the country.

Knudsen and Hahn went right through the district occupied by the tribes of Bethanie and Berseba. They went to Tseib's tribe at Swartmodder[1] as well, and they left no single settlement in this enormous territory unvisited. It would be a waste of time to give

---

[1] Keetmanshoop.

the names of the places for, with the exception of Swartmodder, none of them have developed, and many of the names of those days are no longer known, even to the Namas who live in those parts to-day. Before he entered the mission seminary, Knudsen had been a lithographer and he knew how to paint. Pictures of well-known chiefs of those times, painted by him and mentioned in his reports, are preserved to-day in the archives of the Rhenish Mission Society at Barmen. He went specially to Windhoek, too, to paint Hereros there. Photography was, of course, as yet unknown.

In 1843 Hahn set out from Windhoek to visit the Red Nation at Hoachanas, which had hitherto been known only from hearsay, and he brought back reliable information about them. He, too, was the very first European, so far as is known, to cross the southern boundary of Hereroland. This he did in February of the same year when he visited the Herero kraals, made notes about their customs and ways of living and got to know their principal chiefs. Accompanied by Mr. Stewardson, he journeyed in 1849 into the unknown country to the north, saw the Omatako Mountains and caught a glimpse of the Erongo Mountains in the far distance. In 1847 he went from Otji-kango to Walfish Bay. On this occasion he gave the mountain, which lies half-way between Otjimbingwe and Otjikango, the name of Lievenberg in honour of Prince Lieven of the Baltic Provinces, who supported him financially. It has kept that name up to the present day. He went down the 'Rhein', i.e. the Swakop River, and reached Tsaobis, and from there he did the rest of the journey by Jonker's road. A black rhinoceros crossed his path and a troop of five lions threatened to attack him one night.

When Hahn went to Capetown in 1843, he had a long interview with the Governor of the Cape Colony. He furnished him with a report on Hereroland and he provided the Government officials with a map he had made of the country. A passport in English and Portuguese was made out for him at his own request, in case he should want to enter the Portuguese territory on his future travels.

Whenever he got the opportunity, Hahn did his best to gain information about the northern part of Hereroland and about Ovamboland, by questioning the natives who came from those parts. He learnt that Ovamboland was entirely without any mountains, and that trees without branches, having large leaves and edible fruits grew there, i.e. palms, and that it was an agricultural country. On both sides of Ovamboland were strongly flowing rivers, and beyond these was the strange race of the *Ourontu umiti*, the people of which were reddish in colour, wore clothes and hats, had beards and long hair, and lived in small houses, not unlike those of the missionaries. (Here we have once again the old story of the people in the north with 'long hair and linen clothing', i.e. the Portuguese in Angola.) Beyond the *Ourontu umiti*, however, the world came to an end.

Rath was the explorer of the right bank of the Swakop River between Otjikango and Swakopmund. In 1850 he undertook, too, the exploration of the Erongo Mountains, where he was repeatedly molested by rhinoceroses. On the way back he passed through what is to-day Karibib, where there was then nothing but a spring, on account of which the Hereros had given the place the name of Otjondjomboimue, which means 'the place of the fountain'.

One, McRidgie, the survivor of a shipwreck, who turned up in Rehoboth in 1848, calculated by means of his instruments the geographical situation of the place and found it to be Lat. 23° 46′ S., and Long. 17° 52′ E.

Both sides of Jonker's Bay road became very well known to the numerous traders, who went to Windhoek by it. Although they left no written record behind them, they told their contemporaries quite a lot, and so we can take it that the country was considerably better known than the documentary evidence would lead us to suppose.

Schleppmann crossed the country lying between the lower part of the Swakop's course and the Kuiseb River. He reached Heigamchab, or Kai-gamchab, 'the place where cold water is plentiful', and he went as far as the Roessing Mountains, which had been discovered previously from the sea and had been given the name of Mt. Calquan. Bill of Hamburg was his companion on this journey; he was leading a lonely life in this region as the first farmer on the Swakop River.

Jonker's services in increasing the knowledge of the country ought not to be overlooked. He brought back valuable information from the many journeys he made into the unknown parts of Hereroland. It was from him that the earliest information of the existence of the Erongo Mountains, the Waterberg, and the Sandveld was obtained. From his many raids he brought back, too, much similar information, until, after 1845, he was interested no longer in the places and the country round about them, but only in the grazing grounds, from which he could most easily carry off cattle.

The mission inspector, Dr. Richter, embodied the results of all these journeys, and the information gathered in the course of them, in a map with the scale of about 1 in 6,500,000. He used for the purpose the map of Captain Alexander's journey, drawn by Arrowsmith, and added to it all the topographical material which had been collected since 1837. It was published again in 1918 by Prof. Dr. E. Moritz in his book, *Mitteilungen aus den deutschen Schutzgebieten*.

Native languages and literature

We can hardly imagine to-day the difficulties presented by the Nama language to the men who first imposed upon themselves the task of acquiring, through their research, the indispensable means of enabling them to reach and guide the inner workings of the people's minds. We have to-day grammars, dictionaries, collections of reliably recorded Nama legends, and a small literature to assist us in learning this language. It can be successfully mastered to-day in the study and, if obscurities arise, they can be explained quite easily. Many of the Namas and Bergdamas of the present time know one or more of the European languages, and are perfect interpreters. The men who had to do all the spade work lived, in the early days of their efforts to acquire the language, in ox-wagons, or in mat huts, or trekked about in the open veld with the nomads of whom they had taken charge. Every kind of convenience, which a European really requires to assist him when he has to do difficult mental work, was lacking.

There were, of course, small collections of words used by the Hottentots of the Cape Colony. Most of these were to be found in large scientific works, which were practically unobtainable. They had been carefully collected as curious survivals of long past ages, and this was all there was when Schmelen set about learning the Nama language. Examples of this kind were given by Dapper (1671), Peter Kolbe (1719), Lichtenstein (1811) and others, but these were of no assistance whatsoever. The first missionary to the Hottentots in the Cape Colony, Georg Schmidt, who collected the Hottentots round him at Baviaanskloof between 1737 and 1744, taught them through the medium of the Dutch language, and was unable to find a way of learning their language.

The extent of the assistance which these books afforded was much the same as that which would be gained by a person wishing to learn German or Afrikaans with the following vocabulary as his guide:

German word	English meaning	Translated into Afrikaans as,	Which means in English
Schaum	foam	soom	seam
Heulen	scream	genees	heal
Erle	alder	pêrel	pearl
Schimmel	mildew	hemel	heaven
Bad	bath	pad	road
Springen	jump	sing	sing
Blumentopf	flower-pot	put	well (of water)

These examples are by no manner of means exaggerated; on the contrary much worse ones could and really ought to be selected in order to set out the true position. These, however, should suffice to give some idea of the muddle which existed in these first philological efforts at the time when a beginning was made in South West Africa to study the Nama language.

Schmelen was the first to prove that it was possible for a European adult to learn Nama. He had, however, an opportunity of acquiring it such as seldom comes to any one. His first wife spoke Nama from childhood, and he came into such close daily contact with the Namas, upon all his treks and travels in their company, that, after he had seen no bread for seven years and had finally taken to wearing clothing made from skins, he confessed sorrowfully that he had forgotten 'his beloved mother tongue, German'. His literary activities have been mentioned previously; he published the four gospels in Nama.

Knudsen followed in his footsteps and took up once again, in Bethanie, Schmelen's pioneer labour. He was better trained scientifically and naturally inclined towards research, and he had mastered the language so completely in a few years' time that he was able to publish, in 1846, the Gospel according to St. Luke, with new characters to represent the click sounds, and a reader with a vocabulary, both of which he had printed in Capetown. In addition to this he collected a mass of material about the grammar of Nama, the manuscript of which is preserved to-day in the Grey Collection of the Capetown Public Library. His contributions to the geography and ethnography of the country are likewise to be found in the Grey Collection. His work as an artist has been spoken of before.

Yet this very man, who was doing his utmost to understand and teach the Namas in their own language, underwent the experience that the people in control of affairs at Bethanie refused, in rude and insulting terms, to allow their children to be taught through that medium. They wanted their children to be taught exclusively through the medium of Dutch, for the Europeans in Capetown and the Orlam tribes spoke nothing else. The chief, David Christian, stood up in a stormy meeting, which had been convened to decide the medium of instruction in the schools, waved his arms about and shouted: 'Only Dutch, nothing but Dutch! I despise myself and want to creep into the bushes for very shame when I speak Hottentot.'

Kleinschmidt and Vollmer were at this time working at Rehoboth on a Dutch–Nama dictionary, but it never appeared in print.

The men who began work amongst the Hereros and had to find out all about their language, without anything at all to work upon, had just as hard a time. The only thing they had was a short list of words compiled by Captain Alexander, which was, however, very unreliable, and indeed it could not well be otherwise. Alexander had got from Jonker, in 1857, a young Herero, to whom he had taken a great fancy, had taken him to England and had had him educated in a military school. He came back in 1841, and Haddy, who was in Capetown then, baptized him and took him up to Windhoek as a teacher. Hahn could have received considerable assistance from him, but he arrived in Windhoek too late for Hahn to derive any benefit from his knowledge. Cloete, a half-caste, who had made his way into the country from the Cape, and, from frequent association with the Hereros, knew something of their language, and the faithful Herero, Kamuzandu of Otjikango, were used in work on the language. In the beginning it was very difficult. Hahn soon discovered that both the phonetics and the syntax of the Herero tongue were quite simple, but that it had an enormous number of form variations, and that more than 3,000 different ones had to be sorted out into their various affinities and learnt by rote. The sentences seemed to the unaccustomed ear to consist of one long word. Despite all this, Hahn was able to deliver his first sermon in Herero in 1847 and, when he went to Capetown in 1848, he had made such progress that he was able to have a reader, a Bible history, and a vocabulary of the Herero tongue printed. Rath had had a *Spelling Book and Phonetic Guide to the Herero Language* printed in Capetown the previous year. The time was then past when the Hereros, upon seeing pictures in Hahn's study, inquired whether those people had to be fed too.

But it was not only the words and forms of the language that had to be mastered, for it was very soon apparent that a much more comprehensive knowledge of it was essential. The Herero language is a very poor vehicle for the expression of abstract ideas, while it has an enormous mass of terms for things, qualities, and actions. There are more than a thousand words to describe the different colours and markings on animals, while there are none to convey ideas like the state, gratitude, or cleanliness. New words had to be invented for the ideas which were non-existent by using such materials as the language possessed. By 1849 Hahn had manufactured about a thousand of these and he was working to try and introduce them into the vocabulary, to get the people used to the new forms and to clothe the ideas with meanings, for Kant's admirable saying holds good for South West Africa, too: An idea is useless unless it can be intuitively grasped.

As the time went on it became clearer and clearer that Herero belonged to the great group of the Bantu languages. Oswell's account of the inhabitants of the recently discovered Ngami Lake proved that a dialect very similar to Herero was spoken there too. Examples of Ovambo obtained from natives from that part showed that that language was related to Herero. The speech of a Bechuana, who had been sold as a slave in Mozambique, and then came to Otjikango with a traveller, supported the assumption that the language of these people likewise belonged to the same group. Then, of course, Dr. Bleek of Capetown had not written his comparative grammar of the Bantu languages, and no one had any idea what a large area this language group covered. It was sufficient to know that Herero was not an isolated language, but had its relatives in the north and east. There would be no need to-day for Rath to struggle, in the heat of the African sun, with the learning of Arabia, in the hope that he might find there some assistance in the study of Herero. It is pathetic to see his notes on Arabic, which are still in existence, with their references to supposed similarities to Herero. As the records of 1859 state, the hill was surmounted. A wide prospect opened out owing to the fact that the Hereros could now be approached through the medium of their own language, and a very fine piece of work had been done in getting to know the country and its people.

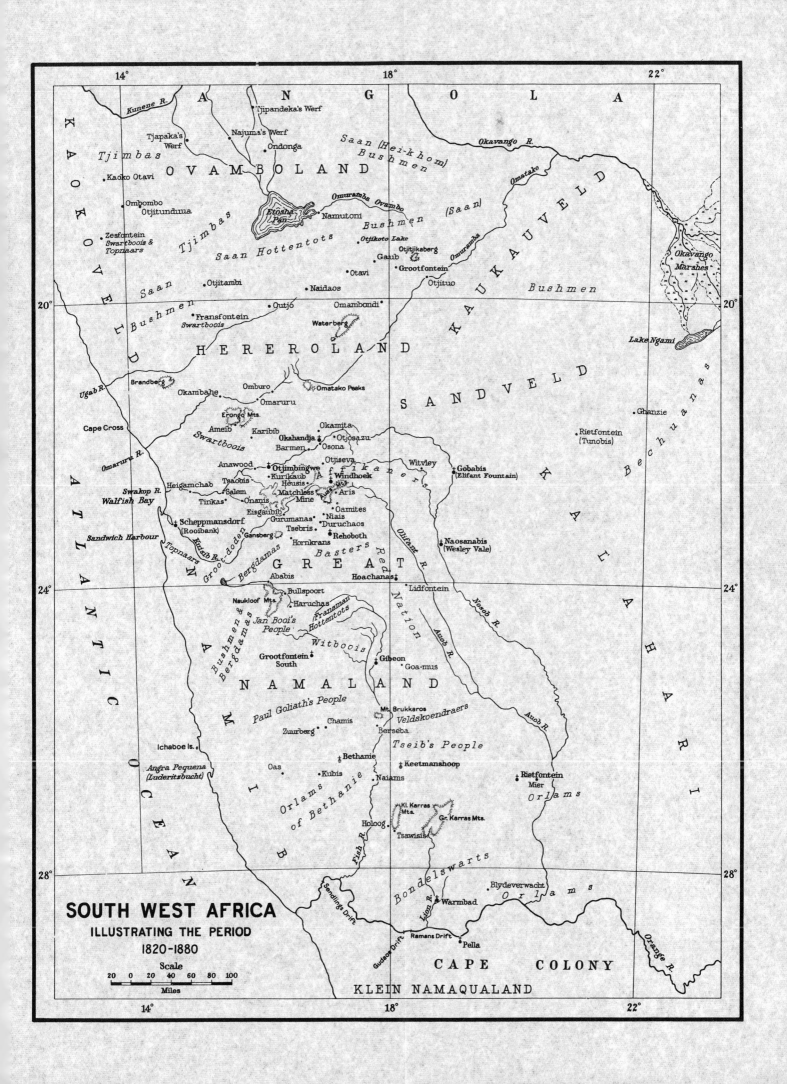

ANGOLA

KAOKOVELD

Kunene R.

Tjipandeka's Werf

Tjapaka's
Werf

Najuma's Werf

Ondonga

*Saan (Hei-khom)
Bushmen*

Okavango R.

Kaoko Otavi

Tjimbas

OVAMBOLAND

Ombombo
Otjitundirua

Tjimbas

Etosha
Pan

Namutoni

Omuramba Ovambo

Omatako

KAUKAUVELD

Zesfontein
Swartboois &
Topnaars

Saan Hottentots

Otjikoto Lake

Gaub

Otjitjikaberg

Bushmen (Saan)

*Okavango
Marshes*

*Saan
Bushmen*

Otjitambi

Naidaos

Otavi

Grootfontein

Otjituo

Bushmen

Transfontein
Swartboois

Outjo

Omambondi

Waterberg

HEREROLAND

Lake Ngami

Ugab R.

Brandberg

Okambahe

Omburo

Omatako Peaks

SANDVELD

Ghanzie

Cape Cross

Swartboois

Erongo Mts.

Omaruru

Rietfontein
(Tunobis)

Omaruru R.

Ameib

Karibib

Okamita

Anawood

Tsaobis

Okahandja

Otjosazu

Barmen

Osona

Bechuanas

Heigamchab

Swakop R.
Walfish Bay

Kurikaub
Heusis

Salem

Matchless
Mine

Otjimbingwe

Afrikaners

Otjiseva

Witvley

Windhoek

Aris

Gobabis
(Elifant Fountain)

KALAHARI

Tinkas

Onanis

Oamites

Niais

Eisgaubib

Gurumanas

Duruchaos

Tsebris

Olifant R.

Naosanabis
(Wesley Vale)

Scheppmansdorf
(Rooibank)

Gansberg

Hornkrans

Rehoboth

Sandwich Harbour

Topnaars

Kuisib R.

Groot-
doden

Bergdamas

Basters

GREAT

Ababis

Hoachanas

Lidfontein

Red

Nation

Bullspoort

Naukloof Mts.

Haruchas

*Fransman
Hottentots*

*Jan Booi's
People*

Witboois

Grootfontein
South

Gibeon

Goa-mus

Noseb R.

Anob R.

*Bushmen &
Bergdamas*

NAMALAND

Paul Goliath's People

Mt. Brukkaros

Veldskoendraers

Chamis

Berseba

Anob R.

Zuurberg

Tseib's People

Ichaboe Is.

Oas

Bethanie

Keetmanshoop

*Angra Pequena
(Luderitzbucht)*

Kubis

Naiams

Rietfontein
Mier

*Orlams
of Bethanie*

*Kl. Karras
Mts.*

Gr. Karras Mts.

Orlams

Holoog

Fish R.

Tsawisis

Bondelswarts

Orlams

Blydeverwacht

Sendlings Drift

Warmbad

Lion R.

Gudeor Drift

Ramans Drift

Pella

CAPE COLONY

KLEIN NAMAQUALAND

ATLANTIC OCEAN

NAMIB

Orange R.

SOUTH WEST AFRICA

ILLUSTRATING THE PERIOD
1820-1880

Scale

20 0   20 40 60 80 100

Miles

III

UNDER THE DOMINATION OF OKAHANDJA
1852–1862

1. THE TEN YEARS OF DECLINE

The Galton peace treaty of Windhoek

ON the 20th August, much at the same time that Jonker massacred the Hereros in Okahandja, an Englishman named Francis Galton landed at Walfish Bay. According to his own description of himself, he was very keen on hunting, exploration, and loved adventure.

Andersson, a Swede, came with him. They wanted to travel to Lake Ngami, which had been discovered early in the year. Ovamboland, which was only known by report, offered a wide field for their investigation. No traveller had yet set his eyes on it. Galton came from Capetown.[1] He had been forced to give up his original intention of entering South West Africa by crossing the Orange River, on account of the opposition of the trek-Boers who were in occupation of the country beyond the river. By reason of this, the roads over the Orange River had all been barred. Besides that, it was known in Capetown that the natives who lived on either side of the Orange River were at war with each other, and that it would be impossible to pass through them and to reach the Hereros and Ovambos. As Galton, however, wished to reach these tribes, he decided to see whether he could find a means of doing so through Walfish Bay.

It was generally thought at the Cape that the interior of South Africa would offer a large and extensive field for colonial trade, seeing that the discovery of Lake Ngami had opened the road to it. Galton writes:

'Hence it was doubly annoying that the emigrant Boers, whose treatment of the blacks was not very many shades better than that of the Orlams, should not only keep us from these countries, but also generate a hatred on the part of the blacks against white faces, which years of intercourse on our part might not efface. His Excellency, the Governor, guided by these views, took advantage of my intended expedition, and also of Mr. Oswell's, who was then in the neighbourhood of Lake Ngami, by formally requesting each of us to

---

[1] Galton left England on the 5th April, 1850, and arrived in Capetown at the end of June.—*Ed.*

establish "friendly relations" on the part of the Cape Government, with the
black tribes, who were subject to the attacks of these marauders. We were
simply to convey expressions of goodwill and strong assurances that the proceedings of the Boers met with no countenance on the part of the colony. I,
therefore, knowing that Jonker still felt some fear and respect for the Cape
Government, wrote him a long letter in legible characters, which I was
assured could be deciphered by some of his people. I told him how much
displeasure the emigrant Boers had caused,—that his actions were as bad as
theirs,—and that therefore he would probably be regarded with the same
displeasure as they, if he persisted in attacking the Damaras, now that he
had been warned. I ended with an assurance that I should call the Damara
Chiefs together, and express to them what I had been requested to do in the
case of the nations threatened by the emigrant Boers.'

Galton dispatched this letter during the course of his journey from
Walfish Bay to Otjikango, and he stayed with Hahn, the missionary,
while waiting for an answer. He waited, in vain, for several weeks.
Jonker was very much opposed to Galton's journey to Ovamboland
and Lake Ngami, and likewise to any conference of Herero chiefs.
The tribal council at Windhoek decided to compel him to turn back
by armed force. Galton, however, was quite right in his assumption
that Jonker still had some respect for the Cape Government, and this
plan was not carried out. To occupy his time Galton went to the
Erongo Mountains, and when he returned to Barmen he found a
letter from Jonker, which had not been sent by messenger, but had
been passed from hand to hand until finally it reached Galton. The
letter was offensive and unsatisfactory. Shortly after the receipt of
this letter Galton heard that Jonker had massacred the inhabitants
of eleven Herero villages close by, and had driven their stock away.

'Now this was too bad; but I determined to have patience for a little
time—a traveller must learn patience—and I wrote Jonker another civil
letter. I took the ground of supposing that he had not understood my last
one, and I explained myself over again. My intentions were simply these: if
he still intended to obstruct the way to Damaraland, in spite of the long,
the carefully worded and well indited letters that I had sent him, and which
explained fairly enough what the feelings were with which the Cape Government regarded marauders like himself, I would try if I could not do something
personally to further my own plans of exploring as I liked. I had no idea of
undertaking a piece of Quixotism in behalf of the Damaras, who are themselves a nation of thieves and cut-throats; but I was determined that Jonker's
contempt of white men should not be carried so far as to jeopardize my own
plans. In fact, if he did not care a straw for me, as the bearer of the wishes

of our common Government, I would take my own line as an individual, who had a few good guns at command, and would do my best to force my point.'

Galton waited therefore until his people arrived from Otjimbingwe. There was, however, no one amongst them who was prepared to accompany him on his dangerous journey to Windhoek. He then sent his wagon to Okahandja and placed it in Andersson's charge, and he took his servants Hans and Morta, whom he had brought from Cape-town, with him, and one of the drivers who spoke Dutch very well, and he went to Jonker.

'I previously gave it out among the Damaras that I was going to make peace between the Hottentots and them. I packed up my red hunting coat, jack-boots, and cords, and rode in my hunting cap; it was a costume unknown in these parts, and would, I expected, aid in producing the effect I desired.'

He set out on the 16th December. As he had no guide, Galton lost his way somewhat, and at the end of a week he arrived at Tjamuaha's deserted werf, from which the Windhoek mountains could be seen. Galton changed his clothes here and towards evening continued his journey to Jonker's place.

'Even Ceylon (my ox) caught the excitement, and snuffled the air like a war-horse. We formed together, gained the corner of the hill; Hans recog-nized Jonker's hut, and we, I cannot say dashed, but jogged right at it. An obstacle occurred and happily was surmounted, which might have discon-certed the assault: it was a ditch or little ravine that a torrent had made; it was rather deep and four feet wide; but I was in hunting costume, and I am sure Ceylon knew it, for he shook his head and took it uncommonly well; in fact, oxen, if you give them time, are not at all bad leapers. The others followed in style. So far all was well. The huts of the place were all in front, and Jonker's much the largest. Everybody saw us and was looking at us. There is great etiquette in these parts about coming to a strange place, but we defied all that, and I rode and rode, until my ox's head not only faced, but actually filled the door of the astonished chief. Conceive the effect. My Dutch was far from fluent, so I rated him in English, and after a while con-descended to use an interpreter. He never dared look me in the face as I glared down upon him from my ox. I then rode away in a huff, and took up my quarters in the village, and received in great state the humble messages which he sent me. . . . I desired Jonker to come to me with his chief people, and I lectured them soundly. We had three or four interviews. I spoke in English, and was interpreted both into Dutch and Hottentot. I saw clearly that I had made a favourable impression upon them. I insisted upon a full and ample apology being written to Mr. Kolbe, and an assurance given of future forbearance and justice being shown towards the Damaras. Jonker begged that Cornelius, the chief of the red people, should be called to his place, and such other people of importance in these parts as could be brought together; and he also mentioned his willingness to enter into any feasible plan for the establishment of better order in the country.'

In the meantime Galton had drawn up a code of laws which he intended to lay before the chiefs for their acceptance. He had it translated by Heinrich Kleinschmidt in Rehoboth into Dutch. In his comments on it Kleinschmidt remarks: 'At present Jonker is afraid of the Englishman, but how long will it last. What will remain if he has no force behind him. Tricks of this kind only do harm.'

When he returned to Windhoek he began negotiations with Jonker, Oasib, and Willem Swartbooi—three interpreters were employed. The meetings lasted long and went off in a very orderly fashion. All kinds of matters were discussed—the disordered condition of the country was proved and admitted. When the desire was expressed that Galton should instruct them how they should govern the country, the right moment had arrived for bringing forward his new code of law. This laid down that the man who stole stock should be punished with a fine of double the number of cattle he had stolen, and it also provided a money fine for the inhabitants of any place who concealed stock thieves in their midst. The code also provided for a treaty between Jonker and Oasib, in terms of which the delinquent was to be punished by the chief in whose territory the crime had been committed. The new laws were accepted by all the chiefs.

Galton had given Jonker a very salutary fright. He did not make a single raid for a full year, but it did not suit him that an Englishman should travel about so freely in the country—that he should go to Ovamboland and come back from there, and then go to Lake Ngami, where his own hunting fields were. It would, however, be no unfriendly action towards the man who could call him to account if he entered into closer relationships with his friend and ally, Tjamuaha, in Okahandja. The man who was in control at Okahandja had the key to the north, and so he decided to put a number of his men in occupation at Okahandja. In order to show that he was respecting the Galton peace treaty he himself retired for a time into the Rehoboth district, but from there he sent three Hereros, who were amongst his retinue, to Tjamuaha at Okahandja. They were by name Harujezu, Kanukua, and Mutimbo, and he sent them to ask whether the old bonds of friendship still held good, and whether he might come up to Okahandja. Tjamuaha was quite willing that he should do so, for the hostility of the rest of the Hereros threatened to bring disaster upon him. Jonker arrived there, and he had the fort at Okahandja erected at the highest spot in the village, at the place where the Church of the Rhenish Mission stands to-day with its old cemetery. The whole place, which was covered with high trees, was laid bare so that the approach of foes could be more quickly discovered. Jonker's relations were not at all pleased that the supremacy of Windhoek should come to an end. David Afrikander and his people set their faces once again in the direction of the Orange River and slowly made their way through Namaland.

Windhoek retrogressed. Jonker did not feel at home there any more. The recollections he had of the place were altogether too unhappy. It was true that a number of Afrikanders and Bergdamas still lived there, but he himself always avoided the place as much as he could, and he went there only when it was necessary to regulate important tribal affairs.

The Hereros' quarrels amongst themselves

The Galton peace treaty gave Jonker breathing space, as it did the Hereros, too, or should we rather say it was the lull before the storm. Oasib worried himself very little about the peace treaty. He was not an English subject like Jonker, who had reason to fear the Cape Government. Every now and then he made a raid into Hereroland and came back with numbers of cattle. The chiefs of the Veldschoendraers, Jan Booi's tribe, and of the Bondelswarts, were of the same opinion. Even if they did not themselves undertake cattle raids, there were quite enough greedy and restless people amongst them to ensure that the Hereros, who lived along the Swakop and to the north of it, were not left in peace. These Namas said as Oasib did—'We have every justification for fighting our old enemies who wanted to take our land away from us, and no Cape Government is going to prevent us from doing so.' It was only David Christian who, when he received the news of Galton's coming, sent a messenger to John Booi in the Kuiseb district to warn him and advise him to be careful.

If the Hereros had stood together it would have been quite easy for them to have brought all this quarrelling speedily to an end, by striking one good blow against the foes, who were themselves weak because they hated each other and fought amongst themselves; but they were not united, and this was not only their weakness but their ruin. Many of the Hereros had gone over to Jonker and had gone on raids for him and with him, and foremost among these were Tjamuaha and his son Maharero. The latter was no longer on friendly terms with Jonker, but his father Tjamuaha was, for he saw that the only way in which he could protect the enormous herds of cattle, which he kept in the vicinity of Okahandja, was to maintain his alliance with Jonker. His one ambition was to increase his cattle and to preserve intact for their use alone, the whole veld of Okahandja. He would not even have his own relations passing through it. He saw with envious eyes that Mungunda still had cattle at Barmen and that there were others who laid claim to grazing rights. He was particularly hostile towards Kahitjene, whose death he had planned, but Jonker had not succeeded in killing him, and Kahitjene still had a number of cattle posts. After the massacre at Okahandja he had retired to the Omatako. Then Mungunda, Kahitjene's uncle, died in Otjimbundja, and Kahitjene, as his nephew, came into control of his estate. Trouble arose over the division of the inheritance, and Kahitjene was accused of having acted unfairly. These accusations annoyed Kahitjene, and he took with him a number of cattle which it was said that he had no right to take. Mungunda's sons went to stay at the Omuramba; Kagee was the most powerful of them. Kahitjene found it necessary to establish some cattle posts on the Omuramba. He sent some cattle there which he had inherited from Mungunda, and he entrusted the supervision of these posts to his son, Kausuva. The latter was killed, together with his herdsmen, by Mungunda's sons, who then appropriated the cattle, which, in their opinion, belonged to them. Kausuva was buried at the Omuramba where Mungunda's tribe lived. Now the customs of the Hereros require that the relatives of anybody who has died shall hasten to the grave at the first possible opportunity and 'view the grave'. If that is not done, some misfortune will overtake them. So Kahitjene made preparations to go and 'view' the grave of his son. He knew what that meant for him, but he had no fear.

On the 12th March, 1851, while he was making these preparations, Francis Galton arrived at his werf, which was at Ombujokaheke, north of Okamita. As Galton's description of this visit gives an excellent insight into the circumstances of the time, we will give it in his own words:

'We had arrived at the place where Kahitjene waited for us. He and about forty magnificently made and well-armed Damaras were standing under the trees. As the wagons came near the men all fell into a single file according to their usual custom, which Kahitjene headed, and they walked up to me. He had quite the manners of a chief, and received me very well. I gave him some gilt ornaments as presents, which, although he was in mourning, he put on in compliment to me; the Damaras strip off their ornaments when in mourning. He had been in great distress of late. After Jonker had attacked him, and scattered his people at Schmelen's Hope, Mungunda's son, who was encamped two days in front of us, followed up the attack, and killed some of his children, and took others prisoners, leaving only one lad with him. The greater number of his oxen were also taken, and he was left almost destitute, with but the remnant of a tribe, and was now about to make a last desperate attack upon his enemy. A few years ago Kahitjene was the most powerful chief in Damaraland, and, like Katjimasha, had once allied himself with, and afterwards had separated from, Jonker. Subsequent to this separation Jonker attacked him, and he made a bold retaliation the next night. Ever since that he had been a marked man with the Hottentots, and werf after werf of his had been swept away, until he was reduced to the condition in which I found him. He was the only friend among the Damaras that the missionaries ever had, and his friendliness and frankness to me and my men interested all of us without exception most thoroughly in his favour.'

Galton offered to go and negotiate with Mungunda's sons, but that he proudly refused 'though he said that he knew his expedition was but a forlorn hope and that he would be killed'. Kahitjene had said nothing to him about his having to go to his son's grave and that the way to it had to be forced open; it was just for this reason that no mediation could be accepted.

Shortly after Galton left him Kahitjene set out with his men to go and visit his son's grave. Mauto, Kavakuna's son, and Tjamuaha's grandson, who was Kahitjene's nephew, and so the principal heir to his property, went with him. Before the party ever reached the grave it was attacked by Mungunda's sons and their followers, and it turned out just as Kahitjene had said—his people deserted him when the danger was at its height. A arrow struck the old warrior down; Mauto ran to him and bent down to help him and to extract the arrow. One of Mungunda's men saw this, and he ran up and stabbed both Mauto and his uncle Kahitjene with a single thrust of his spear.

Kahitjene was dead and his heir was dead too. He had no other heirs in the direct line for they had all been killed in battle. Tjamuaha, however, Kahitjene's bitter enemy, felt that he had been injured through the loss of his nephew Mauto. If only Kahitjene had not taken him on that unfortunate expedition he would not have been killed. This mistake must be atoned for in some way and his loss must be made good, so he promptly appropriated Kahitjene's cattle as compensation and reparation. But what was to be done with Kahitjene's followers? They no longer had a leader. The man who had first claim to recognition as the heir to these people was Zeraua, for Kahitjene was Zeraua's younger brother through one of Zimberuka's many marriages. A message therefore was sent to Zeraua suggesting that he should call Kahitjene's people to him. Zeraua sent back the answer that he had more people than the small number of cattle he possessed could provide with food. He suggested that Maharero, who was Tjamuaha's son and Zeraua's nephew, should adopt these people and become their chief, and this was the arrangement made. So it came about that in 1851—'the year of the peace'—Maharero left Otjimbingwe again and went back to his father Tjamuaha at Okahandja and became a chief; until then he had only been 'Jonker's dog' and 'Tjamuaha's unruly calf'. As Tjamuaha, by virtue of his being Jonker's ally, was still required to look after a great part of Jonker's cattle, it followed, as a matter of course, that the duty of looking after these cattle fell upon Maharero, and this put an end to the ill feeling between Jonker and himself. Jonker was never a man to harbour ill will. If anybody angered him, he 'punished' him speedily and thoroughly, and in doing so he had the knack of touching the spot where it hurt most. When the punishment had been meted out, he could meet his victim in the friendliest possible way, as if nothing at all had happened; but Maharero did nothing more to anger Jonker. Jonker, however, often paid Okahandja visits of longer or shorter duration for the purpose of seeing his Herero friends and looking after the Nama garrison he had placed there. What he really wanted to see was whether his cattle were all there still, and whether his allies were still to be trusted.

Only one picture of the relations of the Hereros amongst themselves is drawn here, but it would be quite easy to multiply them indefinitely. The history of the country would only be burdened with superfluous matter through doing so, without having any further light thrown upon it. We shall refrain from spending any further time over these wretched inter-tribal troubles, through which the noblest members of the race were killed off, and we shall sum up everything of this kind that happened until the time of Tjamuaha's death by quoting this passage from Rohden:

'Whenever the Hereros were not worried by the Orlams and the Namas, they fought all the more fiercely amongst themselves. It was a war of each one against all the rest, and every small chief who had a few cattle plundered and murdered the others who had rather more, and every one who had been despoiled looked for a third at whose expense he could recoup his loss. Blood-shed and misery, murder and horror, were so prevalent throughout the land that people were almost inclined to wish that the times when Jonker inspired universal fear and terror would return. It is much easier to be ready for a lion than to protect oneself against a whole pack of hungry wolves.'

To this let us add—the lion was not dead yet; he had only crept into the bushes in temporary alarm. It was not long before his roar was heard again, and the whole of Hereroland trembled.

Jonker comes back

Galton was still in the country. He visited Windhoek, went to Lake Ngami, came back through Windhoek, and found to his great satisfaction that the peace which he had dictated had not been broken. Secretly, however, it was whispered around that this man had not the power behind him which he had been supposed to have, and that he had no means whatever of enforcing his authority if anybody should disobey him. The Nama tribes had found this out long ago, and, for their part, they had raided the Kuiseb and Swakop areas with their habitual diligence. Now Jonker began to realize that he had been bullied into submission, and was very angry indeed, for he had fallen far behind the Nama chiefs. A whole year of very profitable 'labour' had been lost. He must be more careful than that in the future. He was regarded as an English subject, and this was not the case with the Nama chiefs, with the exception of Amraal and Kido Witbooi, the latter of whom had just left Pella to trek up and down in Namaland in search of pasturage. He had received no invitation from the Nama chiefs, but Jonker had repeatedly asked him to come.

The establishment of outposts and garrisons is a peace measure. Had not Jonker conquered the whole country between the Swakop and the Kuiseb, and had not his actions on the right bank of the Swakop been so effective that no one could possibly contest his rights? That being the case, he was now justified in taking steps to consolidate his authority. He had settled one garrison at Okahandja;

there was a Nama post on the Waterberg right behind the Hereros controlled by him, Otjimbingwe must now receive a garrison at his hands. Anybody coming to Otjimbingwe would, of course, hardly notice that anything particular was happening. Some families who were befriended by Jonker came and settled there. The men were armed with guns, but who could make any objection to that? Jonker himself came now and again and brought his wife Betty and their spoilt daughter with him. Why should he not pay his friends and relations a visit if he wanted to? The men worked as drivers on the transport wagons between Otjimbingwe and the copper mines, and they earned the good wages of 1s. 6d. a day. No one could possibly raise any objection to all that; but Jonker had an observation post which cost him nothing, and when anything happened he was right on the spot.

He went still a step farther. It was a thorn in Tjamuaha's side that a rich Herero had established a cattle post at the hot springs in Klein Barmen, for he could not bear any Herero encroaching upon his pasturage. Here was an opportunity for testing whether a breach of Galton's Peace Treaty would have any untoward consequences. Jonker himself took no part at all in the attack on this post, but a number of Afrikanders from Okahandja, and some volunteers from Windhoek, joined Tjamuaha's people in raiding it. It was decided beforehand that, to prevent any fugitives from raising too great an outcry, the mouths of all adverse witnesses of the deed should straight away be closed. At the break of day, when the Hereros at Klein Barmen were still in their huts, their werf was surrounded. No opportunity was given for any escape or resistance. Tjamuaha's people had more than a hundred guns and the other tribe had not a single one. The captive Hereros who had expected to be shot or clubbed to death with the kirrie were pleasantly surprised when they were not dispatched in this manner, but their elation soon turned to terror. They were driven into a stock kraal, which was surrounded with an impenetrable hedge made of thorn branches and more than six feet high, of the kind that was always constructed in those days to protect the cattle from the lions. When they were all—men, women, and children—in the kraal, it was closed up and set on fire. The dry thorn branches blazed furiously and everybody inside was suffocated in the smoke and heat of the fire. That happened while Galton was still in the country. Little was said about this atrocity, and still less written, but the story of that terrible morning has come down to our own times by word of mouth. Even

Hahn at Barmen, close by, never learned the whole truth. The stock did not pass into Jonker's possession, but Tjamuaha took them for himself. Jonker saw, however, that in spite of the conclusion of peace it was quite possible to carry on the 'trade' of warfare with impunity.

The members of his garrison in Otjimbingwe acted unwisely. They wanted to own something too, and so, soon after this, they made a raid in the same area. They carried off twenty-four cattle from Barmen which were under Hahn's protection. Hahn turned to Jonker for redress and got it. Jonker did not punish his own people, nor did he take the cattle away from them and send them back, but he sent twenty-four cattle of his own to Barmen as compensation. Unfortunately, only eleven reached there, the rest being 'stolen' along the way. Such an honourable way of doing things must surely make a good impression on Hahn and Galton!

When Galton left the country, Jonker broke loose, and set out to make up for the time he had lost in the year 1851. Like a lion he sprang on the Hereros, and these, over-awed and powerless, placed themselves in great numbers under Jonker's protection, which was given them when they were willing to allow themselves to be formed into raiding parties. This they were quite willing to do. Were not their most prominent men, Tjamuaha and Maharero, likewise the vassals, or even perhaps the friends, of this man who was called Mukuru Uouje, which means 'God of the world'?

Tjamuaha, however, must be made to come to heel as well. Jonker had to see to it that he did not wax too great. It was in the first months of the year 1852 that Tjamuaha came to Hahn at Barmen. Tjamuaha was trembling like an aspen leaf. Jonker had wiped out one of his finest cattle posts at Otjosemba, about a day and a half's journey from Barmen, and now Tjamuaha wanted to place himself under Hahn's protection and to come and stay at Barmen. He had promised to do that previously but had never kept his promise. He came there and stayed only for a very short time and then left again. He felt that he was not dealing rightly with his friend Jonker by living in Barmen, and Hahn, too, had to suffer for it. His cattle had already been driven off once in consequence, but Jonker had stopped doing this at Maharero's request, and now Hahn wanted to go to Otjimbingwe, which made Jonker suspicious. He wrote Hahn a letter forbidding him to go there, for in Otjimbingwe, he said, 'my people are living'. Hahn went, nevertheless, and he wrote in his diary, 'the low cut-throat'.

Jonker now turned his hand to Omambondi and the Omuramba. He raided Otjihinamaparero and exterminated Katjikurure's powerful tribe there. He allowed a few of Onguatjindi's cattle posts to remain, so that he could be in a position to start again, for it did not pay to kill all the geese that were laying the golden eggs. We have no desire to tell about his further large expeditions. There were eleven of them, though some people consider that there were fifteen. Andersson, who was on the Omuramba during this period, met one of Jonker's raiding parties and said that it consisted of five hundred fighting men, who had about seventy guns between them, and that about twelve hundred cattle were collected and brought back. A share of them went to the 'warriors' as loot. Jonker kept a further share for himself. Most of them passed into the hands of dealers, who provided Jonker with ammunition and with everything else which he and his people required.

The Cape Government recognized the fact that it had to do something about this unconscionable trade in arms and ammunition, and early in 1852 a warship arrived in Walfish Bay. The Mission had stationed Bam, who was born in Capetown, there as catechist. The captain of the ship went to him and inquired closely into this trade in ammunition. When he heard of the raids made by the Namas, he authorized Bam to stop all English subjects in the Bay from taking any part in this trade, and to continue doing so as long as the natives put the 'ammunition' to such evil uses. If the English subjects opposed him in any way, he was to write to Capetown and a warship would be sent up at once to punish those who disobeyed the order. Some time afterwards, the importation of powder was entirely forbidden. What happened at Luderitzbucht illustrates the way in which this prohibition was circumvented. Three traders, who had an intimate knowledge of the position in South West Africa, and only dared to import and dispose of powder in very small quantities, went to England and bought a ship there. They loaded it with merchandise and some 20,000 lb. of gunpowder, and sailed in it to Angra Pequena, i.e. Luderitzbucht. Some part of the gunpowder got wet. They traded with David Christian at Bethanie, and he gave them a place at Aus in which to store their goods. One of the traders set out to take thirty hundredweights of powder to Jonker. When he came to old Jan Booi, the latter had his wagon searched and he forbade him to go any farther—it did not suit him that Jonker should get this supply of ammunition. In the meantime David Christian had also thought the matter carefully over, and he supported his father-in-law's veto. Then the traders accused Kreft, the missionary in Bethanie, of spoiling their business. Nothing remained for them but to go down to the mouth of the Orange River. There they carried on a brisk trade in gunpowder and brandy, and strenuous efforts were made by all the restless Namas at the Orange River mouth to obtain these two forbidden articles in exchange for cattle which they had stolen. When the traders' wagons reached Jonker's werf the Namas used to say 'let us get busy and go and harvest our crops', meaning the Hereros' cattle posts, and the Hereros used to say 'the traders are the cause of all our troubles'.

Their misery was becoming really unbearable. Famine broke out amongst the Hereros; they had no more milk and no more cattle to slaughter, and many of them died of hunger. Hahn found two small Herero boys in the veld, one of whom was tied to a stone. Their own mother, who had two other children besides these boys, had tried to get rid of them in this way. He brought the boys home with him and fed and raised them in his own house. On another occasion a child was brought to him with its head tied in a skin knapsack by its own mother. She could not feed the child any more and had meant to strangle it.

But Jonker knew no mercy. His Bergdamas were his spies. When a raid was made his Hereros had to attack and carry it through. When this part of the work had been concluded his Afrikanders came on the scene to carry off the loot. At times Maharero himself was forced to be the leader of Jonker's raiders. Hahn tells how one day Jonker passed Barmen on his way to an unknown part of the country towards the north-west. He called Maharero to him and bound his hands behind his back with a riem, and compelled him to lead the way, bound as he was, and to guide him to some hidden Herero werfs. To this he adds with considerable satisfaction, that Jonker's people stood round the crowded cattle kraals at Barmen for some hours, and prowled round the kraals like bees round a honey-pot. 'Their mouths must have watered at the sight of all those cattle which they dared not touch', for Hahn was respected by Jonker as chief of the place and a neutral.

On the 3rd March, 1853, he went personally to Jonker at Windhoek to have an interview with him and to plead with him on behalf of the Hereros. Tjamuaha and Maharero had again moved to Nettlebeck, near Windhoek. About his visit to Maharero he writes as follows: 'The poor fellow is like a mouse in the cat's claws. The Hereros are very anxious as to the result of my visit to Jonker, and they have every reason to be, for they know well enough that, if Jonker listens to me, they are saved, but if he does not, then their doom is sealed.' Jonker knew what could be expected of him. He gave instructions that there was to be peace and quietness in his village, and the noise ceased. From discussions with him and his counsellors, it appeared that Jonker had a considerable grievance against his previous missionary Haddy, a number of whose letters he produced. After his return to Capetown in 1850, Haddy had given the Government information as to what was happening in South West Africa. He regarded this as treachery. Missionaries were traitors to the country and spies of the Cape Government, he said, and he would rather go to hell with his whole people than ever again receive a missionary amongst them. This saying of his spread throughout Namaland, and the missionaries, who had no idea at all of what had happened, passed through a very difficult time, because it engendered distrust amongst the people with whom they had long lived in peace.

Even the Herero, Tjamuaha, became distrustful. Had not Jonker reproached him for betaking himself with his son to the mission station in order to escape his 'friendship' in a neutral place? The idea occurred to him that one of these evenings, when Hahn was working by lamplight, with his windows and doors open, some of his men should creep up to the house and shoot a few poisoned arrows into him, but Kavikunua, Tjamuaha's son, prevented this plan from being executed.

By 1857 Jonker's work in Hereroland could be regarded as complete. The southern part of it was entirely void of people and cattle. Andersson found even the Kaokoveld empty. The Hereros had fled far into the north. Even in the Omuramba he found no cattle in the year 1858. No tongue will ever tell how many people were killed, how many cattle were driven away to Jonker and his traders, and what terrible atrocities were committed. Jonker had stones bound upon the backs of the chiefs he captured, and made them go about so burdened in order to prevent them from getting away. The women and children were kept as slaves.

Jonker had almost reached the goal which he had marked out for himself, i.e. the destruction of the whole Herero nation. He was helped by the Nama hordes, who did not make common cause with him, but were for the greater part his competitors. It seemed more profitable to them to rob and pillage, murder and burn, for their own account, for then they could take home the produce of their 'gardens' themselves, without having to share it with Jonker.

The Namas stay where they are

The holiday which the Galton peace treaty had caused Jonker to keep was never observed by the Namas. For them it seemed right and proper that Jonker should not lift any more cattle. In their hearts they hated him and all his works, but they envied him his success, and the story of the reproof which he had received was told with considerable relish. David Christian of Bethanie, who had first of all been overawed by the reports which came from Windhoek, soon recovered from his fright. Galton had not yet reached Ovamboland before a number of his people had joined with some of Jan Booi's in a foray in the north. Unfortunately Bethanie had no missionary who could check these activities, but soon afterwards Heinrich Kreft came there as missionary. The chief was awed by his quiet determination and evident sincerity. When a further expedition was on foot, he tried to give it an innocent-sounding name, and he talked about a 'hunting expedition' upon which he was going, with the idea of hiding from Kreft what sort of hunting expedition it really was, but Kreft learned from some traders in good time the real meaning of the expression. The chief felt that he had been found out, and he gave up his idea of 'hunting elephants round about Otjimbingwe and Barmen'. But that did not prevent old Jacob Isaak from buying 180 lb. of powder in 1855. Saul Frederik, too, thought it a good idea to bring the loot, which he had acquired in raids of his own) across the Orange River and to exchange it for horses, and then to go and stay with Jan Booi, where one could be free from control and surveillance. Jan Booi, however, who was close to the Hereros and wandered about to the northwards of Bethanie, made one raid after another. Not much is known about his actions, and there is practically no record of them. The 'evil spirit' of Bethanie threatened to infect Berseba too, but there the upright old man, Paul Goliath, was in control of things, and Krönlein's powerful personality afforded him support, so the difference between this Orlam tribe and all the others was that, in spite of temptation, they never took part in any criminal activities. The Veldschoendraers under Hendrik Nanib and a tribe of the Red Nation under Piet Koper acted very badly indeed, for finally they joined Jonker out and out and became part of his garrison in Okahandja. Both of them formed bands, which were joined by the Bondelswarts and other Namas, whose chiefs were too slow and faint-hearted for their liking. In March 1857, however, Hendrik Nanib made an unsuccessful expedition against the Hereros and a considerable number of his men were killed. Not a single one of Amraal's disobedient followers came back. Nine men from Rehoboth were given no share of the small quantity of loot taken, and so they went on a jaunt of their own to the Erongo and despoiled the Bergdamas there of the few animals they possessed. A further march into unknown country (the Kaokoveld) turned out to be fraught with danger, even for men like Hendrik Nanib. He lost his way and spent ten days wandering about in the veld until, with his men weakened by fever and thirst, he managed to find people.

Not long afterwards Piet Koper made an expedition to Bechuana-land and Lake Ngami. At first his Namas did not behave like enemies, but they were pleased to allow the Bechuanas to receive them as friends and guests. When, however, they had enjoyed their hospi-tality to the full, they fell upon their hosts, cut their throats, and carried off their cattle.

Willem Swartbooi in Rehoboth observed the Galton peace treaty faithfully during the first year or two. He was under Kleinschmidt's influence, and he allowed himself to be advised and led by him. He turned a deaf ear to Jonker's persuasive arguments—but it was only one ear, not both! He was constantly casting covetous eyes on the wealth which the others were acquiring so easily, while he was getting nothing. At last he found a simple name for his project and on the 13th November, 1853, he took leave of Kleinschmidt on the pretext that he was going with his people to look for a new watering-place. Kleinschmidt knew very well what the 'watering-place' really meant and, while not refusing to say goodbye to him, he once again made a very strong appeal to his conscience. Some of the serious-minded men of the congregation decided to remain at home. Others said, 'if he is going on a raid, we are not going with him, for he has told no one, not even his counsellors, what his actual plans are'. When he saw that it was not possible to go cattle raiding with people who were of that opinion, he changed his ground and said that he intended to attack Jonker and punish him for his arro-gance. For a considerable time the relations between him and the autocratic Jonker had been very strained. So he went to Windhoek and was very pleased indeed to find that Jonker did not take him seriously, although he was expecting a harsh reception. Jonker killed the fatted calf and they settled their differences at the festive board. Jonker allowed old Willem to depart in peace, and he arrived back at Rehoboth without having achieved anything. He did not forgive Kleinschmidt, however, for having condemned his actions so roundly. In 1857 he still declares, in anger, 'He (Kleinschmidt) tries to keep me humble by using God and His Word against me. All the others are hard at work (raiding) and he prevents me from acquiring any property at all.' He lost his influence with the community entirely, and finally he left Rehoboth and went and lived amongst the Topnaars near Walfish Bay. His people said of him: 'Our chief has become a Bushman.'

Oasib, the Paramount Chief of the ancient Nama tribes, watched the whole disorderly business for a long time without taking any part whatever in it. He took Vollmer as his missionary, and in him he had a man to whose advice he listened, but he was by no means pleased with Jonker, who had been brought into the land by his own people and now behaved as if he were the paramount chief. He could not endure it that this man should gather such an immense amount of wealth, which really belonged to him, for it was his people, and not Jonker, that the Hereros had injured at the time when they had pressed them so severely. Besides this, he had another reason for dissatisfaction. During the disturbances prior to 1850, Tjamuaha's people had, with Jonker's connivance, lifted a large number of cattle from the Fish River, and had so caused the Red Nation very heavy losses. This action called for revenge. He was anxious to attack Tjamuaha, Jonker's friend, and to punish the hated Hereros, while weakening Jonker indirectly and enriching himself at the same time. Jonker was quite able to appreciate ideas of this kind, and when Oasib, with Hendrik Nanib and many other parties of Namas, started out to plunder in 1856, he did not oppose him. It was actually quite in accordance with his plans that Tjamuaha should be kept down. He could allow Oasib to acquire a certain amount of Tjamuaha's property, and then there would be no need to touch him himself. Then, too, Oasib would probably be somewhat reconciled with the position of not being the only lord of the country. When Oasib reached Windhoek, Jonker sent him a friendly message to the effect that he should not put himself out any more, that Tjamuaha had fled and he would not be able to overtake him, and thus Oasib's bold plan came to nothing.

Amraal kept his people well disciplined and controlled, first in Naosanabis and then in Gobabis. He could not, however, prevent a war party being formed amongst the members of his tribe. Once before a number of his tribe had gone on an expedition with Hendrik Nanib and none had ever come back. In 1861 two parties went out without his permission and brought back a great deal of booty, and the old man of ninety had not the power to punish the evil-doers. On this occasion the Veldschoendraers, the Bondelswarts, and a number of men from the Red Nation had joined the expedition.

A real robber chieftain came upon the scene at this time, in the shape of an Orlam named Piet Vaalrug, supported by a number of Hereros under Tjamuaha's son Katjimazepa. He stormed Otjimbingwe on the 3rd April, 1862, and beat the missionary, Rath, and subjected him to severe ill treatment.

The ill-usage which captured Hereros were subjected to in Namaland was exceedingly hard. In 1861 Krönlein says:

'The ill-treatment which the captured Hereros receive at the hands of the Namas is often dreadful. If one goes from Berseba farther into the interior of the country one comes across masters who are really monsters. They do not hesitate to thrash a poor wretch with a sjambok until the skin breaks with every blow, exposing the raw flesh, and sometimes, indeed, the place of chastisement is covered with blood, just as if a sheep had been slaughtered there.'

And Hahn writes in 1859:

'The Red Nation's Herero slaves are treated terribly, and they very often almost die of hunger. We saw some of these wretched creatures, who were nothing more than living skeletons, and whose bodies bore innumerable marks of the sjambok.'

A large number of slaves were taken from the Mbanderus as far down as Warmbad and the Orange River, and even in the copper mines of O'kiep in Klein Namaqualand captured Hereros were to be found.

Oasib against Jonker

Oasib, the chief of the old Nama tribes, was not the same stamp of man as Jonker. How gladly would he not have driven this dangerous fellow out of Windhoek! Jonker, who ought to have been his assistant, was taking away from him all the glamour of his chieftainship, kept all the booty for himself, and laid claim to all the valuable country between Windhoek and Walfish Bay. If only he had somebody who could deal with Jonker and keep him within bounds, or, best of all, force him back across the Orange River. He himself had not the courage to attempt what he so often almost made up his mind to do. Jonker had traders in Windhoek who provided him with ammunition. Oasib had none, and, if one went to him by any chance, he could not get from him the quantity of powder which he needed for a campaign, either because the trader had not enough, or because he could not pay for it, for Oasib was poor according to the circumstances of the time. It did not help him a bit that he had equipped Hoachanas, lying as it did away from the beaten track, with everything modern and convenient for the comfort of visitors. He really ought to have been glad that Jonker left him in peace. He had had the opportunity of causing him considerable loss. It seemed, however, that a certain sense of decency had restrained him from doing so. In spite of this, war between him and Oasib had to come, but it was a war which was carried on with little energy by either side.

A free tribe of the Topnaars lived in the dunes of Walfish Bay and the lower part of the Kuiseb Valley. They had their tribal centre in Rooibank, where the peaceable chief Kichab (Frederick), who had thrown in his lot with Scheppmann, lived, while at the Bay, Kachab, who was very fond of fighting, resided with his barbarous following. Jonker invited both these chiefs to leave the Bay and trek into the interior. He was probably anxious to obtain recruits from this tribe, for he used to save his own Afrikanders when there was serious fighting to be done. About 300 men then went to Jonker and settled in the Auas Mountains. That was in the beginning of the year 1852. By the end of the year most of the members of the Rooibank congregation were back again with Kichab. They could not see the need for the tribe's settling elsewhere. Jonker did not prevent them from returning. The remainder of them, who were under Kachab, found a suitable place to the west of Rehoboth, where they settled temporarily with the small number of cattle they possessed. Kleinschmidt visited them frequently but he found them very unsympathetic.

In August 1852 some men belonging to the Red Nation, who did much as they liked, attacked and robbed these Topnaars and also a family of Hereros, who had placed themselves under Willem Swartbooi's protection. The victims turned to their protector for help, and as he stood under Oasib, he called upon him to support him, arrested the culprits and kept them in custody. Oasib arrived there in September and fixed a date for the trial. The accused were found guilty, and the question arose as to the law under which they should

be dealt with. Galton's code of law was suggested but that did not
meet with Oasib's approval, so the tribal laws of Bethanie, Berseba, and Rehoboth were applied. The marauders were deprived of
fifteen guns and their booty was taken away from them. Oasib divided
a portion of the stolen cattle amongst his counsellors, and the Topnaars received the rest of it back. The Hereros received ten cows
and a bull. Jonker must have taken it amiss that the Topnaars should
have turned to Willem Swartbooi and Oasib for help, for in March
1854 he attacked them and thinned their ranks very considerably.
Willem Swartbooi was very indignant at this action of Jonker's, and
he wanted to go to Windhoek at once and punish Jonker for it.
Kleinschmidt warned him, however, and pointed out to him that he
had no powder. Oasib was just as angry. He made preparations to
leave Hoachanas and to go and stay at Rehoboth, with the idea of
forcing Jonker, through this combination of forces, to recognize his
position as suzerain. The whole tribe was called up. The Hereros
who were living under Willem's protection, however, made up their
minds that, if the Swartboois and the Red Nation went to attack
Jonker, they would take the opportunity of escaping and taking the
tribal herds of both the tribes with them. When their plot was discovered, the Hereros only narrowly escaped being killed. They
fled to Kleinschmidt in terror and hid themselves in his house under
the tables, and in the cupboards, and wherever there was a possible
hiding-place. The missionaries' houses were regarded as neutral
ground and as sanctuaries. Kleinschmidt soothed the angry Swartboois and prevented a massacre. Jonker, however, was very perturbed.
The Swartboois were taking up arms against him, and so were the
Red Nation, Jan Booi's tribe, and any one else who liked a little
fighting. The traders who came to Rehoboth from Windhoek in
April of that year found themselves in an awkward predicament. The
stock that Jonker had lifted from the Topnaars was already in their
possession and was being taken to South Africa. The Topnaars were
very anxious to get it back and Willem Swartbooi intervened. He
made them give back 130 cattle and 300 head of small stock to the
Topnaars, and then told them that they should look to Jonker for
compensation. Emboldened by this, the Topnaars made a raid in
May into Jonker's grazing-grounds and did not come back with
empty hands. Rehoboth was turned into a fortress. A high wall was
built round the houses and cattle kraals. On the 15th May, 400 ox
riders and 30 horsemen, with gun-bearers and bowmen, advanced on

Windhoek, and a fierce battle took place at the hot springs in Windhoek on the 19th. Kachab, the Topnaar chief, was killed. Jonker observed his old tactics and sent his allies, the Hereros, to ward the attack off, and the gunfire of the Namas made wide gaps in their ranks. In the end the men of Rehoboth had no more powder left and so withdrew from the fight. On the way home they took with them any of Jonker's cattle they could find in the veld. The loot was considerable.

Jonker was by no means daunted by the failure of his arms. A Swedish explorer, Professor Wahlberg, was with him at the time, and went from there on the 29th May to Rehoboth. Jonker sent a message with him to the effect that he was considering paying Willem Swartbooi a visit at an early date. Kleinschmidt, however, told him that he need not worry about that as nothing would come of it.

Members of the Red Nation were arriving in Rehoboth in increasing numbers and the place looked like an armed camp, but Jonker bided his time. He had other things to do which paid him better. Besides that, he was very dissatisfied with his Hereros. They had not done their duty properly when they were fighting in the front ranks in the battle of Windhoek. When so many of them were shot down by the Namas, the rest began to flee. Jonker now had all those that ran away shot. He was therefore poorly provided with fighting men who were ready to pluck the chestnuts out of the fire for the Afrikanders. He sent the rest of his Hereros and the Bergdamas time and again into the Rehoboth territory to visit different cattle posts, and there he got back all the cattle that had been taken from him, and very many others with them, until Willem Swartbooi was in utter despair. Meanwhile, Oasib became tired of the whole business. Abraham Bondelswart, the blind chief of Warmbad, had written him a very acrimonious letter, which contained only insults and abuses, without saying plainly why he was so angry with Oasib. All that the latter could understand from it was that some danger was threatening him from this direction. Simon Afrikander, whom Jonker had instructed to keep Oasib in check from the east, became very active. A kind of revolution took place in Rehoboth. The old tribal law was repealed and a new code of law, the so-called 'Law of Sin' was proclaimed on the 3rd April, 1885. The chief provision of this law was to the effect that the women and girls should be free for everybody in future. Kleinschmidt was then compelled to leave and go to Rooibank. Before he went back the more decent part of the people had repealed the 'Law of Sin' again, and Jonker had meanwhile paid Rehoboth a visit and kept it under fire for a whole day. Very little blood flowed, for the wall round the village afforded very efficient protection. During the battle the Red Nation had occupied the mission house and had done dreadful damage to it. When bullets ran short, they had melted up the communion vessels and made them into bullets. Jonker had retired without attempting to storm the place.

Oasib returned to Hoachanas with his Red Nation. It was felt that the war was at an end. Willem Swartbooi, who had not got very far with his 'Law of Sin', collected round him those of the tribe who were of his way of thinking, and went with them to the copper mines, which were on the boundary of Jonker's territory, so that he could live as he chose, free from interference.

The uncertainty of the times made things very unpleasant for the people who were mining the copper. They were dependent upon their oxen for the transport of their copper to the sea. Their trek oxen were repeatedly stolen from them, and likewise their milch cows and small stock. Up to that time they had looked chiefly to Jonker and had thought that he had the right to grant them mining concessions. Willem Swartbooi, however, claimed to have the same right, and so did Oasib, his paramount chief, and this question was by no means one of academic rights, for a considerable income in cash went with the granting of the concession. For every ton of copper ore, which was taken out, the mines paid a round £1 sterling. The time had arrived to determine once and for all to whom this money really belonged. In order to avoid being attacked by one or other of these tribes in the long run, the manager of the mine, Mr. Reid, got into touch with Jonker and succeeded in getting him to invite Willem Swartbooi and Oasib to a peace conference at Kupferberg. 'You are the great paramount chief of the Namas, but I am chief over my own tribe', he wrote to Oasib. On this basis it was possible to negotiate. Oasib brought his missionary, Vollmer, with him, and Willem Swartbooi brought Kleinschmidt along. Amraal came from the eastern side of the country. When Oasib saw the great mass of people who had gathered together prepared to make peace, another idea suddenly came into his head. It seemed to him that Jonker had expressed himself very haughtily in the letter of invitation he had sent. It would not do him any harm if he were to be thoroughly humiliated before peace was concluded. Vollmer told him that that sort of thing was not done amongst civilized people, and that, when any one had agreed to make peace, he had no right at all to take up weapons.

Oasib then submitted. The gathering at the Kupferberg was an impressive one. Jonker was there with a large bodyguard and his counsellors. He went up to Oasib and greeted him very cordially as his 'father to whom he had to be thankful that he was still alive'. After all present had attended the funeral of a miner, who had been accidentally killed, the negotiations began. Oasib put forward the demand that he should be recognized by every one as paramount chief, and that occasioned a lively discussion. This became almost too warm and it was well that Kleinschmidt and Vollmer were there. They persuaded them to discuss the matter quietly and advised the others to give way. They came to an agreement whereby Oasib retained his former position and Jonker likewise kept the rights which he had. To determine what these were, the first thing of all that had to be decided was the right of granting mining concessions. Jonker, however, handled this point very skilfully, so skilfully that a resolution was taken that all boundary questions should be dealt with at a conference to be held later. So the peace of Kupferberg was concluded on the 24th November, 1855, and every one went home except Jonker, who went to Rehoboth to visit his former friends, who had become his friends once more!

Provision had been made in the peace treaty of Kupferberg that a conference of chiefs would be convened to adjust all differences as to boundaries, and to settle the question of the mines. This did not take place until the 22nd April, 1858. Barmen (Otjikango) was selected as the place for the conference. The only people who appeared to discuss the matter were Jonker, Oasib, and the mine manager, Hilder. Hugo Hahn, the missionary in whose house the conference took place, was invited to attend as adviser and witness. The question of precedence was brought up once again. Oasib recognized Jonker as a chief who was his equal in rank and entirely independent of him. Jonker agreed that from then onwards half of the royalties received from the mines in his territory should go to Oasib. The course of the Kuiseb was fixed as the southern boundary of Jonker's tribal territories. Just as the question of the Hereros had been avoided at the peace conference at Kupferberg, so nothing was said about it at the meeting at Barmen.

The peace of Hoachanas

The parties who had entered into the peace treaty at Kupferberg were of the opinion that the peace, which they had concluded, could not be completely effective until it had received universal recognition. For this reason a general peace conference at Hoachanas for the whole of Namaland was proposed. The consent of the two chiefs of Bethanie and Rehoboth, who had taken no part in the negotiations at Kupferberg, was the principal aim. Jonker Afrikander undertook to send out the invitations to attend.

Paul Goliath and David Christian had previously entered into an agreement of mutual support and protection. They met once again to discuss between themselves the conditions under which they would subscribe to the peace at Hoachanas. They agreed upon the following points:

1. The peace should embrace the whole country.
2. The Hereros should be included in the peace.
3. Any one who should steal cattle from the Hereros after the conclusion of peace would be punished by a police force appointed for the purpose by the peace conference.
4. This police force should also be used against any Hereros who encroached upon Namaland, and should take them for punishment to a court of justice appointed by the peace conference.

The two Nama chiefs arrived at Hoachanas but Oasib was not there. He was in fact near by but did not put in an appearance. He sent them a message that the council meeting would take place some days later. They sent him a request that he should come and discuss matters with them personally. He sent the message back 'I have told you you must go home'. As neither Jonker nor Willem Swartbooi nor Amraal was there, the two men left and were back home again by the 19th March. It is unfortunately impossible to explain this remarkable occurrence and to give the real reason for it. After this, there was certainly very little mutual confidence between the people who had concluded the peace treaty of Kupferberg and those who wanted to conclude one at Hoachanas. This appears very clearly from the following occurrence. Kido Witbooi, who had been wandering all over Namaland since 1850, erected huts at numbers of different places, and would not accept from Oasib any fixed dwellingplace. He was inclined to give up this nomadic existence and to accept a missionary to look after his numerous people. Just then he was staying near Kalkfontein. Jonker had summoned him to Windhoek on more than one occasion and had given him exceedingly friendly invitations, for Kido was likewise an Orlam from the Orange River. Up to that time Kido had not accepted the invitation.

Jonker, who had now definitely given up the idea of becoming paramount chief in Namaland, was anxious to negotiate with Kido personally, for the purpose of increasing his strength by combining this powerful tribe with his own. He even considered the possibility of making Kido his successor in Windhoek in the event of his joining forces with him. Jonker still had a number of plans which he was anxious to carry out. We shall hear of these plans and their execution later. Even if the peace of Hoachanas came to pass, and any further despoiling of the Hereros (who had not really much more to lose) should be forbidden him, there was still Ovamboland on the other side of Hereroland. It seemed an attractive goal for his declining years to go with Kido Witbooi to the north, obtain further riches for himself there, and discover a kind of paradise, in which he could settle his tribe. Then the Nama chiefs, who did not want to recognize his authority, could go ahead with their peace of Hoachanas.

In order to reach Kido, however, Jonker had to pass Hoachanas. He sent a message to Oasib that he was coming and told him that he was coming in peace. Oasib was not present when the message arrived, but the missionary Vollmer, who had Oasib's confidence, let Jonker know that he would be welcome. This act did not receive Oasib's approval. He was seized with suspicion and summoned his men together to oppose Jonker by force of arms. Jonker must have learned of this for he never went to Hoachanas but gave it a wide berth. Jonker stayed at Kalkfontein for some considerable time, and on the 26th October, he sent a letter to Oasib inquiring whether he would allow him to go back through his territory to Windhoek. Jonker was uneasy, for there were no mountains round about Hoachanas in which he could take refuge, and there were no Hereros whom he could put into the front line of battle. Oasib sent him a friendly reply and invited him to come and see him. On the 31st October two of Jonker's messengers arrived in Hoachanas, where they were very surprised to find everything so peaceful. Rumour had reached Kalkfontein that the people at Hoachanas were making feverish preparation to fight Jonker. He passed through there and went on to Windhoek unmolested.

The chiefs of Bethanie and Berseba received a letter from Kido Witbooi inviting them to a peace conference. The place and time of the conference were, however, not mentioned. They were both rather taken aback that the invitation should not come from Oasib, or from Jonker, but from an Orlam, who was a complete stranger in the country. This created the impression that the conference was to be a conference of Orlams and not as they wanted—a conference of all the chiefs of the country. On this account they feared that their participation might be regarded with disfavour by other chiefs who were perhaps not invited, and that war instead of peace might be the result. When, however, they received a formal invitation from Oasib in the beginning of December, they laid their scruples aside and set out for Hoachanas. A busy time began for Oasib at Hoachanas, which was usually so quiet. On the 4th December he laid the foundation stone of a large church, which was to mark the termination of his nomadic life. On the 22nd December, Amraal arrived with ten wagons and nearly all his followers. The chiefs of Bethanie and Berseba arrived there during the Christmas holidays. Jonker came on the scene on the 4th January with twenty-seven wagons and one hundred mounted men, and he brought with him a considerable number of other chiefs with their counsellors. The peace negotiations started on the 5th January, immediately after his arrival. The missionary Vollmer, who had likewise been invited to take part in the negotiations, opened them with a religious address. The Griqua, Andries Van Rooi, was chosen as chairman upon the proposal of Jonker, Oasib, Amraal, and Witbooi, for he was recognized as a man who was not mixed up in the numerous political disputes between the chiefs. That was a gesture of goodwill and so was the fact that Tjamuaha, the Herero chief, had been invited as well. He could not, however, be present personally because of his great age, and he sent his three sons as his representatives, and of these the peace treaty makes mention of Jan and Piet Kopervoet. Maharero's name does not appear in it, although he was present. The Namas called Tjamuaha 'Kopervoet' because he wore heavy copper rings round his ankles. His sons' Herero names are not mentioned. At that time anybody with any sort of self-respect adopted some European name by which he was known amongst the Europeans and Orlams. The first and second days of the negotiations were devoted to the settlement of the dissensions and grievances which the individual chiefs had against each other. After the slate had been wiped clean of these, the relations between Jonker and Oasib were discussed in the light of their agreement at Barmen, and they became completely reconciled. The meeting then passed on to the discussion of the general position throughout the land, and the relationship between all the different chiefs and tribes. The result of the decisions was drawn up and recorded in Dutch, and so it was that there came into being the twelve articles of Hoachanas which were signed on the 9th January, 1858, by all the responsible people who took part in the peace conference.

Each of the chiefs went back to his own territory. The twelve articles of Hoachanas furnished excellent proof of the fact that none of them lacked knowledge of what the land really required. The future will show that what was lacking was a strong hand which could carry out the provisions of the treaty.

Jonker and the Ovambo tribes

In 1857 Hugo Hahn and Rath had travelled to Ovamboland in order to learn something about that country and its people, and to investigate the possibilities of founding a mission amongst the Ovambos. The chief Nangoro had received them in a very unfriendly way, and they only narrowly escaped with their lives. On the day of their departure, however, Nangoro died suddenly and his brother Tjikongo assumed the chieftainship. Some of the people were dissatisfied with him as successor and they got into touch with Jonker, hoping that he would help them to put their opposition into effect.

Jonker was only too glad to have an excuse to go amongst the Ovambos. Had not they treated two missionaries who were under his protection very improperly? Had not they even called him into their country to decide their quarrels? Of course the articles of Hoachanas had forbidden raiding, and Jonker had duly subscribed to them, but those articles said nothing at all about Ovamboland, and, besides that, it was always contemplated that chiefs could act as arbitrators in quarrels between other people! Jonker sent one Karuaina, a Herero, to Ovamboland as a spy, and then dispatched an armed force composed in part of Afrikanders under the command of his nephew Jan Jonker, and partly of Hereros under the command of Tjamuaha's son. In order that they might not arouse any suspicion they were provided with goods for trading, so that it might appear that the expedition was a trading one. Jonker's cousin, Simon, likewise took part in the expedition. They entered Ovamboland in the beginning of October, and their success was much greater than had been expected. Eighteen cattle posts were stripped of all their cattle, and two of Nangoro's sons and three of the chief Tjipanga's wives were taken prisoners. All this loot was brought to Windhoek. On the return journey one section of the party made a detour to

Grootfontein, killed a number of Herero cattle-herds in the veld, and took their cattle along.

Tjikongo recognized that he had very little chance against Jonker and the guns with which his men were armed. He sought, therefore, to gain Jonker's favour by peaceable means. In May 1859, when the rainy season was over and it was possible to travel in Ovamboland again, he sent an envoy to Jonker with a large following and a goodly number of presents. He was very anxious to get the release of the prisoners who were in Jonker's hands. With this object in view, there had been included in the company a number of Hereros, who had been captured in Ovamboland whilst stealing cattle. They belonged to Tjamuaha's tribe, and they had been surrendered all the more readily because their comrades had got away with the booty. Jonker did not at all approve of this high-handedness. He summoned his council together and placed Tjamuaha's acts before them. It was decided that Tjamuaha should collect all the stolen cattle and deliver them to Jonker, and that he should replace any that had already been killed out of his own stock. The Ovambos' property was to be returned to them, for Jonker's expedition had been a punitive one, sent because they had failed to ask him as suzerain chief whether he approved of Nangoro's successor, but Tjamuaha had committed the criminal offence of cattle stealing. To Tjamuaha he said: 'The white people (Hahn, Rath, and Green) had to fight for their very lives in Ovamboland and yet they did not go raiding. When they escaped, they did not send out Hereros to steal cattle. You, however, have gone on a cattle stealing expedition without the slightest excuse. It will be said of us throughout the land that we are rogues.' This raid of Tjamuaha's had been conducted by the Herero, Katjiunda. It is not known whether the loot was actually sent back, or whether it stayed in Jonker's kraals.

Jonker handed over the prisoners to Tjikongo's emissaries and let them go back safe and sound. He sent Tjikongo a message, however, that he was coming personally to fix up all the other questions with him. Tjikongo, who knew very well that he had treated Hahn, Rath, and Green very badly, knew too that the chieftainship was not his according to the law of succession, and he had grave doubts as to what the outcome of this visit would be.

It was in July or August 1860 that the story went round the country that Jonker was making ready for a journey to Ovamboland.

His mission was, of course, a peaceful one, for its object was to decide certain quarrels between the Ovambos themselves. Jonker took the road with forty wagons, almost the whole of his fighting men, many of whom were mounted, and a large nunber of followers. Adam Kraai was a member of Jonker's company. A swarm of traders from Otjimbingwe and the surrounding country followed the march to do business.

Tjikongo very soon saw that the objectives of this expedition were anything but peaceable. He took to his heels with all the people who could manage to get away, and left all the cattle behind. No battle was ever fought. The only work that Jonker did was to gather in, and to collect together, all the property that the tribe had left behind, whether it was living or inanimate. He had come prepared for this task—a tremendous quantity of stuff can be loaded on to forty ox-wagons. He stayed in Ovamboland for almost six months. In a good rainy season no ox-wagon can travel through the country during the rainy season, between December and April, because it is flooded. When the rains were past Jonker went back to Windhoek. Andersson reckons that he brought about 20,000 cattle with him and his total losses were two men. But he was not to get any pleasure out of what he had stolen for rinderpest[1] broke out and most of the stolen cattle died. Of the 800 cattle which, according to Andersson's account, one trader had brought with him from Ovamboland, barely a hundred survived. It was said that Jonker had brought the rinderpest with him from Ovamboland; others again said that the trader Chapman, who had at this time passed through on his way from Lake Ngami, had brought it to Otjimbingwe, and that it had spread from there throughout the country.

While Jonker was away in Ovamboland the restless spirits of Namaland had not sat quiet. They grudged Jonker the possession of all this wealth. Several bands of marauders under various leaders set out to despoil other Ovambo tribes. Hendrik Nanib set out; some of Amraal's tribe did so too, and an armed mob of the people of the Red Nation likewise took the road to the north. No one thought any more of the twelve articles of Hoachanas. All were intensely

[1] Rinderpest or lung sickness has swept South Africa from the Zambezi to the Cape several times, and entirely decimated its cattle. Veterinary science has now robbed it of its terrors.—*Ed.*

interested in the success of those who had gone raiding and secretly made up their minds to follow their example. The outbreak of the rinderpest, and then the events which followed it, namely Jonkers' death and the Herero war of freedom, prevented these secret plans from being put into execution.

The inhabitants of Windhoek, however, had during Jonker's absence gone on some cattle stealing expeditions against the Hereros, and this was clearly a breach of the covenant of Hoachanas. When Jonker came back and found out what his Afrikanders had done, he tried them and dealt very severely with them.

Krönlein writes, at the end of this period, in dealing with the general position of affairs in so far as Namaland and its chiefs were concerned:

'Oasib calls himself "the father of his country" but most of his people go on murderous raids without his even punishing them. Amraal is old and has become so powerless that it is very unlikely that the parties of marauders who have set out from Witvley will ever be punished. His son, Lambert, has the reins in his hands, and he is a crafty customer who seems to take after Jonker. Kido Witbooi's son, Moses, who is almost as grey-haired as his father, has established amongst the latter's large following a section of people who are of Jonker's way of thinking, and thus the hands of the old man are tied, and the son acquires more and more power and has thrust his father into the background. Hendrik Nanib, captain of the Veldskoendraers, is an inflated windbag like his whole tribe, who are just a real band of robbers. He has gone raiding at the head of his commando. Aimab and Garib, Oasib's subordinates, are at daggers drawn regarding precedence, each of them claiming to be superior to the other. Willem Swartbooi's dignity and influence have practically disappeared. Jan Booi keeps right away on the boundaries of the inhabited country, because he fears that his son-in-law, Jonker, who has threatened to make "boot-soles out of the thick skin of his neck", may actually carry out his threat. But for this, he would have gone to stay in Ovamboland. Fear prevented him from doing so and has driven him down as far as Bethanie. David Christian is far too much the slave of his good or bad moods. If he is in a good mood, his kindness knows no bounds. If he is in a bad one, then he wants "to punish God himself". That, amongst his very many good points, is his principal fault, and it has caused him to do many a wrong. Paul Goliath, who is old and grey, counts for nothing as a chief, but as a private individual and Christian he exercises a good influence. Compared with him, his brother-in-law, Jacobus Izak, is a good ruler and a strong character. He is just as he appears to be, and that is a trait one seldom finds amongst the Namas.'

The Europeans and the Namas

Up to this time the property rights of the Europeans in South West Africa had been respected. Of course, some troubles had arisen when, for example, stock was being sent through Namaland across the Orange River and the temptation to steal was really too great, but these little irregularities had never become unendurable. In December 1860 some thieving Namas did an unheard-of thing in Otjimbingwe, which aroused the ill feeling of everybody, and was the cause of all the Europeans living in the neighbourhood being called together for their mutual protection. The circumstances were as follows: Two Englishmen, Wilson and Castray, had a cattle post at Anawood, near Otjimbingwe. One day five hundred of their cattle failed to come back from the veld, and the relatives of the cattle-herds reported that they were likewise missing. Inquiries were made, and it came out that four of Wilson's cattle-herds had been locked up in a hut and burned to death, and that two of Castray's servants had been killed. The cattle had been driven off. It was then decided to call a council of all Europeans to decide what steps should be taken. Andersson was chosen as chairman of the meeting. He was very well known and was well liked by both the Europeans and the Hereros. No one knew at that time with any certainty who the thieves were, but it was thought that Hendrik Nanib and a party belonging to the Red Nation were the authors of this impudent outrage, and that Willem Swartbooi and Oasib knew all about it. It was therefore decided to go to Rehoboth and demand from Willem Swartbooi that he should take the matter up. The justification for making this demand was based upon the twelve articles of Hoachanas.

It was decided further that, in case Willem Swartbooi and Oasib should refuse to deal with the matter in the way that was required of them, the forty Europeans present should take up arms, that the wagon drivers and the staff of the copper mines should be armed too, and that the whole force should be strengthened by the addition of Herero volunteers. It was then not only Rehoboth which was to be brought to book, but the idea was to wipe the slate clean and to bring the rest of the Nama tribes to heel. There went hand in hand with these decisions an idea which was not openly discussed, the execution of which was, however, felt to be very desirous and necessary for the peace of the country, in order to enable the Europeans to carry out their work undisturbed. As there was lacking in Namaland a hand strong enough to maintain law and order, and as there was no tribal organization at all amongst the Hereros, it was felt that the time had come for the Europeans to take over the reins of Government in both the north and the south, and that there was no person who was better qualified than Andersson to take upon himself this control. He was the most enterprising of them all, and he was liked by the Hereros and the better disposed Namas, while he enjoyed the confidence of all the Europeans, and no one had any reason whatever to doubt his capabilities and honesty of purpose. Perhaps the time had now come when this excellent idea should be put into practice.

Upon the instructions of this council of war Wilson wrote a letter to Willem Swartbooi. It was signed by the forty Europeans. Willem sent an answer immediately to Otjimbingwe explaining the position and assuring them that neither he nor Oasib, nor any people belonging to the Red Nation, had taken any part in the robbery, but that Hendrik Nanib, the chief of the Veldskoendraers, was the sole culprit. He disapproved of this man entirely, and he was ready to try to get the Europeans' property back for them, so far as laid in his power. He had already sent out a circular letter to all the chiefs allied to Hoachanas.

After receipt of this letter, another council of war was held at Otjimbingwe. It was agreed that they were willing to settle the matter peacefully, but it was decided to demand of the Swartboois that, in the event of it being necessary, they should declare themselves to be prepared to attack Hendrik Nanib jointly with the Europeans.

Four Englishmen took the letter to Rehoboth. Great excitement reigned there and, when they saw the horsemen in the distance, they thought that an attack was going to be made on them. Only when the messengers had entered Kleinschmidt's house did their minds become easy. From there they went to discuss matters with Willem Swartbooi. He declared himself unwilling to go and attack Hendrik Nanib in the company of the Europeans, but he was willing to go up against him alone and to take from him the cattle which he had stolen. When he took objection to the fact that he was being treated as a guilty party, he was told very plainly that it appeared very strange to the Europeans that the traders' transport oxen were not allowed to pass through the territory of the Nama tribes because of the existence of rinderpest, while Hendrik Nanib should be allowed to go through with a number of cattle from an infected area without any hindrance. Willem Swartbooi then tried to intercept Hendrik with his best troops, but the latter had slipped through between Rehoboth and Berseba. At last they found him. As he was no match for Willem's forces, all Wilson's and Castray's stock, which were still in his possession, were taken away from him. It was half of what had been taken—250 head of cattle. Many of the animals had died of lung-sickness and some of the others had perished of thirst along the way. The Europeans had put up their camp on the Rehoboth border, and they were waiting to see what would happen, with the idea of stepping in without any loss of time. Willem Swartbooi returned on the 15th March, 1861, and the Europeans were advised immediately. They entered Rehoboth the following day and Andersson was with them. The 250 cattle were taken over and the owners, Wilson and Castray, declared that they were satisfied, and every one was glad that an affair, which had looked so alarming in the beginning, had righted itself in the end.

Hendrik Nanib, however, demanded compensation from his own subjects for the 250 head of cattle he had lost and he found them exceedingly unwilling to give it. They had the courage to say it was entirely his fault that the raid had turned out badly. He then decided to punish them thoroughly, and he told his neighbour, Kido Witbooi, to keep out of his way so that he could have plenty of elbow room. Kido Witbooi, however, maintained a bold front and nothing came of the threat of punishment.

The death of Jonker Afrikander and of Tjamuaha

Jonker had worried very little about Windhoek since 1854. It is true that a number of his relatives lived there and that it was his head-quarters, and if there was any serious business to be done, which had to be laid before the tribal council, he put in an appearance there for a few days, or perhaps even weeks. During the rest of the time, he was sometimes in Oamites, sometimes in Otjimbingwe, and sometimes in other places. He often stayed with his friend Tjamuaha and his garrison in Okahandja. Upon his return from Ovamboland, he first of all went to Windhoek. Kleinschmidt found him there on the 21st July, 1861, and he little thought that, when he paid him his next visit, he would find him on his death-bed. Shortly after that, Jonker went to Okahandja and when he arrived there he fell ill. He had picked up the germs of his illness in Ovamboland. Tjamuaha fell ill just about the same time. While Jonker was on his raiding expedition Tjamuaha had been to the Kaokoveld to see his old friends and relatives once again. It would seem that he discussed with them a great many things of which very little is known. Maharero could almost certainly have said what they were, but he never did so. He brought with him from the Kaokoveld a chief called Mireti, who later settled with his people in the country round about Omaruru, and he also brought Kaupangua with him. When he got back to Okahandja he felt that his days were numbered. He had likewise brought back with him from this journey the germs of his last illness. Jonker lay in his hut on the west side of the Okahandja river. On the north side, about a hundred yards from there, Tjamuaha lay in his hut. Jonker sent three of his Herero headmen, Kahuueni, Makurupa, and Kanangure, over almost every day to ask how Tjamuaha was. Tjamuaha replied to the inquiry by sending back a messenger of his own. It was a question of honour with Jonker not to die before Tjamuaha, and he would have been only too glad to learn that his ally had passed away. Tjamuaha had the same feelings about the matter, and often asked his messengers 'Is that man, that friend of mine, not dead yet?' When he received an answer in the negative he had a way of saying to himself: 'That is empty talk, you child of Tjipuputa ua Ngombe. I still remain the Karupumbura.'

(In using these words Tjamuaha was trying to maintain his own courage. Katjipuputa was the name of his mother and she was Ngombe's daughter. Out of the word Okupumbura, which means 'to cut the branch off a tree', he invented for himself the name Karupumbura, the prefixing of *ka* to some other word being a way of making names for small children. For this reason one often finds that Katjamuaha or Kamaherero are written in old accounts in place of Tjamuaha and Maherero. It was only in the case of chiefs that the custom was to leave the diminutive prefix out. What he meant to say was, 'I am Karupumba, and therefore I shall survive even when the old branch (Jonker) is chopped down, i.e. I am going to live longer than Jonker.')

Jonker felt that his strength was deserting him and that his end was approaching. He sent for his son and heir, Christian, and said to him: 'When I am dead give Maharero all the things that I have had in my personal use, give him my clothes and my shoes, my pipe and my tobacco pouch, my stick and my old gun, and also my cartridge belt, and everything else of that kind.' Then he had Maharero also summoned to his bedside, while Christian was present, and he gave them both this solemn warning: 'You two have grown up side by side like brothers. See that you treat each other as brothers should. Rule the Namas and the Hereros together and do not quarrel.' Then he took off his right shoe and he gave it to Christian, and he took off his left shoe and he gave it to Maharero, indicating by doing so that both of them were to succeed him in the chieftainship, but that Christian should be first.

After he had said goodbye and put his affairs in order, he sent a man on horseback to Otjimbingwe, where Kleinschmidt happened to be acting as a substitute for the missionaries who were absent on a journey. Jonker had always thought a great deal of Kleinschmidt, while he had hated Hugo Hahn. Just a few weeks before his death he had expressed his opinion of the former to a Nama messenger from Rehoboth as follows:

'I know that neither Willem Swaartbooi nor Oasib can stand Kleinschmidt because he refuses to fall in with their wishes; but when they want to say nasty things about me, when Kleinschmidt is present, he replies, 'You are not a bit better than Jonker.'' That is what I like about him—he never speaks evil about me behind my back, but only when he is alone with me—for he tells me the truth and makes out that I am the only sinner in the whole wide world.'

Kleinschmidt had only come down from Rehoboth and taken over the work at Otjimbingwe on the 2nd August, and directly he received Jonker's request that he should come and help him to die, which was on the 16th August, he started out immediately. His horses, however, were so utterly exhausted that he had to do half the journey on foot. He arrived at Okahandja the following day and found Jonker so weak that he could not talk to him. It was only on the Sunday morning of the 18th August that he was able to have a long talk with him for the first time. Jonker was not unresponsive to the religious comfort he wished to give him, but he utterly refused to admit, before God and man, that the things that he had done were wrong. He was willing to recognize that all human beings were responsible for the sins of the race, but his own personal sins did not worry him a bit. Kleinschmidt then went to hold a service for the Namas who belonged to the garrison in Okahandja and, when the service was over, the news reached him that Jonker had just died. Kleinschmidt could not possibly give him a Christian burial, and his grave was dug under a camel-thorn tree, which stood outside his hut. He lies buried on the mission property at Okahandja, and the cattle have trodden into the ground the few stones with which his grave was marked and protected. A fine church was erected in 1876 by the Rhenish mission on the place where his hut formerly stood.

When Tjamuaha heard that Jonker was dead, he had his relations called to his bedside and he said to them: 'Children, now I am ready to follow the man who was my friend. My friend is waiting for me. Come here that I may give you my blessing.' (The words of a dying man were regarded by the Hereros and the Namas as having magical effect, especially when they were spoken by a man like Tjamuaha, who was the guardian of the sacred fire.) Maharero bent down before his father, and the latter took both his hands between his own and stroked them several times, backwards and forwards, as if he was giving him something, and said, 'Take it, take it! Keep our people together! Be faithful to the service of the sacred fire of your ancestors!' He then spat into Maharero's open mouth and repeated the words, 'Take it, take it!' By doing this he transferred to Maharero at one and the same time his religious powers, his priesthood, and his office as chief. Then he added: 'My child, the things which I have had in my personal use are to be given to Christian when I die.'

Christian too, Jonker's successor, came to say good-bye to Tjamuaha a few days later. He was very anxious to receive Tjamuaha's blessing, for he believed that his last blessing would ensure him success, while his curse would do him a great deal of harm. Tjamuaha summoned Maharero also to his bedside, and said to them both: 'You two have grown up together like brothers and now it is for you to conduct yourselves as such in the future. Govern the Hereros and the Namas together and do not quarrel.' Then he took the shoe from his right foot and gave it to Maharero, and the left one he gave to Christian, to whom he made the promise that all the things which he himself had used should go to him. When Christian then asked for a special blessing, Tjamuaha said that he could not give him that; he could only give him that if he had a large blanket made from fresh lamb skins and brought it to him. Christian went away and made arrangements that sufficient lambs should be slaughtered and that the skins should be brayed and sewn together. This took a considerable time, and Tjamuaha became increasingly weaker. At last the blanket was finished, and Christian went over to Tjamuaha, with a large following, to go and secure his blessing. He spread the blanket out before him and waited for him to speak. Tjamuaha let his eyes wander backwards and forwards over the blanket and was very glad, but not so much because of the blanket as because he had been able, before his death, to cause these Namas, who had so often worried, frightened, and robbed him during his lifetime, very considerable loss, by inducing them to kill so many of their lambs for him. Then he turned round on his bed and turned his back on Christian, shutting one eye, but peeping out of the other to see what impression his action was making on Christian and those who had come with him. Christian knew very well that an insult was intended, and he left the hut in a rage and never entered it again. Just about this time a son was born to Kavezeri, one of Tjamuaha's near relations, and the father gave it the name of 'Uasikeho' which means 'He (Tjamuaha) closed one eye only'.

Tjamuaha, however, said to his sons: 'When I am dead I will free you from the Namas.' It must have been sometime in December 1861 that Tjamuaha closed his eyes for the last time. The exact date is not known.

On the afternoon of the day on which he died, a strong whirlwind sprang up, rushed past the dead man's house, and turned southwards to the place where the Namas lived. There it gained such force that it tore the mats from the Namas' huts and carried them off to the south. Then the Hereros said amongst themselves: 'That is Tjamuaha's spirit. The Namas will have to leave and go and build their huts down in the south, i.e. in Namaland.' Tjamuaha was buried at the entrance of his cattle kraal. The mourning ceremony was duly held and a *kudu* horn was planted on his grave in his memory, for he had belonged to the religious sect of the Kudus, and nothing might be placed on their grave which belonged to the head of an ox. Christian Afrikander was desirous of observing the outward forms of friendship. and sent one of his men on horseback to the burial place to 'view the grave'. He could just as well have gone there on foot, for Christian's werf was not more than five hundred yards away from Tjamuaha's grave. When Christian's representative had 'viewed' the grave he mounted his horse again. The horse, however, threw its rider who was unfortunate enough to break his neck and lie dead where he fell. That was regarded as a bad sign. The Namas did not trust Tjamuaha's spirit and began to hate the Hereros.

The death-knell of the Jonker period

The earth now covered both these men, who had made history in South West Africa during the last twenty or thirty years. Not a single Nama mourned for Jonker. The old lion was dead and every-body breathed again. Nor did a single Herero mourn for Tjamuaha, for he had thrown his own people over for the sake of his cattle, and he had become the willing ally of a foreign tyrant, without having any genuine regard for him. The bonds of friendship are not woven from self-interest, fear, and cunning. To what extent the outward friendship between Christian and Maharero was to hold good still remained to be seen. For the time being they lived peacefully side by side.

Piet Koper supported young Christian with his following and lived with him in Okahandja. Hendrik Nanib thought it advisable to go and stay there too. Piet Koper was quiet and considerate and exer-cised a good influence. Hendrik Nanib, with his gang, was unruly and intractable, and his influence promised to become a great danger to the community. Kleinschmidt was the only missionary in the whole country as far as the tropics, for all the others had been called away. Barmen stood deserted. With Otjimbingwe as his centre he looked after Rehoboth and kept it straight. He went to Okahandja too. He had an idea that Christian, who had for many years up-braided his father for having thrust Hahn and Kleinschmidt to one side in 1844, might be prepared to accept a missionary. In March 1862 he went to Okahandja with seven Nama youths, whom he had trained as teachers. He stayed there for some considerable time, made the young men he had brought with him give the children lessons, and occupied himself in doing the same for the grown-up people amongst the Namas and the Hereros. Life there began to assume a pleasant aspect. Christian was prepared to allow Kleinschmidt to come and stay there as his people's minister. Maharero, who had written to Barmen long before to ask for a missionary, was likewise agreeable. Kleinschmidt, however, had already two congregations to look after. When he returned to Otjimbingwe he received valuable presents. Even Maharero contributed a fat sheep, and the school children of both races insisted on accompanying the wagon as far as the next outspan place, so that they could have their lessons for the last time.

Andersson, too, who was Kleinschmidt's friend, thought it wise to pay a visit to the two young chiefs and set out for Okahandja, taking his wife with him. His good intentions might very well have had a tragic ending. A man named Piet Hartebeest had settled close to the road to Okahandja. He was one of Jonker's relations, but was a rough fellow of no importance. For a long time he had been playing the part of highwayman; he had been robbing all the Hereros who passed that way, ill-treating Bergdamas, and worrying the Europeans. Andersson outspanned close to where he lived and watered his oxen there. Piet came on the scene and started to make trouble. He had heard that Andersson had a box on his wagon, which contained presents for Christian Afrikander, and he demanded this box. In spite of the fact that Mrs. Andersson was sitting in the wagon, he wanted to go and take it forcibly. This made Andersson angry. He ordered his men to leave immediately and tried to mount his horse. Piet snatched at the reins to stop him. One of the reins hit Andersson in the face and injured his eye. Andersson lost his temper, took his gun, and shot Piet dead. He went on and reached Okahandja. There he placed himself at Christian's disposal. As, however, Piet had started the quarrel, and besides that was known to be a good-for-nothing, and no one was sorry that the highwayman was put out of action, the council decided to dismiss the case. Andersson, however, suffered from the effects of this incident to the end of his life. Elephant hunters came to Okahandja, as well, to pay their respects to Christian. They generally brought one or two casks of brandy with them and started carousing with the Afrikanders. Life became wild there and Christian countermanded his request to Kleinschmidt for the missionary, whom he had before been so anxious to get. What still remains to be told about him after 1862 does not belong to the ending of the period which we have just dealt with here, but to the new period between the years 1863 and 1870, when the history of the Hereros' war of freedom comes to be told.

2. THE PROGRESS OF CIVILIZATION AND ITS OBSTACLES

After everything that has been said previously about the political events of the period between 1850 and 1862, it might reasonably be expected that there could be no talk whatever of the progress of civilization, and that, in dealing with the obstacles to civilization, it would suffice merely to point out the condition of things throughout the period, in that it was one which was utterly subversive of the very existence of civilization. But this is not the case. Just as the period between 1830 and 1850 corresponded to the Iron Age, in that it succeeded the Stone Age, so the period with which we are now concerned may be called the Copper Age.

Copper had been discovered in Little Namaqualand, and the copper fever broke out. One company after another was formed to exploit it, and any one who wanted to get rich quickly bought copper shares. Feverish activity broke out from the Buffalo River to the Orange River. Europeans and native labourers hastened to go and live in parts in which not a single person had ever lived before. Mines were established, barrack-like buildings arose, and small villages were built in the wilderness, while ships came and went, and ox wagons toiled backwards and forwards.

Copper in Namaland

The prospectors for copper made their way into South West Africa. Angra Pequena (Luderitzbucht) offered a safe anchorage for ships. If there was copper in the interior, the transport would not be so expensive as to be a bar to its exploitation. The interior of the country must be prospected. We find that by 1852 there was a small settlement of Europeans at Angra Pequena, and that they had put up wooden houses for themselves there. In 1854, the trader, Fielding, got a lease from the chief at Warmbad of a large piece of his territory for the purpose of exploring it for copper, and he paid a considerable sum of money for the concession. Not content with that he leased the rights of the whole country along the Orange River, between its mouth and its confluence to the Fish River, from David Christian at Bethanie. The contract was for thirty-three years, and, if copper should be found, the chief was to receive a payment of £50 a year. Some well-known names appeared on the scene again. A man named van Reenen went to live in a small bay to the south of Angra Pequena. It got the name of van Reenen's Cove, and the prospecting of the dune country was undertaken from there. Slaughter stock and labourers were sent him from Bethanie. As he met with no success, he stopped work in April 1855. A similar attempt was made three years later by another prospector. This bay now has the name of Baker's Cove. About the same time, David Christian leased the whole coast-line between the mouth of the Orange River and Angra Pequena, together with a strip of country five miles broad, to a trader. When, however, an attempt was made to mine for copper at Aus, without a prospecting concession, the chief of Bethanie sent some messengers there with written instructions that the work should stop. The miners decided to leave the place without giving trouble.

To-day one is surprised that a great deal of prospecting for copper was done in an area in which diamonds glittered all over the surface, without any one discovering them. We should, however, not forget to say that at the end of September 1855 the missionary Kreft went from Bethanie to the sea to pay van Reenen a visit, and that he found on his way back some remarkable crystals, which he casually mentions in a letter to the mission authorities in Barmen in the following words: 'I found some small transparent stones, which appear to be crystals, on the hills near Aus.'

Copper mines in the north

Some time before Jonker went to stay at Windhoek he had shown Alexander a copper deposit to the north of Rehoboth and the latter had taken samples of the ore to Capetown with him. After Jonker had constructed his road to the Bay, the possibility of working the deposit arose. A man named Stead went to Hoachanas and Rehoboth to get a concession from the chiefs. He agreed to pay Oasib £1 3s. for every ton of ore he mined and sent away. Jonker, however, claimed that the tax belonged to him. We know from what has gone before that this claim was settled by agreement between Oasib and Jonker at Barmen. A fall-out, which might well have been dangerous, took place between Oasib and the mining authorities, and they stopped payment of the tax in 1857. In the latter period of his life, Willem Swartbooi went and stayed at the mine and he compelled the inspector to pay these moneys to him, on the ground that he was the rightful owner of the property. Oasib did not like that. He appeared on the scene with an armed force of 150 men and demanded his rights. Messrs. Todd and Goodman had a very unpleasant time. On account of the difficulties of transport the workings did not pay and van Reenen came there on the 21st May, 1858, and stopped work and abandoned the mine.

Todd tried to work another deposit of copper very close to Rehoboth. Willem Swartbooi gave him the concession against payment of £1 2s. for each ton of ore removed. Todd arrived there with his people on the 4th November, 1856, and started the preparatory work. Rich ore was discovered on the surface and all that it required was to be loaded up and taken away. The impression, which he got from the surface indications, was so favourable that he went down to Capetown in 1857 to persuade the mining company to go in for operations on a larger scale. In this he was successful and a number of copper miners came from Capetown. Buildings were erected, quantities of stores were brought to the mine, traders came on the scene, and a lively business developed between the Europeans and the natives. If only there had not been that long and difficult road to the sea!

Walfish Bay became a very lively place. In 1854 the Jew, Aaron, came to stay there. He had, previous to this, spent several years fishing in Sandwich Harbour, and had likewise sold gunpowder and brandy in the Bay and had, in addition, worked the guano deposits on the coast quite profitably. Now he landed in the Bay with a very extensive undertaking in view. He brought with him five ox wagons and a large quantity of trade goods. His idea was to go on a trading trip right to Lake Ngami, and to prospect the whole country for minerals. The agreement which he made with Jonker, regarding all copper deposits in the lower Swakop valley, provided that Jonker should receive as tribute a one-eighth share of the value of the copper mined.

The Suffert, Wicks, Enterprise, and Walfish Bay Mining Companies were all now formed. They all had offices, storehouses, and residences for their agents in the Bay. Most of the undertakings never got any farther than the performance of preliminary and prospecting work. The concern which worked on the largest scale was the Walfish Bay Mining Company. They had obtained from Jonker the copper deposit, in the Jonker Mountains, at a place half-way down the Kuiseb valley. Taking Otjimbingwe as the centre of their operations they began work on the mine. The miners arrived at Otjimbingwe in five ox wagons from Walfish Bay the day before Christmas 1854, and houses were built for them there. A large number of oxen were bought for transporting the ore. The manager's name was Wallaston and that of the mine superintendent, who had charge of the transport, was Reid. The Namas and Afrikanders, who belonged to Jonker's garrison, acted as wagon drivers and the Hereros were employed in mining the ore. Unfortunately, in addition to the useful articles which were sold to Europeans and natives in the shops which were started there, a great deal of brandy was sold too, which gave the busy life of the place a lurid hue. They would much rather have got rid of the founder of the place, Rath, the missionary, although he did his best for the mine workers. We have already learned that they finally succeeded in doing so, but Kleinschmidt saw to it that they did not succeed in getting possession of the whole place, and it was with this object that he transferred his residence from Rehoboth to Otjimbingwe after Rath's departure. In 1857, Andersson became the manager of the company's operations. The successful years were already past. The good ore had been taken out and what remained contained only 20 per cent. of copper. Besides that, underground water was encountered in the mine and it would not have paid to erect a large pumping apparatus. Then a further deposit of copper ore was discovered close to Tsaobis and it was worked with good results. A great many things, however, were begun in South West Africa which in the end fell far short of the hope in which they were begun. As time went on, the business ceased to pay its way because the transport of the ore became so costly. Then the rinderpest broke out and nearly all the oxen belonging to the Company died. Mining operations were then stopped and, in April 1860, all the mine labourers returned from the mine to Otjimbingwe. On the 25th April the mine was sold by public auction, and twenty Europeans took part in the bidding. Andersson received for all the buildings in Otjimbingwe and at the mine £1,500. In the village there were a trading store, a wagon-maker's shop and a smithy. Most of the Europeans who had lost their work stayed in the country. Some of them settled in Otjimbingwe and others became traders. Andersson forsook mining and became a business man. For this purpose he had, first of all, to lay in a stock of goods. He collected 4,000 cattle for this purpose and trekked with them through Namaqualand to Capetown. It was a critical time and a very risky undertaking. Long before his arrival in the unsettled part of the country, however, the rumour had spread right throughout it that Andersson was armed with two cannons and poisoned gunpowder. That gained him respect, and that was all he wanted. He considered that it was not of any importance at all to be popular in the country, seeing that it had a population which had so often put obstacles in the way of everything he wanted to do. In August (1862) he reached Bethanie. David Christian felt very much inclined to forbid him to pass through his territory, because it was generally known that the cattle were not free from lung sickness. Fear of the cannons, however, induced him to turn back from Kuinis, and to send Andersson a message that he was not to pass through Bethanie, but to turn aside and go through Aus. Andersson was satisfied with that and reached the end of his journey without molestation. In November 1862 he returned by ship to Walfish Bay and from there went to Otjimbingwe. He brought goods to the value of £5,000 into the country.

Trade and traffic

Although Andersson in Otjimbingwe was now the largest merchant in the whole of South West Africa, he was not the first, nor by any means the only one. Between 1840 and 1850, travelling traders had traversed the length and breadth of the country with their carts and ox wagons and, in the period which followed, their number had increased considerably. War didn't frighten them away. On the contrary, the traders who had the right wares with them were all welcome amongst the Nama tribes, if their prices were not too high. What was most in demand were powder and shot and, although the importation of these articles into South West Africa was strictly forbidden, they both found their way into the country by devious routes. Other things which found a ready sale were brandy, clothing, ironware, trinkets, and bar-iron for the manufacture of iron arrow-points and spears. No money was used in making purchases. It had not yet come into general use. It was only the workers in the mines who were anxious to get their wages in cash, and the wagon drivers received wages at the rate of 1s. 6d. per day. Ivory was a medium of exchange, but, because of the continuous state of war prevailing in the country, there was little opportunity for hunting expeditions on a large scale, and the only time that hunting expeditions were ever spoken about was when a plan was made to go and hunt Herero cattle, for the whole eastern side of the country was more or less Jonker's happy hunting-ground. In Namaland, ostrich feathers were the principal product with which the trader was paid, and hunting ostriches was, therefore, a profitable undertaking. The ostriches were pursued in the midday heat, with fast horses, until they fell down exhausted. That was the favourite way of hunting them because it did not require an expenditure of any powder. If, however, there were no ostrich feathers on hand when the trader arrived on the scene, his customers were forced to have recourse to their sheep or their cattle to pay for their goods. It is on record that, between January and March 1853, nine traders' wagons passed through Rehoboth, and it was the same with other places. Debts were incurred, too, and many of the chiefs owed the traders more than a hundred oxen. The giving of credit was often the cause of a raid into Hereroland so that the debtors' own cattle might remain intact. It was expecting too much of the traders to require them to make inquiries as to the origin of the cattle paid them, although Kleinschmidt once told the traders in Otjimbingwe, in a perfectly friendly way, that there was really very little difference between a man like Jonker, who stole the cattle, and a trader, who accepted them as payment for his goods with full knowledge that they were stolen. Knudsen's point of view was rather a strange one. When in a bad mood he wrote as follows: 'It is only right that the traders should suck the Namas dry so that they can be forced to work. I regard it as a blessing when thousands of oxen pass through Bethanie and when one trader succeeds another.'

Kreft, however, his successor, expresses himself in 1861 as follows: 'It makes me unhappy to hear of the absolute impudence with which some of the people treat the traders, who come here from Angra Pequena. They extort from them just as much as they like.'

We will make a slight digression here, so as to throw some light upon this statement of Kreft's. Shortly before Christmas in 1857, Kleinschmidt heard at Rehoboth that a trader had outspanned close to the village. His name was Letto. As Kleinschmidt's wife had no cotton, he went to him to buy some. He found Letto in despair. One of his wagon wheels had been taken off by the Swartboois, and he was only to get it back if he promised that he would not go to Amraal's people, as he had intended to do. They did not want Amraal to have these goods. The people of Rehoboth had a way of making large purchases and then taking the goods they had bought to distant parts, where no traders ever went, and selling them there again at a considerable profit, and Amraal's people did the same. Willem Swartbooi was sitting on the driving-seat of the wagon with an angry look on his face. Kleinschmidt tried to plead for the trader, but all that he succeeded in doing was to put Willem into a tearing rage. It was only the following day that Petrus Swartbooi produced the wheel, after the people had bought what they wanted and paid just as much as they thought proper. Petrus demanded 4 lb. of flour for the return of the wheel, and he got it.

It is not to be wondered that, under these circumstances, some of the brighter spirits conceived the idea that a toll should be levied upon traders who passed through their ground. The Polsen brothers, who went from Rehoboth to Windhoek with several wagons in 1861, were forced to pay Jonker a tax of 50 lb. of powder for every wagon. Wine or brandy was often demanded as toll.

Thus it happened that both sides were often wrong, and the idea was conceived of introducing a missionary trader, or of establishing a missionary colony, somewhere in the country, with the object of trying to put both sides straight. Hahn writes in 1858 regarding a plan of this kind:

'I recommend that an industrial and farming colony be established with a small capital and that it begin its operations at once. There must be no lack of iron for the smith, or of wood for the wagon-maker, and they must be provided with the proper tools. The stock-farming operations ought to begin with between 100 and 150 head of cattle; between 500 and 1,000 sheep will be required. A European bull must be obtained and a proper number of Merino rams should be imported. It would not be easy to find better herdsmen than the Hereros. If the Missionary Society should see its way clear to establish a mission colony of this kind, it can have some expectation of the Herero mission becoming a success.'

We shall see later how Hahn tried to carry out his ideas of a mission colony for handicraft and trading, and what his experiences with it were. There was a complete lack of European tradesmen in the country. The only blacksmith's shop in existence was one put up by Bassingthwaighte in Rehoboth, and he was kept very busy. He got an apprentice from Capetown and, when his years of apprenticeship were finished, he too settled in the country as a blacksmith. It is interesting to note the way in which the movement of natives was regulated in those times. During 1854 Amraal paid his neighbour Oasib a visit. They discussed the nuisance caused by wandering Namas, who did a great deal of mischief, and they decided that every Nama, who wanted to go into the tribal territory of another chief, must get a pass from his own chief. Any one who did not have a pass was liable to be regarded as a vagrant and was then to be treated as one. The idea was a good one. Unfortunately, it went the way of so many more of Oasib's good ideas. The necessary energy to carry out what the highest authority in the land decreed was lacking. Rehoboth opposed the measure altogether. Willem Swartbooi would have nothing to do with it, but it is not known what the other Nama chiefs had to say about it. It is quite probable that this arrangement of Oasib's never even came to their ears. In any event, any number of Nama vagrants wandered about through the country and paid little attention to their chiefs.

The carriage of mails and goods

The post, as might well be expected in a country which was so very isolated, continued to cause worry and trouble. Of course, as the time went on, it became rather cheaper. There was no longer any need to fear that, when one sent a letter, the person who received it at the end of its long journey would be considerably out of pocket, as was the case some ten years previously, when Knudsen found it necessary to write to the mission authorities as follows: 'You wish us to write to you frequently, and still you say in your letter that the last dispatches from Capetown cost, between there and London only, over £12 and contained only diaries and private letters.'

It was, however, due to Knudsen's departure and the obstinacy of the chief at Bethanie that constant interruptions took place in the regular postal service, which the missionaries had instituted. The minutes of the conference at Rehoboth in 1851 contained the following remark:

'Owing to the unfortunate position in Bethanie it may well happen that our postal connection with the Colony will be endangered, or even come to a complete standstill, and so we are inclined to dispatch our post boys three times a year in future in place of four. What route our letters will take, whether through Wesleyvale (Naosanabis), instead of by way of Nisbet Bath (Warmbad), or direct from here to Komagas, we cannot possibly say. As soon as we are certain about it, we will advise the Colony.'

When the mining of copper had started, and by 1857 a merchant ship was to be expected in Walfish Bay every other month, communications from Rehoboth, Gobabis, and the mission stations along the Swakop became much easier. The sending of individual men across the Orange River was discontinued, and the letters were collected in Otjimbingwe and sent to the Bay. Letters from Barmen in Germany took two and a half months to reach Barmen in South West Africa. It should, however, not be forgotten that the period we are dealing with was one of continuous warfare, and that, in times like those, it was just the letters which were most carefully closed and sealed up that were apt to be objects of suspicion. Just as Willem Swartbooi in Rehoboth had once before thought it necessary that the post should be subjected to censorship by the chiefs, he repeats his suspicion of the secret letter bag in 1853. Kleinschmidt remarks:

'The chief keeps on complaining that I will not read out to him the letters I receive. As a punishment, he and his headmen had to have a lesson in geography, and that about Germany and China, for it was from there that I received the letters from which I read out extracts to them. With a great deal of impatience he waited until I had finished, for he thought that they were government letters which I had received.'

Another instance of censoring letters could have turned out rather badly. In 1857 Kido Witbooi wrote Jonker a letter. For some time past he had been treating with Jonker on the one side, and Oasib on the other, with the object of acquiring his own grazing grounds, and a suitable place for the establishment of a centre for his tribe. The letter went through Hoachanas. Oasib wanted to let it go on. His son, however, who had learned to read and write, was of another opinion. He thought again that no one need send a letter on if he had reason to suppose that the contents of it might do the man, who was sending it on, harm. Vollmer advised him to put his suspicions aside, lest a great deal of trouble might arise through the misunderstanding his action might cause. The future paramount chief refused, however, to listen to the old man's advice. Kido's letter was opened, read, and then sent on to Jonker. Jonker was very annoyed at this treatment. He came with the letter to Hahn at Barmen to inquire how things of that kind could be done in a civilized country. Hahn talked soothingly to him and Jonker left, after giving the assurance that he would do everything in his power to keep the peace between himself and Oasib.

An unexpected increase took place in wagon traffic during the period under review. The wagons from the mines, when coming back empty from Walfish Bay, were only too glad to get loads for the interior. From Otjimbingwe again the owners of the goods had to fetch them with their own wagons. As, however, the price of transport was very high, many people went to the Bay themselves and fetched what was stored in the warehouses there. Namaland got its supplies through Angra Pequena. Even van Reenen went to the trouble of conveying goods into the interior from his bay. In 1856, goods were landed at Alexander Bay, at the mouth of the Orange River, and fetched from there. Every Nama chief made it his aim to have as many ox wagons as possible amongst his people. At the peace conference at Hoachanas in 1856, the reader will remember that a large area was reserved as a parking place for wagons. Of these, ten belonged to Amraal and about twenty-seven to Jonker. The fact, too, that Jonker went to Ovamboland with forty wagons, makes it possible to estimate the number of wagons, which were in the possession of the natives, over and above those which were owned by Europeans. It may be of interest in these days of motor-cars, in which any one can travel from Walfish Bay to Windhoek in a day, to give a table of

DR. HUGO HAHN

Missionary at Windhoek 1842–1844; Barmen 1845–1864
Otjimbingwe 1864–1873
All honour to his name

the times it took to do the same journey in an ox wagon, in the year 1853, compiled very carefully by Hugo Hahn:

From Walfish Bay to Husab	. . . . .	16 hours
„ Husab to Jonkersfontein .	. . . .	5 „
„ Jonkersfontein to Tinkas .	. . . .	10 „
„ Tinkas to Onanis .	. . . .	$8\frac{1}{2}$ „
„ Onanis to Tsaobis .	. . . .	$13\frac{1}{4}$ „
„ Tsaobis to Otjimbingwe .	. . . .	$8\frac{1}{2}$ „
„ Otjimbingwe to Omandjimba .	. . .	$14\frac{1}{4}$ „
„ Omandjimba to Buxton Springs	. . .	4 „
„ Buxton Springs to Barmen	. . . .	4 „
„ Barmen to Windhoek	. . . . .	$17\frac{1}{2}$ „
Total	. . . . . .	101 hours[1]

The settlement of wandering tribes

In a country in which it may happen that the European, whose whole inclination is to settle and establish a permanent home for himself, may be forced temporarily to lead a nomadic existence—the farmers, for instance, who trek with their stock in times of severe drought—it is not to be wondered that the settlement of its Nama population made very slow progress. As soon as it appeared as if the tribe of Bethanie had settled down they started to disperse again. This happened through a quarrel between David Christian and his missionary Knudsen, whom he banished from his country. It was only after long and patient labour that Kreft succeeded in collecting the tribe again and getting its members to come and live at a tribal centre. It may appear to be strange that trade with the natives proved an obstacle to their settlement. One would have supposed that business, which prefers fixed centres and prospers best at such places, would have contributed to the process of tribal centralization. On going into the matter more closely, however, it must be recognized that it is only in accordance with existing conditions that the experiences of one land can be introduced to another, where the circumstances differ. In 1862 Kreft writes about his own experience as follows:

'The traders are coming into the land at present in such numbers that one wonders what is to become of it all. There is such a lust for buying things, particularly in the case of the women and children, and everything is

[1] The average period which a South African wagon travels in a day is 8 hours, so that the journey must have occupied at least 12 days. Galton gives the distance between Walfish Bay and Barmen as $82\frac{3}{4}$ hours, which he regards as representing 207 miles.—*Ed.*

immediately worn to show it off. The poorer people try to ape the richer ones, and that makes them poorer still. It helps very little as yet to warn or try to teach them. The people then think that one is grudging them these things, and they simply will not believe that this aimless buying must reduce them to poverty; when a tremendous number of their cattle are gone they begin to save. The killing of animals stops, and they live entirely on milk, and that makes it necessary for them to trek and wander about once more.'

In spite of all this the tribe of Bethanie was successfully brought back to its centre at Bethanie during this period, and the Swartboois became used to Rehoboth, notwithstanding constant disturbances, while the tribe at Berseba was kept round about its springs. The Red Nation became settled at Hoachanas, despite the urge which arose every now and then to wander, now to Rehoboth, now to Otjimbingwe, and then again to the north. Amraal's people finally established their home in Gobabis. With Jan Booi's tribe nothing could yet be done, and the Witboois still had no tribal territory of their own. It is hardly worth while talking about the Hereros. We see just the beginning of the centralization of their tribes in Barmen and Otjimbingwe. In consequence of Jonker's barbarous actions, their tribal organization had been absolutely broken up. Each individual who still had a few cattle tried to keep them alive and, at the same time, keep them hidden by moving them about wherever it seemed best. They wandered up and down in the north of the Kaokoveld and even as far as the Kunene.

3. PROGRESS IN THE EXPLORATION OF THE COUNTRY

It is the gift and task of Faustic man that he should restlessly strive, explore, elucidate, conquer, and force his way onwards, in eternal dissatisfaction, whether it be in science or in business, in private undertakings, or in the conquest of nations. He marches always in the van of mankind's slow ascent, breaks loose from it now and again, and presses forward alone, to be the first to hear something, which has never been heard before, and to see something which has never before been seen, and to make himself their master—if he can with his fists, but if he cannot, then by applying his mind to it. This is his fate, his reward, and his risk. He breaks the trail and finds the road in every province of life; where there is a new country he is the one who does the pioneering work; the first furrows to be ploughed are generally made by him. No one begrudges him the pleasure of reaping the first harvest, which is often such a poor one; it is a pleasure which he seldom enjoys. Others usually reap the fruits of his labour, and worry little about him when he is dead, for in his lifetime he was often an awkward kind of person, just as the engine of a lorry would be found to be, if it possessed consciousness and thinking capacity. We must, however, not overlook the fact that the lorry consists of engine and body, and that the one would be quite worthless without the other.

South West Africa has much to be thankful for to people who were Faustian by nature. Eighty years ago it was still to a great extent an unknown land, and it is still to-day a new country. The history of South West Africa cannot possibly pass the men by, who forced their way along untravelled roads into its unknown regions, and unveiled their hidden secrets. It would not go beyond the bounds of the appreciation we must bestow on them if we were to give a full account of what they experienced and suffered. Their own detailed accounts, which are amongst the best things that have ever been written about South West Africa, afford us a considerable amount of information. This history cannot content itself with just a few brief remarks about their journeys, their aims, and their successes. Nor is that argument a sound one which slightingly states that they were mostly hunters, traders, and missionaries, who explored the land for the sake of pleasure, profit, and missionary endeavour. We assuredly do not meet, in South West Africa, during the period between 1850 and 1862, with any expeditions equipped for exploration with plenty of money from foreign sources. When hunters and traders set out into an unknown country, with equipment upon which they have spent the last penny they possess, and go and live on meat and wild veld food for months on end, and then, in spite of the dangers with which the bush and the plains threaten them, they return with valuable information, no one ought to try to set their services off against the value of the elephants' tusks, which they have managed to drag to a trading centre with great toil and hardship.

Ovamboland; Galton and Andersson

Dr. Livingstone, who had come up from the south-east, had hardly discovered Lake Ngami before other explorers came on the scene and tried to reach it from the south-west side. Vague rumours about a perennial river in the north had barely been heard, before people were ready to go and see it with their own eyes and to explore its course. A large agricultural nation, which lived to the north of the Namas and Hereros, had hardly been heard of, when the apostles of the missions inspanned their oxen to go and visit this nation, and look for ways and means to commence their work amongst them.

It was Francis Galton who made it his object, in the company of Charles Andersson, to explore Ovamboland and its river, the Kunene. He then intended to push forward into the unknown eastern country, and to prove that the newly discovered Lake Ngami could be reached from the Atlantic Ocean. He had hoped that he would, in this way, be able to fill up the empty places on the map, which, 'lying between the Cape Colony and the western settlements of the Portuguese, stretch far into the interior right up to Lake Ngami'. He landed at Walfish Bay in 1850. The preparations for his journey took quite a long time. Disturbances amongst the natives threatened to frustrate his entire plan. It has previously been told how Jonker Afrikander, who had just about exterminated Kahitjene's tribe at Okahandja, regarded him as a troublesome interloper. Jonker had been informed by a letter from Galton that Ovamboland and Lake Ngami were his objectives. Jonker, however, regarded Ovamboland as his own particular domain. He wanted to do just as he liked in northern Hereroland without any interference, and free from the observation of Europeans. Any foreign influence amongst the Hereros was undesirable. To the east, again, lay Jonker's hunting-grounds. It seemed to him that, if he allowed others to go there, he might lose very heavily. We know already how Galton dealt with Jonker. The strong man was temporarily over-borne by one who was stronger than himself. The Galton peace treaty caused the lion to hide himself in the bush for a whole year, and Galton was free to go where he liked. After he had paid a visit to the Erongo mountains (in December 1850), he set out in January 1851 from Okahandja and travelled in a northerly direction with the intention of first finding Lake Omambonde. This unknown lake was at that time a general topic of conversation amongst the Europeans of South West Africa. According to the accounts of the natives, it was very big, and the amount of game round about it was enormous. This story came into existence through misunderstanding on both sides. Owing to the lack of the proper word for a lake in Herero, questions had been asked about a 'big water' inland, and the Hereros had mentioned the large vlei at Omambonde, which dries up during the rainless period of the year, as being the largest water known to them. An explorer's experiences do not consist only of the pleasures of discovery; he often meets with disappointments on the unbeaten tracks he travels. Galton and Andersson experienced at Omambonde a disappointment of this kind, which was only mitigated through the large quantities of game they found in the neighbourhood. They travelled on in a northerly direction. Thick thorn bush, rocks, deep water-holes in the Omuramba Omatako, long stretches without water—who has not experienced these obstacles when travelling in South West Africa! The travellers met in May a party of Ovambos who were going to trade with the Hereros. They decided to camp for a time to give the trek oxen a chance of recovery. Then the Ovambo traders came back, and Galton decided to attach himself to them, so as to get guides and companions who knew the way. His own original party consisted of fourteen people and twenty-four others now joined him. As, however, all kinds of travellers attached themselves to him along the road, there were finally 170 people with him. Oxen, sheep, and goats, which they had taken with them, were used as food, and these were very often threatened by lions, which were numerous in those parts. Galton's, Andersson's, and Allen's guns were kept hard at work protecting the animals. The travellers reached Lake Otjikoto, near Tsumeb, unexpectedly on the 26th of May. Galton measured its depth at different places and found it to be 180 feet. The natives held the belief that no one who bathed in the lake ever came out of it alive. Galton, Andersson, and Allen swam vigorously up and down in the sight of everybody, and explored the caves, which they found to be the homes of innumerable bats. The fact that they came out of the water alive made their guides distrust them, for they now reckoned that they were sorcerers.

A messenger was sent from the borders of Ovamboland to inform the chief Nangoro of their visit. Some four hours from the northern edge of the flats, they passed the Omumborombonga tree, which was the ancestral tree of the Hereros, and of which mention has already been made. 'The caravan stopped a while, and the savages danced round it with great delight.' (Each individual approaches the tree with grass or leaves in his hands. When he comes to the tree he spits on the grass, rubs his forehead with it, thrusts it into a hole in the bark of the ancient tree, and says, 'Accept my greetings, father. Give me good fortune on my journey.') Now the wooded country was reached. For a long time they had pushed their way through thorn trees, and Galton began to doubt whether Ondonga existed. At last they came out of the bush, and the corn country of Ovamboland lay yellow and broad like a sea before them.

'Fine, dense timber trees, and innumerable palms of all sizes, were scattered over it. Part was bare of pasturage, part was thickly covered in high corn stubble; palisadings, each of which enclosed a homestead, were scattered everywhere over the country. The general appearance was that of a most abundant fertility. It was a land of Goschen to us, and even my phlegmatic wagon-driver burst out into exclamations of delight.'

At the first house they came to, the travellers were brought a dish of hot gruel and a basin of sour milk. Then they continued their journey to the chief Nangoro.

'Ondonga, for that is the name of the land, is most uniform in its appearance, and I should think no stranger could recollect his way for any distance in it. I don't know what we should have done here if I had brought my wagons. We could never have taken them across the Ovambo fields, trespassing everywhere. The roads that the natives and we travelled were only pathways through the stubble, and we were particularly requested to keep to them. There was hardly any grass whatever, it was quite eaten up, and the Ovambo oxen had been sent away to distant cattle posts on every side to get food for the stock. They were now being driven back in small herds to eat off the stubble upon the farms of their owners. By each homestead were five or six cows and a quantity of goats, very small, but yielding a great deal of milk. To give water even to these was a great difficulty, for the wells have to be dug twenty or thirty feet deep through the sandy soil before water is reached, and then it oozes out so slowly that only a very limited supply can be obtained. There had been great trouble in getting even my small drove of cattle watered, but Chik (Galton's guide) 'said that there were some vleis still left, which were Nangoro's property, but to which he would probably allow my oxen to be driven. The Ovambos made a great fuss about water; if I wanted any to drink I had to buy it with beads. I was greatly pleased with the mutual goodwill and cordiality that evidently existed among the Ovambos; they were all plump and well-fed; even the blind old people, who are such wretched objects in Damaraland, were here well tended and fat. Every one was perfectly civil, but I could not go as I liked, nor where I liked; in fact I felt as a savage would feel in England. My red coat was the delight of all the little boys and girls, plump, merry little things, who ran after me, shouting and singing, as happy as could be. The Ovambos took much interest in seeing the oxen packed and ridden; they had never seen them used in that way before, and carefully examined the saddle-bags and the way in which they were put on.'

'At last a particularly fine clump of trees came in sight, and there Chik said we were ordered to stay, Nangoro's palisading being only a quarter of a mile farther. Here we off-packed, and made a kind of encampment. I pitched my tent, and we made as good a screen as we were able with the saddle bags and a few palm branches, but we had hardly any firewood, grass, or water. After a great deal of trouble I made Chik obtain for us the use of some wells close by, but we had to wait half the day till they were disengaged. Then I could find no place to send my oxen to feed. No kind offer was made of a stubble field, and Chik would not bestir himself. He was always saying "You must wait; Nangoro will come down and see you to-morrow and then he will arrange everything". But in the meantime my oxen were starving. The Ovambos kept away from us, and Chik was almost the only person with whom we were allowed to communicate. We all felt uncomfortable; I never for a moment expected any attack from the Ovambos, but I had considerable mis-givings that they purposely intended to keep my oxen in low condition that I might be less independent.'

Nangoro, however, did not come the following day (6th June). On the 7th June, Galton writes in his diary:

'The oxen looked dreadfully thin. I began to fear that they would die, and then we should have to abandon our luggage and get back on foot—an exertion which I had little fancy for. However, about midday Chik came in great excitement to tell me that Nangoro was on his way to me, so I smartened things up and made ready for him. There was a body of men walking towards us, and in the middle of them an amazingly fat old fellow who laboured along; he was very short of breath, and had hardly anything on his person. This was the king himself. He waddled up looking very severe, and stood in the middle of his men staring at us, and leaning on a thin stick very neatly shaped, that he seemed to carry about as a sceptre. I hardly knew what to do or what to say, for he took no notice of the elegant bow I made to him, so I sat down and continued writing my journal till the royal mind was satisfied. After five or six minutes, Nangoro walked up, gave a grunt of approbation, and poked his sceptre into my ribs in a friendly sort of manner, and then sat down. I gave Nangoro the things I had brought as a present for him, regretting excessively that I could spare him nothing better. In fact all my gilt finery was but little cared for by these people. It would look as *outré* for an Ovambo to wear any peculiar ornament as it would for an Englishman to do so. The sway of fashion is quite as strong among the negroes as among the whites, and my position was that of a traveller in Europe, who had nothing to pay his hotel bill with but a box full of cowries and Damara sandals. I would have given anything for £10 worth of the right sort of beads; half of that value would have made a really good present to Nangoro, and franked me into the good graces of all his people. As it was, he was rather sulky, for he considered it a kind of insult to an African chief to visit him, and to make use of his country without commencing acquaintance by sending a tribute. He insisted upon my giving him a cow which I, or rather John Allen, had with me, besides the ox with which I had presented him, and, as there was no help for it, the cow went. We then had a short conversation; he looked at our guns and made us shoot with them, chatted a little, and then left us, saying that we were free to buy and sell with his people as much as we liked.'

This was the moment the inhabitants had been waiting for, and soon they gathered round and a lively trade was in progress. They learned at the performance of some dances, which was held in the evening, that Nangoro had a strong bodyguard of Bushmen, and that these lived close to his kraal.

There was a particular reason for Nangoro's cool reception of them. According to the beliefs of the Ovambos and the Hereros, a stranger who has come from a distance brings with him strange matter which can do his host a great deal of harm. There is, therefore, a custom that a stranger must sit and wait outside a chief's hut until the latter comes to him, and then the first thing he does is to spray the water of that place with his mouth over the guest as he sits on the ground. This custom has two significations: through it the stranger is accepted in the village and community as a welcome guest, and at the same time the village and its people are safeguarded by it, in some mystical way, from any harmful matter which may be clinging to the guest. Galton and his companions had, however, refused to submit to this custom. Nangoro, therefore, mistrusted them. He did not, however, keep out of his way entirely, but afforded him an opportunity for making inquiries about the river, which was Galton's objective, and he learned a great deal about the course of the Kunene and the people who lived on it. He did not, however, permit Galton's oxen to graze on the stubble lands, nor might they be watered until after Nangoro's cattle had drunk their fill, and so they came back thinner and thinner every evening and were a source of considerable anxiety to the travellers. There was no question of making a hasty departure for 'I had been given to understand from the first that I must neither go back nor go on without Nangoro's express permission, so that we were always under some anxiety. Of course, I did all I could to please him; but still, either from want of consideration on his part, or intentionally, things did not go on smoothly.' But permission was not given to go on farther to the north to see the Kunene. What happened was that, on the 13th June, Galton was told that he could still buy and sell that day, but that he would have to take leave of Nangoro the following day and return to Hereroland the day afterwards—without having seen the Kunene; and yet it could easily have been reached in four days.

Galton bartered for beads as much corn as he could get, and prepared himself for the return journey. He took leave of Nangoro on the 15th June and he left the place with his companions, unmolested. They returned along the way by which they had come, and reached the place from which they had set out to go to Ovamboland by the middle of August.

The East: Galton and Andersson

Immediately after their return from Ovamboland, Galton and Andersson commenced their second journey, which was to the east. Their intention was to go right through to Lake Ngami. They went to Windhoek, the residence of the now tamed Jonker Afrikander. Jonker was friendly to them, and Galton did not neglect to express the pleasure that he felt that he had kept his people in order during his, Galton's, absence, and had not allowed them to go cattle-lifting. He found Eyebrett with Jonker, the carpenter and teacher who had been brought there by the Wesleyan mission. Eyebrett had, however, been dismissed by the mission and had been appointed 'Jonker's prime minister'. He spoke Hottentot, had a pleasant personality, and he undertook to guide Galton to Gobabis (Olifantsfontein). It was many years since any wagon had been over this road. It was far too dangerous for traders to travel through this boundary country between the Hereros and the Nama-Orlams. Up to that time Gobabis was the farthest point that was known, and what lay beyond it to the north and east was unexplored country. Amraal, who had taken possession of this area for his Orlam people with Oasib's consent, had ventured to go to the east another forty miles, and had gone even a little farther when on hunting expeditions. With a great deal of difficulty, Galton reached Gobabis and learned from Amraal that broad plains, covered with grass and bushes, were to be found to the eastward, and that beyond them was a desert which could only be crossed on foot after the rains, and thus had the effect of cutting off the countries of the west coast from those of middle Africa proper.

'It was principally with a view to try if this desert were really impassable that I proposed now to travel, and my object was to strike upon some road that led from the colony up to Lake Ngami. The Lake itself I was indifferent about reaching, for it is of no great size, and might prove a very unhealthy place for us, who had been accustomed so long to the pure air of a high plateau.

It was two years since its discovery, and there was every reason to suppose that it was by this time perfectly well known.'

The travellers who had left Windhoek on the 30th August and had arrived at Gobabis on the 14th September, continued their journey on the 19th September. Amraal kept them company. After they had ridden for eleven hours they arrived at Twas, where Galton found a South African named Saul, and took him into his service. Galton says that he was a well-known shot, spoke Hottentot perfectly, and that he was just the man he wanted. On the 28th of September, they reached the farthest point to which Amraal had ever been. Here Bushmanland began and the spoors of elephants were visible. The Bushmen knew Lake Ngami very well indeed. They could describe it, and were able to furnish a great deal of information about the life on its banks. They had in their keeping some articles belonging to European travellers who had gone to the Lake, intending to retrieve them again on their return. They said, however, that it would be impossible for the large company (Amraal had taken forty people with him for Galton's protection) to reach the Lake by way of Tunobis (Otjimbinde) at this time of the year. On the afternoon of the 1st of October Galton set out with Amraal's people for Tunobis. They followed an elephant path which 'was as straight as a Roman road'. They came across large numbers of Bushmen, but they were only able to make themselves understood with difficulty, because their Nama-speaking guide did not know the Bushman language. They reached Tunobis, and they spent the time, until the 10th October, in dangerous and exciting hunting adventures, for there were great numbers of elephants and rhinoceroses there. When, however, his bodyguard got tired of travelling and hunting, Galton decided to return, as there was no prospect at all of being able to reach Lake Ngami at that time of the year. Besides this, he had previously written from Barmen to Capetown that he was prepared to pay a share of the cost, if the ship, which the Missionary Society chartered every second year for Walfish Bay, could be sent earlier, so that he could board it in December.

Galton returned by the Bay road to Heigamchab and Walfish Bay, and had the good fortune, after successful hunting in the lower Swakop valley, that the ship came just at the right time and took him to Capetown in the beginning of January. The results of his two journeys were as follows: The opening of the road to Ovamboland; the partial opening of a road to Lake Ngami; the obtaining of reliable information about the Ovambo people; proof that no lake existed at Omambonde; accurate information regarding northern Hereroland; the discovery of Lake Otjikoto; the discovery of the Etosha Pan; careful triangulation of the area between Walfish Bay and Gobabis.

From Walfish Bay to Lake Ngami: Andersson

What Galton and Andersson had not succeeded in doing together, i.e. reaching the Kunene and Lake Ngami from South West Africa, Andersson was to accomplish alone after Galton's departure. He went right through to Lake Ngami and, in 1867, he found a lonely grave on the southern bank of the Kunene. Here we shall deal only with his journey from Walfish Bay to Lake Ngami, and for that purpose we must go back to the preparations he made for the journey and the events connected with it.

Andersson required for this long journey a great number of things, which he could only get in Capetown. He, therefore, trekked down to the Cape with a bunch of cattle to raise funds. It was in February 1851, just a month after Galton's departure, that he set out for Capetown. He reached Windhoek and made it his business to go and see Jonker. It is well known that Jonker, who had been held on a chain by the Galton peace treaty, commenced cattle-raiding immediately after Galton had left. Andersson, who had passed through Okahandja on his journey to Windhoek, and had spoken with Tjamuaha and other Hereros there, was of the opinion that Jonker's raids in the month of January had brought him in between ten and eleven thousand Herero cattle; he had, at the same time, destroyed about forty Herero werfs. During the time he spent in Windhoek, Andersson did his best to find out what Jonker's forces were, and he estimated that the number of men of the Afrikander tribe, who were capable of bearing arms, numbered about five hundred. In his estimation, however, the tribe had three or four times as many people in their service. These consisted of Bergdamas, Bushmen, and those Hereros who had thrown in their lot with Jonker. A conservative estimate of the number of the inhabitants of Windhoek at that time would be round about 4,000.

The meeting between Andersson and Jonker was not exactly cordial. Andersson said to him: 'Captain Jonker, when I last saw you I shook hands with you; it grieves me that I cannot do so to-day; the cause you must be aware of.' Jonker began to excuse himself. He said that he had acted in self-defence. The Hereros had caused him great losses and, in any event, he had left a large number of cattle still in their hands.

Andersson then went on to Bethanie, crossed the Orange River, and reached Capetown. In the course of his journey he met, at Oasib's place, Amraal, the chief of the eastern country, with whom he was already acquainted. Amraal told him that there was nothing to prevent a properly equipped expedition from reaching Lake Ngami, and that he himself had recently been to the Lake with forty-seven wagons on a hunting expedition. This news encouraged Andersson considerably in making his preparations. He returned from Capetown through Walfish Bay, and from there he sent 360 cattle to the Cape. He began his journey to the Nosob on the 1st April and reached Tunobis, the northernmost point of his first journey, and went off from there to Ghanzie, which lies beyond the present eastern boundary of South West Africa. This place was known already, for Green, the elephant hunter, had been there eighteen months previously. On the 23rd June he left Ghanzie and turned eastwards in the direction of Lake Ngami. He sent messengers to the chief who lived there to announce his arrival, and then went on a hunting trip, upon which he came into contact with the enormous numbers of elephants, giraffes, and rhinoceroses of both kinds, white and black, which were to be found in those parts. He left the horns and ivory he had collected in charge of a Bushman in order to go to the Lake on horseback. Here we had better let him talk himself:

'The return of daylight found us again on the move. The morning being cool and pleasant, and our goal near, the whole party was in high spirits, and we proceeded cheerily on our road. I myself kept well ahead, in hope of obtaining the first glimpse of Ngami. The country hereabout was finely undulated, and in every distant vale with a defined border I thought I saw a lake. At last a blue line of great extent appeared in the distance, and I made sure it was the long-sought object; but I was still doomed to disappointment. It turned out to be merely a large hollow, in the rainy season filled with water, but now dry and covered by saline incrustations. Several valleys, separated from each other by ridges of sand, bearing a rank vegetation, were afterwards crossed. On reaching the top of one of these ridges, the natives, who were in advance of our party, suddenly came to a halt, and, pointing straight before them, exclaimed, "Ngami! Ngami!" In an instant I was with the men. There, indeed, at no very great distance, lay spread before me an immense sheet of water, only bounded by the horizon—the object of my ambition for years, and for which I had abandoned home and friends, and risked my life.

'The first sensation occasioned by this sight was very curious. Long as I had been prepared for that event, it now almost overwhelmed me. It was a mixture of pleasure and pain. My temples throbbed, and my heart beat so violently that I was obliged to dismount and lean against a tree for support until the excitement had subsided. The reader will no doubt think that thus giving way to my feelings was very childish; but "those who know that the first glimpse of some great object, which we have read or dreamed of from earliest recollection, is ever a moment of intense enjoyment, will forgive the transport".

'The Lake was now very low, and, at the point first seen by us, exceedingly shallow. The water, which had a very bitter and disagreeable taste, was only approachabl: in a few places, partly on account of the mud, and partly because of the thick coating of reeds and rushes that lined the shore, and which were a favourite resort of a great variety of water-fowl. Many species new to us were among them; but we had no time to spare for approaching the birds.'

In order not to leave his duty undone, Andersson now hastened to introduce himself to the chief. At the time which had been appointed he donned his best clothes, which consisted of jacket and trousers of fine white duck, a red velvet sash, and a gold embroidered skull cap. He arrived at Letcholetebe's place of residence, and found the Bechuana chief sitting on a wooden chair, inside a stout semicircular palisade, drinking coffee, with about forty to fifty of his subjects grouped round him. He was clothed half in European dress and half in African costume. His feet extruded from a pair of moleskin trousers; on his feet he wore socks and veldskoens, and from his shoulders a fine jackal kaross hung down gracefully. The latter he exchanged almost immediately for a jacket and waistcoat.

As the chief said very little, Andersson soon retired. He struck his camp, and set to work to explore the Lake properly. He crossed it several times in a canoe and he estimated its circumference to be between sixty and seventy English miles and its average breadth seven miles. The Lake swarmed with crocodiles in many parts, and the tsetse fly, which is so dangerous to cattle, was much in evidence. He then made a number of expeditions in the neighbourhood of the Lake, and obtained much information about the parts of the country which he was not able to reach. The ivory which he had collected, and the collection of entomological specimens which he had gathered, made him think about the journey back. He had reached the Lake by means of riding and pack-oxen, but it would require an ox wagon to take his whole collection back. As he could only obtain a wagon in Namaland, he set out, accompanied by one native, on a return

journey of almost a thousand miles. Andersson closes the account of
his travels with the words of one Captain Messum: 'This was the
pleasure of travelling in Africa. It requires the endurance of a camel
and the courage of a lion.'

His endurance, however, proved that Lake Ngami could be reached
from South West Africa. His entomological collection increased the
knowledge of Africa's flora and fauna, and his description of the life
of the natives, especially of the Bechuanas and Bajejes, who were
hitherto unknown, enabled a glimpse to be obtained of the manner
of life amongst these peoples in the interior of Africa.

When he had completed his journey, Andersson went to Europe
for the purpose of getting his book 'Lake Ngami' printed, and he
returned to Capetown towards the end of 1856.

From Ngami to Walfish Bay: James Chapman, 1855

While Andersson proved that it was possible to travel through
South West Africa from the Atlantic Ocean to Lake Ngami, James
Chapman proved that it was possible to travel from the Indian Ocean,
past Lake Ngami, and across South Africa, to Walfish Bay.

Chapman came from England and landed in Natal in 1849. This
was the year in which Livingstone discovered Lake Ngami. Chapman's
intention was to become an official, but he evolved a scheme for
establishing a trade route, with trading centres on it, from Port
Natal, across South Africa, to Walfish Bay. For this purpose he
became an explorer, hunter, and trader. The hunting and trading
were to cover the expenses of his expedition. It was possible to do
that at that time, because ivory could be obtained very cheaply from
the natives and sold at a high price. Andersson relates that he saw a
chief at Ngami give a large elephant tusk for three quite ordinary
copper mugs, and he heard that, at the time the Lake was discovered,
a native had paid for a musket 1,200 lb. of ivory, which was worth at
least £240.

Chapman accompanied by a man named Edwards travelled through
Kuruman in a northerly direction and reached Ngami after many
dangers and difficulties. He hunted there and obtained such a mass
of ivory through trading that he decided not to take it to the south,
along the unsafe way by which he had come, but to take it on to
Walfish Bay, seeing that this route offered new possibilities for exploration. Green, whose name we have already come across, one of the
greatest and most successful elephant hunters of those days, was just

then in the country round about the Lake. He transferred to Chapman some Hereros, who had been his guides up to then, and were very anxious to go back to their own country. Professor Wahlberg, who was staying in Green's camp, provided him with another interpreter and helped him to accomplish his journey, by supplying him with some sketch maps of eastern Hereroland, in which he had hunted.

Chapman set out on the 1st August, 1855, and passed through Ghanzie to Tunobis. He reached Amraal's territory on the 14th September and saw the 'elephant kloof or valley', i.e. Gobabis, which was the most easterly point of the country under Amraal's control, for the old chief had handed over the eastern part of his domains to his son Lambert. He found there a mission house in ruins, with a small church in front of it, and a Herero village. Here the former cattle owners, who once called the whole of the eastern territory their property, lived in abject poverty. They were forced to live on roots and tubers like Bushmen, for the Namas had taken all their property and had killed large numbers of their fellow tribesmen. They regarded themselves as the slaves of the Orlams, who exercised over them absolute control of life and death. Amraal himself, a venerable old man with white hair, made an excellent impression. He was too old to be able to enforce his principles amongst his people. Chapman learned that Amraal's ancestors had been Hottentot chiefs of the tribe of the Cham-gan, or 'Lion-hairs', in the neighbourhood of Worcester. He had in his youth lived in Capetown as a slave, had taken part in the battle of Blaauberg, and had then gradually raised himself to the position of an Orlam chief. After he had roamed about in Namaland for a long time, he had settled his tribe, which consisted of about 1,200 Orlams and Namas, in the eastern part of the country.

Chapman went from Gobabis to Witvlei, where he came across some very low class Hottentots, who belonged to Amraal's people. He experienced a great deal of trouble with them. They wanted powder and shot from him, and he could not afford to give them any. They tried to prevent him going on, but he got through to the Nosob, and from there to Windhoek. The hey-day of Windhoek was passed. All that remained from past times were a church and mission house, which had fallen into ruins, and a wall of stones at the springs, which was a relic of a battle between Jonker and the Red Nation. Passing through Barmen, he found two Herero women there with their feet cut off, and then he found Europeans again at Otjimbingwe—one named Rath, who questioned him closely about his

experiences amongst the natives in the east, and one named Hoerne-
mann, who, according to his own account, was working himself to
death trying to teach the Hereros the art of cultivating the soil. He
met there, too, the officials of the mines, who suspected that Chapman
had an idea of becoming their competitor. They arranged,therefore,
with Jonker Afrikander, that he should order him to leave the place.
Chapman took no notice of this order, and very soon afterwards
Jonker himself appeared on the scene, made excuses for having issued
it, and said that they had made him drunk, and then placed before
him a document for his signature, of the contents of which he was
quite ignorant. He invited Chapman to come and stay with him.
He said he was free to go where he would in the country.

Chapman, however, felt no inclination at all to go and stay in
Jonker's country. His opinion of the Hereros was that they had
completely lost their nationality, and he made haste to get to Walfish
Bay, because he had several thousand pounds worth of ivory with him.
He went through Tsaobis to Rooibank with seven wagons from the
copper mines, each of which carried a load of 1,200 lb. of ore. At Rooibank he enjoyed to the utmost, after his long trek, Bam's hospitality,
without dreaming that the latter would die in his arms in a few weeks
time, and that he would have to dig his grave and read his funeral
service. The only inhabitants he found at the Bay were the Latham
family, who received him very hospitably. His hopes of finding a
ship at the Bay, with which he could proceed to England, were not
fulfilled. He therefore sailed with the *Eblana* to Capetown on the
21st January, 1856, and arrived in Table Bay on the 1st March.
Something will be told later of Chapman's return to Walfish Bay and
his journey back to Lake Ngami in 1861. It is not possible to appreciate fully the significance of Chapman's successful journey from this
short sketch. In its comprehensive form Chapman's book was published in London in 1868, under the title *Travels in the Interior of
South Africa, comprising Fifteen Years' Hunting and Trading*. In this
work appear numerous observations dealing with plant, animal, and
human life. Chapman's education enabled him to observe and describe very many things which had escaped the notice of many
travellers whose training had not been so good. His affable nature
enabled him to find the key to many secrets, which remained hidden
to other people. He was especially interested in the plants of South
West Africa, and he imported the first photographic apparatus into
the country, in 1861, for the purpose of obtaining pictures of them.

Even if his plan to establish a trade route between Port Natal and Walfish Bay never materialized in the way in which he had conceived it, he, nevertheless, opened the way along which trade could advance, and the comprehensive description he gives of his journey enables us to get a clear picture of South West Africa, as it was in the year 1855.

Ovamboland: Hahn, Rath, and Green

Galton's account of Ovamboland was received with a great deal of interest, especially in mission circles. The question which Galton had previously answered with an emphatic 'yes', whether, after all the failures amongst the Hereros, the Ovambo tribe would not more readily embrace Christianity, now arose. In order to decide this question, it was necessary that some one should go to Ovamboland to investigate matters, and Hahn, accompanied by his colleague Rath, was prepared to undertake this mission. This is the proper place to deal with their journey. It should not be included in an account of the work of the missions for the reason that this, and a subsequent journey of Hahn's to Ovamboland, contributed very materially to the knowledge of that country and its people.

The conference of the Rhenish missionaries, which lasted from the 10th to the 13th March, 1856, at Otjimbingwe, had previously considered the question of the Ovambos. We find these remarks in its minutes:

'The Herero race has, so far as we know, ceased to exist. There are now only individuals left, without any kind of link between them, who wander about in a state of the greatest misery.

We have no knowledge at all of the state of affairs in the north. Whether there are still tribes there, as some people say, or whether it is a poor, almost unpopulated country, as others seem to think, it is impossible for us to judge. It seems more probable that this latter position is correct, for if the former were the case, it is hardly thinkable that any of those tribes could have escaped the destroyer (Jonker).

That is the position, and all we can say is this: the mission among the Hereros has come to an end, and it cannot form a foundation for any efforts among the tribes who live in the north. At the very most the two stations, Otjimbingwe and Barmen, might serve as places from which communications might be maintained with northern and eastern stations, if the latter could be reached from there. The only possible starting point for a mission in the north would be a bay situated in the north. If the country ever gets back to safe security, order, and work, we believe that the Hereros may well

recover, and that they may acquire once more a relatively independent
existence, if not perhaps, as a race, at least as a working class. Naturally,
nothing of that kind can be expected to take place while the Namas have
control.'

Hahn and Rath made ready to undertake the expedition upon
which they had been instructed to go, and they left Otjikango on
the 20th May, 1857. Their company consisted of Hahn's house
servant Kamuzandu, the marksman Gertse, who was a Baster, and
the guide Katjikamba, who very seldom knew the road. In addition
to these were the Hereros Kahikuna, Kambahunga, Kamuvanga and
Kapeja, 'who professed to be able to shoot, but for whom the game
have not the slightest need to be frightened'. An Herero, called
Kahingua, was the leader of the oxen, and Kambararapeke was cook,
and it was his duty to walk behind the wagon and to see that nothing
was lost. Amongst them was August, whom they could only trust
as long as he was under their eyes, and likewise a mixed company of
all kinds of characters, occupying all kinds of positions. This company
set out on its journey from Barmen on the 20th May, 1857. They
viewed in Okahandja the place of the massacre, where Kahitjene's
people were surrounded by Jonker's men on the 23rd August, 1850,
and slaughtered. Hahn found the bones of the victims still there.
The journey to Okarumumbonde on the Omuramba Omatako was
by way of Okamita. In the distance were the Omatako mountains,
out of which the Hereros used to get their ochre, which they mixed
with butter to make the paint which they were so fond of rubbing
on their bodies, and on the skins they wore. The remains of large
numbers of wells in the bed of the Omuramba showed that numerous
Hereros had stayed there in earlier times, but now there was not a
single trace to be found of any cattle, or their herdsmen. Following
the Omuramba to the north they saw the Waterberg in the distance,
and, on the 15th June, they reached the palm belt on the wide flats
of Grootfontein. They expected to find Green's camp in this neighbourhood, and they found it at Otjituo on the 20th June. Green had
been hunting with Bonfield in the Omuramba, and had discovered
that it debouched into a sandy plain forty miles farther on at Ka-
tjoruu. Green provided fresh oxen as wheelers, and decided to go
with them to Ovamboland. After resting for a time in the shade of
a palm tree, they set out for the Otjitjikaberg. They were now in
Bushmanland and Hahn made efforts to find out as much as he could
about the Bushmen. A Bushman boy was engaged as wagon leader,

and his father was taken on to do odd jobs. That very evening, however, a lion carried the father off, and Hahn, who hastened to the
scene directly he heard the screaming, only found one arm and part
of the Bushman's entrails. An elephant gun loaded with sixteen
pistol bullets was set as a spring gun for the purpose of killing this
lion, but, unfortunately, all that fell into the trap was a hyena. To
everybody's joy, Green soon afterwards killed an elephant, which
served as a welcome contribution to the food-supply.

On the 17th July they saw Ovambos for the first time. These were
coming up from the south with copper, probably from the neighbourhood of Otavi. Two of them approached very shyly. After a
Herero had been sent to them, they came along more readily, and a
pipe of tobacco, which they smoked in long horn pipes, made them
quite talkative. Hahn writes:

'Their faces are pleasant, and the shape of their heads more like that of a
European than is the case with the Hereros. Their bodies are slender but
not at all muscular, and they are of more than medium height. They are
darker in colour than the Hereros, and their hair is cut short, with a tuft on
the crown of the head. They likewise smear their bodies with ochre and fat.
They wear round their waist a girdle, between six and nine inches wide, in
which they carry a dagger. A piece of the stomach of an ox, which has been
worked soft, hangs down from the girdle in front, while they wear a small
apron made of leather behind.'

The travellers passed the old dead Omumborombonga tree, of
which mention has already been made, on the 18th July, having come
unexpectedly upon the Etosha Pan a few days before. Hahn's account
of the journey contains the following statement about it under the
date of the 12th July:

'I thought that I could see a stretch of water in the west, and I called the
attention of Rath and Green to it. The latter said he was certain it was
only a mirage. I thereupon called the Bushman guide, who laughingly said
that it was water which never dried up, and that many fish were to be found
in it. The elephants were in the habit of bathing there in the summer time.

'We decided to ride over to it the next day, and we did so, very interested
to see what the water was like. When we reached a slight elevation, after we
had been riding for half an hour, there lay before us a stretch of water that
was in all respects a lake. It was a surprising sight. Innumerable flamingos
were busy catching fish. We could not see how long it was from the north-
east to the south-west. We rode for a full hour along the bank, but could
not see the western end of the water from there, for it was misty in that
direction. The Omuramba widens out to form this lake, but another river

runs into it from the north-east. I have seen a number of lakes in my life-time and reckon that this one was about thirty miles in circumference, that is to say, the circumference of that part which we were able to see. It is more than probable that it is closely connected with Galton's Etosha.'

Hahn's company reached Ovamboland, after they had crossed a waterless plain and had forced their way through the thickly wooded belt. The travellers did not find it to be as Galton's descriptions had led them to expect. The country gave an impression of desolation. Camp was pitched close to Nangoro's head-quarters. He had pre-viously sent them a messenger to tell them that he was expecting them. A second one brought a message to the effect that Nangoro expected his guests to take part in a raid against Kasima, with whom he had recently made a temporary peace. He added that the tribe was only a small one. Hahn had, of course, to refuse, and that brought him into disfavour with Nangoro from the very beginning. The latter sent back the 12 lb. of beads which had been sent him as a present, with the message that he expected that all the presents should be handed over at once. Hahn sent a message back that he would hand over the presents when the chief himself came to greet the travellers. That evening he sent over some burning embers to the camp, and asked that their own camp fire should be extinguished and that only Nangoro's fire should burn in the camp. Hahn, who knew the Herero custom of the sacred fire, was of the opinion that it was not proper for a missionary to take any part in a heathen religious practice. They also made no secret of the fact that they did not want to be sprayed with water according to the custom of the country, and they advised Nangoro of their refusal in courteous terms. On the 24th July the camp was moved to Nangoro's place. Up to the Sunday evening of the 26th July, Nangoro had not yet shown himself. That evening a dance took place very close to their camp and lasted right into the night. The travellers were tired and wanted to sleep, and they sent an interpreter to ask the dancers to go and enjoy themselves a little farther from the camp. The request was misunderstood. One of Hahn's Hereros, who had been listening to the dancers' chant, then called out to the dancers: 'Why are you cursing the strangers, and saying: "How dare these slaves, who have come to be killed, interfere with our dance?".' Hahn understood him and became anxious; his people became frightened; Green felt un-comfortable.

Nangoro did not appear on the Monday, but towards evening he sent a bowl of beans over and said they were for Hahn's dogs, meaning his Herero servants. Hahn, Rath, and Green then decided that they would rather leave this inhospitable place than allow themselves to be treated with discourtesy any longer, and remain in doubt as to what further developments might take place. The plan to reach the Kunene with Nangoro's assistance had to be abandoned. The trek oxen were in a very bad condition from lack of grazing, and no further risk could be taken with them. Furthermore, it seemed to be out of the question that Nangoro would give them permission to travel on to the Kunene, seeing that Galton, who had been received in a much more friendly manner, had not obtained it. The position seemed to change on the 28th July. A movement amongst the natives, round about ten o'clock, told them that Nangoro was coming. He arrived. About three hundred armed warriors accompanied him. One of his sons carried a chair for him, and he sat down under a palm tree. The travellers were summoned and sat down opposite him. He stared at the strangers with a mixture of affected contempt, dignity, and curiosity on his face. Hahn spoke for the company, and told him what they wanted. Nangoro said nothing in reply, but asked where the presents were. Upon being asked whether he wanted them brought there, he said he would go himself and have a look at them. Hahn and Green then went over to their wagons. When everything was ready, Nangoro came there. Hahn gave him two young cows, a fat sheep, a piece of blue print, a red woollen cap, a piece of cloth, a tin mug, a bar of iron, a bar of thin hoop iron, five knives, a tinder box, two axes, two files, two German saws, some wire, and some other small articles. He looked at all this with utter contempt and told Hahn that he could not use any of those things; he wanted beads. Hahn replied that he would very gladly give him beads, if these things were useless to him, for they were very useful to him, Hahn. It appeared, however, that the presents were not as useless to him as he made out, for it proved very difficult for him to decide which of these articles he did not really want. In the end he gave the iron back and received in place of it some pounds of the most expensive glass beads. Hahn was willing to give him an ox in addition. Now the old man was satisfied, and he honoured Hahn with the title 'Muhona-uandje' meaning 'My Lord', and then he went to Green's wagon. There things went no better, despite the fact that the present was even more valuable in that a gun was included in it. Nangoro refused everything and asked for beads, and these Green gave him with the addition of three cows, a young ox, some goats, and other things.

Nangoro was now ready to talk. It appeared that he could speak Herero fluently. When Hahn thought, however, the time had now come to make his request for permission to go to the Kunene, and to the Kuanlama tribe, he found out his mistake. Nangoro declared roundly that there could be no talk of anything of that kind. He then started looking at the wagon and asked them for everything he saw, especially Rath's dog, but took the refusals quite calmly. After he had been there about two hours, he asked that the guns should be fired, so that he could hear them. When, however, the shooting was about to take place, he crept behind a tree in fright. After several shots had been fired, and Green had fired off his two revolvers as well, Nangoro went home satisfied.

Preparations for the return journey were then made. Hahn had bought as much corn as possible from the people. Green's attempt to trade for ivory was unsuccessful. They brought him very little, and they wanted such enormous prices for the little they did bring as to make it quite unprofitable to take it. They discussed the plan of going back as far as the Omuramba and then going out in a north-easterly direction from there. Schipepa was sent to Nangoro on the 29th July to tell him of their departure, which was to take place next day. Luckily Schipepa only took the message over the following day. Hahn and Green had noticed that, for some days past, all the Ovambos who came to the wagon were armed. The people in charge of the wagons therefore thought it necessary to carry their weapons as well.

Hahn, Rath, and Green regarded it as improper for a guest to do this, and as a breach of the customs of the country. They went everywhere unarmed and ordered their wagon attendants to do the same, but the latter paid very little attention to the order, until Green threatened to take their weapons away from them. At dawn on the morning of the 30th July the wagons were inspanned and the slaughter stock sent off ahead. As the first rays of the sun came over the horizon, the trek commenced. Then Mbapupua ran to the chief's residence and called out, 'Why are you still asleep; our foes are riding off?' Shortly afterwards the travellers realized that they were being followed by a large company of armed men. Hahn stayed behind the wagons and waited until they came up. They were under the leadership of one of Nangoro's sons (Nangoro had about 106 wives and about 70 sons). Hahn asked quietly what the warriors' war cries meant. Their leader replied that they were only amusing themselves. Hahn knew very well that something very different was intended, and replied that, if this was merely a form of amusement, he had better tell them to leave the war cries out; he had come in peace and he wanted to leave in peace. Those who were in his immediate neighbourhood kept quiet and some of the others hung back. Suddenly Kahingua, Hahn's driver, who was standing behind the wagon, called to him to look-out, as Nangoro's son intended to stab him with the spear, which he had raised above his head. Green, too, who had ridden on ahead, came rushing back and saw the danger and warned Hahn. Hahn went and sat on the driver's seat in the wagon, and told his driver that he was to walk beside the wagon and not behind it. At the same moment Kahingua screamed. Hahn turned round and was appalled to see that the chief's son had stabbed the wagon driver, as he was bending down, in the back with his spear, and that this was sticking right through his shoulder. Kahingua, who was carrying a double-barrelled musket, immediately fired both barrels, and the chief's son, and another member of Nangoro's family, fell to the ground severely wounded. The wounded Herero was lifted on to the wagon and died half an hour later.

The greatest confusion arose amongst the travellers. Green wanted to form a square with the four wagons, making a kind of a fort out of them and defending it. The Hereros proposed that they should break into one of the homesteads along the road and resume hostilities from there. Hahn insisted that, if the wagons were to proceed alongside each other over the flats, the journey could be continued, and they would not give the impression that they were running away. In this way the trek oxen were protected from the arrows of the pursuers, who, while remaining at a respectful distance, kept up a regular fusilade. The wagons were driven to a water-hole, and the water casks filled up right in the face of the enemy, and then they went on. The pursuers continually increased in numbers. Green rode up and down the line. He had donned all his weapons. With his revolver in his hand, his hunting knife in his belt, and his sword handy, he took charge of the defence. He was determined to sell his life as dearly as possible. No one had any hope that they would escape. Fighting became general. Well directed arrows fell all about them. Special attention was paid to Hahn and Green. Green ordered an irregular but well directed fire to be maintained. Whenever the Ovambos tried to storm the wagons, Green himself shot the leader down. During a short pause in the fighting he exchanged his revolver for his long-range elephant gun. Green's comrade, Bonfield, shot one of the leaders in the forehead. According to his reckoning, that was the eleventh who fell that morning, and that made an impression. With every shot, the Ovambos immediately fell on the ground, so one could never be certain how many of them were wounded. The Ovambos had often mocked at the guns during the last few days, but now they began to be frightened of them. After the battle had lasted about two hours, they began to realize that it was better for them to keep as far away as possible. Separate groups of them began to retire. Every attempt to advance was accompanied by new casualties. With the exception of Kahingua, none of those in the wagons had been touched. There were more than 800 Ovambo warriors. The whole party with the wagons consisted of thirty people, and only eight of those knew how to handle a gun. At the end of three hours, not a single pursuer was to be seen. If they had only made a concerted attack, it would have been very easy indeed for this mass of people to have surrounded the wagons and massacred everybody. Green writes as follows about these hours, which were so fraught with danger: 'It really seems incredible that we managed to escape from such a dangerous position. It must be attributed entirely to the help of the Almighty and His good providence.'

What had actually happened in these hours of peril only became known later. Nangoro heard the firing. The news of the death of his son, and of many more of his leading men, was communicated to him immediately, and that probably gave him such a shock that he had a stroke and died immediately. Nangoro was dead before his warriors got back. The news of his death was conveyed to those who were taking part in the battle. They regarded it as due to the intervention of higher powers, and they gave up the pursuit. His successor was, however, not his brother, but Tjikongo, who was disposed to be friendly and afterwards sent Hahn an invitation to visit him, and gave Hahn his son to educate.

It came out later that it was not so much the refusal of the fire and the water rites, nor the refusal to take part in a raid, which was the reason for Nangoro's fateful decision, but that it was the deliberate consideration of the fact that the possession of four ox-wagons would be a wonderful means of getting iron and copper ore from Angola and Otavi, with very little trouble, which was the motive for the attack.

On their journey southwards, the travellers met a number of
Ovambo copper miners, who were going to Nangoro's brother. Hahn
told them what had happened to him at Nangoro's place, and gave
them exact information about his intentions and purposes in Ovamboland. The journey was then continued by the way they had come,
and they reached the Omuramba Omatako. Green remained behind
at Omevaomengo, with the intention of continuing the elephant
hunt, which the journey to Ovamboland had interrupted. Hahn and
Rath got back home to Barmen on the 11th September, 1857, without
further mishap.

Hahn had undertaken this journey as a preliminary step to the
prosecution of a new missionary effort, and from this point of view
it proved entirely fruitless. What had been gained, however, was a
closer knowledge of circumstances in the northern part of Hereroland,
and also an insight into the tribal conditions, language, and distribution of the Bushmen of the north. The glowing account, which
Galton gave regarding Ovamboland, could be commented on and
supplemented from his own observations. The second discovery of
the Etosha Pan resulted in the knowledge of the country being en-
riched through a detailed description of it, and a fairly accurate
sketch of it being made.

The Okavango: Charles John Andersson

Andersson was in Capetown at the end of 1856, and he met
Frederick Green, the elephant hunter, there. They planned a journey together to explore the interior of South West Africa. They
would go to the Kunene, for Galton had not succeeded in getting
through to this northern boundary of South West Africa in 1851. As
Andersson had many preparations to make, Green went ahead to
wait in South West Africa until his companion arrived. When Andersson, however, got there, Green was nowhere to be found. He had
gone with Wilson to Lake Ngami, and from there to Libebe.[1]

After Andersson had waited in vain for two months for Green's
return, or some news of his whereabouts, he decided to accept the
offer of the Walfish Bay Mining Company for the time being, and to
become the manager of their affairs in Otjimbingwe. It was during
this time that Hahn and Rath went to Ovamboland and met Green

[1] An account of this expedition was published in the *Eastern Province Magazine*
in 1857.

on the way, and the latter joined them in the hope that he would reach the Kunene. We have learned that this object was never achieved. When Andersson's contract expired, he gave up his position with the mining company and went to Capetown for the purpose of fitting himself out in the best possible manner for a journey to the Kunene.

His entourage consisted of John Mortar, a native of Madeira, who had previously travelled with Galton, John Pereira from Malabar, who had had an unusually good education, for he spoke English, Dutch, Portuguese, Chinese, and several Indian dialects, and understood Latin well. In addition to these, there were nine natives. He took with him an ox-wagon, thirty trek oxen, five riding and pack oxen, five young oxen, eleven mules, one 'old' horse (that means a horse which has survived horse sickness, and was therefore not likely to die in the rainy season), seventy sheep and goats for food, and a dozen dogs for hunting purposes.

Andersson now had to decide what route he was going to take. There were two ways of reaching the Kunene. By travelling in a northerly direction through the western side of the country, it could be reached through the Kaokoveld. The Hereros of Omaruru used to take this route when they went on trading expeditions. On the eastern side, however, it was possible to travel by well-known roads down the Omuramba Omatako, to follow this in such a way as to avoid the dangers of Ondonga, to find more friendly Ovambo tribes, and to reach the Kunene through their territory. Andersson much preferred to travel unknown roads, and thus to pass through country which had not yet been explored. In spite of all warnings, he decided to go through the Kaokoveld.

He left Otjimbingwe on the 22nd March, 1859. He reached the Omaruru River and rested for a time on its banks. There he wrote in his diary:

'When a heavy sea-fog rests on these uncouth and rugged surfaces—and it does so very often—a place fitter to represent the infernal regions could scarcely, in searching the world round, be found. A shudder, amounting almost to fear, came over me when its frightful desolation first suddenly broke upon my view. 'Death', I exclaimed, 'would be preferable to banishment to such a country'.

If the resting-place proved so undesirable, things got worse the farther they went. They were forced to make a road through a hundred miles of thorn bush. His riding horse, which had his gun in its gun bucket, ran away. It was only found again after a three days' search, and the gun was badly damaged. He hurt his knees and arms badly through an unlucky fall, and finally his ox-wagon capsized and he thought it was entirely wrecked. He was, however, able to get it on its wheels again, and he went on to Otjitambi, which was a kind of tribal centre for the Hereros in former days. Andersson found a spring there and a number of old wells, but no human beings, not even one whom he could employ as a guide, for Hottentots had been in this neighbourhood, about a year before, raiding Herero cattle. The Hereros, however, had defended themselves despérately, and had defeated the Veldskoendraers. The latter were forced to flee to the south without any loot. They murdered a number of Berg-damas in the Erongo mountains, and took from the Swakop valley the booty which the Kaokoveld had refused them. The Hereros, however, had driven their stock into the northern Kaokoveld, and left the southern part, through which Andersson travelled, totally uninhabited.

Andersson went on from Otjitambi to Okaua. The oxen had now been five days without water. No one knew the way, and he realized that he would have to go back. Back he went to the barren Omaruru River and this time he found a better camping place. He sent a mes-senger to Otjimbingwe to let his friends there know what he was doing, and to fetch his post. He then pointed his wagon shaft east-wards and, on the 20th July, 1859, he reached the Omuramba Oma-tako, and set out to reach the Kunene by the eastern road, which had been constantly used before.

Andersson came to the Otjirukaku mountains in December, and here he met a caravan of Hereros, the conductor of which was a man named Karoinene, one of Tjamuaha's sons. They had been prevented from entering Ovamboland but they had attacked and robbed the Ovambos' southern outposts on the Etosha Pan. They had robbed the Bushmen too, and had beaten the Bushmen women terribly. One came crying to Andersson and begged him to help him, and he forced the Hereros to give back what they had stolen.

He learned from the Hereros that it was known in Ovamboland that he was on the way, and that the Ovambo chiefs had taken refuge at a Bushmen werf out of sheer fright. As is well known, the Ovambo chiefs generally kept Bushmen as their bodyguards. That seemed to Andersson to be a very bad sign. As Karoinene professed to know the country to the east, Andersson engaged him as guide and then took an easterly direction, with the idea of making as wide a detour as possible to avoid Ovamboland, in the expectation of reaching the Kunene notwithstanding.

The last weeks of the year 1859 were taken up with hunting, and, on New Year's day, 1860, we find the explorer back at Omambonde. again. Messengers arrived from Otjimbingwe and he set out again on the 5th January. He had heard from Green about the Omuramba Ovambo, which he reckoned to be a tributary of the Kunene, and his idea was to make for it. By following it, he figured that he must at last reach the river, which was the goal of his journey. Passing Okanambuti, he came close to the Otjitjika mountains, where he found Hahn's old wagon spoor of 1857, which he followed for a time, turning then to the east. He dismissed Tjamuaha's son, who proved to be utterly useless. On the 16th January he reached the Omuramba Ovambo without recognizing it, but the Bushmen told him where he was. They were willing and obliging, because they had not forgotten the good treatment which they had received from Hahn and Green, and they were not the least bit timid. The end of the journey was in sight, and we shall now leave Andersson to tell his own story:

'The bush became, if possible, more and more dense, harassing, and re-tarding to our march. It would be wearisome to dwell on our wretched progress; whilst to add to our embarrassment, our discontented and suspicious guides threatened to leave us. It was, however, to us of the utmost impor-tance at present to retain their services, as the difficulty of finding both way and water increased daily. I therefore earnestly requested them to stay with us, at least till other Bushmen could be found. But no persuasions or offers of handsome rewards, could induce them to remain, and one day they unex-pectedly decamped, leaving us to grope our way out as best we could.

'Elephant paths now became exceedingly numerous, crossing and re-crossing the country in every possible direction. Sometimes half a dozen or more of these paths might be seen converging towards some particular point, i.e. a vlei; it was impossible therefore to know how to select the proper one. Yet we dared not neglect them altogether, as by following them on we could alone find water. At one time one of these tracks actually led us back towards Damaraland. This, however, would have mattered little had I known the exact course to pursue; but the Bushmen had so contradicted each other's statements, that I felt completely puzzled. At times these per-plexing conductors would point to the north, at others to the north-east, and some even said that due east was our proper route for finding the river. In this uncertainty, cruising about day after day in the intricate bush with our cumbersome vehicle, was distressing in the extreme; I therefore, after a while, determined on leaving the wagon at some vlei and proceeding with a few draught and carriage oxen ahead, to explore the country, and, if possible, discover the river.

'To dispatch this business quickly, with some chance of success, I packed up the smallest quantity of necessaries possible, and, selecting a few of the most light-footed and enduring of my native attendants, started on the expedition. That same day, at about sunset, we perceived a small column of smoke issuing from a cluster of trees, and by sending part of my people in a roundabout way in advance, we succeeded in capturing all the inmates of a small Bushman werf. The whole party captured consisted but of a few women and children, and two or three grown-up men. The poor people were of course desperately frightened, and I soon pacified them by presents of meat and tobacco. Thinking it inadvisable at the time to make any mention of my need of guides, I merely gave them to understand that I was en route for the river. I was determined, however, should they not decamp during the night, to secure a couple of the men on the following morning. My mode of proceeding answered well, for at an early hour the next day, on going to their werf (we bivouacked at a pool of water hard by), we found them enjoying themselves, in all security, by a roaring fire. Without a moment's delay I ordered two of them to rise and to accompany us. They were extremely loth to comply, but I soon gave them to understand that obey they must—that they had no alternative.

'Late in the afternoon of this day we came upon several pretty fresh tracks of Bushmen, and, following them steadily, espied after a while a woman digging for roots. She was soon secured, but until addressed by our guide she was in great trepidation. Five minutes' farther walk brought us to a werf consisting of between twenty and thirty huts.

'Whilst my men were here making everything snug for the night, I had some conversation with the chief of the place, a fine intelligent young fellow. He told us that, by smart travelling, we might reach the river in a day and a half. This was cheerful news, the more so as he promised to conduct us thither personally. I lay down to rest consequently that night more contented than I had been for many a day, and in much better spirits.

'At break of day we were afoot, but, the morning air being raw and sharp, I had at first some difficulty in getting the guides along. After about six hours' journeying at a rapid rate, these Bushmen suddenly stopped short, and each of them, drawing from his quiver two or three arrows, carefully concealed them amongst the trees. On demanding an explanation of this singular proceeding, I was simply told that the Ovaquangari were a very unscrupulous set of men, who, whenever they thought themselves strong enough, would take forcible possession of anything that struck their fancy, and, as the concealed missiles were new, and of some value to the Bushmen, they were, they said, loth to lose them. They also warned me to be on my guard, as the natives, whose villages we were now fast approaching, were fierce and savage. This was an old tale, and though I did not despise the warning, I conjectured that our sudden and unannounced arrival amongst them would cause rather fright and consternation than any demonstration of hostility on their part.

'After this little delay we again proceeded, but had not gone far before I perceived on the faraway horizon a distinct dark blue line. "Ah ha!" I exclaimed to myself, "in the valley of which that line evidently forms the border, there is surely something more than a mere periodical watercourse." A few minutes afterwards, catching a glimpse of an immense sheet of water in the distance, my anticipation was realized to its utmost. A cry of joy and satisfaction escaped me at this glorious sight. Twenty minutes more brought us to the banks of a truly noble river, at this point at least 200 yards wide. This was then, in all probability, the Mukuru Mukovanja of the Ovambo, which these people had given us to understand flowed westward. Taking it for granted that their statement was in this respect correct, I had stood some time by the water before I became aware of my mistake. "By heavens!" I suddenly exclaimed, "the water flows towards the heart of the continent, instead of emptying itself into the Atlantic!" For a moment I felt amazed at the discovery. "East!" I continued to soliloquise; "why, what stream *can* this then be, in this latitude and longitude? Tioughe? No; that channel alone is much too insignificant to form the outlet for such a mighty flow of water. Well, then, it must be one of the chief branches of that magnificent river, the Chobe." This was my first impression, which was to some extent corroborated by the natives, who described this river, called by the Ovaquangari "Okavango", as forking off in two directions in the neighbourhood of Libebe, one branch forming the said Tioughe, the other finding its way to the Chobe. But on more mature consideration, I strongly question the correctness both of my own impression and of the account of the natives.'

Andersson had gone in search of the Kunene and he had discovered the Okavango, but he did not give up hope of reaching the Kunene. He sent a messenger to the Ovambo chief Tjikongo, and went on a hunting expedition until he returned, but fever worried him continually. In spite of this, he went to see Tjikongo, who was perfectly friendly to him. He had been attacked by the Makololos, who had been quite peaceful while Livingstone stayed with them, but had resumed their robber existence after he had left them. Andersson returned to his camp on the Okavango on the 6th June, 1861. As he could not get rid of the fever, it was impossible for him to hunt, and the slaughter stock were getting fewer day by day, so he sent Pereira with two men and two pack animals back to Otjimbingwe to fetch fresh provisions and his post. The messengers came back on the 17th November, and brought with them the unexpected news that Green was near at hand for the purpose of coming to his assistance. He had heard in Matabeleland that the chief Tjipanga had sent his warriors out to kill Andersson. He had therefore set out with all possible speed to go to his assistance. Andersson wrote him a letter, suggesting that while he was coming up from the south, he, Andersson, would come from the north to meet him. Andersson broke up his camp on the 23rd November and went as far as Orujo. Further he could not get, for there was no water between that place and the Omuramba Ovambo, and Green found him there.

'Most deeply was I affected by this noble deed. Indeed, this single act of devotion was to me infinitely more gratifying than would be all the wealth the world has to bestow. It was heart-warming to know that at least one human bosom beat genuinely for the solitary wanderer. Dear Green! an approving conscience must be your greatest reward; but should these lines ever reach you,—and God grant they may ere long:—I beg you will here accept my poor but warm and sincere thanks for your spirited resolve to come to my rescue when dangers so great, of which I was unaware, encompassed me. Believe me, this one act of heroic friendship has, in my own estimation, much more than outweighed any trifling service it has been in my power to render you.'

Soon after Pereira's return, Andersson learnt that the expedition which had been sent against him had actually arrived in the vicinity, but that, for some unknown reason, its leader had decided to abandon his murderous purposes and to leave the country.

The importance of Andersson's journey to the Okavango lies, in the first place, in the fact that he discovered the river, sailed on it, and brought back with him the first reliable information about its course and the country on its banks. He journeyed through the southern Kaokoveld, and his book, *The Okavango River*, will remain of lasting value for all those who are, or will allow themselves to become, interested in the story of South West Africa, and the life of those early days. Attention should be drawn to the fact that Andersson was the very first person to give to the land between the Orange and the Kunene rivers, which had up to then had no other name but 'Namaland', 'Damaraland' and 'Ovamboland', the comprehensive name of South West Africa, and use this name in the books he published.

PART III

HEREROLAND AGAINST NAMALAND

I

THE HERERO WAR OF FREEDOM AND
THE ORLAM WAR

1. THE HERERO WAR OF FREEDOM

BEFORE we begin to describe the events of the two wars, which turned the whole of South West Africa, from 1863 to 1870, into a theatre of war, it is desirable to make some acquaintance with the people who played a leading part in those wars.

The Herero leaders

Zeraua had been able to stay at Otjimbingwe under the protection of the mission and the copper mines. Tjiseseta, one of Zeraua's relations, was living in the veld of Omaruru. Mbandjou, who was related to Tjiseseta, lived sometimes in the Kaokoveld, and sometimes in the veld to the east of Omaruru. Ndjiharine, who subsequently became the chief of Omburo near Omaruru, belonged to the same family. These were the family ties between the Herero chiefs of the west, who recognized Zeraua of Otjimbingwe, not as a paramount chief, but as an influential man to whom one could turn for help in times of need, especially as he was on very good terms with the Europeans at Otjimbingwe.

Alongside this family bond there existed a second one, which was grouped around Tjamuaha and Maharero. The principal members of this were Kambazembi, who had come in from the Kaokoveld after Tjamuaha's death and taken possession of the country round the Waterberg, Mungunda, of whose death we read previously, Kahitjene, whom Jonker persecuted and Mungunda's sons killed, and many others. Now Maharero's mother, Otjoruzumo, Tjamuaha's principal wife, was Kambazembi's sister, and Kambazembi's mother was the daughter of Tjirue, Maharero's grandfather. Then Kambazembi married Ndomo, Maharero's sister, and Maharero, again, took Katundure, Kambazembi's sister, as an additional wife.

The chiefs' family circle was completed owing to the fact that Maharero's mother, Otjoruzumo, was a younger sister of the principal wife of Zeraua at Otjimbingwe. In this way all the Herero chiefs were related to each other, and Maharero saw to it that the bonds were strengthened by numerous additional marriages, and that, in this way, any chiefs who had been outside the circle were drawn into it. (On the 26th December, 1863, Maharero took his ninth wife, and in his later years he had more than sixty.)

The eastern Hereros, the Mbanderus, did not belong to this circle, for the Hereros and Mbanderus never intermarried. Their most prominent chief was Kahimemua. The Hereros under Nicodemus, who was the son of Kavikunua, the son of Tjamuaha, must be distinguished from the Mbanderus. This is important for the sake of the history of a later period, in connexion with the execution of the the chiefs of both these tribes under martial law at Okahandja in 1896. Amongst Maharero's near relations were Hirarapi, his eldest brother, who was killed at the battle of Otjimbingwe in 1863, and his brother Kavikunua, Nicodemus's father, who ruled such of the eastern Hereros as were not Mbanderus. Maharero had a half-brother named Riarua, who was a man of parts, and became the leader of his army. He was the son of Otjipeze, one of Tjamuaha's later wives, and a sister of Otjoruzumo, who is mentioned above. Another of Tjamuaha's sons, who became of considerable importance later, was Kavezeri. One can see how close the ties of relationship between all the important Hereros were in 1862. The reason why Maharero occupied such a prominent position amongst all the chiefs was that he was the guardian of the sacred fire of their ancestors, and that there was hardly a single guardian left amongst the other tribes, because Jonker had killed them all. Even Zeraua at Otjimbingwe possessed no true sacred fire. It is true that he was an Omuhona, i.e. a rich man and a chief, but he lacked the most important thing of all—the mysterious power inherited from his ancestors, of being able to kindle and tend a true ancestral fire. The other Herero chiefs came to get the sacred fire from Maharero after Tjamuaha's death. In that way the road to the paramount chieftainship was opened up. Even if he was not by any means the most powerful chief, he was clothed with a religious prestige which the other chiefs did not possess—and that entirely through the last blessing bestowed on him by Tjamuaha: 'Take it! Take it!'

The Nama leaders

After Jonker's death his eldest son, Christian, became the chief of the Afrikander tribe, which had its tribal centre in Windhoek, although Christian preferred to live in Okahandja for the time being. The Hottentots of Jan Booi's tribe, who belonged to the northern part of Bethanie, stayed with Christian. Jan Booi, the leader of this tribe, which was really a branch of the tribe of Bethanie, and stood under David Christian of Bethanie, although it took little notice of him, was Jonker Afrikander's father-in-law. Jan's son Jacobus Booi, was the father-in-law of Jan Jonker, who was Christian's successor after the latter fell in the battle of Otjimbingwe, in 1863. Jacobus Booi attracted a large part of the tribe to himself while his father, Jan, was still alive, and he allied himself to the Afrikanders. In addition to this, there belonged to this northern alliance, which was in close proximity to the Hereros, the Topnaars of Walfish Bay, the Grootdodens along the Kuiseb under Aimab, the Veldskoendraers in the country round Keetmanshoop under Hendrik Ses, or Nanib, and the warlike part of Amraal's people in Gobabis. From time to time Oasib, too, the paramount chief of the old Nama tribes at Hoachanas, joined the northern alliance as well.

In contrast to this warlike northern alliance, there gradually formed a southern alliance, which was more peacefully inclined. To this there belonged the tribe of Bethanie under David Christian, the tribe of Berseba under Paul Goliath, the Witboois of Gibeon under Kido Witbooi, the Swartboois under Frederick Willem of Rehoboth, and the better disposed part of Amraal's people in Gobabis. Abraham Bondelswart, however, the chief of the Bondelswarts in Warmbad, and Piet Koper, the chief of the Fransman Hottentots on the Auob, belonged neither to the northern alliance, nor to the southern. Both these tribes retire into the background in the history of the events between 1863 and 1870, although their neutral attitude was not by any means to be relied upon.

After Tjamuaha's death

Tjamuaha was dead. He had been buried at the entrance of his cattle kraal just at the end of 1861. Late every afternoon the lament began and continued far into the night. In accordance with tribal custom, every member of the family had to come and 'view' the grave within a year of his death. An animal had to be killed with every new arrival, and with every new arrival the lamentations had to start again. The men were not allowed to do anything at all during this time. As a sign of mourning the women turned their leather head-dresses round and wore them back to front. The men turned their finely woven leather belts, and wore them inside out. The children of both sexes were given bibs of calf skin, the lower edge of which was cut into a fringe. All this was done as a sign of mourning for the departed.

Directly Tjamuaha had died, his sacred fire had been allowed to go out, by refraining from putting wood on it. It was necessary, however, that the daily supply of milk should be consecrated for use. Tjamuaha's quiver was brought out, and his kindling-stick with which he had once kindled a new sacred fire in the days of his youth after Tjirue's death taken out of it. This stick served to represent the deceased. The meat which was prepared for the funeral feast was hung on it; it was dipped into the milk which was drunk day by day. When, however, all the relations who were expected, had arrived, Maharero had made a new kindling-stick out of Omuvapu wood. With this he went out beyond his father's grave in a northerly direction. The men of importance followed him. There was an open space about a thousand yards away. There he sat down on the ground, held the lower part of the kindling-stick between his feet, put it in the hole which had been made for it, and started to give it a fast twirling movement by running his hands continuously up and down it. While doing this, his face was turned towards Tjamuaha's grave, for the latter had been buried lying from east to west and on his left side, so that his face looked towards the north. Maharero did not say a long prayer to his forefathers. It was short and to the point: '*Tate, matu zeja omuriro uarue omupe, ete ku matu oto,*' which means, 'Father, we are kindling another new fire at which we desire to warm ourselves'; and out of Maharero's mouth came his father's consent: '*Ii, jakiseje!*' i.e. 'that is right, kindle it.'

By doing this, Maharero had actually taken over the control of the Herero people. All the old huts were now deserted, and new ones erected around the new sacred fire. All the old fires had now to be extinguished, and every one who wanted to have a fire of his own in his hut had to fetch burning embers and light it from Maharero's fire. All the relations, too, who were now returning home, had to take some embers with them on their journey. There was any quantity of dry wood along the road, with which the dying embers could be renewed. What really mattered was that the fire itself, and not the embers, should be taken by each one to his own werf. From then onwards, Maharero sat day by day at the sacred fire and tasted himself the daily milk-supply of his dependants, and Tjamuaha's twirling-stick was placed in the bundle of the other ancestral sticks, with which there was a piece of wood from the ancestral Omu-

mborombonga tree amongst the other objects which had been collected through the centuries as sacred ancestral heirlooms. These
were carefully hidden from the gaze of the curious in a hut lying to
the east of the sacred fire. In times of need or religious ceremonial
they were taken out and placed round the sacred fire. Tjamuaha's
nephew, who had seen the bundle himself, said that it was so thick
that his two hands could not go round it. Christian Afrikander watched
everything that was happening with no inconsiderable anxiety. The
numbers of Hereros who were streaming in from all sides showed him
how large Maharero's family was. Besides, signs were not lacking
that there were forces working amongst the Hereros which he had
thought were entirely extinct. It was reported from Gobabis that
even the Mbanderus were beginning to throw aside their slavish submissiveness, and either to resist their oppressors openly, or to disappear in the night with the stock of which they had been given charge.
Christian's flocks were under Maharero's superintendence, and
were herded by his own herdsmen. They numbered about 5,000
head, and there were more than 1,000 fat wethers amongst them. He
was beset with all kinds of fears and oppressed by his suspicions. Why
was it that Maharero had not handed over to him the inheritance
which Tjamuaha had promised him on his death-bed? He sent a
messenger to ask Maharero for the old things which his father had
worn on his person. Maharero sent back the answer that he knew
perfectly well that it was a custom of the Hereros that an inheritance
of that kind should not be handed over until all the relations had
'viewed' the grave. They had not all been there yet, and he was
expecting a great many more.

Christian had, too, a great deal of trouble with his Afrikanders,
whose chief he was. He had come into possession of the estate of his
father Jonker, and now there were members of his family, who
accused him of unfairness, and wanted to make out that his division
of the inheritance was wrong. His brother, Jan Jonker, Jacobus
Booi's son-in-law, who was clever and courageous and a splendid
horseman, was very dissatisfied indeed, for he had been totally excluded from all share in the estate. With that Jan could not possibly
remain satisfied, for he knew very well that Jonker had thought a lot
of him on account of his bravery and prudence. This had, however,
greatly annoyed his half-sister, Jan Arie's wife, and she and Jan Arie
were the moving spirits in getting Jan left out. But still it was not a
pleasant thing to see that Maharero never went to Christian, but

stayed in Jan's hut till far into the night and had private talks with
him. Nobody could have any idea what these two found to talk
about. Innocent folk might have said: 'Jan Jonker and Maharero
have been friends from boyhood. In Windhoek they hatched many
a plot and carried it out. These friends like to be together.' Maharero, however, used to say in after years, when he and Jan had been
fighting each other for a long time: 'Jan cannot get the better of me.
I am just as cunning as he is. We drank milk from the same goat,
he on the one side and I on the other.' Christian and his Afrikanders
were suspicious, however, and they had every right to assume that
something was going on between Jan and Maharero, but what it was
they did not know. Thus the year 1862 came to a close, and twelve
months had passed since Tjamuaha had gone to his grave. It was the
duty of an Herero chief to go once more, during this month, with all
the members of the family who were within reach, to his father's
grave, and to offer up a sacrifice and to tell his late parent that, as
the year of mourning was past, the family would now take up their
residence in a new place, in accordance with ancient custom. It was
not only all the people, old and young, who had to attend this ceremony at the grave, but all the deceased's cattle had to be brought
there too. This ceremony took place, and Philip Katjimune from
Otjimbingwe was present, as Zeraua's representative, with a large
number of men, who were all armed with guns. Philip had been
robbed by the Namas in his youth. Hahn, the missionary, had found
him at Steinkopf, in 1843, and had brought him back with him. He
was a clever, reliable man, and, although he could not speak Herero,
but only Nama and Dutch, he enjoyed the confidence of Zeraua and
of the Europeans who lived at Otjimbingwe.

When the period of mourning was past, there was nothing to
prevent the departure from the old werf and the establishment of a
new one, either near by or some distance away. Maharero chose for
the purpose the plateau on the Kaiser Wilhelm Mountain, which lies
to the east of Okahandja, half-way up the mountain side. He was
now separated from Christian and the Afrikanders by the Okahandja
River and a small piece of level country on the west, but from his
mountain he could see everything that was going on in the plain
below. Christian sent and asked Maharero what this strange action
meant. Maharero sent word back that it was the usual custom for
Hereros to change their dwelling-places when the days of mourning
were past. The weather was extraordinarily favourable to Maha-

rero's early efforts, for in December already there had been heavy rains, and by January 1863 the veld was green in every direction, and marvellously green, such as it had hardly ever been before, and so Maharero's cattle lacked neither water nor grazing. He drove them into the eastern mountains and kept them well guarded.

It then came to Christian's ears that the Herero women and children had left the werf on the mountain and gone to Otjimbingwe in the company of Philip and his Hereros, and that they had taken a number of milch cows with them. Maharero, however, sent Christian a message to the effect that he was not to let this disturb him. The milch cows were intended to provide the women and children with food, and they had just gone to Otjimbingwe for a visit. His head wife Kataree was still with him on the mountain. Christian, however, was a prey to evil thoughts, and he feared for his stock, and considered whether it would not be wiser to send for them.

Christian gave up the idea and sent two neutral men from Otji-kango, the Basters, Samuel Gertse and Daniel Cloete, to Maharero with this message: 'Child of my father, when your father died he said: live together like brothers; why have you now left me? Come down from your mountain, let us talk matters over, and let us live together.' Maharero replied, 'You are quite right; I will come. I, however, have become a chief, and as a chief I have the duties of a chief to perform. The first of these duties was the removal of my werf. When everything connected with that has been done I shall come to you.'

The two men left. As they were going down the mountain Daniel Cloete said to Samuel Gertse: 'I quite forgot to give Maharero some of the tobacco which we grow in Barmen. You go on and I will follow you shortly.' Daniel went quickly back to Maharero and said to him: 'Maharero, if you go and meet Christian, you will be a dead man, for Christian and his whole council have decided to get you into their hands and kill you.'

Maharero sent Christian a message to tell him that he thought it necessary to send the rest of his cattle to Otjimbingwe as the bellowing interfered with his father Tjamuaha's rest, and that Christian should come and take the stock that belonged to him, if he feared that he was being defrauded of it through its removal to Otjimbingwe. Christian made no move.

Maharero, however had not been inactive. He had sent messages to all Hereros living within a reasonable distance, asking them to come to him on the mountain, or to assemble at Otjimbingwe. In this way a large camp was gradually established on the mountain, and the cattle which were still there were collected behind it. All the cattle, and Christian's 5,000 head of small stock with them, were taken off to Otjimbingwe by degrees under cover of night with a strong guard. Christian let the removal of the cattle proceed without interference. When Maharero got the news that everything that he possessed was safe, he gave orders to load all the guns. He had round about one hundred guns amongst his people, some of which he had received from Jonker, and some of which he had bought from traders at Otjimbingwe. Then the Hereros came down from the mountain to commence their fight for freedom.

Christian had seen what was afoot. Hendrik Ses, the chief of the Veldskoendraers, who was staying with him, was likewise watching the proceedings. It was not long before the Namas and Hereros stood opposite each other near enough to hear each other's shouts. The Hereros shouted: 'Here are Jonker's guns. Will you not come and wrest them from us?' Then Hendrik Ses went and fetched a white cloth, which he fastened to Christian's hat, and waved it in the air. Maharero said: 'They do not want to fight, so we ought not to shoot at them. The least we can do is to say goodbye to them. Then they all fired their guns by way of greeting, and marched in a westerly direction to Otjimbingwe. But the Afrikanders never moved for they had lost their courage. A few Herero stragglers, who came from Osona in the south and tried to join the march, were attacked and killed. Amongst these were Tjihundju and Karuaina, the son of Kanjama.

At Otjimbingwe

Since the time that Rath had settled there, and, afterwards, the copper miners had come to live there, Otjimbingwe had become quite a busy place, but now, with the addition of Maharero's subjects, it became the most populous place in the whole of South West Africa. More than a hundred huts were quickly erected on the level ground, right up to the limestone ridges on the west and north sides of the village. The place actually consisted of two parts, which were separated from each other by the Omuseme River. To the east of the Omuseme were the mission buildings, and Kleinschmidt was doing his best to keep the work going in Otjimbingwe, Rehoboth, Barmen, and Rooibank, from here, for all the other missionaries had either

been called away or transferred. On the western side were situated
the mining company's building, a mile or two away, in which Andersson had established his workshops and stores. There, too, were the
werfs of the earlier mine workers, who had formerly been supported
by Jonker, and during the time when Jonker was interested in the
mines, had acted as labourers and a garrison at the same time. In the
course of time they had acquired guns out of their earnings, and as
they were Hereros, they now proved to be valuable allies for Maharero. There stood there, as well, a small Nama werf, that of Jonker's
old garrison of Afrikanders, who had worked as wagon drivers for the
mine. Zeraua, who had long been irked by the fact that the Afrikanders treated his child Maharero so badly, had long ago suggested
to Tjamuaha that it would be advisable to bring his people to
Otjimbingwe when a favourable occasion offered, for Andersson and
all the Europeans would certainly help the Hereros, and arms and
ammunition could be got through Andersson at any time. Andersson
had returned to Otjimbingwe in December 1862 after a long absence,
and had filled his stores with such a variety of goods as had never
yet been seen in South West Africa. The two famous cannons, which
served to protect his neutrality and to show his independence, stood
in front of his house. The Hereros hoped that, should the necessity
arise, he would let them speak in their favour. They had the assurance
of all the Europeans that they would help them, so far as was consis-
tent with their duties as neutrals. All the Europeans and missionaries
in both the north and the south were regarded as neutrals in those
days. This was the only possible position that they could take up, if
they did not wish their numbers to be reduced to nothing, through
their being involved in numerous attacks and affrays. Maharero made
thorough preparations, expecting that the Afrikanders would unite
with the Nama tribes to make war upon him. He sent his messengers
as far as the Kaokoveld to summon all the Herero warriors from there.
The number of Hereros grew larger and larger. Otjimbingwe, however, was like one big garden, for it rained in 1863 as it had not rained
for the last thirty years. The heavy rains only ceased in April, and
so they were in a position to graze the cattle which they had removed
from Jonker's vicinity in the veld round Otjimbingwe.

Christian, too, was making his preparations. He wrote letters and
sent messages to all the chiefs of Namaland and asked them to come
and fight the Hereros with him. It had been Jonker's ambition to
become paramount chief of all the Nama tribes, and it was Christian's

opinion that he occupied this position by virtue of his being his father's heir. He was to find out very soon that his opinion was wrong. Hendrik Ses, the chief of the Veldskoendraers, was naturally on Christian's side, for he hoped that he would now, once and for all, succeed in securing a great deal of booty. Oasib was in such a tremendous hurry after he had received this summons, that he did not even wait for the arrival of his secretary, Saul Sheppard, but, disregarding all Vollmer's warnings, he set out with his men and joined the Afrikanders. He demanded that Willem Swaartbooi at Rehoboth should provide him, as his paramount chief, with an armed force, but Willem Swartbooi had always given the Hereros sanctuary in Rehoboth from their oppressors and had no inclination to allow himself to be involved in this venture. Berseba and Bethanie were entirely in agreement with him. Amraal, too, received a summons. He had long been aware that the eastern Hereros were restless, and that they would not put up with the cruelty of their Nama masters any longer. He, however, took up the position that the Hereros likewise had the right to be regarded as human beings, and that they ought not to be treated merely as Jonker's 'dogs, herdsmen, and pipe lighters'. He thought, too, that it was wrong that the summons stated that the 'baboons' had got wild again, that the 'dogs' had run away, and that they had to be fetched back from Otjimbingwe. Amraal went, therefore, with his men to Okahandja, with the idea of bringing Christian to his senses and preventing a catastrophe. He only reached Barmen, however, and there he was persuaded to turn back, and so, in the end, Christian only had the Afrikanders, Hendrik Ses, and Oasib on his side, and besides them a mixed rabble from the other Nama tribes, who joined up as volunteers.

It is a remarkable fact that, with almost all the Nama tribes, the urge always became stronger to move their tribal centres farther to the north. The tribe at Bethanie had been debating for more than ten years whether they should not go and settle at Otjimbingwe and along the lower Swakop valley. A branch of this tribe, Jacobus Booi's followers, were not satisfied with merely considering the question, but worked their way farther and farther north. The Bondelswarts were utterly dissatisfied with Warmbad. The Swartboois thought seriously of going to Otjimbingwe with Kleinschmidt and giving up Rehoboth. Oasib wanted to leave Hoachanas. He had previously consulted Jonker as to whether he might not be allowed to settle in Barmen, but Jonker had refused his request on the ground that the place was too small for his own people. Then he directed his attention to Otjimbingwe, for it was known throughout the land what fine crops could be grown there, and he recognized, too, that to have a trading establishment in the village was something very different from having traders merely passing through. So it happened that all eyes were fixed on Otjimbingwe, and it became the centre of almost every one's desires. The tribes at Bethanie, Berseba, and Rehoboth, who were bound together by a common legal code felt, however, that to obey Christian's summons would imply an abandonment of the code and a breach of the treaty of Hoachanas, and they knew, moreover, that the Afrikanders had always rewarded their allies very poorly. They therefore stayed where they were.

The battle of Otjimbingwe

On Sunday, the 14th June, Kleinschmidt, who had just recovered from a long illness, held a service again for the first time, and Andersson also attended it. After the service a messenger arrived from Christian Jonker. He brought a letter from Christian which was addressed to Kleinschmidt, Andersson, and Maharero. It was couched in courteous terms, and stated that Christian was on the way to Otjimbingwe, accompanied by Oasib, Amraal, and Piet Koper. He expected to arrive there on Tuesday, but that they had no reason to be uneasy. His intention was to discuss things with Maharero in a friendly way. Maharero had still some stock belonging to the Afrikanders under his care, and they were coming to fetch it. Maharero, who had himself invited them to come and fetch it, should therefore be told to have the stock collected. The letter ended with the words: 'We have shed enough Herero blood, and this must now come to an end.'

No one trusted the professions of peace this letter contained, and least of all Maharero. It was not on the Tuesday, but at dawn on the Monday that two Nama horsemen entered Otjimbingwe. They were Christian's messengers. He demanded that Maharero should send him some of his responsible men to negotiate with him, but that was merely a ruse. Christian wanted Maharero to refuse. Kleinschmidt, who really believed that Amraal had come with them, and did not know that he had turned back from Barmen, was just getting ready to conduct negotiations, as nobody else was prepared to do it. He was on the point of leaving his house when Christian's horsemen and the Namas broke into the place. The mission was stormed. Maharero lay behind the walls of the threshing-floor. Philip had taken up a position in front of the mission house. He had assured Kleinschmidt the previous evening that no Nama should set his foot in the mission house except over his dead body. Philip was one of the first to be laid low by a Nama bullet, and with him fell Hirarapi, Maharero's brother. The mission house was riddled with bullets. Herero women and children had taken refuge in it. Two Namas lighted a fire with the object of throwing burning brands on the thatched roof of the house. It was easy to see what they meant to do. Just as they were about to apply the fire to the roof, they were shot down by a well-directed volley from the Hereros. Then the attackers tried to storm Maharero's werf. This consisted principally of the threshing-floor in which his men were posted. The horsemen came on in an orderly formation. Maharero ordered every one to keep absolutely still and to wait until they were at close range. The riders rushed on. They received a volley the effect of which hardly anybody escaped. Christian Jonker, his brother David, his uncle Jager, his councillor Timothy, and his uncle Jonas Afrikander, and very many more fell to the ground. The leaders were killed, but the fight went on. They were determined to take the European quarter, and they launched three fierce attacks against it. Three times were they driven back with heavy loss by the Hereros in Andersson's service. Then the attackers took to their heels with the Hereros always close behind. Up to then only those who had guns could take part in the fighting, but now those who were armed merely with kerries and assegais also joined in the rout. They killed every one they could lay their hands on. Oasib had not been taking much notice of what was happening, for he was quite sure of victory. He had been sitting behind a bush making coffee. His attention was called to the danger which threatened him by the Namas who passed him in flight. Without any hat on his head, he jumped on to the horse of a fleeing horseman and escaped. Many of the horses had to carry three men on their backs, and the weary Hottentots were even holding on to their tails. Any one who came into the Hereros' hands was killed. They pursued the flying mob as far as Otjikango, and the bodies of those who were killed marked the way they had gone. It was not only Oasib, the Afrikanders and Piet Koper who were defeated, but also a big body of Bergdamas who were in Christian's service. Many of them were left on the field of battle, and the Topnaars of Walfish Bay, too, received a hard knock. The enemy left more than two hundred dead behind, while the Hereros lost sixty men, amongst whom were some of Maharero's near relations; amongst the dead was Hakane, the son of chief Mureti of Omaruru.

Kleinschmidt went out to collect the wounded, but he did not find very many. His house was turned into a hospital. After he had tended the wounded, he began to bury the dead. In due course Maharero returned from the pursuit and asked: 'Who are you burying? Black people or red (Hereros or Namas)?' Kleinschmidt took the opportunity of impressing upon him that they all had to be buried after a battle, and he asked him to bring some of his people to help him. He came the following morning and made a start with Christian and his relatives, and with Piet Vaalrug, who had once struck Rath and now had met his fate at the very same place.

The Afrikanders had not succeeded in doing what they had meant to do. Their plan had been to destroy Otjimbingwe utterly. All the Hereros were to have been killed, and Andersson especially was to have been got rid of. The other Europeans were to have been sent back to Walfish Bay.

About a month afterwards, Krönlein was going on his official rounds to Gobabis and passed through Hoachanas. Oasib was there, but he would not let any one see him, and he persistently kept out of Krönlein's way. Krönlein went to him and took him severely to task. He had expected to find a humble man, but instead of that he found a foe who could think of nothing else but revenge and of collecting forces for a new attack.

After the fight at Otjimbingwe

Christian, the Afrikander chief, had fallen at Otjimbingwe, and so the tribe was faced with the necessity of electing a new one. According to the custom of the Afrikanders, Christian's son ought to have become chief. As he was not of age, Christian's brother Jan Jonker, assumed the chieftainship, with the assurance that he would resign directly his nephew came of age. Part of the tribe, in fact the better part, which was inclined to make peace with Maharero after the heavy blow they had received at Otjimbingwe, agreed with this arrangement. The war party, however, did not trust Jonker, but regarded him as Maharero's secret ally. They turned to Kido Witbooi, who was on the point of giving up his nomadic existence and settling in Gibeon, with the proposal that he should come to Windhoek and become chief of the Afrikanders and Witboois. Kido was an

old man, and he refused the offer. The Afrikanders' suspicion of Jan
was probably not entirely without foundation. His Nama name was
Hoa-arab, which meant Cat-ribs, and it seems that his cat-like traits
made their appearance quite early in his life. We recollect how that
there were nightly interviews between Maharero and Jan during the
critical time at Okahandja and how they were then regarded with
distrust. Now, after the defeat of the Afrikanders, Jan approached
Maharero and asked him to send back his 5,000 head of small stock.
Maharero sent some of them back, and let him know that he would
have sent them all, but that as no single word regarding peace and
friendship had as yet come to his ears, he was going to retain the rest
until Jan was ready to make peace with him. It may be assumed that
Jan was quite prepared to do so. The war party, however, refused
to allow him to act according to his convictions. Kleinschmidt, for
whom there was no longer any necessity to stay at Otjimbingwe,
seeing that Hahn had arrived there accompanied by several mission
colonists, was desirous of returning to Rehoboth, and he made
strenuous efforts to strengthen Jan's hand and to bring about a
speedy conclusion of peace. He found, however, that Andersson and
the other Europeans at Otjimbingwe did not fall in with this idea.
They were convinced that no lasting peace could be brought about
until the Afrikanders had been properly humbled. Then Willem
Swartbooi went to Windhoek to try to persuade the Afrikanders to
make peace, but he came back to Rehoboth without having effected
anything. By December 1863 Jan had pledged himself so far to the
war party that he told Brincker, who paid him a visit, that he was
going to take good care to keep the Hereros in their proper place.
Some Griquas had arrived in Windhoek and had assumed the role of
advisers. They had brought matters to such a pitch that the Afrikanders announced: 'We do not want to see either a white thing or a
black thing in front of our eyes. Either they are all going to die or
we are. We are now, once and for all, scallywags, and we are determined to get the whole land under our control, happen what will.'

Just about this time a miserable old Bushman appeared at Windhoek as a prophet, and ran about the werf at nights shouting 'Woe
to you Afrikanders, your judgment day is approaching!' He was
beaten unmercifully; Jan Aries' wife, Jonker's sister, scored him all
over with a burning branch, but he never ceased his nightly wanderings and predictions. Brincker saw this dreadful looking creature,
and found his whole body a mass of burns and festers, and he died

very soon afterwards. Jan Jonker, however, swaggered round Windhoek in an officer's red uniform, listening to the advice of his Griqua counsellors, and casting round for new allies. As he was of opinion that Weber, the missionary at Gobabis, had influenced the old chief Amraal against joining the Afrikanders in their attack on Maharero, and in desiring peace, he wrote him the following letter:

'I know all about your advice and your groans over us Afrikanders, but what you really want to do is to destroy us. Did not the Missionary Society dispatch you to shed our blood? We have lost a great many people through following your advice. You are a traitor to your country. You do your best to prevent unity and promote the shedding of blood. I tell you to keep your nose out of these things, otherwise I shall come and deal with you. Do you not know that we are a nation?

I am the paramount chief of Hereroland,
Jan Afrikander.'

There seemed to be very little chance of making peace with a man who was beaten, and felt himself no longer safe in Windhoek, but withdrew to Witvlei in order to seek to strengthen his own position by going and living under the protection of the war party at Gobabis, and yet, despite all this, still called himself 'the paramount chief of Hereroland'.

In Otjimbingwe, however, they were fairly certain that the war would go on, and that there would be a sudden attack by the Namas. It was well known that Jan Jonker and Oasib intended to destroy the European settlement entirely, and if it were possible, to kill Andersson. Hahn, the missionary, who had returned from Germany, was likewise hated by them. As Maharero was taking no steps to ward off the danger that was threatening, Andersson and Green took the initiative. The Herero people ought to be combined and brought under a common paramount chief. It was of no use that every man who possessed a number of cattle should be able to claim that he was a free and independent chief. Maharero and Zeraua were not opposed to this idea, for the Hereros could hardly find any breathing space, because jealousy and greed arose time and again and set them to robbing each other. Then a new evil was added to the old one. The Hereros, who until then had left alcohol alone altogether, began to drink brandy, and unpleasant scenes occurred in Otjimbingwe.

It was arranged that a chief should be elected, and Zeraua, who was the oldest chief, was chosen as paramount chief. This was quite a good choice, for Zeraua had much more energy than Maharero. But Zeraua refused and proposed Maharero. Nobody felt very sympathetic towards Maharero, for it was well known that he and his men had not been responsible for the victory in the battle of the 15th June, but that the Hereros belonging to the mines were the real victors. It was well known, too, that Maharero was avaricious—a characteristic which is not to be admired in a chief; it was noticed as well that Maharero was enervated through having so many wives. This very circumstance, however, that he had so many wives connected him with all the Hereros of importance, wherever they might be. Maharero was chosen as paramount chief, and the people pledged themselves to obey him.

Andersson had now a man with whom he could do something. Even if this man had no great ideas of his own, and lacked the energy required of a leader in dangerous times, this defect could be remedied by inspiration on Andersson's part. It was not very long before Andersson had in his possession a document which read as follows:

'Notice is hereby given that we, the undersigned, chiefs and councillors of Hereroland, have appointed, of our own free will and accord, Charles John Andersson as regent and military commander for the period of his natural life, or for as long as he desires to hold office. We promise to be faithful to him, and to obey him unconditionally in all matters concerning his control over the internal and external circumstances of the country. Charles John Andersson is to be responsible only to God and his own conscience.'

With a deed of appointment like that in his pocket, a man ought to be able to do something. The first important measure which was required, was the securing of the southern border of Hereroland against surprise attacks by the Nama tribes. The Swartboois at Rehoboth were the people who lived closest to the southern border. Andersson had already had dealings with them. He knew that Willem Swartbooi was friendly towards the Hereros, and had received them when they were fugitives. If one could only make a kind of buffer state of Rehoboth, and get Willem Swartbooi as an ally for the Hereros, one could lay upon him the task of keeping in check the restless northern tribes, i.e. the Topnaars, Booi, Aimib, Oasib, and Hendrik Ses. The alliance went through. Willem Swartbooi and Maharero became friends. It could not be denied that Rehoboth's position became very difficult in consequence. In fact, this alliance implied its desertion from the paramount chief, Oasib, and the Red Nation—and the Swartboois could not possibly forget that they were a branch of the Red Nation.

The eventful year 1863 came to an end with the conclusion of this alliance, and 1864 was heralded by excellent rains. Dry years are not favourable to undertakings of any magnitude in South West Africa. Good years and warfare go together, because then there is water everywhere for man and beast. Andersson had come to the conclusion that a peace with Jan Jonker could never really be concluded, unless the Afrikanders were forced to make it from dire necessity, and that necessity would only arise if the Afrikanders were stripped of their natural resources, i.e. their flocks and herds. Andersson, therefore, decided to go and take the Afrikanders' stock away from them before they could prepare themselves against attack. As he was ill himself, he entrusted the command of a fighting force, consisting of 1,400 of Maharero's Hereros, to Green. On the 5th March, 1864, when the rains were almost finished, this force took the field against the Afri-kanders, who had united with the Topnaars and felt that they were reasonably safe at Witvlei, east of Windhoek. They were taken by surprise, and the results were exceedingly successful. Without losing a single man in the fight, Green returned to Otjimbingwe, on the 21st March, with all the Afrikanders' stock. They consisted of more than 3,000 cattle, a still larger number of small stock, in addition to their gunpowder and their household utensils. Jan Arie, Jan Jonker's brother-in-law, was amongst the killed.

The loot was fairly distributed at Otjimbingwe. Andersson, who had himself defrayed the greater part of the cost of equipping the force, and was therefore entitled to a lion's share of the booty, refused to accept it, and allowed it to be given to the Hereros who were poor. When, however, some Hereros could not resist stealing some of the booty surreptitiously, he had them brought up and court-martialled. Green pronounced judgement on them and sen-tenced them to be shot.

Andersson's battle

Green's bold and short campaign had done the Afrikanders con-siderable damage. Not only had Jan Arie been killed, but likewise Jan Jonker's wife, who was Jacobus Booi's daughter, had lost her life, and, in addition to this, the tribe was weakened by the loss of another forty of their men. Jan Jonker then wrote a pathetic letter to Maharero, in which he said that he wanted to come personally to

Otjimbingwe and make peace. Whether he was killed there or made a servant was a matter of indifference to him; he wanted peace at all cost. More plainly than that he could not express his willingness to throw himself unconditionally on Maharero's mercy.

But Jan never put in an appearance. The war party amongst his Afrikanders were not in agreement with his plans. Oasib, too, had no idea of making peace. He organized a tribal alliance, directed against Rehoboth in the first place. Willem Swartbooi was to be forced to give up his alliance with the Hereros and to march against them with Oasib, or otherwise to leave Rehoboth with his whole tribe. The members of the alliance were the Red Nation under Oasib, the Afrikanders under Jonker, the Veldskoendraers under Hendrik Ses, the Grootdodens under Aimab, and with them the Topnaars and a commando from Garib. They worried the Swartboois at Rehoboth with threats of storming the village and began stealing their stock. The people in Rehoboth commenced to fortify the village. The stock kraals were removed into the village itself and the whole place was surrounded with a loop-holed wall. Kleinschmidt was absent in March, for his official duties had taken him to Otjimbingwe, and Schroeder of Keetmanshoop had also gone there. They both wanted to leave Otjimbingwe by ox-wagon on the 7th April, and return to Rehoboth and Keetmanshoop respectively. Andersson then decided to send with them two carts and two wagons as well, for he wished to send some 1,400 cattle, and a large flock of small stock across the Orange River to Cape Town.

Green was the leader of this trek. A large number of guards, drivers, and herdsmen accompanied the wagons and the stock. The long procession had reached the boundaries of the Rehoboth territory safely by the 18th April. They considered themselves safe, seeing that the territory belonging to the dangerous Afrikanders lay behind them. The missionaries and Green thought, therefore, that they were free to go ahead to Rehoboth. A South African had, however, settled close to the border; he had formerly been in Andersson's service, and had been dismissed by him. This man wanted to get even for the wrong which he considered had been done him, and so he sent a message to Jan Jonker, informing him of the position, for he was on friendly terms with Jan, who had done him many a service. Jan Jonker turned to Willem Swartbooi, requesting him to permit his, Jan's, allies to go through his tribal territory. Willem refused emphatically, for the alliance into which he had entered with the

Hereros required of him to prevent any other Nama tribes from combining with the Afrikanders. Jan then suggested to Oasib that he should pretend to invest Rehoboth with his forces without actually attacking them, and in this way prevent Willem Swartbooi from coming in between when he got the news that alarming things were happening in the northern part of his territory. Green and Klein-schmidt knew nothing at all about this. They reached Rehoboth, and, on the 21st April, they were sitting unsuspectingly together, discussing ways of making Otjimbingwe safer. Then they heard firing. Willem Swartbooi called his men together immediately. Green and a hundred Swartbois rode out in the direction from whence the noise of fighting had come. Three European employees of Andersson's, who had been left behind with the wagons and the live stock, came running towards them. They brought the news that nearly all the herdsmen had been shot down by the Afrikanders, and all the cattle carried off.

The fact that sham fights had been taking place round about Rehoboth had enabled the Afrikanders to pass through without hindrance, and had given the Topnaars an opportunity of joining them. Now European fugitives from the neighbourhood filled the mission house at Rehoboth. Green gave up the idea of pursuing the Afrikanders. He had to be careful that Oasib, who was still in the neighbourhood, did not attack him in the rear. He therefore returned to Otjimbingwe with the few men he had left. Half of Oasib's men were tired of war, so they returned to Hoachanas, and Oasib had to give up the idea of forcing the Swartbois to give up their present alliance and link up with him. He began to consider ways and means of exterminating them, with his allies' assistance. Great excitement reigned in Otjimbingwe when Green unexpectedly appeared upon the scene with the news of the disaster. Andersson was not the man to let the Afrikanders do as they pleased with him. He made energetic preparations for a quick counter-attack. On the 25th April, 1864, he obtained the following order for traders, signed by Maharero and his councillors: 'It is hereby made publicly known that all persons, who travel round for the purpose of trading, while the Afrikander tribe or other Nama tribes are at war with me shall not supply the enemy with ammunition, guns, or any other weapons. They will receive no permission from me to pass through my country. Every person who contravenes this order will lose his goods.' This order was signed by Maharero and the councillors, Willem Zeraua, April,

James Kaene, Padmaker Kazombaue, Onesimus, Kaviandje, and Karira. Andersson's signature is missing.

Something else happened too. Maharero gave an order for a general mobilization. Herero warriors streamed in quickly from all sides. They came with guns, spears, and bows and arrows, and they all had dangerous kerries in their belts. On their heads war plumes, made of ostrich feathers, waved wildly in the breeze; some again had caps made of jackal skins with the tails hanging down. Many of them had leopard skins slung across their shoulders. The meeting-place for the troops was an hour's journey south of Otjimbingwe. Thither went Andersson, too, with his friend, Green, and his assistants Haybittel, Newton, and Birmingham, and some coloured vagrants from the colony who had taken some part in the Kaffir wars, and a number of half-breeds. Hahn went there, too, with his wife and the painter Baines, who wanted to paint a picture of the Hereros marching away. Here was an opportunity of seeing how Herero fighters prepared for battle. They marched past Maharero's sacred fire in endless columns. Each of them took a little ash from the fireplace and rubbed it on his right cheek and temple, as that guaranteed a safe return. Of the men who marched past, six hundred had good rifles, two thousand more had guns of a poorer quality and their old Herero weapons, while four hundred others were only partly armed. Andersson was in command, therefore, of about three thousand warriors. As, however, Otjimbingwe could not be left entirely without protection, a thousand other fighting men, armed with two hundred guns, were left behind. Hahn made a rough calculation that for every fighting man he could reckon at least five other people who were wives, children, or parents, and that thus the number of people who had survived the years of persecution must be in all about 24,000. Hahn now mounted the driving-seat of his ox-wagon and addressed the gathering, and Baines painted the scene. This oil painting was, and is probably still to-day, in the possession of the Andersson family in Capetown.

After saying good-bye, Maharero mounted his horse. He wore a long cloak over which a guardsman's sword was buckled. Any one who looked closely enough could see that the cloak was Brincker's nightgown, which Maharero had persuaded him to give him. Kataree, his principal wife, quickly tied into a corner of this cloak a small quantity of earth taken from her husband's sleeping-place, for that guaranteed him a safe return. As, however, a double seam holds better, she picked up the dust in which her husband's last footprint had been made, wrapped it in a rag, and put it away in the sacred hut with the staffs of his ancestors. Maharero, Andersson, and Green placed themselves at the head of the marching army, and went off in the direction of Rehoboth to look for the Afrikanders.

On the 15th June, 1864, Andersson's army arrived at Duruchaos on the borders of the district of Rehoboth. Willem Swartbooi and his councillors came to meet them. The alliance, which had previously been made, was renewed in Duruchaos and the entrance into Rehoboth took place on the 17th, when the troops of the Swartboois joined up with them. After service for the troops had been held in the church, the march to Oamites commenced the following day. A blue flag with a red cross on a white ground was borne at the head of the column. They made Seeis their objective, for they expected the Afrikanders to be there. They discovered them in a kloof, which was called by the Hereros Otjonguere, and by the Namas Gam-Gam (Two Waters), because there was a little stream high up on the mountain in the rocks, in which the water ran for a long time, and a second supply about half-way up the mountain side. Two mountain ridges met at this place, and the Afrikanders had made a werf here, and had built fortifications round it. Andersson and his troops came suddenly upon the enemy on the morning of the 22nd of June. Andersson wanted to storm their position immediately. He was received, however, both from the fortifications and from the mountain slopes on either side, with such a fierce fire that his troops fell back, and Andersson received a bullet in the knee, which put him out of action. Green knew nothing about his being wounded, and was trying to attack the foe from the rear. Andersson therefore lay in a thorn bush, from 10 o'clock in the morning till 3 o'clock in the afternoon, without any assistance. After an exceedingly stubborn resistance, the Afrikanders were, however, compelled to take to their heels and to leave their mountain fortress and all their possessions behind. It was only then that Andersson was found and that first aid was administered to him.

The booty was considerable. Twenty-two ox-wagons belonging to the Afrikanders were burnt on the spot. A thousand pounds of gunpowder exploded during the fight, and a further thousand pounds fell into the hands of the victors. Over a thousand cattle and the Afrikander's flocks of sheep and goats, as well as their domestic possessions, were captured. Jan Jonker, however, and his brother escaped, and Adam Kraai and his followers had not even been engaged in the fight.

The Hereros brought Andersson back to Oamites on a litter made of branches. Kleinschmidt heard what had happened and hastened to go and see him and to take him back to Rehoboth with him. Andersson, however, knew how dangerous Rehoboth's position was and insisted upon being taken to Barmen. He advised Kleinschmidt not to oppose the departure of the Swartboois from Rehoboth, but to accompany them to Otjimbingwe until the times changed. Andersson bade his faithful friend an affectionate farewell, and little did he think that he would see him again in a few weeks' time as a dying fugitive. Hahn and Brincker went to meet Andersson, and Brincker took charge of the wounded man. His leg never recovered completely. After the wound was healed it was shorter than the other and a tiresome lameness remained. As Barmen, too, was not safe enough, the patient was taken to Otjimbingwe. Andersson had never expected that things would turn out as they did. He had not even got back the full number of stock which had been stolen from him. In acknowledgement of his services, however, Maharero made him a present of Otjimbingwe. The Afrikanders were now quite impoverished and defeated, but their spirit was not broken. They were angrier than before. The Hereros, however, had been thoroughly frightened by the hail of bullets on the mountain-side, and declared that they would not fight another battle under European leadership. These methods of fighting might be all right for wars against Europeans, but in a war against the Namas, other tactics ought to be adopted.

As there was no longer any source of income in Otjimbingwe, most of the Europeans left. Amongst them, too, Andersson's actions did not meet with unanimous approval. Some of them agreed with him, but others, who had been trading with the Afrikanders and the Namas, and were annoyed because the miserly Hereros showed so little inclination to trade, saw that their businesses were ruined. The prohibition against the importation of arms and ammunition was specially injurious and irksome to them. Andersson soon tired of the position he held, and revolved in his mind the idea of selling his property in Otjimbingwe and settling at Walfish Bay. Maharero, however, after his return from the greatest battle of his life, had himself a house of stone built at Otjimbingwe, and Zeraua followed his example.

The end of Rehoboth

In Andersson's battle on the 22nd June, 1864, the Swartboois of Rehoboth had fought bravely by his side, and had helped the Hereros to win. Several of Rehoboth's most important men were killed. Jan Jonker was exceedingly angry with them and sent the following message to Rehoboth: 'Hitherto we have done nothing at all to harm you, but now we are going to begin.' The Swartboois then saw that they would not be able to hold their fortified village against attack. Andersson was ill, Maharero would not promise to send any troops to help them, but advised them to leave the place. He wanted to establish the Swartboois in the country along the lower course of the Swakop river. He offered the whole country between the Swakop and the Omaruru rivers to his allies as their tribal territory. They decided in this time of dire necessity that the step, which they had often discussed in times of peace, should be carried out before it was too late, and so the ox-wagons and carts were put into repair and loaded up. Oasib did not feel at all inclined to fall in with Jonker's request to join him in a swift attack on the Swartboois. A great part of the Red Nation sided with Vollmer, who was always impressing upon Oasib that he should bury the axe of war and put his hand to the spade instead. There was also, however, a war party in Hoachanas. When Oasib turned his back on the whole business and went to the Fish River, the war party joined Hendrik Ses, the chief of the Veldskoendraers, who was aiming to join forces with Jan Jonker, for Hendrik Ses had an old grudge against the Swartboois. His father had been attacked and killed by the Swartboois in the thirties. The Swartboois had then made a fire, and had burned the women and children of the Veldskoendraers to death. A blood feud never becomes prescribed, and it now pressed its claims with a force increased by time in his now aged son, when a good opportunity of revenging himself occurred.

The preparations for departure went slowly ahead in Rehoboth. On the 18th July, Kleinschmidt began to celebrate his silver jubilee as a missionary. Out of the twenty-five years, he had devoted nineteen to the congregation at Rehoboth, which he had built up from the very smallest beginnings. They marched away on the 25th July. The caravan proceeded very slowly indeed for it had to overcome many difficulties caused both by the road and the wagons. The idea was to follow the road along the Kuiseb to the west, in order to avoid Jan Jonker, and then to turn eastwards and to get to the Swakop, in order to settle first of all in Otjimbingwe. A distance, which normally took four days to cover, took them four weeks. Kleinschmidt was advised to go on ahead with his wagon and family, but he could not make up his mind to do so. The bed of the Kuiseb River was reached on the 16th August, and there the news reached them that Jonker was on their track. At daybreak on the 18th August he appeared on the scene. The Swartboois had already made a fortified lager out of twenty-five ox-wagons. All their possessions and their women and children, too, were in the wagons. They took up protected positions behind the wagons. The position they had taken up was not a good one. The mountains close by offered a more favourable battle-ground, and a number of the defenders took up their positions there. Kleinschmidt took his wife and children there too. There were many, however, who preferred to remain within the protection of the wagons. The pursuers numbered 800 and the Swartboois 200, and the latter were driven farther and farther along the foot of the mountain, and farther and farther from the wagons.

Long dry grass stood all about, for the rains had been specially good during 1864. Then Hendrik Ses set fire to the dry grass. The wind was blowing strongly and it drove the flames into the wagon fortress. The wagons caught alight and almost every one who had felt himself secure behind them was suffocated in the smoke and flames. Then the men fled. The camp fell into the hands of the enemy and in a few hours the Swartboois had been stripped of everything they possessed. Kleinschmidt and his family were forced to try and reach Otjimbingwe on foot over the mountains of the Khomas Highlands. He spent three days and four nights on the road. Six Hereros, who had fought for the others in the morning, joined him, and provided him and his family with water and food from the veld. He arrived with his family at Otjimbingwe on Sunday, the 31st August. The Swartboois who had escaped went there as well. They were taken to Anawood, near Otjimbingwe, which Hahn had bought from an Englishman. Hahn had heard that the Swartboois were approaching, and he had gone to meet them. As he did not find them, he returned again, and there he found Kleinschmidt in his house very ill. His friend died in his arms on the 2nd September, and he buried him the following day, when he wrote in his diary: 'I have lost my dearest friend, and the mission its most faithful worker'. He might have added: 'and the Namas and the Hereros their most upright counsellor and minister.'

The day of Eis-gaob was a day of terror for the Swartboois, for it was thus that they named the place where their pursuers attacked them, with the intention (*eis*) in their hearts (*gaob*) to destroy the whole tribe. About thirty women and children succumbed in the flames, and the number of men who were killed was never ascertained. Where were the Swartboois to go and live now? Maharero and his people and Zeraua and his people were living in Otjimbingwe. As a preliminary measure they had to try to grow enough food for themselves by tilling the soil, until such time as their own cattle which had run away could be collected one by one, and Anawood had not sufficient agricultural land for this. Attention was then drawn to the mission station at Salem, in the lower Swakop valley, where the soil was good. Jacobus Booi's people had gone there, with the idea of making it their tribal centre, and the missionary Bohm had gone to live with them. Large gardens had been laid out, but they had never been kept in order, and the young plants had been destroyed by the cattle. The Boois very soon got tired of this way of living, and after a few months of it, they decided to resume their old profession as highwaymen and marauders. The Swartboois now took their place, and there they found, for a number of years, a new home and Bohm found a new congregation.

The Herero rising in Gobabis

After his defeat by Andersson at Two Waters, Jan Jonker was like an enraged lion. It is true that his wrath against the Swartboois had been assuaged, but that did not bring him any great satisfaction. His settlement with the Swartboois was merely one stage along the road which he intended to travel, and his road led him into Hereroland, more especially to Otjimbingwe, for it was there that his greatest enemies, Maharero and Andersson, lived. But his tribe had been very much weakened, and he had to find support from some source or other. If Oasib refused, there was still a strong war party in Gobabis, and this had increased in strength since the death of Amraal, who had been of a peaceful disposition.

A position of anarchy had supervened after Amraal's death. He had transferred the leadership of the tribe to his son Lambert. Lambert, however, was sixty years of age and he fell a victim to small-pox barely fifteen days after the death of his ninety-year-old father, and that very day his son Willem, who was to have taken over the chieftainship, died also. Gobabis was therefore left without a chief. A full year passed before the tribe agreed to appoint Andries Lambert. The war party, however, would have nothing to do with it, and clung to Frederick Vlermuis, as they had always done. It made no difference that Krapohl tried to help the impoverished folk by trading honestly with them, and that the missionary Weber gave them lessons in gardening, and showed them how they could make a living by hard work without plundering and murdering. A trader named Forsythe arrived at Gobabis with a well-laden cart, and the quantity of the goods he had brought with him aroused the cupidity of the people. Forsythe was seized and, as he refused to give up his merchandise voluntarily, they cut his throat and distributed his goods. Some of the Christians belonging to Weber's congregation were amongst the receivers of the stolen goods, and he adopted a stern attitude towards them. Even if civil law and order did not exist in the place, he was going to maintain order in his congregation. He therefore excluded these people from his congregation. This made the war party intensely angry, but Weber did not allow himself to be intimidated.

For a considerable time Jan Afrikander had not felt himself comfortable in the neighbourhood of the Hereros. He, therefore, went to Gobabis and he found the field well prepared for the seed he wanted to sow. The war party was greatly encouraged through his influence. They began to conceive marvellous plans. All superfluous Hereros and Mbanderus were to be killed; all the Europeans were to be driven out of the country; then the Hereros were to be forced to resume again their former servitude. Jan Jonker was to be the master of the country, and Frederick Vlermuis the second man in his empire, and this was to stretch from the Orange to the Kunene. Naturally all the tribes which had been subdued were to pay regular tribute, and from this they would live comfortably without working.

The Hereros and Mbanderus heard all this loud talk. It seemed to them that the time was not exactly ripe for trying to carry out plans of that kind, when there was in Otjimbingwe a man like Maharero keeping a careful eye on the Afrikanders and dealing them heavy blows whenever it was necessary. They got together, therefore, and before the inhabitants of Gobabis realized it, a Herero rebellion had broken out. Many of the Orlams lost their lives, and many of them lost all their stock. The attack was over almost as quickly as it had been made, directly the cattle had been carried off to a safe place, for it was only made with the object of keeping the Orlam inhabitants in check until this had been done.

During the attack Weber and Krapohl were not turned out of their houses, nor did a single Herero come upon their premises. The members of the war party, however, and those who had suffered loss, alleged that Weber had hidden Hereros in his house. They then made a search of the mission house, but it did not stop at searching, and a great many articles were either damaged, destroyed, or taken away. Even though the Hereros had taken Weber's milch cows along with the rest, the Namas took the 400 cattle belonging to the mission, which had been acquired through honest trading. Weber and Krapohl were forced to leave Gobabis. Weber was allowed to depart unmolested, but Krapohl was repeatedly robbed along the road. It only now became clear to them why Jan Jonker had shown such an interest in Krapohl's cattle that he had asked to see them, and had not hesitated to go out to the cattle post personally for this purpose. Weber went to Berseba and Krapohl started his own business at Steinkopf. After the departure of the missionaries, who represented the only vestige of conscience which Gobabis had left, war broke out between the Hereros and the Mbanderus·on the one side, and the Orlams and Jan Jonker on the other. Thus it was that the Hereros of Hereroland, and the inhabitants of Otjimbingwe were given a breathing-space for a half-year. Jan Jonker was so pleased with conditions in the east, that he discussed with Frederick Vlermuis and his followers a plan for going and settling far out in that direction. It came to nothing, however, for the means of existence which the far eastern country could provide were not inexhaustible.

The attack on Otjimbingwe of 3rd September, 1865

It came to Jan Jonker's ears that Hendrik Ses had made preparations to go and attack the Hereros at Otjimbingwe, and he felt that it was impossible for him to allow Hendrik to go alone. If Hendrik were successful in his enterprise, the danger might well arise of his jeopardizing Jan's claim to be paramount chief. He therefore set out with his Afrikanders with the intention of combining with Hendrik Ses's force in the proposed attack. Jan, who had chivalrous instincts, sent and let Brincker at Barmen know that he and Hendrik Ses would arrive at Barmen very shortly, and then go on to attack Otjimbingwe. It would be better for him to leave the mission, for Hendrik Ses was in command, and he, Jan, could not be responsible for what might happen. Brincker decided to stay, and he gives the following account of the arrival of the Hottentot fighters:

'The 31st August arrived. We had heard nothing more of the Namas. It was remarkably quiet. Early in the morning a Herero came running up to me holding something in his hand, and said: "Look here, teacher." He had fresh horse dung in his hand. There were no horses for many miles around, and it was apparent that Nama spies had been in the place during the night, and this was a sure sign that there was a commando close at hand. In less than half an hour the whole place was deserted. All the Hereros had taken to their heels. Ourselves, the Cloetes, and the Gertses, had to stay, for at sunrise a big body of armed Namas, numbering more than 800 men, entered the place. A Herero and his wife stayed with us in danger of their lives, and likewise an old woman. Before they fled the Hereros had hidden away an old blind woman in our kitchen under some lumber, and she kept on talking as if she were mad.

'It was not very long before a whole troop of people made for my house with Hendrik Nanib or Ses at the head of them. He is the cheekiest and nastiest Hottentot I have ever seen. He never looks any one in the face. His manners and conduct, which were intended to show what a great and worthy man he was, were really disgusting. He came along with an interpreter, who came from Griqualand, and started every sentence he had to say with the words: "I, who am the mouthpiece of the great captain Hendrik Ses." Seven of his officers came into the house with him, without greeting me. They threw themselves roughly down on the chairs, which cracked under them, and then the trouble started. Hendrik Ses: "I have come here with a big army, do you see that, Mister?" I: "That I can see." Ses: "What are you doing here in the country?" I: "I am these people's minister, and my work is to preach God's word to them for the salvation of their souls." Ses: "That I will not allow. The 'baboons' (Hereros) have no need of it. You want to baptize them with water, but now I, Hendrik Ses, am here, and I am going to baptize them with blood, do you hear? Now I want so much ammunition, so much tobacco, clothes, coffee, sugar, tea, salt, and so on." I replied: "You can get all that in Capetown, and a great deal more, but you cannot get it from me." Ses: "But I am going to have it from you, otherwise I shall kill you." I: "God's will be done! As you see, I am quite defenceless."

'In the meantime more and more people arrived. They pulled the old blind woman out of the kitchen and killed her in front of the door, putting several shots into her. Hell was let loose in the house itself. Everything was smashed up, and what was not nailed absolutely fast was taken away. My wife was in the bedroom with our little child, and three Hereros lay hidden under the bed. Jan Jonker, the chief of the Afrikanders, was influenced by the fact that I had visited him in Windhoek several times. He pushed his way into the bedroom with some of his people, and protected my wife and child from interference. Although he discovered the people under the bed, he said nothing about them, but kept the howling mob off. Meanwhile a number of them put me in their midst and pressed round me so closely that I could not move. Some of them broke the window panes and stuck the barrels of their guns into the house, while others shouted: "Shoot the minister! We want to see whether the heavens will fall if we do." That went on until evening, when the Hottentots got tired, and we were still alive. During the night numbers of bullets whistled about the house. Under cover of darkness we removed the body of the murdered woman to the back of the house. Next day only a few of them came along and that was to ask for medicine for a horrid disease. The others knew very well that there was nothing more to be got from us. The leaders, too, had found honey in the possession of the Cloetes and the Gertses, and this kept them away from me. Honey beer was brewed and drunk the night through in the Nama way. In the afternoon of the third day, Hendrik Ses's people took me down to their camp. I had to witness the shooting of a Herero prisoner. His hands were bound behind his back and the poor wretch was kicked continuously forward. About fifty Namas followed him. They kept this up for a distance, and then each of them fired a bullet into the Herero, and they let him lie where he fell. I was then allowed to go home again. On the morning of the 2nd September we experienced an hour of terror. The horde stormed down on our house with fearful yells, and took up their positions before it with their guns loaded. I stood in the doorway with Samuel Gertse, and they pointed their guns at us. Then Jan Jonker, drunk as he was, came running up with his men, and lashed those in front in the face with his riding-whip, saying: "What has the minister done to you? Go and shoot the Hereros. Get out of here." Then they marched off to Otjimbingwe. Hendrik Ses had given orders to shoot us, because we had hidden Hereros in the house. Besides that, a fierce quarrel had arisen between Jan Jonker and Hendrik Ses at the beer drink the night before, over the question which of them was greater, and they had very nearly decided the matter by fighting a duel. When Hendrik Ses had left with his troops Jan Jonker came to us with some of his men. He was still a little bit intoxicated, but he could understand what he was doing. He wanted me to play a hymn on the harmonium, and asked us to sing as well. The fighters marched on to Otjimbingwe and the place was attacked on the afternoon of Sunday, the 3rd September. This was contrary to the Namas' usual habits for it was customary for them to attack in the early morning. Hendrik Ses had, however, insisted that the baptism of blood should take place on a Sunday afternoon. Careful preparations had been made in Otjimbingwe. The Swartbois, who were living close at hand, had hastened to its assistance, and every one who had a gun held it ready to give the Namas a reception. The greeting they received was so hearty that the Namas fled with great losses, without fighting and without shedding a single drop of Herero blood, throwing away in their flight everything they had looted in Barmen. Hendrik Ses fled through Barmen to Windhoek, and from there southwards. When the Hereros and Swartboois saw that Jan Jonker would not fight, they went after Hendrik Ses, and they overtook the Veldskoendraers just north of Rehoboth. The fight which developed went very badly for the Namas. Hendrik Ses received a bullet through the mouth. His tongue was torn by the bullet and hung out of his mouth, and it was thus that the Swartboois found him. He motioned them with his hand and made signs to them, begging them to spare his life. The Swartboois then left him alone, but when some Hereros discovered him they stabbed him with their assegais, cut him up, and scattered the pieces of his body all over the veld. The blow which the Namas had received was such a heavy one that it was a full year before they could take any further steps against the Hereros. Jan Jonker, who had lost his strongest ally, went back to Rehoboth. He wanted peace again but he did not dare to say so, for there was a conspiracy to kill him if he should go back upon the war party.'

'He was so anxious to make peace that he wrote a letter to Hahn at Otjimbingwe asking him to act as go-between with Maharero, and inviting him to meet him at Otjikango for a preliminary discussion. Hahn was quite prepared to go, but Maharero said he could not let Hahn go alone. If, however, he insisted on going, he and his council would accompany him. Hahn was afraid that fresh discords might arise, and decided to abandon his journey. He replied by letter, however, making Jan Jonker certain suggestions, and giving him some advice, which he was, however, not able to profit by, because the war party of Afrikanders and Gobabis people were only prepared to follow him if he did what they wanted.'

A separate peace was, however, concluded between Maharero and the Topnaars before the end of the year, 1865. This affected the war-weary part of the tribe, which had formerly lived at Walfish Bay, and had been transplanted by Jonker Afrikander to the vicinity of Rehoboth. They had then fallen out with Jonker, and now they had every reason to wish to live quietly at Erongo, for otherwise they would inevitably be ground to powder between the upper and the nether millstones. The embassy which they sent to ask Maharero to make peace was received by him courteously, and peace was concluded.

Another separate peace came to be concluded before trouble broke out again. It was Oasib who was anxious to bury the hatchet. He had too much on his hands in his own country. The chiefs of Bethanie and Berseba, and likewise the Witboois, to whom he had recently given Gibeon, occasioned him trouble and difficulty. Once before he had written Maharero a letter, asking him to make a separate peace, but this letter had been intercepted by the Afrikanders. Some further efforts had been ineffectual. Then Vollmer, Oasib's missionary, went to Otjimbingwe in May 1866, and took the opportunity of negotiating with Maharero. He told him about Oasib's abortive efforts. Maharero had a friendly letter written to Oasib and gave it into the safe hands of Vollmer, who delivered it. The letter pleased him exceedingly, for Maharero had not laid down any humiliating conditions. All he asked was that his former enemy should keep quiet and not undertake any more expeditions against the Hereros. Oasib agreed and asked Maharero to come to his help in case he was attacked by his enemies, as he expected to be.

This separate peace of June 1866, between Maharero and the Red Nation, was looked upon by the other Nama tribes with the greatest suspicion. What angered them especially was the arrangement that Oasib should receive the assistance of Herero troops. The story is told of a conference of several Nama chiefs, which was convened for considering a new campaign against Maharero, and at which Oasib was present. When Oasib gave them clearly to understand that he was not in favour of any expedition against the Hereros, one of the chiefs stood up in the conference and said: 'Why are we sitting here and talking about a campaign against the Hereros, who live far away in the north? Is not there a man sitting here amongst us who has himself become a Herero? Let us get busy and fight the Hereros who are living in our midst?' So it very nearly came to a war between the Nama tribes and their paramount chief Oasib.

The attack upon Otjimbingwe and the plundering of Walfish Bay

It would almost seem as if the Hereros' war of freedom, which had been commenced with such a tremendous amount of energy, was dying down through the exhaustion of their foes. The year 1866 passed without any great alarums or excursions. The Hereros, at any rate, suffered no damage of any consequence. The national feeling amongst all the different tribes gradually increased in strength. Maharero conducted friendly negotiations with the chiefs of the Ovambos, with the idea of making an alliance with them in the event of a general peace with the Nama tribes proving impossible. Hahn made a second journey to Ovamboland, and returned with great expectations and new plans for the future. The flames of war could very easily have flared up again at Gobabis, for a Baster named Samuel had done a great deal of mischief there. He had fallen upon some travellers and robbed them of six wagons loaded with ivory, and one of the Europeans was killed. A Herero commando followed Samuel's wagon spoors to Gobabis. While its war party was away hunting, the Hereros did a great deal of damage. They were pursued immediately, however, and practically exterminated. In revenge the Hereros returned with a very much greater force, and practically exterminated the whole war party at Gobabis. The result of this was that the Mbanderus freed themselves entirely from the domination of Amraal's people. They went westwards, and finally found a new home close to Otjikango. When that happened, however, the nest in which Jan Jonker had so long been so safe and snug, was entirely destroyed.

He was heard of again in November 1867. He had entered into a close alliance with Jacobus Booi. It has been told how the latter had tried to adopt a new way of life at Salem in the lower Swakop valley, and how he had not succeeded. After that he had gone back again to the place where his father Jan Booi was living, in the northern part of Bethanie district and along the Kuiseb River. After Jan Jonker and his father-in-law Jacobus Booi got together once more they started on a series of new exploits.

They advanced from the west together, with a considerable force, against Otjimbingwe. Maharero knew about it, but he was not the least bit afraid. Hahn was quite anxious when he found that Maharero had such a strong feeling of security. Zeraua was of the opinion that his little finger was strong enough to put the Namas to flight. Hahn then had ramparts and trenches made, for Andersson was no longer in command.

He had sold his whole interest to the Rhenish Mission and had gone to Walfish Bay, where he had set up a shop and a warehouse. Then, with the object of improving his financial position, he had set out for Ovamboland with a load of goods and war material, with the idea of exchanging it for ostrich feathers and ivory. Young Axel Erikson went with him as his assistant. He hoped on this journey that he would at last reach the Kunene. He did reach it, but he was very ill indeed when he got there, and died at Ukuambi on the 5th July, 1867.

Just before dawn on the morning of the 14th December the Namas broke into Otjimbingwe. They had crept unobserved into the very outskirts of the village, lying on the ground and concealing themselves behind every little rise, and they began to shoot just as dawn showed in the sky. The Hereros rushed out of their huts in the greatest confusion, and the best and bravest of them were shot down before they could lay their hands on their guns. The women and children took refuge in the newly erected church, which had been built with specially thick walls for occasions such as these. Hahn, who had established a mission colony, which will be mentioned later, had his hands very full. The colonists had to mould bullets and fill powder horns, but to keep a sharp eye on things to see that the Hereros did not divert the ammunition to their own private purposes but used it in the fight. Towards evening, when the attackers had expended all their ammunition, they retired in a westerly direction. Neither side dared to bring matters to a final decision by resorting to storming tactics. A second attack was expected the following day.

'Everything around us was in a sorry state, for the courage of the Hereros had fallen to zero, as the bravest of them had either been killed or wounded. Some thought that, if they only had a cannon, the enemy would become respectful and would not dare to attack again. Others thought again that the mere firing of a cannon would scare them away from where they were camped. Then some enterprising individual conceived the idea of making a cannon. They got hold of a thick tree trunk to which a pump had been fixed, and the blacksmith put a number of bands round it, and so on. Then the terrible shot had to be fired. One of the colonists stuck the lint on the end of a long reed, and held it to the touch-hole. An alarming crackling took place and then the cannon went up into the air in hundreds of pieces; there never was such a bang before. Everybody ran home as hard as they possibly could' (Brincker).

The expected attack never came, and now all the wounded had to be attended to. The colonists set to work to do it. None of them had shot at the enemy, and neither had Green, who was present in the village. It was thought to be better to allow the Hereros and the Namas to fight the matter out between themselves, in order not to endanger the whole place. After the fight Jan Jonker had made for Anawood, and from there he took Hahn's carts, and thirty bags of wheat which had just been harvested. It was very difficult to induce the Hereros to follow the enemy up. It was only after they had been provided with a large quantity of ammunition that they took up the pursuit. On the night of the 22nd December they surrounded the camp of their unsuspecting foes at Salem, and next day they inflicted very heavy losses on them, until at last they broke through their attackers and escaped to Tsaobis. The loot, consisting of wheat and the contents of the store at Anawood, together with the stock belonging to the trader there, remained in the fugitives' possession. Jan Jonker and Jacobus Booi, who were not as yet satisfied, then made for Heigamchab on the Swakop River. There Eggert was living; he had a large storehouse in which he stored all the missionaries' goods which arrived in the Bay, and then saw to their being transported into the interior. There were two Englishmen staying with him at the time. Eggert's herdsman was killed, his stock driven off, and the Europeans were threatened with death. Eggert fled with his family over the dunes to Sandwich Harbour where he found a ship and sailed to Capetown.

Jan Jonker, however, went on with his father-in-law to Walfish Bay. The shop belonging to Andersson's widow was stripped of everything it contained, but no harm was done to her. Iverson, however, who had settled in the Bay as a trader, was murdered.

The marauders, still unsatisfied, marched on to Rooibank to see whether they could find anything useful there. They destroyed the small printing press belonging to the mission and took the type for making bullets, and then they settled down to share the spoils. Jan Booi, Jacobus's father, had received the news of his son's success, and made all speed from Bethanie to attend the distribution of the loot. Seeing that each of the three relatives wanted the lion's share for himself, they quarrelled very seriously between themselves, and the men who had helped them to get the booty hardly received anything at all.

This bold and impudent attack on Otjimbingwe and the plundering of the stores at Anawood, Heigamchab, and Walfish Bay, had a sequel. Mrs. Andersson and Eggert went to Capetown and they reported the happenings in South West Africa. Letters and requests from South Africans poured in upon the Cape Government. Ritter, the Treasurer-General of the Rhenish mission in Capetown, likewise presented a petition to Sir P. C. Wodehouse. The Governor then authorized a warship to be sent to Walfish Bay, and it anchored there on the 18th June, 1868. As, however, there was nobody at Walfish Bay, and so no one to show them the road to the interior, it came back after a short stay. In July, however, the warship appeared there for the second time with Eggert on board. A show of military force was made. The English flag was hoisted at Rooibank, and search was made for Iverson's murderers. When they could not be found, the commander said a few plain words to the effect that every one who laid hands on the life and property of Europeans would be hanged in future. Everybody understood what that meant, and everybody in Namaland heard of it and discussed it freely. Sir P. C. Wodehouse did something more. He wrote a letter to David Christian at Bethanie demanding of him that he should bring his subjects, Jan Booi and his son Jacobus, to justice, and should take steps to ensure the observance of law and order. David Christian acquired respect through this, and he immediately sent out messengers with summonses for both the malefactors. When, however, they refused to go to Bethanie, the chief left matters as they were.

Maharero, too, let his voice be heard. He got Hahn to write a strongly worded letter to David Christian inquiring of him whether he was prepared to undertake the punishment of these marauders as a competent chief should do, for if he was not, he, Maharero, would take matters in hand with his Hereros.

A war cannot be waged with nothing but loud talk, neither can a victor be rendered happy merely by the fact that he has secured a great deal of booty. Jacobus Booi and his men fell ill. Whether he liked it or not, he was forced to go to Bethanie. The commando was so weak that David Christian had to send some ox-wagons to go and meet them, and bring them in. The idea of making him stand his trial had fallen through, seeing that no inquiries had been received from Capetown regarding the manner in which the instructions which had been given had been carried out. Besides this, David had lost a great deal of his influence and standing with his own people. He had been a heavy drinker for over three years, and had, in his drunken bouts, wronged his subjects and failed to look after his tribe's welfare. Then his opponents forced him to appear before the council, where the simple question was put to him whether he would give up drinking and remain chief, or whether he would continue to drink and be deposed. He gave up drinking and recovered his influence.

Maharero, however, was unable to carry out the threat he had made against David Christian, for, after the excellent rains which fell between 1863 and 1866, the rain grew less and less each year, and the increasing drought prevented any expedition on a large scale.

The last events of the war of freedom

The veld round Otjimbingwe was entirely grazed off. Zeraua's and Maharero's people could not agree any more, and Zeraua left and went to live on the Omaruru River. He left Maharero to defend himself unaided against the Namas and Jan Jonker, and that meant that he was very much weakened. Besides that, there was not sufficient grazing for the immense number of cattle he had. In the district of Otjimbingwe the veld was bare, and the beginning of the new year, 1868, did not bring with it the long expected rains. Maharero looked round for the cause of his misfortunes. His witchdoctors told him: 'Your father Tjamuaha is angry with you in his grave at Okahandja. You have deserted him and have not made him any sacrifices. Instead of this you have been listening to missionaries. Tjamuaha must now be propitiated, and that can only be done if you go to his grave accompanied by all your people.' To Maharero this pronouncement seemed to be right. Of course, he could not give Otjimbingwe up altogether, and leave it without protection to the mercy of Nama thieves, for that would be very poor thanks to Hahn, who had always helped him with good advice. He, therefore, left behind a number of young men, from the best families, who were being taught by Hahn, and amongst these were his eldest son, Willem, and his younger son, Samuel. Hahn then had forty young Hereros to protect the place and, in addition, a number of Herero Christians of both tribes, who preferred not to leave, but to stay with their minister. With their help he built a protecting wall round the whole place; he instituted a night watch, patrolled the cattle posts when danger was afoot, and likewise carried out his duties as missionary and principal of the mission colony.

Maharero, however, took the road up the Swakop, with all that he possessed, and reached Barmen. The Mbanderus had settled there and he concluded an alliance with their chief Aponda, who accompanied him to Tjamuaha's grave at Okahandja.

The grave of his father is the most sacred place that the Herero knows. It is true that he knows about Ndjambi, the God of Heaven, but he possesses no sanctuary on the earth, and a human being cannot reach him through prayer. Deceased ancestors, however, act as mediators. Death takes them close to Ndjambi, so that they can have speech with him, and can beseech him for blessings for their children and grandchildren, and pass these on when they have obtained them. According to Herero ideas, all blessings come from their ancestors, and any one who neglects them can expect punishments in the shape of drought, ill health, and misfortune amongst his cattle. When it was necessary to propitiate an ancestor and to pray for his help, the whole tribe with its women, children, and cattle had to assemble at the grave, and then the guardian of the sacred ancestral fire, as the representative of the tribe, kneeling at the north side of the grave, had to confess their faults aloud, and proffer their requests.

Maharero and his people acted in accordance with this ancient custom. The grave and the ground all about it were covered with thick grass, for Okahandja had been uninhabited for the last six years. Through the carelessness of some of the women, burning embers fell into the grass, and in an instant, a big grass fire started. The grass on the grave was burnt down as well, and then the witch doctors declared that Tjamuaha was no longer in the grave. His ghost had probably fled into the grassy plains, and there Maharero ought to go and look for him.

Maharero did not know what to do. He knew perfectly well that the grassy plains were not at Otjimbingwe, and he had a very strong suspicion that the witch-doctors wanted to use him for their own purposes. He therefore stayed where he was. Maharero's move from Otjimbingwe to Okahandja took place in January 1868.

During the month Maharero left Otjimbingwe, Hahn received a letter from Jan Jonker, written in red ink. This informed him that the writer had given up all ideas of peace and was going to make an end of Maharero. He was considering destroying Otjimbingwe as well, and if any of the Europeans were desirous of avoiding disaster, they had better leave the place, for he would spare no one at all. Hahn heard from another source that Jan had said that he was going to kill Hahn, the missionary, because he was no friend of the Namas. He was going to give all the other missionaries a good thrashing, and then give each one his work under his own supervision. This was plain speaking. Protecting walls, ramparts, outposts, and a keen supervision became the order of the day at Otjimbingwe.

Jacobus Booi, Jan Jonker's father-in-law, was well again, and he was quite ready to join him once more. Karel Ses, Hendrik Ses's brother and successor, joined him too. These three allies prepared themselves for a campaign which had three objects in view, namely: to bring the Herero nation back under the Afrikanders' yoke; to drive all the Europeans and missionaries out of the country; and to take vengeance for Hendrik Ses's death. The fighting men were assembled at Rehoboth. The idea was, on this occasion, not to attack the Hereros from the south, through Windhoek, but from the west. But month after month went past and the expected attack never came, and so Maharero made no special preparations.

On the 5th November a Bergdama called Nawasib arrived at Otjimbingwe. He had been present in Rehoboth and seen the troops assemble there, but he had run away and he was now able to tell them that the Namas were on the march. A messenger was quickly sent to Maharero at Okahandja. He did not wait for the enemy to come to him, but advanced against the Namas with all his forces. The Nama spies discovered this and when they came to a place on the western side of Okahandja, where there were a great many Omukaru trees standing, and where there was a kloof which offered a good defensive position, they decided to wait there until the Hereros came up. Jan Jonker posted his forces amongst the rocks of the kloof, and Jacobus Booi's and Karel Ses's warriors concealed themselves in a position which was protected by almost impenetrable thorn bush. The Hereros came on, and they discovered very soon that they had to deal with two groups of enemies. They therefore attacked on both sides, and very soon routed Jan Jonker's people. When Jan Jonker himself saw that, he got safely away before it was too late. Jacobus Booi had followed him, after giving his men instructions that they were to fight to the bitter end. The instructions were really unnecessary for there was very soon no chance of escape. The Hereros surrounded the bushy spot, which was not very large, and not a single man escaped. Jan Booi's tribe was utterly exterminated, and it disappears from history. Jacobus, himself, died of enteric fever soon after this defeat, and his widow and children went to live with another tribe.

About a month later Hahn and Brincker passed Omukaru on their way to Okahandja, and the place presented a horrible appearance. The whole area looked as if it had been sown with skulls and gnawed bones. They made one big grave and buried more than a hundred Namas in it. Over a hundred more lay scattered about in bushes, and they had not sufficient time to collect them. Maharero heard about this queer proceeding on the part of the white people and reckoned that they had taken all that trouble for nothing. Jan Jonker heard about it, and his anger against Hahn abated.

After the battle of Omukaru, Maharero decided to bring these seven years of warfare to an end; seeing that Jan Jonker had lost his chief supporter and that the Namas were greatly weakened, he must surely succeed in forcing them to make peace. His witch-doctors prophesied that his wishes would be fulfilled, and that his plans would have a successful outcome. Tjamuaha's spirit, they said, had returned again, and he would lead his son on the last campaign into Namaland and bestow peace upon his people.

Maharero made his preparations, but the drought continued. The Namas heard that he was getting ready for war, and partly from fear of the Hereros, and partly from lack of grazing, they scattered in all directions, and went to outlying parts where grass and water were still to be found. In July 1869 the Hereros marched out from Barmen, through Windhoek into Namaland. Aponda's Mbanderus went with them. Maharero had taken no food with him for his men. The Namas' fat sheep were supposed to provide them with food, but they could not find these fat sheep anywhere. The whole of Namaland lay as if it were dead. One division went westwards and found a few wretched Hottentots, whom they killed. The women and children were allowed to escape, for Maharero had learnt that it was not decent for a civilized army to kill women and children. He had repeatedly promised Hahn, too, that he would not loot any more cattle in warfare. The principal force marched to Gibeon where the Witboois lived. As they had remained neutral in the war against Jan Jonker neither they nor their stock were touched. The Witboois later requited this consideration with base ingratitude.

From day to day the hunger of the Hereros increased. They tried to satisfy it with roots, tubers, and the bark of trees, but roots and tubers only grow in Namaland in years when good rains fall, and Namaland is very poorly provided with trees which have edible bark. Ever hollower grew their cheeks. It was hopeless to make further marches and to fight great battles with half-starved men like these. Maharero, therefore, gave the order to return to Barmen, and he sent messengers ahead ordering that a number of his own oxen should be slaughtered, and a good meal of meat prepared. When the weary men reached Barmen, the enormous flesh-pots were bubbling on dozens of fires, but no one dared to eat anything. First of all they had to sit down in long rows on the ground, with their faces turned towards the fires and the flesh-pots. Maharero had a large wooden trough filled with water, into which were put ashes from the sacred fire and small branches of the Omurangu bush, and then he sprinkled each warrior individually with this water on his brow and breast. With that they were cleansed from every evil which they had brought with them from Namaland, and now the meal began. This was the end of the last campaign of the Hereros' war for freedom.

The Hereros did not regard the whole war from 1863 to 1869 as one continuous campaign. They gave different phases of it special names, as if they were separate wars. The first phase, the most important event of which was the battle of Otjimbingwe on the 15th July, 1863, was called the 'Battle of the dappled grey oxen', for when Maharero was expecting the Namas, and was preparing to give them a warm reception, he had a dappled grey ox belonging to his sacred herd killed and roasted the night before the battle, so that every one of his warriors could partake of it with special religious ceremonies. The last phase of the war was given the name of 'The scorpion campaign' for, when the Hereros were starving in Namaland, they had picked up scorpions from under many a stone and had roasted and eaten them.

We ought now to deal with the conclusion of peace. The events which preceded the peace of Okahandja of 1870 were so involved, however, that it cannot as yet be dealt with. What happened in Namaland during the years when the Hereros were fighting for freedom must be told, and more especially what happened amongst those tribes who were hardly engaged at all in Jan Jonker's war against the Hereros. The following chapter must therefore be devoted to the Orlam War.

2. THE WITBOOI OR ORLAM WAR

The Witboois

The reader will remember that, in the year 1800, the country south of the Orange River, as far as the Kuiseb River, was occupied by a number of Nama tribes, each of which had its own chief, but that, with the exception of the Bondelswarts at Warmbad and the Topnaars at Walfish Bay, they were all under paramountcy of the chief of the Red Nation, which occupied the country round about Hoachanas. These tribes led a nomadic life on the big river courses of this country, which was so vast that the grazing it provided could not possibly be used up by their cattle, and there was no necessity for fixing precise boundaries for the different tribal areas. What really mattered was not the outside limits of the territory, but the river courses, on the banks of which wells could easily be made to provide water for man and beast.

The position became very different, however, when Orlam tribes from the Cape Colony, who were related to the Nama nation, came into the country from the other side of the Orange River. The first one to come was the chief of Bethanie with his followers. He made arrangements with the paramount chief at Hoachanas, and received a grant of the western part of Namaland as his tribal territory. The territory of Bethanie stretched from the Orange to the Kuiseb, and David Christian occupied the southern and middle parts of it, while his relative Jan Booi and his son Jacobus occupied the northern part.

At that time, the chief, Kido Witbooi, had been living in Pella on the south bank of the Orange River for many years. He had important chiefs under him, that is to say, well-to-do heads of Orlam families who had collected large followings of pure-blooded Namas and Orlam half-breeds. Amongst these sub-chiefs was Paul Goliath, who crossed the Orange River in order to join his relations in Bethanie, and settled temporarily in Bethanie and along the Fish River, but established a home for his tribe in Berseba in 1850. Another one was Amraal, who took the same road and settled afterwards in Naosanabis and Gobabis. It has already been told how Jonker Afrikander and his Afrikander people found their way into the country. The Red Nation had called them in to help them against the Hereros, and had promised them that they could choose a tribal territory, wherever they liked, as the reward for their assistance. Their choice fell on Windhoek and the area between the Kuiseb and the Swakop, down to the lower part of the courses of both these rivers, where the Topnaars' country began. This territory had previously been re-garded as a sort of no-man's land, which was grazed at one time by the Nama and at another by the Herero cattle.

Before Jonker Afrikander came to South West Africa and took up the struggle against the Hereros, he was in close touch with Kido Witbooi in Pella. They had become very great friends, and had entered into a treaty of which only one condition is known. This condition was to the effect that, in the event of either of them dying and leaving the tribe without a chief, the other should adopt the tribe which had lost its chief and amalgamate it with his own. This bond between them must be borne in mind in order that the history of the Witboois may be understood. According to their historical past, they were actually the overlords of the Orlams in Bethanie, Berseba, and Gobabis, and the allies of the Afrikanders, in the event of the latter's chief dying without a legitimate successor. This explains why Jonker Afrikander made three requests for Kido Witbooi and his people to come and settle at Windhoek, with the object of strengthening his own position through them. We can likewise understand how he came to entertain the idea of appointing Kido Witbooi as his successor. Kido Witbooi, had, however, subscribed to the treaty of Hoachanas in 1858, and that contained the condition that the Hereros were to be left in peace. The Witboois had been under the influence of Christianity from the time when they lived in Pella, and this influence did not cease when they went trekking about in Namaland. After a nomadic existence, which lasted thirteen years, they succeeded in obtaining a tribal home for themselves at Gibeon. Oasib, to whom Gibeon belonged, had had such unpleasant experiences with the Orlams (the sheep hunters and hat-wearers), that he was but little inclined to take up with a new tribe. Besides this, the Witboois were not very greatly in love with Gibeon, the place which Kido had decided upon, and to which he gave this name. The first inhabitants, the Bergdamas, had called the place Goregu-ra-as, which means 'the spot where the zebras drink', and the Namas had called it Khacha-tsus, meaning 'the spot where the fighters had a hard time'. Kido's son Moses, who was likewise called Little Kido, found it very difficult to decide to join his father with his followers. He preferred to go and settle at Goa-mus (the bubbling spring), and Goa-mus actually retained its importance as well as Gibeon. The fact, however, that the missionary, Knauer, went to live with Kido after the latter had complied with the condition that he should choose a tribal centre for his tribe, and that a church and school should be erected there, assured Gibeon pride of place.

Oasib, the paramount chief of Hoachanas, had thus provided the Witboois with a place to live in, much, however, against his will. He was forced to recognize that the Orlams were powerful, and he realized that it would be better to accept them as his guests by a friendly arrangement, rather than be compelled to fight for house and home. He hoped, too, that Kido would not refuse him assistance in times of trouble.

Times of trouble were not long in coming. Kido had decided to settle in Gibeon in April 1863, and the missionary Knauer went and joined him directly he got there. A few weeks later Oasib received a message from Christian Afrikander that 'Jonker's dogs had run away', and that he was to come and help to bring them back from Otjimbingwe. Christian Afrikander was an Orlam, as were the Witboois. Oasib had brought the former into the country, and had provided the latter with a territory for his tribe; seeing that Christian Afrikander had called for assistance against the Hereros, it was only natural that Kido Witbooi should help too.

But this was where Oasib erred. Not only did the Swartboois of Rehoboth, who were a branch of his own tribe, refuse to supply him with troops, but Kido Witbooi refused to give him any assistance as well, for he felt that the terms of the conference of Hoachanas of 1857 bound him not to take up arms against the Hereros. The chiefs of Berseba and Bethanie, and Amraal of Gobabis all held that they were bound by these provisions, too.

We have already learnt that Oasib never forgave the Swartboois. He tried by friendly methods and by force of arms to get them on to his side, and make them obey him. His efforts ended with the departure of the Swartboois and their partial destruction by Jan Jonker.

The Witboois were doomed to suffer the same fate. Oasib allied himself with Hendrik Ses, the chief of the Veldskoendraers of the lower Fish Valley, and likewise with Aimab, the chief of the Grootdodens in north Namaland, and he gathered round him every one in Namaland, who had any inclination for looting and fighting. Kido Witbooi was accused of having acted contrary to the treaty of Hoachanas, which made it incumbent upon all the Nama chiefs to stand firmly together, and that, moreover, he had kept back traders who had wanted to go to Hoachanas with powder and shot, in order to weaken the Red Nation. He was also accused of having said that the time was not very far distant when the old Nama tribes would have to go about in leather aprons once more. By this he must be taken to have meant that he was going to work for the downfall of the old tribes, with the object of making himself the paramount chief of the country. Oasib had not sucked all this out of his thumb. Even old Amraal had made an effort to have a conference of chiefs called, with the idea of deposing Oasib and appointing a real chief in his place.

In any event precautionary measures were taken, and the chiefs of Bethanie, Berseba, Gibeon, and Gobabis, entered into an offensive and defensive alliance. By the end of 1864 Oasib's preparations for war were so far advanced that Kido demanded help from Berseba and Bethanie, for he feared that he was going to be attacked.

The first attack on Gibeon

The fears of the Witboois, and their cry for help to Berseba and Bethanie were not without foundation. On the 3rd December, 1864, a strong force under Oasib, Aimab, and Hendrik Ses advanced against Gibeon. Kido sent two messengers to the enemy with the request that he might be informed as to their intentions and reasons for coming. The messengers had their guns taken away, and they did not come back, but in their stead the enemy sent a messenger to Kido, with the request that he would send delegates to enter into negotiations. This message had hardly arrived when it was seen that the enemy had taken possession of all the high positions round the village, and the fight began. Knauer had all the women and children brought into the mission house; a bullet actually grazed his arm. The battle lasted for two days, but as neither side would risk the lives of their men, neither a sortie nor storming tactics were resorted to. At last the Witboois' ammunition was exhausted. They had been making bullets out of bar iron throughout the nights. That same night the besiegers drove away the cattle, sheep, and goats. The Witboois' deserted huts were plundered, too, for the battle had not taken place on the werf but at the mission house, which was close to the spring. On the third day Kido and Knauer went into the enemy's camp to start negotiations. Kido spoke to Oasib and the latter demanded complete surrender: 'Whoever wants to live in my country must be my servant.' Knauer went to see Hendrik Ses, and the way in which he expressed himself was: 'I shall not rest until I have driven all the missionaries out of the country, for they are the cause of all the trouble. By means of their prayers they deflect our bullets and we cannot hit anybody.' They both went back without having effected anything. Gibeon's forty-two guns had not been able to keep the foe at bay. The cornfields and gardens which they had made were trampled down. Fifteen horses which had been put in Knauer's garden for safety's sake were shot down. Fire was applied to the mat huts on the werf. At nine o'clock in the evening Oasib and Hendrik Ses appeared and called for Kido saying that they had come to say good-bye to him. Kido sent an answer back to the effect that he was not in the habit of receiving anybody at that time of night. The foe left on the 6th December without having said good-bye. Gibeon was in ruins and the inhabitants reduced to poverty. Kido's son and subsequent successor, Moses, was not in the village, nor was he able to save any part of the tribe's property as he and his people were at a distant outpost at the time.

Where were the allies with their assistance? In Berseba they had waited for a commando from Bethanie with the intention of combining with it. David Christian in Bethanie had, however, received Gibeon's request for ammunition and men when befuddled by liquor. He had sent his son, Joseph, with an ox-wagon to Luderitzbucht to fetch some more liquor. When the latter returned to Bethanie with several barrels of brandy, which Sinclair had given him for mining concessions, his father held a New Year's celebration which lasted for four days. Only then was Joseph sent at the head of a commando through Berseba to Gibeon. Naturally there was nothing more to be done, so the ally's commando just went back home again.

The second attack on Gibeon

The measure of success in Nama warfare is not the number of people killed, nor even the distance which the defeated foe is driven back, but simply the quantity of stock which is captured. Whoever gets possession of his enemy's cattle has gained in two ways: he has appreciably strengthened his own position, and can get fighting men to come and help him, and he can buy arms and ammunition. The enemy, moreover, has been deprived of his means of existence, and so very considerably weakened. Any people who are helping him are forced to leave him, and he has been deprived of the means of buying ammunition for a further campaign.

Seeing that one-half of the Witbooi tribe had been robbed of all their stock in the first attack, Kido felt that he must make an effort to recover what had been lost. Bethanie and Berseba were of the same opinion, and both these tribes sent a commando to Gibeon. As, however, they were frightened that horse-sickness would break out with the beginning of the rains, they did not want to start a campaign in January, and this brought about dissension between the chiefs. Witbooi and Paul Goliath wanted to force the enemy to make peace, but David Christian favoured milder measures. He wanted to negotiate with the enemy and to make peace with him without fighting, if only he would consent to restore the stolen stock, for the majority of the Witboois' cattle had been driven off by

David's relative, Hendrik Ses. In the end it was decided to wait for the end of the rainy season and to take the field in June.

It was very soon apparent that David Christian was utterly worthless as an ally. He went back on the promise that he had made, and elected to remain neutral. As a neutral he had every right to sit at home alongside the brandy cask, and to acquire by doing so the reputation of a man of peace. This is exactly what he did. All Kreft's sad experiences during this period bear witness of the truth of it.

The allies had hardly left Gibeon at the end of January, when their enemies, who had waited for them to leave, came on the scene again and carried off all the stock which the inhabitants of Gibeon had received from their relations for their support, and whatever had been fortunate enough to escape the first attack. Their allies from Berseba came back immediately, and having joined up with Gibeon's forces they succeeded, not only in pursuing the raiders to Hoachanas and Rehoboth, but in recovering from them everything they had stolen.

Now Oasib was in difficulties, for he had no ammunition left. Precautions were taken in Bethanie and Berseba to see that no trader, who had any powder with him, reached Hoachanas. Then a trader from Walfish Bay ventured to take ammunition to Amraal. He was very much afraid of coming into contact with Oasib, for he had very often treated traders badly. When Oasib heard that he was near at hand he forced him to turn out of his way and to come to him. The trader was forced, not only to leave behind him all his powder and shot, but likewise to pay a heavy toll for taking the other goods through Oasib's territory; then he let him go on. That was at the end of March 1865. It might be asked whether it is worth while mentioning incidents of that kind, but it is necessary to do so in order to follow the sequence of events. Oasib now felt that he was strong enough to start the ball rolling again.

Vollmer, Oasib's missionary, saw that more trouble was brewing, and so he set out for Gibeon for the purpose of advising Kido to make peace with Oasib in good time. Kido was, however, of opinion that he had lost too much, and that the time for peace negotiations had not yet arrived. Kido knew, too, that he could expect a strong commando from Berseba. Signs of impending danger showed themselves on the 5th June. Messengers brought the news to Gibeon on Whit-Monday that the stock on the north side of the village had been stolen. The raiders were pursued but they escaped with their booty. The stock on the south side was carried off the following day and, though they were pursued immediately, the thieves likewise escaped. Then Paul Goliath arrived on the 17th July with his commando from Berseba to help them in their need. The men of Gibeon got ready at once and on the 20th July they set out to pursue the raiders. They left a few men in Gibeon to protect the village. Their opponents had waited for the others to march out, for they knew everything that was going on at Gibeon. In the afternoon of the same day they came out of their hiding-places. The garrison ran to take up defensive positions. They were ready to defend the place, but the enemy refused to fight. They contented themselves with collecting and driving off the stock, which was wandering about unguarded.

There was a special reason why the enemy treated Gibeon's inhabitants so gently. Just at the time for which the attack had been planned, an Irish trader appeared with his ox-wagon close to the village. He was bringing the Witboois five horses, some ammunition. and tobacco. The arrival of this wagon diverted the attention of Oasib's band of robbers, which was composed of all kinds of riff-raff. One part of the forces busied itself with collecting the stock, while the other part robbed the trader's wagon and divided the spoils between them. They did no harm to the trader himself, but took all his clothes off him, and sent him to Knauer, the missionary, in Gibeon. The latter took him in, gave him new clothes, and helped him on his way.

Gibeon's troops got news that very night of what had happened during their short absence. While the Berseba commando and some of the Witboois set out in pursuit of the foe, the rest went back to Gibeon to protect the place from further attacks. This time the pursuit was not in vain, and the pursuers brought back with them twenty-two riding oxen, six horses, and ten guns. Another expedition was made on the 28th July. A large werf at Oas belonging to Oasib was attacked and taken without opposition, and all the stock brought to Gibeon. When this large amount of booty came to be divided, a quarrel arose between the Witboois and their allies. The men of Berseba claimed the larger share, and even took away with them some cattle, which had probably first belonged to the Witboois, and then been taken away from them by Oasib. Oasib was now tired of the whole business. His ally, Hendrik Ses, was dead. The Hereros had cut him to pieces. He had lost his richest werf in the night.

He wanted peace, so he wrote a pathetic letter to Kido Witbooi and offered to make peace with him. Kido replied that a man like Oasib must ask for peace three times before it would be granted him. In these difficult circumstances, a peace proposal was made to him from a direction from which he had not expected it, for Jan Jonker took a hand in the affairs of the Namas and the Orlams in the year 1866, which was such a peaceful one for the Hereros. In March 1866 Oasib had thanked the chief of Bethanie for his neutral attitude, and had asked him to maintain it. In June of the same year Jan Jonker had sent a friendly letter to David Christian and told him that he intended to pay him a visit in the near future. In it he frankly admitted that he was coming to beg, for he was without everything that he required. He had neither horses, nor ammunition, and he was even without clothing and small stock. He trusted that David Christian would provide him with all these, and then he would discuss the position in Namaland with him. Jan Jonker had an idea of negotiating peace between the Namas and the Orlams, and then getting them to join him in dealing the Hereros a heavy blow. Jan Jonker arrived at Bethanie, and there they gave him the cold shoulder. He stayed there for eight days, but David Christian left without worrying himself about Jan, or providing him with any equipment.

Then Jan took his new scheme to Oasib. What Oasib really wanted was to make peace with the Witboois and to get them to join him in a joint campaign against the Hereros, and thus enable him to improve his own financial position, and so Jan quickly won him over to his scheme. Aimab was likewise taken into their confidence, and he was willing to stand in with them. The Veldskoendraers were informed of the plan and they were agreeable to it. Gaibis was fixed as the place where the peace conference was to take place, and two Veldskoendraers were appointed to go to Gibeon and invite Kido to take part. Kido did not refuse this time, but he was so suspicious that he did not go without a strong bodyguard. When he arrived at Gaibis he saw at once that there was no intention of making peace with him by means of friendly negotiations, but that force was to be used to persuade him. That did not suit him at all. He promptly attacked the camp with considerable success. He captured Aimab, the chief of the Grootdodens, and twenty-two of his men. He took them to Gibeon with riems round their necks and kept them prisoners there.

It is, however, tiresome and costly to keep prisoners for a considerable time when one has no prison and food is scarce. Aimab knew that too and so he begged Kido, in friendly terms, to restore him and his people to liberty. He was prepared to make any promises which were desired of him. Kido allowed himself to be persuaded, and accepted a promise from his enemy that he would not take part in any further raids, and that he would have nothing to do with any further warlike enterprises. Aimab made all the promises which were required of him, and he and his twenty-two men were set at liberty.

The third attack on Gibeon

Aimab had no intention whatsoever of keeping his promises; all he thought of was revenge, and he found Oasib in a similar frame of mind. They joined forces again to go and attack the Witboois. This time they were going to do things carefully and to employ strategy as well as force. The people in Gibeon had heard a rumour that a new attack was pending, and arrangements had been made with Berseba to secure its help, but no one had any idea that the danger was so close. Kido Witbooi intended to go and visit his son Moses in Goa-mus, and a number of his men were going with him; so Gibeon would once again be left without proper defence. This Oasib knew, for he had received detailed information of everything that was happening in Gibeon from a Bushman woman. A plan was now made, by which Aimab was to attack Kido wherever he could on his journey to Goa-mus, and to kill him and his following, and then to turn against Moses Witbooi in Goa-mus and to kill him too. Oasib, however, intended to attack the weaker portion of the tribe at Gibeon.

Kido Witbooi set out and suddenly, on the 25th September, Oasib appeared before Gibeon with a big force. The men who were left there hurriedly took up defensive positions, but Oasib would not allow any fighting to take place. He said that he had come not to make war but peace. His only enemy was Kido, but Kido was away, and he therefore had nothing at all against the inhabitants of Gibeon. Some of the men must come to his camp and convince themselves with their own eyes that his intentions were peaceable. Talk of this kind was quite unexpected and it worked wonderfully well. Three of the men laid their suspicions aside and went to his camp. They were treated kindly and sent back with the message that, if Gibeon would surrender without fighting, the lives and possessions of its inhabitants would be spared. If this friendly proposal proved acceptable, the messengers were to tell the women and children to assemble in the church, but the men were to come over to the camp. The messengers returned unharmed. They were the manifest proof of the honesty of Oasib's words. Thirty men then went to Oasib's camp, while the Witbooi's women and children gathered in the church. Knauer, the missionary, was away from home. He had gone to Berseba and Bethanie to fetch a load of goods from the Bay. Directly the thirty men reached the camp they were surrounded by Oasib's men, who pointed their loaded guns at them and ordered them to take their clothes off. When they had done that they were shot. Then Oasib and his men arrived at the church. The women and children who had gathered there were likewise forced to take their clothes off, and were then taken off to the camp, and given over to the pleasure of the troops. Two of the men, however, Petrus Roman and Andries van Saal, succeeded in escaping and in bringing the news of what had happened to Kido Witbooi at Goa-mus. Oasib moved his camp to Gibeon. The women were brought to the village with riems round their necks. First of all the mission house was plundered, and everything which could not be taken away was smashed up. Then the werf was plundered and the huts were burned. On the 1st October, Oasib left Gibeon with nine wagons, all the women and children, and all the stock. He had accomplished more by cunning than he could have done by valour.

Aimab's march to Goa-mus was not such a bloodless business. It was very unfortunate for him that he did not intercept Kido's wagon on the road. When he arrived at Goa-mus, he was received with such heavy fire that he had to retreat as quickly as he could, if he did not want to run the risk of having his whole force wiped out. The two men who had escaped from Gibeon had arrived just in time to warn the Witboois, and their rage at Oasib's treacherous conduct led them to fight against Aimab like lions.

Meanwhile Knauer had arrived in Berseba on his return journey, and there he heard of the destruction of Gibeon. Paul Goliath sent a commando with him for his protection and for the Witboois' assistance. When, however, they found Gibeon in ruins and deserted they returned to Berseba. Knauer, who now had neither a home nor a congregation, accepted Kido's invitation to accompany the forces which he had hastily collected in order to follow up Oasib and Aimab.

Oasib, however, had left Hoachanas and had compelled his missionary Vollmer to go with him on his march, for Oasib set out for the Fish River not only with his forces, but with all his people, in order to put his booty in a safe place. Vollmer was suffering from malaria, but he had no option, and had to follow Oasib, with all his family, in his own ox-wagon. Thus the two missionaries suddenly found themselves army chaplains in opposing forces.

In the third week of October, the Witboois saw Oasib's camp fires from the top of a mountain. The following day, some ox-wagons loaded with loot, which had been deserted by their drivers, fell into their hands. They approached Oasib's fortified camp where Aimab also was. Paul Goliath, old as he was, appeared on the scene with fresh troops from Berseba to help the Witboois. A demand was sent to Oasib that he should surrender the women and children he had captured. When he refused his defences were stormed, and then the opponents lay opposite each other for more than a week without doing anything. Messengers were sent backwards and forwards. Knauer paid his sick colleague a visit in the enemy's camp. The two chaplains did their best to reconcile the combatants. The captured women and children ran away at night, and when, at last, only one sickly woman and a few children were still left, Oasib sent them back to the Witboois of his own accord. On the 21st October Kido, Paul, and Oasib met in conference. Aimab held aloof from the negotiations. Paul Goliath did not spare Oasib, but told him some plain truths about his methods of fighting. Kido treated him very courteously, and said all kinds of flattering things to him. They then discussed the prevailing shortage of tobacco and it was decided to enter into peace negotiations the following day. When the conference met, the Witboois saw that Aimab's 200 men had crept close to the place of the conference with loaded guns. They took up positions opposite to them, but neither did an outbreak of hostilities occur, nor was there any conclusion of peace. Oasib would very much have liked to have had Knauer's head, for he believed a lie which had been circulated to the effect that Knauer had said that he would like to have Oasib's head in pickle. The two parties separated in due course, but there was no talk of peace. Kido had to see that the women and children, who had escaped from captivity, reached Gibeon, and after that he resumed the pursuit of Oasib. The latter was utterly defeated and put to flight. He left Vollmer, who was very ill indeed, and his family without warning or protection. Vollmer's wagon fell into Paul Goliath's hands. Paul took charge of the sick man, but on the 3rd February he died on the road, and Paul Goliath buried him at Hei-guru-aos on the Tsaob River. Since then the place has had the name of 'The Missionary's Grave', and a simple monument stands there in memory of the tragic ending of a life of self-sacrifice. Paul Goliath helped the widow and children to get to Berseba as soon as circumstances permitted, for, first of all, the pursuit of Oasib had to be continued. The latter had retired to Rehoboth. After the Swartboois had left it, a number of Topnaars from Walfish Bay, who had formerly had a werf in the vicinity, entered into occupation of it. Some Afrikanders had settled there too. On this occasion, however, a commando of the Afrikanders came out against Oasib—for Jan Jonker had made up his mind to put an end to the fighting in Namaland—with the object of attacking the Hereros with the forces of the combined Namas. What Jan Jonker, however, had decided in his tribal council, was betrayed to Oasib by his relative Adam Kraai. It was then decided that Oasib should make an attack on the Witboois, and that the Hereros, who were present in his camp as servants, should fight in the front rank of his forces. He, too, had learnt something of Jonker Afrikander's tactics. The Topnaars were to oppose the Afrikanders, and Aimab with his Grootdodens was to give battle to the men of Berseba.

Just before dawn the Witboois commenced the last battle of the Orlam war. Before Oasib realized it, his defences were in the hands of an enemy storming party. A bloody struggle ensued. Oasib's principal men were quickly shot down. Frederick, the chief of the Topnaars, fell. The fighting men and allies of the Red Nation were scattered in absolute rout. Oasib and his son Barnabas hid behind a thorn bush, and the Witboois rushed past without seeing them. The women and children of the Red Nation were all captured, and all their stock carried off. The wretchedness of the prisoners, who had suddenly lost everything they possessed and their means of existence, affected Paul Goliath so greatly that he drove out of the captured herds as many milch cows as were necessary to feed them, and had them restored to them on their release. That did not meet with Kido's approval at all. The victors returned to Gibeon and Berseba. The booty was sufficient to make up for all the losses Gibeon had suffered through the attacks.

Oasib went back to Hoachanas and its neighbourhood. When he heard of Vollmer's death, he said: 'It is a very bad sign for us that our minister is dead.' Soon afterwards he fell ill himself and his illness quickly sapped the little strength he had. He died, and no one made any record of the date of his death. He was buried, but no one can say with any certainty where his grave lies. His son Barnabas, who was peacefully inclined, became chief of the Red Nation in his stead. This happened in the middle of 1867.

The peace of Gibeon

Paul Goliath and his brother-in-law David Christian of Bethanie recognized that a defeated enemy, with whom no peace has been made, can become unexpectedly dangerous. They therefore decided to do everything in their power to bring about a peace conference at Gibeon. When Jan Jonker saw, however, that this peace would not result in an agreement to carry out his own plans against the Hereros, he wrote a furious letter to David Christian and advised him that he was going to pay him a second visit, when he would 'teach the inhabitants of Bethanie how to do something else than drink coffee all day'.

He went personally to Barnabas, the chief of the Red Nation, and warned him not to go to Gibeon as the idea was to tempt him into a trap and kill him. Barnabas was therefore very frightened, and when the chiefs of Bethanie and Berseba went to Gibeon, he did not put in an appearance, although he had begged Kido to make peace with him. They were forced, therefore, to go home, and the conference was convened again in November. Barnabas, however, was still very reluctant, for a large part of his people had secretly ranged themselves on Jonker's side, and had promised to follow him in a campaign to Hereroland. Barnabas had, therefore, a guilty conscience. Kido had his difficulties too. His son-in-law, Paul Visser, had been strongly opposed to the war with the Red Nation, and now he wanted to have nothing to do with the peace treaty. The quarrel grew so fierce that it seemed as if a resort to arms was unavoidable. The peacemakers of Berseba and Bethanie were confronted with this unpropitious state of affairs. Kido had actually called up an armed force, and was letting them make a demonstration on horseback in order to inspire his stiff-necked son-in-law with respect, when these two chiefs arrived with their councillors. The long war had made everybody suspicious of each other, and so they naturally came to the conclusion that this warlike reception was intended for them, and, although this was almost certainly not the case, Berseba long maintained this wrong impression. Messengers were sent to Barnabas at Hoachanas, and he finally ventured to put in an appearance. It was made perfectly clear during the discussion that the suzerainty of the Red Nation, and the paramount chieftainship of Oasib's successor, was no longer in keeping with the times. An alliance of the tribes of Gibeon, Berseba, and Bethanie was concluded, with the object of guaranteeing the general peace of the whole country and, on the 19th December, 1867, the peace treaty was signed.

Barnabas had no alternative but to submit. The suspicious display of military force at Gibeon created bad blood at Berseba and Bethanie. A serious quarrel arose between Kido and his two allies, which almost led to a new war against Gibeon, especially as Kido expressed his disapproval of Paul Goliath's kindly action towards the helpless women and children of the defeated enemy. He was of opinion, too, that as he was formerly the chief of Pella, he had now become the paramount chief of the Namas, and thus Paul Goliath and David Christian were subordinate to him. David Christian, however, was of opinion that the peace treaty, even if it did not expressly say so, had really conferred upon him the paramount chieftainship, seeing that he was the author of the peace. The story of this dispute does not, however, require to be recorded, as it is of no importance to the history of the country.

Old Paul Goliath did not live very much longer after the conclusion of peace at Gibeon. He died, mourned by his whole tribe, on the 15th April, 1869. He was born at Ebenezer on the Oliphants River in the Cape Colony, and escaped to the Orange River as a fugitive from the system of slavery in vogue in the Cape. He was received by Ebner into the Christian congregation at Pella and, at the age of eighty years, he was buried in Berseba, where his grave is still greatly revered. After his death, a Nama poet belonging to his tribe composed a song in the style of the ancient Nama songs. It was sung a great deal and gave expression to the regard in which the whole tribe held its aged chief. Jacobus Isaak, who had hitherto been senior judge and assistant chief, became Paul Goliath's successor. His disposition was almost the opposite of that of his predecessor; he was domineering and energetic, quick to decide, regardless of consequences, but open to conviction when his anger had spent itself. As the tribe of Berseba centred round the two families of the

Goliaths and the Isaaks, provision was made in the laws of the tribe that, from now onwards, the chiefs should be taken alternatively from the Goliath family and the Isaak family.

3. THE INTERVENTION OF THE CAPE GOVERNMENT

The petitions

In Jonker's wars against the Hereros Europeans had always been regarded as neutral and had hardly ever been molested. In the beginning of the Hereros' war of freedom, the combatants had hesitated to attack European settlements or to endanger their lives and property. Then Andersson had openly ranged himself on the Hereros' side, and had fought with his European employees and his native labourers against the Orlams and Namas. That was never forgotten. All the Europeans in Otjimbingwe, which was the biggest settlement in the country, were regarded by the Namas as more or less acknowledged enemies. This hostility reached its highest point with Jan Jonker's demands that the place should be abandoned, because he intended to destroy it. He was, however, afraid to take the lives of Europeans, although his father Jonker had said, shortly before his death, that he intended to go to Otjimbingwe and clean the place up thoroughly. The robber bands under the command of Jacobus Booi and his friends had actually commenced hostilities against the Europeans, by carrying off cattle belonging to white people living in Otjimbingwe, by plundering a shop in Anawood, by threatening Eggert and two Englishmen at Heigamchab with death, by plundering Andersson's widow's store at Walfish Bay, and by killing the Dane, Iverson.

On the 7th June, 1868, the Europeans in Otjimbingwe and its neighbourhood held, therefore, a meeting to decide how a stop could be put to these outrages. It was decided to send a petition to Sir Philip Wodehouse, the Governor of the Cape Colony. This petition bore the signatures of thirty-one European men, whose wives and children numbered eighty-seven. Twenty-five natives signed it, too, for Maharero had likewise taken part in the conference. It was sent down with William Coates Palgrave, whose name we shall often come across in the next period of our history.

The answer to this petition was the dispatch of the two warships to Walfish Bay, an account of which was given in the first section of this chapter. The warships were dispatched for the purpose of inspiring the natives with respect, and the military march from Walfish

Bay to Rooibank, the search for Iverson's murderer, and the threat to hang the robbers, were not without effect. A further purpose was to give the Europeans, who did not want to stay any longer in a country where they had no protection, the opportunity of leaving it.

Something else happened. The management of the Rhenish Mission at Barmen got into touch with von Bismarck, the Chancellor of the North German Confederation, and requested the Government's protection for their missionaries in South West Africa. The Government could not see its way clear to protect German subjects in so distant a land, and advised the presentation of a petition to the British Government in London. Dr. Fabri, the Director of the Missionary Society, then lodged a petition with Lord Stanley, the British Minister for Foreign Affairs, in which he set out the position in so far as Europeans were concerned, gave the names of those who had been murdered, namely Kendendo, Charles Collins, and Iverson, and added that the dispatch of the warships in June 1868 had only made the position of the Europeans more precarious, because the demonstration had not been followed by any further action. Annexed to the petition was a circumstantial account of the general position in South West Africa. As Lord Stanley had in these circumstances to get into touch with the Governor of Cape Colony, Dr. Fabri's petition received no reply in the first instance. In September, therefore, he went back to the Chancellor of the North German Confederation with the request 'that His Highness would most graciously communicate the accompanying representation and request for intervention and protection of the lives and property of the German missionaries in Namaland and Hereroland to the Foreign Office in London, and give it his whole-hearted support'. In the annexures, reference was made to the fact that 'the Cape Press had already reviewed the possibility of the direct and active intervention of Prussia and the North German Confederation'.

This referred to an article in the newspaper *Vriend des Volks* in Capetown, dated the 8th July, 1868, which read as follows:

'An unconfirmed report is being circulated in the newspapers that Prussia is desirous of acquiring colonies, and is trying to obtain possession of the Portuguese settlements in Africa. Nothing could be more advantageous for those unhappy countries, in which the slave trade is still carried on, than the control of a state like Prussia. Who knows, however, whether Bismarck may not perhaps cast his eye on Walfish Bay. In that case the British Government might feel itself compelled to consider very earnestly whether it would not really be worth while to hoist the British flag over Namaland and Hereroland. We shall anxiously await any proposal which the Governor may think it advisable to send to England when the *Petrel* comes back.'

Dr. Fabri likewise approached the King of Prussia:

'May it please your Royal Majesty to instruct the Chancellory of the North German Confederation, by special command, to support, as strongly as possible, the petition sent to the Foreign Office in London by the undersigned, requesting that Government's intervention and the protection of the lives and property of the German missionaries in Namaland and Hereroland.'

On the 30th October, the King of Prussia gave Dr. Fabri an audience, in the course of which he readily promised his support for the petition to the British Government, and expressed his regret that he could not intervene himself. On the 6th November, a memorandum on the matter was presented to Lord Stanley by the Cape missionary, Esselen of Worcester, who was on leave in Germany. The memorandum was handed over in the presence of some members of the English nobility who were acquainted with the country. Lord Stanley promised to discuss matters with Berlin and then to issue instructions to the Cape Government. When, after several weeks had passed Dr. Fabri received no answer, he approached Count von Bernstorff, the Ambassador of the North German Confederation in London, in the hope that his intercession might bring matters to a head.

Any one reading to-day the petition to Lord Stanley, and the memorial annexed to it, can make a shrewd guess as to why the petition met with such reluctant response. It contains the following request:

'Your Excellency will, in the same manner as you did recently in the case of the French Missionaries in Basutoland, instruct the Government of the Cape Colony, to intervene actively in the state of warfare which has prevailed throughout Namaland and Hereroland for the last six years, and has year by year imperilled more and more the life and property of all the European residents, and to see that the Rhenish missionaries and mission stations, which have been robbed, shall be awarded as much compensation as possible.'

The following amounts were given as the amount of damages suffered:

Gobabis	.	.	.	£2,000	Scheppmannsdorf-Heigamchab		£300
Rehoboth	.	.	.	£2,000	Otjimbingwe	. . .	£5,000
Hoachanas	.	.	.	£300			

The damages which other Europeans had suffered were put at a still higher figure.

Piers as Government Commissioner at Bethanie

These different petitions had no effect. It was not as if the Cape Government took no interest at all in South West Africa. It was afraid of a costly undertaking, which it had reason to believe from its previous experiences and the inquiries it made, it might have to pay for itself. In actual fact the land had been declared to be under English jurisdiction as far as the 25th degree of latitude by Sir George Napier. But official recognition had not as yet been accorded to this declaration. It was likewise a fact that, in 1866, an English warship had not only hoisted the English flag upon all the islands lying off Angra Pequena, but had taken possession of the Bay itself, and had altered the name 'Angra Pequena' into 'Penguin Harbour'. Moreover, the copper mines, which had recently been opened by Sinclair in the district of Bethanie, had attracted the attention of the Government. Sinclair had suffered a great deal of inconvenience from marauding Bushmen, and had on this account approached the Cape Government. In the end, however, he had taken the punishment of the thieves into his own hands, thereby incurring the displeasure of David Christian at Bethanie, who regarded his action as an encroachment on his privileges. The Cape Government then announced that a Government Commissioner would visit the country to investigate on the spot all the complaints which had been made and to admonish the allied chiefs of Bethanie, Berseba, and Gibeon to use all their influence to ensure that peace was restored throughout the whole land. Kido Witbooi took not the slightest notice of the invitation to be present. He went on a long journey for the purpose of collecting some scattered members of his tribe, who were still living along the lower Fish River. When Piers arrived at Bethanie on the 9th October, 1868, he found the chiefs of Bethanie and Berseba present. A number of Europeans were likewise present at the proceedings. Piers presented his credentials and had the complaints of the different parties explained to him. Like the skilful official that he was, he gave his decisions in such a way that he administered reproofs, now to the Europeans, and now to the natives, without hurting any one's feelings. 'He knew how to tell his own countrymen who were present, as well as the Namas, the plain truth without arousing their anger', writes Krönlein, who was present at the proceedings.

Both the chiefs came next day with the suggestion that a friendly alliance should be concluded between their tribes and the Cape Government. Piers thereupon drew up a memorandum on the subject, but stated that he had no authority to enter into an alliance; he would, however, convey their wishes to the Government in Capetown.

Piers left on his return journey, and at Aus he received letters from his Government, which contained reports of fresh outrages in the north and disturbances on the Orange River. On the ground that they had sought an alliance with the Cape Government, he immediately instructed the chiefs of Bethanie and Berseba to take steps, with all their power and without delay, against the evildoers in the north and south. If they did that, the Cape Government would reward them for their trouble by giving them a plentiful supply of ammunition. If they did not do so, then they would have to be regarded as enemies, and the importation of ammunition would have to be forbidden entirely.

Berseba and Bethanie had thus been commissioned to provide that, under all circumstances, peace and order should be restored in the country. In order, however, to be able to undertake this task, Kido Witbooi's assistance was necessary. He had never taken the trouble to come to Bethanie, and the feeling between Gibeon and Berseba was so bad that the chief of Berseba was seriously considering whether he had not better drive the Witboois back over the Orange River. This position imposed upon Kreft of Bethanie, Krönlein of Berseba, and Schroeder of Keetmanshoop, a very difficult task. Although they did not readily interfere, by virtue of their position, in the political relations of the natives, they could not very well hold themselves aloof when it became necessary to make peace between the tribes. They therefore went to Gibeon as quickly as they could, and succeeded in clearing up the misunderstanding and exposing some people who had been telling malicious lies. The culprits were brought back to Berseba and were forced to make a public confession of the lies they had been telling. That cleared the air, and by the beginning of April 1869 the ground had been so well prepared on both sides that Kido Witbooi came to Berseba and after a full discussion, renewed the alliance which he had previously entered into with his neighbours.

Bethanie was not subsequently required to concern itself with Bushman disturbances on the Orange River, for the Magistrate at Springbokfontein made an agreement with the chief of Warmbad, by virtue of which he had to take all possible steps 'to suppress disturbances, to prevent robbery and theft, and to preserve peace and order along the Orange River'. For this he received a yearly payment of £50.

The Cape Government's letters to the chiefs

With the object of doing everything possible to ensure peace in South West Africa, the Governor of the Cape Colony wrote several letters to the Nama chiefs. On the 9th January, 1869, he requested the chiefs of Bethanie and Berseba to co-operate with the colonial forces against the Koranas, and to refuse to harbour Korana cattle-thieves in their territories. Kido Witbooi received a warning not to go back on his agreement. Jacobus Booi, who had written to the Governor with the object of pleading extenuating circumstances for the crimes he had committed at Otjimbingwe, Anawood, Heigamchab, and Walfish Bay, by representing that Hahn and the other Europeans at Otjimbingwe had violated their position as neutrals, received an answer to the effect that it was well known at the Cape that it was Hahn who had actually protected him from Herero attacks on two occasions.

On the 11th January, 1868, Sir Philip Wodehouse wrote to Jan Jonker very plainly, for the latter had tried to clear himself in the Governor's eyes by writing him a letter in August 1868 saying that he could not understand why hunters and traders were avoiding his territory, seeing that he had always treated them well. He was reminded that an elephant hunter was murdered in March 1865 by Samuel, one of Jan's relations. In May 1868 this self-same Samuel had attacked three other hunters, wounded one of them, taken all their clothes off them, robbed them of their wagons, horses, and guns, and then forced them to make their way to the nearest station, which was more than three hundred miles away, without any food at all. In the same month he had attacked another hunter, who had lost six of his people in the fight, and had been forced to turn back. If all that was true, there were very good reasons for taking steps against Jan Jonker. Andersson and Green had only attacked him after they had been robbed by him. If he was anxious that travellers should not shun his territory, things of that kind must stop. It was remarkable that Europeans could travel unmolested in the southern part of the country and amongst the Swartboois, a thing which was quite impossible in Jan's territory. Charles Collins, likewise, had been robbed and murdered. The letter closed with these words: 'I shall be very pleased to hear that the fighting between you and the Namas, Hereros, and Europeans, has come to an end. In the hope that this may very soon take place. . . .'

There is no doubt that the dispatch of an armed force would have made a much greater impression upon the combatants than the sending of a second warship, an official, and a few letters. Who knows, however, whether, with the position as it was, armed intervention in a country which was not yet occupied would not perhaps have made the confusion still greater than it was before, and who could foresee what the cost of an expedition of that sort might not have been—it would probably have been so great that the whole of South West Africa, as it was then known, would not have been worth the expenditure.

4. THE PEACE OF OKAHANDJA

Hugo Hahn as peacemaker

In order that we may bring to its appointed end the account of the Hereros' war of freedom which was given in the first chapter, we must just call to mind the position in South West Africa in the year 1869. Maharero's 'scorpion campaign' had come to an end without reflecting any glory on him. He had marched out to destroy his Nama foes and to force them to make peace, but his warriors had returned to Barmen with hollow cheeks, without having even seen the Namas. A terrible drought had the whole country in its grip. The Nama tribes had scattered to the very farthest borders of the country to enable man and beast to survive. Jan Jonker's tribe was utterly impoverished and his supporters had gone. Jacobus Booi, his strongest ally, had fallen ill and died. His people were starving. Without outside assistance to help him to fight, and without being able to steal other people's cattle for food, he could achieve just as little as Maharero with his better equipped folk had done. Every day some of the women and children died of starvation. Then Jan Jonker turned to Hugo Hahn at Otjimbingwe with the request that he would act as his intermediary in making peace with Maharero. He even went personally to Otjimbingwe to talk the matter over. Jan was prepared to agree to anything, if only Maharero would give him back the same number of stock as he had retained, when he gave up his position as manager of Jonker's flocks after the battle of Otjimbingwe in June 1863, and had never given back. It would clearly be to Jonker's advantage if an arrangement of that kind could be carried out. Hahn felt, however, that Maharero would not agree to it, and he did his best to persuade Jan Jonker not to persist in this demand. Hahn and his colleague Brincker then went to see Maharero. He was staying at an outpost called Otumama, between Otjimbingwe and Windhoek. Maharero was not disinclined to make peace with Jan, but he was of opinion that it was Jan who wanted peace, not he, Maharero. If Jan wanted it he should take the trouble of coming to him personally and talking matters over with him. Maharero thought himself a big man again. He had given himself a new title, and was having himself addressed by the full name 'Maharero the Great, the Rich, and All-powerful'. Hahn informed Jan what Maharero's decision was, and he wrote to Krönlein that the time was ripe for persuading the chiefs of the triple alliance in Namaland to attend a conference with Maharero, as the latter did not intend to enter into any peace with Jan Jonker unless the neutral chiefs would stand security for his keeping it.

Krönlein as peacemaker.

Krönlein and his colleague Kreft of Bethanie had no easy task in persuading David Christian of Bethanie, Jacobus Isaak of Berseba, and Kido Witbooi, to undertake the journey to Maharero. David Christian reckoned that he could not afford the time. He had just returned from his Bushman hunt, and had received a cask of brandy from Sinclair, as the reward for his having inflicted punishment on the Bushmen; for many years he had abstained from alcohol entirely. He began once again to give way to his old craving and had no more interest for anything else. Besides that, Jacobus Booi, his rival, was dead. Although Jacobus was his relative he was secretly glad to be rid of him, and he felt that any danger which threatened him had been very much decreased through the death of this dangerous robber, who was Jan Jonker's father-in-law. The persistence of Kreft and Krönlein was successful in the end in inducing David Christian to undertake the long journey to Maharero in the company of the chief of Berseba and Kido Witbooi of Gibeon, and they reached Gibeon. Kido was old and could not very well make the long journey. He therefore furnished his son Moses, or Klein Kido, who was already quite grey, with written credentials, and arranged that he should go to Okahandja. The preparations for the journey had not as yet been completed and there were no trek oxen at Gibeon. The chiefs of Bethanie and Berseba went on ahead to Rehoboth, where they intended to go hunting and wait for Moses Witbooi.

This was the arrangement, but after waiting for several weeks, Moses did not turn up. Then David Christian felt a very strong urge to return to Bethanie. We can guess what that urge was. He turned back and reached home on the 7th January, 1870, without having done anything.

Moses Witbooi's subterfuges

Moses Witbooi, furnished with all the powers of a chief and accompanied by a number of his father's councillors, had made a detour to avoid the chiefs of Bethanie and Berseba at Rehoboth. It did not interest him at all to go and meet them, so he went through to Windhoek with the object of seeing Jan Jonker, who was, however, absent from home. The Afrikanders thought that the Witboois had come to march with them against the Hereros, and they were somewhat disappointed when they discovered that the purpose of their journey was to make peace. Moses Witbooi, however, told them a story which made them prick up their ears. Of course they knew that the chiefs of the south were expected, and that they were coming to negotiate with Maharero, and that Jan Jonker had also been invited to the conference. Moses told them now, however, that these very chiefs were trying to collect an armed force in order to induce Maharero to make peace, not by negotiations, but by force, after they had inflicted a decisive defeat upon him. What could be more welcome to the Afrikanders than news of this sort! Moses wrote a letter from Windhoek to his father, in which he tried to conceal his trickery from the people of Gibeon. It stated: 'I do not know why Jacobus Isaak has collected so many of his people. I do not trust the position. I am therefore not going to wait for him and for the conference, but am going to negotiate by myself and then return.'

That Jacobus Isaak was 'collecting so many of his people' was an entire fabrication. Credence was, however, attached to the statement, and so Moses's arbitrary action was justified, and a separate peace with Maharero warranted. Moses had some personal objects, which he was not certain of attaining if his allies should be present. He left his wagon south of Windhoek and reached Okahandja on the 26th October, 1869. Maharero had made an express request to the chiefs of the south that none of them should come with a large bodyguard. He was not too certain about all this peace talk, and feared lest a big body of wagon attendants might very easily be converted into a fighting force, in case the Namas should think it necessary to enforce their demands by ways other than peaceable.

Maharero's distrust was increased through Moses Witbooi's telling him that he had not come in the company of the southern chiefs, but had come on ahead of them, because David Christian intended to arrive with a strong force, and to bring about peace through force of arms. This friendly communication made Moses appear to Maharero to be a true friend, and he treated him accordingly by making the Witboois a present of Windhoek as a residence, and of the surrounding veld as pasture lands. That was more than Moses had expected. He wrote a second letter to his father in which he said: 'The people of Berseba are anxious to make war and the Hereros do not trust them, but the Hereros have received me kindly and have given me Windhoek.'

The letter, however, never got to Gibeon but to Berseba. It was opened and read, and then Bethanie and Berseba knew where they stood. Jacobus Isaak sent ten of his people to Hahn at Otjimbingwe to inquire from him what the true position was. Hahn got into communication with Maharero. Moses Witbooi, and with him Saul Sheppard, the Herero mentioned before who had gone from Hoachanas to Berseba and from there had gone to stay at Gibeon, went to Otjimbingwe, stayed there for two weeks, and returned to Okahandja on the 4th December. There, too, they told the story of the Nama chiefs' preparations, of Maharero's gift to them, and of their fear that Jan Jonker and Jacobus Isaak would probably attack them on their return journey to Gibeon.

The position of affairs in Hereroland was already known in Berseba. It was known too, that Saul Sheppard had been to Otjimbingwe and that no one other than he could have spread the lying report about Berseba. From the period he had spent in Berseba, he knew that the actions of the Hereros in Gobabis, and their cruelty towards the Orlam relations who lived there, had been resented. The matter had been mooted that, at any future peace conference, Maharero should be made to compensate the Orlams of Gobabis. These statements were now maliciously passed on to Maharero with a number of additions, and Berseba as well as Bethanie came under the grave suspicion that it intended to play a dishonest game with its so-called efforts for peace.

On the 23rd January, 1870, Moses went back to Gibeon. There was great rejoicing amongst one section of the tribe over the news that Windhoek was to be their future tribal territory. Their hopes were renewed once more. If they went to Windhoek then they were so much nearer well-stocked hunting-grounds, for hunting was no longer very profitable in Namaland; then perhaps they would be able to pay off the heavy debts which they had incurred with Duncan for arms and ammunition and, in addition, there would be no need to endure the humiliation of being subordinate to the chiefs of Berseba and Bethanie. This latter position was especially galling, seeing that the people of Bethanie were reckoned as Hottentots, while the people of Berseba were formerly regarded as the Orlam subjects of the Witboois at Pella.

This web of falsehood was very soon to be torn to shreds. It was not long before the full truth became known, not only in Berseba and Bethanie, but in Gibeon as well. The name of the Witboois stank throughout the whole country. Kido declared that he would never go to Windhoek with his tribe. Even Moses's followers, who had been prepared to dismantle their huts and to trek to Windhoek immediately, had hardly a word to say. The scorn of the better-disposed part of the tribe rested heavily on them.

The feeling in Okahandja before Moses Witbooi arrived, and while the chiefs of Bethanie and Berseba were expected, was very good. After Moses's departure Maharero very soon found out the truth about the intentions of the southern chiefs, and stated that he realized that Moses had deceived him, and that he had been the cause of the chiefs of Bethanie and Berseba returning home again. If, however, there was to be any conclusion of peace both those chiefs would still have to come and see him.

Jan Jonker's subterfuges

Hugo Hahn had been asked by Jan Jonker to act as his intermediary with Maharero, but at the same time he had been Maharero's confidential adviser from the time he had come to live at Otjimbingwe. Hahn, therefore, thought it his duty to see that the two chiefs met, and succeeded in arranging a conference between Maharero and Jan Jonker for the 27th May, 1870. The meeting between them, and the discussion, were arranged to take place in the missionary's house at Barmen. As Maharero had, a little while before, accepted the missionaries Diehl and Irle for Okahandja, he took them with him to Barmen. Boehm and Viehe went there too. Hahn, however, did not put in an appearance, so that he might neither disturb nor influence the discussion. The missionaries, too, held aloof from the proceedings. It was only at the end, when they were asked to record the individual points of the treaty in writing, that Brincker, the local missionary, became the recorder of the transactions.

Brincker, who had every opportunity for observing what went on, writes as follows regarding this first meeting between Jan and Maharero:

'The meeting between Maharero and Jan was quite a simple affair. Maharero sat on a chair. The Mbanderu chief, Aponda, acted as master of ceremonies. Viehe and I sat in front of Maharero. Aponda brought in Jan Afrikander and his people, who had in the meantime been waiting in an Herero hut, walking in a very ceremonious way at the head of Jan Afrikander's procession, until Jan stood face to face with Maharero, and then he stepped back. Jan gave Maharero his hand and then everybody who was with him did the same. While this was going on the chief remained sitting in his chair, with his head bent forward because he could hardly refrain from laughing. Now, however, the Herero ranks came to Jan, and he had to shake hands with a thousand Hereros, whom Maharero had brought with him for his protection, each of them saying "Morro! Morro!" With their guns on their shoulders and their assegais in their hands they marched past Jan with this greeting and a handshake. According to Herero custom, when this ceremony was at an end, peace was concluded.'

Here we have an instance of a peace concluded without any negotiations. The negotiations then took place between Jan and Maharero, and the result of them appears from Brincker's record. Jan accompanied Maharero to Okahandja. He could not expect more than he had been given, although he put his own interpretation on the agreement made at Barmen, and that was that he had become paramount chief of Namaland and Hereroland once again. Maharero, however, thought that Jan was going to help him to remove existing difficulties, more particularly those with the Europeans, and that then there would be a conference of all the chiefs, where the last word would be said and the final conditions drawn up. Olpp at Gibeon probably had a true grasp of the position when he wrote about this peace on the 28th May to the following effect: 'The peace which was concluded between Maharero and Jan Afrikander in May is nothing more than pure child's play.' Maharero, too, was very soon to realize that this was the case.

Very soon after concluding peace so light-heartedly, Jan issued a manifesto and had it published throughout the country. It was directed to all Europeans who were living in Hereroland. He threatened all those who had provided the Hereros during the past years of warfare with arms and ammunition with the severest punishment. No traders would in future be entitled to the right of residence. The prices of goods were no longer to be fixed by the sellers but by him. The missionaries, too, were in future to be under the control of the tribal chiefs.

He issued a second order to the chiefs of Namaland. The hunting of ostriches was strictly forbidden them, and the Basters, who had recently immigrated from the Cape Colony, some of whom had settled in Rehoboth, were forbidden to live there.

Maharero was very much annoyed by the issue of these decrees. He informed Jan Jonker in a letter, written on the 25th July, that he reserved to himself all rights of punishing Europeans in Hereroland.

Jan Jonker did not return to Windhoek after the conclusion of peace in Barmen and his visit to Okahandja. He had an idea that he had exposed his cards too soon, and he withdrew into the Auas Mountains and the mountains of the Kuiseb. When the settlement that had taken place became known, thunder-clouds gathered over the whole land, and the Europeans feared the worst. No one trusted anybody else, and every one longed for a 'real peace'.

The 'real' peace

Hugo Hahn was convinced that the circumstances required the personal intervention of the missionaries, and that it would not be enough merely to bring the opposing parties together. He therefore got into touch with his colleagues in Namaland and with Maharero, and many messages were sent to and fro. The Nama chiefs were earnestly exhorted to come to Okahandja, and Jan Jonker was invited again. By the beginning of August the arrangements were so far advanced that the last days of September could be fixed for the conference.

Maharero invited the chiefs of the Herero tribes and, as guardian of the sacred fire, he prepared his people for the great event. A trough full of water was placed on the ashes of the sacred fire, and herbs of various kinds were immersed in it. Every man had to kneel down and drink water out of the trough. Maharero stood next to it and, as each one of them drank, he sprinkled him with holy water, which he held in his mouth and sprayed over all his fellow tribesmen. Then a kind of a mud was made with water, earth from Tjamuaha's grave and ashes from the sacred fire, and their breasts and arms were smeared with it.

Then the report came in that the Nama chiefs were advancing

with a large number of wagons and that they were outspanned to the south of Windhoek. Willem Swartbooi, Maharero's ally when the times had been very difficult, sent two messages to him to warn him not to trust these chiefs. He was of opinion that they were coming with a large following to attack Maharero. The Hereros paid very careful attention to this warning. Jan Jonker, too, who had passed through Rehoboth, sent a message to tell Maharero that he had found so many Namas in Rehoboth that the water from the springs, plentiful though it was, had not been sufficient for them all. This caused considerable consternation. Maharero offered up a sacrifice at his father's grave and summoned all the fighting men of southern Hereroland. Hahn wrote a letter to the unsuspecting chieftains of the south, and he went over to Barmen on the 23rd August. He arrived at Okahandja on the 27th August and went to see Maharero. Guards had been posted and scouts sent out, but when nothing suspicious happened the anxiety subsided. Towards the middle of September the ox-wagons reached the Okahandja flats. The place had never yet witnessed a procession of this size. Of the missionaries, Krönlein of Berseba appeared as the leader of the chiefs of the fourfold alliance, Hugo Hahn as Jan Jonker's intermediary and Maharero's confidential adviser, Olpp, the missionary from Gibeon, Brincker from Otjikango, Diehl and Irle from Okahandja, and seven missionaries belonging to the Finnish Mission to represent Ovamboland, together with Conrath as the representative of the commercial community. The Nama chiefs who were there were David Christian of Bethanie, Jacobus Isaak of Berseba, Kido Witbooi of Gibeon, and Jan Jonker of Windhoek.

Maharero's supporters were: Zeraua of Omaruru, Aponda of Otjikango, and besides these Kahuiko, Kavinjoko, Tjetjo, Kanambano, and Katjinonjungu, while Abraham Swartbooi was present as well.

Hahn was virtually appointed chairman of the proceedings while Viehe of Otjimbingwe acted as Maharero's legal representative. The negotiations passed off quite well during the first two days. The Hereros were inclined to be a little bit arrogant at times, and the sensitive Namas apt to take offence, but Hahn was always successful in pouring oil on the troubled waters. By the third day matters had progressed so well that the parties' representatives were in a position to draft a treaty. This treaty had, however, to contain a provision for Jan Jonker's future place of residence. Maharero tried very hard to arrange that the Nama chiefs should take Jan Jonker with them and assign him a place to live in in Namaland, but to this the chiefs would not under any circumstances agree. Things came to such a pass that the Hereros left the meeting and sent a message to the effect that the others could all go home immediately, for, if Jan Jonker were to stay in Windhoek, a real peace was out of the question.

What was now required was really sound advice. Hahn went hurriedly backwards and forwards between Maharero and the Namas, but no one could find a real solution. Things looked very black for the Namas. It was a bitter pill for them that they had to experience treatment of this kind from 'Jonker's dogs', from 'these escaped baboons and Namas' pipe-lighters'. Hahn, at last, found a way out. He suggested to Maharero that he should give Jan Jonker the village and district of Windhoek 'on feudal tenure'. The Hereros did not understand the term and took it to mean on temporary loan. Maharero agreed that, if the success of the negotiations was to turn on a single phrase, it could be put into the treaty that Maharero gave Jan Jonker Windhoek 'on feudal tenure'. The treaty could now be finally drawn up.

The original peace treaty, which is in the archives of the Herero Mission, bears the marks of the chiefs David Christian, David (Kido) Witbooi, and Jacobus Isaak, as intermediaries.

Then follow the marks of the paramount chief, Maharero, and the chiefs Zeraua, Aponda, Katjihuiko, Kavinjoko, Tjetjo, Kanambano, and Katjinonjungu. Under this again appears the mark of Abraham Swartbooi, who signs himself as the chief of the Rehobothers.

Jan Jonker signed his name to it, he being the only one amongst them who was able to write, and under his signature stand the signatures of C. H. Hahn, Ph. Diehl, and C. Conrath as witnesses to the marks.

When the treaty had been drawn up and was about to be signed, some of the Herero chiefs said to Hahn: 'We are allowing you to subscribe to the treaty on our behalf to-day, for we cannot write ourselves, but you will see that Windhoek will still cost us a great deal of blood.'

5. THE WORK AND PROGRESS OF CIVILIZATION

In an account of the work of civilization which was carried on in South West Africa between 1863 and 1870, it is quite unnecessary to enumerate and discuss the obstacles which lay in its path. The whole political position was as inimical to civilization as possible, and many excellent things, which were planted with affection and were nursed and protected with solicitude, came to a sudden end in the fierce storms of the Hereros' war of freedom and the Orlam War in Namaland. Thanks are due to the persevering and hopeful labours of the missionaries that any civilizing work was done, and whether there can be any talk at all of the progress of civilization must be gathered from the account that follows.

It has already been stated that it is practically impossible to raise a nomadic people in the scale of civilization, and strenuous efforts were, therefore, made to get the Namas, Orlams, and Hereros to settle down. Bitter experience had shown that something more than a good water-supply and the goodwill of the tribe were necessary to this end, for good and sufficient garden ground and good rainy seasons were just as much indispensable conditions. If there was plenty of good soil for cultivation but the rain stayed away and the air remained hot and dry, then the families belonging to the tribe were forced to scatter, even in favoured places like Bethanie, Berseba, Warmbad, Gibeon, and Hoachanas. Then the missionary who had set his mind upon getting the people settled at one spot, could be glad if those who were living far out in the veld were able to send animals from the cattle-posts, to provide milk for the old people and children who had stayed behind at the mission station, so that the tribal centre need not be utterly deserted. Since this difficulty has been previously discussed, we shall only deal here with the settlement of certain tribes, which had either had no tribal centre up to that time, or had lost the one they formerly had.

The wandering Namas

Tseib, who lived with his tribe in the country round about Keet-manshoop, had for many years had his eye on Swartmodder as a centre for his tribe. Although some traders had settled there, he had never entered into occupation of the place but, in 1866, when Schroeder went there, he kept his promise of going to live there with his tribe. Some families from the tribe of the Veldskoendraers came and joined him. Although it was difficult to stay in the village during dry years the tribal centre was never entirely deserted.

The tribe of the Afrikanders, which had had Windhoek as a tribal centre since Jonker's time, gradually resolved itself into separate groups. Adam Kraai and his people wandered up and down in the northern part of the Rehoboth district and showed some preference for the western part of the Gobabis district. Jan Jonker himself only stayed in Windhoek temporarily, and generally spent long periods of time either in Gobabis or with Jacobus Booi. His allies, the Top-naars, tried to make deserted Rehoboth their home, but they did not succeed, and Amraal's tribe, in so far as it belonged to the war party, looked upon a fixed place of residence with disinclination, although, in Gobabis itself, a large dam had been constructed and provided sufficient water for the cultivation of vegetables. Oasib, too, and his Red Nation, although they made a good beginning and maintained it for several years, found that they were not sufficiently certain of things in Hoachanas. Time and again he returned to the Fish River, partly on account of the grazing and partly out of fear of his foes, who could find him very easily in Hoachanas but could only lay hands on him with great difficulty at the Fish River. His successor, Barnabas, succeeded in gathering together the tribe, which had run utterly wild, and tried to revive the old tribal centre once more. How, after years of effort, the wandering Witboois were induced to settle in Gibeon has been told before, so the early history of this tribe and its wanderings may be passed over here.

The Basters[1] as wanderers

This seems to be the best opportunity for turning our attention to the immigration of a small race, of which hardly anything has yet been said, i.e. the Baster race. By the word 'Baster' we, in South West Africa, do not mean all the people of mixed race who had their origin in the association of European men with native women. We call the product of associations of that kind 'half-castes'. It is, how-ever, by no means easy to state where the difference between half-castes and Basters lies. It might be said that the people of mixed race living within the boundaries of South West Africa, who have become a united whole and possess a history of their own, are called 'Basters', while half-castes are the product of miscegenation, in that they are not connected by any tie, but have remained attached to their mother's tribe and so possess no history. This, however, would be

[1] The German text of the book uses the word 'Bastards' throughout. These people, however, call themselves 'Basters' and this name, although it is a corruption of the opprobrious term 'Bastards' has, for them, so far lost all the significance of its origin that they are quite proud of it. The term used in the German text for people of mixed race is 'half-whites', but South African people refer to these un-fortunate individuals as 'half-castes'.—*Ed.*

only partially correct. It therefore appears to us to be necessary to go into the origin of the Baster people, and to trace where they came from in the Cape Colony.

Round about 1750 there lived in Capetown some 4,000 Europeans, of whom fully a third were officials of the Dutch East India Company. There were amongst them large numbers of slaves, who had first of all been brought from the East Indies, Madagascar, and Moçambique, but had later been recruited from the South African Hottentot tribes. Through the association of European sailors with this mixed coloured population there arose the peculiar coloured population of the Cape Colony, which has neither tribes nor chiefs. Out of this mixture one particular Hottentot tribe was formed; it was called the Giriguas, or Jackal tribe, and lived close to Table Bay. The descendants of these half-caste Giriguas became the forefathers of the Griqua tribe, which came together under the leadership of Adam Kok, wandered about in the neighbourhood of the Orange River, and acquired considerable importance there. It is not a part of our task to follow up the history of these people any farther, as they were never in South West Africa.

The completion of the settlement and occupation of South Africa now took place in different stages, under conditions which continually repeated themselves so far as the manner in which they affected the Europeans and the natives was concerned, and were as follows:

1. A number of Europeans[1] wandered about beyond the boundary of the colony, with large or small flocks, built their huts where it pleased them, and chose whatever grazing was convenient to them. They fought against the Bushmen and the Hottentots who were ill-disposed towards them, and took as their wives the daughters of those Hottentots with whom they stood on a friendly footing. It is easy to understand why they did so, for the borders were so unsafe at that time, and life was so very hard there, that European women could not possibly have stood it. This miscegenation met with very strong disapproval from the Europeans who lived within the boundaries of the colony. The Europeans who had married Hottentot women were utterly despised amongst them, and their descendants were refused recognition. They were, therefore, forced to cohabit with new arrivals amongst the adventure- and freedom-loving Europeans, or even to marry them, or to marry Hottentots. Association

---

[1] They were generally fugitives from justice, or deserters from the Company's troops or from ships in Table Bay.—Ed.

OVAMBO DANCE

By courtesy of F. Nink, Windhoek

with a European was regarded as very desirable and it was called 'breeding progressively' while connexion with Hottentots was called 'breeding retrogressively'.

2. The Bushmen and Hottentot tribes were driven northwards through the pressure exerted by these Europeans and Basters and, when the boundary areas appeared to be sufficiently settled, the Government extended by a process of occupation the northern boundaries of the colony, had the country surveyed, leased pasture land and sold farms to Europeans.

3. The Europeans and their bastard descendants, who lived on the boundaries, were very fond of their free life, and they found control under fixed laws so irksome that they decided to continue their wandering life, so they trekked farther to the north, into the country which lay beyond the new boundaries, where the same process repeated itself in due course. In 1824, a law was made to the effect that, for the future, the Europeans of the border country would not be allowed to change their places of residence without the permission of the Government, but that did not make any difference. At the end of three years the law was withdrawn as being quite impracticable. It was only when the Orange River was proclaimed as the northern boundary of Cape Colony, in 1847, that the existence of free territory on the southern side of the river came to an end.

The Basters whom we have in South West Africa, had their actual home in the Karee Mountains, on the edge of the so-called Bushmanland south of the Orange River. According to the traditions of one or two of the families, it appears that they can trace their origin back to some thirty Europeans who married Hottentot women. The fathers saw that the children got some slight schooling, and in many cases even taught them to read and write and, although most of the children were never baptized, they got a smattering of Christianity. While the Baster children regarded the Hottentots with disdain, they could not associate with actual Europeans and their families, and thus there developed amongst them an extraordinary pride in the fact that they were Basters. They married amongst themselves and attained a measure of prosperity, and the veld of the Karee mountains was sufficient for them in the early days. Numbers of them joined the Griquas and came under the command of Berend Berend, but the others had, in the beginning, no chief. They were received into the missions, and settlements of them were formed at Kommagas, Amandelboom (now Williston), Pella, and Die Tuin. Pella's history is known to us already. Founded in 1800 by the Wesleyan Missionary Society, it became the sanctuary of the Bondelswarts in 1811, when Jager Afrikander sacked Warmbad. When the Bondelswarts went back to Warmbad, Kido Witbooi and his people lived there for many years; then Basters began to collect there. In 1841, the missionary, Schroeder, belonging to the Rhenish Mission, resumed work at the deserted mission station. Drought and Bushman raids were the cause of Pella becoming entirely deserted in 1851. In spite of this, a congregation of 420 members existed there in the course of the following decade. When Schroeder died in 1868, Johann Christian Friedrich Heidmann from Luebeck became the Basters' missionary. He had worked amongst them previously at Die Tuin and Skietfontein.[1] Die Tuin, which means 'the garden', and was so called because a European had settled there in the early days and had laid out a garden there, lay nearest to the territory occupied by the Bushmen, and suffered very greatly at their hands. For that reason the Government promised its protection, for the granting of which the Basters had sent in numerous petitions, and dispatched several deputations. The advancing European occupation limited the veld, and it was necessary that the Basters' stock should be taken to other pastures, if the Europeans were to be able to make a living on their farms. The Basters did not succeed in managing to purchase any considerable extent of ground. Life in Pella and Die Tuin became impossible for them. In February 1868 the majority of the tribe, consisting of about 90 families, decided, therefore, to cross the Orange River, and thus to follow in the footsteps of the Orlam tribes in seeking a new home in South West Africa. Heidmann decided to accompany his flock. He was in close touch with his colleagues of the Rhenish Mission who were working in Namaland, and this enabled him to get the tribe of Berseba to promise to receive the Basters as guests in its territory for two years. Then preparations were made for the trek. Hermanus van Wyk was elected chief and leader and, just before the new year, they crossed the Orange River and stopped at Warmbad for a short rest. The tribe at Warmbad granted them the right of trekking through free, but the Afrikander tribe of Blydeverwacht warned the chief of Bethanie about it, and requested him to refuse them the right to trek through his territory, for they were heading for Bethanie. As, however, Berseba had come to the Basters' assistance, Bethanie was not prepared to offer any opposition, and they stayed at Chamis

[1] To-day known as Carnarvon. — *Ed.*

for several months. Hahn invited the Basters to come to Rooibank which lay deserted and, seeing that they were inclined to settle along the lower course of the Swakop, he would gladly have put them in the Topnaars' former territory. Jan Jonker, again, would have been glad to see them join his tribe and come to Windhoek, but he demanded the resignation of their chief, Hermanus van Wyk, and required them to place themselves entirely under his authority. Rehoboth, however, had been deserted since 1864 and there were a church and a mission house belonging to the Rhenish Mission, there was a good supply of water, and the veld was known to be good. The Basters, therefore, went and occupied Rehoboth and, as the tribes in the north and south were weary of war and were busy with peace negotiations, and as the country was suffering from a severe drought, nobody stopped them.

Hermanus van Wyk took part in the peace conference of Okahandja and there he met Willem Swartbooi, the chief of the Swartboois, who had formerly lived in Rehoboth, and asked him for permission for the Basters to continue to live there until the Swartboois required it again themselves. It was arranged that one horse a year should be given to the Swartboois in recognition of their rights. Thus the Basters' two years of wandering came to an end, and Heidmann stayed with them in Rehoboth as their missionary, teacher, doctor, lawyer, and their confidential adviser in all matters concerning the congregation and the tribe.

Some small fragments split off from the Basters of Die Tuin and Pella who crossed the Orange River towards the end of 1868, and found a refuge in other places. A few families actually remained behind at Warmbad, with the result that Warmbad still has a small Baster population to-day. When the trek went through the Bethanie territory, Klaas Swart and his following left it because he would not submit to the chief, Hermanus van Wyk. He stayed behind at Grootfontein South with about twenty families. Some of these families went to Rehoboth afterwards and others to Keetmanshoop. A few other families left the main body and went eastwards to where Dirk Filander had previously formed a settlement of Basters at Mier and Haas, beyond the boundary of South West Africa, and they joined him.

The half-castes in South West Africa may well be defined as the children of a native mother, who have no father, although they have a European progenitor. The Basters might then be defined, so as to distinguish them from the half-castes, in this way: Basters are the descendants of Hottentot mothers, who grew up under the influence of their European fathers, and then, after creating under the pressure of circumstances, an economic existence of their own and a tribal bond of their own, established a tribal home at Rehoboth to fit in with their tribal ideals. The surnames of the European ancestors have been faithfully adhered to through many generations, and family traditions are wonderfully reliable with some of the families and go quite far back. These traditions were collected with praiseworthy diligence by Dr. E. Fisher in his book *The Rehoboth Bastards*. The names of the principal families are as follows: Benz, Beukes, Bezuidenhout, van der Byl, Claasen, Cloete, Coetsee, Diergaart, Dragoener, Engelbrecht, de Klerk, Koopman, Morkel, Steenkamp, Mouton, Slenger, Swart, Vries, Vrey, and van Wyk.

Colonization, trade and business

The most outstanding feature of the period was Hugo Hahn's well thought out plan to establish a European colony, for the purpose of carrying on handicraft and business at Otjimbingwe under the control of the mission. The Hereros were to be given the opportunity of actually seeing the life of a Christian congregation in a Christian colony; they were to learn the virtue of hard work from workers who were inspired by Christianity, and were to be trained by them. A business organization connected with the colony was to help the home society to bear the financial burden of all the missionary work in South West Africa. The plan was an excellent one and the idea a noble one; it was difficult to carry it out, and its success was doubtful. After a great deal of opposition the missionary administration gave its consent. When Hahn returned from Germany in 1864, he brought the first colonists out with him. Those amongst them who deserve special mention are Edward Haelbich, and Wilhelm Redecker, who came a little later. Andersson was anxious to leave Otjimbingwe and to go and live at Walfish Bay. Hahn purchased all his ground and buildings for £600, and so came into possession of a large dwelling-house, a blacksmith's shop, a wagon-building shop, a storehouse, a butcher's shop, and several small dwelling-houses. There now arose a hammering and a sawing, a planing and a filing, such as the place had never seen before. The Hereros were astonished—but, as they could live upon sour milk and without effort of any kind, all this work had no practical effect upon them. Trade was brisk. A pound of ostrich feathers still cost £45, and there were still large numbers of ostriches. The plans that were made were very far-reaching. It was thought that Walfish Bay would certainly develop into a place of export for Herero cattle to St. Helena, that preserved beef in hermetically sealed boxes would open up a new market, and that the salt deposits near the sea would become a useful asset. There was, however, no money available for new undertakings of a commercial nature. Then the Wuppertal Trading Society was formed at Elberfeld and Barmen; it found the necessary money, sent out a commercial manager named Conrath, and took over the mission colony's trading concern at Otjimbingwe. One-half of the net profit was to be paid to the mission, and the other half was to go to the shareholders. Branches were established at Okahandja, Rehoboth, Warmbad, and other places. The store was to take the place of the travelling trader. If South West Africa had only not been South West Africa, an organization of this kind might well have gone ahead, but what happened to it was what happens to the plants which spring up quickly and come into full bloom overnight; they wither in the burning heat of the next day's sun. Ostrich feathers grew scarcer, and ivory disappeared altogether as an article of commerce. The days of mighty hunting in a country full of game were over. The natives were impoverished by long years of warfare and they were the only customers. The principles of the organization itself forbade any trade in liquor or weapons. At last the trading company died a natural death and there were no mourners at its funeral. Haelbich took over one part of the business establishment, while Redecker stayed on and founded his own business; Baumann joined the actual mission itself, Fanem went to Waterberg as a farmer and died there, and Felling went to the Transvaal. The administration of the mission had learnt not to go in for any schemes, however well intended they might be, when it had not at its disposal the power and means for carrying them out. Their work lay in another direction and their aims had nothing to do with making money. Krapohl, who was to conduct the business in Gobabis, wrote in 1864: 'Trading is in every respect the hardest occupation which any one can take up in this country, because it is bound up with trouble, care, annoyance, and unpleasantness, to an extent that could never be imagined under European conditions.'

The mission ought, therefore, not to be reproached with the failure of an undertaking which was so well intended. Experience cannot be acquired in a new country merely by theoretical reflection. It was only through actual trading that it was possible to discover what could and what could not be done. It was a pity about the sixty shares of a thousand thalers each.[1] If the money had been used for other purposes, it would probably have benefited South West Africa very much more.

Copper-mining too was unsuccessful. By 1863 already, it had been ascertained that the Pomona mine contained too little copper and silver to enable it to be worked profitably. Sinclair then made a treaty with the chief of Bethanie, granting him the mineral rights of his whole territory for ever. The period was afterwards reduced to forty years, and David Christian showed him a copper outcrop which had been kept secret until then. He worked it from 1864 onwards, but there, too, he had the same experience, but he did not give up the mine at once, because it was possible to carry it on in conjunction with trading.

The mining of copper in Hereroland was entirely suspended. New schemes were, however, made and, in 1866, Maharero gave the Walfish Bay Mining Company written permission to travel about in Hereroland with their wagons and their attendants, whenever and wherever they chose. He was guaranteed £1 for every wagon load of copper, the tax being payable in Walfish Bay. In consideration of this, Maharero had to provide wood for the smelting of the ore and grass and grazing for the trek oxen, free of charge.

The founding of the Augustineum

It is in the nature of missionary work that native assistants should be trained and appointed to help in the work of schools and congregations as soon as possible. Kleinschmidt and Hugo Hahn had this object in view from the very start and, when Kleinschmidt had made sufficient progress at Rehoboth, he took seven boys and gave them special instruction, with the idea of sending them to the teachers' seminary at Genadendal in the Cape Colony. The number increased to twelve afterwards and the parents were so taken with Kleinschmidt's idea that, when he went to stay at Otjimbingwe in 1861, they provided him with cows, from which their children could derive nourishment, and some of the parents even brought the money for the journey by sea to Capetown. Information came from Gobabis

[1] The total amount of the share capital was equivalent to a sum of between £15,000 and £20,000 in the money of the present day.—*Ed.*

to the effect that there were young people there who were anxious for further education, and the same was the position amongst the young people in Namaland. Sending these boys to Genadendal did not prove successful, for the change of climate, the alteration in their way of living, and the performance of a daily task, made a number of the scholars sickly, and some amongst them died. It was, however, absolutely necessary to have native assistants. The tribes were still partly nomads, for whom one had to have travelling teachers and, at the mission stations, the missionary, who had so much to do, could not possibly spend all his time in teaching children. The development of teaching capacity out of the native population itself was a problem which required urgently to be solved.

Here, too, Hugo Hahn brought a scheme to fruition. When he returned from Germany in 1864, he was certain of the money for establishing an institution for the training of native teachers. In many of his discourses, he had emphasized the urgent necessity for an undertaking of this kind, and had asked for money for that purpose. Then Princess Augusta of Lippe sent him 3,500 thalers. Prince Ernst von Schoeneburg and Princess Mathilde of Rudolstadt added their subscriptions to hers 'as the first bricks for the erection of a native training institute in Hereroland'. It was built in Otjimbingwe and opened in 1866. Two of Maharero's sons, Wilhelm and Samuel, were amongst the first pupils. Two of the Ovambo chief, Tjikongo's, sons entered the school the following year. The institute was called 'The Augustineum' in honour of Princess Augusta of Lippe. It was transferred to Okahandja in 1890 for reasons of convenience.

THE TEN YEARS OF PEACE: 1870 TO 1880

1. THE POLITICAL POSITION

Maharero and the Hereros

AFTER Maharero and his warriors had visited Tjamuaha's grave in 1869, the tribes went back to their distant dwelling-places and left the paramount chief and his subjects in and about Okahandja to settle matters with the Namas. A number of the important chiefs did not even attend the peace conference in 1870. The difficult times were past and the cattle were no longer in danger. Those of the chieftains who did not live on the border were devoting all their efforts to increasing their stock. Maharero, however, lived right on the border and so he had to take upon himself its entire protection. The other chiefs left, therefore, to him the regulation of all the political relationships amongst the allies, for they did not like this man at all, and, rich though he was, they regarded him as far too greedy for a paramount chief. There ought, long ago, to have been a proper fixing of the boundaries of their pasturage between the different chiefs, and there ought, long ago, to have been an agreement as to the rights of the paramount chief, and representatives of the other chiefs should have been appointed on his council, but nothing of the sort had been done. Maharero felt how necessary it was to keep up his connexions with other tribes and took steps to do so. Amongst his many wives, he married in 1871 one of Kambazembi's daughters, for Kambazembi's wealth and power were well worth courting. He likewise made a number of visits to different parts of the country, but these were seldom returned.

Maharero knew very well that, in times of crisis, he would have to depend entirely upon his own tribe, and acted accordingly. He sent his brothers and half-brothers and other reliable members of his family to the southern boundary of his territory. This was for the time being to the north of Windhoek, for the district of Windhoek had, of course, been given to Jan Jonker and his Afrikanders as a fief. The boundary line ended somewhere near Gobabis on the eastern side. The cattle posts on this boundary line served likewise as boundary posts, and his cattle-herds were given the duty of guarding the boundary also.

The newly established village of Otjizeva, with the veld belonging to it, which was between Windhoek and Okahandja, was treated differently. Otjizeva lay nearest to the Afrikander tribe and, if any cattle stealing was to take place, it was this boundary post which was most in danger. It is proof of Maharero's political good sense that he did not put his relatives in occupation of this post, but garrisoned it with Herero prisoners, who had been for very many years in Namaland and had suffered a great deal of ill treatment there; some of them could not even speak Herero, but they had certainly no affection for their oppressors. It was agreed at the peace of Okahandja that all the Herero prisoners in Namaland should be released, and Maharero settled in Otjizeva the majority of these tribesmen. Friedrich Eich was appointed as their missionary and, for the time being, Otjizeva gained considerable importance.

The number of Maharero's outposts increased from year to year. His herds of cattle grew larger and, when the rain stayed away, there was insufficient grazing for them. Then Maharero began to consider the position arising from the fact that the district of Windhoek had only been given to the Afrikanders 'on loan'. By that he understood that it was lent to them until such time as the loan was cancelled. He most certainly did not want to cancel the conditions of the peace treaty, for that would have undoubtedly caused trouble with the other Nama chiefs who had subscribed to the treaty. Jacobus Isaak, the quarrelsome and touchy chief of Berseba, did not allow himself to be played with. He had hardly been chosen as chief in 1872, when he went to the border to investigate the position, for Jan had complained to him about Maharero's want of consideration. It is true that he stated that he was only hunting at Seeis and paying Windhoek a visit. Maharero, however, was clever enough to realize that he was being watched. Jacobus Isaak was therefore compelled at Seeis to abandon his hunting trip, and Maharero sent him a message that, if he did not turn back immediately, he would have him killed like a dog. Open hostilities very nearly broke out again in consequence. The Nama tribes, however, were for the time being weary of war, and the chief of Berseba did not feel himself strong enough, even with the support of the Afrikanders, to try conclusions with Maharero. The matter was therefore arranged by means of rather angry negotiations in Okahandja, and Jacobus Isaak returned to Berseba in a towering rage.

The years became drier, while Maharero's cattle increased and grazing became scarcer. Whither was Maharero to go? To the north? There were the tribal territories of the people whose paramount chief he was, and their chiefs were not particularly fond of him. Would it not make their relationships still more strained, if he sent his enormous herds into the country between their cattle posts? That prospect did not please him. Had not the Herero cattle formerly grazed in Rehoboth and west of Rehoboth in the Kuiseb valley? According to law, this territory belonged, therefore, to the Hereros. Admittedly they had been driven out of it by Jonker Afrikander fifty years before, and since then no Herero cattle-herd had ventured as far as the Kuiseb. As, however, Jonker's successor, Jan, had been defeated by him in war, the former position was surely restored. In any case, why should he worry about the small Nama tribes who possessed so few cattle that they could hardly live on them. Did not old Jan Booi, of whom he was formerly afraid, occupy the western part of the country, practically without followers or stock? All that he had kept over from his raids was two cows! The Grootdodens, too, with their young chief were nothing to be afraid of. The Basters in Rehoboth had to thank him for their new settlement, for he had given the Swartboois, who were the owners of Rehoboth, a residence in Hereroland, and so Rehoboth really belonged to him. That the Basters acknowledged, too, by referring all their legal difficulties to Maharero and respecting his position as paramount chief. What could prevent him from placing his border posts in the Baster's territory, and on the Kuiseb?

Something then occurred which had the effect of confirming Maharero in this opinion. In 1876 W. C. Palgrave came to South West Africa as Government Commissioner, for the purpose of entering into an agreement with the Hereros and Namas for establishing a protectorate. Palgrave prepared a map, on which the boundaries between the two races were clearly laid down. This boundary line passed through Rehoboth to Gobabis. Maharero signed the treaty, and was very anxious indeed that Palgrave should have the boundary line marked with a plough, from the Namib desert as far as to Gobabis, for it seemed to him that a line on paper was too uncertain, and he was only convinced, with a great deal of difficulty, that a boundary line on a map was much more effective than one which was made with a plough. What had up to now merely been the object of Maharero's desires received, through this map, the impress of being his legal rights, and he was only too anxious to put these legal rights of his to good use. He, therefore, sent his best stock, consisting of horses, cattle, and sheep, to Gurumanas, on the western side of Rehoboth. This would surely arouse the covetousness of the Namas, who had lost everything through their own lack of foresight, and was certain to annoy them intensely. It was Jan Jonker, however, who would have to suffer most through this inconsiderate action.

Maharero and Jan Jonker

Jan Jonker had been forced to listen to some very unpleasant things at the peace conference. It had been said that the best thing to do with Jan Jonker was to hang him on the camel-thorn tree next to the church. It was only after a great deal of begging that he had induced Maharero to allow him to continue to live in Windhoek. The Hereros had been very reluctant indeed even to consider it, and they had only given their consent to Jan being granted Windhoek as a fief, in order that the conclusion of peace might not be utterly endangered. The chiefs from the south had purposely avoided raising the question of the boundary line, and Maharero had not brought it up either. He preferred that no boundary-line should be fixed. Jan Jonker then went back to Windhoek again with his Afrikanders. In order to show how peacefully inclined he was, he applied for a missionary, and Johann Schroeder, who had already worked in Berseba and Keetmanshoop since 1863, and therefore knew the country and its people well, was sent to him as such. Jan wanted to have a storekeeper as well. A trader named Babie was prepared to go and live there. Jan asked Maharero on the 20th April, 1871, whether he had anything against it and added: 'I shall do nothing without your permission, and so I expect an answer to my question.' He got his storekeeper, but he had to guarantee that he would protect him properly. Hereros came again and again to visit Windhoek. They got Jan to entertain them, made careful observations of everything that he was doing, and intended to do, and then gave Maharero careful reports, which were not always entirely unbiased. The behaviour of these visitors was sometimes of such a nature that Jan found little pleasure in having them as his guests. Jan complained to Maharero of their lack of consideration: 'What your people do is this: they come on to my werf and eat the meat I have roasted for them, and then they go back to you and tell tales about me. My people never go to your werf, but yours are always coming to mine, and they speak badly of me and make charges against me and my people.' It may well be that Herero boastfulness led them to utter many an impudent threat; it is even possible that some of them let the cat out of Maharero's bag for, as early as 1871, Jan wrote to Maharero: 'Hereros who come here tell us that we ought to pull out our dagga and tobacco, and leave this place and go to Rehoboth.' The worst thing of all for Jan was, however, that he was on several occasions prevented from going on a hunting trip which he had planned, and it was from hunting that he and all his followers had to derive a considerable part of their sustenance, for the Afrikanders' cattle were very few.

It would seem as if Jan had a certain amount of confidence in Maharero, and regarded the inconsiderate actions of the Hereros as excesses, for which he would take his subjects to task. He, therefore, decided to discuss his evil plight with Maharero, and went to Okahandja in January 1872. Maharero treated his neighbour and guest very courteously and even went so far as to promise him some cattle, with which he could buy a new wagon for himself. He received, however, only half of what had been promised, and the inconsiderate attitude of the Hereros towards the Afrikanders continued. Then Jan wrote a letter to all the Nama chiefs, laying his hopeless position before them and asking them to come to Windhoek on the 15th May, 1872, to 'ratify the peace', i.e. to revise the peace treaty of Okahandja. The latter knew very well that a revision could only be effected by force, and they had no ammunition. The chief of Bethanie, moreover, had no desire at all to get mixed up with Jan's troubles, and the chief of Warmbad was in the pay and under the control of the Cape Government. The Witboois had a scheme of their own, which was to leave Gibeon and settle in some northern paradise. It was the chief of Berseba who showed, in keeping with his fiery temperament, most inclination to force the Hereros to be moderate, the more so because of the very unpleasant experience he had had with them the Christmas before. For these reasons no conference of chiefs took place, but Maharero heard all sorts of strange rumours to the effect that the Namas were coming, and inquired of Jan if there was any truth in them. The latter answered:

'We all know that, if the chiefs of the south come, they will come to ratify the peace which they concluded. The first peace was really only an armistice and not a proper peace. If the first peace had been a proper peace, then I should not be in the position of being continually driven back from the hunting-grounds. The chiefs have therefore realized that a real peace is still to be made, and they have agreed to come back again. I will advise you when they are coming, for I am certain that they will come. I am not thinking, however, of going to war, dear friend.'

The revision of the treaty never came to pass, and the order preventing Jan from hunting, which had in the meantime been extended to apply to the remaining Nama tribes, remained in full force and effect. The Orlams of Gobabis suffered under it, too, and Kido Witbooi saw that it closed against him the door to the new country which he wished to seek. Old as he was, he took the long journey to Maharero, in order to put in a good word for his fellow tribesmen in Gobabis and to ask that the eastern hunting-grounds should be opened to them. Kido returned, and no one found out from him what Maharero had said. In any case, no relief was given. It did not help one iota that the missionary Diehl in Okahandja pleaded Jan's cause. Maharero said to him: 'The cattle posts which I have established on the border to graze our former boundaries are my feelers. I do not trust the Namas at all. So far as I am concerned I want to live in peace, but I am always on my guard. If any one touches my posts in the border lands I know what I shall do.'

A letter which Jan wrote to Maharero on the 3rd January, 1874, read like the cry of one fighting for his life, and it is worth while preserving it, word for word as it was written:

'My brother Chief Maharero,

I made peace with the intention of leading a quiet life, going my own way, going out hunting, digging tubers in the veld, and bringing up my children in a godly fashion, and I took a missionary to stay with me. Since the conclusion of peace, however, things have happened which have caused friction between us, and of these you are not ignorant because I have brought them to your notice, so I will not mention them again. I hope that you have power over your own subjects and can tell them to do things, or not to do things, and that they will do as you tell them, although they are heathens.

There has, however, been no improvement up to this fourth year. The more complaints I bring you, the more difficult things are made for me, and the more I ask you for freedom, the more do I find that all the roads are closed to me. At last it has come to this that I have no idea at all where I can go to.

Now I want you to understand clearly what I think and want to say: You know from your own experience that a bird becomes tame when it is prevented from flying, and the same is the position with a man when he is treated kindly, for then he becomes at ease. If you can tell me what the end of all this is to be, and how I can get out of this position to my satisfaction, without your calling your people back, then I shall be satisfied, but if you do not know what to do yourself, and only withdraw them slightly, I cannot tell you what I shall do and what the end of the whole matter is to be.

You once told me that you wanted to act and live in the way that the Governor had advised you. Now I ask you what did he say; did he tell you that you need not bother yourself with Jan's troubles, but were to let him suffer and hem him in, and that, if he resisted in any way, you were to get up and beat him for it? I do not believe that he said anything of the sort. I understand that the law which we established by our peace treaty was that a woman should be able to go from the Colony to Ovamboland, quite alone with a stick in her hand, without being molested; that is what I understood.

But these things cannot be left as they are—that is no use at all. Tell me now whether you have anything against me for, if you are satisfied with me, then I think that your subjects would likewise be satisfied with me, but let me tell you that you are the responsible party, for where the leader goes his subjects follow. Now please tell me what I am to do for a living. For Heaven's sake allow me to live.

With this I close my letter;

With kind regards, I remain,

Your brother,

Chief J. Jan Afrikander.'

Maharero received the letter, acquainted himself with the contents, and left it for safe keeping with the rest of his letters in the mission house at Okahandja, but he did not alter one whit in his attitude towards Jan. The Herero cattle grazed the veld of Windhoek, and Maharero excused himself by saying that he could not get sufficient water for his cattle elsewhere. When the veld was absolutely bare, however, the cattle trekked away, and it became perfectly plain that sufficient water was to be found for them elsewhere. Jan went to Warmbad on the Orange River to try and get the Bondelswarts and his relations in Blydeverwacht to help him, but that brought him no relief and had the effect of bringing him under suspicion. Then two of the Nama chiefs, upon whose support he was relying, died. Kido Witbooi died at Gibeon on the 31st December, 1875, in his ninety-fourth year, and his son Moses, who was already sixty-eight years of age, succeeded him as chief. On the 21st May, 1877, the chief, Barnabas, died of tuberculosis at Hoachanas and, on the 4th November of the same year, his son Petrus was solemnly installed as his successor. The old tribal council resigned and a new one was elected. Maharero sent the young chief a letter congratulating him, and impressed upon the keepers of his cattle posts that they should conduct themselves decently in the territory of the Red Nation.

CHARLES JOHN ANDERSSON

Pioneer, Explorer and Gentleman Adventurer. Hereroland
Ovamboland and Ngamiland. 1850–1867

All honour to his name

They obeyed his instructions and always asked courteously for permission to water their cattle, whenever they were forced by circumstances to do so there.

Jan now turned to Moses Witbooi and asked for his help against the Hereros, but Moses Witbooi told him that it was only the triple alliance (Gibeon, Berseba, and Bethanie), which could deal with the position, and that Gibeon had no right to march against the Hereros by itself.

The position of the Afrikanders was truly a very unenviable one. They, who had formerly lived in luxury as the rulers of the country, had hardly any property left, and the few cattle which they still possessed could not find anything to eat in the neighbourhood of Windhoek. The miserable food of the Bergdamas, such as berries and roots, with the addition of the produce of their gardens in Klein Windhoek, formed their principal food. They had to give up the usual Nama custom of going on long hunting expeditions every year, and coming back with large quantities of dried meat, for, on six occasions, they were prevented by the Hereros from carrying out their plans.

The Hereros' inconsiderate conduct towards the Afrikanders often took other forms, which, under other circumstances, would have led to an immediate outbreak of war. In the last year of peace, the missionary Traugott Richter was murdered in Windhoek by the Hereros. Bergdamas, who were Jan's servants, were beaten without mercy by Maharero's herdsmen and, when Jan complained to Maharero about it, the offenders were not even brought before the tribal court. One can well understand Jan's cry for help to the chief of Berseba: 'Come quickly! Let us rise and come to the help of our country before the evil gets too great, for the Hereros have killed more than 100 people.'

Maharero, Jan Jonker, and the Basters

The Basters had lived in Chamis until the conclusion of peace at Okahandja, and their stock had grazed in the upper Fish River valley and along the Kuiseb. Hermanus van Wyk was the leader of the tribe and Piet Beukes was an influential man on the council of the elders. Rooibank, Sesfontein in the Kaokoveld, and other places came under consideration as permanent homes. Finally, they decided upon Rehoboth, which had stood empty since the Swartboois had left it.

The Red Nation regarded it as a matter of course that Rehoboth belonged to them after the Swartboois left. The Swartboois, however, claimed that their former village and pasture-lands still remained their property. Maharero based his claim to it on the grounds that he had given Ameib to the Swartboois, and that, as long as they remained in his country, Rehoboth naturally belonged to him. Jan Jonker based his claim on the right of conquest. He said that he had conquered the Swartboois in warfare and driven them out. What they took with them belonged to them according to the laws of war, but what they had left behind, and had thus fallen into his hands, belonged to him by the laws of war. Rehoboth had fallen into his hands and consequently it belonged to him.

Hermanus van Wyk made up his mind to bring his tribe's wishes regarding Rehoboth under discussion at the peace conference at Okahandja, and he asked Hahn for his support. Hahn, however, was not successful in getting anything out of Maharero. Jan Jonker and the other Nama chiefs, too, were prejudiced against the Basters. Hahn then advised Hermanus van Wyk to apply to Abraham Swartbooi, and he came to a settlement with him very quickly. Abraham handed Rehoboth over to the Basters until he himself wanted to reoccupy it, and Hermanus had to pay a horse a year in recognition of his rights. Hermanus van Wyk now acquainted the chief of the Red Nation with the arrangement. He raised no difficulties and communicated the result of the private agreement to the other chiefs, who fell in with the scheme as well. Hermanus then presented Abraham Swartbooi and Maharero each with a horse, and as he had no more with him, he promised one to Aponda, the chief of the Mbanderus, and others to Jan and the chief of the Red Nation. These promises were speedily fulfilled, and the Basters entered into occupation of Rehoboth. A document dealing with the transfer of the territory was not drawn up. Abraham Swartbooi actually asked Hermanus to draw up an agreement and offered to sign it, but the matter remained where it was.

As Jan's life in Windhoek began to get impossible, he thought of Rehoboth as he felt that it would be better for him if he got a little farther away from the Hereros. He therefore made a request that the Basters should be forced to leave 'his property' and, when he did not succeed, he asked Abraham Swartbooi to come and visit him at Rehoboth. Maharero heard about it and at once asked him what he wanted to discuss at Rehoboth with Abraham Swartbooi, who lived in his country. Jan replied as follows on the 17th February, 1872:

'I have sent for Abraham Swartbooi because of the position which has arisen between the three of us (Hermanus, Jan, and Abraham), for the district of Rehoboth was not given to Hermanus van Wyk as his property, but he is very pleased with the place and he does not want to leave it. It is for this reason that I have summoned Abraham, and not with the object of making war against you.'

Hermanus van Wyk, however, insisted on his rights and wrote to Maharero as follows: 'I advise you that I intend coming to see you, in order to find out who is entitled to make laws in this country besides you.' It speaks for itself that Maharero would not acknowledge that either Jan, or his guest Abraham Swartbooi, had any right of this kind, and Hermanus acted accordingly. When he was in difficulties he always turned immediately to his protector, Maharero. We shall see later how this alliance with the Hereros was regarded by the Namas, and more especially by Jan, as treachery, and was treated accordingly. When the Basters began to develop the place, and necessity compelled them to open the water-supply by blasting, and they saw that they were faced with a considerable outlay, they went to the Swartboois once more and offered to buy it, but the Swartboois would not hear of selling it. Thus the yearly dispatch of a horse in recognition of the Swartboois' rights continued.

It was not long before the question of the ownership of Rehoboth was brought up from two different directions. Erikson of Omaruru went to the Swartboois and offered them 120 horses and five new wagons for Ameib. Of course they had no right, as guests in the Herero territory, to sell Ameib, but it was called a purchase price, and directly the Basters heard of it they went and offered the same price for Rehoboth. Hermanus and Abraham came to an agreement that Rehoboth was to be sold to no one except the Basters. For the time being matters were to remain unchanged but, if circumstances made it necessary that their agreement should be brought into effect, the purchase price of Rehoboth would be 120 horses and five wagons. The agreement was reduced to writing and signed. By doing this, the Basters recognized the Swartboois as the owners of Rehoboth. Even if this agreement had been entered into without causing trouble, and the question of the ownership of Rehoboth had been answered without any protest from the other chiefs, there were Europeans who were gravely dissatisfied with this turn of affairs. The circumstances were as follows:

'Several traders had settled at Rehoboth. They had not bought the ground on which they had erected their houses; it had been placed at their disposal by the Baster council in accordance with the usual custom of the country. As burghers of Rehoboth, the European merchants had to pay £25 a year for every shop and, in addition, the very much smaller sum which every burgher had to pay by way of local taxation. One of the Europeans was the storekeeper and contractor, Dr. Theophilus Hahn, who must not be confused with the missionary, Dr. Hugo Hahn. He and his business associate Steyn applied to the Baster council at its sitting on 12th January, 1876, for the reduction of the taxes to £10 12s. a year and, besides this, they made a proposal that, in court cases between Basters and Europeans, the court should consist of one-half Europeans and not, as hitherto, solely of Basters. An angry altercation ensued and it ended with Dr. Hahn and Steyn being ordered to leave the place. The latter had not waited for the end of the council session, but had walked out in a rage. Then the following council resolution was sent to them:

"I write to ask you who gave you the right to dig wells here and build houses and make dams? From to-day you are forbidden to turn another spadeful of earth and to place one stone more upon another. I tell you further that, from to-day, you must look for some place to live in other than Rehoboth. You will not submit to my authority, so I cannot allow you to stay. I mean both of you, Hahn and Steyn. For you, Hahn, want to summon a hundred Boers into the district of Rehoboth. From me, Hermanus van Wyk, Captain, in the presence of my council."

Upon receipt of this order of ejectment, Hahn wrote at once to the chief of the Red Nation, to whom Rehoboth had formerly belonged, recognizing him as the owner of Rehoboth, and asking him for permission to stay there. Hermanus van Wyk, however, wrote letters of protest to all the Nama chiefs in order to get them to recognize his right of ownership. As time went on the storm subsided. No action was taken by any of the parties to whom an appeal had been made.'

The proximity of the Bergdamas, the trespassing of Herero cattle, and the Afrikanders in Windhoek, were matters of far greater consequence to the Basters than was unpleasantness with the Europeans. From the very beginning, cattle were lost every now and again owing to thefts by the Bergdamas. Very little fuss was made about it, but Jan Jonker was requested to prohibit encroachments of this kind, for the Bergdamas living in the Aus Mountains and along the Kuiseb were under Jan Jonker's authority. These thefts increased, however, to an alarming extent in the years 1877 and 1878. The Basters hesitated to take up arms against the Bergdamas, as they did not wish to infringe upon Jan's rights of jurisdiction. When, however, a Bergdama leader called Naiseb formed a robber band, which went in for stock theft on a large scale, the Basters captured him and his band and brought them before Jan's court at Windhoek. There the Basters were very astonished to see that Jan's assurances were not followed by action of any kind, and they began to get suspicious. The real position was that Jan was trying, through the medium of his Bergdamas, to drive the Basters out of Rehoboth, with the idea of getting possession of the place for himself. Petrus Swartbooi, the energetic assistant chief of the Swartboois in Ameib, was summoned, so that he might personally make it perfectly clear that the Basters were living at Rehoboth with his permission. He came on the scene, was exceedingly cautious, and went back to Ameib without doing anything. The stealing became very much worse and the Hereros took a hand in the game. It was not that Maharero had himself anything to do with stealing stock from the Basters, but the advance of his posts to Gurumanas was a source of continual danger. The herdsmen took a few cattle at different places and times, and they knew how to hide them so well that the Basters could never find them again,—and Maharero closed his eyes to it. The old Nama tribes of northern Namaland began to grow envious. If other people were going to grow rich on the Basters' stock, they were going to have a share too. Topnaars and Bergdamas concealed themselves in the Gansberg and stole and slaughtered everything they could get hold of, and when they saw that the Basters whom they had despoiled pursued them on horseback, they made it their special business to take their horses away. In quite a short time Rehoboth lost twenty horses, which were slaughtered and eaten by the Topnaars. And so the 'ten years of peace' came to an end which found the Basters in absolute despair. Jonker was trying to annoy them so as to compel them to leave; Maharero's herdsmen were watering their cattle at the wells the Basters had sunk as if they belonged to them, were stealing their stock and were very impudent when search was made for missing animals. Bergdama and Nama hordes carried off entire herds and Maharero would not move in the matter, while the chiefs of the triple alliance would not worry their heads about the sorely-tried Basters. How was a peace of this kind to end?

The Orlams of Gobabis

In Amraal's time there had existed amongst the Orlams of Gobabis, who were related to the Orlams of Berseba, an unruly war party, which had caused him much worry and trouble. After his death they got the upper hand entirely. After the missionary, Weber, had given up his work in Gobabis as hopeless in 1865, the missionary, Judt, made a further attempt, during the years 1876 to 1880, to christianize the tribe. Most of them knew the difference between good and evil very well, but the propensity towards evil was overpowering. This incident will serve as an illustration: Judt had a few cattle and suspected that his milk was being stolen at night. One Sunday morning he got up before daybreak and actually found a man stealing milk in his cattle kraal, but, when he saw that he was discovered, he managed to get away. Judt threw a stone at him but did not hit him, and then he went and laid a charge with the chief against the offender. The former held a court and investigated the matter and the judgment was as follows: 'The missionary has laid himself open to punishment, for he has thrown a stone on a Sunday and that is a desecration of the Sabbath according to what he has taught us himself, and it is proper for us to judge Europeans according to European law.'

Alcohol was to no small extent to blame for their lapse into barbarism, for traders, who had no conscience, brought it in in large quantities with the idea of getting rich; but they very often suffered heavy losses. Unfortunately, other traders had to suffer with them. The sum of £5 had to be paid for every wagon, which went through the territory of Gobabis in the direction of Lake Ngami, as a toll for free passage, water, and grazing. No exemption was given to traders who could prove that they had already obtained a trading licence from Maharero. The inhabitants of Gobabis strengthened their ranks with Griquas and Zulus, who were of the same mind as themselves, and became highway robbers, so that, in the end, traders did not dare to enter their territory. Nevertheless, they were anxious to have a shop in Gobabis. They invited Redecker of Otjimbingwe to open one there. Redecker went to them, but stopped first in Witvlei and, as it was Sunday and he found some Christians there, he held a simple service. Directly they heard about this in Gobabis, they decided that they would rather not have a storekeeper in the place at all than have one who wanted to live according to Christian principles.

Axel Erikson sent his trader, Ferry, out from Omaruru with goods to the value of £500. He came back with ostrich feathers worth £150. The goods which had not been paid for he had been forced to leave behind at Gobabis. He had received a promise that, if he would come back with a similar load, he would receive payment in full for all his goods. Erikson hoped to get his money if he complied with the condition, so he sent Ferry again with another load. When he arrived at Gobabis, he found that they had neither ostrich feathers nor ivory, so he wanted to go back again. The people of Gobabis would not allow that, however, and they insisted that all the goods should be given them on credit, to which Ferry would not agree. They then took two-thirds of the goods he had brought with him by force, until finally he took up his position on the seat of his wagon, with his knife in his hand, and threatened to kill anybody who touched anything more. It was only then that they allowed Ferry to leave with the rest of his wares. Erikson estimated his loss at £800. The same thing happened to the trader, Kleinghardt, of Rehoboth and many others. A technical expression was invented to denote the robbing of a trader; in Gobabis they talked about 'off-loading wagons'. Of course, when these robberies took place, fierce quarrels often arose, and it is on record that some traders, who used strong language on these occasions, were sentenced by the tribal court to a whipping for 'improper conduct and insulting language' and the sentence was carried out over the trader's wagon pole. An old account tells how one trader was fastened with riems underneath his wagon until it had been 'off-loaded', and he was only released when all his goods had been carried away.

Maharero knew very well what was going on in Gobabis. He instructed Kanagati, who was a valiant fighting man and a large cattle owner, to trek to Witvlei with his cattle, and he made the Mbanderu chief, Kahimemua, take up a position quite close to Gobabis. How were the Orlams of Gobabis to stay there if all the veld round about was destroyed by the Herero cattle? The inhabitants of the place were exceedingly annoyed at Maharero's unfriendly action, but they did not dare to oppose it actively. When Kahimemua had placed his posts right up against Gobabis, he sent a message to the chief saying: 'Here are my oxen and cows. Come and take them, and buy powder and shot with them.' Neither he, nor any of his subjects, dared to lay hands on the Herero cattle, but many of the families went with all they possessed to the southern part of the country.

2. THE TREK-BOERS

The trekking about of the Transvaal Boers, who were present in
the far east of South West Africa between 1870 and 1880, cannot be
ignored in this story, for exaggerated rumours about them created
anxiety in everybody's minds, and they caused decisions to be taken
and things to be done, which were to have a far-reaching importance
for the history of South West Africa. It is most certainly no part of
our task to write an account of the wanderings, successes and misfortunes, trials and sufferings of these men and women, who left their
old home to seek a new one in the unknown country of the distant
west. All that should be recorded here is as much as is necessary to
elucidate the history of South West Africa. A short survey of this
peculiar national characteristic will serve as an introduction.

Andries Pretorius had raised the Republican flag in Natal in 1839,
but was forced to trek again when Natal became British territory.
On the other side of the Drakensberg, several families of his fellow
Boers were living in independence and freedom. He and his followers
went to visit them, and finally settled to the north of the Vaal River.
The battle of Boomplaats caused him and his followers to join up
with his other fellow countrymen. Andries Pretorius died and, in
1856, his son, Martinus Wessels Pretorius, was elected as President
of the newly founded Boer Republic. His successor was Theodore
Frederick Burgers. Burgers did not possess the confidence and support of many of the more conservative Boers, who were annoyed,
not so much at the way in which he carried out his duties as President, as by the fact that he gave up his religion. A man who had
formerly been a minister, and then became a Freemason and a free-
thinker, was not a man whom they could trust. Rumours broke out
of a threatened intervention by the British Government. Both these
things had the effect of influencing many freedom-loving and God-
fearing farmers to go on trek and look for a more ideal home. On the
wide surface of Africa there must surely be a place for them; no one
knew where it was, so they must go and look for it.

On the 20th May, 1874, Gert Alberts' tent-wagon stood ready for
the road on his farm near Pretoria. Three other families joined him
on the journey to the north. By the following year he had twelve
families with him. They formed themselves into an organized community and chose Gert Alberts as their commandant. If anybody
wanted to join the trek, he had to submit to its laws. Alberts took

his people in small groups to Lake Ngami. It was impossible for them all to trek together because of the waterless Kalahari, the 'Thirstland', with its occasional water-holes, where there were water and grazing for but few trek oxen at a time. On the 28th January, 1876, the trek from Lake Ngami arrived in Rietfontein, on the edge of the Kalahari and on the borders of South West Africa. As the water-supply in Rietfontein was good and there was sufficient grazing, Alberts decided to stay there for a time. To which of the chiefs was he to go in order to get grazing rights and remain there without being interfered with?

A hundred years before the whole of the eastern part of South West Africa had been the undisputed territory of the Mbanderu people. Then the Namas had thrust their way into it while hunting, and the Orlams, who came with them, had oppressed and enslaved the Mbanderus, settled in Gobabis, and taken possession of the whole of the east. The Mbanderus had then, during the Herero war of freedom, thrown off the Orlam yoke and regained their freedom, and had then gone to Hereroland with all their possessions. Maharero, however, claimed the ownership of Gobabis and Rietfontein, basing it on the peace of Okahandja in 1870. Aponda recognized him as the paramount chief, who had made peace with the Namas on behalf of all the other chiefs. Maharero's idea was that, in the same way as Jonker had received Windhoek from him as a fief, Andries Lambert too, the chief of Gobabis and Rietfontein, held his land under similar tenure, and so had no right of free disposal over his tribal territory.

Gert Alberts knew nothing about these confused ideas as to ownership, and he went to Andries Lambert to ask him whether he would allow him to stay temporarily in Rietfontein. Neighbours of this kind were very welcome to Lambert. The Orlams of Gobabis had become entirely impoverished through adverse economic conditions, and they promised themselves all kinds of advantages from the European settlers in Rietfontein. Andries Lambert, therefore, wrote Alberts a letter on the 17th April, 1876, in which he gave him the right of staying at Rietfontein, and of using the water and the grazing, and of hunting as much as he chose. As, however, he did not feel quite sure, and did not know what the Cape Government would have to say if he took British subjects into his territory, he wrote the same day to the Governor of the Cape Colony, explaining to him the motives that had actuated him in giving the Trek-Boers a place in which to stay. He said that the Orlams at Gobabis could learn from the Boers how to manage their affairs better, and the Boers could likewise protect them against their foes, who had almost exterminated his people, besides which the Boers were known to him as a peace-loving people. As the Commissioner of the Cape Government, Palgrave, was still in the country, Andries Lambert forwarded his letter through him.

When Maharero got to learn of the arbitrary way in which the Orlams in Gobabis were acting, he at once sent a threatening letter to Andries Lambert, instructing him to see that Alberts left his territory, and he told him that in case he disobeyed the order he would attack him. Alberts got to know of this letter and went to Maharero and assured him that he would do nothing without his permission, and that he had no intention of buying land, and he asked his consent to his staying in the country for the time being.

Gert Alberts stayed at Rietfontein for some time, and was not bothered by anybody. On the 16th May, 1877, he received a call for help from some other Trek-Boers which caused him to leave Rietfontein. A man named Louw du Plessis had left the Crocodile River on the 28th May, 1875, and had likewise trekked in a northerly direction. Jan Greyling had gone with him as leader, and the others with him were Gert Meyer, Diederik Prinsloo, and Lukas van Rensburg. They had not done as Gert Alberts had done, but had tried to cross the broad waterless plains in one party with all their wagons and cattle, with the result that they had come to utter disaster. One hundred and twenty-eight wagons were standing in 'Thirstland' and the people and animals were suffering dreadfully. To add to their misery, the tsetse fly was doing great damage amongst the trek oxen and many of the people had fallen victims to malaria. Gert Alberts, who had been asked to send 200 trek oxen, went with them to Lake Ngami. There Lukas van Rensburg formed a separate trek with which he reached the Okavango, and his party was almost entirely wiped out by fever in the marshes of the Okavango Delta. Gert Alberts went to look for them in January 1878, and became their helper and saviour. The few that were left joined him and the election of a new leader was held, when Botha was chosen as commandant. He led the trek through Kuring-Kuru to the Etosha Pan. From there scouts were sent into the Kaokoveld, for the Commissioner, Palgrave, had opposed their settling in South West Africa and had advised them to go and settle in the Kaokoveld. We shall see in the next chapter his reasons for giving this advice. The scouts came back with satisfactory information, and the trek passed successfully through rather waterless territory. The wanderers came to rest at the fine springs at Otjitunduua, Ombombo, and Kaoko-Otavi. They erected some quite good stone buildings in close proximity to the water, laid out gardens, and went elephant hunting. The ruins of these buildings are still there to-day.

Erikson of Omaruru came into contact with the Trek-Boers. Their hapless condition moved him to get the Cape press to appeal to the public to assist them. Within a short time the sum of £3,000 was collected and the Government decided to send the two Government ships, *Swallow* and *Carolina*, loaded with foodstuffs, ammunition, and clothing, and to land their cargoes in some northerly bay, as near as possible to the place where the new inhabitants of the Kaokoveld were living. As Maharero had ceded the Kaokoveld by treaty to the Cape Government, it intended to settle the Boers there permanently, and Palgrave went with the ships to the north. They could not, however, find a landing-place high up on the coast of the Kaokoveld, so they had to turn back and land their cargoes at Walfish Bay. All those who needed help were then advised, and they came and fetched the goods from Walfish Bay in their own or hired wagons. After the Boers had been in the Kaokoveld for two years, they found that it was not suitable for permanent settlement. Good grazing must go side by side with a good water-supply, and, owing to its scanty rainfall, there was no good grazing in the Kaokoveld. Then Willem Jordaan drew their attention to southern Angola. Jordaan was well known to them and as a trader, hunter, and a man who knew the land thoroughly, he possessed considerable influence with Europeans and natives both in South West Africa and beyond its borders. He could speak Dutch, English, and French and he had stayed in various places. He was acquainted with the northern part of South West Africa, had been in Ovamboland, and had travelled through South Angola, where he had a number of friends. He knew, too, that the Portuguese Government had been fighting the native races for the last 400 years, and that they were not unwilling to strengthen their position by establishing a European colony somewhere in Humpata. Jordaan was authorized to enter into negotiations with the Portuguese Government, and these proved to be successful. The Trek-Boers crossed the Kunene and Humpata became their new home for two generations. The first wagons reached it on the 4th January, 1881, and on the 23rd November, 1882, the immigrants were naturalized as Portuguese subjects.

Jordaan undertook to provide the inhabitants of Humpata with

trade goods. It was not very long before a number of them proved
to be dissatisfied with their new home. Jordaan proposed to them
that they should accompany him to a district in the north of South
West Africa, where the country was to their liking. He was thinking
of the district comprising the Waterberg, Otavi, and Grootfontein
North. The Waterberg was unquestionably part of Maharero's territory, for Kambazembi, Maharero's father-in-law, was in occupation
of it. Nobody quite knew who the owner of Grootfontein and Otavi
was. Maharero's claim was that the whole country belonged to him
and, on the principle that wherever Herero cattle had grazed was
to be regarded as Herero territory, he was right. Kambonde of Ondonga, however, likewise claimed that he was the chief of this
area, on the ground that it was the Ovambos who had opposed and
slaughtered the Katauu when they invaded this territory, and they
were very much averse to having any Hereros at the place where
they got valuable supplies of copper ore. An agreement was now
made between Kambonde and Jordaan, by which the latter was
given the district of Otavi and Grootfontein, and those of the Boers
who had returned from Angola entered into occupation of the Otavi
valley. This was the last thing that Maharero desired. He regarded
this action as an infringement of his ownership rights and of his right
to grant leave to settle. For some time he had been looking for a
man who could deal with the difficult positions which arose through
European immigration to his satisfaction. It was for this reason that
he had asked the Cape Government for an official and had been given
Palgrave. The latter had, however, left the country in 1880 without
having satisfied Maharero in this respect. Now he considered that
he had found the right man in Lewis. The two men knew each other
well. They had lived next to each other in Barmen where Lewis had
opened a shop. He spoke Herero and he had done Maharero many a
service when steps had to be taken which he did not want to discuss
with his missionaries. Now, when Maharero heard that Boers had
settled in the north, and intended to found the Republic of Uping-
tonia under Jordaan's auspices in a part of the country to which he
laid claim, he instructed Lewis to make suitable arrangements to prevent it, and he promised him the district of Otavi as a reward for his
services. Lewis went to Otavi when Jordaan was away. He represented to the Boers that it would be dangerous for them to stay there
against Maharero's will. They were immediately prepared to leave
Otavi and go to Grootfontein, where Green and Erikson had had

their head-quarters for their elephant hunting as early as 1860. The Hereros called the place 'Otjivanda Tjongue' which means 'The Leopard Flats', but the Bushmen and Saan had named it after the strong springs there 'Gei-ous' which means 'large spring'. It was afterwards called Grootfontein, which was a literal translation of the Bushman name.

Lewis was by no means certain of his case. It was quite possible that he had incurred Maharero's displeasure, because he had achieved nothing more than an arrangement whereby the Boers were to settle in Grootfontein for the time being. There was still Jordaan to be reckoned with, and Jordaan was in possession of a document, which stated that he was the legal owner of Otavi and Grootfontein, and this document was signed by several Europeans as witnesses. This might easily cause considerable trouble. Jordaan had gone to Angola again but he was expected back from there, and the veil of secrecy has never been lifted so as to reveal what happened then. All that can be told here is the stories that have come down from both the Europeans and the natives. Maharero is supposed to have sent a letter to Kambonde at Ondonga, containing a request that he should kill Jordaan. Kambonde, however, was afraid and he passed the instructions on to his brother Nehale. (When Maharero was questioned afterwards he denied strenuously that he had had anything to do with Jordaan's murder, and he took steps to see that Jordaan's possessions were fetched from Ovamboland and delivered to his heirs.)

Jordaan came back from Angola with his trek wagons and outspanned at Nehale's place. He spent the night there and Nehale came to the wagon the following morning under the pretext of selling him an elephant tusk. When he saw that Jordaan was having his morning wash and was unarmed, he shot him dead on the spot. His servant ran to the wagon to get a gun but he, too, was killed immediately. Nehale took Jordaan's goods for himself.

When the Boers of Grootfontein heard of Jordaan's death, they broke up. Some went back to Angola and others went back again to the Transvaal, while a few of them remained in Hereroland, where they found work as wagon-builders.

3. THE CAPE GOVERNMENT IN SOUTH WEST AFRICA

Introduction

The peace of Okahandja in 1870 had brought the country rest. The Namas were exhausted and impoverished and could, for the time being, not even think of going to war with the Hereros. The Hereros were war-weary and could think of nothing else but increasing the number of their cattle. Even the most powerful chiefs left Maharero to manage the political situation. They were not at all anxious to be mixed up in things which they did not understand. It was not because of their confidence in their paramount chief's wisdom that they had retired to their pasture lands, but because of the fact that Maharero was living on the boundary, and that, therefore, if any danger threatened them, he would be the first one whose enormous herds of cattle would suffer. They would, of course, be on their guard, so that they could run away promptly should misfortune overtake him. Vassals of this kind made the position of the guardian of the border a difficult one. He could not reckon on the active support of all his vassals. He was entirely dependent on his own tribe, which numbered about 20,000 people, in times of trouble. One could never know what Jan Jonker, the friend of his youth, was up to. It was likewise very plain to him that the Nama and Orlam tribes did not love him, and that the increasing number of his cattle offered them a perpetual temptation, while they were a constant source of danger to their owner. Experience had taught him that a letter from the Governor of the Cape Colony to the Nama chiefs, or an emissary like Piers, or an impressive message from a strong Government like that of the Cape, was worth a great deal to him. How would it be if he could in some manner make use of the European Government in Capetown?

These ideas were not in the nature of a new discovery. He knew well enough what many of the South African hunters and traders, who came regularly every year to Hereroland, wanted, for they made cautious suggestions to him of this kind: 'How safely you could live and how your cattle and your people would prosper, if you were under the protection of the Cape Government.' Were he to subject himself to a foreign Government, however, it appeared to him as if he might well be pushed to one side, and no one could prophesy where it would lead. Saul Sheppard, his private secretary, whom Captain Alexander had given a good education in an English military school, advised him that it was in his interest to approach the Cape Government. His missionaries, who were Maharero's confidential advisers, had had a number of differences with this Government and it was well known that they had always been prejudiced against it. It was necessary to act cautiously and Maharero did so. Experience had made him distrust everybody and act with the greatest caution. Disputes between individual Europeans and Hereros increased tremendously and so did disputes between the Europeans themselves, and Maharero was very often entirely at a loss how to satisfy the disputants, when they came to him for a decision. He felt that his decisions were no longer true judgments, in the real sense of the term, but were rather in the nature of diplomatic attempts to settle matters in such a way that he did not fall out with either of the parties. If he pronounced judgment against the Europeans, he offended the traders upon whom he was dependent for arms and ammunition, from whom he received considerable revenues and advantages, and through whom his whole people obtained the imported articles they required. If he fell out with the Hereros, he made enemies of his own subjects, and he heard it said that he was looking after the foreigners better than after his own people. How would it be if he could obtain a Government official to deal with all disputes between white and black, one who would support Maharero in his position as paramount chief, would handle the cases so skilfully that he would divert the antagonism of the parties to himself, and thereby relieve him of the trouble of dealing with matters which were too difficult for him? Then all sorts of rumours to the effect that people were attempting to come and settle in the country were current. It was said that more than a hundred Trek-Boers' wagons were on the march in the north and north-eastern parts, and that their owners intended to settle in Namaland or at the Waterberg. It was said that the Griquas, who were subject to the control of the Cape Government, were very anxious to escape from that control by emigrating to South West Africa. It was said that a whole host of diamond diggers were approaching with the idea of conquering South West Africa. Were not all these people subject in some way or other to the Cape Government? Would not an official of the Cape Government, if he were liberally paid, be better able to deal with these people than a chief, who had never been outside the country, would be able to do?

In 1872 Maharero ventured to take the first step in this direction. Like a careful diplomat, he caused a letter to be written to Sir Henry Barkly, the Governor of the Cape, in which he did not express his own ideas and intentions but merely asked if 'the illustrious British Government would give him some advice as to how to govern his poor land better; it might perhaps give his people a helping hand by offering them good advice and telling them what to do when the

Namas would not leave them in peace'. Together with this letter
Saul Sheppard sent a long screed to the Government, giving him an
account of his own career and also the history of the Herero nation.
It is probable that Maharero knew nothing about this letter, and it is
reasonable to suppose that Saul, by reason of his education and knowledge of the world, wanted to give the Governor a hint as to the way
in which he could best comply with Maharero's wishes.

Some notice was taken of Maharero's letter in Capetown. Krönlein, who was staying in Capetown, was given an audience with the
Governor on the 4th March, 1872, when the latter showed him
Maharero's letter and handed Saul Sheppard's memorandum over to
him. Interest in South West Africa was aroused and *The Argus* suggested, in a leading article, that the Governor should pay South West
Africa a visit in order to convince himself of the value of the west
coast to the Government. Sir Henry Barkly was, however, just as
careful as Maharero and, as a preliminary measure, he sent a letter
to the Nama chiefs, warning them to observe the peace treaty.

The rumours regarding the immigration of the Boers persisted.
There was proof enough that there was some truth in them. In the
previous chapter an account was given of what actually happened.
Maharero went to Omaruru and took his father-in-law Kambazembi
with him, for the purpose of talking matters over with Zeraua and
the Europeans living there. Seeing that his first letter to the Cape
Government had had no perceptible effect, he wanted to make a fresh
attempt, with the assistance of the other chiefs who were closely
related to him. The second letter, which he wrote on the 21st June,
1874, constituted a turning-point in the history of South West Africa.

The only answer, which Maharero had received to his first letter
to the Cape Government, was to the effect that the Government
hoped that his difficulties had solved themselves in the meantime,
and that there was at that time no officer available for Hereroland,
but that Maharero would be immediately advised if any prospect of
appointing one arose; meanwhile he was not to believe anybody who
gave out that he had been sent as a representative of the Cape
Government. The second letter, however, caused Sir Henry Barkly
to look round for somebody qualified to investigate the circumstances
in South West Africa, in the capacity of special Government Commissioner, and to make some concrete proposals. The best person to
do that would, of course, be a man who knew the country well, and
his choice fell upon the surgeon, W. C. Palgrave.

W. Coates Palgrave, the Special Commissioner

Palgrave was no stranger to South West Africa. During the 'sixties, he had made long journeys throughout the country, and had been amongst the Ovambo tribes prior to Hugo Hahn's second visit to Ovamboland in 1866. He had met some Portuguese emissaries there and had learned from their leader, Nunes da Malta, that the Portuguese had fixed the Kunene as the southern boundary of their territory. As an explorer, hunter, and trader he got to know both Hereroland and Namaland very well. On the 5th July, 1867, Maharero had furnished him with a document granting him the right of travelling everywhere throughout Hereroland for a period of twenty-one years. He and his companions were to be supplied with water, grazing, and wood, free of charge. For copper, or any mineral of that kind which he exported through Walfish Bay or any other port, Maharero was to receive £1 for each wagon-load. He had an unpleasant encounter with some of the Booi tribe in the veld north of Bethanie. They made a raid on him and he defended himself. The Namas spread the report that Palgrave shot several Boois in the fight, and took from them two horses, some riding oxen and a number of guns. For this reason Palgrave stood well with the Hereros, but his relations with the Namas were from the very start somewhat strained. In order to understand the history of his mission, it is most important to know the way in which he himself was regarded by the natives of South West Africa, and what really matters is the general opinion of the population regarding him, and not whether that opinion was justified.

W. C. Palgrave received his appointment as Special Commissioner for Hereroland and Namaland on the 16th March, 1876, and the instructions which were given him were of such a general nature as to afford him the greatest freedom of action. The principal thing which he was to impress upon the chiefs was that the protection of the Government which they had asked for would only be granted them, if all illegal acts and offences against Europeans and against each other stopped.

Palgrave arrived at Walfish Bay by the *Themis* on the 25th April, 1876. He found there five Europeans and two shops, one of which belonged to the Swedish firm of Erikson & Company, and the other to the Wuppertal Trading Company. For the last nine years the water of the Kuiseb had never reached the sea. There was no pasturage nearer the sea than Otjimbingwe.

Palgrave and the Hereros

Palgrave first rode through Hereroland to investigate matters and to learn what the Herero tribes thought about things. He passed through Tsaobis on his way to Otjimbingwe and Barmen, with the intention of getting into touch with Maharero at Okahandja. Here the traders Grendon, Cain, and Irons had decorated the town with flags in honour of his arrival, and Maharero's troops took up a position in the river-bed, and fired a salute as a greeting to the Government's envoy. The preliminary discussion with Maharero went off well, and Palgrave wanted to set out for the Waterberg to get into touch with Kambazembi. Maharero would not agree to that, so Palgrave altered his plans and went to Omaruru. He found the country between Oka-handja and Omaruru covered with enormous herds of cattle, and Omaruru itself was evidently the trading centre of northern Herero-land, from which Ovamboland, too, was provided with goods. He learnt here of the tremendous hold which the trade in arms and ammu-nition had taken on the country, for the traders had in stock 6,000 guns, 20 tons of gunpowder, and a corresponding supply of lead. The European population presented the Government Commissioner with an address. The old chief, Zeraua, was ill and Palgrave had to go to his hut. Zeraua asked him if anything had happened in conse-quence of the letter which had been written to the Governor in 1874, and Palgrave told him that he had been sent to South West Africa in consequence of it. No detailed discussion took place, for Zeraua said that he alone could not speak for all the Hereros, but that he would attend a conference at Okahandja and give his opinion, after he had discussed matters with Maharero and Aponda.

As Petrus Swartbooi, the assistant chief of the Swartboois at Ameib, had come to Omaruru to fetch the Commissioner, the latter went back with him to Ameib, where he discussed matters with the most influential representatives of the tribe. They assured him that the Swartbooi tribe would be very glad to get an English magistrate, but that they had not the means to support one. For the rest, they would write and tell Maharero how they regarded things. This they did a few days afterwards, and they advised their protector that the Swart-boois desired to be associated with any treaty the Hereros saw fit to make with the Cape Government.

As Palgrave had arranged with Maharero that a conference of all the Herero chiefs was to be held in Okahandja, he hurried back through Otjimbingwe and Barmen to the Herero head-quarters. The chiefs of Otjimbingwe and Omaruru were already there, but Kambazembi, and likewise Mureti, had sent their sons to represent them, while the chief of Omburo did not even trouble to send a message. This conference, which was attended by some eighty influential Hereros in addition to the chiefs, took place at Okahandja on the 29th and 30th July, and Brincker, the missionary from Barmen, acted as interpreter. After Palgrave had referred to the proposal which they had made to the Government in 1874, and had explained very clearly the purpose of his mission, he asked the chiefs to discuss the matter and to come to a decision. Maharero thought, however, that the business on hand required that all the chiefs should be present in person. It was of the utmost importance to send for Kambazembi and Mureti, who were then in the Omuramba Omatako, and Palgrave expressed his agreement. He had so many disputes between Europeans and natives to settle that an adjournment of the meeting caused him no inconvenience, and it gave him time to make a number of points, which were not thoroughly understood, clear to the natives.

The conference of the chiefs was then fixed for the 8th and 9th September, but Kambazembi was not present, and his sons had come back. Maharero expressed his wishes in the following sentence:

'I wish to tell the Governor that I want an official as the chief of my country, and that I desire that you (Palgrave) shall be appointed as that chief. The Portuguese are our enemies. The Boers are our enemies. The Griquas are our enemies. If I am to place myself under the Government's protection, I do not wish to have a stranger in the country and, because I know you, I would like to have you.'

Then particular questions were discussed. The Commissioner was given jurisdiction over Europeans and natives and a promise was made him that the chiefs would work hand in hand with him to support him in carrying out the law. Palgrave was of opinion that the official who was to be appointed should have jurisdiction over Europeans only, and that the administration of justice amongst the natives should remain in the hands of their chiefs, but Maharero would not agree with that. The granting of hunting rights was also to be placed under the official's control: 'I wish to leave this matter to you,' said Maharero, 'for people go out hunting and stay out until they have driven all the game away, and then we have to suffer for it.' Coming back to the question of judicial matters, Maharero thought it better that he should reserve to himself jurisdiction in cases between Hereros, and that only those cases which were between Europeans themselves, or between Europeans and natives, should be left to the Commissioner.

The payment of the officials presented a difficulty. Maharero proposed to present the Government with a large piece of territory, with which it could do just as it pleased, and the expenses of governing the country could be covered by the income of mines and the hiring out of grazing rights. Palgrave said that he was satisfied with the proposal and got Maharero to fix the boundaries of this Government Reserve. An agreement was then made that the boundary of the reserve should run from Walfish Bay to Otjimbingwe, and from there fifteen miles to the west of Omaruru as far north as the Kunene, and from the southern boundary of Ovamboland southwards, with a line running from west to east through the Waterberg to the farthest eastern point of Hereroland. According to this the following country was then to fall into the reserve: the whole of the Namib, the Kaokoveld, and the country north of the Waterberg with Otavi, Grootfontein, Tsumeb, and Outjo, to within a five days' journey of Ondonga. The extension of the southern boundary, however, was to run through Rehoboth to Gobabis. It appears that the author of this idea was the trader Lewis, who took part in the discussions. When Palgrave requested Maharero to state the boundaries of the proposed reserve, the latter got Lewis to fix the various boundary lines, and when he had done so, Maharero said, 'those are the boundaries; Mr. Lewis has pointed them out correctly, and he has fixed the boundaries of the country, which we wish to retain for our own use, just as accurately', meaning the southern boundary through Rehoboth and Gobabis to the far east. It is important to bear this in mind in order to understand things which happened later, for this boundary gave Maharero the apparent right of advancing his cattle posts up to the line which had been marked. This matter was referred to previously.

On the 9th September, an important document, through which Hereroland was placed under the protection of the Cape Government was executed.

The actual document was signed with the mark of Maharero the paramount chief, of Willem Zeraua, the chief of Otjimbingwe, and of Solomon Aponda, the Mbanderu chief of Barmen, while Maharero's eldest son and prospective successor, Wilhelm Maharero, was the only one who was able to sign his name to the document. The missionary, Brincker, the shopkeeper, Kleinschmidt, the Finnish missionary, Bjoerlund, the missionary, Hegner, and the traders, Lewis and Christian, signed as witnesses. Besides this the request bore the marks of fifty-four Hereros, some of whom belonged to the tribal council of different tribes, and some of whom had merely attended the conference as spectators.

The night the conference broke up, Palgrave prepared, with the assistance of Lewis and Cain, a map of the whole of Hereroland, which showed the boundaries of the Government Reserve and the Hereros' pasture lands, and he annexed this map to the record of the proposals made at the conference, and sent them both to his Government. The only respect in which the matter was not quite in order was that Maharero had overlooked the fact that the Namib did not belong to him, that the territory to the east of Walfish Bay was still recognized as the property of the Topnaars, that the Kuiseb district in Rehoboth and the whole of the high country round Rehoboth belonged to the Hereros only so far as their wishes went, but in actual fact not at all, and that he had never agreed upon any fixed boundary line in the course of his negotiations with the Nama chiefs.

Palgrave and the Namas

During the course of the negotiations in Okahandja, Palgrave received advice that 300 Boer families had gathered at the Crocodile River, and that a considerable portion of this trek was coming to South West Africa. At Maharero's request he wrote a letter to Alberts at Rietfontein, advising him that Rietfontein was Herero territory, and that any one who wanted to settle there must get Maharero's permission. Alberts replied that he was thinking of leaving. Palgrave sent another letter to the Trek-Boers, in which he said that the Government had a large reserve at its disposal. He invited them to settle in the Kaokoveld, and advised them of the conditions under which they could live there. We learnt previously that these people refused his proposal and directed their trek to Angola. One of the grounds for their doing so may have been that the Commissioner's letter stated that the Kaokoveld was under British rule, which was something for which they had no inclination.

After his work in Hereroland was finished for the time being, Palgrave left Okahandja on the 15th October, 1876, to go and visit the chiefs of Windhoek, Rehoboth, Berseba, and Warmbad. His plan was first of all to discuss matters with the chiefs individually, and then to convene a conference of all the chiefs, for the purpose of getting them to make a joint request to the Government for the establishment of a Protectorate, and the appointment of officials as resident magistrates in the principal places in the country. The conference was fixed for the 20th November at Berseba and all the chiefs were invited to it. The discussion with Jan Jonker and his council took place on the 23rd September, and it did not lead, at first, to their giving their consent to the new plans. It was only some weeks later that Jan wrote to Palgrave that he agreed to the appointment of a magistrate at Windhoek. His great trouble was the position regarding his pasture lands, and the quarrels with Maharero's herdsmen about it, and he wanted his boundaries clearly defined. In Okahandja, however, the boundary which had been laid down made provision that Windhoek should fall entirely within Hereroland. Palgrave had already spoken to Maharero, and pointed out that the foreign tribes who lived inside the fixed boundaries, i.e. the Afrikanders and Swartboois, ought to be allowed to stay there undisturbed, as long as they obeyed the laws of the country, but this was not at all to Maharero's liking, for he would gladly have seen Jan in some part of the country other than Windhoek. Palgrave therefore made provision that, under certain conditions, Jan should get compensation from the Government, in the shape of stock, and should be transferred to another part of the country. Any one who read the complaints against the Hereros which Jan put in his petition, would think that he had every right to expect a change in his wretched position, if he came under the protection of the Cape Government. His representation of the history of his tribe was, however, entirely one-sided, for it did not say a single word about the things which his father Jonker had done to the Hereros. Jan's initial hesitation was to be traced to the influence of a Griqua, named Piet Beukes, who was considered in Jan's council as a very clever and careful adviser; Jan had given him three farms near Aris in consideration for which he had to supply Jan with brandy. Piet Beukes was afraid that he would lose his influence directly the British Government took over the country. As Jacobus Isaak, the chief of Berseba, happened to be in Windhoek as well, it was decided that the chiefs' conference should be held at Berseba, and Palgrave left for Rehoboth. He arrived at Rehoboth on the 5th October and found that he had two chiefs to deal with, namely Hermanus van Wyk, the captain of the Basters, and Abraham Swartbooi, the chief of the Swartboois of Ameib, who were the former owners of Rehoboth but had handed it over to the Basters against a yearly payment in recognition of their rights. Abraham had gone to Windhoek to arrange matters so far as Ameib was concerned, and from there he accompanied Palgrave to Rehoboth, in order to arrange matters with the Commissioner and the Basters on the spot. The Swartboois wanted either to return to Rehoboth again, or to sell Ameib so that they could look for another place in which to live. Palgrave dissuaded them from both these steps, and showed them how the sale of Ameib would enable Maharero to demand a much higher purchase price for Rehoboth from the Basters. Hermanus van Wyk complained that he could not depend either on the Hereros or on the Namas, and that he would, therefore, be glad to see the Government taking a hand in the matter, although he was unable to take any steps in opposition to the rest of the tribes. On the very day that Palgrave arrived the stormy council meeting in connexion with Dr. Theophilus Hahn's actions had taken place, and Hahn had received instructions to leave the place. Palgrave advised the council to let the matter rest until the Government should send a commissioner to put the whole matter straight.

Palgrave reached Berseba on the 20th November. As the conference had been convened for a week later, he took the opportunity of visiting Klaas Swart's Basters at Grootfontein South. Upon his return to Berseba he found that the chiefs, Jacobus Isaak of Berseba, David Christian of Bethanie, Simon Koper of Haruchas, and Tseib of Keetmanshoop had arrived. Moses Witbooi was apparently hurt because the Commissioner had not visited him, and he only put in an appearance afterwards. Barnabas of Hoachanas was very ill and asked to be excused. Jan Jonker, however, and the chiefs of Gobabis and Warmbad, stayed away without giving any reasons for doing so.

Two matters had to be dealt with at the conference at Berseba on the 22nd November. The first was the question of the establishment of a protectorate over Namaland, and the second the complaints of traders as to unfair treatment the Namas meted out to them, when they went round trading. Jacobus Isaak was the principal speaker and he said that he was in a position to rule his country without any help. If resident magistrates were to be appointed over the chiefs, a chief would be of no more consequence or importance. Besides, it was necessary to hear the opinion of all the chiefs about so important a matter, and he proposed a conference at Hoachanas, to which all the chiefs must come without exception. It was very easy for Palgrave to prove to them that their capacity to rule the country themselves could not be very great, for all these cases of plundering European traders could not possibly have occurred, if the chiefs knew how to govern the country. They answered him by saying that the traders who had reason to complain of ill treatment had only to go to competent chiefs to get their rights. Palgrave then stated that he would give all the traders notice to that effect, and that he expected that each of the chiefs would keep proper order in his territory. If they should show themselves too weak to do so, the Government would step in, and then it could well happen that the chieftainships would be entirely abolished. The day after the meeting, the Commissioner received an assurance that the chiefs would do everything they could to comply with the Government's requirements. Palgrave sent his secretary, Christian, back from Berseba to visit each of the chiefs who had not been present, in order to acquaint them with the discussion which had taken place and to prevent the circulation of false rumours. He himself went to Warmbad, arriving there on the 22nd December, 1876. The chief Willem Christian had been for many years in the pay of the Cape Government. He received a yearly pension of £50, for which he undertook to surrender all criminals from the south who took refuge in his tribal territory, and to keep the Bushmen and Koranas in check. He had actually undertaken very much more than he was able to perform, for he was not a sufficiently strong man to keep a proper watch along the boundary. He succeeded in arresting a few fugitives and killing a few more, but he was not the least bit concerned when his people clothed themselves from a passing trader's stock, without paying for it, or 'off-loaded' his brandy casks, without asking him or giving him anything in return. Willem Christian consented to the appointment of a magistrate at Warmbad. From the Government's point of view this remote spot, which is of little importance to the history of South West Africa, was by no means valueless. The country could only be entered from two directions, i.e. from Walfish Bay and from Warmbad.

At the end of the year Palgrave returned to Windhoek and Hereroland. His two journeys had resulted in preparing the way for the establishment of a protectorate over Hereroland. The only ones amongst the Nama tribes, who were prepared to accept a Government official, were the Afrikanders at Windhoek, the Basters at Rehoboth, and the Bondelswarts of Warmbad. He sailed for Capetown to make a verbal report and to receive fresh instructions. His recommendations to the Government may be summarized as follows:

1. The Government ought to give instructions that Walfish Bay, together with the whole north coast, should be proclaimed British territory, for that would prevent the extension of Portuguese sovereignty to the south, and it would further cut off anybody who considered founding a republic to the north of Hereroland from access to the sea, thereby enabling the whole trade of the interior to be properly controlled.

2. The Government should send a magistrate to Okahandja. He should serve as Maharero's adviser, and should have jurisdiction in all disputes which arose between non-Hereros, or between a non-Herero and a Herero. For this purpose it would be advisable to hold courts on fixed days at Omaruru and Rehoboth as well. A field cornet should be stationed with every native tribe.

3. The expense which would be incurred must be covered by customs dues and trading licences, and by ground rent which could be collected from the Basters, since they were living on borrowed land which belonged to Maharero, because he had provided the rightful owners with a place of residence at Ameib. It was probable that the harbour dues would amount to £2,000 a year in the beginning, and that £600 a year could be collected as ground-rent from the Basters. When the Government's reserve was given out to settlers, the Government's revenue would be considerably increased. It should not prove difficult to find new landing-places for the Kaokoveld. Their discovery was only a question of time and could be left to the enterprise of the settlers. He thought that there was sufficient land for about 400 settlers.

With regard to his first mission, Palgrave expressed himself subsequently in the following terms:

'It must not be overlooked that the object of my first mission was to get a hold on the country between the Orange River and the Portuguese settlements on the west coast, in such a way as might lead to annexation, if the inhabitants desired it and our own interests made such a course desirable.' (Extract from a letter dated the 12th February, 1879.)

The Cape Government's first measures

During Palgrave's absence, the Cape Government took the first steps to get a firm foothold in South West Africa. The British warship *Industry* appeared in Walfish Bay on the 6th March, 1878, and the whole of the ship's company landed the following morning. Parade uniforms were worn and, at 11.15, the British flag was hoisted and a proclamation was read, by which Walfish Bay and Rooibank and the north coast, as far as the mouth of the Swakop to a depth of fifteen English miles, was proclaimed as the territory of the British Crown.

An official was stationed at Walfish Bay to issue trading licences and collect customs. A duty of £1 was levied on every gun imported. The Wuppertal Trading Company had to disburse £65 for the year 1878. These were preliminary steps and, after the Commissioner's return, the Government taxes were to be revised.

Palgrave stayed longer than had been expected in Capetown. It was only on the 2nd August, 1877, that he wrote to Maharero as follows:

'I am now in the position of being able to advise you that it has pleased His Excellency the Governor and the Government of the Cape of Good Hope to give your request for protection and my return to you its careful consideration. I am writing you to acquaint you of the fact that I shall be coming back to you for a while, and that I sincerely hope to be back in Hereroland in six weeks' time.'

He landed at Walfish Bay in October 1877, not as Special Commissioner but as Civil Commissioner, and he went to stay temporarily at Okahandja.

The Civil Commissioner and the Hereros

The Commissioner's long absence had not in any way prejudiced Maharero against the new plans. Jan Jonker had argued with him about it and said that the Government was digging a pit for him, and that he was going to fall into it, but Maharero had replied:

'That may well be, but I know you and the Namas and I know, too, that you are my enemies. You stay where you are and leave me alone. If I have got to fall into a pit, I would much rather fall into the Government's pit than into the hands of people like you, who have been my enemies from the very earliest days.'

Palgrave was anxious to hold a general conference of chiefs, in order to discuss various matters of importance. One was convened for the 31st December, 1878, and Palgrave could not help saying to Maharero: 'The Hereros are at present like a span of oxen who pull first to one side and then to the other, and in this respect your own people are the worst.' He was very displeased with a number of the things which Maharero was doing, or had done. He noticed that the other Herero chiefs generally took up a non-committal attitude, and so he asked the chief, Tjiharine of Omburo, why this was. The latter replied that Maharero had ordered them to keep their ears open at the conference but to say nothing. That made the Commissioner's task considerably more difficult, for he did not know where he stood, even if he had Maharero's consent to a proposal. He had already realized that Maharero's paramount chieftainship was more of a courtesy title than an actual fact. Only Maharero's son, Wilhelm, Tjiharine of Omburo, Aponda of Barmen, Mureti of the Omuramba, and Kambazembi of Waterberg attended the conference on the 31st December. All the others stayed away.

The introduction of a tax was strenuously opposed by the meeting. Maharero's plan was to levy a payment on the werfs and huts of the individual chiefs. Since Palgrave had said that a magistrate for Oka-handja would cost about £900 a year, he was prepared to collect £450 in cattle from the chiefs. Opinions differed very much as to how the other £450 was to be raised. It had been previously agreed that it should come out of the territory reserved to the Government, but it was something new and unpleasant for Maharero to hear that the Commissioner had, without his knowledge, gone so far as to tax hunting and trade. He had always said that he wished to bear the cost of government himself. The traders, hunters, and other Euro-peans were to have nothing to do with it. Now, however, they could go about the country showing their tax receipt and saying: 'The country belongs to us; we have bought it with this piece of paper.' Things came to such a pass that Palgrave said that his work for the last twelve months had been useless, and Maharero must not be sur-prised if the Government were to say one day: 'Come back Palgrave! We do not trust you any more Maharero, for you said that taxation was a thing which you did not understand, and that you left that to the Government.' Maharero replied: 'All this trouble has been caused by the fact that you are always travelling instead of staying in Okahandja. It is my intention that the Hereros should pay every-thing and, if they cannot do so, then and then only are the Europeans to be approached.'

He then said that he was tired of the whole business, and that he wanted to go and rest in the shade of a tree. He handed over the conduct of further negotiations to Riarua, the captain of his troops, and made him responsible for all further misunderstandings.

It was decided that the Herero territory should remain the unalienable property of the Herero tribe. If a European wished to live within its borders, he could only do so with express permission from the paramount chief, and the same permission had to be obtained for building a house. The Bergdamas and Bushmen living in the Government Reserve were in future to be under the control of the Government.

Palgrave had been to Windhoek and had seen Jan Jonker's sorry state, so he put in a good word for him with the chiefs and said to them: 'Nothing is so true as the saying "as a man sows so shall he reap". The time has now arrived for you to decide what is to be sown. If violence and murder is sown by the Hereros, they will reap the very same in due course of time. I have said to the Afrikanders "what you have sown, you are reaping now" but now I say to you "what you are sowing now, you will reap later".'[1] As there had been some talk that Wilhelm Maharero and his brother Samuel were to accompany the Commissioner on a journey to Capetown, Palgrave urged Riarua to relieve the pressure on the Afrikanders in Windhoek before Wilhelm's departure. The Hereros ought to remember what their own position was like, when Jonker had his stranglehold upon them, and they ought not to do the same kind of thing to Jan's people and his Bergdamas.

When the discussion turned upon Rehoboth and the Basters, and the Swartboois of Ameib, Palgrave said:

'The Basters had settled there prior to 1876. If that had not been the case the Commissioner would not have given them permission to stay there. Whatever else the position may be, they are actually living there, and what really are their rights? Their rights are the same as those of other settlers, namely, the rights which the Hereros have given them of living there, and that is the sum total of the rights they have.'

The Civil Commissioner and the Namas

In the same way as the Hereros, the Nama chiefs were likewise advised of the Commissioner's return to South West Africa. The opportunity was taken of impressing upon the chiefs of Gibeon, Berseba, and Bethanie, i.e. the triple alliance, that they must stop

[1] This prophecy was fulfilled in a more terrible fashion than Palgrave could ever have conceived when the German campaigns reduced the Herero nation from 85,000 to 12,000.—Ed.

the raiding in the Rehoboth territory, and see that peace and order were maintained. If they failed to do this, it might become necessary to cut off their supply of ammunition, and to disarm those who caused trouble, for guns and ammunition were only to be imported when they were to be used for the purpose of hunting game. Palgrave himself wrote to Jacobus Isaak at Berseba on the 8th August, 1878, and told him that the north-eastern part of Namaland, which was under his control, was in an absolute state of chaos, and that it was desirable that a conference should be held either in Berseba or Gibeon.

The triple alliance agreed to hold a general conference of all the chiefs at Hoachanas, where they had intended to meet in 1876. This conference was held in June 1878. With the exception of Chief Petrus of Hoachanas, the only other people to turn up were Jan Jonker of Windhoek and Arisemab of the Veldskoendraers. They waited for five weeks for the representatives of the triple alliance, consumed all the slaughter stock which had been collected for the purpose of the conference, drank up two bags of coffee, and then entered into an agreement to drive the Basters out of Rehoboth, and to take their territory for themselves. They then went home, without having said a single word about the safety of the country.

About the same time, however, Jacobus Isaak and Moses Witbooi, who had suggested and convened the conference in Hoachanas but never attended it, wrote a letter to Maharero in the following terms:

'We should very much like to know what your real opinion is as to Palgrave's intentions and the arrangement he wants to make with you. We should be very pleased indeed to hear from you that you distrust him entirely, for we are determined to keep our land and country for ourselves. We are going to defend our country to a man and that is why we are writing to you. We give you a friendly invitation to come to Oas and discuss with us the affairs of the country. We hear that a letter was written to you, representing that the object of our meeting was to work in opposition to you, but do not believe it. It is not true; people are trying to keep us apart. It is thus our friendly and earnest desire that you should come to Oas on the 15th October.'

This letter was dated at Hoachanas on the 19th June, 1878.

The previous day the same two had sent a letter to Hermanus van Wyk at Rehoboth containing the following warning:

'You have no right to take any part in important matters without our consent, for that is contrary to our agreement. . . . If you want to surrender to the English, it cannot be done without our consent; if you want to make a treaty with them, it cannot be done without our consent; if you want to part with your land, that cannot be done without our consent.'

In spite of this, a discussion between Palgrave and David Christian took place at Rehoboth. David Christian stated that he was prepared to afford the Basters some relief from their discomfort by calling the Boois out of the Kuiseb. He could do nothing, however, against the raiders of the Red Nation. Careful investigation of the robberies which had taken place, and the losses which they had occasioned, revealed that, in the year 1877, 236 cattle, 676 head of small stock and two horses had been stolen from the Basters, besides the stock which the traders had lost. As Jan Jonker had appeared on the scene, too, the investigation took a very unpleasant turn for him, for it was proved that he had a secret arrangement with the robbers that they should make Rehoboth so impossible for the Basters that they would be forced to leave, so that he could then go and settle there himself, and thus escape to some extent from the importunities of the Hereros. The proof of his complicity in Rehoboth's sorry condition brought him into very bad odour, and, from then onwards, Namaland turned a deaf ear towards his complaints. The danger that the Swartboois would demand Rehoboth back was over for the present, for they were trying to get a new place to live in in the Kaokoveld, although Palgrave did not want them there at any price, as no native tribes were to be allowed to establish themselves in the Government Reserve. Palgrave thought that the best settlement of the Rehoboth land question would be for the Government to take over the district, and to lease it to the Basters on a 99-year lease. The Bergdamas, Bushmen, and Topnaars living in the Government Reserve were to be transferred to seven or eight places on the lower Swakop, and to form a labour reservoir for the European settlers in the Government Reserve, and for the labour market of the Cape Colony.

It was not with unalloyed pleasure that Palgrave could look back on the results of his second mission. He had discovered that the Hereros were beginning to distrust him, and that it was only Wilhelm Maharero who had any sympathy with his outlook and plans. The Namas, too, with the exception of Bethanie, Warmbad, and the Basters of Rehoboth, persisted in maintaining their independent attitude, owing largely to the bad influence of the rebellious Griquas amongst them. The chief opponents to any change were, however, the chiefs of Berseba and Gibeon. Palgrave wrote, therefore, to the Government that, if peace was to be maintained in Namaland, the chiefs would have to be deprived of their authority, so that they could not continue to attack their neighbours. When the time arrived Namaland would have to be invaded by Government forces, which need not be very large, but they should not be supported by Herero auxiliaries. That would also serve as a lesson for the Hereros, for Maharero was always urging that the Government ought to display more power. With this the Commissioner was in full agreement, but for quite another reason, and that was that the military force ought 'to be large enough to inspire fear on the one side and confidence on the other'. So that everything which he had built up so carefully should not be lost, he proposed to the Government that he should be authorized to arrest and deport the most notorious law-breakers.

Palgrave returned to Capetown early in January 1879, and Maharero's two sons, Wilhelm and Samuel, went with him. Wilhelm, as his father's future successor, was not only to get to know the Cape Colony, but was likewise to acquire some knowledge of the system of Government in vogue there. He was an able man with an excellent character. He had been educated at the Augustineum and he had laid the foundations of a Christian community at Okahandja. Contrary to the custom of his people, he had contracted the first love match amongst the Hereros, by marrying Magdalena, a Herero woman with Bergdama blood in her veins, who had been trained as a teacher at Stellenbosch. He was the hope of every one who had the interests of the Herero at heart, and he was the terror of those who were fond of crooked dealing. He did not hesitate to stand up for what was right, even in opposition to his own father, when it was necessary. Once, when Maharero had had a Bergdama executed without sufficient reason, his action had aroused Wilhelm's displeasure to such an extent that the old man barricaded himself in his hut for three days, until Wilhelm's anger had subsided.

Palgrave's third mission

Palgrave returned from Capetown in January 1880 as magistrate of Walfish Bay and Commissioner for Hereroland, and Wilhelm and Samuel Maharero came back with him. Palgrave went to live at Walfish Bay, and used to go to Okahandja, or other places, only when the chiefs requested him to do so. Manning, Resident Magistrate of Okahandja, was in charge of the Government's interests there, so far as they concerned Maharero. His position was by no means an easy one. The Bergdamas in the Otjimbingwe mountains stole stock from the Hereros, and the Hereros pursued the thieves, and shot fourteen of them dead instead of bringing them before the court. Manning, therefore, threatened to put the Hereros in jail. That would, however, have created a difficult position, so Manning was recalled and Major B. D. Musgrave was appointed in his place. The latter was a wise and sensible man, who had served in the Indian Army, and had spent a considerable amount of time travelling in Germany and other countries. His duties were merely to advise Maharero and to correspond with the Government, for the latter had reduced its activities amongst the Hereros to a considerable extent. It had decided to do nothing more than was provided for in the treaty, and that was to provide Maharero with a magistrate. This decision was to be traced to dissension between the Europeans in Hereroland and Palgrave, for they did not agree with the measures he had introduced. Ohlsen, Erikson, and Pilgram went to Capetown, and got into touch with some members of Parliament, who made things difficult for the Government. On the 9th January, 1880, only two days before Palgrave's departure for South West Africa, they had had an audience with the Governor in Capetown and complained about the taxes which had been levied upon all traders since 1878. They asked that the Government should supply police and a military force for the protection of the lives and property of the Europeans, failing which they were not going to pay any more taxes. Parliament had thereupon forbidden any further intervention in affairs in Hereroland, and had expressed the view that, if protection in this sense was required, the Resident Magistrate of Okahandja ought to be recalled, and the country left to its own fate.

Much at the same time, the Minister for Native Affairs made the following statement to the missionary, Brincker: 'So far as Hereroland is concerned it is a question of time. While Parliament is in its present mood we cannot do more for Hereroland than we are doing. The only reason why all connection with it is not broken off is that the Government is hoping for a change of opinion in Parliament.'

Palgrave went steadily on with his work. He gave up, for the time being, his idea of settling the lower Swakop valley with Bergdamas from the Government Reserve, and he collected a number of labourers from amongst them in order to send them to Capetown. In this way he hoped to free the Government Reserve entirely for European settlement. When he went to Maharero at Okahandja, the latter received him with these unfriendly words: 'I thought that you were going to add to my power, but now I see that some of the power which I have is to be taken away from me.' Palgrave pacified him by saying: 'For the power which I take away from you, I will give you something much better.'

The Nama chiefs still maintained their independent attitude, and then, in the middle of 1880, the trek-boer van Zyl was robbed, ill treated, and sentenced to death at Gobabis, and Erikson's traders were robbed there too. Here was an affair which had to be dealt with, for it concerned British subjects and Europeans. Palgrave went to Okahandja. When he heard that the Rhenish missionaries of Namaland were on the point of holding their yearly conference at Hoachanas, he went there too. Amongst other things, the conference had to decide what was to be done in regard to the case of van Zyl, who had been staying as a guest in the missionary Judt's house, and it was decided, that Judt should, under no circumstances, return to Gobabis until this stain on its character had been removed. Palgrave asked the missionaries to use their influence to persuade the chiefs of Namaland to come to Gobabis, for the chief, Frederick Vlermuis, had written him a letter from there asking him 'for God's sake' to come to Gobabis, and to introduce some order into the confusion which reigned there. Invitations were sent out and the chiefs promised to go to Gobabis. Palgrave returned to Windhoek through Gibeon. He took with him as his interpreter and secretary, David Christian, the teacher and subsequent chief of Berseba, who wrote a very good hand. In Windhoek he was able to see once more to what a state of wretchedness the Afrikanders had been reduced, for their small flocks of goats were starving, because the Hereros had grazed all the pasturelands round about utterly bare, by establishing thirty-nine cattle posts there with between 5,000 and 6,000 head of cattle. He saw that all his efforts to move Maharero to a more generous attitude towards Jan Jonker had been quite in vain.

When Palgrave arrived at Gobabis, none of the Nama chiefs were there, and even Frederick Vlermuis, who had begged him so urgently to come, did not put in an appearance during the first week. They had reached Hoachanas and had stayed there to discuss matters. When, however, a message from Palgrave informed them that the

Commissioner had been waiting for them for several days, they set out for Gobabis without delay.

Palgrave stayed in Gobabis for twenty-seven days. Besides the chief Andries Lambert and the leader of the opposition party, Frederick Vlermuis, both of whom were of Gobabis, the chiefs, Jacobus Christian of Berseba, Moses Witbooi of Gibeon, David Christian of Bethanie, and Petrus of Hoachanas, took part in the conference. Palgrave's idea was to see that the actions of the Gobabis people should be condemned by the other chiefs. He hoped that they would make some arrangements whereby law and order would be restored again, but his hope was not fulfilled. The Nama chiefs and the triple alliance stated that they could do nothing so far as the robbing of van Zyl was concerned, and that they had no power to prevent traders from being robbed. Andries Lambert was willing to give Palgrave his last penny if he could tell him who was the real chief in Gobabis, Frederick Vlermuis or himself. When, however, Palgrave got tired of talking, and asked for a definite answer which he could lay before his Government, Paul Visser, Moses Witbooi's brother-in-law, who had been taking a leading part in the proceedings, and Frederick Vlermuis remarked: 'What is the Government? Let us kill that thing (Palgrave) or throw him out, and then see what the Government is and what it can do.' An attack on the Commissioner was actually planned. The chief of Bethanie got to know of it and opposed it strenuously, while he urged Palgrave to leave Gobabis as quickly as possible.

Then something occurred which will be related in full in the following chapter. The ten years of peace came to an end on the 23rd August, 1880. For some time past there had been talk of the war which was threatening between the Hereros and the Namas. Inflammable matter enough had been collected during those ten years, and now the spark had fallen into the powder barrel while the chiefs of the Nama tribes were present in Gobabis. The Hereros organized a great massacre of the inhabitants of Gobabis, who were forced to leave the place and flee to the south. Palgrave, however, returned to Hereroland on the 3rd September, and what happened to him there will be told later on. He hurried back to Walfish Bay, and the Resident Magistrate of Okahandja likewise left the village and went to the Bay with his secretary. That was the end of the efforts of a man, who was held in the highest esteem, and worked for four long years to make South West Africa a protectorate under the Cape Government. Maharero, however, in looking back upon this period, re-marked: 'The British flag flew here. It waved this way and that; we attached ourselves to it and we were waved backwards and forwards with it.'

4. CULTURAL ADVANCEMENT

It has been said that the degree of culture to which a nation has attained is to be judged by the quantity of soap it uses. This test was not applicable in South West Africa, but the proper measure to be adopted is the extent to which cotton material was used. The ten years of peace saw the old way of tending the body disappear, namely the continuous anointing of the naked body with a salve made of rancid fat or butter mixed with powdered iron ore. Water and soap began to be used by the Herero for cleaning himself, instead of fresh cow dung as previously. The skin clothing gradually disappeared when the men and women of the small Christian congregation began to clothe themselves in European fashion, for the clothes which the Europeans wore constituted the only pattern they had, but it is still questionable whether these are really suitable for the natives of South West Africa. No other form of clothing could be introduced, for the natives of the Cape Colony had likewise followed the European fashion. The styles worn by the missionaries' wives at the time served as the general pattern for the women's clothing, and the Hereros have remained true to this style for more than sixty years, up to the present day, which is an outward sign of the extraordinarily strong conservatism of the race. The married women's leather head-dresses, with their heavy pendants of iron beads and their three leather points, were banished from the villages to the cattle-posts, and the cloth used by the Namas as a head-dress became the fashion, although in a much more elevated form. Her sense of modesty, which had been strong during the time when the leather head-dresses were worn, did not permit a woman, even when the fancy cloth for the head had become the fashion, to be seen by anybody without it.

Another thing which was closely bound up with the requirements of the natives, was, naturally, the trade which supplied them with the things they required. Cotton goods had to be provided in place of guns and gunpowder. It was mentioned previously that, during the ten years of peace, about 100 wagons and carts traversed the land every year, trading. In Rehoboth alone there were the businesses of Dr. Hahn, Steyn & Co., Jordan & Gunning, and the Wuppertal

Trading Company. Haelbich and Redecker both opened shops at Otjimbingwe. Erikson's store was at Omaruru and, from there, he sent out his wagons to the eastern boundary of Hereroland and as far as Lake Ngami. There was, of course, very little money in the country, but the natives bartered goods for cattle, as well as for ostrich feathers and ivory. Palgrave calculated that, in 1876 alone, 34,500 lbs. of ivory and 5,800 lbs. of ostrich feathers were exported, and that this brought into the country an amount of £45,000. In 1878, the traders and storekeepers introduced the first stock brands, in order to distinguish the cattle they had traded in from those of the natives. It should be mentioned that, in all the places where there were congregations, cemeteries were established, and the Christians and the most prominent of the heathens began to be buried in coffins.

No sales of land to Europeans had as yet taken place. In 1873, however, the chief Willem Christian of Warmbad sold the farm, Haruchas, to the farmer and trader Rittmann for £215, and he like-wise sold the farms Tsawisis, Holoog, and Groendoorn to the trader, Hill, for £800. Maharero allowed Europeans to settle with any of the tribes, but he took very great care that no one obtained any right to lay claim to a single square foot of Hereroland on the ground that he had purchased it.

We will leave Pieter Heinrich Brincker to state what the general position was; he was in a position to make personal observations for many years and he wrote as follows:

'In a land, which is situated at a great distance from any other civilized country, which has hardly any products of its own, and is therefore compelled to acquire, at great expense and with considerable risk, all its civilized re-quirements, it follows that the cost of production for the few things which the land still produces ought to be less than what it is in richer countries. In Hereroland, however, everything is the other way about. For instance, a bag of wheat, 200 lbs. in weight, which has been produced here, costs £4, while the price for the same quantity of wheat in Capetown is about £1 10s. A large ox can only be bought from the Hereros, with a great deal of haggling, for between £5 and £6, and generally not even for that. Under favourable circumstances, one can get for this ox, after driving it 150 miles, about £7, but generally rather less in Capetown. The worst of it all is that no actual money can be brought into circulation in Hereroland. Directly any money is introduced, it is sent back to Capetown at the very first opportunity by the shopkeepers, to take the place of the produce which they have not on hand for export.

'When, in the so-called good times, ostrich feathers and ivory could be exported in sufficient quantities, nobody thought that in a few years' time ostriches and elephants would almost entirely have disappeared. Competition in purchasing trek oxen and slaughter stock is so keen that the natives become accustomed to receive prices, which are out of all proportion to the position and circumstances of the country. During the last eight years, the Hereros have acquired such enormous wealth in the shape of cattle' (Brincker is writing of the end of the ten years of peace) 'that their very number ought to have had the effect of bringing the price down, if only the Herero did not idolize his cattle, and therefore, when he has at last made up his mind to part with a particular animal, a lordly price has to be paid for it. As things are at the present moment, the trade of Hereroland is utterly worthless.

'Through the stupid, or rather inhuman, way in which ostriches have been hunted during the last few years, they have been almost exterminated, or they are so difficult to find that it is seldom that any one succeeds in killing one. Enterprising English and Swedish traders go trading right to the other side of Ovamboland and to the Okavango. They still get from there a fair quantity of ivory and feathers through trading and hunting themselves, in a way which many people would not care to undertake. The Hereros cannot be induced to breed ostriches, for where there are no laws, and no means of carrying out any law which might be made, any one would be free to come and pluck the tame ostriches, or to shoot them down, without anybody else worrying their head about it. I am not putting things too strongly, nor am I being unduly pessimistic, when I say that Hereroland has been ruined for business purposes, and that this state of things has been brought about through the ostrich feather trade.

'Another undesirable feature is the fact that there was, from the beginning, no fixity of wages, and that there was no proper standard at all, and this was something of which the natives learnt very quickly to take advantage. When the poorest labourer, who could not do a third of the work which a labourer in the Colony could do, received just as high a wage as the latter, and when, upon payment of the wage agreed upon, the labourer had the audacity to demand from the "big people", who were, in such circumstances, apt to get false conceptions of what was equitable, double what he had agreed to take and, when he got it, still be dissatisfied, one cannot wonder that very little could be done to civilize the native, and that every European tried to get on alone as best he could. The wages for all necessary labour are in fact so high in the country that one is always afraid of taking a long journey, because of the enormous amount which is swallowed up by wages alone on such a journey. Still one must be fair. The wages are only high to us. The people get very little in the way of goods for the large sums we pay them, when one reckons that everything costs them from 100 to 150 per cent. more here than in Capetown.

'Hereros would rather not work at all, or at least only until they have acquired a few cows or some small stock. The Bergdamas do very much the same. When they have grown fat through good feeding, they go off with their wages into the mountains, and then they live by stealing as the opportunity offers, and for this they are never punished, as long as they confine their thefts to the property of Europeans.'

That was how matters stood in South West Africa in 1880, when the Europeans' seven fat years were past and it was thought wise to leave the country to itself, chiefly because the outbreak of war, after ten years of peace, had wrecked business entirely, and then most of the Europeans left the country.

III

THE TEN YEARS OF WAR: 1880 TO 1890

1. THE WAR OF THE SWAKOP BOUNDARY

The cause of the war

HUMAN nature seems to be so constituted that it can never learn any lesson from the past, but prefers to follow the chances of an irregular sort of existence, which it provides with a fine new name, when its object is to set ancient hates and quarrels, new schemes and plans, the lust for power and the will to conquer on the throne. At the beginning of the century, the Herero herdsmen had, with a total disregard of what was right, grazed and trodden down the pastures of Namaland, as if there were no such thing as a Nama nation, which had the right to put its own cattle to graze in the veld of its own country and to water them at the drinking places, to which their fathers and their grandfathers had always driven their herds. Jonker Afrikander had come to the Namas' assistance, when they were sorely in need, and had driven the Hereros back to the Swakop in several fierce battles. Jonker was not satisfied with that so he settled in Windhoek, where the Namas had hunted in times gone by and where, too, the Herero cattle had grazed since ancient days. From Windhoek, and afterwards from Okahandja, he had sent his robber bands farther and farther north, carried off innumerable cattle, and so impoverished and oppressed the Hereros that they ceased to be a nation at all. Then followed the recovery of the Hereros in 1863, when Jonker's son, Christian, lost his life and his brother Jan Jonker became chief of the Afrikander tribe. The Hereros and the Nama matched their strength against each other in a struggle which lasted seven years, until general war-weariness brought about the peace of Okahandja in 1870, as a result of which Windhoek was given to the Afrikanders as a fief. No boundary lines were fixed by the peace treaty of Okahandja, for the peace negotiations would certainly have broken down had boundary questions been brought under discussion, and so the parties separated without having settled a most important question. The Namas thought that, because Windhoek had been granted to Jan Jonker, the Swakop was the northern boundary of Namaland. Maharero thought that, as he had only given the Afrikanders Windhoek as a fief, and as he had provided the Swartboois with a new place to live, Ameib, in exchange for Rehoboth, the southern boundary of Hereroland consisted in a line drawn from west to east, passing through Rehoboth. As this line was not clearly marked by the course of a river or a range of mountains, he tried to persuade Palgrave, the Cape Government's Commissioner, to have it ploughed, because, to a man who could not read and write, the thin line appearing on the Commissioner's map seemed to be far too indefinite. Now the same old game began once again, if almost imperceptibly. Maharero sent large herds of cattle to Windhoek and set up his cattle posts to the south of it. When complaints were lodged, he made the existing drought his excuse, and said that he was forced to take possession of the pasture lands to the south. In actual fact, his cattle posts operated as guards for the boundary line, and this the Namas knew very well. The ancient disregard for the rights of others made itself felt along the whole border. Without even asking, the Hereros watered their cattle at wells which the Namas had sunk, and any one who tried to resist them was ruthlessly beaten to death with their knobkerries. In the end, Jan Jonker calculated that 118 of his people had been killed by Maharero's herdsmen. This was, of course, not always without fault on their side, for it was in the blood of the Namas, and the Bergdamas who served them, to drive off cattle by stealth whenever they could.

In the beginning, the Nama tribes who lived in the south turned a deaf ear to all Jan's requests for assistance. It appeared to them as if he had taken over from his father the idea of becoming paramount chief of all the Nama tribes, and that, if they hastened to his assistance, it might be reckoned as an act of obedience and recognition of his exaggerated claims. They were, however, gradually compelled to recognize that it was not only Jan, who was threatened with danger, but the southern tribes as well. If only the Basters were not in Rehoboth! These immigrants, who felt so much more drawn to the Hereros than to the Namas! How was one to get at the Hereros, when the necessity arose, if the Basters remained neutral? The process by which the Swartboois were driven out of Rehoboth, when they became the Hereros' allies, was duly repeated, and an effort was made to make the Basters tire of Rehoboth, by persistently stealing their stock and so forcing them to return to the Orange River. Maharero did nothing for them. If the Basters left Rehoboth, it became free and it belonged to him. He felt that he was strong enough to hold his own, not only with Jan, whom he had decided to squeeze gradually out of Windhoek, but with the other chiefs as well. His boundary guards knew exactly what was in his mind, and they were apt to express themselves rather more frankly than their diplomatically inclined master was wont to do in his letters or in his replies to deputations. They told the disconcerted Namas perfectly plainly that their intention was to water the Herero cattle at the Orange River, and then to wash the blood off their assegais in the same river, for there would be no peace between the north and the south, until the Namas had found their proper place as the servants and shepherds of the Hereros. Maharero's cattle posts remained at Gurumanas, west of Rehoboth, and Witvlei on the road to Gobabis, and in the veld of Gobabis itself, and served to guard the border. Kahimemua, the Mbanderu chief, acted as guardian of the border at Gobabis. Maharero could not have put a better man there, for it was in Kahimemua's own interest to protect the country, which had belonged to his own ancestors until the Orlams of Gobabis had enslaved them and had taken away their cattle and grazing grounds.

There existed, therefore, in the first days of the year 1880, a dangerous tension between the Hereros and the Namas, and it did not help matters at all that Palgrave hastened to Gobabis to see that justice was done between white and black. Nor did it help matters that the management of the Rhenish mission asked the German Government to exert pressure upon England, to induce her to maintain law and order in South West Africa. The British Government replied that it would take no responsibility at all for anything that happened beyond the boundaries of Walfish Bay, for the Orange River was the boundary of the Cape Colony. With that Palgrave's hands were tied, and the cannons and the small body of soldiers, which he would have been so pleased to see in the country, remained but a pious and unattainable wish, which he did not even dare to submit to the Cape Government, for there was no desire at Capetown to engage in an adventure in South West Africa, which might cost a great deal of money, while no one could safely predict how it would end.

Thunder-clouds were gathering over the whole country. A number of Hereros, who had earned a few cattle in Namaland, were trekking northwards past Hoachanas with their few possessions. Some of the Red Nation then said: 'Why should we let the Hereros live when the Hereros are killing the Namas?' The Hereros fled in the night to the missionary, Heider, at Hoachanas and hid in his wagon house, and it was only through the active intervention of Heider, who succeeded in getting the chief, Petrus, on to his side, that a tragedy was prevented. Petrus kept his blood- and cattle-thirsty subjects under control, saying: 'No one shall dare to touch these Hereros, for they are under my protection. If any one wants to go and fight the Hereros, let them go and attack their fighting men, but they are not going to kill peaceful people who have been living amongst us.' The same kind of thing happened at other places, and Heider wrote to his relations in July 1880 saying that it seemed to him that war was only a question of time.

This was recognized both in the north and the south. The black thunder-clouds were gathering and the sultriness of the atmosphere depressed everybody. No one knew when and where the first flash of lightning would strike, and neither Jan nor Maharero had any idea that the thunders of war would roll for ten long years, and that it would only terminate with the shot from his own son's gun which put an end to Jan's life in 1889, and with the thud of the clods of earth which filled up Maharero's own grave at Okahandja in 1890.

The evening of blood at Gurumanas

Maharero and his half-brother, Riarua, were well aware that the veld at Rehoboth was excellent, not only for horses but likewise for cattle and sheep. They had therefore established a post at Gurumanas, westwards of Rehoboth, with 1,500 selected cattle, several thousand sheep, and a number of horses. The head overseer, who commanded a large number of herdsmen, was called Karuvingo, which means 'The Red Ant'. Now there was at Gurumanas a Nama werf, in which there lived a number of people belonging to various Nama tribes, such as the Topnaars, Afrikanders, Jan Booi's tribe, and so on. Their leader was a Nama called Nu-Nanub, which means 'The Black Cloud'. As was naturally to be expected, the Namas were very much annoyed with the Herero invaders, and the Hereros did nothing to improve matters by their attitude. For example, in the early days of August, a Nama had made a saddle for a Herero to the latter's order. When he delivered the saddle and asked for payment, it did not please the Herero, and the Nama said: 'You need not take it if you do not like it.' The Herero lost his temper and said: 'So you made the saddle badly, intending that I should not like it. I'll make you pay for that.' That constituted a threat to Nama ears and everybody was very sensitive at that time. In the second week of August Karuvingo discovered one evening, when the cattle returned from the veld, that a cow which was in calf was missing, and he immediately suspected the Namas. A number of strong men betook themselves to The Black Cloud's hut, tied him up with a riem, thrashed him, and took away his cattle, which were standing in the kraal next to the hut. That had hardly happened when the missing cow was seen coming out of the veld with her calf. It was clear to everybody that an injustice had been done to The Black Cloud. The Hereros, however, did not trouble to apologize, and also persisted in refusing to give him his cattle back. Then they started fighting and, in the fight, both Karuvingo and Nu-Nanub were killed. The Namas, however, were forced to retire. During the night, the Namas took their wives and children to a safe place in the mountains, and then returned to settle matters with the Hereros. The latter had decided to attack the Nama werf at daybreak. According to their usual tactics, they shot into the Nama huts, in order to throw the sleeping people into confusion and frighten them out, thus making them incapable of resisting. They did not know that the huts were empty. The Namas guessed, however, that the Hereros would act in this way, and they took up good positions and started shooting into the rows of Hereros, who were surrounding the werf. A fierce battle developed and Maharero's best herdsmen fell. They left thirty dead behind, while there were very few casualties on the Nama side. Now Maharero's cattle had no herdsmen, for all the Hereros who had not taken part in the battle had taken to their heels. The Topnaars, Boois, and Afrikanders knew, from years of practice, what was to be done with cattle under those circumstances. They were driven off and the previous inhabitants of Gurumanas scattered, each one with his share of the booty, into the farthest corners of Namaland, for it stood to reason that Maharero would revenge himself. The lightning had struck, and it had set the country on fire.

The night of blood at Okahandja

Jan Jonker at Windhoek received the news of what had happened at Gurumanas on the 21st August. It seems that the fight had taken place on the 20th August, which was a Saturday. The following day he had all his fortifications, which had been built long years ago, put into proper order and manned. The missionary, Schroeder, tried to pacify the people, and so did Hegner, who was on a visit to Windhoek from Berseba, but Jan knew very well what Maharero's anger meant, and his conscience was not entirely clean. Had not his father Jonker been the cause of dreadful bloodshed in Okahandja in August 1850, when the war clouds had hung over the country as they were doing now, and had he not then exterminated a whole tribe in his rage, so that for years the hills of Okahandja were strewn with their bleaching bones? Alas, when an old blood-feud is resuscitated and joins forces with desires for vengeance of more recent growth! Jan's nearest relatives were in Okahandja with Maharero. They had been summoned there by the resident magistrate's clerk in connexion with a court case.

On the 22nd August, a Herero horseman arrived at Otjizeva, saying that the Afrikanders in Windhoek had made ready to fight and that they were already on their way. The Hereros of Otjizeva believed the report and seized their weapons. They fell upon a Nama werf, lying to the north of Windhoek, and shot down every one they could find; it was chiefly the women and children whom they killed, for the men had gone hurriedly to Windhoek to learn what was happening in the country. When they returned and saw what the Hereros had done, they set out in pursuit and shot down the greater part of the Herero commando, and took 1,200 cattle belonging to these Hereros back with them. They even burnt the beams which were intended for the church at Otjizeva.

The same day Maharero heard the ominous reports as to what had happened in Gurumanas, Windhoek, and Otjizeva, but it was only towards evening on the 23rd August that Daniel Kavezeri brought him reliable information as to the extent of his losses at Rehoboth. The Resident Magistrate, Musgrave, and his clerk were that day at Okahandja, and likewise Pabst, the missionary, who was passing through, and Spiecker, Lutz, and Bam, who had arrived from the south. Diehl, the missionary in charge of the mission station, was in Capetown. None of these heard anything of what had happened. This was a matter with which Maharero wanted to deal by himself.

It was stated before that Musgrave's clerk had summoned a number of Namas from Windhoek to Okahandja, in connexion with a case, and amongst them was Joseph, Jan Jonker's brother, to whom Maharero had always been very friendly, treating him as his child, and even calling him so. Jan Arie, Jan Jonker's brother-in-law, was there too. There were about seven people in all from Windhoek and, in

addition to them, there were about twenty other Namas in Okahandja, who had nothing to do with the case, some of whom did
not even belong to the Afrikander tribe. Maharero issued secret
instructions that all the Namas present in Okahandja were to be
murdered during the night of the 23rd August. The latter had no
suspicion that anything was amiss. Maharero had treated them very
well, so that there had been no need for them to go to sleep
hungry round the fire, as was so often the case in Windhoek. When
the whole of Okahandja was asleep, the chief's orders were carried
out. All the Namas were seized and those who resisted were killed
on the spot, while the rest were taken off to a deep hole at the foot
of the Kaiser Wilhelmberg and finished off there. (The missionaries,
Diehl and Irle, climbed this mountain for the first time, in 1871, in
order to celebrate the formation of the German Empire, and had then
given it this name.) The corpses were thrown into the hole, which
was the place where Maharero's executioners were wont to dispatch
their victims. Then messengers were sent throughout Hereroland,
with orders to kill all the Namas in the country, and these instructions
were carried out. Over 200 Namas lost their lives. The Namas of
Otjosazu were hidden and protected by the Christians there. A large
number of Bergdamas were likewise killed. The land had to be
cleaned up. A Bergdama boy, who had come to Okahandja with the
Namas from Windhoek, received a timely warning from his friends,
and fled to Windhoek during the night of the massacre and brought
the dreadful news.

The Europeans in Okahandja did not find out what had happened
until the 24th August, when everything was over. Perhaps the connexion between the 23rd August, 1850, and the 23rd August, 1880,
did not occur to anybody. Maharero, certainly, did not worry his
head about the date being a historical one. He kept out of sight.
Hermanus van Wyk, who was with Spiecker and Lutz, lost all confidence in Maharero. He returned to Rehoboth immediately. Spiecker
and Lutz went on to Otjimbingwe the same day. Pabst, however,
stayed behind, and warned Maharero not to go too far. He reminded
Maharero of the Swartbois, who were living in Hereroland as Maharero's friends, and pointed out the danger with which they were
threatened by the order to kill the Namas. Maharero immediately
sent further messengers to overtake the first ones, with instructions
that no harm was to be done to the Swartbois. At the same time
he sent their chief, Abraham Swartbooi, a present.

Hendrik Witbooi's first revelation

Maharero's instructions for the massacre had almost cost the life of a man, whose name had until now been almost unknown, but was to become very famous later. This was Hendrik Witbooi, the son of the chief, Moses Witbooi, of Gibeon. When Moses set out for Gobabis to attend the conference of chiefs and the discussion with the Commissioner, Palgrave, his son, Hendrik, made preparations to go through Rehoboth to Hereroland, for the purpose of fetching some oxen from there, which he had left behind with friends on a previous journey. He reached Haobetsaus and was stopped by some Hereros there on the pretext that they wanted to exchange the horses, which he and his companions were riding, for oxen. Hendrik soon saw, however, that all they wanted to do was to hold him prisoner, and then they told him plainly that Maharero had given instructions that all Namas were to be killed. Their horses and guns were taken away from him and his companions and the chief's orders were upon the point of being carried out. Then a Herero, who had previously stayed at Gibeon as a prisoner-of-war, intervened on Hendrik's behalf. He had been treated fairly well as a servant in the chief's family and had come to like Hendrik. Upon this man's intercession, Hendrik's horse and gun were returned to him and he hastened back to Gibeon. He had just escaped death, and he was riding through the mountain pass of Khani-gukha, when he heard a voice which said three mysterious things to him: 'It has come to pass!'—'The road lies open!'—'I lay on you a heavy burden!' Hendrik told nobody about his strange experience. It was only years afterwards that he wrote about it to his former teacher, the missionary Olpp, after the latter had returned to Germany. From this time onwards, however, he regarded himself as called by God to be the conqueror of the Hereros and the paramount chief of the Nama nation.

The end of Windhoek

Jan Jonker knew that Maharero intended to destroy him utterly and, for that reason, he had no intention of waiting for the arrival of the Herero forces. As he had no ammunition, he did not dare to fight. He decided to leave Windhoek and go to the south, and this decision was put into effect on the 25th August. When they came to the Auas Mountains, Jan sent the women and children into the mountain kloofs. He and his men crossed the mountains, fought a fierce battle with the Hereros who tried to bar their way, and reached Rehoboth in a sorry state. There they did everything for him which their duty as Christians required, but they were very pleased when he went off and established a laager in Tsebris. Here he received information from Walfish Bay that the magistrate was prepared to supply him with ammunition, seeing that the transport of ammunition through Otjimbingwe had been stopped by the Hereros.

The Afrikander tribe had only just got safely away, when Kanaimba's Hereros from the Nosob entered Windhoek for the purpose of finishing them off. They found the nest absolutely empty, for even the missionary, Schroeder, had gone to Okahandja. In their rage, they set fire to the werf and destroyed the mission house, stealing everything they could use and smashing up everything they could not take with them. Kanaimba himself broke Schroeder's harmonium to pieces with a blacksmith's hammer. When Wilhelm Maharero arrived, on the 13th September, to take the property of the mission to Okahandja, he found hardly anything left which was worth taking, and Maharero, who was angry with his Hereros for doing a thing of this kind, promised that he would compensate the mission in full.

On the night of the massacre, Wilhelm Maharero had been out in the hunting-grounds beyond Gobabis and, when he received news that war had broken out, he wanted to proceed to Okahandja with all possible speed. Palgrave, however, who was in Gobabis and was likewise on the point of leaving, stopped him and then went with him. Wilhelm was very much annoyed at his father's action and said to him: 'You will see that this innocent Nama blood that you have shed will cost me my own life,' and Palgrave told Maharero how disappointed he was with the way in which he had acted. He said that this would bring the name of the Hereros into very bad odour in Capetown. He would only say a good word for him there, on condition that Wilhelm was appointed for the future as his adviser and as the protector of the Europeans. Palgrave then closed the magistrate's office at Okahandja and returned to Walfish Bay. Wilhelm, however, gave instructions for the withdrawal of all his cattle posts which lay south of the Swakop. He ordered Otjizeva to be evacuated, so as not to expose it to a Nama attack, and he gathered around him the Christian Hereros, while Riarua assembled all the heathens in his commando. Kanaimba and Kahimemua, however, led their own commandos against the Namas.

The first battles

Palgrave had set out from Gobabis on the 26th August, and the end of the place came four days later. The chief of Bethanie and his followers had left. Jacobus Isaak, however, whose tribe was related to that of Gobabis, for which reason he was anxious to regulate tribal matters amongst these trouble-makers, remained behind. Then Kahimemua brought his Hereros close to the village, without being seen, and attacked the werf in the middle of the night. Every one who fell into the hands of the Hereros was slaughtered. It was too late to offer any resistance. The men of Berseba just managed to save the lives of their chief and his relations, and escape to the south. The Hereros started a simultaneous massacre at Witvlei, where about thirty Namas had gone to buy horses, and not a single one escaped. Peace had been brought to the unruly corner of South West Africa more expeditiously than Palgrave had expected and more harshly than he would have desired! Jacobus Isaak sent letters throughout the whole of Namaland in the following terms: 'Help, help, my brothers. Citizens and friends come quickly! No one dare stay at home! Come with every horse that can run! We are in the greatest need. Tell old Tseib in Keetmanshoop and Willem Christian in Warmbad.'

The alarm did not fail to work. The Namas of all the tribes assembled and soon formed a fine army. Those who could not go out immediately, put their weapons in order at home. The chiefs bought provisions and ammunition from the stores. It was true that they could not pay immediately, but the promissory notes which they gave read: 'The Hereros will pay everything', and it was not long before the first herds of Herero cattle began to arrive. On the 12th September, Jacobus Isaak and Andries Lambert fought the Hereros at Khoa-gaos and were successful. On the 26th September, Jan Jonker sent Maharero a declaration of war, and advised him that he would be in Okahandja in October. On the 27th September, Jan captured a large cattle post from the Hereros, which had not been withdrawn from the border quickly enough. Wilhelm Maharero's commando went out to recapture the stock but, when their heathen comrades refused to take the field, came back on the 2nd October without effecting anything. A battle was fought at Kubakob on the 15th and 16th October and eighty Hereros were killed. The fiercest battle of all took place on the 28th October, on the Olifant's River near Okangondo, where the Hereros lost 230 men and many thousands of cattle, which were quickly sent into Namaland. When Samuel Maharero brought the news of this defeat to Okahandja, Maharero lost heart. He decided not to send out any more commandos but to wait for his foes at home.

The latter assembled at Rehoboth. It is true that Rehoboth was neutral territory but nobody worried about that. Jacobus Isaak went through Namaland and personally summoned the tribes to war. His argument was that Maharero must be compelled to recognize boundary lines. The chief of Bethanie wrote stating that he was agreeable that Jan Jonker should receive support from everybody, 'but I beg you not to attack Maharero before I arrive, for on the day that he is captured I want to be present'. Hermanus van Wyk was in a difficult position. His trust in Maharero had received a blow from which it could not recover. The Namas urged him to join up and march with them. He did not know what to do. The fact that he lived in Rehoboth made him Maharero's vassal. What would happen to him if the Namas, who were so sure of victory, did not turn out to be victorious? What would happen if they actually did win? He would lose Rehoboth if Maharero won, for he would never forgive disloyalty. If the Namas won, he would probably lose Rehoboth too for the events of the last few months had furnished him with clear proof that the Namas did not like his being there, and Jan Jonker least of all. Then news arrived, which induced him to decide to join the Namas and to take the field with them against Maharero.

A hunter, named McNab, was hunting in the Waterberg with six Basters, and they were there with their trek-wagon when Maharero's instructions to kill went out to all the Herero werfs. Some Hereros followed the wagon spoor and found the hunters sleeping at their fire, and took them for Namas. They had supposed that McNab was in the wagon, and so they killed all those who were sleeping. They only discovered next day that the people they had killed were Basters, and that McNab was lying amongst them and had been killed too. The missionary, Irle, saw that McNab's wagon and goods were brought to Okahandja, for Maharero had acquainted him with what had happened. Maharero likewise advised Hermanus van Wyk about it and expressed his regrets, but, as some Basters had been killed at Gobabis as well, Hermanus van Wyk abandoned his neutral attitude and, on the 10th November he set out with his men for Jan Jonker's camp at Windhoek, for Jan Jonker had gone back there with the idea of attacking Maharero from the south by the shortest possible road. He had with him the Veldskoendraers, Petrus of Hoachanas with his men, Jacobus Isaak of Berseba, David Christian of Bethanie, and now the Basters of Rehoboth as well. A second encampment had been established at Seeis and this had given rise to differences of opinion amongst the leaders. Moses Witbooi had expressed this opinion in the council of war:

'We are not in a position to carry the war, for which the Hereros have so long been prepared, into Hereroland. We ought rather to stay on the boundary and then to fight every battle which is offered to us, and to drive off as much booty as possible. The rainy season is not far away and the time for horse sickness is approaching. It is not wise to force our way into Hereroland.'

Jan Jonker's opinion was different:

'The taking of booty is not the most important thing, which is to humble Maharero and to do it as quickly as possible, and to make him promise to observe the boundaries. Windhoek must remain in the possession of the Afrikanders and, for that reason, we must establish our head-quarters in Windhoek. The number of stock we take from Maharero is of secondary importance, so long as he is forced to pay the costs of the war.'

They could not agree, and Jan and his supporters got their way, and Moses Witbooi, together with the Grootdodens and Andries Lambert of Gobabis marched to Seeis, in order to make an encircling movement and to attack Okahandja from the east. This plan would, despite the fact that it had been born of dissension, have been by no means a bad one, if the two leaders had co-operated. They would then have caught Maharero between them, and probably effected his downfall. In describing the further course of the hostilities we have therefore to do with the southern force, which marched through Windhoek and was under Jan's command, and with the eastern force, which was under Moses Witbooi's command.

The operations of the southern forces

Aponda, the Mbanderu chief of Barmen, announced that by the beginning of December Jan's army had marched from Windhoek to Otjizeva. From there Jan wrote the following letter to Maharero:

Otjizeva, 3rd December, 1880.

To Paramount Chief Maharero,

With these lines I ask you what your intention is regarding the war, whether you want to continue it, or whether we shall make peace. The southern chiefs, who came together at Okahandja in 1870 to make peace between us, and succeeded in doing so, want to hear from you which of us it is, whether you or I, who has broken the peace of 1870. They would all like to have an answer from you and hear your opinion on the matter. You have treated me disgracefully without any reason, and not only have you murdered my people, but you have repeatedly made war on me. That is why I am now asking you to say what you think, as to whether this unpeaceful state should be changed to a state of peace, or whether you want actual warfare. I am fully equipped, I may tell you, to defend myself in every possible way. Let me hear what you think.

Yours faithfully,
J. Jonker Afrikander
Captain.

Simultaneously with the letter to Maharero, a letter from Jan reached Bam, who was then staying at Okahandja with the trading company there. Jan begged him not to take Hereros into his house when he came to Okahandja. He had nothing at all against the Europeans and did not want them to suffer any harm. 'When we reach Osona you can safely come and see us. I repeat once more the white man has no cause for anxiety, for I have to do with the Hereros only, and not with the missionaries and traders.' On a separate piece of paper Jan wrote that he would be very thankful if Bam would give him some news as to the 'circumstances of the country'.

When he got to know the contents of these two letters, Wilhelm Maharero said: 'In his letter to us Jan talks of making peace, while in his letter to Bam he talks of making war. We shall get ready for war.'

Certain of victory, Jan set out on the 10th December with three carts and twenty-five wagons for Barmen, for he regarded Barmen as the key to Okahandja. He did not share the opinion of some of the leaders that he was acting imprudently in taking all the wagons, and that, as the result of the expedition was uncertain, it would be better to take only so many as were absolutely required. Maharero had ordered Aponda to hold Barmen as long as possible, and had promised to help. Barmen was attacked, but the assistance was not forthcoming. Aponda held out till the evening, and then fled with all his people. All the cattle at Barmen fell into the hands of the Namas. After sufficient had been killed to provide them all with food, and the fire for roasting the meat had been lighted, the captured animals were divided up and sent to Rehoboth that same night.

Messengers, too, were sent to Namaland to spread the news of the victory. After this business had been finished, the Namas set out to make themselves comfortable. They took off their coats, relieved themselves of their equipment, made coffee and cooked rice, of which a plentiful supply had been brought in the wagons, and then stretched themselves out beside the fires to rest after an excellent meal. Sentries were not posted and, when some of the men said that they had shot away all their ammunition, and that they ought to be served with a fresh supply, they were told to go to sleep. The following day would be time enough for anything of that sort.

The following day had not yet dawned when Wilhelm Maharero, with some 800 Hereros, crept up very close to the wagons and the sleeping troops. The attack was made from three sides. Wilhelm's commando had undertaken the most difficult part of it. The Namas were awakened by the Herero volleys and terror seized them. Most of them ran off without coats or hats. The flight became infectious and terrible confusion ensued. In vain Jan tried to stay the rout, but nothing could stop it. The chief of Bethanie was the only man who tried to defend the wagons. He had to pay for his bravery with his life, as did all those whom he persuaded to fight with him. Thirty of his men fell beside him. Wilhelm Maharero, who commanded the right wing, wanted to cut off the fugitives. He and his Christians had almost succeeded in surrounding them, when a Nama bullet from an ambush hit him, and he was carried to the mission-house in a dying condition. If only the Hereros had confined their attentions to the enemy, instead of securing the booty and plundering the twenty-five wagons, there would have been no escape for the Namas. The Hereros had bought their victory dearly, for Wilhelm Maharero died in the night. The storekeeper Bam and Magdalena, Wilhelm's wife, came by night from Okahandja to fetch the body. He was buried alongside the church at Okahandja and, from that day onwards, his father, Maharero, never entered the church again. Kukuri of Otjosazu had three of his sons killed, and the elder, Karl, and the teacher, Petrus Kandjii of Okahandja, fell too. On the Nama side the chief of Bethanie and his youngest son were killed, besides Petrus of Hoachanas and many others, who were not killed in the battle, but were struck down while they were running away. Petrus was the last of Oasib's race, but it was subsequently disclosed that it had not been a Herero bullet which had ended his life, but a Nama one, which had been paid for by a man who aspired to the chieftainship of the Red Nation, his successor, Manasse.

The defeated Namas passed through Rehoboth in a sorry state. Jacobus Isaak of Berseba had to pursue the long road back to Berseba, hatless and on foot. There was a report that two Europeans, du Toits, father and son, fell on the Namas' side in this battle on the 12th December, but there is no confirmation of this. One thing is certain, and that is that the defeated Namas had by no means lost heart. The Basters said: 'We have been defeated and, had we not been mixed up amongst the Namas, we could have kept the Hereros back with our volleys and given the Namas a chance to recover.' The Namas said: 'Our defeat was caused through our own negligence. If we had posted sentries and had given out ammunition at the proper time, we should have come out of the fight as victors. That must be managed better next time.' Jan said nothing, but he took the road to Walfish Bay to buy some more ammunition. The Cape Government, however, had prohibited its importation. He could therefore get it only from Jordan, but Jordan was away and Jan had to wait for a long time until he returned. In the end he got so little that it was very doubtful whether the war could be continued. He then resorted to intrigue. In an evil moment, the idea occurred to him: how would it be if Maharero were to be removed by the Hereros as Petrus of Hoachanas had been by his rival? He, therefore, wrote the following letter to Riarua, the commander of Maharero's troops, suggesting that he should murder Maharero.

From the fact that the letter was found among the papers which Maharero left, it is clear that Riarua never had any intention of entertaining a proposal of this kind. From Tsebris, the place where his father, Jonker, had been so comfortably established when Captain Alexander visited him there, Jan went into the Gansberg. He and his Afrikanders had fallen on evil days. He had grown poor in Windhoek through Maharero's persecution. The rest of his property had been traded for ammunition, and this ammunition had fallen into the enemy's hands through his own negligence, when they captured all his wagons at Barmen. What were he and his people to live upon? 'If I make peace I must starve. If I make war I have meat, which my cattle-herds, the Hereros, fatten up for me,' he said, and he devoted himself to the least dangerous form of warfare, namely, cattle raiding. This he could have done with much less trouble from

Tsebris, but there he was always in danger of being caught. In the Gansberg he could hide himself and his loot in its impenetrable kloofs. It is no task of ours to concern ourselves with the history of Jan's cattle raids, or to describe them.

The operations of the eastern forces

Moses Witbooi, who commanded the eastern forces, had been joined by the Red Nation of Hoachanas, the Orlams of Gobabis, and the Grootdodens, and hoped to capture a great deal of cattle in the Nosob in the course of his raid, but his hopes were not fulfilled. Wherever he went, he found the country deserted by man and beast. His troops finally got so desperate that they had to kill and eat their own riding oxen. All the Hereros had withdrawn in the direction of Okahandja. In the end, he came across some Hereros and was successful in defeating them and taking their cattle away from them, and this relieved his necessities for a short time. The cattle which had been driven to Okahandja could not get used to the place. The grazing became increasingly worse and, with considerable dismay, the Hereros saw whole herds of them running back to their old grazing grounds, to which their owners did not dare to follow them unless they wanted to fall into the hands of the Namas. Kanaimba, who had accomplished the destruction of Windhoek, became so desperate over the position that he went mad.

Before he left for Barmen, Jan had received a letter from Moses Witbooi, advising him that he expected to be at Okahandja on the 27th December. When he attacked Okahandja from the east, Jan was to attack it from the south. This letter was with other letters which fell into the hands of the Hereros after the unfortunate battle of Barmen, and thus Maharero got to know something of which he had hitherto not been aware. A strong force of 800 men was sent to Otjosazu, for it was known that Moses Witbooi was encamped at Katjapia, east of that place. After a number of skirmishes, a battle took place on the 23rd and 24th December. The Hereros surrounded the whole camp and their opponents defended themselves half-heartedly. By evening they were not beaten, but their ammunition was exhausted. The Hereros waited quietly for the following morning to complete their victory over Moses Witbooi. In the night, however, the Namas found a gap in the encircling troops, and made a noiseless escape while the Hereros slept. When the 24th December dawned the Hereros found the camp empty. Moses Witbooi and his army returned to Gibeon very subdued, tattered and torn, without horses, riding oxen, and wagons, and without any ammunition. It was enough to reduce them to despair.

Moses Witbooi, however, was by no means in despair. Despair on account of failure is the trait of a weak character; strong characters recover and anger lends them new strength. Moses Witbooi was a strong character. He knew how to get ammunition, to collect people round him, to encourage Jan Jonker to march with him again and, while Maharero was waiting in Okahandja to see what would happen, when he could have marched right to Gibeon and beyond it without the slightest danger, Moses had succeeded in fitting out quite a large force. He did not want to fall upon Maharero unawares; oh no! He had in mind a Maharero, who knew everything which was going to happen, and was going to meet the inevitable doom which he so richly deserved. He was going to make him feel the pain of it to the very last stroke. He therefore sent him a long declaration of war, for which there was not the slightest necessity, for the war had been going on quite a long time and Moses had already one campaign behind him.

Moses was a long time coming, but at last he set out with a very strong force, certain that he was going to win, but he never reached Okahandja and did not drink from Okahandja's springs. Maharero, too, had collected a very large number of men. He let Moses and Jan come right to Osona and there the greatest battle which had yet been fought in South West Africa took place, that is, the greatest from the point of view of the number of combatants on both sides. The struggle lasted throughout the 22nd and 23rd November and ended in Moses losing all his wagons, horses, and ammunition, and a large number of his men. The road to Windhoek and even beyond Windhoek was strewn with Namas, who had died of their wounds. Utterly defeated, he went back to his 'royal throne' at Gibeon, and Jan went and hid himself again in the Gansberg.

Dr. Hugo Hahn's mission

Since 1874 Hugo Hahn, the founder of the Herero mission and director of the mission colony in Otjimbingwe, had been working in Capetown as the pastor of the German Lutheran Church. (In recognition of his philological work he had in the meantime received a doctor's degree honoris causa.) He had advised the Government on many difficult questions in connexion with circumstances in Hereroland. Now it approached him with the request that he would go as commissioner to Walfish Bay, to investigate the position there and to work for peace. The administration of the Rhenish Missionary Society had already prepared the way. It addressed a long letter to Maharero and the Christian community of Hereroland on the 15th November, 1881, which contained an earnest exhortation to peace, and likewise a practical proposal as to the way in which negotiations might be set in train. The missionaries Diehl and Eich were to be appointed as representatives and mediators for the Hereros, while Krönlein of Stellenbosch in the Cape Colony and Heidmann of Rehoboth were to perform the same service for the Namas.

After his arrival in Walfish Bay in February 1882, Dr. Hahn got into touch with Abraham Swartbooi. Abraham, who had taken up arms with the Namas against Maharero, was tired of war. He was prepared to desist from any further attacks, if he could be provided with a place in which to live, where he would be safe from both the Hereros and the Namas. He wanted to call together his scattered people, especially those who were with his brother Petrus, and then to go and stay with his whole tribe in the tribal territory which Maharero would allot them. Until then, however, there must be an armistice between him and the Hereros. Dr. Hahn's success with the Swartboois necessitated a journey through Otji-mbingwe to Okahandja so as to discuss with Maharero the question of the dwelling-place, an armistice, and, if possible, an independent peace. Maharero was of the fixed opinion that it was no use making peace with one's enemies; the only thing to do with them was to kill them. He agreed, however, that the Swartboois might trek to Fransfontein or Sesfontein, to the west of Outjo, and on the 3rd March, 1882, a separate peace was made between him and Abraham Swartbooi. Shortly afterwards the Swartboois went to Fransfontein, where they are still living to-day.

Maharero had now one troublesome enemy less in the west. On the 15th February the missionary, Heidmann, and Hermanus van Wyk had come to him from Rehoboth to ask for a separate peace, and had been granted it straight away, so it seemed as if there was a break in the war clouds, and there was room for hope.

Dr. Hahn's mission was performed. Walfish Bay was no longer threatened. He set out on his return journey to Capetown and he met, in Walfish Bay, Captain Windus, who performed his duties as magistrate wisely and impartially. An entire stop was put to the importation of ammunition, which had to be smuggled from then onwards through Sandwich Harbour.

Krönlein's mission

When Hermanus van Wyk and the missionary, Heidmann, returned to Rehoboth, at the end of 1882, they found J. G. Krönlein, the missionary from Stellenbosch, and Hegner of Berseba there. Krönlein had received instructions from the Rhenish Missionary Society to go to Namaland and to try and bring about peace. An attempt had been made by the Society to clear the way for him, by means of a letter written to all the chiefs in the country. He wrote letters of invitation to all the tribes, and it was expected that peace would soon be made. When, however, the conditions under which the Basters had made the peace with the Hereros became known, namely, the recognition of the line fixed by Palgrave as the southern boundary of Hereroland, the Nama chiefs saw no possibility of engaging even in preliminary discussions, for they wanted to see the southern boundary line drawn through Otjizeva and northwards of Windhoek. In spite of this, only a few of them refused to come to Rehoboth, but they demanded that Maharero must first ask for peace and must come to the conference himself. Maharero had not the slightest idea of going there personally. He appointed some of his councillors to attend. With the idea of making good use of the time which must elapse before the chiefs arrived, and principally with the object of getting Jan Jonker to attend the conference, Krönlein and Hegner decided to visit him in his mountain stronghold, which was, in Krönlein's words, 'a natural fortress, which the most up-to-date free-booter could not have selected and devised better for the protection of himself and his loot'.

Jan had been advised that Krönlein was coming and so he received a very ceremonious reception. In the front rank stood his Bergdamas fully equipped; behind them his 'burgher' force; and behind these the women folk. Jan himself did not put in an appearance. His suspicions led him to assume that the Basters might follow behind Krönlein's cart and trap him. It was only after sunset that he came on the scene. After they had greeted him, the conversation turned upon the prospective peace negotiations. Jan flew into a rage and said that there would be no such thing as peace in the country until all the missionaries were driven out, for they were the real cause of all the trouble. Next morning he was more amenable, and he promised to go to Rehoboth. Krönlein and Hegner left, but Jan made them wait for him in vain, for he never turned up at all. In the end Jacobus Isaak arrived as the representative of Berseba and Bethanie. He was prepared to make peace with Maharero, as were Manasse of Hoachanas, Kol, and Hermanus van Wyk, and he wrote to Maharero asking him to reconsider his decision to send others to represent him and not to appear in person. Maharero never answered. Jacobus was of opinion that Maharero must first of all be humbled to the dust, and Moses Witbooi announced that peace negotiations with the Hereros could only take one form, and that was that all the chiefs should march together like one man 'to bring about peace at the point of their guns'. In the meantime Maharero's ideas about conditions of peace became known. They consisted of five points:

1. There could be no talk of peace while the old Nama chiefs were alive.
2. Jan must go back to the country where he came from.
3. The boundary line should be drawn with a plough in the position where Palgrave had marked it on the paper.
4. The Basters were to be permitted to live at Rehoboth.
5. If the Swartboois were more respectable people, they could have lived at Rehoboth too, but as nobody could tell where he stood with them, it would be advisable to send them farther south. (From point 5 it would seem as if Maharero regarded the settlement of the Swartboois at Fransfontein merely as a temporary measure, which could be altered when a general peace was concluded.)

When it was apparent that there was no object in waiting any longer, seeing that Moses Witbooi was not to be persuaded to come to Rehoboth, Maharero's delegates met the missionaries, Eich and Diehl, and peace negotiations were commenced on the 8th June, 1882. On the side of the Namas, Jacobus Isaak of Berseba, Manasse of Hoachanas, and Hendrik Windstaan, alias Kol of the tribe of the Grootdodens, took part. Maharero's representatives were the Hereros, Saul Sheppard, Johannes and Martin, as well as Constantine and Johannes from Otjizeva. The Namas were very anxious to bring up the question of blame, so that they could humble the Hereros, and this was the first matter raised in the conference. Krönlein made it very clear indeed that they had come together to discuss not the question of blame but the question of peace. After several weeks of discussion, an agreement was arrived at and a document containing ten points was signed on the 13th June, 1882.

Krönlein returned to Stellenbosch. Even if he had not achieved everything he had hoped for, he had at least made a good beginning with the pacification of Namaland. It was a pity that Jan Jonker, Moses Witbooi, and the other chiefs had not put in an appearance. It was, however, to be hoped that they would become parties to the peace of Rehoboth in course of time. Jacobus Isaak decided to go personally to Jan Jonker in the Gansberg. What he could not get over was that Hermanus van Wyk had made a separate peace with Maharero, and so he was anxious to bring him back again to the side of the Nama chiefs. As Hermanus knew that Jan was just as annoyed with the Basters for having done this, he was not at all pleased with Isaak's visit to the Gansberg, but he could do nothing to stop it. Jan Jonker assured Jacobus that he was entirely innocent so far as the Basters' misfortunes were concerned, but that he did not think it was right that a chief at Rehoboth should side with the Hereros, and he regarded any association of this kind as deserving of punishment. He therefore intended to inflict that punishment very shortly. Jacobus knew very well what that meant when Jan said it. When he went back to Rehoboth he did not say a single word of what was in his mind, nor did he disclose what had happened. One of Jacobus's companions, however, talked about what he had seen and heard. In his distress, Hermanus turned to Maharero with the request that he would come quickly to his assistance. Maharero agreed and sent a strong force under Riarua to Rehoboth. When Jacobus Isaak saw that, he mounted his horse in a rage and returned to Berseba.

Jan let them wait longer for him than could have been anticipated from the indications he had given. If he was to fight the Basters and Hereros together he must first look round for an ally. Part of the tribe of the Grootdodens and Abraham Swartbooi, the former occupier of Rehoboth offered to join him. Riarua had invited Jacobus Christian to stay so that he could show him how to deal with Jan Jonker, but, when Jan stayed away, Riarua went home again. Then Jan came on the scene, burnt down half of Rehoboth, took all the stock he could find, and disappeared with it into the Gansberg. Abraham Swartbooi was seriously wounded in this attack on Rehoboth. He was brought to the district of Bethanie, where he died from his wounds.

Maharero's regulation of the boundary

The peace of Rehoboth, which was also binding upon Maharero, had left the boundary dispute, round which everything really turned, unsettled. A commission was to decide it. The boundary claimed by Maharero, however, was so different from that claimed by the Namas that there seemed no prospect of any agreement being reached through negotiations. Maharero decided, therefore, to fix the boundary himself, in such a manner, that every one understood him and in such a way that his actions strengthened his legal claim. He did not say a word to anybody as to what his purpose was. He left other people to think what they pleased. In the beginning of the year 1883, he gave the order to abandon Okahandja; the order applied not only to Riarua and his fighting men but to his whole tribe. The departure took place without haste and in good order, and only he knew where they were going. The fact that he took with him not only all the women and children and all the cattle, but that he per- suaded his missionary, Eich, to go too, made it plain that he meant to leave Okahandja for a long time. He was providing the Christians among his people with an adviser and minister, for Maharero was fond of the Christians. They had helped him on many an occasion when he could not rely upon the heathen section of his people. He took two Herero teachers with him on his excursion, so that the children should not have to go without instruction. Thus Okahandja stood empty in 1883 and Barmen and Otjizeva were filled with people.

Maharero marched to Windhoek and camped there for a consider- able time. Then he went on to Aris and, after that, he made his camp to the south of Aris. There the Grootdodens attacked him twice but he destroyed their werf and scattered the little Nama tribe. Velds- koendraers, who were in league with the Witboois, worried him, but Maharero repulsed them in a way which left them with very little spirit to attack him again. Accompanied by his enormous herds of cattle and the women and children, he set up another camp in Onguheva. His last camp was fixed at Gurumanas, the place where 1,500 of his sacred oxen had been carried off three years before. Until then Jan had been in the habit of coming down from the Gansberg whenever he felt inclined for some of the Basters' stock. The house of the trader, Carew, stood at Gurumanas. It was immediately put into commission by Eich as a church and school, and he was very glad to have a roof over his head again. When Eich asked the old man what his purpose was with this wonderful trek, Maharero used to say: 'I want to spare the Namas the trouble of going such a long way to look for my oxen.' Things went very pleasantly in Maharero's camp. Many of the women returned to Okahandja and Osona in September and October to work in the gardens and, after their work was finished, they came back to their families at Gurumanas.

For a long time the fact that Maharero was staying in Basterland with his whole tribe was a thorn in the side of Jan Jonker. He knew well enough that a Herero warrior when far from his home was very easily discouraged, but that he would fight like a lion when he was near his property. He did not dare, therefore, to arouse Maharero by stealing his cattle, but his own people must eat. Where were they to get food? He helped himself to the Basters' stock. Maharero knew what his duty was. He marched with his warriors against Jan, and the Basters joined him. Jan's hiding-place was traced. For a whole day they exchanged shots without doing any great damage, but in the end Jan was surrounded. He could not get out any more and he was cut off from water. Without any further fighting he could have been left to die of thirst. The Hereros argued however that they had enough booty, seeing that they had taken 40 horses, 250 cattle, and 50 lb. of powder, and marched away in spite of the Basters' expostulations. Jan and his men went and drank their fill of water. They then pursued the Hereros, robbed them of 1,300 cattle, and disappeared into the Gansberg.

Maharero felt that his work was finished. He had indicated the boundary line which he thought should be fixed between Hereroland and Namaland more plainly than it could have been marked with an iron plough-share. That the western boundary line was fixed in Gurumanas, where he had stopped so long, must now be clear to everybody. He left there and trekked slowly along the boundary line to the east. No one knew how long he meant to pursue this course with his cattle and his whole tribe. In any case, he established his camp in Onguheva for the time being. It seems probable that he would have trekked, little by little, right to Gobabis and Rietfontein, if, while he was at Onguheva, a man had not come upon the scene and compelled him to turn northwards and go back to Okahandja. He entered it again on the 1st September, 1884. The man, who caused him to do this, was the man about whom history will have a great deal to relate during the years that follow, for his name was in everybody's mouth; he was called Hendrik Witbooi.

2. HENDRIK WITBOOI'S WAR

Hendrik Witbooi's youth

The most difficult problem of all is the human being. Only when the regions of man's inner consciousness have been explored, as the land and sea of the external world have been, will it perhaps be possible really to understand and rightly to judge those exceptional individuals, who are wont to appear from time to time in all the races of the earth. Until then, it is advisable to reserve judgement and to record their deeds as truly as possible in the archives of history. Hendrik Witbooi was an exceptional individual of this kind, a riddle for his contemporaries and a riddle for history.

The history of the tribe of which he was a member has already been told. His father was Moses Witbooi, with whose temperamental disposition, which was capable of attaining impassioned heights, we have already become acquainted. His grandfather was Kido Witbooi, who had been the chief of Pella at the beginning of the century, and then had led a nomadic life for a long time, until, in 1863, he had settled in Gibeon under pressure from the mission and at the desire of the women of his tribe. That he was also possessed of a certain amount of psychic force seems possible, and the name of the place shows that this force carried him beyond the bounds of the commonplace. The place where he wanted to pass his old age was to be called Gibeon. For just as the sun restlessly takes her course across the broad expanse of the sky, day in and day out, so had he trekked around for ten restless years with his tribe and, just as Joshua of old had bidden the sun to stand still in Gibeon, so was he giving heed to the words of God's messenger, the missionary, and so to God's voice, in finding a resting-place for himself and his tribe, even if it was only a temporary one, for the Witboois thought that they ought to go northwards, and that there they would find a beautiful paradise. This fitted in, too, with the story of Joshua, for after the sun had stood still the Israelites continued their wandering. It required quite a bold flight of imagination to bring the sun and a Nama chief into such close association! On the Orange River, Hendrik's duty was to herd his father's goats like any other Nama boy. Kido was not a Christian and Hendrik, too, grew up unbaptized.

In the year 1863, when the Hereros' war of freedom broke out, Hendrik went to stay at Gibeon with his father and grandfather. He was then a young man of about twenty-five years of age. There he experienced the terrors of the war between the Witbois and the Red Nation of Hoachanas, and he lost the thumb of his right hand through an enemy's bullet. When he learnt to write later, he must have held the pen between his index and middle fingers, but, in spite of this, he wrote an excellent hand, especially in his younger years. After the peace in 1867, which brought the Orlam war to an end, Hendrik was by no means a man of property. He had married and the children came rapidly, until finally he had seven sons and five daughters, and he had a hard struggle to keep this family in food. He could not, as many others did, enrich himself by stealing stock.

Olpp asked for candidates for a class he was starting for those who wished to be baptized. Hendrik's wife gave in her name and several of Hendrik's sisters too, and even his grey-haired, old grandfather, Kido, who was over eighty years of age, sat down on the school bench and asked to be instructed for baptism. Hendrik did not come and so Olpp asked his wife why. She replied: 'He will come later but he is not quite ready yet.' He did not want to be in a hurry about taking the first step to Christianity, or to do it, simply because his family wanted him to, and Olpp was pleased about that. But Hendrik came in the end and on the 15th March, 1868, Olpp writes as follows:

'A grandson of the old captain, named Hendrik, came this evening and joined the class for baptism. If there is any one amongst them who is really earnest, it is this young man. Up to now he has been one of my best scholars. He reads Dutch and Nama fairly readily and he is taking enormous pains to learn to write a fair hand, although he lost the thumb of his right hand in the war.'

Hendrik's instruction was interrupted. The old chief sent his son-in-law and field cornet, Paul Visser, with twenty men and five wagons, into the territory of the Bondelswarts to go and fetch some members of the tribe who had remained behind there, and to bring them to Gibeon, and Hendrik had to accompany them on their journey. The losses he had had in the war were to be made up in this way, for Gibeon had always to be on its guard against its Nama neighbours and the Hereros. There were stories current about Basters, who were likewise anxious to come to South West Africa, and Kido was afraid that they might take it into their heads to conquer Gibeon and to take it for themselves. This was all the more likely because it was known that the Red Nation, to whom Gibeon had formerly belonged, was not fond of the Witbois, although it had made peace with them. Hendrik was in charge of the trek on the return journey. When he reached Goa-mus he left his post and hurried home to Gibeon. Who could take that amiss of a father who had so many children? Next day Paul Visser arrived with the newcomers.

Paul Visser was not a man to be satisfied with any one who went his own way without asking his permission, and he laid a charge against Hendrik for disobeying orders. A tribal court was convened, and Paul Visser succeeded in getting a fine imposed upon Hendrik and likewise a thrashing. A few days later, however, the chief sent a commando out to shoot the wild dogs, which ran about in packs in the veld, and did enormous damage amongst the sheep. Some of the judges had to take part in the hunt, but Hendrik was given charge of the commando in accordance with his grandfather's wishes. Now he was in command and the men who had been his judges a few days before had now to obey him. This they thought unnecessary, and they did as Hendrik told them with the greatest indifference. Hendrik said nothing, but upon his return to Gibeon he did not hesitate to take them to task for their dereliction of duty, in a quiet and serious way. In spite of all their eloquence, he succeeded in getting each of the culprits sentenced to pay a fine. There appeared to be more in Hendrik, quiet and reserved as he was, than was apparent to the eye, and people were surprised.

Just about this time, Stephenson, the strange scholar, who was trying to walk through Africa, from the Cape to Cairo, without a wagon and without any companion, arrived at Gibeon in the course of his travels. He wanted some one to go along with him and show him the way, and to help him to carry his bundle. Hendrik became his companion and they probably talked along the road. Hendrik knew quite well that his father's and his grandfather's hopes were centred on the north, and that they regarded Gibeon merely as a halting place on their journey. What they talked about is not known. With a man of Hendrik's mentality, however, it may be taken that this lonely, highly-educated wanderer from the north aroused in him feelings and ideas, which crystallized in his inmost consciousness in the predominant idea 'northwards'.

Hendrik was baptized. Contrary to the usual custom, which was to take a new name at this turning point in life, he clung to his old name. This was a good sign with a Nama, for it is a characteristic trait of the race to turn to things which are new and high-sounding.

When Moses Witbooi returned from his journey to Okahandja in 1870, and brought back a message to the effect that Maharero had offered Windhoek to the Witboois there was great excitement and rejoicing throughout the tribe. Everybody wanted to take down their mat huts immediately and to trek to the north. It required all the energy and persuasion of the missionary to restrain the Witboois from this unconsidered step, and only when he declared that he would, under no circumstances, accompany them, but that he was minded to stay in Gibeon, did many of them come to their senses. Hendrik's name was mentioned as one of those who wanted to leave. When Olpp asked him what he had decided, he replied: 'The people say that I am anxious to go with them, but I give them no answer when they ask me. I do not know what I shall do. I cannot be without my teacher, for he is the only comforter I have.' This was not mere flattery, for the relationship between him and Olpp could not possibly have been better.

Olpp dismissed his Herero herdsmen, and Hendrik did him an excellent service by getting Nama herdsmen for him, and persuading reliable people to undertake the work. He himself took charge of the largest cattle post and supervised all the others. In this way, he not only obtained milk for his numerous family, but likewise a share of the increase, so that he soon began to have a small flock of his own. He kept accounts himself of the increases and decreases, and there were never any irregularities at the cattle post of which he was personally in charge.

Once he had acquired some property, he became very desirous of occupying a stone house in place of a reed one. He asked Olpp for a plan, and the latter gladly gave him assistance, for the building of a substantial house seemed to him to be the best guarantee that Hendrik had given up his idea of going to the unknown country in the far north. When, however, the site of the building was pegged out on the ground, it appeared that Hendrik had chosen for himself the very place which Olpp had selected for the building of a new church. It was only necessary to explain this to him to cause him to select another building site close by, and he laboured, day in and day out, with industry and skill, at the building, which consisted of two large rooms with windows and doors.

Olpp was very anxious to have a man of this kind as church elder, and Hendrik and his brother Isaak stood as rival candidates for election. Hendrik received a majority of votes but he resigned in favour of his elder brother. Two years later there was a new election and this time he received a unanimous vote and he accepted the appointment.

Olpp was, however, not in good health, and he could not continue to do his work. He had a nervous break-down and decided to go to Germany. When Hendrik heard that his teacher wanted to under-take this journey, he insisted upon going with him and taking charge of everything. He went to Steinkopf with Olpp, and there he took leave of the man whom he loved like a father. He never dreamt that his own father would one day reproach him bitterly because of this journey and his sojourn in Steinkopf. Moses Witbooi, who was very proud of his chieftainship and, despite his great age, very jealous, and so was obsessed with the idea that his son was aspiring to the position, had found out that Hendrik had a document in his Bible which he guarded as if it were sacred. It was actually only a picture, with Olpp's inscription on it, which he had given to his faithful Elder as a parting present. In Moses's jealous imagination this was an important document, and he believed that Olpp had 'anointed' him as chief of the Witboois, as Samuel did in the case of Jesse's son at Bethlehem, when the evil spirit came upon Saul. This matter will, however, be referred to again in its proper place. The eventful year, 1880, commenced. Moses Witbooi was summoned by Palgrave to Gobabis, for what his brother-in-law and field cornet, Paul Visser, had been doing there required a certain amount of adjustment. Hendrik went to Hereroland, much at the same time, to fetch some oxen from Otjizeva and to buy some horses and, on this journey, the things we have told happened to him, and these things influenced his whole life. He entered upon a new phase of life, in which many of his actions would have seemed incomprehensible were they not regarded in the light of what happened to him then. It was only after four years had passed that Hendrik took his new minister, Rust, into his confidence. During this time he had evolved a fixed plan in accordance with his own interpretation of the three things which had been said to him. What had happened was the outbreak of the war, which people had been dreading for such a long time. The way which was opened was the way to the north to which old Kido's desire had always turned, and whence a new call had come. Thither his brother Isaak had gone some years before, and he had never re-turned. Rumour had it that he had been killed by Bushmen, and then a sign had been received from him that he was still living, and Hendrik had been very eager to go and join him. After the receipt of the sign nothing more was heard of him until a young man appeared and said that he had been with Isaak and that they had reached a fine country. The young man was to lead the Witboois to it. The country was very good; there were large numbers of game there; hippopotami wandered about in troops. The land had very few inhabitants and these were friendly people. Gold was used in place of iron; at least all the implements, such as axes, knives, &c., were made of a metal which appeared to be gold, for when it was put into a blacksmith's fire it melted.

In order to get to this land, however, there was a difficult obstacle to be surmounted: it was necessary to conquer the Hereros, for they barred the road. Hendrik was of the opinion that he had subsequently received an explanation of the duty, which had been laid upon him in the course of the revelation, to the effect that he was chosen to kill Maharero, and that only two members of his tribe would lose their lives in the undertaking. Hendrik had become a fanatic. He spent long hours at night in quiet meditation at his grandfather's grave. What the people gleaned from his remarks led them to hope that Hendrik was going to lead them to a better country and to improve their position. The number of people who began to talk of dreams, visions, and revelations, began to increase. Rust worked with all his power to banish these fantastic ideas, and he especially tried to influence Hendrik, but all in vain. Hendrik received at his grandfather's grave some new instructions, which were of a somewhat dangerous kind. Beginning in his own werf and then going farther afield, he was to kill a number of people. He was to drive the Red Nation out of Hoachanas. Two chiefs were to fall by his hand at Rehoboth, and the Basters were to be driven out. Should he refuse to carry out these commands, it would cost him his life. Rust tried to arouse Hendrik's conscience and to get him to see clearly. Hendrik asked Rust not to ask him any more questions, nor to trouble him with warnings and admonitions. He was certain of his way and he was going to follow it, whatever the missionaries, whom he still honoured and respected, might say when he set out. 'When we left Pella', he said, 'we came to Gibeon, without any intention of staying here permanently, for our inclinations were urging us northwards. Gibeon was only a camping-place for us up to the time of my grandfather's death; now it is time for us to go on. It would be better that I should die than leave this task undone.'

An alienist would not have regarded Hendrik as mentally deranged. He was obsessed with a great idea. So far as his revelations are concerned we should reserve judgment; the human mind has depths which cannot be plumbed.

Hendrik Witbooi and his father

The reader will remember that Moses declared war on Maharero, and the lamentable result of the campaign which followed it. Moses's pride was not broken by the disaster, but he was afraid that Maharero would come and revenge himself on him at Gibeon, and so he resorted to strategy. He put on an honest air and went to Rust, and asked him to write to Maharero, at his dictation, asking for peace, and saying how very anxious he was to make peace. His idea was to acquire a new supply of ammunition while the negotiations were in progress, and then to attempt a new campaign which he hoped would have better results. Not dreaming that anything was wrong, Rust wrote the letter, and Maharero answered it promptly on the 23rd October, 1883, in the following terms:

'I agree with you that enough blood has been shed, and that we have both suffered enough losses in the three years we have been at war. I am therefore prepared to make peace with you, if that is your honest wish, and you intend to keep peace as faithfully as Manasse of Hoachanas and Captain Hermanus van Wyk of Rehoboth have done up to now. If it is really your desire to conclude peace with me, let me know at once. I shall then regard you as a chief with whom I am at peace, as I do the chiefs, Manasse and Hermanus van Wyk. I am, Maharero Tjamuaha.'

Moses never answered this letter. He had gained time and strengthened his position in the meanwhile and, besides this, something else happened which claimed his entire attention. His brother-in-law, Paul Visser, who was friendly with the war party in Gobabis, those successful robbers of the east, had gone to Lidfontein. Some Basters were living in the place, which was in Manasse's territory, and amongst them was Arie van Wyk, who was quite a wealthy man. He had trekked there with his own stock, with a view to protecting them from Jan Jonker's raids, and a number of the Basters at Rehoboth had entrusted their stock to him, so that they should not lose them when Jan made his frequent forays. This stock had grazed in veld belonging to Gibeon, and that gave Paul Visser an excuse to seize it and drive it off. Moses Witbooi was privy to this action. He really had no liking for Paul for several reasons, but now that the latter had

HENDRIK WITBOOI

The Hottentot Chief

By courtesy of F. Nink, Windhoek

brought some loot home with him, he did not inquire too closely into its origins; but he was very dissatisfied when Paul wanted to give him a smaller share than that to which he was entitled as chief. Such a furious quarrel ensued that the danger arose of their deciding it with their guns. Hendrik Witbooi and the Christian congregation at Gibeon were very dissatisfied with Moses's and Paul's attitude. Hendrik wanted all the stolen stock to be given back to the Basters, and the majority of the Witboois supported him. When Moses refused, Hendrik called a meeting of the congregation and laid the circumstances before them. Sixty of them, who owned cattle, declared themselves ready to contribute sufficient cattle to make up the number which had been taken from the Basters, and to deliver these to the people of Rehoboth. When Moses saw that he had so little support, he gave way and instructed Hendrik to put matters straight. Hendrik's cattle kraal got fuller every day. Every animal which was driven into the kraal seemed to Moses to be a vote of censure on his actions. He cancelled his own instructions, and based this cancellation on the excuse that Hendrik was setting himself up as chief of Gibeon. Hendrik had a clear conscience and did not worry about his father's having countermanded the instructions. When Moses saw that he had lost all prestige in Gibeon, he went to stay at an outpost and gave himself over to evil cogitations. Suddenly there were rumours in Gibeon that he was coming to attack the place. Hendrik left the werf, accompanied by his large body of supporters, and went into laager in front of Gibeon. The rumours were not without substance, for Moses had written to Manasse of Hoachanas, asking him to come over secretly with an armed force and to help him against his son Hendrik, 'who wanted to rob him of his royal throne'.

Judt, the missionary at Hoachanas, got wind of this demand, and used his influence to prevent Manasse from going. At the same time, he and Rust wrote letters to Hegner, the president of the Nama mission, and the latter came to Gibeon immediately accompanied by Jacobus Isaak, the chief of Berseba, to investigate matters; Jacobus came because Gibeon belonged to the triple alliance, and Hegner came because Hendrik was the Elder of the congregation. Moses and Paul Visser were asked to attend, and did so, and now it came out that Moses supposed Hendrik to have a document in his Bible, which proved that Olpp had 'anointed' Hendrik at Steinkopf as chief of the Witboois. This suspicion was founded on the general custom of the time that a newly-elected chief should be installed in his office with a religious ceremony, to show clearly that the Christians regarded themselves as subject to him. The entire groundlessness of the accusation was proved without any difficulty at all, but suspicion is a plant which grows without roots, and no reconciliation between father and son took place.

Hendrik had now to declare what his further plans were. If he was not seeking to become chief, people wanted to know why he had established himself in a laager outside the village. That he had asked his father for ammunition and had been refused, that he had gathered all his followers round him, and that he had managed to procure ammunition from one source or other, all these things were very suspicious circumstances. Hendrik refused to give any information at all about 'his business'. This looked very much like rebellion. Moses and Simon Koper, who had hastened to assist him, would very much liked to have taught the 'rebels' a lesson, but they did not dare to do so because Hendrik was very much stronger than they were. Hendrik's attitude, however, was not that of a rebel. He kept his own counsel, but he continually declared that he had no intention of attacking his father, but that his plan was to leave Gibeon. He told no one where he meant to go, not even his own people, and on the 14th May he received the following message: 'Seeing that you will not listen either to your father or mother, nor to your missionary, you may go your own way.' Immediately after this Moses inspanned and drove off. Hendrik asked his father to come to his laager to discuss matters with him privately. Moses replied: 'If you want anything from me you can come to me; I am keeping out of your way.'

Whenever any discussion took place Hendrik always spoke about 'his business'. It was clear to nobody what he meant by it. His father was suspicious, and felt absolutely convinced that he meant to attack him and deprive him of the chieftainship of the Witboois. Rust and Hegner thought that 'the business' embraced the return of the stolen stock to the Rehoboth Basters, for Hendrik had taken this matter in hand so energetically, but they gradually came to recognize that it could not possibly refer to this matter alone. As Hendrik would say nothing, they tried to find out his intentions from his people, but all that these knew was that Hendrik was going to ensure them future happiness somewhere or other. Hegner and Jacobus Isaak returned to Berseba on the 15th May. The following day Hendrik set out and marched northwards, whither, no one knew.

The day of Onguheva

Was it Hendrik's intention to engage in a campaign against the Basters? Gibeon had never been fond of Rehoboth. Did Hendrik, supposing Maharero to be in Gurumanas, intend to break through to the north, while Maharero was not in a position to prevent him, or did he want to attack Maharero himself? On the 4th May, before the conference in Gibeon, Hendrik had written to his father as follows:

'My dear father, I have received your letter but can give no reply to it. There is no particular reason why I cannot reply, except that I have given you a sufficient answer before. I have put my hand to the plough and I cannot turn back. I now request you to open the doors to the people who want to go with me, so that they may be able to go, and to give them all horses and ammunition to help them on their way. You have no cause for anxiety. I am your son and I am going to act fairly towards you, for it is no small matter which I now intend to undertake.'

When Hegner and Rust visited him on the day before his departure, and pressed him once more to abandon the prosecution of his mysterious plans and then wrote him a letter in the very same terms, he wrote back:

'I beg you spare me the indignity of having to sit in front of you and tell you something which you do not believe. I still stand where I have always stood.'

On his northward march, Hendrik believed that he was led by a bright light, like the rays of the sun reflected from a mirror. When he took the road to Gurumanas, where he supposed Maharero to be, the light went out. Hendrik turned back in the direction of Rehoboth and it came back again. Considerable excitement was caused at Rehoboth when the horsemen were seen approaching. All the men ran to get their guns and took up their positions in the fortifications. When they saw the excellent order with which the riders approached, that they were waving a white flag, and that they had white crests on their hats, which were shaped like combs, they knew that these were the 'Whitecombs', as the Witboois were called, and they thought that Hendrik Witbooi had come to bring them back their stolen stock.

Hendrik dismounted and went to Hermanus van Wyk, who had just returned from a visit to Maharero. The latter was at Onguheva, which the Namas called Hu-guis, which means 'The jutting cliff', on account of the shape of the mountain. He had been discussing with him the campaign against Jan, and Maharero had promised to give him adequate support. Hendrik now revealed his plans to Hermanus. He had come to make peace with Maharero, and even to compel him to make peace by force of arms. The Basters should go with him, for the separate peace which they had made with the Hereros was an unseasonable one, and therefore required some further adjustment. Hermanus reminded Hendrik of his father's letter, in which he had asked for peace. Hendrik said that the letter had not been meant seriously. His father had only wanted to gain time in order to renew his equipment and, besides this, he had a quarrel with Paul Visser, and had feared that the Hereros would attack him while he was in this difficult position. If Hermanus absolutely refused to join him in attacking Maharero, Hendrik would not take it amiss. He withdrew his horsemen and pitched his camp near Rehoboth. He asked Hermanus to write to Maharero, telling him to expect him and to make his preparations. A messenger was sent to Maharero. Stragglers came from Gibeon and other places to join the Whitecombs. The Basters, however, remained in their positions day and night, for they did not trust Hendrik at all.

A week later, Hendrik and his troops moved off in the direction of Onguheva, south of Aris. In spite of the warning, Maharero had not made any preparations, but he had Hendrik's troop of horsemen very carefully watched by his Hereros. Hendrik did not advance to the attack, but tried to get past Maharero. He was expecting to be reinforced by Guwusib, Manasse's half-brother, who was going to bring with him a body of men, equal in number to Hendrik's own. On the 24th June, 1884, the Hereros attacked, and the shooting lasted the whole day. Only two men fell on Hendrik's side, while Maharero's losses were very slight. Both sides had taken good cover. They lay so closely together that the men could taunt each other. Then a Bergdama on Maharero's side recognized a Nama called Gamab, whom he had met previously in Hendrik's ranks. He called out to him: 'Gamab, you have come a long way, why do you come as an enemy? We have heard good of you and expected that you would come in peace.' The Nama shouted back: 'We, too, want peace, but as your chief is so arrogant and refuses to open the gates to us, we have come to open them by force.'

This talk of peace from both sides was partially caught up without the full import of the conversation being understood, and then

Hendrik gave the order to cease fire, and Maharero had an announcement made that, if an unarmed Nama would come out into the open between the combatants, he would send someone, also, to negotiate. Hendrik put to Maharero the question whether he was prepared to make peace, saying that otherwise he would go to Okahandja and compel him to do so. Maharero sent back an answer: 'I am Okahandja; there is no need for you to go there. Let there be peace between us.'

Maharero apparently agreed with all Hendrik's proposals, but he made no promises. He would, however, have nothing to do with giving Hendrik's troops provisions for their march back to Rehoboth. He gave Hendrik three oxen, however, and the latter promised him that he would use his influence with the southern chiefs to induce them to negotiate for peace as well. While these negotiations were going on, the Namas, whose arrival Hendrik had been expecting, and of whom Maharero knew nothing at all, had caused the Hereros a great deal of damage at Aris, where they had carried off all the cattle. News of these losses reached Maharero. Hendrik heard about them and was very much perturbed. He suggested to Maharero that, as they had made peace, he would follow up the raiders and return the stolen stock to him. With that Maharero agreed. Hendrik, therefore, mounted his horse and went after the 'thieves' with a number of his people. He caught them up and brought the stolen stock back to Maharero. Hendrik however, took, the thieves into his camp and thus increased his strength twofold.

Hendrick returned to Gibeon as victor and peacemaker. On the 17th July, Moses Witbooi had entered once again the 'place of his royal throne', which had not proved a very difficult undertaking, for nobody offered any opposition, and then he had gone away again.

Maharero left Onguheva and went back to Windhoek, where he intended his cattle to stay for a long time. By this he wanted to show that he still made a claim to Windhoek's springs and grazing ground, for Hendrik's letter had merely demanded the restoration of the village, without making any conditions as to its future occupier. Maharero himself was going on a visit to Kambazembi in the Waterberg. He had hardly left Windhoek when his Hereros left, too, and trekked to Otjizeva. Windhoek seemed too dangerous to them and, as Riarua, the commander of the troops, was ill, they would under no circumstances remain there. Maharero came back and his people urged him to go and live at Okahandja again. He gave in, and so he entered his old place of residence once again on the 1st September, 1884, after many months of patrölling his boundary line.

'The year of lies'

Hendrik returned from Onguheva to Gibeon as a victor, and, what was more, he, who was not a chief, had succeeded in a very short time in doing what the Nama chiefs had been trying to do for years, that is to say, to make peace with Maharero, and he had done it virtually without loss of life. Things had turned out just as he had predicted, and he had lost only two men. The confidence which his followers had in him became stronger. They became more attached to him than ever. As Moses held aloof, Hendrik was the hero of the day. People went to him whenever they were in difficulties, and Hendrik performed the duties which the chief usually performed. Meanwhile, he made preparations for his march to the unknown promised land in the north. He bought wagons and provisions, and his friend Duncan at Keetmanshoop obtained guns, powder, and shot for him. He could actually have got any quantity of ammunition at Bethanie for half the price, for Lüderitz from Bremen had come into the country, had purchased the sea coast from the chief of Bethanie, and had established a trading store, where ammunition could be bought at extraordinarily cheap prices, while no ammunition at all could be imported through Walfish Bay. Hendrik did not want to run the risk of getting into the German's clutches. He had heard that German officials had come to make treaties with the chiefs, whereby they put themselves under German protection. It seemed to him to be a similar kind of arrangement to that which Palgrave had made, and he had left the country four years before when the war broke out, and had never been heard of again. He was suddenly heard of again in January 1885, when he arrived at Walfish Bay and summoned Jan Jonker to him. What passed between them no one knew. It had likewise come to Hendrik's ears that the German consul Vogelsang had been to Rehoboth early in the year, and had sent Jan Jonker a letter, asking him to come and discuss matters with him at Bethanie, for he had something important to tell him which would be to his advantage. Jan had not accepted the invitation, but had replied that he was receiving no orders from a pedlar. He was annoyed because Vogelsang had hinted in his letter that Jan had better not make any more raids against the Basters of Rehoboth, because they were now under the protection of the German Empire, and Hermanus van Wyk received an equally unpleasant letter from Jan, suggesting that, as he had given his territory away, he had better go back to the Colony from which he had come.

This did not please Hendrik at all. All his preparations were completed and he intended to set out for the north in the middle of the year. He wanted to take with him all his followers, including the old and the sick. If his missionary, Rust, did not want to go with him, his son, Hendrik, would see to the teaching of the children, and Samuel Isaak would undertake the instruction of the adults. In the middle of his final preparations, there reached him a letter from the head of the mission at Barmen, in which he was given an earnest and friendly warning to abandon his project, but this letter had no effect at all. Hendrik was convinced that he had been called by God. The revelations which he had received counted with him more than the opinions of any human beings, and more than the actual words of the Bible itself. Hendrik had to give up his office as elder of the church, and he did so without any ill feeling. He felt that he was misunderstood and he was sure that his minister would come to understand him later on.

In the middle of July 1885 he set out, with all his people, in the direction of Rehoboth. He did not hurry at all and, when he reached Rehoboth, he went into camp. Heidmann warned him not to march on Okahandja with an armed force, as that would be likely to occasion trouble with Maharero, or, at the very least, to make him distrust him. Hermanus van Wyk offered to act as an intermediary between him and Maharero. All this was to no purpose. Excellent order was kept in the Witbooi's camp, and not a single goat was stolen from the Basters. Maharero sent a messenger to ask whether Hendrik was coming in peace or war. Hendrik wrote to Maharero stating that he was coming to confirm the peace of Onguheva, and to pass through to the north, in accordance with the promise which Maharero had given him. Maharero, however, did not trust Hendrik, and the fact that he was advancing with 600 armed men aroused his suspicions. He collected as many Hereros at Okahandja as he could. Messages were sent in all directions. Maharero wrote back saying that he was fully prepared to stand by the agreement made at Onguheva, but that he was surprised that Hendrik had not kept his promise. He had promised him that he would do his best to get the other Nama chiefs to make peace with him, but not a single one had appeared. If he was coming with honest intentions, he would point out a place at Osona where he could pitch his camp, and from there they could negotiate further.

Hendrik arrived àt Otjizeva close to Osona and Okahandja. Eich, the missionary, advised Hendrik not to ask too much of Maharero. Hendrik's son was of the opinion that, with God's help, ten men would be enough to overcome Maharero's Hereros, if it became necessary to force a passage.

The expedition arrived at Osona on the afternoon of the 14th October. Hendrik was shown a gorge alongside the Swakop where he could put his wagons and pitch his camp. The camp was so placed that its occupants could only get to the water by passing through a large number of Hereros, who were encamped in the bed of the Swakop in front of the gardens. The two chiefs greeted each other in a friendly manner. They were very careful in the way in which they treated each other, but they smoked the same pipe and, when Hendrik asked for tea, coffee, and sugar, Maharero sent some one to Okahandja immediately to fetch it. For the moment everything went well. A few days before Dr. Goering,[1] Pastor Buettner, and six other Germans had been to see Maharero, to negotiate with him with a view to getting him to place himself under the protection of the German Empire, and they had gladly given him whatever he asked for from their own supplies. Coffee and tea, however, are of no use without water, and Maharero had said nothing about water. Hendrik meant to speak about the water when Maharero's peace offering was given him, but the latter had left by then. Then the Witboois asked that they might be permitted to go and get water, whereupon the Hereros crowded together and allowed them only to draw sufficient for their immediate requirements. They would not, however, allow the horses and trek oxen to be watered at all. The following day the scarcity of water became serious. Maharero gave instructions as to how the wagons had to be driven. He then left the approach to the water open, but insisted that, after the water casks had been filled, the trek oxen and horses were to be watered immediately. That implied that he was not willing to give them free access to the watering-place, so that they could go and fetch water right throughout the day as they required it. Hendrik took the precaution of having his ammunition unpacked.

Suddenly trouble arose at the waterhole. It went against the grain with the Witboois who were drawing water to be ordered about by

[1] Dr. Goering was the father of General Goering the Nazi War Minister.—*Ed.*

the Hereros. Those who were drawing water tried to take possession of the waterhole and the Hereros beat them back. In a moment there was a fight in progress, and a number of Witboois lay dead on the ground. Hendrik immediately ordered his men to fire, and large numbers of Hereros fell. He received, however, a sharp fire from both sides, for the Hereros at the water were only the central body, other armed Hereros having been posted on both sides of them. It now became impossible to stop the fighting and, if the Witboois did not wish to be overwhelmed by a force which was twice as large as their own, they were forced to flee. They fled and were pursued. Their wagons, trek oxen, and horses all fell into the hands of the Hereros.

In Okahandja, the German visitors were given some unusual work to do. The wounded Hereros were brought into the village, and they were engaged in dressing their wounds until after midnight. That made an excellent impression upon Maharero and his men, and expedited the negotiations of the following day. On the 21st October, four days after the battle of Osona, the treaty with the German Government was signed.

Hendrik did not return through Rehoboth. On the 5th September Hermanus van Wyk had entered into a similar treaty, and Hendrik did not want to show his face there in his defeat. He reached Gurumanas in a wretched state. Two of his sons had been killed and a third had a shattered arm. His men had suffered heavy losses and all his possessions were gone. Shortly after his arrival he wrote to Heidmann: 'You warned me to keep the peace, and now I have fallen into the hands of Maharero's murderers, and you knew all along, for you knew that he was a murderer. Now the gates of war are open and the gates of peace are closed.' He asked for food for the many wounded men he had with him and he received it. He wrote to Hermanus van Wyk: 'I ask you as a friend to keep away from the Hereros, for our enmity is greater than it has ever been before. Let us conquer the Hereros, for the Lord will certainly deliver them into our hands.' He asked for ammunition, too, saying: 'I do not want to wait any longer. I have two steps behind me, and I want to ascend the third one quickly. Formerly I begged you not to take back those of your men, who were staying with the Hereros as burghers, again. Now I say to you "let them stay there and drink with Maharero out of the same cup".' To Maharero he wrote as follows:

Gurumanas, 19th October, 1885.

You know that I came there (Osona) in peace, but you deceived me and brought me into your kraal and murdered my men under the cloak of peace, and all that I did was to defend myself. You know very well what happened that day. I left because I had no more ammunition. You know very well that you never conquered me. My people never retreated at all, but I had to leave because of the lack of ammunition. Now I have prepared myself for war. I shall be with you again very shortly. Sit and wait for me. For with the peace of Onguheva you tied my hands, and you have now untied them again with the war you have made. I have now made every preparation, as I did the first time, and I have opened all the gates of war. I tell you plainly that you are now going to be attacked from every side. You know that, when I made peace with you, I closed all the doors, but you know too how you murdered my men through treachery. Truly the Lord will judge between us. I remain, the insulted and deceived Hendrik Witbooi.

It is very difficult to solve the riddle of the fight at Osona. It would appear that Maharero was prepared to negotiate peace with Hendrik, and to bring to a conclusion what had been put in train at Onguheva. It likewise appears that Hendrik had no intention of fighting Maharero, if the latter had given him a free passage to the north. Both sides, however, were so suspicious that the fight can only be regarded as having arisen by accident.

As the Hereros believed that Hendrik had lied to them, they call the year 1885 'the year of lies' to this very day.

Hendrik's third step

All kinds of things were happening at Gibeon while Hendrik was making preparations for a third campaign against Maharero, with the object of forcing a passage to the north. Pastor Buettner, the German Government's Commissioner, had let Moses know that he was coming to discuss a Protectorate with him. Moses went off as quickly as possible, and only stopped when he got to Warmbad, where he stayed until the end of the year. Five prominent Witboois, however, placed themselves and their families under German protection at their own risk. These were all members of the tribal council. On the 5th December, Dr. Goering arrived there with the same object, but as Moses was not back yet, he had to continue his journey without effecting anything. Then the old chief turned up and vented his wrath on the five councillors. They were sentenced to a fine of both money and stock and, besides that, they were tied up with riems and forced to lie on the floor of their huts for three days and two nights, without being able to move, which was the old form of imprisonment. Moses was angry, too, with Rust, the missionary, for Dr. Goering had stayed at his house, and had gone to church with him one Sunday in full uniform, which was something that had made a great impression upon the Witboois. Moses prohibited the holding of church services, and Rust was forced to collect his congregation under the green trees in front of his house until the president, Hegner of Berseba, appeared on the 18th February, 1886, and the quarrel was, to some extent, patched up. In the meantime, Paul Visser had allowed himself to be 'anointed' as chief, for he was of the opinion that a chief ought to pay some attention to his tribe and not to spend all his time elsewhere. Moses, who had declared war upon him some time previously, wanted now to go and attack him in all earnest. He called upon all the Nama chiefs to come and help to restore him to his 'royal throne', but no one appeared. The only one who was at all inclined to help him was Manasse of Hoachanas. Judt, however, who had a clear insight into things, warned him, saying: 'If you go, you admit by doing so that you are Moses Witbooi's subject, for in his summons he calls himself "the King of Great Namaland" and, in a previous letter to you, he described you as "Chief by favour",' the position being that Manasse had obtained his position not by public vote, but through the favour of two of the councillors. Judt prevailed, and so even Manasse had no dealings with Gibeon. Moses Witbooi was determined to fight, so what he wanted above everything else was money with which to buy arms and ammunition and to pay mercenaries. He decided to sell one of his finest farms, Goa-mus, which many people had wanted to buy from him. He first sold the place to one Spangenberg from South Africa, and then to Sinclair and, not satisfied with that, he sold it again to Krabbenhoeft at Keetmanshoop, taking £15 worth of goods to close the bargain. The two other chiefs of the triple alliance heard of these land sales and demanded a conference at Gibeon. Moses opposed it, but could do nothing to prevent it. Before they arrived, he dismissed the tribal council which had advised him so badly, and wrote a letter to the 'magistrate of the Boers at Kenna', telling him that the hundred families which he had intended to settle at Goa-mus should stay where they were. There was a mistake in what their foreman, Spangenberg, had told them, for he could not sell land without the consent of the other chiefs. The horses which Spangenberg had given him should be regarded as borrowed by him for hunting purposes. When the chiefs, accompanied by Dr. Goering, came on the scene there was nothing more to be done. Moses lied about the land sales, which Dr. Goering had

viewed very favourably, for he cherished ideas of settlement and
would gladly have seen the Boers established in the territory of
Gibeon. From the second day onwards Moses took no part in the
conference.

Nothing was seen of Hendrik. He was preparing for the third step,
which, as he had written Maharero, he was anxious to ascend. His
son, Hendrik, paid Gibeon a visit, and he said that his father's followers still believed firmly in his mission, in spite of his serious defeat
at Osona. Hendrik's son went to Berseba and Bethanie to look for
volunteers and to buy ammunition from Duncan. Hendrik had joined
up with Jan Jonker and had gathered round him the Topnaars, Grootdodens, Boois, Veldskoendraers, and the unruly elements amongst the
Basters, and had set up his laager at Nauas. Jan himself was not
there, for it was against his nature to fight under anybody else's
command.

Maharero had been expecting Hendrik's return for a considerable
time. He had collected a body of men who were always eager to
fight and were accustomed to war. Fortifications were built on the
southern side of Okahandja, and it was decided to repel Hendrik's
attack as sharply as possible. In spite of the fact that Hendrik had
been expected daily for months, he took Maharero by surprise in the
end. On the 17th April, 1888, the sleeping inhabitants of Okahandja
were wakened by shooting, as the day dawned. Hendrik had arrived.
From the two hills on the south of the place, his Witboois were
shooting right into the huts. He had expected to cause a great deal
of confusion and, through profiting by it, to gain a victory over
Maharero, but he had made a miscalculation. In a few moments the
Hereros were in the fortifications; they opened fire, drove the Witboois out of the hills, thrust them back towards the south, took
position after position away from them, and, towards evening, surrounded them completely. The following morning they were going
to make an end of them. It was moonlight, however, and this enabled
the Witboois to find a gap through which they escaped unnoticed.
The Hereros were very angry when they discovered this, and set out
to pursue the fleeing foe. The latter had broken up into separate
groups. Other fights took place at Otjizeva, Otjihavera, and at
Okapuka. The Hereros would not desist, but followed the Witboois
into their laager at Nauas. The camp was empty, but their wagons
and household utensils were still there, and they took everything
with them. The occupants of the laager had fled in the direction

of Hoachanas, and they were pursued as far as there. This persistence in pursuing the enemy was something unheard of, for, until then, the Hereros had always left a defeated enemy when they had chased him far enough away. Hendrik was now absolutely poor again. The third step had brought him no advancement, but he did not give in. While the Hereros returned home and devoted themselves to breeding cattle, Hendrik went back to the Gansberg, where Jan Jonker had long ago proved that it was possible to become the owner of a large number of cattle without breeding them. Hendrik, too, was forced to adopt Jan's methods. The warrior, who had believed himself to be called and led by God, became the captain of a robber band, which went forth no longer to win battles, or to conquer a distant land, but to steal cattle to enable its members to lead a life of misery, privations, and danger, and to acquire, with some portion of their loot, the ammunition that was necessary to enable them to steal. To Maharero, however, he wrote as follows: 'You have robbed me; I shall do the same to you. I am now going to make war against you in the same way that Jan Jonker does.'

Hendrik's petty warfare against the Hereros

Hendrik Witbooi did as he had promised. He had noticed that some Hereros from Otjimbingwe had fought against him at Oka-handja. He knew, too, that Basters from Rehoboth were living in Otjimbingwe, and tending gardens there which the Hereros had handed over to them. The reader will remember the letters to Her-manus van Wyk and Maharero, in which Hendrik had declared that the Basters who lived with the Hereros would in future drink out of the same cup as the Hereros. The cup which he gave them to drink was very bitter. He took from the inhabitants of Otjimbingwe every-thing which they had acquired through years of careful industry. On the 24th April, 1887, he attacked the unguarded village, where the representative of the German Empire, Dr. Goering, had taken up residence in the old Augustineum. One section of his men took the horses of the Europeans, amongst which was Goering's horse, from the grazing-grounds at Ameib, while another division fetched the cattle from Karibib. Otjimbingwe itself was surrounded and kept under fire until the loot, which consisted of more than 1,000 cattle, a large number of horses, and a big flock of small stock, had been driven off. At the time of the attack Dr. Goering was at Walfish Bay. He demanded his horse back and got it, as did the other Europeans. A pursuit, which was started too late, met with no success. The Hereros who were sent out returned with whole skins but empty hands. When Hendrik came out to meet them, their courage evaporated.

Another attack was made on the 3rd June. This time the place was under fire from early morning until late in the afternoon. The losses were not serious, but a herd of cattle was carried off. The Witboois actually attempted to storm Dr. Goering's house, but were repulsed by the Hereros, and they withdrew through Tsaobis during the night.

Maharero saw how things stood. He had a hornless ox killed, so that his witch-doctors could foretell the future by examining its entrails. They told him that it was useless to undertake a campaign against Hendrik, but in spite of that, he decided to put an end to this scandalous state of things. His most skilful captain went out with 250 men to look for Hendrik. They reached the Gansberg and, towards evening, they saw his camp fire burning in the distance, between two mountain ranges. The Hereros crept noiselessly to the spot, with the intention of joining battle as soon as day broke. When the day dawned, however, they found neither huts nor people, but only some burning and smoking tree stumps, which Hendrik had lighted in order to entice the Hereros to the place where he wanted them. The Hereros were annoyed and continued farther in the same direction, which was what Hendrik wanted. Maharero's warriors suddenly found themselves surrounded, and under a sharp fire from every side. They managed to defend themselves until nightfall, when they escaped. They returned despondently to Okahandja and said that they were being pursued. The inhabitants of Osona left their fine gardens to look after themselves and fled to Okahandja. The people were frightened of Hendrik and his Witboois, and Maharero's warriors declared that they would never march out against them again into that terrible neighbourhood. Diehl of Okahandja wrote, however, in his diary:

'Oh, what a weak race these Hereros are! They cannot help themselves and the treaty of friendship with the German Government has been reduced to writing and is patiently abiding the time when German help may be expected. We have said to them repeatedly: It is an absolute disgrace that you should ask for assistance to suppress this handful of Namas. Pull yourselves together! You are strong enough to render them harmless.'

It is not our task to follow Hendrik in his subsequent raids to the north and east. Those things concern the history of individual places, not of the country as a whole. Thousands of Herero cattle were driven into Hendrik's mountain fastnesses, and were either eaten there, or driven off to Keetmanshoop and traded for fresh supplies of ammunition. The Nama chiefs, who had bound themselves to see to the preservation of peace and order, never opposed him, while many of them supplied him secretly with ammunition. Jan Afrikander bestirred himself too, and tried to 'reap the Hereros' gardens', as the saying was in former years when the northern boundary was crossed. Between Hendrik and Jan, however, no great friendship existed.

Naturally the reader's thoughts will turn to the German Government's representative, who had now been five years in South West Africa. Why was nothing done to counter attacks of this kind by Hendrik against a tribe, which had a protective treaty with the German Government and possessed the flag of the German Empire? The only answer to this is that Germany repeated the mistake which the Cape Government had made ten years before, i.e. the tribes of South West Africa were to be brought under the authority of a foreign Government without the application of force. Palgrave's indefatigable labour miscarried because his desire for a small police force was not complied with. Dr. Goering's efforts came to nothing for the very same reason, for, in 1888, Maharero cancelled the treaty he had made with him, and produced another one which he had made with the trader, Lewis. Maharero had hoped that the promised protection would safeguard him particularly against Hendrik's attacks. When he saw that he was deceived in this respect, he refused to have anything more to do with protection, and Dr. Goering and his officials had to leave. The description of these events belongs, however, to 'German South West Africa' and so can be referred to here only in the briefest possible manner. As far as it was possible, Dr. Goering made efforts to protect those who had entered into formal written contracts with him. After the attack on Otjimbingwe in July 1887 he sent, with the Hereros' permission, his Secretary, Nels, accompanied by Herr von Goldammer and Hendrik Kleinschmidt, out into the veld to find Hendrik. The latter received them very courteously and assured them that he wished to live in peace with the Europeans. He immediately gave them back the stock he had stolen, including Dr. Goering's horse. He would, however, not listen to any suggestions of peace with the Hereros, and all subsequent attempts at mediation proved unavailing. It was only natural and seems no more than right that Dr. Goering's attitude was subjected to strong criticism, that a petition was sent to Berlin, and that the doings of the German officials were deplored in German newspapers. What could a few German officials do, however, when the German Parliament was not supporting them, and what was the good of their making laws when they were refused the means of enforcing them properly? They could not accomplish anything more than Palgrave when he found himself deserted by the Cape Parliament.

3. THE END OF EARLY SOUTH WEST AFRICA

Moses Witbooi's death

As long ago as the 19th December, 1867, when the peace of Gibeon had brought the Orlam war to an end, it was apparent that there was some tension between Kido Witbooi and his brother-in-law, Paul Visser. Paul had taken no part in the Orlam war and so he would have nothing to do with the peace of Hoachanas. It will be remembered that the peace conditions laid down that the chief of Hoachanas was no longer to be regarded as the paramount chief of the Nama race. The chiefs of Bethanie, Berseba, and Gibeon were to exercise the paramountcy jointly.

In the course of years, the relationship between Kido and Paul Visser, who was the commander of the Witbooi forces, had not improved, and when Moses Witbooi became his father's successor matters became very much worse. Open hostility broke out on different occasions. We know that Paul Visser went and stayed at Gobabis with his followers for a time, in order to have a free hand, and that, by doing so, he added considerably to the troubles which arose in 1880. It finally came to a declaration of war by Moses Witbooi against Paul Visser, and a fierce battle was fought between them, which ended in Moses being taken prisoner. In a pathetic letter, which he wrote to Manasse of Hoachanas in August 1887, he begged him to come and help him, for Moses regarded Manasse as his subordinate. The latter came on the scene but found that intervention from his side was no longer necessary. Forced to it by his defeat, Moses had resigned his chieftainship in favour of his brother-in-law. Moses did not even thank his helpers from Hoachanas for coming, in fact, he did not even greet them. After his release, he mounted his horse and rode off to Gibeon shouting 'Hurrah'.

Hendrik Witbooi was so occupied with his 'business' that he could not go to his father's assistance, but he stood to lose a great deal by it.

By abdicating the chieftainship in favour of Paul Visser, Hendrik's prospects for the future as Moses' son and legal successor were ruined. Hendrik therefore went to Fritz, the opposition chief of Hoachanas, and to Nasemab, the leader of the disloyal section of the Red Nation, and induced them to attack Paul Visser. This proceeding was naturally very unwelcome to Manasse, who had been passed over, and he wrote to Hendrik that he was advising his people to disobey his instructions and to rebel. Hendrik replied: 'You are an upstart and not the son of a chief at all. What do you want? You are a rebel yourself! Go and look for your equals amongst the wild dogs of the veld!' He sent a number of his Witboois to reinforce Fritz's and Nasemab's troops, expecting that they would get the better of Paul Visser. The old commander who had just become a chief, was, however, more than a match for them, and he defeated his opponents in several fights. Then Fritz and Nasemab went their respective ways and left it to Hendrik to fight for 'the royal throne of Gibeon'. Hendrik then tried to gain an advantage by trickery. He wrote a submissive letter to Paul, stating that he had done him wrong, and asking him for peace. Paul Visser summoned Manasse to come to him. He was quite prepared to negotiate for peace, but he soon saw through Hendrik's trick and realized that his submissiveness was only due to a shortage of ammunition, so he attacked Hendrik. The latter had to take to his heels and make for the upper Fish River valley, where he did not neglect to carry off stock belonging to the Namas living there. Paul went after him and dealt him another heavy blow. He took away from him the stock he had stolen and nineteen horses as well, and then returned to Girichas where he had his werf.

Hendrik, who had hitherto been reluctant to buy his ammunition at Lüderitz's store at Bethanie, decided, in his dilemma, to try to get some from the Germans, for which purpose he went to Walfish Bay. He went with his request to one of the chief German officials, von Goldammer, and received from him an answer which was not at all to his liking. Von Goldammer told him that he would not get as much powder as he could put in the corner of his eye. Hendrik replied angrily that, from then onwards, he would 'unload' every wagon which went from Walfish Bay to the interior. In many cases, he actually carried out his threat. He then went to Bethanie and got what he wanted.

On his return, he told the people at Gibeon that he was coming there to be present at the enthronement, and he actually did so, but the ceremony was put off, for Paul Visser was wide awake. He took, however, the harmonium belonging to the church away with him, and he went to attack the Grootdodens, who had offended him. He destroyed their three werfs and took away all their stock; he spared neither women nor children, and even had the dogs killed, thereby practically exterminating this unruly inconstant tribe. He then went to Arisemab, the chief of the Veldskoendraers, who was an ally of Paul Visser's. Arisemab had not the slightest suspicion that there was any-thing amiss, and did not even have his gun handy. His werf was stormed, both he and his wife were wounded, and his son killed. The wounded chieftain begged Hendrik to spare his life, but the latter put a bullet through his heart with his own hand.

Paul Visser came on the scene and attacked Hendrik. The latter had not expected him so soon, and he suffered a severe defeat which compelled him to retreat. The Veldskoendraers, however, urged Paul to march against Moses as well in the veld of Bethanie. They pointed out that they, who were his allies, had lost their chief Arise-mab, simply because he had left them in the lurch and had not come to their assistance in good time. He was responsible, therefore, for Arisemab's death, and only when Moses' blood was offered to satisfy their lust for revenge, would they absolve Paul Visser from his blood-guiltiness.

Persuaded by these arguments, Paul Visser marched with his men into the territory of Berseba. The chief of Berseba got wind of it and sent his people out to bring Moses to Berseba. When they came on the scene he had already been placed bound on a cart and taken off to Gibeon. The captured chief reached Gibeon on the 22nd Febru-ary, 1888. Adam Klaase, who had been one of his councillors, was taken prisoner with him, and the two men were now put on their trial. The principal charge was that Moses Witbooi had called upon his son Hendrik for assistance immediately after he had surrendered his chieftainship to Paul Visser. By doing so, he had made himself guilty of high treason and his adviser Adam had done the same. Sen-tence of death was passed on both of them. A young Orlam, named Gottlieb Vlermuis, who happened to be passing through Gibeon, thought it very wrong that no one should prepare the condemned men for their death, although there were people competent to do it at the school centre, where the sentence had been imposed. When he drew attention to the fact that this office should be performed, he received the answer that no one understood how to do it. Gottlieb then looked for a Bible and, when he found one, he read the 57th Psalm to the condemned men and prayed with them, without anybody raising any objection. Then the two unfortunates were taken off to the cemetery where a new grave had been made next to Kido's. When Moses and his councillor reached the grave, they were made to sit down on the heap of earth which had been taken out of the hole; they were given a few moments to collect their thoughts and then shot dead.

Moses had shed a great deal of blood in his lifetime, especially in his old age, and he fell a victim to a blood feud. He and Paul Visser had hatched and carried out many a plot together and, in the end, Paul Visser's plots against him cost the old man of over seventy years the 'royal throne of Gibeon', and his life.

Paul Visser's death

When Jan Jonker heard the news of Moses' death he wrote joyfully to Paul Visser that he would now put everything else aside and join him in an attack on the Hereros. It was necessary to humble them thoroughly before they got into closer association with the Germans. After that, he proposed a joint campaign against Hendrik Witbooi.

From now onwards Paul Visser subscribed his letters as 'Captain of the whole of Great Namaland'. He spent his time in the territory of Berseba, collecting scattered Witboois who had left Gibeon to get away from all that was happening there. When he went to Berseba on this occasion he got such a cool reception that he left again immediately.

Hendrik, however, formally reported the death of his father to the German Commissioner, Dr. Goering, and added that he had now become chief of the Witboois. He went to Gibeon on the 3rd July, 1888, and visited his father's grave. He had come to take revenge on Paul Visser for the death of his father, and to remove his rival from his office as chief. Paul Visser knew the fate that was hanging over his head, and set out from Girichas for Gibeon. He did not know, however, that Hendrik was on his way to him with a strong force. Hendrik discovered Paul's commando first and placed his men under cover on either side of the road by which Paul had to come. Paul Visser suspected nothing, for he thought that Hendrik was at Gibeon. Suddenly his whole column was under fire and Paul Visser was the first man to be hit by Hendrik's bullet. Paul's men, who were now without their leader, rallied under cover of a hill and resumed the fight, but they were put to flight with heavy losses and Hendrik entered Girichas. He destroyed the werf, took with him everything useful, and set fire to whatever was left behind, and then went after the fugitives and killed two more parties of them. This took place on the 12th July, 1888. He then returned to Gibeon 'where not even a dog had lived since the beginning of the year' and held a funeral feast for his father. He had his horses newly shod and went off again to carry on 'his work'.

Jan Jonker's death

A special history of the tribe of the Witbois, or the story of Hendrik's life, would be the proper place for giving a detailed account of Hendrik's doings after Paul Visser's death, but the readers of this book would only be wearied by it. Hendrik was now chief of the Witbois and there were two principal things which he had to provide, namely, a safe place in which the tribe could live, for he did not consider Gibeon safe, and ammunition. Ammunition, however, had to be bought and so he rounded up 4,000 Herero cattle in December 1888, and Duncan of Keetmanshoop, a Scotsman who had been thirty years in the country and had taken one of Hendrik's relations as a wife, made provision for war materials. Hendrik received 70,000 cartridges, 1,200 lb. of powder, 7,000 lb. of lead, and an enormous number of percussion caps. With that something could be done.

But where was he to find a safe place in which he could live in security with his tribe and his troops, and prepare himself for new expeditions without being disturbed. The Gansberg did not attract him. Jan Jonker was there, and Jan was no longer his friend. Amongst Paul Visser's papers Hendrik had found the letter which Jan had written to him, and there it stood, in black and white, that Jan had the intention of turning his weapons against him. Besides this, Jan had taken people into his company with whom Hendrik was annoyed, and that was not at all to his liking. Last of all, Jan was the sort of man who wanted to command himself and would submit to no control, and Hendrik was of the same way of thinking. He decided, therefore, to go to Hornkrans just west of Rehoboth, seeing that Hornkrans was very suitable for the establishment of a fortified encampment. Water, grazing, and mountain kloofs were there in abundance. Hendrik's diary, in which no new entries had been made since October 1885, mentions the fact that he was living at Hornkrans on the 10th March, 1889.

On the 22nd March, Hendrik wrote to Dr. Goering. A personal meeting between Goering and Hendrik did not have the desired effect. After Hendrik had explained to him his position, Goering was forced to come to the conclusion that the time for making peace was not yet ripe, and he offered his services as intermediary when the proper time should come.

Jan Jonker knew that he was next on the list to be dealt with by Hendrik. Things were going badly with him. All his raiding had failed to make him rich. His best Afrikanders had left him and gone over to Hendrik, for it was said of him that he had shot one of his nearest relatives when out hunting with him, and that another of them, whom he believed to be aspiring to the chieftainship, had been killed in a fight at his instigation. Even his own illegitimate son, Phanuel, and Moses Jager were in Hendrik Witbooi's camp. Jan had only thirty fighting men left and so he decided not to come to grips with Hendrik, but to escape to Hereroland and to join the Swartboois at Otjimbingwe and Anawood. In the beginning of August, 1889, Jan set out with all his belongings to escape Hendrik's anger, but Hendrik heard of his flight and went after him. His diary contains these few remarks about what happened:

'On the 6th August, we went out after Jan Afrikander. We followed his tracks, which went in the direction of Hereroland, and after four days we caught him up at Gugu-ameb (near Tsaobis on the Swakop). On the 10th August we attacked him. Many of Jan's men were killed and many of them were wounded, and he, the chief Jan Jonker Afrikander, fell on that same day too, in the battle of the 10th August, but our men returned home unhurt.'

As a story was immediately spread, and was even set down in the records of the time, to the effect that Hendrik Witbooi had enticed Jan to his camp and treacherously shot him, the true facts, which have been carefully investigated, should be set out here. Hendrik Witbooi caught Jan up to the west of Tsaobis, and surrounded his camp in the night. Next morning a fierce fight took place, in which thirteen men and three women were killed on Jan's side and a number of others were wounded. Jan sent a child to Hendrik's camp with a letter which was full of reproaches for the way in which he had treated him. He said that a great many wrongs had been done to him but that he had always forgiven them. It was not right for Hendrik to persecute him so persistently. Hendrik's answer was to the effect that he was prepared to give Jan an hour's armistice. During this time he might consider whether he would ask for peace in a proper fashion. Jan thereupon asked Hendrik to discuss matters with him; his own people had urged him to abandon his opposition before the whole Afrikander tribe was destroyed. Hendrik agreed to the discussion and Jan went to him. Moses Jager and Jan's illegitimate son, Phanuel, urged Hendrik, however, to have Jan shot down immediately, as any discussion with him would bring about fresh dissension. Hendrik watched Jan approach and gave no reply to what Phanuel said. When Jan was close to the camp, he put his gun down and walked up to Hendrik and, at that very moment, Phanuel's bullet laid him low. Hendrik walked to the body, looked at it for a moment in silence, and then turned away without saying anything. He did not praise Phanuel for what he had done, but neither did he take him to task for it.

The tiny remnant of the formerly so powerful Afrikander tribe fled into Hereroland, and Maharero gave them Kaundua in which to live. They stayed there until 1897, when almost all of them died of malaria.

It was in the month of August 1864 that the Swartboois had fled before Jan Jonker and his Afrikanders from Rehoboth, to find safety at Otjimbingwe. Jan Jonker caused a terrible massacre of them and robbed them of everything they possessed. Kleinschmidt, the Swartbooi's missionary, died of a broken heart as a result. In the month of August, just twenty-five years later, the self-same Jan Jonker, with the remnant of his Afrikander tribe, set out for Otjimbingwe, in order to take refuge with the very Swartboois whom he had formerly persecuted, and then Hendrik Witbooi came down upon him and brought his bloodstained career to an end.

The missionary Brincker wrote as follows about Hendrik Witbooi:

'One may look at the man in whatever way one will, but it must be recognized that he had his task to perform. This task consisted of cleaning up the country and ridding it of a horde of Nama vagrants, whom a life of warfare and robbery had made incorrigible. It consisted, too, in executing judgment on the Jonker Afrikanders and in instilling into the Hereros, once again, a certain amount of respect for other people, which was something that they had almost lost. Finally, he must have afforded all the other Namas convincing proof of the fact that war brings them to beggary, and that it is far better for them to stay and work the poor ground which belongs to them, and to give up all hope of reaching and taking possession of a Land of Cocaigne in the distant north.

Maharero's death

Maharero felt old age approaching, but he busied himself with everything and wanted to be consulted in every way. Shortly after his return from his long trek along the southern boundary, Dr. Hoepfner came to negotiate with him about a treaty with the German Government. He achieved nothing, for Maharero had become suspicious. What had become of the treaty which he had made with Palgrave and the Cape Government? Where was Palgrave all this time? On Maharero's instructions, Lewis wrote a letter to the Cape Government, and Palgrave came back once more. Shortly before the German consul Vogelsang reached Okahandja, Palgrave was there to make a new treaty with Maharero. When he had done this, he went back again, for a hint from the English Government had caused the Cape Government to call Palgrave back, and Maharero received notice that it could not recognize the treaty, and that it had decided not to have anything more to do with South West Africa. The Cape Government's representative left in February 1885. In October of the same year, Dr. Büttner, who had previously been a missionary and the Director of the Augustineum at Otjimbingwe, arrived at Okahandja. The German Government had sent him to South West Africa because he knew the country and its languages, and had entrusted him with the conduct of negotiations with the different chiefs. Dr. Goering, whose duty it was, as Commissioner for the Empire, to enter into treaties, arrived almost at the same time from Walfish Bay with his staff. There was still a third person who came on the scene, and that was Hendrik Witbooi, who wanted to confirm the peace treaty he had made, but actually started the war afresh at Osona, and gave the German officials the opportunity of binding up the Herero's wounds until far into the night. This made such a good impression on Maharero that, on the 21st October, he and his people voluntarily placed themselves under the protection of the German Government. In doing this, however, he had caused his friend Lewis great disappointment. This was the man who had gone to the Trek-Boers in the Waterberg and at Otavi at Maharero's instance, to persuade them to leave Hereroland. Lewis advised them to withdraw to Grootfontein, for, as a trader, he was interested in not losing them altogether. Maharero was dissatisfied with this, but his dissatisfaction passed away, for he was of the opinion that he could not get on without

Lewis. Nobody was so well acquainted and skilled in the problem of the Trek-Boers as he was. It was to be Lewis's task to do what Maharero had wanted the Cape Government's representative to do. If the German Government protected him against Hendrik and Jan Jonker, and Lewis helped him to deal with the Trek-Boers, he had got what he wanted. The German Government, however, sent no soldiers. It is true that the Colonial Association sent out two officers and five non-commissioned officers, who were to form a small protective force at Otjimbingwe, which was to be recruited from amongst the Basters. But that did not help Maharero at all.

The letters which Dr. Goering sent to Hendrik Witbooi and Jan to tell them to behave themselves helped him just as little. Maharero had expected that matters would turn out very differently. Hendrik Witbooi stole his cattle, as he had always done, and nobody laid a finger on him. When the importation of ammunition was prohibited for a time, his suspicions increased to such an extent that he feared that: 'a pit was being dug for him' and that he would one day fall into it. It seemed to him very wrong, too, that his missionary at Otjimbingwe should sell the old Augustineum to Dr. Goering, so as to enable him to put up a new building at Okahandja, for the raw brick and wood in the building belonged to him. He had given them both, with the idea that young Hereros should be trained as teachers for his people in a house which was built with his bricks and wood, and now an official of the German Empire was living in this house, and had even bought it for money, and Maharero had not even been consulted about it. (No one had ever thought of asking him, for no one ever dreamt that Maharero could claim any right of ownership in the building.)

In 1888 Lewis arrived at Okahandja, with a staff of fifteen, in the employ of a Kimberley Syndicate, and Dr. Goering arrived there, too, in his capacity as the highest official of the Protectorate. Then, on the 3rd October, 1888, Maharero formally denounced the treaty of the 21st October, 1885, and Lewis produced a treaty which was dated the 9th September, 1885, in which Maharero transferred almost all his rights as chief to him. It was thus a few weeks older than the treaty with the German Empire. Dr. Goering then went back to Germany. Was South West Africa once again unprotected? For a considerable time it seemed as if it was. Maharero, however, came to reconsider the question. In July 1889, Captain Curt von François arrived with a small troop of twenty-one men. He occupied Otjimbingwe, erected the Wilhelms Fort at Tsaobis, received reinforce-

ments for his troop, and in May 1890 he visited Maharero at Okahandja and the latter did not refuse to renew his old treaty.

As in the case of a chain one link fits into another, similarly the
history of early South West Africa is linked with the history of
German South West Africa, and German South West Africa had its
origin in the conclusion of treaties with individual chiefs in the
days which really belong to 'the early times'. The detailed history
of the way in which the German Protectorate came into existence
can only be dealt with when a history of German South West Africa
comes to be written. A short summary of these beginnings will perhaps not be out of place here.

After the British Government had declared, in 1880, that it had
decided to restrict its possessions to Walfish Bay, the merchant
F. A. E. Lüderitz of Bremen worked out a scheme for the acquisition
of land in South West Africa, between lat. 22 and 28 S., and for the
purchase of trading stations, laid it before the Foreign Office in
Berlin, and asked the protection of the German Government for the
property he intended to acquire.

Lüderitz bought the whole strip of dune country from the chiefs
of Bethanie and Walfish Bay and, on the 24th April, 1884, he tele-
graphed to von Bismarck, the Chancellor of the German Empire,
and to the German Consul in Capetown as follows: 'We wish it to
be officially declared that Lüderitz and his settlement are under the
protection of the German Government.' It was thus that Germany's
protectorate in South West Africa began.

The next step was the dispatch of Dr. Nachtigall, as Consul-
General for the West Coast of Africa, to supplement the deed of
purchase by which Lüderitz had acquired a right to part of the dune-
lands along the coast from the chiefs, by making treaties for protection
with these same chiefs. In this way the latter came under the protection of the German Empire, while retaining jurisdiction over
their own subjects, exclusive of their quarrels between Europeans,
and they agreed to allow German traders and settlers to come into
the country.

The third step was accomplished by Dr. Goering, Dr. Büttner,
and others, and this was the conclusion of protective treaties with
the Herero and Nama chiefs. These were concluded in the following
sequence, viz.:

On the 2nd September, 1885, with Manasse of Hoachanas;

On the 15th September, 1885, with Hermanus van Wyk of Rehoboth;

On the 21st October, 1885, with Maharero at Okahandja;

On the 3rd November, 1885, with Manasse of Omaruru.

The treaty with Willem Christian of Warmbad and Jan Hendriks of Keetmanshoop was not concluded until the 21st August, 1890. Simon Koper of Gochas and the Swartboois of Fransfontein asked for, and were granted, their treaties only in 1894. Hendrik Witbooi, however, refused to make any treaty at all, but went on with 'his work', and had to be forced by von François and his successor, Governor Leutwein, to surrender and to return to Gibeon.

When von François went to Okahandja to visit Maharero in 1889, something occurred which caused a great disturbance amongst the Hereros. He never even knew about it, and to many people it may well appear to be ridiculous. Von François had brought some camels with him, and a camel was a thing which had not as yet been seen in South West Africa. What appeared to be most extraordinary to the Hereros about this large animal was its lack of horns. Now Maharero belonged to the religious Society of the Kudu, or Ohorongo, which was distinguished from other similar societies by the fact that its members were forbidden to eat the flesh of any ox, goat, or other animal, which had no horns. If any one did so accidentally he was a dead man unless his life could be saved by the efforts of the witch-doctors. As the camel had no horns, the heathen Hereros thought that it was an animal which might be dangerous to Maharero. The danger, however, was not very great, for it was only harmful if its flesh was eaten. One morning early, however, just as the sun rose, a camel was seen close to Maharero's house. There stood the sacred ancestral fire, upon which the food which only men of the Kudu Society might eat was always cooked in large earthenware pots. Maharero's ancestors would probably take revenge for any desecration of this holy place, on his family and his whole tribe. It was now noticed that the camel's shadow fell on the ashes of the sacred fire in such a way that the shadow of its hornless head was right on the fire-place, where the priestess of the sacred fire was going to kindle a new fire with the embers which she had carefully kept over in her hut from the previous day, and thus give the sign for the milking of the cows to commence. This was immediately recognized as a bad omen and sacrilege, and every one was agreed that Maharero had not long to live, for the camel had bewitched him. It was impossible to conceal what had happened from the old chief, and he discussed the question of his successor with his half-brother and general, Riarua, more earnestly than before. His eldest son, Wilhelm, who had been given a good education at the Augustineum in the expectation that he would become his successor, had been killed in 1880 in a battle with the Namas. According to Herero law, his eldest son, Samuel, had to inherit the sacred fire, with all the cattle connected with it, but the eldest son of his eldest sister was the heir to all the rest of his property, and it was property which made a man a chief amongst the Hereros, not the sacred fire, unless a large number of cattle went with it. Maharero's eldest sister was called Outjina. She had married Kandjii, and her eldest son's name was Tjetjo, a man of a quiet disposition, without any particular ambition, who was satisfied with the large herds of cattle which he owned.

Maharero did not want his son, Samuel, to succeed him to the chieftainship, for he was very much addicted to liquor. He could not be his successor at the sacred fire, for Samuel had been baptized a Christian. It is true that he had been put under censure by the church and that he had no rights whatsoever in the congregation, but the ancestral staffs could not be handed over to him, nor could he perform the duties of the sacred fire, as the waters of baptism had deprived him of his qualifications. He did not want to see his nephew, Tjetjo, as his successor either, but what he had against him has never been discovered.

As Maharero himself did not know what to do, and as others could give him no advice, his principal wife, Kataree, Samuel's mother, took matters in hand. She impressed upon her husband that he had become a German subject through his treaty with the German Emperor, and that he should make his decision according to German law and custom. In Germany it was always the Emperor's eldest son who succeeded him on the throne, and therefore her son, Samuel, was the only person who had a right to succeed Maharero. After pressure had been brought to bear on him, and some of his councillors had signified their consent, he gave in at last, and, when German officers passed through Okahandja, Samuel did not fail to introduce himself to them as his father's successor.

Kataree was in great perplexity. She was afraid that Maharero would go back on his undertaking some day and appoint some one else as his successor; this second choice would then be effective, unless people were prepared to expose themselves to revenge by Maharero's spirit after his death. Things must be managed so that Maharero did not go back on what he had said. Maharero must not be allowed to die of old age, nor must he be allowed to die after a long illness, for both these things might have an undesirable effect upon his decision upon the important question of the succession. It, therefore, seemed best that he should die soon and in such a way that he lost consciousness first. Von François' camel was a source of inspiration. With great secrecy, Samuel was sent out by his mother to fetch a hornless goat and this was slaughtered in the night. Early in the morning, Kataree cooked the meat and brought it to Maharero's hut. At that moment Riarua came on the scene. He warned her, saying: 'Maharero will smell it.' She replied: 'He will not smell it. He eats like a wolf.' A little while later Riarua went into Maharero's hut. He found him eating greedily and he sat down. Maharero went on eating and said nothing, but he gave his half-brother none of the food as it was customary to do. When he had eaten everything Riarua said to him: 'Why did you give me nothing to-day.' Then Maharero began to speak: 'I am giving you nothing because I do not want to do you harm. I know exactly what Kataree and Samuel are doing to me. Samuel will become chief after me, but I tell you that it will only be for a very short time and that he will die in a distant land. We two, however, will stay here and be buried here. You have become a Christian and you will find your grave in the Christian churchyard. I have remained a heathen, and so I must be buried in the heathen manner. It is right that things should be done in this way. All your life you have been like a dove and all my life I have been like a snake, and a dove and a snake ought not to be gathered together in the same place.'

As far as is known, those were Maharero's last words, and they were preserved by the Hereros very carefully, all the more so because great weight and effect are attached to the words of a dying man. They wanted to summon the witch-doctors when convulsions set in, but Maharero would not allow it. The only medicine he took was some which he obtained from his missionary, Diehl. He then ordered them to take him to the grave of his father, Tjamuaha, where he sat down and spent a long time, deep in thought, without saying a word. They carried him back to his hut as if he were dead. His strength ebbed quickly. He lost consciousness and died early in the morning on the 7th October, 1890.

He was buried beside his father, Tjamuaha, with great ceremony and much lamentation. The ancestral staffs, which, according to his decision, were to be buried with him, were kept back. They were given to Kavezeri, who destroyed them when he became a Christian. Samuel Maharero followed his father in the chieftainship and after fourteen years he was forced to take refuge in British territory, where he died on the 14th March, 1923. His body was brought to Okahandja in a metal coffin, and was buried in a grave alongside those of his father and grandfather. A tombstone was erected with an inscription significantly written in three languages, which reads as follows:

THE HERERO CHIEFS
Tjamuaha gestorben 1859
und sein Sohn Maharero gestorben 5. Okt. 1890.
Samuel Maharero
geb. 1856. Gest. 14. März 1923.
Imba pa suva ovahona vetatu, mba ungurire
mouhona namouingona, nu ngamba va koka ave ri ovahona tjiri.

The following is a translation:—

Tjamuaha, died 1859, and his son Maharero, died 5th October, 1890; Samuel Maharero, born 1856, died 14th March, 1923.

Here lie three chieftains at rest. They ruled the country for the good of the Herero people, but now they are dead. They were chiefs indeed.

With Maharero's death on the 7th October, 1890, 'Early South West Africa' came to an end. On the 18th October, 1890, von François laid the foundation stone of the first building in Windhoek, the capital of German South West Africa, and, since the World War, of the Mandated Territory of South West Africa.

LITERATURE

ALEXANDER, Sir J. E. *An Expedition of Discovery into the Interior of Africa.* Two vols. London, 1838.

ANDERSSON, C. J. *Lake Ngami or Exploration and Discoveries during Four Years Wanderings in the Wilds of South Western Africa.* London, 1856.
—— *Notes of Travel in South Africa.* London, 1875.
—— *The Okavango River. A Narrative of Travel, Exploration and Adventure.* London, 1861.

BAINES, T. *Explorations in South West Africa.* London, 1864.

Barmen Missionsblatt, seit 1840. Barmen, Missionshaus.

BRINCKER, Dr. P. H. Th. *Aus dem Hererolande.* Barmen, 1896.

BÜTTNER, Dr. C. G. *Das Hinterland von Walfischbai und Angra Pequena.* Heidelberg, 1884.

CAMPBELL, JOHN. *Travels in South Africa.* London, 1815.

CHAPMAN, JAMES. *Travels in the Interior of South Africa.* Two vols. London, 1868.

COOK, EDWARD. *The Modern Missionary.* 1849.

DANCKELMANN, FREIHERR VON. *Mitteilungen von Forschungsreisenden und Gelehrten aus den deutschen Schutzgebieten.* (Missionschaftliche Beihefte zum *Deutschen Kolonialblatt.*)

DANNERT, E. *Zum Rechte der Herero.* Berlin, 1906.

DRIESSLER, H. *Die Rheinische Mission in Südwestafrika.* Gütersloh, 1932.

EBNER, J. L. *Reise nach Südafrika.* Berlin, 1829.

Eingeborenenrecht—Beantwortung des Fragebogens über dasselbe. Mit Beiträgen von Baumann, Wandres, Elger, Brockmann, Irle und Vedder. Berlin, 1912. Weiter bearbeitet in: *Das Eingeborenenrecht.* Abschnitt Südwestafrika. Stuttgart, 1930.

FABRI, Dr. F. *Angra Pequena und Südwestafrika.* Elberfeld, 1884.
—— *Bedarf Deutschland der Kolonien?* 1879.
—— *Fünf Jahre deutscher Kolonialpolitik.* Gotha, 1884.

FISCHER, Dr. EUGEN. *Die Rehobother Bastards und das Bastardierungsproblem beim Menschen.* Jena, 1913.

FRANÇOIS, C. von. *Deutsche Südwest-Afrika. Geschichte der Kolonization bis zum Ausbruch des Krieges mit Witbooi.* Berlin, 1899.
—— *Kriegführung in Südafrika.* 1900.

FRITSCH, G. *Drei Jahre in Südafrika.* 1868.
—— *Die Eingeborenen Südafrikas, ethnographisch und anatomisch beschrieben.* Mit Atlas. Breslau, 1872.

GALTON, FRANCIS. *Interior of South Africa.* London, 1852.
—— *The Narrative of an Explorer in Tropical South Africa.* London, 1853.

GÜRICH, G. *Deutsch-Südwestafrika. Reisebilder und Skizzen aus den Jahren*

1888 und 1889. Mitteilungen der geographischen Gesellschaft in Hamburg, 1891–92.

HAARHOFF, B. J. *Die Bantustamme Süd-Afrikas. Eine ethnologisch-mythologische Studie.* Leipzig, 1890.

HAHN, J. *'Die Ovaherero.'* Zeitschrift der Gesellschaft für Erdkunde. Berlin, 1869.

HAHN Dr. THEOPHILUS. *Report and Proceedings with Appendices of the Government Commission on Native Laws and Customs.* Capetown, 1883.

HENOCH, H. ADOLF. *Lüderitz. Eine biographische Skizze.* Berlin, 1909. (Koloniale Abhandlungen, Heft 25.)

HEFFE, HERMANN, Dr. jur. *Die Schutzverträge in Südwest-Afrika.* Berlin, 1905.

IRLE, J. *Die Herero.* Gütersloh, 1906.

KINGON, W. L. *The Germans in Damaraland.* Capetown, 1889.

KLEINSCHMIDT, H. *Ein Missionarsleben aus Süd-Afrika.* Barmen, Missionshaus, 1897.

KNUDSEN. *Gross-Namaqualand.* Barmen, 1848.

KÖHLER, Prof. Dr. A. *Der deutsche Anteil an der Entdeckung und Erforschung der Erdteile. Teil I: Afrika.* 1929.

KÖLBE, PETER. *Caput Bonae Spei hodiernum.* German edition Nürnberg, 1719; Dutch edition 1727; English edition 1731.

KÜLZ, Dr. *Deutsch-Südwestafrika im 25. Jahre deutscher Schutzheerschaft.* Berlin, 1909.

MEINHOF, E. *Afrikanische Religionen.* Berlin, 1912.

MEYER, F. *Wirtschaft und Recht der Herero.* Berlin, 1905.

MOFFAT, R. *Missionary Labours and Scenes in Southern Africa.* 1846.

MORITZ, E. *Die ältesten Reiseberichte über Deutsch-Südwestafrika.* Berlin, 1916.

MORREL. *Narrative of a Voyage to the South and West Coast of Africa.* London, 1844.

OLPP, J. sen. *Angra Pequena und Gross-Namaland.* Elberfeld, 1884.

—— *Erlebnisse im Hinterlande von Angra Pequena.* Barmen, 1906.

PALGRAVE, W. C. *His Mission to Damaraland and Great Namaqualand in 1876.* Capetown, 1877.

Palgrave, W. C. and H. Hahn's Missions. Reports presented to both Houses of Parliament, 1877, 1880, 1881, 1882. Capetown.

PECHUEL-LÖSCHE. *'Zur Kenntnis des Hererolandes.'* Ausland, Bd. LIX. 1886.

RIDSDALE, B. *Great Namaqualand.* 1883.

ROHDEN, L. von. *Geschichte der Rheinischen Missionsgesellschaft.* Barmen, 1888.

SANDER, Dr. L. *Geschichte der deutschen Kolonialgesellschaft.* Berlin, 1912.

SCHINZ, J. *Deutsch-Südwestafrika. Forschungsreisen 1884–1887 durch die deutschen Schutzgebiete*. Leipzig, 1891.

SCHREIBER, Dr. A. *Kurze Übersicht über die 50jährige Missionsarbeit im Hererolande*. Barmen, 1894.

THEAL, G. McCALL. *History of South Africa*. Vols. i–vi. London, 1888–1902.

TINDALL, HENRY. *Great Namaqualand*. 1856.

VEDDER, H. und E. MEIER. *Quellen zur Geschichte von Südwestafrika*. Manuscript 28 vols., Parliamentary Library, Windhoek.

VEDDER, H. '*Die Bergdama*.' *Abhandlungen des Hamburger Kolonialinstitutes. Teil I und II*. Hamburg, 1923.

Wissenschaftliche Vereinigung für Südwestafrika. *Veröffentlichungen von 1927 an*.

Witbooi, Hendrik, Die Dagboek van. Van Riebeeck Society, Capetown, 1932.

INDEX

Witch-doctors, 76, 504.
Wobma, Capt. C. Th., of the *Bode*, 10.
Wodehouse, Sir P. C., and David
  Christian, 359; petition to, for pro-
  tection, 379.
Women, Bushman and Hottentot, stea-
  topygy of, 80.
Women and wives, clothing, status and
  duties of, Bergdama, 62; Bushman,
  81; Herero, 45, 46, 48, 49, 55; Nama,
  53, 55; Ovambo, 68–9, 70–1, 77.
Wuppertal Trading Society, 401, 436, 457.

Xosa race, kinship of, with the Damas,
  114, 116.

'Year of lies, the', 484 ff.
Yellow-skinned races in South West
  Africa, 119.

Zeraua, 325, 336; elected paramount
  chief, 339–40; and his gun, 144; letter
  to, from Cloete, 217; and Palgrave,
  428.